Lecture Notes in Computer Science 1012

Edited by G. Goos, J. Hartmanis and J. van Leeuwen

Advisory Board: W. Brauer   D. Gries   J. Stoer

D1221827

Springer
Berlin
Heidelberg
New York
Barcelona
Budapest
Hong Kong
London
Milan
Paris
Santa Clara
Singapore
Tokyo

Miroslav Bartošek   Jan Staudek
Jiří Wiedermann (Eds.)

SOFSEM '95:
Theory and Practice
of Informatics

22nd Seminar on Current Trends
in Theory and Practice of Informatics
Milovy, Czech Republic
November 23 - December 1, 1995
Proceedings

 Springer

Series Editors

Gerhard Goos
Universität Karlsruhe
Vincenz-Priessnitz-Straße 3, D-76128 Karlsruhe, Germany

Juris Hartmanis
Department of Computer Science, Cornell University
4130 Upson Hall, Ithaca, NY 14853, USA

Jan van Leeuwen
Department of Computer Science,Utrecht University
Padualaan 14, 3584 CH Utrecht,The Netherlands

Volume Editors

Miroslav Bartošek, Institute of Computer Science
Jan Staudek, Faculty of Informatics
Masaryk University, Burešova 20
602 00 Brno, Czech Republic

Jiří Wiedermann
Institute of Computer Science, Academy of Sciences of the Czech Republic
Pod vodárenskou věží 2, 182 07 Prague, Czech Republic

Cataloging-in-Publication data applied for

Die Deutsche Bibliothek - CIP-Einheitsaufnahme

Theory and practice of informatics ; proceedings / SOFSEM
'95, 22nd Seminar on Current Trends in Theory and Practice of
Informatics, Milovy, Czech Republic, November 23 -
December 1, 1995 / Miroslav Bartošek ... (ed.). - Berlin ;
Heidelberg ; New York ; Barcelona ; Budapest ; Hong Kong ;
London ; Milan ; Paris ; Tokyo : Springer, 1995
  (Lecture notes in computer science ; Vol. 1012)
  ISBN 3-540-60609-2
NE: Bartošek, Miroslav [Hrsg.]; SOFSEM <22, 1995, Milovice>; GT

CR Subject Classification (1991): D.1-4, H.1-3,F.1, F.4, H.5

ISBN 3-540-60609-2 Springer-Verlag Berlin Heidelberg New York

© Springer-Verlag Berlin Heidelberg 1995
Printed in Germany

Typesetting: Camera-ready by author
SPIN 10487212   06/3142 – 5 4 3 2 1 0   Printed on acid-free paper

Foreword

The international Seminar on Current Trends in the Theory and Practice of Informatics SOFSEM'95 was held November 23–December 1, 1995, in the conference facilities of the Devět skal (i.e., Nine Rocks) Hotel, Milovy, the Czech Republic. It was already the 22nd annual meeting in the series of SOFSEM seminars organized in the Czech Republic or in the Slovak Republic.

SOFSEM is a seminar with a long term tradition that has been evolving into its present form for more than 20 years. Founded in 1974, SOFSEM (which stands for SOFtware SEMinar) initially arose through the efforts of Jozef Gruska from the Computing Research Center, Bratislava, and Jiří Hořejš from the Central Computing Center of Masaryk University, Brno. Gruska served as the program committee chairman for the first 10 years of SOFSEM's existence.

Soon after its establishing, SOFSEM became the foremost Czechoslovak seminar devoted to theoretical and practical problems of software systems. In fact, during those early days of computer science and technology, SOFSEM supplemented the university education and academic research by mediating a fast transfer of the latest relevant knowledge to the SOFSEM audience. Traditionally, this audience consisted of university professors, academic researchers, university teaching staff, advanced students, and professionals from the field. First local and later on also international experts have been invited. Each of them was to present a series of lectures related to some recent topics in computer science. The basic format of each SOFSEM consisted of several series of invited talks. Each of them had the duration of 3 to 5 hours. This was complemented by selected contributions of participants presented during two half–days in two parallel sessions. Until 1994, the total duration of SOFSEMs was two weeks.

The most substantial changes concerning SOFSEM have been realized since the 'velvet' revolution in Czechoslovakia in 1989. SOFSEM has been transformed from a mainly national seminar into a truly international conference. In 1993, an international advisory board was created to provide assistance to the program committee in the preparation of a scientific program. Beginning with SOFSEM'95, after two years of exhaustive discussions, SOFSEM was shortened to eight days while almost preserving the number of invited lectures. This was achieved mostly at the expense of shortening the basic lecturing unit from 60 minutes down to 45 minutes and of getting rid of a single free day during the seminar. At the same time SOFSEM proceedings now appear as a volume in the Springer–Verlag series Lecture Notes in Computer Science. Also after the split of Czechoslovakia in 1993 it is still assumed that SOFSEM will continue to be held in either the Czech Republic or the Slovak Republic.

Thus, through its numerous invited papers and selected contributed papers as well as its excellent working atmosphere, the current SOFSEM is a mix of a winter school, a conference, and an advanced workshop. Driven by an international advisory board in reflecting the recent trends both in theory and practice, the current SOFSEM prolongs its tradition in striving for multidisciplinarity and generalizations in informatics. At the same time it intends to foster international co-operation among professionals working in various areas of computer science.

The present volume of proceedings contains 17 invited papers by renowned researchers and prominent academic professionals. These papers offer a unique opportunity to gain a comprehensive and up-to-date survey over the latest issues in selected areas of informatics such as parallel machine models, fuzzy logics, databases, and software engineering (tools and methods, parallel scientific computing, networked multimedia systems, and geographic information systems). The invited papers are accompanied by 22 contributed papers, selected from 52 submissions. They relate mostly to topics treated in the invited papers, thereby providing a still larger context. Rather than to specialists in any particular area, the proceedings are directed at computer professionals, researchers, and advanced students who hold an interest in the recent state, trends, and hot topics in the field of informatics.

We are grateful to the members of the Advisory Board for their proposals for the scientific program of SOFSEM'95. We also wish to thank everyone who submitted a paper for consideration, all Program Committee members for their meritorious work in evaluating the papers, as well as to all subreferees who assisted the Program Committee members in the selection process. We are deeply indebted to all authors of the invited papers and of the accepted contributed papers who prepared their manuscripts according to the specified guidelines with LNCS LATEX style.

Miroslav Bartošek and Lenka Motyčková, in their roles of SOFSEM'95 Program Committee Secretaries, deserve special thanks for their enormous help in the preparation of the present proceedings for publication.

Many thanks are due to the members of the Organizing Committee who did an excellent job in preparing and conducting SOFSEM'95, as usual. We regret to announce that Tomáš Havlát — our colleague, our friend, and the head of the Organizing Committee — died this summer at the age of 49 following a lengthy disease. Tom served as the chairperson of SOFSEM Organizing Committee for more than 10 years. He contributed significantly to the success of SOFSEM, and we will always acknowledge Tom's efforts.

We also thank all institutions that took part in organizing SOFSEM'95 and all sponsors who, through financial support, permitted the invited speakers and advanced students to participate.

Last, but not least, we want to thank Jan van Leeuwen, one of the editors of the LNCS series, for his trust in SOFSEM and the people around it. His involvement eventually led, for the first time, to the appearance of these proceedings as a volume in the Springer–Verlag LNCS series. The assistance of Springer–Verlag in the preparation of the volume is highly appreciated as well.

Brno, Prague, September 1995   Jan Staudek, Jiří Wiedermann

SOFSEM '95 :≡

Advisory Board:

Dines Bjørner	United Nations University, IIST, Macau
Peter van Emde Boas	University of Amsterdam, the Netherlands
Manfred Broy	Technical University Munich, Germany
Michal Chytil	Arthur D. Little Int., Prague, Czech Republic
Georg Gottlob	Technical University Vienna, Austria
Keith Jeffery	Rutherford Appleton Laboratory, Oxon, UK
Maria Zemánková	NSF, Washington DC, USA

Program Committe:

Chair:

Jan Staudek	Faculty of Informatics, Masaryk University, Brno
Jiří Wiedermann	Institut of Computer Science, Academy of Sciences of the Czech Republic, Prague

Secretary:

Miroslav Bartošek	Institute of Computer Science, MU Brno
Lenka Motyčková	Faculty of Informatics, Masaryk University, Brno

Members:

Jaroslav Král	Faculty of Informatics, Masaryk University, Brno
Jan Pavelka	Software Engineering Department, Charles University, Prague
František Plášil	Software Engineering Department, Charles University, Prague
Igor Prívara	Institute of Informatics and Statistics, Bratislava
Bronislav Rovan	Department of Computer Science, Comenius University, Bratislava
Jiří Zlatuška	Faculty of Informatics, Masaryk University, Brno

SOFSEM '95

organized by	Czech Society for Computer Science Slovak Society for Computer Science Czech ACM Chapter
in cooperation with	Faculty of Informatics, Masaryk University Brno Institute of Computer Science, MU Brno Department of Computer Science and Engineering, TU Brno Department of Computer Science, Comenius University, Bratislava Institute of Computer Science, Academy of Sciences of the Czech Republic, Prague
sponsored by	ApS Brno s.r.o. Arthur D.Little Digital Equipment s.r.o., Czech Republic Help Service s.r.o. Hewlett Packard s.r.o., Czech Republic IBM Czech Republic s.r.o. Oracle Czech s.r.o. Da-Lite Liesegang SOFTEC Bratislava

Organizing Committe   T. Havlát *(chair)*

J. Staudek *(vice-chair)*	Z. Malčík
Z. Walletzká *(secretary)*	P. Přikryl
Z. Botek	B. Rovan
P. Hanáček	J. Sochor
T. Hruška	P. Sojka
J. Kohoutková	T. Staudek

Contents

Invited Papers

FUNDAMENTALS

Parallel Machine Models: How They Are and Where Are They Going 1
  J. Wiedermann

Fuzzy Logic From the Logical Point of View 31
  P. Hájek

Sense of Direction in Processor Networks 50
  G. Tel

Welcoming the Super Turing Theories 83
  H.T. Siegelmann

What NARX Networks Can Compute 95
  B.G. Horne, H.T. Siegelmann, C.L. Giles

DATABASES

Database : Introduction to Problems 103
  K.G. Jeffery

Distributed Information Systems 120
  J. Grimson

Extending Database Technology 146
  N.W. Paton

SOFTWARE ENGINEERING

Introducing SSADM4+ and PRINCE 166
  A.J.G. Betts

Formal Methods in Practice: A Comparison of two Support Systems
for Proof 184
  J.C. Bicarregui, B.M. Matthews

Development of Safety-Critical Real-Time Systems 206
  H. Rischel, J. Cuellar, S. Mørk, A.P. Ravn, I. Wildgruber

Why Use Evolving Algebras for Hardware and Software Engineering? 236
  E. Börger

PARALLEL & DISTRIBUTED SYSTEMS, SCIENTIFIC COMPUTING

Experience with Chorus 272
  C. Bac, G. Bernard, D. Conan, Q.H. Nguyen, C. Taconet

High-Level Languages for Parallel Scientific Computing 292
  B. Chapman, P. Mehrotra, H.P. Zima

MULTIMEDIA, HYPERTEX

On Some New Aspects of Networked Multimedia Systems 315
  H. Maurer

Quo Vadis GIS: From GIS to GIMS and Open GIS 334
  A. Limpouch, K. Charvát

WWW – The World Wide Web 350
  V.A. Marshall

Contributed Papers

Implementation of Higher-Order Unification
Based on Calculus of Explicit Substitution 363
  P. Borovanský

A Modular History-Oriented Access Structure
for Bitemporal Relational Databases 369
  A. Cappelli, C. De Castro, M.R. Scalas

Software Engineering Meets Human-Computer Interaction: Integrating
User Interface Design in an Object-Oriented Methodology 375
  H.-W. Gellersen

Parsing of Free-Word-Order Languages 379
  T. Holan, V. Kuboň, M. Plátek

Distributed Algorithm for Finding a Core of a Tree Network 385
  E. Jennings

Stepwise Synthesis of Reactive Programs 391
  P. Kozák

A Simple and Efficient Incremental LL(1) Parsing 399
  W.X. Li

Fundamentals of Contex-Sensitive Rewriting 405
  S. Lucas

Constraint Logic Programming with Fuzzy Sets 413
  L. Matyska, H. Bureš

Parallel Processing of Image Database Queries 419
  F. Meunier, P. Zemánek

Maximum Flow Problem in Distributed Environment 425
  L. Motyčková

Fuzzy Set Theory and Medical Expert Systems: Survey and Model 431
  N.H. Phuong

The Fusion Object-Oriented Method: an Evaluation 437
  A. Pirotte, T. van den Berghe, E. Zimanyi

Integration of Object-Oriented Analysis and Algebraic Specifications 443
  Z. Repaská

On the Implementation of Some Residual
Minimizing Krylov Space Methods 449
  M. Rozložník, Z. Strakoš

A Formal Lazy Replication Regime for Spreading Conversion Functions
Over Objectbases 455
  C. Smith, C.A. Tau

Hopfield Languages 461
  J. Šíma

Inconsitency Conflict Resolution 469
  J. Štuller

A Methodology for Performance and Scalability Analysis 475
  E. Tambouris, P. van Santen

On the Efficiency of Superscalar and Vector Computer
for Some Problems in Scientific Computing 481
  M. Tůma, M. Rozložník

Logic Programming in RPL and RQL 487
  P. Vojtáš, L. Paulík

Recognition of Handwritten Characters
Using Instance-Based Learning Algorithms 493
  J. Žižka, I. Šnajdárková

Author Index   499

Parallel Machine Models:
How They Are and Where Are They Going

Jiří Wiedermann*

Institute of Computer Science
Academy of Sciences of the Czech Republic
Pod vodárenskou věží 2 , 182 07 Prague 8
Czech Republic
e–mail: wieder@uivt.cas.cz

Abstract. The practice of parallel computing seems to be in a crises. The parallel processing has not become a common matter and the "second computer revolution" that should have been caused by the replacement of sequential computers by parallel ones is not to happen in near future. The only hope for overcoming the parallel computing crisis lays in the development of computational complexity theory. This offers a good opportunity to survey the respective results and trends in this theory and to discuss its reactions to the changing needs, both, in theory and practice of parallel computing. To provide an adequate answer to the current parallel computing crisis, building on the top of the respective theory, the focus in computer science is currently shifting from purely theoretically motivated problems also towards more practical ones, determined by the potential of hardware technologies today. As a result, computer science is looking for the "right" model of a parallel computer — namely for such a model that would present a reasonable design framework for algorithmic problem solving, would be elegant enough from a mathematical viewpoint and, last but not least, would allow for an efficient hardware realization. Despite the rather extensive effort, only partial success can be reported thus far.

1 Introduction

1.1 Motivation

The fact that there have always been problems which cannot be solved even on the most powerful existing computer systems is a great challenge, both for computer science and computer technology.

Except for the undecidable problems without any algorithmic solutions the reason of practical unsolvability of other problems stems from the computational complexity of the underlying algorithms.

Even in cases in which the computational complexity of a problem grows relatively slowly along with the input size it is clear that for sufficiently large

* This research was supported by GA ČR Grant No. 201/95/0976 "HYPERCOMPLEX — Complexity Issues in High Performance Computing"

inputs we can always arrive at problem instances that cannot be solved in a reasonable amount of time (or space) on a given computer.

By increasing the computational speed of the underlying computing system, the computational complexity barrier can be overcome to some extend. Increasing the speed of elementary computing operations is a technological matter. Nevertheless, it is clear that a speed limit that cannot be surpassed exists for every computing technology. Even worse — there is an ultimate limit that cannot be surpassed by any technology whatever. It is given by the finite speed of signal transmission in physical media. In any real computing system a non–zero time is needed to transmit a signal between any two of its communicating parts (e.g., say between its input and output) and, moreover, this time depends linearly on the distance of these two parts. It is amusing to observe that from this simple consideration it follows that the faster a computer is the smaller it should be — the trend that can be readily observed by a naked eye in the recent development of sequential computers.

There is another possibility how to accelerate the computational speed of computational systems, even under the assumption of fixed speed of their components. This possibility is offered by parallelism. The idea of parallelism is very natural and very tempting. By enhancing the machine with several processors, we let it to perform more than one computational operation at a time in hopes that the larger the amount of parallelism involved the larger the speed up w.r.t the sequential case could be expected. In order to make the speed up really attractive from an asymptotical point of view it seems reasonable to allow that the number of operations, which are to be performed in parallel, can depend on the problem size. Providing that the problem at hand can be split into subproblems which can be solved independently — and hence also in parallel — there is a good chance that by making use of parallelism we could solve the problem faster.

The first ideas about building parallel computers have appeared soon after the first real sequential computers have been built. In spite of this, even after more than a half of a century of computer development, real parallel computers are still rare, expensive and idiosyncratic machines with a cumbersome programming tools, mostly used for very specific purposes. On the other hand, the investigation of parallelism presents a rich and increasingly flourishing field that consumes most of research capacities in complexity theory.

Confronted with such a paradoxical situation, some people start to speak about the crisis of parallel computing [17] and push as far as trying to blame computer science for a failure in this respect.

Are they right? In this paper we shall address this issue from the viewpoint of a respective part of computational complexity theory. We shall make the use of this opportunity in order to survey the related results and trends in the theory of parallel machine models so that we can illustrate how it is reacting to the changing needs, both, in the theory and the practice of parallel computing.

1.2 The Contents of the Paper

The main methodological approach of the paper will be to chronologically survey the development in the field of the theory of parallel machine models. This development is seen as a continuous interplay between the internal needs of the computational complexity theory on one hand and the external stimuli caused by the recent technological achievements on the other. At the same time this approach will offer the opportunity to screen the main representatives of existing abstract models of parallel computers in order to discuss their design motivations and to evaluate their contribution, both, to the theory as well as in the practice of parallel computing.

The degree of fulfillment of the three basic general requirements that any good abstract computer model should satisfy will be considered as the main criterion of a "quality" of the design of a machine model. These requirements will be specified in Section 2.

In Section 3, the basic theoretical complexity characterization of the family of sequential computers (so–called *first machine class*) will be briefly mentioned. It will serve as the basis for the subsequent comparison and characterization of the computational efficiency of theoretically very powerful class of parallel computers.

The respective class of idealized parallel computers — so–called *second machine class* — will be surveyed in Section 4.

In Section 5, it will be shown that the previous class of parallel machines is physically infeasible — i.e., their real models, operating with the performance assumed in the complexity theory, for arbitrary large inputs, cannot exist. This will be identified as the turning point of the theory at which its results and achievements have been re–evaluated and new goals have been set up. Also, this is the key point where the prevailing discrepancy between the best of the theory and of the present day practice starts.

In the next two sections two possible ways out of the trap of the physical infeasibility of parallel machines will be sketched.

The first of the two considers the impact of fundamental physical laws from an asymptotic point of view in which the size of processors and the speed of inter-processor communication approach their theoretical limits. The corresponding ultimate class of the so–called *scalable parallel machines*, which are physically feasible also in the asymptotic sense, will be introduced and characterized in Section 6.

The second way out of the two (a "practical one") is based on the assumption that, in practice, we do not process arbitrarily large inputs and that the performance characteristics of current parallel computers are still quite far from their theoretical limits. In such a situation the proof of the physical infeasibility of the respective machine fails. These ideas lead to the currently intensively investigated class of the so–called *realistic parallel machines* which will be discussed in Section 7.

Due to the limited size of the paper it cannot achieve its objectives as sketched above without severely restricting the level of detail in some places. This remark is concerned mainly with the description of machine models involved. The paper assumes some preliminary acquaintance with the fundamental machine models of, both, parallel and sequential computers, e.g., ones within the scope of basic courses in complexity theory. Therefore, the most of the commonly known models will be only briefly mentioned along with references to original papers. Only less known models or models of some specific interest will be described in more detail which will be vital for the sake of the discussion. As an excellent introductory paper, the chapter "Machine Models and Simulations" by Peter van Emde Boas, from the handbook [37] is highly recommended. A recent paper [51] by the present author can also be useful as a suitable preliminary reading.

2 Abstract Machine Models

In order to avoid any future misunderstandings when speaking about an abstract model of a computer, we shall implicitly assume that the model is always given by its *architecture*, by its *instruction repertoire* and by the related *complexity measures*. We shall not try to formalize the previous three notions. For our purposes, especially in connection with a concrete abstract computer model, they can be considered as self explanatory. We have mentioned these notions only because they enable us to stress that according to this point of view two models will be considered as different if they differ not only in their architecture. They will be considered as different also if they differ, e.g., in their respective complexity measures (think about two RAMs, one with a uniform cost measure and the other one with a logarithmic cost measure) or in their instruction repertoire (think again about two RAMs, one with the complete repertoire of arithmetic instructions, the other one with the same repertoire except for the instructions of multiplication and division that are missing).

Now we shall formulate certain informal necessary and sufficient conditions which any reasonable abstract model of a general purpose computer should simultaneously satisfy in order to be considered as the "right" model:

(i) the "programming language" associated with the respective instruction repertoire should present a natural conceptual framework for the design and development of algorithms

(ii) from a mathematical point of view it should be simple and elegant enough, equipped with complexity measures that would allow for a complexity analysis of the respective algorithms

(iii) it should enable its efficient hardware realization in such a way that the complexity analysis of the respective algorithms, as implied by the abstract model, would correspond to its performance on the hardware model.

The first condition ensures, in a sense, that the model can also serve well in supporting the *software model* in which the algorithms can be implemented.

The second condition ensures that the model could be formalized with the help of a standard mathematical apparatus, and that the resulting formal model will not be too cumbersome. It should be amenable for further formal treatment, e.g., for program correctness proofs or for complexity analysis of related algorithms.

The last condition assumes that the model is realistic, i.e., is physically feasible — the corresponding real incarnation of the model exists.

Thus, the first and the last condition assure a certain practicability of the model while the second one opens the possibility of formal and rigorous treatment of the related matters, and, hence, for building a meaningful theory related to the model at hand.

Note that in formulating the above prerequisites, the "mode" of computation, whether sequential or parallel, was not mentioned at all.

3 Models of Sequential Computers

3.1 Fundamental Models of Sequential Computers

When trying to speak about general pros and cons of parallelism, the only reasonable way seems to be offered by its comparison to sequential computing. For the sake of the subsequent discussion and also for inspiration we shall briefly review the situation in the field of sequential computing.

A prime example of a sequential computer model is the *random access machine* — RAM, as it was introduced by Cook and Reckhow in 1973 [10]. Let us see how this model performs w.r.t. the three above mentioned "reasonability" criteria.

Clearly, any common "sequential" programming language enables to write programs that can be translated into the sequence of RAM instructions straightforwardly. The complexity of such a program can be analyzed in terms of cost of individual RAM instructions and there are no doubts that the resulting efficiency estimates correspond well with the performance of real programs which are implemented on real instances of von Neumann computers.

This is also the reason why a RAM presents a paradigmatic instance of a sequential computer against which the efficiency of all other sequential computer models is compared.

The situation is somewhat different with another model of a sequential computer, namely with a Turing machine. This model can be by no means considered a practical and realistic model: nobody will seriously think about designing practical algorithms for such a machine (but for the exception see [30]), and nobody will really be interested in its hardware realization (although some early computers with a small internal memory and with tape units in place of external memory resembled the Turing machine quite closely). Nevertheless, nobody would deny that the Turing machine presents a very elegant mathematical model of computation that, *in principle*, can be implemented easily.

3.2 The First Machine Class

What makes the models of RAMs and Turing machines almost equally interesting from the viewpoint of computer science is their equivalence as far as the efficiency of computation is concerned. It is a well known fact that these two models, equipped with proper complexity measures, can simulate each other with only a polynomial lost in time efficiency and linear lost in space efficiency.

Based on this observation, Slot and van Emde Boas have formulated the notion of the so–called *first machine class*, which is denoted as C_1 and consists of deterministic Turing machines and of all machines that satisfy the following invariance thesis:

Definition 3.1 (Invariance Thesis, [32]) *Reasonable machines simulate each other with polynomially bounded overhead in time and with constant factor overhead in space (both simulations involved can be mutually different).*

The introduction of this class has had a far reaching methodological consequence on the complexity theory. First, it has characterized, in theoretical complexity terms, the class of computers of which all can be considered as reasonable models of sequential computers. Second, it has shown that the well known hierarchy of fundamental complexity classes, originally derived from Turing machine complexity,

$$LOGSPACE \subseteq PTIME \subseteq PSPACE \subseteq EXPTIME \subseteq EXPSPACE \ldots$$

is in fact machine independent since it captures the efficiency properties that are shared by all machines within the first machine class.

In order to achieve this effect, the ingenious idea was to insist on mutually polynomial time and linear space simulation of machines within C_1. This ensures that both polynomial (and higher) time complexity classes and also $LOGSPACE$ are invariant w.r.t. all models in C_1. By the way, proving that a RAM with the logarithmic cost space measure can be simulated in linear space by a TM depends heavily on the way how this measure is defined for the RAM at hand. For the detailed discussion of this problem see [32] and [46]. For the currently best simulations among TMs and RAMs, see [22], [43], [50].

4 Idealized Models of Parallel Computers

4.1 Designing Parallel Computer Models

It is to be expected that when looking for a reasonable model of a parallel computer the experience from the realm of sequential computations would be helpful. After all, since sequential models are but a special case of parallel ones, one may expect that by a suitable generalization of the former ones one can arrive at useful models of the latter ones. Indeed, this was the avenue taken by early pioneers of research in complexity theory during the seventies when practically no real parallel computers existed.

The two basic ideas were either to consider a number of processors and let them somehow cooperate in solving a common task or to allow one "smart" processor to manipulate arbitrary large structured entities within a single computational step.

Nevertheless, when thinking more thoroughly about the realization of this idea, several crucial problems arise. How will the processors communicate? What should be their computational power? How shall we escape the influence of the finite speed of light on the computational efficiency of the resulting parallel computers? And, once answering the former questions, most naturally by providing a certain abstract model (or set of models), we may ask further concrete questions concerning those models. What will be the computational efficiency of the resulting models? What will be the class of problems amenable for solving on such models? Will the resulting models preserve complexity class hierarchy in the same way as the sequential machine did?

Thus, finding the right abstract model of a parallel computer, or a couple of such models, seems to be the key to the investigation of the benefits and the limits of parallelism.

4.2 A Quick Tour to Parallel Machine Models

The large design space for parallel computer modelling which is offered by additional dimensions of the problem, namely by the number of processors, their computational power and the way they communicate, has lead to the explosion of parallel machine model proposals. Nowadays we know, from literature, tens of parallel machine models that differ mainly in their architectural features. Next, we shall briefly review the basic representatives of these machines just to illustrate the variety of possible architectures of such models. It is quite difficult to introduce something other than "genealogical" taxonomy into the plethora of parallel machine models. This taxonomy is based on the similarity of parallel models to their sequential relatives. Therefore, we shall next distinguish among parallel machine models that appear to be the generalizations of a RAM model (SUPERRAMs and parallel RAMs), Turing machines (alternating and synchronous TMs) and combinatorial circuits (conglomerates, neural networks, etc.).

Parallelized RAMs

SUPERRAMs. Under this generic name we shall understand the class of parallel machines that retain the features of (sequential) RAM family computers. The difference being that in a single computational step they manipulate arbitrarily large data objects, vectors or (integer) numbers.

The vector manipulating machines are equipped for this purpose by a set of instructions allowing the transfer of the vectors from the given memory address to the accumulator and vice versa. Also, there is a set of operations defined over vectors. The vectors can be either *Boolean*, as in the *vector machine* designed by Pratt and Stockmayer [28], or have integer components, as in the *Array Processing Machine* designed by van Leeuwen and Wiedermann [38]. The effect of parallelism is thus achieved by allowing the operations over all off the (or over only suitably selected) components of a vector in parallel in a single computational step. From the programming point of view, this calls for a special approach in which the task at hand must be solved solely in terms of vector operations. The vectors should be as long as possible in order to make efficient use of parallelism. However, this is quite natural in many cases (e.g., in problems in linear algebra), while in others it is somewhat cumbersome (e.g., in sorting).

A special position among SUPERRAMs is taken by the so–called *arithmetic RAM — ARAM* by Bertoni et al [2]. Formally, ARAM is equal to an ordinary, unit cost RAM with a complete set of all four basic arithmetic operations $(+, -, \times, :)$. Hence, the effect of parallelism is hidden here in allowing the realization of arithmetic operations over arbitrary large integers in unit time. It goes without saying that, except for certain numerical algorithms, the realization of parallel algorithms in this way is very unnatural. Therefore, ARAM should be considered rather as a proof that RAM with a unit cost presents, in fact, a very powerful parallel computer, or curiosity, rather than a serious attempt to design a viable model of a parallel machine.

The last interesting example that we shall mention here is presented by the so–called EDITRAM proposed by Peter van Emde Boas et al. [33], [37]. It is in fact a model of an idealized word processor that can, in a single computational step, perform any operation over (text) files that editors usually provide such as appending or splitting files, inserting/deleting new symbols into/from files, systematic replacing of a given pattern by an other one, etc. After seeing the previous models, it is probably no longer surprising that also this model can be seen as an efficient universal parallel computer.

Parallel RAMs. Parallel RAMs present a family of parallel machine models that is created by a set of cooperating ordinary RAMs. Parallel RAMs appear basically in two different variants depending on the way in which these "local RAMs" cooperate.

In the basic model, called originally SIMDAG (i.e., Single Instruction, Multiple Data, Global Memory) by L. Goldschlager in [18], the individual RAMs are indexed by natural numbers. There is one central processor that in each parallel step is issuing instructions for the first k local RAMs (the value of k may be changed during the computation). In each parallel step the same instruction is issued for all RAMs. This instruction can be realized either over the local RAM memory, or can ask for a read from, or a write to, a common global memory that is also realized as a potentially infinite array. Since the local RAMs have access to their own indices, they are able to address different parts of the global memory.

Consequently, although all processors realize the same instructions, it can be carried out over different operands. Therefore, according to the so–called Flynn's classification [16] one speaks of a SIMD (Single Instruction, Multiple Data) machine.

The next variant of a parallel RAM is represented by Savitch and Stimson's model of a *parallel recursive RAM* (PRRAM) [29]. When a function or procedure call is encountered during a PRRAM computation, a special RAM dedicated solely to the execution of this call can be activated. Without waiting for the results of the call, the original computation can go on as the subordinate RAM reports the results of its computations along with their finishing time back to the calling RAM. In this way one can achieve a parallel realization of different instructions by different RAMs and, therefore, according to Flynn's classification mentioned above the resulting device is a typical MIMD (Multiple Instruction, Multiple Data) machine.

At the present a single generic model seems to have emerged out of the two previously mentioned earlier parallel RAM models. This generic model is known under the name *Parallel RAM* (PRAM) and is inspired by the most natural intuitive idea regarding the operational capabilities of an ideal "mental" (as Papadimitriou put it nicely in [25]) parallel computer. PRAM consists of several independent sequential processors, each one equipped with its own private memory. They communicate with one another through a global memory. In one unit of time each processor can read one global or local memory location, execute a single RAM operation or write into one global or local memory location. It can appear either as a SIMD, or a MIMD machine.

It is assumed that all processors work synchronously, performing any operation in a unit time.

Nevertheless, without any further provisions it may very well happen that two or more processors of a PRAM try to access the same global memory cell. If this is allowed both for read and write instructions we speak about *Concurrent Read, Concurrent Write PRAM* — a CRCW–PRAM. All other combinations of concurrent/exclusive read/write PRAMs have been studied in the literature and they all differ to some extend as far as their efficiency in solving some (classes of) problems is concerned.

A PRAM presents a very flexible and natural tool for designing parallel programs and most of the programs described in the literature are designed for PRAMs of this type [21]. Nevertheless, as we shall see in Section 5, the assumption on "instant" access of any processor to any global memory address, not speaking of concurrent accesses, is an unrealistic one from an engineering point of view. In fact there are no real counterparts of these machines known to be in operation.

Parallelized Turing Machines

Alternating Turing Machines. An Alternating Turing Machine (ATM) [6] differs from the standard model of a nondeterministic Turing machine by allowing the machine to enter, besides nondeterministic (i.e., *existential*) states, also the so-called *universal states*. While in an existential state, the machine has to make a choice from several possible continuations of its computation. The continuation chosen has to lead into an accepting state. In a universal state the alternating machine proceeds differently. It creates as many copies of itself as is the number of possible continuations of its computations from the configuration at hand and each copy follows one of the possible computational paths. However, this time all paths must lead into an accepting state. The time complexity of an accepting computation is defined as the depth of the respective computation tree which emerges in the course of a computation (one takes a minimum over all accepting trees of maxima over all inputs of length n, of course). The space complexity is given by the space complexity of the largest configuration encountered during the accepting computation.

When, during a computation, an ATM changes its state from an existential one to a universal one, or vice versa, we say that an *alternation* has been performed. In general, an ATM can perform an arbitrary number of alternations during its computation. Since ATMs are generalizations of standard nondeterministic TMs, they are well suited to be compared with the latter machines via mutual simulations. Thus, from computational complexity point of view they present a natural theoretical tool for the investigation of a computational power and efficiency of parallel machines. In this respect, alternating machines with bounded number of alternations are studied as well and their study leads to a better understanding of the nature of parallel computations [20].

Obviously, since it is the case with nondeterministic TMs in general, ATMs do not represent a realistic model of a parallel computer. For instance, it is not clear at all what would be the right definition of the "hardware" complexity in this case [9].

Synchronized TMs. Synchronized TMs are further generalizations of ATMs. They have been introduced, both, simultaneously and independently by two authors — J. Hromkovič and J. Wiedermann [19], [45]. Their idea was to enhance the computational abilities of ATMs by allowing a restricted kind of communication among the processors during a computation and to see whether the resulting machines will obtain more computational power this way. Although completely different mechanisms for the implementation of such a communication have been proposed by the above authors, it turned out that the resulting machines were equivalent as far as their computational power and time and space efficiency was concerned. It has been shown that these machines make optimal use of their space [13], [45] — any $S(n)$ space bounded computation of any nondeterministic TM can be performed in space $O(\log S(n))$ by an STM. Moreover, any $O(T(n))$ time bounded computation of an STM can be performed in space $O(\log T(n))$ by a machine of the same type.

The previous results also point to a certain robustness of the notion of synchronousness since they hold for both kinds of STMs at the same time.

Networks of Machines

Networks of machines are models of parallel machines that consist of a number of processors that are connected by a connection network with a fixed topology. Thus, there is no global memory and therefore these models seem to be closer to reality because information is being exchanged along "wires". The individual models within this category differ not only w.r.t. to the topology of the underlying network but also by the computational power of their respective processors.

At the one end of the respective spectrum we have machines consisting of RAMs connected by certain kind of "uniform" graphs (i.e., graphs that can be generated by a TM in a polynomial time). The processors communicate with each other via exchanging the appropriate messages along the graph edges in a constant time per unit message per edge traversal. It seems a good idea to have graphs with a small diameter that would allow for fast communication between any two processors. Further, in order to allow many processors to communicate in parallel, there should not be "bottlenecks" in the graphs through which all messages should pass (like in trees where a lot of messages should pass via its root). Therefore the *hypercubes, cube connected cycles, shuffle exchange networks* and even *random graphs* have been proposed and studied in place of communication graphs [21], [40].

At the other end of the spectrum of parallel network machines are networks with very simple processors.

For instance, the uniform families of standard combinatorial circuits, when computing in a synchronized parallel mode, also represent a class of universal parallel devices [9]. This is an important result showing that from practical point of view parallel computers can be built from the same "components" as sequential computers.

Dymond [14] has studied the class of finite automata networks called *hardware modification machine*. They were able to change the interconnection topology during a computation. Nevertheless, their efficiency is comparable to that of previously mentioned combinatorial circuits.

Last but not least, the (uniform) networks of bounded and unbounded degree which consist of *discrete neurons* have also been investigated [26], [49] in this context.

4.3   The Second Machine Class

Fortunately for the theory it soon appeared that in spite of their different appearance, all previously mentioned parallel machine models — with the exception of unbounded degree (neural) networks — have about the same computational efficiency. They all represent universal parallel computers that are polynomially time equivalent. The respective family of parallel computers is nowadays known as the so–called *second machine class* [37]. It does not matter which of the previous models we take as the "basic" one in the following definition of the respective machine class. In our case the ATM has been chosen because of its simplest formal definition (cf. the fundamental paper about ATMs [6]) and for the consistency with the definition of the first machine class (see Section 3.2):

Definition 4.1 (The Second Machine Class) *The second machine class C_2 consists of all machine models that are polynomially time equivalent to the Alternating Turing Machine.*

The polynomial time equivalency within the C_2 can be proven by direct simulations of the respective machines. An example of such a simulation can be found, e.g., in [38]. In a similar way it can be proven that all parallel machine models mentioned in Section 4.2 belong to the second machine class.

The Parallel Computation Thesis

An immediate question is, of course, how do we know that $C_1 \neq C_2$? The answer is somewhat surprising because in fact, we do not know! To see the reasons we have to compare the computational power of the machines within C_1 with those within C_2. An interesting relationship manifests itself here. Namely, it appears that the respective machine classes are neatly related as stated in the following theorem.

Theorem 4.1 *The class of space bounded computations on the first machine class is polynomially related to the class of time bounded computations on the second class machines.*

From historical reasons this theorem is sometimes called the *"parallel computation thesis"* (PCT) [18]. Thus, the PCT formally translates into the equality //PTIME=PSPACE by denoting the class of problems solvable on the second class machines in (parallel) polynomial time as //PTIME. It follows that we do not know for sure whether $C_1 \neq C_2$, since in theory we do not know whether PTIME$\neq$PSPACE. Thus, $C_1 = C_2$ iff PTIME=PSPACE.

Providing that PTIME$\neq$PSPACE, as it is generally assumed, C_2 represents a class of very powerful machines that can solve any PSPACE–complete (and hence any PTIME–complete) problem in polynomial time.

Note also that it follows from the validity of the PCT for any two different parallel machines that the machines at hand are polynomially time related.

Proving Membership to C_2. The best way to see where the source of a great computational efficiency of the second class machines comes from and what is the price that must be paid for such an efficiency is offered by the investigation of the respective simulation proof of the previous theorem. Although the simulations involved depend heavily on the specific machines that are simulating each other, the main ideas can be distilled out in a less formal way as seen from the following sketch of the respective simulations.

Fast Parallel Simulation of Sequential Space. In proving the validity of the inclusion PSPACE$\subseteq$//PTIME, for the sake of definiteness we shall describe the simulation of a $p(n)$ space bounded computation of an (in general nondeterministic) TM M_1, for an arbitrary polynomial $p(n)$, by an arbitrary PRAM–like second class machine M_2. At the same time this simulation will demonstrate that at least M_2 does really belong to C_2 and hence, $C_2 \neq \emptyset$.

The course of a computation of M_1 on a given input of length n can be viewed with the help of a computational tree T. The initial configuration of M_1 finds itself in the root of T, while the configurations reachable in a single move are recorded in all of its subsequent offsprings. Some (or all) paths in this tree are either infinite or else they end in accepting states at a certain depth.

Clearly, since the computation of M_1 is $p(n)$ space bounded, there are at most $D(n) = c^{p(n)}$ of different configurations which can be represented in the given space for a suitable constant c. Hence, w.l.o.g. we can restrict the depth of T to D(n) since some accepting states must be reached within this depth if at all.

The aim of the simulating machine M_2 is to discover whether there is at least one accepting computational path in T.

To do it efficiently, M_2 in a divide–and–conquer manner, in (parallel) time $O(p(n))$ initializes with zeros a $D(n) \times D(n)$ Boolean matrix G in which rows and columns correspond to all $p(n)$ space bounded configurations of M_1. The respective configurations are sorted lexicographically.

Then, again in parallel, making use of $D^2(n)$ of its processors, M_2 inspects all pairs of configurations of form (c_i, c_j) and writes a 1 into those entries of G for which c_j follows from c_i (denoted as $c_i \vdash c_j$) (or vice versa) in zero or one computational step of M_1.

In this way the graph of T is represented in G by the matrix of incident vertices. Now the idea is to compute the transitive closure of G to see whether there are some paths in T connecting its root with some accepting configuration.

This is again done in parallel with the help of $D^3(n)$ processors. All triples of form (c_i, c_j, c_k) of configuration of M_1 are fetched, each by extra processor of M_2 and it is verified whether $c_i \vdash c_j$ and simultaneously $c_j \vdash c_k$. In the positive case a 1 is written in the entry corresponding to the pair (c_i, c_k). This step is repeated $p(n)$ times.

Clearly, at the end of this procedure the transitive closure of T is represented in G, since after each parallel step to each path of length 2 in G the respective "shortcut" of length 1 is also added to G.

To see whether there was a path from the root to some accepting configuration of M_1, it is enough to inspect, in parallel, all of the pairs of configurations in G and to see whether there is a 1 in the respective entries.

Thus, M_2 is indeed capable to simulate the computation of M_2 in a polynomial time $O(p(n))$ using up to $c^{3p(n)}$ processors. To store and verify the respective configurations in each processor space of order $O(p(n))$ is needed. Nevertheless, the size of the global memory is $c^{2p(n)}$. Moreover, note that there are no access conflicts in the previous algorithm and that the matrix G is simultaneously accessed by at most $c^{3p(n)}$ processors. Thus the *bandwidth* of the parallelism is $O(c^{3p(n)})$.

Simulating Parallel Machines in Small Sequential Space. The proof of the inclusion //PTIME$\subseteq$ PSPACE seems to be more involved that the previous proof of the opposite inclusion. Therefore, we shall merely sketch its basic idea.

As it is seen, e.g., from the previous simulation, the problem here is that due to space reasons in the sequential machine C_1 machine M_1 (think, e.g., about a RAM) we cannot afford to represent the whole contents of the global memory and of all local memories of a C_2 machine M_2 (of a PRAM, say) in a given moment. Thus, we have to give up the idea of simulating one parallel step of M_2 after the other by making use of instantaneous description of the whole machine M_2. Rather, we shall simulate all actions of each PRAM processor, one by one. In general, to simulate in the t–th step of M_2 a specific instruction of the i–th processor of M_2 that accesses the global memory word x_j and the local memory word y_k, say, we have to know the contents of these particular words in time t. These contents are computed with the help of the two recursive procedures $GLOBAL(x_j, t)$ and $LOCAL(i, x_k, t)$. The respective procedures compute the required values recursively from the values of the corresponding variables in time $t - 1$ that are combined according to the instruction at hand. When the time complexity of the parallel machine is $T(n)$ then the depth of the recursion is bounded by $T(n)$ and therefore all of the necessary computations can be done in space polynomial in $T(n)$. The time complexity of this simulation is exponential w.r.t. $T(n)$.

4.4 The Complexity Class NC

While the PCT postulates a great theoretical efficiency of C_2 machines, the respective simulations proving membership to C_2 also reveal their weakness. The weakness is a high price which must be paid for their efficiency in terms of hardware complexity. Clearly, an exponential number of processors is unacceptable by even stronger arguments that are used against the computations of exponential time complexity. To build a machine with an exponential number of processors requires an exponential effort and an exponential space. While in operation the resulting machine consumes (and dissipates) an exponential amount of energy. Therefore the whole class //PTIME is infeasible (also because of its equality with PSPACE) and one should look for some of its subsets that could be feasible.

A good idea might be to consider the class of problems from //PLOGTIME. This is the class of problems whose time complexity on C_2 machines is of polylogarithmic time complexity (i.e., of complexity $O(\log^k n)$, for a fixed $k > 0$). Such a class would be interesting since it would capture the class of problems that on C_2 machines could be solved substantially faster than C_1 machines.

Unfortunately, solving some problems from this class on C_2 machines could still require more than a polynomial number of processors since $c^{\log^k n}$ grows faster than a polynomial. Therefore, the condition requiring a polynomial number of processors must also be included in the definition of the complexity class of problems feasible for C_2 machines.

The resulting complexity class of problems that are solvable on C_2 machines satisfying simultaneously both previous conditions is known as class NC (for a more exact definition, cf. [9] or [21]).

Thus, the class NC can be viewed as the class of problems that admit the efficient parallel solution within C_2. It contains many important algorithms. Among them there are, for example, the basic arithmetic operations, the transitive closure and the Boolean matrix multiplication, the computation of the determinant, the rank or inverse of a matrix, the integer sorting, etc. [21].

Clearly, NC⊆PTIME, since sequential simulation of one parallel step of an NC computation requires only polynomial time and there is a polylogarithmic number of these steps to be simulated. We do not know whether NC=PTIME. The positive answer to this question would mean that all problems within PTIME that are considered to be sequentially feasible, would also be efficiently parallelizable within C_2. The least likely candidates from P for the membership in NC are P–complete problems (cf. [21]).

It is possible to introduce a hierarchy within the class NC [20]. For instance, circuits with unbounded fan–in and fan–out of polynomial size and of constant depth present a very attractive subclass of computing devices within NC that are the subjects of a very vivid recent research.

The practical importance of NC algorithms will be discussed in Section 7.3.1 and 7.4.

Also other, less restrictive parallel complexity classes than NC have been proposed and studied. The idea is not to force the number of processors to be unreasonable large (i.e., exponential) w.r.t. to the parallel computational time and to be be happy with *any* nontrivial speed up. For instance, in [42] the class $\mathcal{PC}$ consisting of those problems from PTIME that can be speeded up by more than a constant factor by use of parallelism has been introduced. A similar stronger class is the class $\mathcal{PC}^*$ in which the speed up is linearly proportional to the number of processors. Surprisingly, it has been shown in [42] that the previous classes contain some problems that are known to be P–complete and thus considered as not parallelizable ones (e.g., path systems accessibility and related problems).

5 The Physical Infeasibility of the Idealized Machine Models

Shortly after the appearance of the first models from C_2 results pointing to physical infeasibility of the related models have appeared. These result are specifying that it is impossible to build realistic parallel machine models whose asymptotic performance would match the theoretical performance of the C_2 machines.

The respective results have been inspired by recent (in those times) progress in computer technology — namely by VLSI (Very Large Scale Integration) technology. The miniaturization and the density of computing elements on a single chip have approached their limits when the size of semiconductor elements, their switching time, the length and the thickness of wires started to play a crucial role in the performance of resulting devices [23]. On such a technological scale one must at least count on the finite speed of signal propagation along the wires and on a certain lower bound on the minimal volume that any processor must occupy. Under such assumptions, no matter how tightly we pack n processors into a spherical body, its diameter would be of the order of $n^{1/3}$. This means that there must be processors at about the same distance and thus, the communication between such pairs of processors will take the time proportional to $n^{1/3}$.

This result immediately says that in reality an exponential number of processors cannot be activated in polynomial time, as it was the case in the proof of PSPACE$\subseteq$//PTIME. Unless PTIME=PSPACE, the parallel computation thesis cannot be fulfilled by any real machine. From this point of view the class NC is also not well defined.

Thus, the class $\mathcal{C}_2$ seems to be doomed to remain just a class of interesting mathematical objects with a computational behaviour that cannot be realized in practice. Hence their alternative name *"idealized computers"*.

Providing only a fixed degree of the underlying communication graph, under similar assumptions as above it has even been proven that asymptotically any realistic three–dimensional parallel machine of time complexity $T(n)$ can be simulated by a multitape TM in time $T^8(n)$ [7]. The idea of the corresponding simulation is astonishingly simple.

First of all observe that due to our assumptions there are approximately $T^3(n)$ processors in our parallel machine. On its tapes the TM represents an adjacency matrix of the communication graph of the parallel machine to be simulated as well as the memory configuration of the respective processors. In this way, it can simulate one parallel step by a series of sequential steps, appropriately updating the configurations of all processors which in the given parallel step communicate with the processor at hand, for each processor. To do so, it must traverse the communication graph represented on its (linear) tapes in which the distance between any two processors is of order $O(T^3(n))$. Updating the respective configurations also requires traversing over all of $O(T^3(n))$ configurations, each of them being of size $O(T(n))$. Since in one parallel step all of $O(T^3(n))$ processors can communicate with a fixed number of their neighbours the simulation of one parallel step takes time $O(T^7(n))$. The final result will be obtained when all of $T(n)$ parallel steps are simulated by the TM.

Thus, w.r.t. the first machine class at most polynomial asymptotical speedup can be achieved by any parallel machine obeying the fundamental physical laws. This certainly comes as a bad news.

The understanding that in order for the models of parallel machines to be realistic they must faithfully reflect the basic physical laws has brought the respective theory to the reevaluation of its results and goals.

First of all, in the theory of machine models the class $\mathcal{C}_2$ has started to play a similar role as the completeness results do in the field of algorithms design. The membership of some machine model in this class can be interpreted as an infeasibility result concerning the model at hand. Nevertheless, this does not mean that the respective parallel algorithms, especially in the class NC, have entirely lost their value. They still present a valuable reservoir of basic ideas, tricks and techniques that can be used in the design of parallel algorithms for realistic models of parallel computers (see the discussion in Section 7.3.1).

Subsequently, within the parallel machine models the new field of research has been opened targeting the design and study of realistic parallel machine models. On one hand, they should be physically feasible and on the other hand, they should still be substantially faster than sequential machines, albeit not necessarily in the asymptotic sense.

The respective development will be discussed in the next two sections.

6 The Ultimate Parallel Machines

6.1 Scalable Parallel Machines

Scalable parallel machines are abstract machine models that take into consideration, very seriously, the ultimate impact of fundamental physical limitations to computations, as was already mentioned in Section 5. Thus, their performance must be tightly related to the performance of realistic, physically buildable machines that obviously are obeying the restrictions resulting from physical laws.

Definition 6.1 *A family $\mathcal{F}$ of abstract computational devices $\{\mathcal{F}_n\}_{n\geq 1}$, with time complexity measure $T_F(n)$, where each $\mathcal{F}_n$ is capable of processing any input of size n, is called* scalable *if there exist such a physical realization $\mathcal{R} = \{\mathcal{R}_n\}_{n\geq 1}$ of $\mathcal{F}$ that for each n the maximal duration of any computational step (measured in any real unit of time) on $\mathcal{R}_n$ is of order $O(T_F(n))$. In the case of $T_F(n) = O(1)$ we speak about* strict scalability.

Intuitively, the notion of scalability captures the requirement that parallel machines of arbitrary size (i.e., those capable to process arbitrary long inputs) can be considered and that there will always exist their physical realization, preserving their time complexity measure.

Examples of strictly scalable machines include cellular automata [3], systolic machines [47], space machines [15] and multitape or multihead TMs [50].

Surprisingly, a RAM with a logarithmic cost is not scalable since the access to its first $S(n)$ registers of size $O(\log S(n))$ each requires time of order $\Omega(\sqrt{S(n)}\log S(n))$ when the memory is laid down in the two dimensional plane and cannot be done in time $O(log S(n))$ as the logarithmic criterion assumes.

It has been shown elsewhere that communication structures used in the design of second class machines — like hypercubes, binary trees, cube connected cycles, butterflies, etc., cf. [35], are not strictly scalable. Despite the low topological diameter of the respective graphs, in any physical realization of them in two dimensions, there will always appear an edge of length of at least $\Omega(\sqrt{n}/\log n)$. This destroys the assumption on the unit cost of communication along the edges of the underlying graphs [39]. This is true even for random graphs with a low diameter [40].

The conclusion from all of the above negative results is that practically the only strictly scalable structures are orthogonal meshes. Other similar scalable graph structures like tridiagonal or hexagonal meshes can be emulated in real time on orthogonal meshes. Presently there is a common consensus that mesh–connected architectures may be the ultimate solution for interconnecting the extremely large computer complexes of the future [39], [3]. Indeed, some recent proposals of realistic parallel machine models are based just on these ideas (see Section 7.4).

6.2 Weak Parallel Machines

The computational efficiency of scalable parallel machines in relation to classes $\mathcal{C}_1$ and $\mathcal{C}_2$ has been investigated by the present author in [44] and [47]. A so–

called *parallel Turing machine* (PTM) has been proposed as a representative of the respective strictly scalable machines.

This machine looks like a nondeterministic multitape TM. However, its computational behaviour is different. Initially, the machine starts in the initial configuration as any TM. When, during its computation the PTM enters a configuration from which $d > 1$ next moves are possible, it multiplies the number of its finite control units (including the respective heads). It then creates d identical "copies" of them (the so–called processors of a PTM). Then each of the d processors executes a different move from altogether d different moves that are to be performed, *still working on the same tape contents.* Further on each processor behaves independently. Combinatorial arguments can demonstrate that during a computation of length $T(n)$ at the most a polynomial number (in $T(n)$) of different processors can emerge.

Thus, starting with a single processor a PTM can repeatedly create new processors that all compute over the same tapes. An input is accepted when all processors enter into accepting states.

The author of this model has shown that a single–tape PTM is strictly scalable or, as he has expressed it, is physically feasible — in real time it can simulate any VLSI–like circuit obeying the physical laws and vice versa. It is linearly time equivalent to any strictly scalable machine model that we have mentioned in this section. From the computational point of view, it can serve as a joint representative of all these models.

The key idea in the discovery of the true computational power of PTMs and of all other similar devices, lies in making use of their limited polynomial parallelism for processing of not only a single input but rather of *a sequence of inputs.* It appears that the main difference between these machines and the first class machines is that the former can be programmed to process any sequence of inputs of the same size to the same problem in a *pipelined manner.* For this purpose, the machines must be equipped with an input mechanism which ensures that after reading for example the k–th bit of an input the k–th bit of the *next input* can be read for all of $1 \le k \le n$. Thus, several inputs in parallel can be read at the same time. Moreover, there must be some output mechanism that prints the results which correspond with individual inputs. The PTM equipped with such an input and output mechanism is called a *pipelined PTM.*

For these particular machines the *period* of a computation can be defined as the time elapsed between starting the reading of the i–th input and printing the corresponding answer (as usual, we take the maximum over all inputs of the given length).

Let PERIOD(F(n)) be the class of all problems that can be solved by a pipelined single–tape PTM within the period of F(n), let PPERIOD be the class of all problems that can be solved on the same machine with a polynomial period. In [44] it was shown that PPERIOD=PSPACE, i.e., polynomially space bounded computations of TMs are equivalent with polynomially period bounded computations of single–tape pipelined PTMs. This may be appropriately called the *pipelined computation thesis.* From the parallel computation thesis it follows that PPERIOD$=//$PTIME. Thus, the class of computational devices that are equivalent to single–tape pipelined PTMs (i.e., the class of strictly scalable machines) is in a interesting way, via the period of the computation, polynomially related both to the first and the second machine class. In [47] the respective machine class satisfying the pipelined computation thesis is also called the class of *weakly parallel machines*.

As a matter of fact, it has been shown in [47] that while a nonpipelined version of a single–tape PTM belongs to C_1, the nonpipelined version of a multitape PTM does not belong to C_1 because it is not linearly space equivalent to a TM. It also does not belong to C_2 since it can achieve at most a polynomial speedup w.r.t. a DTM. The latter machine is also not strictly scalable.

For an overview of all known results about PTMs see the paper [47].

7 Realistic Parallel Machines

7.1 Motivation

As it was to be expected, soon after the appearance of the first commercially available parallel computers during the eighties, it turned out publicly that most of the new computers have little in common with their would–be abstract models from C_2.

There was perhaps one early honourable exception – viz. *Array Processing Machine* (APM) mentioned in Section 4.3 that has been developed in 1984 by van Leeuwen and Wiedermann. Its development has been inspired by existing array, or vector, processors ("number crunchers" as the respective machines have been called in those times). The aim was to design a parallel machine model that would play a similar role in C_2 as RAM does in C_1. In [38] it was shown that APM with a unit cost measure does belong to C_2. Nevertheless, with the proper cost measure that would reflect the lengths of vectors to be processed, the APM starts to be a realistic model of vectorized parallel computers that make an intensive use of pipelining in realizing the vector operations. With the latter cost measure the APM seems to be the only realistic model of parallel computers that is oriented towards vector processing, known until now.

But for most of the real parallel computers it appeared that in striving for the mathematical and programming elegance, the abstract models from the second class have been based on a gross oversimplification of physical reality. As a result, parallel algorithms designed for abstract models could not be straightforwardly implemented on real computers. Since the performance parameters of real parallel computers did not correspond to those assumed at their theoretical counterparts, also complexity analysis of algorithms, based on abstract model, has lost its practical value.

Nevertheless, any expectation that C_2 models could aspire for being at the same time realistic models of parallel computers presents a great misunderstanding: this has never been the goal of the respective theory. Its motivation was completely different, aiming at discovering a robust theoretical notion of parallelism and studying its properties. This is completely understandable since no real parallel machines have been around when the corresponding theory started to develop. After all, it was also the theory itself which recognized the physical infeasibility of C_2 models.

As a consequence, by the previously mentioned development both in the theory and practice of parallel computing the question of the right (in the sense of requirements from Section 2) parallel machine model has been re–opened again. This time there is a high degree of urgency. It is not only the scientific curiosity, but economical necessity that is driving the respective research.

In answering the above question theory offers two possible answers. The first answer is based on the assumption that in practice we are still quite far from the ultimate limits on parallel computer performance imposed by basic physical laws as explained in Section 5. We also do not strive for solving arbitrary large problem instances on our computers. The resulting class of machines is called also *bridging models of parallel computers*. The second answer is inspired by the previous considerations on scalable machines and consequently the class of "almost scalable" *meshes of processors* is considered.

7.2 Towards a Bridging Model of a Parallel Computer

As seen from the previous overview of second class machines none of them fulfills all three conditions as required for an abstract model to be a "reasonable" one as in Section 2 . Especially, results from Section 5 show that unless PTIME=PSPACE none of the above mentioned models can be realized in hardware, by whatever technology. Moreover, since the underlying models vary wildly as far as their architecture and the level of abstraction is concerned, they do not even offer any unifying framework which would be suitable for parallel program development, not speaking about the respective efficiency analysis.

Thus, the situation in parallel computing is substantially different from that in the realm of sequential computing. Here, the practical success of the RAM, or von Neumann, model is ascribable to the fact that it is an efficient bridge between software and hardware. One one hand, high–level languages can be efficiently compiled onto this model. On the other hand, it can be efficiently implemented in hardware. Valiant [34] seem to be the first one who pointed to the importance of designing an analogous unifying *bridging model* for parallel computation. A major purpose of such a model would be to act as a standard on which people can agree. Last, but not least, it should also provide a suitable framework for a realistic complexity analysis of the respective parallel algorithms. Hence, what is required from such a model is a complete fulfillment of all three conditions from Section 2 which we have required from any reasonable machine model.

It appears that a bridging model cannot be based on some fixed parallel machine architecture since virtually any possible architecture has some advantages and some disadvantages over the other. From all we know about the C_2 machines it seems that such a decision would severely restrict the architectural flexibility and at the same time severely restrict the programming style of the underlying machine. In fact the same also holds true for existing, more or less experimental parallel computers. The possibility of simulating one machine on the other is also of no help since the necessary simulation overheads are too large to make such an approach practical.

The best we can probably hope for is that we shall arrive at a suitably parametrized model. With a suitable setting of its parameters it will be able to cover a variety of the most common architectures of parallel machines encountered in practice.

In practice, on one hand, one can already trace out some kind of a partial consensus concerning the main architectural features of a realistic parallel computer. On the other hand, one can even identify the architectural features where no consensus is emerging and perhaps never will. According to the authors of [11] the situation in practice of parallel computing looks as follows.

First of all, there seems to be a consensus that computers with hundreds (or in a foreseeable future with thousands) of processors, each of them equipped with a sizeable internal memory are well within reach considering the present (or foreseeable) technology.

Second of all, it seems that these processors will be connected by some kind of a fast, point–to–point communication network. The only problem is that the interconnection topology of this network is the point of departure where the consensus is missing. The networks of new commercial parallel machines are different from their predecessors and from each other. Moreover, to guarantee the robustness of the resulting parallel system it is required that the physical connection among processors on a single system may vary over time to avoid broken components. Fortunately, this necessity goes hand in hand in recent progress in adaptive routing techniques that are becoming increasingly practical.

In this situation, when one cannot stick to a certain fixed interconnection network one still can postulate its main task: it should enable a connection between any source and any target processors. By a different treatment of this basic simple idea two recent models of realistic parallel computers have emerged.

Bulk–Synchronous Parallel Computer

In looking for a bridging model, Valiant's viewpoint was to see the computation as performed by a parallel computer, as a sequence of so–called *supersteps* [34]. During a superstep each processor performs a combination of local computational steps, message sending as well as message receiving. These activities are subject to the following conditions: (a) the local computation may depend only on data present in the local memory of the processor at the beginning of the superstep, (b) a processor may send at most h messages and receive at most h messages in a superstep. This type of communication pattern is called an *h–relation*.

The architecture of Valiant's *Bulk–Synchronous Parallel Computer* (BSPC) supports this view of parallel processing. The BSPC consists of three main components:

- A certain number P of processors, each performing processing and/or memory functions;

- A *router* that delivers messages point to point between pairs of components; and
- Facilities for synchronizing all or a subset of the processors at regular intervals of I time units where I is the *periodicity* parameter. A computation consists of a sequence of above mentioned supersteps. After each period of I time units, a global check is made to determine whether the superstep has been completed by all the processors. If it has, the machine proceeds to the next superstep. Otherwise, the next period of I units is allocated to the unfinished superstep.

Thus, the role of a communication network is taken over by the router. Its basic task is to realize the h–relations over the selected subsets of processors. The idea is to charge $\bar{f}h + L$ time units for realizing such an h–relation. Here $\bar{f}$ defines the basic throughput of the router when in continuous use, and L defines the latency or startup cost (i.e., the maximum time needed for a single data item to be transmitted from its source to its destination within the network). We shall always assume that h is large enough that $\bar{f}h$ is at least of comparable magnitude to L. If $\bar{f}h \geq L$, for example, and we let $f = 2\bar{f}$, then we can simply charge fh time units for an h–relation and this will be an overestimate (by a factor of 2). Thus, we can define a parameter f such that h–relations can be always realized in time fh for h larger than some h_0.

This parameter f in fact characterizes the performance of our router. Valiant argues that even in a fixed technology it can be kept low by using more pipelining or by having wider communication channels. Keeping f low or fixed as the machine size P scales up incurs extra costs. In particular, as the machine scales up, the hardware investment for communication needs to grow faster than for computation. Valiant's theses is that if these costs are paid, machines of a new level of efficiency and programmability can be attained.

The LogP Computer

In Valiant's model two pieces of specialized hardware are required. One is the router that realizes arbitrary h–relations over selected subsets of processors. The second one must perform synchronization in barrier–like style of all processors that are involved in the particular h–relation at the end of each superstep. Such hardware is not a common matter on many parallel machines. Moreover, the notion of supersteps imposes a certain communication discipline on the design of the respective parallel algorithms that in some cases may be too restrictive. For example, messages sent at the beginning of a superstep can only be used by the target processor in the next superstep, even though it has been assumed that the duration of the superstep exceeds the latency time.

In striving for still more flexibility, generality and realism in the design of parallel machines the authors Culler et all. [11] have concentrated on the identification of further lower level details that are common to all kinds of communication network. Again the idea was to consider a single communication operation between any source and target processor. Depending on the kind of network (and routing algorithm) one will assign a certain cost to this operation.

In a more detailed look this cost consists of two parts. The first one is due to the transition time itself — a so–called *delay* or *latency* — denoted as L (we assume transmission of a single data item — let us say, of a single word per operation). The second one comes from the fact that there is a certain *overhead* o at the sender and receiver during which a processor is sending/receiving its data and cannot be engaged in performing other operations.

Also, there are some other technological constraints common to all kinds of interconnection networks. The most important of them is that there is a certain minimal time interval (called *a gap* and denoted as g) between consecutive message transmissions or consecutive message receptions at a processor. Furthermore, it is to be assumed that the network has a *finite capacity*, such that at most $\lceil L/g \rceil$ messages can be in transit from or to any processor at any time. The reciprocal of g corresponds to available per–processor communication bandwidth.

The parameters L, o and g are measured as multiples of processor cycle. The network is asynchronous, i.e., processors work asynchronously and the latency experienced by any message is unpredictable, but always bounded by L. Because of variations in latency, the messages directed to a given target processor may not arrive in the same order as they are sent.

The last important parameter of a network is P — the number of its nodes (processors).

The previous four parameters can be considered as the main ingredients of the so–called *LogP model* [11]. Its authors claim that by a suitable setting of each of these parameters they are able to faithfully model most of the existing parallel machine models.

For example, it is possible to see a PRAM as a special instance of their model. PRAM is a LogP computer assuming an arbitrary number of processors that work with interprocessor communication having unbounded bandwidth, zero latency and zero overhead. Hence, the PRAM does not discourage the design of asynchronous algorithms with an excessive amount of both processors and interprocessor communication.

To achieve a BSPC model, one has to "manually" program the realization of h–relations and the synchronization actions at the end of each superstep. In this way we gain the possibility of having supersteps with a variable length, with dynamically varying h in the respective h–relations during a computation.

7.3 Programming Realistic Parallel Computers

Basic Approach. Undoubtedly, designing parallel algorithms is a more demanding task than designing sequential algorithms, by order of magnitude. This is due to the fact that one must keep track of dynamically changing parallel running processes and maintain their correct cooperation. This task becomes even more difficult when memory and communication management must be explicitly programmed, as in the case of realistic parallel machines.

Except for a few trivial cases any attempts to provide some sort of automatic translators of sequential programs into parallel ones is deemed to failure. This is due to the undecidability of problems related to the automatic detection of parts of programs that could run in parallel.

Just the opposite approach seems to work: instead of automatic parallelization of sequential programs, one can design a kind of automatic partial *deparallelization* of originally highly parallel programs.

According to Valiant [34] the idea is to design programs with sufficient *parallel slackness*. This means that programs are written for v virtual parallel processes (like for a PRAM) to run on P physical processors (of a BSPC, or LogP computer, for instance) where v is rather larger than P (e.g., $v = P \log P$). The slack is exploited by the computer to schedule and pipeline computation and communication efficiently. The high level languages that could be compiled in this mode could allow virtual shared address space. The program would have to be so expressed that v parallel instruction streams could be compiled from it.

In designing the previous programs several virtual processes must be mapped onto one physical processor whose task is to simulate the actions of these processes sequentially. Here, one makes use of the large memory space available in each processor. To optimize the time efficiency it is desirable to map the processes that frequently communicate onto a single processor and simultaneously to decrease the interprocessor communication by balancing the number of accesses to each processor memory module. Then, within one processor the processes can communicate without making any use of the network communication facilities. To make an optimal use of the parallelism available it is important to design parallel algorithms with the right *"granularity"* — i.e., such where the time spent in internal computation within processors is roughly balanced by the communication time. In the BSPC model this can be achieved by suitably choosing the parameter I during which one can proceed in internal processor computation without waiting for results from other processors. In the LogP computer the supersteps must be programmed and controlled explicitly by the program.

Thus, the programs for realistic parallel computers must be designed so as to work optimally within the spectrum of possible values of the respective parameters that characterize the underlying model. The standard approach is that one starts, say, from a PRAM program that makes use of unbounded parallelism. It is exactly here where the benefits of studying and designing efficient PRAM, or NC algorithms can pay for themselves. Next, one looks for the possibilities of restricting the amount of parallelism down to the number P of available processors by introducing an appropriate level of granularity into the algorithm. The complexity of the resulting algorithm can be then analysed in terms of parameters of the underlying realistic parallel machine model. These parameters take concrete values on a concrete parallel computer. As a result one is able to predict the practical efficiency of the algorithm at hand within a certain range of, both, its parameters and its input size. The asymptotic analysis is more or less only of academic interest since, as explained in Section 5 and 6, the respective machines are not scalable.

It is important to observe that the ideas of bridging models do not enforce any particular programming style. They are equally suitable to shared–memory, message passing and data parallel paradigms. Programs written in any of these styles can be compiled into the instructions of the underlying bridging model that can be mapped further to real parallel machines.

Automatic Distribution of Memory Accesses. It has been already mentioned that the main "art" in designing efficient realistic parallel algorithms is to find an appropriate mapping of a larger number of virtual parallel processes to a smaller number of physical processors. In doing so a specific problem to parallel computing arises. There is the primary problem of allocating the virtual processes into the physical processors in such a way that the computation will not be unnecessarily slowed down by memory accesses of processes realized in one particular processor to other processors. When possible, these accesses must be minimized and should not be made unevenly, overloading thus individual memory units.

This, of course, can be made manually by making use of a natural locality of references that is the property of certain algorithms (cf. standard algorithms for matrix multiplication). However, it appears that there is also a general approach that works under the assumption that if the memory words are distributed among the memory units randomly, independently of the program, then the accesses to various units should be about equally frequent. The most promising method used to realize this idea is offered by hashing. Hash functions for this parallel context has been proposed by several authors (cf. [24], [12]). For their efficient use a certain degree of parallel slackness is necessary.

To see this, observe the main result from the theory of hashing which states that when only P accesses are made to P memory units at random, there is a high probability that one unit will get about $\log P / \log \log P$ accesses and some get none. However, if about $P \log P$ random accesses are to be made, there is a high probability that each component will get no more than about $3 \log P$ accesses which is about 3 times the expected number.

This phenomenon can be exploited as follows in the context of realistic parallel machine models. Suppose that we have to simulate v virtual processes, with $v \geq P \log P$, on P physical processors, each of them being equipped by a sufficient size memory. Allocate $v/P \geq \log P$ virtual processes at random to each processor. Then the v memory requests of one parallel step of our simulated virtual PRAM (say) will be spread almost evenly, about v/P per processor and hence the machine will be able to execute this (super)step using an optimal number $O(v/P)$ of its parallel steps. Hashing functions of relatively simple form (basically polynomials of degree $O(\log P)$ in arithmetic modulo m, where m is the total size of the address space) have been described in the theory. The frequent re–evaluation of such a hashing function can be replaced by a look–up into a precomputed table.

Note that the previous scheme works with a predicted efficiency thanks to the fact that we have assumed the parallel slack greater than $\log P$.

For more details see the original papers by [34], [12] and [11]. For recent results concerning efficient realization of h–relations see [1].

7.4 Meshes of Processors

The other class of realistic parallel computers that is considered in the literature is inspired by the class of scalable machines from Section 6. The idea is to consider "almost strictly scalable" machines that are created by two–dimensional orthogonal square meshes of processors. Full RAMs are usually considered in the place of processors. With the exception of outer processors, each RAM is connected with its four neighbours. Each of the n processors is addressable by a pair (i, j) that determines the position of processor within the mesh. What makes the resulting computer strictly non–scalable is the fact that the size of internal processor's memory grows with the size of the mesh since each processor must be able to store at least its address that is of size $\Theta(\log n)$. While this asymptotically violates the scalability, since the area of the resulting mesh computer grows faster than the number of its processors, in practice the respective machines can be considered strictly scalable in a relatively large scope. This is because within the existing technology the speed of internal processor computations exceeds by far the overall time of message transfers (inclusively all communication overheads) between neighbouring processors. The discrepancy between the respective times is so large that it even leaves room for sizeable internal processor memories. Roughly, the size of internal memory can grow as long as the corresponding memory access time is less than total communication time between any two neighbors. For the detailed discussion of the related issues see the excellent paper [3].

To make the maximal use of the parallelism of mesh–connected parallel computers, special parallel algorithms tailored to the underlying mesh architecture must be designed. Nevertheless, there is again a theoretically based approach that in practice makes the mesh–connected computers more versatile than one might think at the first sight. The idea is to design efficient algorithms simulating any n processor PRAM on an n–node mesh. This will enable efficient realization of PRAM programs on meshes. Clearly, due to the mesh diameter, an $\Omega(\sqrt{n})$ lower bound applies to the simulation of any single PRAM operation. Therefore the simulated PRAM programs will be slowed down by the same factor. Fortunately, it appears that in many cases the optimal or almost optimal slowdown is achievable (cf. [27]). The underlying algorithms are quite complicated and often probabilistic or randomized ones.

To illustrate the main related problem note that by a few PRAM operations one can, in a constant time, realize any h–relation. On a mesh connected computer this translates into the problem of correctly routing all of the respective variables from their home processors to their target processors. Clearly, this requires at least $\Omega(\sqrt{n})$ moves. To achieve this bound schemes using only local information available in individual processors and minimizing the delays and contentions when more messages need to pass through a given processor must be devised. Despite of a quite intensive research no definitive solutions to such problems have been found so far.

Though a slowdown of order $\Theta(\sqrt{n})$ seems to be quite high in the case of certain NC algorithms it can still lead to algorithms from the class $\mathcal{PC}$ (see Section

4.4) that are of sublinear time complexity and therefore, supersede the sequential computations. This again brings further support to the study of idealized parallel machine models and to the design of the corresponding efficient parallel algorithms.

The computational efficiency of, in a sense, similar parallel model as above that, however, has a simpler topological structure and consists of less efficient processors has been studied in [48]. In this case a so–called *Ring Turing Machine* (essentially a ring network of Turing machines communicating via message exchanges) has been proposed. Its efficiency has been investigated w.r.t. its ability to simulate nondeterministic computations. It has been shown that within a certain range, the speed up proportional to the number of processors can be achieved.

An other interesting recent parallel machine model that is created by an $n \times n$ mesh of memory modules over which n processors with the ability of "instantaneous" access to a selected module in each column or in each row are operating has been proposed in [8]. From our point of view this model of the so–called *PADAM — Parallel Alternating Direction Access Machine*, seems to be somewhere between realistic, scalable (because of the underlying mesh structure) and idealized machine models (because the fast column or row access is a non–scalable feature).

7.5   Towards Complexity Theory of Realistic Parallel Computing

Looking for efficient simulations of PRAMs on realistic parallel machines seems to be one of the most promising immediate trends in the respective theory that could contribute substantially to the practice of parallel computing. In doing so the attention should be paid to the problems of simulating PRAMs on realistic models of parallel machines with a fixed number of processors. This would correspond to the most common situation in practice.

While the proposed models of realistic parallel machines seem to be well tailored to current practical needs, especially for "machine independent" program design and analysis it is not yet clear whether they are also suitable to serve as a basis for building the respective complexity theory of realistic parallel computing. This theory should clearly be different from that for C_2 machines by considering computational resources that have been so far neglected in the existing theory but that are vital for realistic parallel computing (like the number of processors, bandwidth of the parallelism, latency, parallel slackness, etc.). One has the feeling that to build such a theory the "right", abstract, but realistic parallel machine model has to be still discovered.

8   Conclusions

The current theory of parallel machine models develops stormily at all open ends.

From practical point of view, the research in realistic machine models is expected to be the most rewarding one. The parallel computer industry and various kinds of national and international research programs are ready to pay a lot of money for the respective research. Therefore, many current research projects are focused onto "high performance computing", or onto "affordable parallel computing" as the recent technical jargon for the realistic parallel computing seems to be. As it is also seen from our survey a promising platform has been already created. The final practical solution seems to be within the reach. It is expected that practical solutions based on the notion of bridging parallel computers will appear soon. E.g., compilers of high–level programming languages and libraries of programs for such machines are under development.

From a theoretical point of view the corresponding complexity theory of realistic parallel computing has to be still developed. A particularly interesting related research is the research involved with machine models whose computation is based on other than "traditional" (mechanical, electrical) principles of classical physics. Especially the models of *quantum computing* deserve a special attention [5] among the respective models. The first attempts in *molecular* or *protein* computing are in sight [4]. Last but not least, via the recent results in *neurocomputing* (cf. [31]) models of *brain–like computing* are announcing their advent (cf. [36]).

All these "non–standard" ways of computing call for discovering of new relationships between the world of physics and the world of computing [41] and thus present an unprecedented challenge for computer science.

References

1. Adler, M. — Byers, J.W. — Karp, R.M.: Scheduling Parallel Communication: The *h*–Relation Problem. Proc. 20th International Symposium MFCS'95, LNCS Vol. **969**, Springer Verlag, Berlin, 1995, pp. 1–16

2. Bertoni, A. — Mauri, G. — Sabadini, N.: Simulations Among Classes of Random Access Machines and Equivalence Among Numbers Succinctly Represented. Ann. Discr. Math., Vol. **25**, 1985, pp. 65–90

3. Billardi, G. — Preparata, F. P.: Horizons of Parallel Computing. Universita di Padova, TR No. CS–93–20, May 1993

4. Birge, R.R.: Protein–Based Computers. Scientific American, March 1995, pp. 66–71

5. Brassard, G.: A Quantum Jump in Computer Science. In: Current Trends in Computer Science, J. van Leeuwen, Editor, LNCS Vol. **1000**, Springer Verlag, Heidelberg, 1995

6. Chandra, A.K. — Kozen, D.C. — Stockmeyer, L.J.: Alternation. J. Assoc. Comp. Mach., Vol. **28**, 1982, pp. 114–133

7. Chazelle, B. — Menier, L.: A Model of Computation for VLSI with Related Complexity Results. JACM, Vol. **32**, 1985, pp. 573–588

8. Chlebus, B. S. — Czumaj, A. — Gasieniec, L. — Kowaluk, M. — Plandowski, W.: Parallel Alternating–Direction Access Machine. Proceedings of Abstracts of ALTEC IV International Workshop, Charles University, Prague, March 1995

9. Cook, S. A.: Towards Complexity Theory of Synchronous Parallel Computation. L'Enseignement Mathématique, Vol. **27**, 1980, pp. 99–102

10. Cook, S. — Reckhow, R.A.: Time Bounded Random Access Machines. J. Comput. Syst. Sci., Vol. **7**, 1973, pp. 354–375

11. Culler, D. — Karp, R. — Patterson, D. — Sahay, A. — Schauser, K.E. — Santos, E. — Subramonian, R. — von Eicken, T.: LogP: Towards a Realistic Model of Parallel Computation. Proc. 4th ACM PPOPP, May 1993, California, USA

12. Czumaj, A. — Meyer auf der Heide, F. — Stemann, V.: Hashing Strategies for Simulating Shared Memory on Distributed Memory Machines. Proceedings of Abstracts of ALTEC IV International Workshop, Charles University, Prague, March 1995

13. Dassow, J. — Hromkovič, J. — Karhumäki, J. — Rovan, B. — Slobodová, A.: On the Power of Synchronization in Parallel Computations. Proc. 12-th Internat. Symp. MFCS'89, LNCS Vol. **739**, Springer Verlag, Berlin, 1989,

14. Dymond, P.: Simultaneous Resource Bounds and Parallel Computation. Ph.D. Thesis, Uni. of Toronto, Dept. of Comp. Sci., 1980

15. Feldman, Y. — Shapiro, E.: Spatial Machines: a More Realistic Approach to Parallel Computing. CACM, Vol. **35**, No. 10, 1992, pp. 61–73

16. Flynn, M.J.: Some Computer Organizations and Their Effectiveness. IEEE Trans. Comput., Vol. **C–21**, 1972, pp. 947–960

17. Furht, B.: Parallel Computing: Glory and Collapse. COMPUTER, November 1994, pp. 74–75

18. Goldschlager, L.G.: A Universal Interconnection Pattern for Parallel Computers. J. Assoc. Comput. Mach. , Vol. **29**, 1982, pp. 1073–1086

19. Hromkovič, J.: Synchronization. Unpublished Manuscript, 1986

20. Johnson, D.S.: A Catalog of Complexity Classes. Handbook of Theoretical Computer Science (Edited by Jan van Leeuwen), Vol. **A**, Elsevier Science Publishers B.V., 1990

21. Karp, R.M. — Ramachandran, V.: Parallel Algorithms for Shared–Memory Machines. Handbook of Theoretical Computer Science (Edited by Jan van Leeuwen), Vol. **A**, Elsevier Science Publishers B.V., 1990

22. Katajainen, J. — Penttonen, M. — van Leeuwen, J.: Fast Simulation of Turing Machines by Random Access Machines. SIAM J. Comput, Vol. **17**, 1988, pp 77–88

23. Mead, C. — Conway, L.: Introduction to VLSI Systems. Addison–Wesley, 1980

24. Mehlhorn, K. — Vishkin, U.: Randomized and Deterministic Simulations of PRAMs by Parallel Machines with Restricted Granularity of Parallel Memories. Acta Inf. Vol. **21**, 1984, pp. 339–374

25. Papadimitriou, Ch. H.: Computational Complexity. Addison–Wesley, New York 1994

26. Parberry, I.: Circuit Complexity and Neural Networks. The MIT Press, Cambridge, Mass., 1994, 270 p

27. Pietracaprina, A. — Pucci, G.: Improved Deterministic PRAM Simulation on the Mesh. Proc. ICALP'95, LNCS Vol. **966**, Springer Verlag, 1995, pp. 372–383

28. Pratt, V. — Stockmeyer, L.J.: A Characterization of the Power of Vector Machines. J. Comput. Syst. Sci., Vol. **12**, 1976, pp. 198–221

29. Savitch, W.J. — Stimson, M.J.: Time Bounded Random Access Machines with Parallel Processing. J. Assoc. Comp. Mach., Vol. **26**, 1979, pp. 103–118

30. Schönhage, A. — Grotefeld. A.F.W. — Vetter.E.: Fast Algorithms — A Multitape Turing Machine Implementation. Wissenschaftsverlag, Mannheim, 1994, 297 p.

31. Siegelmann, H.: Neural Networks as a Computational Model. In: Current Trends in Computer Science, J. van Leeuwen, Editor, LNCS Vol. **1000**, Springer Verlag, Heidelberg, 1995
32. Slot, C. — van Emde Boas. P.: The Problem of Space Invariance for Sequential Machines. Inf. and Comp., Vol. **77**, 1988, pp. 93–122
33. Stegwee, R.A. — Torenvliet, L. — van Emde Boas, P.: The Power of Your Editor. Rep. IBM Research, RJ 4711 (50179), May 1985
34. Valiant, L.G.: A Bridging Model for Parallel Computation. CACM Vol. **33**, No.8., 1990
35. Valiant, L.G.: General Purpose Parallel Architectures. Handbook of Theoretical Computer Science (Edited by Jan van Leeuwen), Vol. **A**, Elsevier Science Publishers B.V., 1990
36. Valiant, L.: Circuits of the Mind. Oxford University Pres, New York, 1994, 237 p.
37. van Emde Boas, P.: Machine Models and Simulations. Handbook of Theoretical Computer Science (Edited by Jan van Leeuwen), Vol. **A**, Elsevier Science Publishers B.V., 1990
38. van Leeuwen, J. — Wiedermann, J.: Array Processing Machines: An Abstract Model. BIT Vol. **27**, 1987, pp. 25–43
39. Vitányi, P.: Locality, Communication and Interconnect Length in Multicomputers. SIAM J. Comput., Vol. **17**, No. 4., 1988, pp. 659–672
40. Vitányi, P.: Multiprocessor Architectures and Physical Laws. Proc. PhysComp94, IEEE Computer Society Press, 1994
41. Vitányi, P.: Physics and the New Computation. Proc. 20th International Symposium MFCS'95, LNCS Vol. **969**, Springer Verlag, Berlin, 1995, pp. 108–130
42. Vitter, J. S. — Simons, R.A.: New Classes for Parallel Complexity: A Study of Unification and Other Problems Complete for $\mathcal{P}$. IEEE Trans. on Computers, Vol. **C–35**, No. 5, May 1986
43. Wiedermann, J.: Deterministic and Nondeterministic Simulation of the RAM by the Turing Machine. In: R.E.A. Mason, Ed., Information Processing '83, Proceedings of the 9-th IFIP World Computer Congress, Paris 1983. North–Holland, Amsterdam, 1983, pp. 163–168
44. Wiedermann, J.: Parallel Turing Machines. TR RUU–CS–84–11, Dept. of Comp. Sci., Utrecht University, Utrecht, 1984
45. Wiedermann, J.: On The Power of Synchronization. J. Inf. Process. Cybern. EIK Vol. **25**, 1989, pp. 499–506
46. Wiedermann, J.: Normalizing and Accelerating RAM Computations and the Problem of Reasonable Space Measures. Proceedings of ICALP'90, LNCS Vol. **464**, Springer Verlag, Berlin, 1990, pp. 125–138
47. Wiedermann, J.: Weak Parallel Machines: A New Class of Physically Feasible Parallel Machine Models. Proc. Math. Found. of Comp. Sci., LNCS Vol. **629**, Springer Verlag, Berlin, 1992, pp. 95–111
48. Wiedermann, J.: Fast Sequential and Parallel Simulation of Nondeterministic Computations. Computers and Artificial Intelligence, Vol. **13**, No. 6, 1994, pp. 521–536
49. Wiedermann, J. Complexity Issues in Discrete Neurocomputing. Neural Network World, No.1, 1994, pp. 99–119
50. Wiedermann, J.: Five New Simulation Results on Turing Machines. Technical Report V–631, Institute of Computer Science, Prague, 1995
51. Wiedermann, J.: Quo Vadetis Parallel Machine Models. In: Current Trends in Computer Science, J. van Leeuwen, Editor, LNCS Vol. **1000**, Springer Verlag, Heidelberg, 1995

Fuzzy logic from the logical point of view

Petr Hájek

Institute of Computer Science Academy of Sciences, 182 07 Prague, Czech Republic,
e-mail:hajek@uivt.cas.cz

Abstract. Fuzzy logic is analyzed from the point of view of formal logic;
the underlying calculi and their proporties are surveyed and applications
are discussed.

1   Introduction

(1) *Fuzzy logic is popular.* The number of papers dealing, in some sense, with
fuzzy logic and its applications is immense, and the success in applications is
evident, in particular in fuzzy control. From numerous books we mention at least
[37], [9], [23]. As stated in the introduction to [23], in 1991 there were about 1400
papers dealing with fuzzy systems. Naturally, in this immense literature quality
varies; a mathematician (logician) browsing in it is sometimes bothered by papers
that are mathematically poor (and he/she may easily overlook those few that one
mathematically excellent). This should not lead to a quick refusal of the domain.
Let us quote Zadeh, the inventor of fuzzy sets ([23], Preface): "Although some of
the earlier controversies regarding the applicability of fuzzy logic have abated,
there are still influential voices which are critical and/or skeptical. Some take
the position that anything that can be done with fuzzy logic can be done equally
well without it. Some are trying to prove that fuzzy logic is wrong. And some are
bothered by what they perceive to be exaggerated expectations. That may well
be the case but, as Jules Verne had noted at the turn of the century, scientific
progress is driven by exaggerated expectations."

I mention a recent paper [5] whose author claimed to prove that fuzzy logic is
impossible (his "proof" was based on an evident misunderstanding; nevertheless,
it had lead to a big discussion, mainly contained in a special volume [20]. To
get insight into the domain let us first ask three questions: what is logic, what
is fuzziness and what meaning(s) has the term "fuzzy logic".

(2) *Logic studies the notion(s) of consequence.* It deals with proppositions
(sentences), sets of propositions and the relation of consequence among them.
The task of formal logic is to represent all this by means of well-defined logical
calculi admitting exact investigation. Various calculi differ in their definitions
of sentences and notion(s) of consequence (propositional logics, predicate logics, modal propositional/predicate logics, many-valued propositional/predicate
logics etc.). Often a logical calculus has *two* notions of consequence: syntactical
(based on a notion of proof) and semantical (based on a notion of truth); then the
natural questions of soundness (does provability imply truth?) and completeness
(does truth imply provability?) pose themselves.

(3) *Fuzziness is impreciseness (vagueness); a fuzzy proposition may be true in some degree.* The word "crisp" is used as meaning "non-fuzzy". Standard examples of fuzzy propositions use *linquistic variable* [35] as e.g. *age* with possible values *young, medium, old* or similar. The sentence "The patient is young" is true in some degree - the less is the age of the patient (measured e.g. in years), the more true is the sentence. *Truth of a fuzzy proposition is a matter of degree.*

I recommend to everybody interested in fuzzy logic to sharply distinguish fuzziness from uncertainty as degree of belief (e.g. probability). Compare the last proposition with the proposition "The patient will survive next week". This may well be considered as a crisp proposition which is either (absolutely) true or (absolutely) false; but we do not know which is the case. We may have some *probability* (chance, degree of belief) that the sentence is true; but probability is *not* degree of truth. (We shall discuss the relation of fuzziness and probability later on.)

(4) *The term "fuzzy logic" has two different meanings - wide and narrow.* This is a very useful distinction, made by Zadeh; we again quote from [23], preface: "In a narrow sense, fuzzy logic, FLn, is a logical system which aims at a formalization of approximate reasoning. In this sense, FLn is an extension of multivalued logic. However, the agenda of FLn is quite different from that of traditional multivalued logics. In particular, such key concepts in FLn as the concept of a linguistic variable, canonical form, fuzzy if-then rule, fuzzy quantification and defuzzification, predicate modification, truth qualification, the extension principle, the compositional rule of inference and interpolative reasoning, among others, are not addressed in traditional systems. This is the reason why FLn has a much wider range of applications than traditional systems.

In its wide sense, fuzzy logic, FLw, is fuzzily synonymous with fuzzy set theory, FST, which is the theory of classes with unsharp boundaries. FST is much broader than FLn and includes the latter as one of its branches."

Let me add two comments: first, in the wide sense, everything dealing with fuzziness may be (and seems to be) called "fuzzy logic". Second, even if I degree with Zadeh's distinction between many-valued logic and fuzzy logic in the narrow sense, I consider (and hope Zadeh would agree) formal calculi of many-valued logic (including non-"traditional", of course) to be the kernel or base of fuzzy logic in narrow sense and the task to explain things Zadeh mentions by means of these calculi to be a very promising task (not yet finished).

(5) *This paper about the fuzzy logic in the narrow sense.* Our main aim is to survey strictly logical properties of the most important many-valued logics whose set of truth values is the unit interval [0,1] and then discuss, from the logical point of view, some applications. In Section 2, we survey propositional calculi; in Section 3 predicate calculi. We pay main attention to Łukasiewicz's and Gödel's logics (for the reasons made clear in Sect. 2), as well as a graded form (extension) of Łukasiewicz's logic invented by Pavelka. Section 4 is devoted to a very general notion of a fuzzy logic. In Section 5 we comment on applications and we and by some conclusions and open problems.

The reader is asumed to have at least a partial experience with the classical (two-valued) propositional calculus; some knowledge of predicate calculus is very helpful. (The Czech speaking sofsemist may consult my [10].) I hope that the reader will agree, after having read the paper, that fuzzy logic is *not* (better: need not be) simple-minded poor man's logic but a powerful and interesting logical calculus.

Acknowledgemens. This work has been partially supported by the grant No. 130 108 of the Grant Agency of the Academy of Sciences of the Czech Republic. The paper is a substantially revised and extended successor of my [13].

2 Propositional logics

2.1 Classical logic

We quickly review notions and facts assumed to be known to the reader. There are two *truth* values:1 and 0 (1 stands for *truth*, 0 for *falsity*). The *language* of the classical propositional calculus consists of a list of *propositional variables* $p, q, \ldots$ and connectives $\rightarrow$ (implication and $\neg$ (negation); each propositional variable is a *formula*; if φ as a formula then $\neg \varphi$ is a formula; if φ and ψ are formulas then $\varphi \rightarrow \psi$ is a formula. A *truth evaluation* is a mapping e assigning to each propositional variable p a truth value $e(p)$ (0 or 1). Each truth evaluation extends uniquely to an evaluation of all formulas, using the truth functions of connectives (which we denote by the symbol of the connective with a dot): $\neg^{\bullet} 0 = 1, \ \neg^{\bullet} 1 = 0;$
$1 \rightarrow^{\bullet} 1 = 0 \rightarrow^{\bullet} 1 = 0 \rightarrow^{\bullet} 0 = 1, \ 1 \rightarrow^{\bullet} 0 = 0.$

(It is customary to represent this by *truth tables*:)

$\neg^{\bullet}$	
1	0
0	1

$\rightarrow^{\bullet}$	1	0
1	1	0
0	1	1

Thus e.g. if $e(p) = 1$ and $e(q) = 0$ then $e(\neg q) = 1$, $e(p \rightarrow \neg q) = 1$, $e(\neg q \rightarrow p) = 0$, $e(\neg(\neg q \rightarrow p)) = 0$, $e((p \rightarrow \neg q) \rightarrow \neg(\neg q \rightarrow p)) = 0$.

Other connectives may be used as abbrevations: if φ and ψ are formulas then

$$\varphi \ \& \ \psi \text{ is an abbrevation for } \neg(\varphi \rightarrow \neg\psi),$$

$$\varphi \vee \psi \text{ is an abbrevation for } \neg\varphi \rightarrow \psi,$$

$$\varphi \equiv \psi \text{ is an abbrevation for } (\varphi \rightarrow \neg\psi) \rightarrow \neg(\neg\psi \rightarrow \varphi).$$

If we compute the corresponding truth tables we get

$\&^{\bullet}$	1	0
1	1	0
0	0	0

$\vee^{\bullet}$	1	0
1	1	1
0	1	0

$\equiv^{\bullet}$	1	0
1	1	0
0	0	1

(We computed the value $(1 \equiv^\bullet 0) = 0$ above.)

A formula φ is a *tautology* if $e(\varphi) = 1$ for each truth evaluation e (i.e. φ is identically true).

The following formulas are *axioms* of the predicate calculus:

$$p \to (q \to p) \tag{1}$$

$$(p \to (q \to r)) \to ((p \to q) \to (p \to r)) \tag{2}$$

$$(\neg p \to \neg q) \to (q \to p) \tag{3}$$

One easily verifies that for each φ, ψ, the formulas (1), (2), (3) are tautologies. *Modus ponens* is the following deduction rule: from φ and $\varphi \to \psi$ derive ψ.

A proof in propositional calculus is an arbitrary sequence $\varphi_1, \ldots, \varphi_n$ of formulas such that, for each $i = 1, \ldots, n$, either φ_i is an axiom or φ_i follows from some preceding formulas φ_j, φ_k $(j, k < i)$ by modus ponens. A formula is *provable* in propositional calculus if it is the last element of a proof.

It is easy to show that if φ and $\varphi \to \psi$ are tautologies then φ is also a tautology; we say that modus pones preserves tautologicity. Therefore each provable formula is a tautology (soundness); conversely, we have *completeness*: each tautology is provable. (The *completeness theorem* says that the calculus is sound and complete, i.e. provable formulas are exactly all tautologies.)

A *theory* is a set T of formulas called *special axioms* of T. A *proof from* T is defined as above but with the additional possibility that φ_i may be an element of T. We write $T \vdash \varphi$ if φ is provable from T (is the least element of a proof from T). The *deduction theorem* says that for each theory T and formulas φ, ψ, $T \vdash \varphi \to \psi$ iff $(T \cup \{\varphi\}) \vdash \psi$.

An evaluation is a *model* of a theory T if it assigns 1 to each special axiom of T (makes all the axioms true). *Strong completeness theorem* says that $T \vdash \varphi$ iff φ is true in each model of T. For details on propositional logic set any textbook of Mathematical logic, e.g. [24].

2.2 More values and truth-functionality

We have good reasons to generalize the two-valued logic to logics having more truth values and undoubtedly this can be done in many ways. To grasp degree of truth let us decide that our set of truth values will be linearly ordered, with 1 as maximum and 0 as minimum. The most obvious choice is the unit interval $[0,1]$ of reals and *this will be our choice* throughout.

Needless to say, other choices are possible; notably one often works will a finite set of truth values. But this will not be studied here.

As we have seen, the classical propositional logic is *truth-functional*, i.e. the truth value of a composed formula can be computed from the truth values of its components, thanks to the truth functions of connectives.

Should our many-valued logics be also truth-functional? I.e. should the truth-value of a formula be determined by the truth values of its atoms via truth-functions of connectives, now assigning, e.g. for implication $\to$, to each pair of the values $x, y \in [0,1]$ a truth value $(x \to^{\bullet} y) \in [0,1]$? Most systems of fuzzy logic are truth-functional (e.g. one usually takes $x \wedge^{\bullet} y = min(x,y)$ for the truth-function of conjunction). Our main attention will be paid to truth-functional systems; but note that the systems of Section 4 will not be.

The reader should observe that there is nothing wrong on truth-functionality: the truth degree of a component formula is just *defined* by the truth functions. But one has to be careful: on then *cannot* interpret truth degrees of formulas e.g. as their probabilities, since probability is *not* truth-functional, as everybody knows. It is also not counter-intuitive that if you interpret conjunction by minimum and negation as $\neg^{\bullet} x = 1 - x$ (also a very popular choice) then $e(\varphi \wedge \neg\varphi)$ may be (and often is) positive. My favourite example is of φ saying "I am old". It is rather true, but still the truth degree is (I hope) less than 1. Thus "I am not old" has a (small) positive value. And the conjunction "I am old and I am not old" (or: "I am old - yes and no") has a small but positive truth degree. This is impossible for crisp propositions, needless to say.

2.3 Where are truth-functions of connectives from?

Obviously, the truth-functions should behave classically on extremal truth values 0,1 and should satisfy some natural monotonicities (the truth function of conjunction (disjunction) should be non-decreasing in both arguments; the truth function of implication should be non-decreasing in the second argument but non-increasing in the first, i.g. the less true is the antecedent φ and the more is true the succedent ψ the more is true the implication $\varphi \to \psi$. $\neg^{\bullet}$ should be non-increasing.) This leads to the notion of a t-norm: (cf. [32]) this is an operation $t : [0,1]^2 \to [0,1]$ which is commutative and associative, non-decreasing in both arguments and having 1 as unit element and 0 as zero element, i.c.

$$t(x,y) = t(y,x)$$

$$t(t(x,y),z) = t(x,t(y,z))$$

$$x \le x' \text{ and } y \le y' \text{ implies } t(x,y) \le \in (x',y')$$

$$t(1,x) = x, \ t(0,x) = 0.$$

We shall only work with *continuous* t-norms as good candidates for truth functions of a conjunction. Each t-norm t determines uniquely its corresponding implication i (not necessarily continuous) satisfying, for all $x, y, z \in [0,1]$

$$z \le i(x,y) \text{ iff } t(x,z) \le y.$$

For each such system we define an *evaluation* to be a mapping e assigning to each atom p its truth degree $e(p)$, $0 \le e(p) \le 1$; a *1-tautology* is a formula whose value is 1 for each evaluation. We shall try to find a simple set of axioms (particular 1-tautologies) and a notion of proof such that we have *completeness*: a formula is a 1-tautology iff it is provable.

It is useful to introduce two special formulas 1 and 0 (truth and falsity) having the value 1 and 0 respectively in each evaluation; then one can define negation $\neg\varphi$ as $\varphi \to 0$.

We present three outstanding examples:

(1) *Łukasiewicz's logic* [22] with the conjunction $x \,\&^\bullet\, y = max(x + y - 1, 0)$ and the corresponding implication $x \to_1^\bullet y = 1$ for $x \leq y$ and $x \to_L^\bullet y = 1 - x + y$ otherwise;

(2) *Gödel's logic* [7] will the conjunction $x \wedge^\bullet y = min(x, y)$ and the corresponding implication $x \to_2^\bullet y = 1$ iff $x \leq y$ and $x \to_2^\bullet y = y$ otherwise;

(3) *Product logic* will the conjunction $x \odot y = x.y$ (product) and $x \to_3^\bullet y = 1$ iff $x \leq y$, $x \to_3^\bullet y = y/x$ otherwise.

One can show (see e.g. [27]) that each t-norm is composed in a certain way from these three examples. Thus our question reads: what is the logic of these examples?

2.4 Łukasiewicz's logic

Similarly as classical logic, Łukasiewicz'logic Ł may be developed from implication $\to$ and negation $\neg$ (or just from $\to$ and 0); the truth function of negation is $\neg^\bullet x = x \to^\bullet 0 = 1 - x$. We can define two different conjunctions and disjunctions:

$\varphi \,\&\, \psi$ is $\neg(\varphi \to \neg\psi)$, $\quad x \,\&^\bullet y = max(x + y - 1, 0)$

$\varphi\underline{\vee}\psi$ is $\neg(\neg\varphi \,\&\, \neg\psi)$, $\quad x \vee^\bullet y = min(x + y, 1)$

$\varphi \vee \psi$ is $(\varphi \to \psi) \to \psi$, $\quad x \vee^\bullet y = max(x.y)$

$\varphi \wedge \psi$ is $\neg(\neg\varphi \vee \neg\psi)$, $\quad x \wedge^\bullet y = min(x, y)$

The following are axioms of Łukasiewicz's logic:

$$\varphi \to (\psi \to \varphi) \tag{1}$$

$$(\varphi \to \psi) \to ((\psi \to \chi) \to (\varphi \to \chi)) \tag{2}$$

$$(\neg\psi \to \neg\varphi) \to (\varphi \to \psi) \tag{3}$$

$$((\varphi \to \psi) \to \psi) \to ((\psi \to \varphi) \to \varphi) \tag{4}$$

The only deduction rule is modus ponens; the definition of a proof is as in classical logic (relative to our set of axioms).

Completeness of this set of axioms was conjectured by Łukasiewicz in Thirties, but first proved by Rose and Rosser [30]; a good proof can be found in [8]. The proof is by no means easy, but very elucidating. The method is general and we describe it roughly here. One defines an approriate class of algebras (here: MV-algebras) one of them being the unit interval [0,1] with truth functions of connectives as operations. One shows that another example is the algebra of classes of provably equivalent formulas $[\varphi] = \{\varphi \mid \vdash (\varphi \to \psi) \wedge (\psi \to \varphi)\}$; operations defined through representatives, i.e. $[\varphi \,\&\, \psi] = [\varphi] \,\&\, [\psi]$ etc.). A partial order is defined in each algebra; in particular, for classes of formulas, $[\varphi] \leq [\psi]$ iff $[\varphi \to \psi] = [1]$; for $[0,1]$; $\leq$ is the usual *linear* order of reals. One shows that

(i) each algebra is a subalgebra of the direct product of some linearly ordered algebras,

(ii) if an identity $\tau = \sigma$ is valid in the algebra $[0,1]$ then it is valid in all linearly ordered algebras (and hence, by (i), in all algebras).

Thus if φ is a 1-tautology and τ_φ is the term resulting from φ by understanding propositional variables as variables for elements of an algebra and understanding connectives as operations in the algebra then $\tau_\varphi = 1$ is valid in $[0,1]$ and hence in all algebras, in particular in the algebra of classes of formulas, which means $[\varphi] = [1]$, i.e. φ is a provable formula.

Needless to say, details are non-trivial and laborious but the structure is the same in all our three logics.

Note that *deduction theorem fails* in Ł (since the formula $(\varphi \to (\psi \to \chi)) \to ((\varphi \to \psi) \to (\varphi \to \chi))$ is not a 1-tautology in Ł); but are have a variant of deduction theorem valid for t.

Deduction theorem for Ł: [25] $T \cup \{\varphi\} \vdash \psi$ if there is an n such that $T \vdash \varphi \to (\varphi \to \ldots (\varphi \to \psi) \ldots)$ (n copies of φ). (An equivalent condition is: $T \vdash \varphi^n \to \psi$, where φ^n is $\varphi \& \ldots \& \varphi$, n copies of φ.)

Decidability: The set of all 1-tautologies of Ł is recursive. (This follows from the definability of truth-functions is certain axiomatic theory of reals known as Tarski's algebra and known to be decidable; the same applies to 1-tautologies of our two other propositional calculi.)

2.5 Gödel's logic

Kurt Gödel (born 1906 in Brno, now Czech Republic), probably the most important mathematical logician, published in 1932 an extremely short paper [7] concerning intuitionistic logic (a subsystem of classical logic with a different meaning of connectives; e.g. $\varphi \vee \neg\varphi$ is not provable). Gödel's aim was to show that there is no finitely valued logic for which axioms of intuitionistic logic would be complete. For this purpose he created a semantics of (possibly infinite-valued) propositional calculus which is now called Gödel's logic G. (Needless to say, this was more than three decedes before fuzzy sets have been defined.

Gödel's logic has the following (not interdefinable) connectives: $\to, \wedge, \vee, \neg$ (implication, conjunction, disjunction, negation; negation may be replaced by 0). The semantics is as follows:

$x \to^\bullet y = 1$ if $x \leq y$, $x \to^\bullet y = y$ otherwise,
$x \wedge^\bullet y = min(x,y)$,
$x \vee^\bullet y = max(x,y)$,
$\neg^\bullet x = 1$ for $x = 0$, $\neg^\bullet x = 0$ for $x > 0$.

The axioms are as follows (G1 - G11 are axioms of intuitionistic logic, G12 is an axiom of "linearity"):

(G1) $(\varphi \to \psi) \to ((\psi \to \chi) \to (\varphi \to \chi))$
(G2) $\varphi \to (\varphi \vee \psi)$
(G3) $\psi \to (\varphi \vee \psi)$

(G4) $(\varphi \to \chi) \to ((\psi \to \chi) \to ((\varphi \vee \psi) \to \chi)))$
(G5) $(\varphi \wedge \psi) \to \varphi$
(G6) $(\varphi \wedge \psi) \to \psi$
(G7) $(\chi \to \varphi) \to ((\chi \to \psi) \to (\chi \to (\varphi \wedge \psi)))$
(G8) $(\varphi \to (\psi \to \chi)) \to ((\varphi \wedge \psi) \to \chi)$
(G9) $((\varphi \wedge \psi) \to \chi) \to (\varphi \to (\psi \to \chi))$
(G10) $(\varphi \wedge \neg\varphi) \to \psi$
(G11) $(\varphi \to (\varphi \wedge \neg\varphi)) \to \neg\varphi$.
(G12) $(\varphi \to \psi) \vee (\psi \to \varphi)$

It is an easy checking to show that all these are 1-tautologies. The deduction rule is modus ponens; this defines the notion of a proof.

Completeness theorem: Each 1-tautology is provable. Again here the proof is rather non-trivial and follows the sketch given above; of course with a different class of algebras, called Heyting algebras or pseudo-boolean algebras. We have no room for details; [8] is recommended for a readable elaborated proof.

Deduction theorem is valid for G: $T \cup \{\varphi\} \vdash \psi$ iff $T \vdash (\varphi \to \psi)$. Note that G is *the only* many-valued logic having the deduction theorem, more precisely: if a logic contains a conjunction given by a t-norm and the corresponding implication $\to$, is completely axiomatized and satisfies the deduction theorem then the t-norm is minimum and hence $\to$ is Gödel's implication.

Gödels logic satisfies the following form of *strong completeness*: Say that a theory *semantically entails* φ if for each evaluation e there is a conjunction α of finitely many axioms of T such that $e(\alpha) \leq e(\varphi)$. (Observe that in classical logic this is equivalent to saying that φ is true in each model of T.)

Strong completeness: For each theory T and formula φ, $T \vdash \varphi$ iff T semantically entails φ.

Note that the easy part of this equivalent (soudness) implies that if $T \vdash \varphi$ and $e(\alpha) \geq r$ for each axiom α of T then $e(\alpha) \geq r$. The difficult part can be obtained by combining the (normal) completeness of G with the techniques of Takeuti and Titani [34].

2.6 Product logic

The logic based on the product t-norm has been considerably less investigated them the two preceding ones (see [2]). The paper [15], just finished, investigates the logic whose primitives are $\odot$ (product conjunction), $\to$ (the corresponding implication) and 0; we get $\neg$ as Gödel's negation and both $\wedge$ (minimum conjunction) and $\vee$ (maximum disjunction) are definable. The paper presents 12 axioms and proves completeness theorem using a class of algebras called *product algebras*. There are many open problems related to this (rather interesting and unjustly overlooked) logic.

2.7 Rational Pavelka's logic

Till now we have been interested almost exclusively only in axiomatizing 1-tautologies, i.e. proving formulas that are absolutely true. But in fuzzy logic we are interested in deriving consequences from assumptions that are only partially true, true in some degree. (We met a result of this type at the end of 2.5 - for Gödel's logic.) Logics of partial truth were studied, in a very general manner, as early as in the seventies by the Czech mathematician Jan Pavelka [28] and since then have been substatially simplified; I refer to [11] but here we describe a still simpler version. It is very different from the original Pavelka's version and looks as an "innocent" extension of Lukasiewicz's Ł; but the main completeness result of Pavelka still holds.

The idea is as follows: assume that $e(\varphi) = r$; then for each φ, $e(\psi) \geq r$ iff $e(\varphi \to \psi) = 1$. Thus if φ is a formula whose value is r in *all* evaluations then the axiom $\varphi \to \psi$ would just postulate that ψ is at least r-true.

Thus we extend the language of Ł by adding truth constant $\bar{r}$ for some $r \in [0,1]$ as new atomic formulas, postulating that $e(\bar{r}) = r$ for each evaluation (we already have had $\bar{0}$ and $\bar{1}$). Our choice will be to add truth constants $\bar{r}$ for each *rational* $r \in [0,1]$ (thus we have truth constants for a countable dense recursirely representable set of reals from $[0,1]$, this is all we need).

Thus for example if φ, ψ are formulas then $(\varphi \to \overline{0.7})$ & $(\overline{0.4} \to \neg\psi)$ is a formula. We have some obvious tautologies like $\neg\overline{0.7} \equiv \overline{0.3}$ and $\overline{0.7} \to \overline{0.5} \equiv \overline{0.8}$; in general, for each rational $r, s \in [0,1]$ we have

(P1) $\qquad\qquad\qquad \neg\bar{r} \equiv \overline{\neg^{\bullet} r},$

(P2) $\qquad\qquad\qquad (\bar{r} \to \bar{s}) \equiv \overline{r \to^{\bullet} s}$

We add these schemas as new logical axioms; the resulting logic (with the language extended by truth constants and axioms extended by (P1), (P2)) will by called RPL (rational propositional logic or rational Pavelka's logic). The only deduction rule is modus ponens.

If φ is a formula and $r \in [0,1]$ is rational then (φ, r) denotes just the formula $(\bar{r} \to \varphi)$ (saying that φ is at least r-true). We have same derived deduction rules.

Lemma. Let T be a theory in RPL (a set of special axioms); for each formula α, $T \vdash \alpha$ means that α is provable in T.

(1) If $T \vdash (\varphi, r)$ and $T \vdash (\varphi \to \psi, s)$, then $T \vdash (\psi, r \,\&\, s)$.

(2) If $T \vdash (\varphi, r)$ then $T \vdash (\bar{s} \to \varphi, s \to^{\bullet} r)$.

Definition. Let T be a theory in RPL. (1) The *truth degree* of φ in T is $\|\varphi\|_T = \inf\{e(\varphi) \mid e \text{ is a model of } T\}$.

(2) *The provability degree* of φ in T is

$$|\varphi|_T = \sup\{r \mid T \vdash (\varphi, r)\}.$$

Thus $\| \varphi \|_T$ is the infimum of values of φ in models of T; $| \varphi |_T$ is the supremum of rationals r such that $T \vdash \bar{r} \to \varphi$.

Completeness theorem for RPL: Let T be a theory in RPL; then, for each formulace, $\|\varphi\|_T = |\varphi|_T$.

This is a very pleasing and elegant result (invented originally by Pavelka); the proof is moderately difficult (much easier than the proof of completeness of Ł, but using the fact that we have the Rose-Rosser's complete axiom system for Ł).

Remarks. (1) A *fuzzy theory* is a fuzzy set of formulas, i.e. a mapping T associating to each formula φ the degree $T(\varphi)$ of being an axiom. An evaluation e is a *model* of T of for each φ, $e(\varphi) \geq, T(\varphi)$, i.e. each formula is at least as much true, as the theory demands. It is natural to assume that each $T(\varphi)$ is a rational number. The notion of a fuzzy theory is central in Pavelka's approach but we see that it is superfluouns; if you define $T' = \{(\varphi, T(\varphi)) \mid \varphi \text{ formula}\}$ (thus for each φ, if $T(\varphi) = r$ we put $(\overline{r} \to \varphi)$ into T') then T' is a (crisp) theory having the same models as T.

(2) The set of all formulas is a recursive set and the syntax is recursive; thus we may call a theory T *recursive* if T is a recursive set of formulas. Note that $|\varphi|_T$ may be irrational; on the other hand, if $r > 0$ is rational then we can construct a recursive theory T such that the set of all φ such that $|\varphi|_T \geq r$ is "badly" non-recursive (for experts: it may be Π_2-complete; see [11] for details).

(3) We can similarly other logics, e.g. Gödel's logic or product logic but unfortunately we cannot hope for Pavelka style completeness (as Pavelka himself tells us) since the truth function of implication is not contuous in these logics. To see this take the theory $T = \{p \to (\frac{\overline{1}}{n}) \mid n \text{ natural }\}$; then

$\|p \to 0\|_T = 1$ for each of L, G, P;

$|/!p \to 0|_T = 1$ for Ł but $|p \to 0|_T = 0$ for both G and P (verify).

Note that RPL satisfies the same generalized deduction theorem as Ł (and of course does not satisfy the classical deduction theorem).

3 Predicate calculi

3.1 The classical predicate calculus

In the present section we assume the reader to have some basic knowledge of the classical predicate calculus. In this subsection we survey the basic notions and facts, for comparison with their many-valued generalizations. We shall restrict ourselves to calculi without function symbols. Details may be found e.g. in [24].

A *language* consists of *predicates* $P, Q, \ldots$, *object constants* $c, d, \ldots$, *object variables* $x, y, \ldots$. Each predicate is assigned a positive natural number as its *arity*. If P is an *n*-ary predicate and $t_1, \ldots, t_n$ are variables and/or constants then $P(t_1, \ldots, t_n)$ is an atomic *formula*. Non-atomic formulas are from atomic ones using *connectives* $\to, \neg$ and the *universal quantifier* $\forall$: if φ, ψ are formulas and x is an object variable then $\varphi \to \psi$, $\neg\varphi$, $(\forall x)\varphi$ are *formulas*. The variable x is bound in $(\forall x)\varphi$; other variables are free/bound in φ iff they are free/bound in $(\forall x)\varphi$. A variable is free/bound in $\neg\varphi$ iff of is such in φ; it is free/bound in $\varphi \to \psi$ iff it is such in φ or in ψ. A formula is *closed* of it has no free variable.

Other connectives are introduced as abbreviations as in propositional quantifier; the *existential quantifies* $\exists$ is defined thus: $(\exists x)\varphi$ abbreviates $\neg(\forall x)\neg\varphi$.

An *interpretaion* of a language L is given by the following:

- a non-empty *domains* M,
- for each n-ary predicate P, an n-ary *relation* $r_P \subseteq M^n$ (set of n-tuples of elements of M)

– for each constant c, an element $m_c \in M$.

The interpretation is *witnessed* if each element $m \in M$ is the meaning of a constant c, $m = m_c$. (This can be achieved by extending the language by some additional constants.) For each closed formula φ and each interpretation

$$\mathbf{M} = \langle M, (r_P)_{P \text{ predicate}}, (m_c)_{c \text{ constant}} \rangle,$$

The *truth value* of φ in $\mathbf{M}$ is defined as follows:

– If $P(c, \ldots, d)$ is a closed atomic formula then $\| P(c, \ldots, d) \|_{\mathbf{M}} = 1$ iff $\langle m_c, \ldots, m_d \rangle \in r_P$ (the tuple of meanings of $c, \ldots, d$ is in the relation r_p which is the meaning of P); otherwise $\| P(c, \ldots, d) \|_{\mathbf{M}} = 0$;
– $\| \varphi \to \psi \|_{\mathbf{M}} = \| \varphi \| \mathbf{M} \to^{\bullet} \| \psi \|_{\mathbf{M}}$, $\| \neg \varphi \|_{\mathbf{M}} = \neg^{\bullet} \| \varphi \|_{\mathbf{M}}$;
– $\| (\forall x)\varphi \|_{\mathbf{M}} = min_c \| \varphi(c) \|_{\mathbf{M}}$, where $\varphi(c)$ results from φ by substituting the constant c for (free occurences of) x.

We write $M \models \varphi$ for $\| \varphi \|_{\mathbf{M}} = 1$ and read: φ is true in $\mathbf{M}$. If φ is not closed then $\mathbf{M} \models \varphi$ means that $M \models (\forall x_1) \ldots (\forall x_n)\varphi$, where $x_1, \ldots x_n$ are the variables free in φ.

A *theory* is a set of formulas (special axioms). $\mathbf{M}$ is a *model* of a T if each $\varphi \in T$ is true in $\mathbf{M}$.

Logical axioms: axioms of classical propositional calculus plus
(A1) $(\forall x)\varphi \to \varphi(t)$

where t is either a constant or an object variable free for x in φ (this is a simple condition preventing "clash of free and bound variables") - the *substitution* axiom,
(A2) $(\forall x)(\nu \to \varphi) \to (\nu \to (\forall x)\varphi)$
where ν is a formula in which x is not free.

Deduction rules: Modus ponens and *generalization*: from φ derive $(\forall x)\varphi$.

A *proof* in a theory T is a sequence $\varphi_1, \ldots, \varphi_n$ of formulas (not necessarily closed) such that each φ_i either is a logical axiom or belongs to T (is a special axiom) or results from some previous formulas(s) using one of the deduction rules. A formula φ is *provable* in T (notation: $T \vdash \varphi$) if φ is the last member of a proof in T.

Gödel's completeness theorem: $T \vdash \varphi$ iff φ is true in each model of T. In particular, φ is a tautology (true in all interpretations) iff $\vdash \varphi$ (φ is provable using only logical axioms).

3.2   Łukasiewicz's predicate logic

: A *language* consists of predicates, object variables and object constants as above. Then we have the *connectives* (in Łukasiewicz's logic just $\neg, \to$) and quantifier(s) - $\forall$. We define some derived connectives (in Ł: $\&, \wedge, \underline{\vee}, \vee, \equiv$) and quantifiers (here: $\exists$ as $\neg\forall\neg$ - as above). A *many valued interpretation* is a structury

$$\mathbf{M} = \langle M, (r_P)_P, (m_c)_c \rangle$$

where everything is as above except for r_P; r_P is a fuzzy many relation on M, i.e. a mapping of M^n into the unit interval $[0,1]$. (Each tuple is in the relation in some degree). The *truth degree* $\|\varphi\|_{\mathbf{M}}$ of a formula φ is defined as follows:

- If φ is atomic, $P(c,\ldots,d)$, then $\|\varphi\|_{\mathbf{M}} = r_P(m_c,\ldots,m_d)$ (the degree in which the tuple of meanings of constants is in the fuzzy relation r_p);
- $\|\varphi \to \psi\|_{\mathbf{M}} = \|\varphi\|_{\mathbf{M}} \to^\bullet \|\psi\|_{\mathbf{M}}$, $\|\neg\varphi\|_{\mathbf{M}} = \neg^\bullet \|\varphi\|_{\mathbf{M}}$;
- $\|(\forall x)\varphi\|_{\mathbf{M}} = \inf_c(\|\varphi(c)\|_{\mathbf{M}})$.

The attempts to find an effective (recursive) systems of logical axioms and deduction rules complete with respect to 1-tautologies were unsuccessful; finally, Scarpellini [31] has shown that no such axiomatization exists: the set of 1-tautologies is not recursively enumerable. (For experts: Goldstern has announced a result saying that the set of all 1-tautologies of Łukasiewicz's predicate logic is Π-complete - personal commucation.)

But we shall show in the next subsection that it is profitable to extend à la Pavelka; then we may say more. This is done in the next section.

3.3 Rational quantification logic

We extend Łukasiewicz's predicate logic by propositional constants $\bar{r}$ for each rational $r \in [0,1]$; for each $\mathbf{M}$, $\|\bar{r}\|_{\mathbf{M}} = r$. The *axioms* of RQL are those of RPL plus (A1), (A2) from 3.1 plus

(A3) $\qquad\qquad (\nu \to (\exists x)\varphi) \to (\exists x)(\nu \to \varphi)$

where x is not free in ν.

One easily sees that all axioms are 1-tautologies of our logic; (A3) is provable in classical logic but here we have to postulate it. We introduce (φ, r) as abbreviation of $(\bar{r} \to \varphi)$ as above; given a theory T, we define the provability degree and truth degree as above:

$$|\varphi|_T = \sup\{r \mid T \vdash (r \to \varphi)\},$$

$$\|\varphi\|_T = \inf\{\|\varphi\|_{\mathbf{M}} \mid M \text{ a model of } T\}.$$

(We should say that for a non-closed φ, $\|\varphi\|_{\mathbf{M}}$ is defined as $\|(\forall x_n)\ldots(\forall x_n)\varphi\|_{\mathbf{M}}$ analogously as above; $\mathbf{M}$ is a *model* of T if $\|\varphi\|_{\mathbf{M}} = 1$ for each $\varphi \in T$.

We have the following Pavelka-style

Completeness theorem (see [12]). For each theory T and formula φ,

$$\|\varphi\|_T = |\varphi|_T,$$

i.e. the truth degree equals the provability degree. Let T be a recursive theory. For each positive $r \in [0,1]$, the set $Pr(T,r)$ of all φ such that $|\varphi|_T \geq r$ is Π_2;

there is a recursive theory T such that $Pr(T, 1)$ is Π_2-complete. (See again [12]; but the announced Goldstern's result is better.)

Thus RQL is an elegant fuzzy predicate calculus with truth degree equal to provability degree; on the other hand, it badly undecidable. For details see [12] and its predecessors, in particular, [25].

3.4 Gödel's predicate logic

This logic is, in contradistinction to Łukasiewicz's logic, recursively axiomatizable. We present a variant of the system discovered by Takeuti and Titani [34], adapted to be as similar to the systems we have had till now as possible.

One extends the notion of a language to contain *propositional* variables, thus: atomic formulas are either of the from $P(s, \ldots, t)$ when $s, \ldots, t$ are object variables or object constants or just z where z is a propositional variable. An other formulas are built using connectives $\rightarrow, \neg, \wedge, \vee$ and quantifiers $\forall, \exists$. An *interpretation* has the form

$$\mathbf{M} = \langle M, (r_P)_{P \text{ predicate}}, (m_c)_{c \text{ constant}}, (t_z)_{z \text{ prop.var}} \rangle$$

where for each propositional variable $z, t_z, \in [0, 1]$ (a truth-value).

Clearly, $\|z\|_{\mathbf{M}} = t_z$; $\|\varphi\|_M$ for other formulas is defined in the obvious way, using truth functions of Gödel's logic,

$$(\|(\exists x)\varphi\|_{\mathbf{M}} = \sup_c \|\varphi(c)\|_{\mathbf{M}}).$$

Logical axioms are those of Gödel's propositional logic (see 2.5) plus the axioms (A1), (A2) of classical predicate logic (see 3.1) plus

(A3) $(\forall x)(\varphi \rightarrow \nu) \rightarrow ((\exists x)\varphi \rightarrow \nu)$
(A4) $\varphi(t) \rightarrow (\exists x)\varphi$
(B1) $(\forall x)(\nu \vee \varphi) \rightarrow (\nu \vee (\forall x)\varphi)$
(B2) $((\forall x)\varphi \rightarrow \nu) \rightarrow ((\exists x)(\varphi \rightarrow \eta) \vee (\eta \rightarrow \nu))$

where x is not free in ν, η and t is free for x in φ.

Deduction rules are modus ponens, generalization and the following rule called (TT) after Takeuti-Titani: from $\chi \vee (\varphi \rightarrow z) \vee (z \rightarrow \psi)$ infer $\chi \vee (\varphi \rightarrow \psi)$. Here φ, ψ, χ are formulas and z is a propositional variable; conditions of use are incorporated into the notion of a proof in a theory T:

Let T be a theory. A sequence $\varphi_1, \ldots, \varphi_n$ of formulas is a *proof* in T of each φ_i either is a logical axiom or is an element of T (special axiom) or results from some previous elements of the sequence by modus ponens or generalization *or* [φ_i results from some previous φ_j by (TT) and *the critical variable occurs neither in χ, φ, ψ nor in any previous φ_j which is a member of T* (is a special axiom)].

This is rather tricky and elegant notion of a proof. It is *sound* in the following sense: if $T \vdash \varphi$ then for each M there is a conjunction α of finitely many elements of T such that $\| \alpha \|_T \leq \| \varphi \|_T$. It follows that if all axioms of T are 1-true in M ($\| \alpha \|_{\mathbf{M}} = 1$) and $T \vdash \varphi$ then $\| \varphi \|_{\mathbf{M}} = 1$ too. Moreover, if M is such that $\| \alpha \|_{\mathbf{M}} \geq r$ for some r and all $\alpha \in T$ and if $T \vdash \varphi$ then $\| \varphi \|_{\mathbf{M}} \geq r$.

And, by [34], we have completeness; $T \vdash \varphi$ iff for each M there is a conjunction α of finitely many elements of T such that $\| \alpha \|_{\mathbf{M}} \leq \| \varphi \|_{\mathbf{M}}$. In particular, φ is a 1-tautology ($\| \varphi \|_{\mathbf{M}} = 1$ for all $\mathbf{M}$ iff $\vdash \varphi$).

Hence, in contradistinction to Łukasiewicz's predicate logic (and Rational Quantification Logic), the set of all 1-tautologies of Gödel's predicate logic is recursively enumerable.

We have surveyed two main systems of fuzzy predicate calculus: Łukasiewicz's calculus (with its extension RQL à la Pavelka-Novák) and Gödel's calculus (à la Takeuti-Titani). The investigation of a predicate calculus based on the product conjunction remains to be a future task. Notice that both RQL and Gödel's calculus may be used to derive conclusions that are only partially true, but in different ways.

4 General fuzzy logics

In this section we describe a very general approach to the syntax and semantics of fuzzy logics, developed by Pavelka [28]. This approach does not assume any truth functionality.

4.1 Formulas and models

We have a set *Form* of *formulas*. These may be formulas of some propositional logic, predicate logic, or quite abstract entities. *Semantics* is given by a set S whose element are called *models*. Each model is a mapping $M : Form \to [0,1]$; thus M assigns to each formula the degree in which it is true (in the model).

For example, *Form* consists of formulas of Łukasiewicz's propositional calculus and S consists of all $e : Form \to [0,1]$ obeying the truth functions of connectives, i.e. $e(\varphi \to \psi) = e(\varphi) \to^{\bullet} e(\psi)$, $e(\neg \varphi) = \neg^{\bullet} e(\varphi)$.

Any $T : Form \to [0,1]$ may be understood as a *fuzzy theory*; $T(\varphi)$ is the degree in which φ is an axiom. An $M \in S$ is a *model of* T if, for each φ, $M(\varphi) \geq T(\varphi)$ (each formula is at least as true as the theory T demands).

For each fuzzy theory T and formula φ, let $\| \varphi \|_T = \inf \{ M(\varphi) \mid M$ is a model of $T \}$ (the truth degree of φ for T).

4.2 Provability

We shall work with *graded formulas*, i.e. pairs (φ, x) where φ is a formula and $x \in [0,1]$. An n-ary *deduction rule* assigns to some n-tuples $(\varphi_1, x_1, \ldots (\varphi_n, x_n)$ of graded formulas a graded formula $(r'(\varphi_1, \ldots, \varphi_n), r''(x_1, \ldots, x_n))$ (r', r'' are appropriate functions).

The function r'' is assumed to preserve all (infinite) suprema, i.e. if $\sup_{n \in I}(x_n) = y$ then $\sup_{n \in I}(r''(\ldots, x_n, \ldots)) = r''(\ldots, \sup_{n \in I} x_n, \ldots)$.

For example, recall the *fuzzy modus ponens* in Łukasiewicz's logic:

$$\frac{(\varphi, x), (\varphi \to \psi, y)}{(\psi, x \,\&^{\bullet} y)}.$$

A theory T is *closed under* the rule (r', r'') if for each tuple $\varphi_1, \ldots, \varphi_n$ of formulas, $T(r'(\varphi_1, \ldots, \varphi_n)) \geq r''(T(\varphi_1), \ldots T(\varphi_n))$, i.e. if $T(\varphi_i) = x_i$ and $T(r'(\varphi_1, \ldots, \varphi_n)) = y$ then from $(\varphi_1, x_1), \ldots, (\varphi_n, x_n)$ the rule derives $(r'(\varphi_1, \ldots, \varphi_n), r''(x_1, \ldots, x_n))$ and T demands $r'(\varphi_1, \ldots \varphi_n)$ to be at least y-true, $y \geq r''(x_1, \ldots, x_n))$.

A *deductive structure* is given by a fuzzy theory A (of logical axioms) and a set $\mathcal{R}$ of deduction rules. For each fuzzy theory T, there is a unique theory $T' \supseteq T$ such that $T \supseteq A$ and T is closed under each rule from $\mathcal{R}$. T' is denoted $Cn_{A,\mathcal{R}}(T)$.

A *graded proof* in T (given $A, \mathcal{R}$) is a set of graded formulas $(\varphi_1, x_1), \ldots, (\varphi_n, x_n)$ such that each (φ_i, x_i) either is a logical axiom $(A(\varphi_i) = x_i)$ or is an axiom of T ($T(\varphi_i) = x_i$) or (φ_i, x_i) results by a rule $R \in \mathcal{R}$ from some previous graded formulas. The *provability* degree $|\varphi|_T$ is $\sup\{r \mid T \vdash (\varphi, x)\}$ (where $T \vdash (\varphi, x)$ obviously means that (φ, x) is the last member of a proof.

The condition of *sup* preservation guarrantees that for each φ
$|\varphi|_T = Cn_{AS}(T)(\varphi)$.

The deductive structure $(A, \mathcal{R})$ is *sound* for the semantics $\mathcal{S}$ if for each theory T and each formula $\varphi, |\varphi|_T \leq \|\varphi\|_T$ ($|\varphi|_T$ being defined using $(A, \mathcal{R})$, $\|\varphi\|_T$ using $\mathcal{S}$). It is *complete* if $|\varphi|_T = \|\varphi\|_T$.

We shall meet an interesting example of a non-truth-functional semantics and a corresponding deductive structure in subsection 5.3.

5 Applications; relation to probability

5.1 Max-min inference

The term "max-min inference" is used for the following: let X, Y be two finite domains and let $\mathcal{R}$ be a *fuzzy relation* on $X \times Y$, i.e. $\mathcal{R}$ maps $X \times Y$ into [0,1]. For each fuzzy subset A of X (i.e. $A : X \to [0, 1]$) we define the *image* of A by $\mathcal{R}$ as the fuzzy subset B of Y defined as follows:

$$B(y) = \max_{x \in X}(A(x) \wedge R(x, y))$$

($\wedge$ is minimum). Thus R defines a mapping of fuzzy subsets of X into fuzzy subsets of Y, that's all. Is here any logic? If we want we may get some logic as follows: consider elements $p \in X$, $q \in y$ as propositional variables and take a graded version of Gödel's logic, i.e. a fuzzy theory consists of graded formulas (φ, X); the following fuzzy deduction rule is sound.

$$\frac{(\varphi, x), \ (\varphi \to \psi, y)}{\psi, x \wedge^\bullet y}$$

($\wedge^\bullet$ is minimum).

$T_{A,R}$ let be the following fuzzy theory:

$$T_{A,R} = \{((p \to q), \ R(p,q)\} \cup \{(p, A(p))\}.$$

Then for each p, $T_{A,R} \vdash (q, A(p) \wedge R(p,q))$, thus $|q|_T \geq \max(A(p) \wedge R(p,q)$ and one easily sees that in fact $|q|_T = \max(A(p) \wedge R(p,q))$. Thus the desired fuzzy set B satisfies $B(q) = |q|_T$. (Admittedly, this is as not much logic; see [21] for further investigation.) This kind of inference is used at least in fuzzy control and fuzzy expert systems; we comment on them.

5.2 Fuzzy controllers

We describe a simplified but typical case. X is the controlled variable, Y the control; the dependence is described by "fuzzy IF-THEN rules" of the form

$$\text{IF } X \text{ is } A_i \text{ THEN } Y \text{ is } B_i$$

$i = 1, \ldots, n$ where A_i is a fuzzy sebset of X, B_i of Y. (Typically: A_i may say "very big" and similar.) This is used to construct a fuzzy relation R:

$$R(x,y) = \max_i (A_i(x) \wedge B_i(y)).$$

Thus the rule is *not* understood as any "implication" among "X is A_i", "Y is B_i"; rather, it is understood as "fuzzy point" in the space $X \times Y$ and the max-min inference of B from A is a sort of "interpolation" of the point (A,B) among the points (A_i, B_i). See [9] for a degree analysis.

Note that fuzzy control has several aspects unrelated to any logic: given the knowledge R (given by fuzzy rules) and a crisp numeric input a, it first converts a into a fuzzy subset A of X (fuzzification), then constructs B and finally converts B into a crisp number (defuzzification). The mechanism appears suprisingly simple but using all this to approximate a crisp numerical function one has to carefully "tune" the exact definitions of A_i, B_i (as mappings of X or Y into [0,1]) and carefully select a method of fuzzification and defuzzification. Thus fuzzy control is fuzzy logic more in a wide sense. See [3] for move information.

5.3 Fuzy expert systems

A prominent example is CADIAG-2 [1]. Think of elements of X as symptoms, elements of Y as diseases. A fuzzy subsset A of X presents imprecise data about the patient: for each symptom $S \in X$, $A(S)$ is the degree in which it is true that the patient has the symptom. Similarly, B is a fuzzy set of diagnoses. So far so good; but the main trouble is that in systems like CADIAG, the value $R(S,D)$ is set to be something like conditional probability of D given S (or relative frequence obtained from data). This is *very questionable* since it remains rather dark what is the meaning of the "inferred" fuzzy set B. For example, if the data about the patient satisfy $A(S_1) = A(S_2 = 1$ (the patient has (fully) S_1 and S_2 and $A(S_i) = 0$ otherwise, $P(D \mid S_1) = P(D \mid S_2) = 0.7$ then $B(D) = 0.7$; but this absolutely need not be $P(D \mid S_1 \wedge S_2)$. It may not be; but *what* the computed B is, remains dark. For example, $P(D \mid S_1 \wedge S_2)$ may be 0,3; but if you add $S_1 \wedge S_2$ as a new element of X and define $R(S_1 \wedge S_2, D) = 0.3$ you will still get $B(D \mid S_1 \wedge S_2) = 0.7$. Cf. [16] for some discussion.

The reader should see that "max-min inference" is O.K. and admits a simple logical presentation; but its use for deriving *degrees of certainty* is denbtful. See also [19].

5.4 Fuzzy logic and probability

Let us now discuss the relation of fuzzy logic to probability theory. We stressed at the beginning the *difference* betwęen fuzzziness and randomness: fuzzy logic deals with degree of truth (and may well be truth-functional), whereas probability theory (or any probabilistic logic) deals with degrees of (uncertainty and surely is *not truth functional*.

But, first, we do have non-truth functional fuzzy logics, as we saw in the preceding section. Let *Form* be the set of all formulas of classical propositional logic and let S be the set of all *probabilies* as Form; each such probability satisfies $P(1) = 1$, $P(0) = 0$, $P(\varphi \vee \psi) = P(\varphi) + P(\psi)$ if $\neg(\varphi \ \& \ \psi)$ is a boolean tautology, $P(\varphi) = P(\psi)$ if $\varphi \equiv \psi$ is a boolean tautology.

Observe that the fuzzy modus ponens of Łukasiewicz's logic

$$\frac{(\varphi, x), \ (\varphi \rightarrow \psi, y)}{(\psi, x \ \&^\bullet \ y)}$$

is sound, i.e. if $P(\varphi) \geq x$ and $P(\varphi \rightarrow \psi) = P(\neg\varphi \vee \psi) \geq y$ then $P(\psi) \geq max(x + y - 1, 0)$. Thus inferences in this sort of graded logic *preserve lower formals of probabilies*. But one should not forget that $P(\varphi \rightarrow \psi)$ is $P(\neg\varphi \vee \psi)$, thus $1 - P(\varphi \ \& \ \neg\psi)$, *not* any conditional probability $P(\psi \mid \varphi)$. See [16]. For a complete axiomatization see [6].

There is a second way, mentioned in [16] and elaborated in [14]: Probability is a quantity (on formulas of boolean logic); and we associate to each boolean formula φ a fuzzy proposition saying "φ is provable". This is a new proppositional variable of fuzzy logic – and $P(\varphi)$ may be taken to be its degree of truth. In [14] we present a theory FP in RPL such that an evaluation e of the variables f_φ (φ boolean) is a model of FP iff the function $P(\varphi) = e(f_\varphi)$ is a (finitely additive) probability. There are just few axioms:

(FP1) $(f_\varphi, 1)$ for φ being an axiom of classical propositional logic (the obvious three schemes),
(FP2) $(f_{\varphi \rightarrow \psi} \rightarrow (f_\varphi \rightarrow f_\psi), 1)$ for all φ, ψ,
(FP3) $(f_{\neg\varphi} \leftrightarrow \neg f_\varphi, 1)$ for each φ,
(FP4) $(f_{\varphi \vee \psi} \leftrightarrow [(f_\varphi \rightarrow f_{\varphi \wedge \psi}) \rightarrow f_\psi], 1)$ for each φ, ψ.

The important thing is: $f_\varphi \wedge f_\psi$ is *not* equivalent to $f_{(\varphi \wedge \psi)}$ ("φ is provable and ψ is provable" does not imply "$\varphi \wedge \psi$ is provable").

6 Conclusion

I hope that I have shown the following:

- *Fuzzy logic is neither a poor man's logic nor poor man's probability.* Fuzzy logic (in the narrow sense) is a reasonably deep theory.
- *Fuzzy logic is a logic.* It has its syntax and semantic and notion of consequence. It is a study of consequence.
- *There are various systems of fuzzy logic, not just one.* The main two most developedp systems are those of Łukasiewicz and of Gödel, the first together with its extension à la Pavelka.

In addition, I claim the following:

- *Further logical investigations of fuzzy logic are possible.* In particular, one has to apply the theory of generalized quantifiers to fuzzy logic and go further in a strictly logical analysis of things pointed out by Zadeh as "particular agenda of fuzzy logic". Cf also [4].
- *To construct combined calculi of vagueness and of uncertainty is possible.* See [17, 18] for information; one gets many-valued modal logics.
- *Fuzzy logic in the narrow sense is a beautiful logic, but also is important for applications:* it offers foundations.

References

1. ADLASSNIG, K.-P. CADIAG: Approaches to Computer-Assisted Medical Diagnosis. *Computers in Biology and Medicine* 15, 315-335.
2. ALSINA C., TRILLAS E. AND VALVERDE L. On some logical connectives for fuzzy set theory. *J. Math. Anal. Appl.* 93 (1983), 15-26.
3. DRIANKOV D., HELLENDORF H., REINFRANK M. *An Introduction to Fuzzy Control.* Springer-Verlag 1993
4. DUBOIS, D., PRADE, H. Fuzzy sets in approximate reasoning II (Logical approaches). *Fuzzy sets and systems* 40 (1991), 203-244
5. ELKAN, C. The paradoxical success of fuzzy logic. *Proceedings of the Eleventh National Conference on Artificial Intelligence* (AAAI'93), MIT Press 1993, 698-703
6. GERLA, G. Inferences in probability logic. *Artificial Intelligence 70* (1994), 33–52.
7. GÖDEL, K. Zum intuitionistischen Aussagenkalkül. Anzeiger Akademie der Wissenschaften Wien, Math. - naturwissensch. Klasse 69, 65-66, 1932. Also in Ergebnisse eines matematischen Kolloquiums 4 (1933), 40.
8. GOTTWALD, S. *Mehrwertige Logik.* Akademie-Verlag, Berlin, 1988.
9. GOTTWALD, S. *Fuzzy Sets and Fuzzy Logic* Vieweg 1993.
10. HÁJEK P. Úvod do logiky. Proc. *SOFSEM'89* Magura 1989, p. 81-92.
11. HÁJEK, P. Fuzzy logic and arithmetical hierarchy. *Fuzzy Sets and Systems* (to appear).
12. HÁJEK, P. Fuzzy logic and arithmetical hierarchy, II. Studia Logica (to appear).
13. HÁJEK, P. Fuzzy logic as logic. Proc. Mathematical Models of Handling Partial Knowledge (Erice, Italy, 1994 (to appear).
14. HÁJEK, P., GODO, L., AND ESTEVA, F. Fuzzy logic and probability. *Uncertainty in Artifical Intelligence*, 1995 (to appear)
15. HÁJEK, P., GODO, L., AND ESTEVA, F. A complete many-valued logic with product-conjunction. Submitted.

16. HÁJEK P., HARMANCOVÁ D. Medical fuzzy expert systems and reasoning about beliefs. *Proc. AIME'95*, Lecture Notes in Computer Science, Springer-Verlag 1995

17. HÁJEK P., HARMANCOVÁ D. VERBRUGGE R.L. A qualitative fuzzy possibilistic logic. *Int. J. of Approximate Reasoning*, 12 (1995) , 1-19

18. HÁJEK P., HARMANCOVÁ D., ESTEVA F., GARCÍA P., GODO L. On modal logics for qualitative possibility in a fuzzy environment, *Uncertainty in AI '94*, L. de Mantaras and D. Poole, ed., Morgan-Kaufmann Publ. 1994, p.278-285

19. HÁJEK, P., NGUYEN, HOANG PHUONG CADIAG-2 and MYCIN-like systems. Submitted.

20. IEEE EXPERT August 1994 (special issue "A fuzzy logic symposium").

21. KLAWONN, F., NOVÁK, V. The relation between inference and interpolation in the framework of fuzzy systems. Submitted.

22. LUKASIEWICZ, J. *Selected works*. North-Holland Publ. Comp. 1970.

23. MARKS II, R., J. *Fuzzy Logic Technology and Applications.* IEEE Technical Activities Board, 1994

24. MENDELSON, E. *Introduction to Mathematical Logic.* Van Nostrand 1964

25. NOVÁK, V. On the syntactico-semantical completeness of first-order fuzzy logic I, II. *Kybernetika* 26 (1990), 47-26, 134-152.

26. NOVÁK, V. Fuzzy control from the logical point of view. *Fuzzy sets and Systems* 66 (1994) 159-173

27. PARIS, J.B. The uncertain reasoner's companion – a mathematical perspective. Cambridge University Press, 1994.

28. PAVELKA, J. On fuzzy logic I, II, III. *Zeitschr. f. Math. Logik und Grundl. der Math.* 25 (1979), 45-52, 119-134, 447-464

29. RASIOWA, H., SIKORSKI, R. *The mathematics of metamathematics.* Warszawa 1963

30. ROSE, A. AND ROSSER, J. B. Fragments of many-valued statement calculi. *Trans. A.M.S.* 87 (1958), 1-53.

31. SCARPELINI, B. Die Nichtaxiomatisierbarkeit des unendlichwertigen Prädikatenkalküls von Lukasiewicz. *Journ. Symb. Log.* 27 (1962), 159-170.

32. SCHWEIZER, B. AND SKLAR, A. Associative functions and abstract semi-groups. *Publ. Math. Debrecen* 10 (1963), 69-81

33. SCHWEIZER, B. AND SKLAR, A. *Probabilistic metric spaces.* North Holland, Amsterdam, 1983.

34. TAKEUTI G. AND TITANI S. Fuzzy Logic and fuzzy set theory. *Anal. Math. Logic* 32, pp. 1-32, 1992.

35. ZADEH L. The concept of a linguistic variable and its application to approximate reasoning. *Information Sciences* 8 (1975), 199-245, 301-357

36. ZADEH, L. Fuzzy logic. *IEEE Computer 1:83* (1988).

37. ZIMMERMANN, H.J. *Fuzzy Set Theory and its Applications.* Kluwer, Nijhof, second edition 1991.

Sense of Direction in Processor Networks

Gerard Tel[*1]

Department of Computer Science, Utrecht University,
P.O. Box 80.089, 3508 TB Utrecht, The Netherlands.
Email: gerard@cs.ruu.nl

Abstract. We discuss recent research evaluating the benefits of certain link labellings in processor networks. Such a labelling, called *Sense of Direction* or SoD, allows processors to communicate more efficiently with each other, and to exploit topological properties of the network algorithmically.

We shall define sense of direction for several specific classes of network, and show how the election problem on rings can be solved more efficiently if chords and a sense of direction are available. We shall show that elections can be performed with linear complexity in Hypercubes and Cliques if SoD is available, but also that a randomised algorithm can achieve the same complexity without using SoD. Algorithms to compute an SoD in networks were none is given will also be presented.

Some results in this paper were previously unpublished or only presented in technical reports.

1. The group definition and characterisation of Sense of Direction; see Subsection 1.3.
2. Some results (e.g., Theorems 6 and 28, Algorithm 4) are stated more generally than they were before.
3. Improved performance of Attiya's election algorithm; see Subsection 2.3.
4. The linear chordal ring algorithm with one chord; see Subsection 2.4.

The work reported in Subsections 2.3 and 2.4 was done with Andreas Fabri.

1 Introduction

Computation intensive tasks, such as weather forecasting and aerodynamical simulations, are usually implemented on parallel computers, structured as processor networks. Each processor can be programmed, like a conventional uniprocessor computer, but in addition to the classical instruction set there are *communication* instructions for sending and receiving messages. Operands of these instructions are the data to be sent or received, and the local name of the connection for which the instruction is carried out. Alternative designs where processors

---

[*] The work of this author was supported by ESPRIT Basic Research Action No. 7141 (project ALCOM II: *Algorithms and Complexity*) and by the Netherlands Organisation for Scientific Research (NWO) under contract NF 62-376 (NFI project ALADDIN: *Algorithmic Aspects of Parallel and Distributed Systems*).

communicate by sharing registers are also common, but in this article we shall assume message based communications.

To study the distributed aspects of these computations, the network is conveniently modelled as a graph, where the processors constitute the nodes and an edge exists between nodes that are connected physically. For example, Inmos produces so-called Transputers, which are powerful processors with four ports to allow connection to four other Transputers. It is possible to connect 16 Transputers in a four-dimensional cube shape as depicted in Figure 1. The system on the left would have no connection to the outside world, so it would not be possible to load programs or inputs, or learn about the outputs of the computation. The processor network must be connected to a host, as depicted on the right, for example by "inserting" the host between two processors that are directly connected in the "idealised" picture on the left. After down loading the programs and inputs, the host computer simply relays all communication between the two processors. We shall ignore the host or other means of communication with the outside world in the rest of the paper.

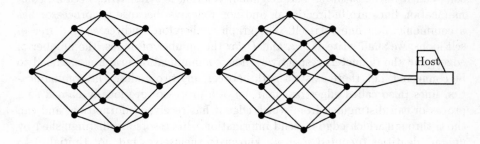

Figure 1 Hypercube network of degree four.

Large scale computer networks (such as the Internet) or local area networks often have an arbitrary graph as their topology, because they have evolved gradually from a small network by adding sites on incidental basis. Processor networks, however, are usually constructed with a regular, symmetric topology, and the local names of the connections of a processor are meaningful with respect to the position of the edge in the network. If connection names are meaningful we say the network is equipped with a sense of direction. The goal of this paper is to give insight in how a sense of direction can be exploited, by presenting efficient algorithms that rely critically on sense of direction.

Overview of the paper. This section introduces some general notions and problems further discussed in later sections. Subsection 1.1 explains the model used for processor networks. Subsection 1.2 introduces the sense of direction informally, and Subsection 1.3 provides some formal definitions. Subsection 1.4 describes how a message can be broadcast efficiently using a *uniform* sense of direction. Subsection 1.5 briefly introduces the election problem, which will serve as a comparison benchmark in the rest of the paper.

Then Section 2 presents some old and new results regarding elections in rings and chordal rings with sense of direction; the new results improve on the node degree necessary to allow linear message election algorithms in chordal rings.

Section 3 discusses the benefits of sense of direction in hypercubes and cliques; especially the situation in hypercubes deserves attention because the complexity of election *without* sense of direction is not completely known.

Section 4 discusses some algorithms to compute a sense of direction in unlabelled networks; these algorithms were previously published [Tel94b]. We end the paper with discussion and open questions (Section 5).

1.1 The Model of Processor Networks

A processor network is a collection of autonomous processors, each capable of executing a local program and communicating with a subset of the other processors, called its *neighbours*. The neighbour relation is symmetric, because communication lines are bidirectional, and non-reflexive, because no processor has a communication line to itself. The graph is therefore undirected and free of self-loops; we shall write N, m, and D for the number of nodes, the number of edges, and the diameter, respectively. The communication graph is assumed to be connected, i.e., there exists a path between any two nodes. The communication lines (also called edges or channels) of a processor are locally named so a processor can distinguish from which edge it has received information, and can chose through which edge to send information. Processors are distinguished by unique identities (denoted p, q, r), known to themselves but not (initially) to the other processors. These identities are uninterpreted numbers, and have no topological significance.

Processors and communication lines are *not* synchronised. That is, between two steps of one processor, another processor can make an arbitrary number of steps. Also, there is no bound on the time that can elapse between sending a message and its receipt by the sender's neighbour.

For the purpose of our study we shall assume (which is not very advisable in practical situations) that the network is reliable, that is, no processor ever goes defective, and every message sent will eventually arrive. We use a Pascal-like pseudo code notation to express algorithms where a variable subscript (as in lbl_p) denotes the processor (p) where the variable is located.

1.2 Exploiting Sense of Direction

Consider a network where the processors share a resource (such as a file or special permission), which is always located in one processor but can move on request. The processors do not have accurate information about the current location of the resource, but each processor keeps a pointer to the neighbour from which it

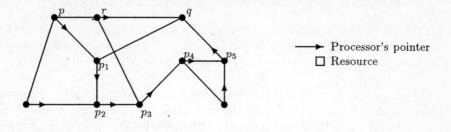

Figure 2 Resource location without sense of direction.

most recently heard about the resource. Using the pointers, requests for using the resource are routed towards the resource location.

In Figure 2 the request of processor p is forwarded via p_1 through p_5, and arrives at q holding the resource. In order to get the resource at p, each of the intermediate processors remembers from which neighbour it received p's request, and the resource follows the request path in the reverse direction. (The pointer is updated in the intermediate processors.) This seems to be a waste, because processors q and p are connected via r, and in fact only at distance 2 from each other. In unlabelled networks, this waste is difficult to avoid because q does not know of the existence of the shorter path.

Figure 3 shows the same principle in a torus network (SoD assumed!). Again q receives the request via five intermediate processors, but observes that the request was sent to the west, the north, the north, the east, the east, and the south. The directions allow q to send the reply via the shorter path through r (south and west). We shall show in Subsection 1.4 how to generalise the principle to other network topologies.

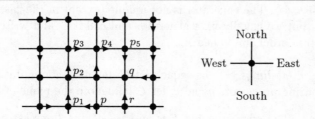

Figure 3 Resource location with sense of direction.

In Subsection 1.4 it will be demonstrated that sense of direction also helps to reduce the complexity of broadcasting information.

1.3 Definition and Characterisation of Sense of Direction

Although sense of direction has received quite some attention in the recent years, no easy definition of what it is has been agreed upon. Several instances were defined [Tel94b], and classes of sense of direction were identified [FMS95].

The group definition. In this article we shall follow a group-theoretical approach and therefore we recall some group theory notions first. A commutative or abelian *group* is a set G with special *zero* element 0 and a binary operator $+$, satisfying the following requirements.

1. *Closure:* For all x, $y \in G$, $(x + y) \in G$.
2. *Identity:* For all $x \in G$, $0 + x = x + 0 = x$.
3. *Inverse:* For all $x \in G$ there exists a $y \in G$ such that $x + y = y + x = 0$.
4. *Associativity:* For all x, y, $z \in G$, $(x + y) + z = x + (y + z)$.
5. *Commutativity:* For all x, y, $x + y = y + x$.

Because of associativity we may omit parenthesis in summations; we write $-x$ for x's inverse, and if $s \in \mathbb{Z}$, $s.x$ denotes the sum of s x's.

The number of elements in G is called its *order*; it is assumed finite in this article. In finite groups, for each x there are positive numbers k such that $k.x = 0$; the smallest such number is the *order* of x, and it divides the order of the group.

For elements g_1 through g_k, consider the set of elements that can be written as a sum of g_i:

$$S = \{x \mid \exists s_1, ..., s_k : x = \sum_{i=1}^{k} s_i.g_i\}.$$

This set is itself a group, called the *subgroup generated by g_1 through g_k* and denoted $\langle g_1, ..., g_k \rangle$. For $y \in G$, the set $T = S + y = \{y + x \mid x \in S\}$ is called an *orbit* of S or of g_1 through g_k. All orbits of S are of the same size, and orbits $S + y_1$ and $S + y_2$ are either equal or disjoint, hence the orbits of S partition G.

The group is *cyclic* if it is generated by one single element, i.e., there is a g such that $G = \langle g \rangle$. The generator is not unique (except in the case of the group of order 2), but we usually fix a generator and call it 1, and write i for $i.1$; the cyclic group of order k is called $\mathbb{Z}_k$.

Networks and labellings. In the sequel, let G denote a commutative group and for neighbouring processors p and q, let $\mathcal{L}_p[q]$ denote the name of link pq at p.

Definition 1. The edge labelling $\mathcal{L}$ is a *sense of direction (based on G)* if the edge labels are elements of G, and there exists a bijection $\mathcal{N}$ from the nodes to G such that for all neighbours p and q, $\mathcal{N}(q) = \mathcal{N}(p) + \mathcal{L}_p[q]$.

Given a sense of direction $\mathcal{L}$, a node labelling as specified in the definition is called a *witnessing labelling* or *witness* for $\mathcal{L}$. The processors know the link labels $\mathcal{L}$, but a witnessing node labelling is not required or assumed to be known to the processors and is *not* part of the sense of direction.

Observe that an SoD does not contain the label 0 (because node labels of neighbours differ) and that an SoD satisfies the *anti-symmetry* property $\mathcal{L}_p[q] + \mathcal{L}_q[p] = 0$, or, equivalently, $\mathcal{L}_p[q] = -\mathcal{L}_q[p]$.

Lemma 2. *If a network has a sense of direction based on G then the order of G equals N.*

Proof. The definition requires a bijection from the network to the group. □

Lemma 3. *If $\mathcal{L}$ is a sense of direction there are exactly N node labellings witnessing this.*

Proof. As $\mathcal{L}$ is a sense of direction, there is a witness; let $\mathcal{N}$ be one, i.e., for neighbours p and q we have $\mathcal{N}(q) = \mathcal{N}(p) + \mathcal{L}_p[q]$.

First, for an arbitrary g in G, define the function $\mathcal{N}^{(g)}$ by $\mathcal{N}^{(g)}(p) = \mathcal{N}(p) + g$. For neighbours p and q we have

$$
\begin{aligned}
\mathcal{N}^{(g)}(q) &= \mathcal{N}(q) + g && \text{by definition of } \mathcal{N}^{(g)} \\
&= \mathcal{N}(p) + \mathcal{L}_p[q] + g && \text{because } \mathcal{N} \text{ is a witness} \\
&= \mathcal{N}(p) + g + \mathcal{L}_p[q] && \text{by commutativity} \\
&= \mathcal{N}^{(g)}(p) + \mathcal{L}_p[q] && \text{by definition of } \mathcal{N}^{(g)},
\end{aligned}
$$

showing that $\mathcal{N}^{(g)}$ is also a witness.

On the other hand, let $\mathcal{N}'$ be a witness for $\mathcal{L}$; pick an arbitrary processor p_0 and define $g = \mathcal{N}'(p_0) - \mathcal{N}(p_0)$; we show that $\mathcal{N}'(q) = \mathcal{N}^{(g)}(q)$ for every q. Let q be given, and consider a path $\langle p_0, \ldots, p_k \rangle$ with $p_k = q$; we show $\mathcal{N}'(p_i)) = \mathcal{N}^{(g)}(p_i)$ by induction on i. For $i = 0$, $\mathcal{N}'(p_0) = \mathcal{N}(p) + g = \mathcal{N}^{(g)}(p_0)$ is already known. Assuming $\mathcal{N}'(p_i) = \mathcal{N}^{(g)}(p_i)$, find

$$
\begin{aligned}
\mathcal{N}'(p_{i+1}) &= \mathcal{N}'(p_i) + \mathcal{L}_{p_i}[p_{i+1}] && \text{because } \mathcal{N}' \text{ is a witness} \\
&= \mathcal{N}^{(g)}(p_i) + \mathcal{L}_{p_i}[p_{i+1}] && \text{induct. hyp. for } p_i \\
&= \mathcal{N}(p_i) + \mathcal{L}_{p_i}[p_{i+1}] + g && \text{expand } \mathcal{N}^{(g)} \text{ and rewrite} \\
&= \mathcal{N}(p_{i+1}) + g && \text{because } \mathcal{N} \text{ is a witness} \\
&= \mathcal{N}^{(g)}(p_{i+1}) .
\end{aligned}
$$

The witnesses for $\mathcal{L}$ have been characterised as the functions $\mathcal{N}^{(g)}$, of which there are exactly $|G|$; with Lemma 2 this proves the result. □

Corollary 4. *A network has $(N-1)!$ different edge labellings that constitute a sense of direction.*

Proof. Every bijection $\mathcal{N}$ from the nodes to G witnesses for a labelling to be a sense of direction, namely the labelling obtained by $\mathcal{L}_p[q] = \mathcal{N}(q) - \mathcal{N}(p)$. As there are $N!$ bijections, and N of them witness for every sense of direction, there are $N!/N = (N-1)!$ different senses of direction. □

Definition using closed paths. Sense of direction can also be characterised without reference to witnessing node labellings by studying the properties of closed paths. A path $P = \langle p_0, \ldots, p_k \rangle$ is *closed* if $p_0 = p_k$; let $\mathcal{L}$ label ports with elements from G and define $SUM_{\mathcal{L}}(P)$ as $\mathcal{L}_{p_0}[p_1] + \ldots + \mathcal{L}_{p_{k-1}}[p_k]$.

Definition 5. The labelling $\mathcal{L}$ has the *closed path property* (CPP) if for all paths P, P is closed if and only if $SUM_{\mathcal{L}}(P) = 0$.

Theorem 6. *The following two statements are equivalent.*

1. *$\mathcal{L}$ is a sense of direction.*
2. *$\mathcal{L}$ has the closed path property.*

Proof. To prove that (1) implies (2), assume that $\mathcal{L}$ is a sense of direction; let $\mathcal{N}$ be a witness for $\mathcal{L}$, and consider any path $P = \langle p_0, \ldots, p_k \rangle$. It can be shown by induction on i that $\mathcal{N}(p_i) = \mathcal{N}(p_0) + \mathcal{L}_{p_0}[p_1] + \ldots + \mathcal{L}_{p_{i-1}}[p_i]$, hence $\mathcal{N}(p_k) = \mathcal{N}(p_0) + SUM_{\mathcal{L}}(P)$. This implies that $p_0 = p_k$ if and only if $SUM_{\mathcal{L}}(P) = 0$, and shows that $\mathcal{L}$ has the closed path property.

To prove that (2) implies (1), assume that $\mathcal{L}$ has the closed path property. For $P = \langle p_0, \ldots, p_k \rangle$, let the *reversed path* $P^{\mathbf{R}}$ be $\langle p_k, \ldots, p_0 \rangle$ and because P concatenated with $P^{\mathbf{R}}$ is a closed path we have $SUM_{\mathcal{L}}(P \cdot P^{\mathbf{R}}) = SUM_{\mathcal{L}}(P) + SUM_{\mathcal{L}}(P^{\mathbf{R}}) = 0$.

We construct a witnessing node labelling for $\mathcal{L}$ as follows. First fix an arbitrary node p_0, and to label q, choose any path P from p_0 to q and set $\mathcal{N}(q) = SUM_{\mathcal{L}}(P)$. Soundness of this definition requires that for any two paths P and Q from p to q, $SUM_{\mathcal{L}}(P) = SUM_{\mathcal{L}}(Q)$; but this follows from closedness of $Q \cdot P^{\mathbf{R}}$, so $SUM_{\mathcal{L}}(Q) + SUM_{\mathcal{L}}(P^{\mathbf{R}}) = 0$. To show that $\mathcal{N}$ witnesses for $\mathcal{L}$, let p and q be neighbours. For a path P from p_0 to p, $P \cdot \langle p, q \rangle$ is a path from p_0 to q, so

$$\begin{aligned}
\mathcal{N}(q) &= SUM_{\mathcal{L}}(P \cdot \langle p, q \rangle) \text{ by definition of } \mathcal{N} \\
&= SUM_{\mathcal{L}}(P) + \mathcal{L}_p[q] \\
&= \mathcal{N}(p) + \mathcal{L}_p[q],
\end{aligned}$$

which completes the proof. $\qquad\square$

An important property of sense of direction is that it allows processors to refer to the other processors by locally unique names, which can be translated from one processor to the other. Processor p refers to r as $\mathcal{N}(r) - \mathcal{N}(p)$ (observe that no witnessing node labelling need be known for this, because the difference is the same for all witnesses), or, equivalently, as $SUM_{\mathcal{L}}(P)$ for some path P from p to r. The local names can be translated; the processor referred to as x by p is referred to as $x + \mathcal{L}_q[p]$ by its neighbour q. The local name of a neighbour equals, of course, the label of the incident link.

Even though the ability to refer to the processors in this way does not provide a means to route messages efficiently, it was shown by Flocchini *et al.* [FMS95] that it allows to solve the election problem in general networks using only $O(N \lg N)$ (long) messages.

Uniformity. The processors in a parallel computer are usually connected in a structure that is symmetric (i.e., the graph "looks the same" from all processors) and known; both symmetry and topological knowledge are implicit in uniform sense of direction.

Definition 7. A sense of direction is *uniform* if each processor has the same collection of local labels.

Let L be the common set of link labels; some properties of uniform sense of direction are immediate.

1. If $g \in L$, then so is $-g$: a link labelled g is labelled $-g$ at the other end.
2. L generates G, because for each $g \in G$ a path P with $SUM_{\mathcal{L}}(P) = g$ exists.
3. For a $g \in G$ a shortest path P with $SUM_{\mathcal{L}}(P) = g$ can be locally computed by a generalised version of the *coin exchange problem*. It suffices to compute a minimal sequence of labels in L with sum g and, because every processor has these labels, this sequence defines a path in the network. This is used in Figure 3.

We describe a network with uniform sense of direction by the set of labels in a processor, often omitting inverses.

Examples. Several examples of sense of direction are found in the literature, most of which are instances of our definition; let $\mathbb{Z}_k$ denote the cyclic group of order k.

Flocchini *et al.* [FMS95] define *chordal* sense of direction. A chordal sense of direction is any sense of direction over $\mathbb{Z}_N$. Of special interest are Uniform Chordal SoD where 1 (or any other generator) is among the labels.

Definition 8. A *chordal ring* $C_N(c_1, \ldots, c_k)$ is a network for which there exists a uniform chordal sense of direction with

$$L = \{-c_k, \ldots, -c_1, -1, 1, c_1, \ldots, c_k\};$$

here k is called the number of chords.

The requirement that a generator of the group occurs as a label is crucial; a $k \times l$ torus, for example, with wraparound and k and l coprime has a uniform chordal sense of direction, but it is not a chordal ring.

Definition 9. An $n \times n$-*torus* is a network for which there exists a uniform SoD over $\mathbb{Z}_n \times \mathbb{Z}_n$ and $L = \{(0,1), (0,-1), (1,0), (-1,0)\}$. (The labels are conveniently referred to as *N, S, E, W.*)

Definition 10. An n-dimensional hypercube is a network for which there exists a uniform sense of direction with base $(\mathbb{Z}_2)^n$ and n labels $i = (0, .., 1, .., 0)$ for $i = 0..n - 1$.

Definition 11. A clique is a network for which there exists a uniform SoD with base $\mathbb{Z}_N$ and $L = \mathbb{Z}_N \setminus \{0\}$.

For the initiator:
> **for** $i = 1$ **to** k
>> **do if** $n_i > 1$ **then** send $\langle \mathbf{info}, n_i - 1 \rangle$ via link g_i

Upon receiving $\langle \mathbf{info}, s \rangle$ via link $-g_j$:
> **if** $s > 1$ **then** send $\langle \mathbf{info}, s - 1 \rangle$ via link g_i ;
> **for** $i = j + 1$ **to** k
>> **do if** $s_i > 1$ **then** send $\langle \mathbf{info}, s - 1 \rangle$ via link g_i

Algorithm 4 BROADCASTING WITH UNIFORM SENSE OF DIRECTION.

1.4   Broadcasting with Uniform Sense of Direction

In distributed systems it frequently occurs that some information must be *broadcast* from one processor to all processors. If no topological information is available, a broadcast requires the exchange of at least one message through every channel [Tel94a], hence has $\Omega(m)$ message complexity. Uniform sense of direction allows the processors to determine a spanning tree of the network "on the fly" and send the broadcast message through it, achieving the broadcast in exactly $N - 1$ messages. This number is optimal, because each of the $N - 1$ processors different from the initiator of the broadcast must learn the information by receiving a message.

Call the labels g_1 through g_k (omitting inverses) in any order, and define n_1 through n_k as follows: First, n_1 is the order of g_1. Then, let n_2 be the order of g_2 in $G/\langle g_1 \rangle$, this is the smallest number for which $n_2.g_2$ is a multiple of g_1. Further, let n_i be the order of g_i in $G/\langle g_1, ..., g_{i-1} \rangle$, this is the smallest number for which g_i can be written as a sum of elements from $\{g_1, ..., g_{i-1}\}$. The n_i have the following properties: their product equals N, and each g in G can be *uniquely* written as

$$g = \sum_{i=1}^{k} s_i.g_i \quad \text{with } 0 \le s_i < n_i.$$

Algorithm 4 sends the information in direction g_1 over $n_1 - 1$ hops, serving all processors that differ from the initiator by a multiple of g_1. The initiator and all processors receiving the message from direction $-g_1$ send it in direction g_2 over $n_2 - 1$ hops, serving all processors that differ from the initiator by a multiple of g_1 plus a multiple of g_2. In general, the initiator and all processors receiving the information through direction $-g_1$ through $-g_{i-1}$ forward it in direction g_i over $n_i - 1$ hops. Because every processor different from the initiator receives the information exactly once, Algorithm 4 exchanges exactly $N - 1$ messages.

If such is required, the non-initiators can store the link through which they received the message to build a spanning tree of the network with the initiator as the root. The tree can be used for sending information back to the initiator; see Subsection 3.2. The depth of the spanning tree employed by the algorithm is $\sum_{i=1}^{k}(n_i - 1)$; if required the depth can be influenced by the order in which $g_1, ..., g_k$ lists the labels in L. We shall not pursue this issue (which is related to the *time complexity* of the broadcast) further here.

1.5 The Election Problem

An election algorithm must be used in a processor network if a special task must be carried out by exactly one processor, but no processor is a priori assigned the task. Starting from a configuration where all processors are in a similar ("initial") state, the system should reach a configuration where exactly one processor is in the "elected" state and all others in the "defeated" state. LeLann [LeL77] posed the problem and proposed a $\Theta(N^2)$ message solution in a ring of processors; subsequent ring algorithms used only $O(N \log N)$ messages [DKR82], which is optimal [PKR84]. For networks of arbitrary, but unknown and connected topology the algorithm of Gallager *et al.* [GHS83] is optimal with $O(N \log N + m)$ messages.

The lower bounds can be beaten if the topology is known or a sense of direction is given. For example, for cliques an $O(N \log N)$ message algorithm can be given, and if sense of direction is given in addition, the complexity is further reduced to $O(N)$ [LMW86].

In this article we shall discuss primarily election in chordal rings, in cliques, and in hypercubes.

2 Election in Rings and Chordal Rings

The election problem on rings and chordal rings has a long history. LeLann [LeL77] gave a solution using $O(N^2)$ messages, which was substantially improved by Chang and Roberts [CR79] who gave a solution using $O(N \lg N)$ messages in the *average* case. Franklin [Fra82] was the first to give a solution with a worst case $O(N \lg N)$ message complexity; his algorithm will be explained in Subsection 2.1 because it is the basis of linear algorithms for chordal rings. Further research [PKR84] was aimed at proving matching lower bounds and improving the implicit constant [HP93].

Attiya *et al.* [ALSZ89] improved the complexity using chords added (uniformly) to the ring; a linear complexity is possible with a very small number of chords as will be shown in Subsections 2.2 and 2.3. But because the algorithm is based too heavily on the ring structure, it does not use the chords in the most efficient way; we shall give a one-chord linear algorithm in Subsection 2.4.

2.1 Franklin's Algorithm

Franklin's algorithm distinguishes *active* and *relay* processors and uses a succession of rounds. Before the first round, every processor is active. A round starting with *more than one* active processor will turn at least half of them, and at most all but one of them, into relay processors, and will be followed by another

---

$state_p := active$;
while $state_p = active$ **do**
      begin send $\langle$ **name**, $p \rangle$ to left ; send $\langle$ **name**, $p \rangle$ to right ;
           receive $\langle$ **name**, $x \rangle$ from right ; receive $\langle$ **name**, $y \rangle$ from left ;
           if $x = p$ **and** $y = p$ **then** $state_p := elected$;
           if $x > p$ **or** $y > p$ **then** $state_p := relay$
      end

Algorithm 5 FRANKLIN'S RING ELECTION ALGORITHM.

---

round. A round starting with one active processor elects this processor and is the last round. Thus, the number of rounds is at most $\lfloor \log N \rfloor + 1$, and because each round takes exactly $2N$ messages, the message complexity is approximately $2N \log N$ in the worst case.

In each round, active processors exchange their name with the nearest active processor to the left and to the right. If a processor is its own "nearest active processor", it is the only active processor and becomes elected. Otherwise it survives the round only if its name is larger than both its right and left "active neighbour", a condition that is true in at least one processor (the largest active processor) and at most half of them (because it fails in both neighbours of a "survivor"). An active processor with a larger nearest active neighbour becomes a relay. Relay processors forward all messages they receive in the opposite direction; this is not shown in Alg. 5.

2.2 Attiya's Amelioration

As the number of active processors halves in each round, the *sum over the* $\lg N$ *rounds* of the number of active processors participating in it is bounded by $2N$. Because an active processor sends two messages in a round, the number of messages sent by active processors is linear: $4N$. However, the messages are relayed over successively larger distances, because after round i, successive active processors are spaced at least 2^i positions apart. Concluding, the relaying of messages by passive processors accounts for almost the entire message complexity.

Attiya *et al.* [ALSZ89] improved the algorithm assuming the ring network is extended to become a chordal ring with uniform sense of direction. At the beginning of each round an active processor knows the relative position of its nearest active colleagues to the left and the right, and sends its name via a shortest path. We assume the topology of the network to be exploited in primitives $Send(message, g)$ and $Receive(message, g)$. The first primitive forwards *message* via a shortest path with $SUM_{\mathcal{L}} = g$, and the latter one receives such a message. The procedure to forward the message (executed in intermediate processors) is straightforward and not shown.

At the end of a round the surviving active processors find the relative position

---

$state_p := active$; $Left_p := -1$; $Right_p := +1$;
while $state_p = active$ **do**
　　begin $Send(\langle \textbf{name}, p \rangle, Left)$; $Send(\langle \textbf{name}, p \rangle, Right)$;
　　　　　$Receive(\langle \textbf{name}, x \rangle, Right)$; $Receive(\langle \textbf{name}, y \rangle, Left)$;
　　　　　if $p \geq x$ **and** $p \geq y$ **then**
　　　　　　begin $Send(\langle \textbf{pos}, 0 \rangle, Left)$; $Send(\langle \textbf{pos}, 0 \rangle, Right)$;
　　　　　　　　　$Receive(\langle \textbf{pos}, r \rangle, Right)$; $Right := Right + r$;
　　　　　　　　　$Receive(\langle \textbf{pos}, l \rangle, Left)$; $Left := Left + l$;
　　　　　　　　　if $Left_p = 0$ **then** $state_p := elected$
　　　　　　end
　　　　　else
　　　　　　begin (* relay the $\langle \textbf{pos}, . \rangle$ messages *)
　　　　　　　　　$Receive(\langle \textbf{pos}, r \rangle, Right)$; $Send(\langle \textbf{pos}, r + Right \rangle, Left)$;
　　　　　　　　　$Receive(\langle \textbf{pos}, l \rangle, Left)$; $Send(\langle \textbf{pos}, l + Left \rangle, Right)$
　　　　　　end
　　end
end

Algorithm 6 ATTIYA'S CHORDAL RING ELECTION ALGORITHM.

---

of the closest active processors by passing a $\langle \textbf{pos}, . \rangle$ message through a chain of processors that became relay in this round. Leadership is detected at the end of the round with one survivor, by the processor finding it is its own neighbour ($Left = 0$).

The new algorithm differs from Franklin's only in the way active processors communicate; the sum over the rounds of the number of active processors is still $2N$. Now the number of messages sent in each round by active processors is 4, so the number of *Send* operations in the entire algorithm is bounded by $8N$. In the case of a clique, each *Send* operation uses a path of length one, and the overall complexity is bounded by $8N$ messages.

For the general case of a chordal ring Attiya defines the *message cost function* F as the smallest monotone and convex function for which $Send(message, g)$ requires at most $F(g)$ message exchanges. (Informally, F is the cost of sending a message to a processor g ring hops away.) In the worst case, round i starts with $N/(2^{i-1})$ active processors spaced 2^{i-1} hops apart, and thus uses $\frac{N}{2^{i-1}} \times 4 \times F(2^{i-1})$ messages.

Lemma 12. *Alg. 6 uses* $4N \cdot \sum_{i=0}^{n-1} \frac{F(2^i)}{2^i}$ *messages in the worst case.*

Attiya *et al.* showed that a logarithmic number of chords suffices to bound the sum by a constant, for example in the chordal ring $C_N(2, 3, 4, ..., \lg N)$; we shall not repeat the computation here.

2.3　Minimising the Number of Chords

Attiya's result determined the complexity of election on chordal rings to be linear; attention focused on the minimal number of chords necessary to obtain this complexity. In this section we shall determine the number of chords needed asymptotically by Attiya's algorithm using "backward graph engineering" from mathematical formulae. But we also show that Attiya's algorithm is not the best way to exploit the chordal ring structure. Indeed, it needs $\Theta(\lg^* N)$ chords for linear election, while the algorithm of Subsection 2.4 achieves linear election with a single chord! The work reported here was done with Andreas Fabri.

The sum is a geometric series. As a geometric series (with growth rate smaller than 1) has a bounded sum we shall first investigate how many chords we need to bound $\frac{F(2^i)}{2^i}$ by some c^i for $c < 1$.

Consider the sequence of chords $L = \{2, 4, 16, 256, ...\}$, where each next chord is the square of the previous one; chords are of the form 2^{2^i} and the number of chords is $\log \log N$.

Lemma 13. $F(d) \leq 2 \cdot \sqrt{d}$.

Proof. By induction on d; the proof uses *greedy* routing, where a path of sum d starts with the *largest chord* l that fits in d, and proceeds with a path of length $d - l$. First, $F(1) = 1 \leq 2\sqrt{1}$.

Now assume $d > 0$ but the result is true for $d' < d$. The chords construction implies that the longest chord that fits in d has length l s.t. $\sqrt{d} < l \leq q$ and we find $F(d) \leq 1 + F(d - l) \leq 1 + 2\sqrt{d - l} < 1 + 2\sqrt{d - \sqrt{d}} < 2\sqrt{d}$. □

So $\frac{F(2^i)}{2^i}$ is bounded by $2 \cdot (\frac{1}{\sqrt{2}})^i$ and this implies that linear election is possible with $O(\log \log N)$ chords. It turns out, that $\Omega(\log \log N)$ chords are also necessary (if greedy routing is used) to make the summation a geometric series!

Lemma 14. *If there is a constant $c < 1$ such that with greedy routing $\frac{F(2^i)}{2^i} < c^i$, then the number of chords is $\Omega(\log \log N)$.*

Proof. For each $i < \log N$, $F(2^i) < c^i.2^i$, which implies that a chord of length at least $(1/c)^i$ is used, and by the greedy routing strategy this chord is at most 2^i. Consequently, for each i there is a chord with length in the interval $(1/c)^i \ldots 2^i$; observe that if $i' = i \cdot (^{1/c}\log 2)$ the intervals for i and i' are disjoint. Consequently, for the $(^{1/c}\log 2) \log(^2\log N)$ different values $i_r = (^{1/c}\log 2)^r$ (here $r < (^{1/c}\log 2) \log(^2\log N)$) we have a collection of disjoint intervals $(1/c)^{i_r} \ldots 2^{i_r}$, each containing a chord length. □

Allowing other routing strategies probably does not improve this result any more than by a constant factor; the proof of this is left as an open question. Determining F from L is related to the *Coin Exchange Problem*, asking to pay some amount using coins from a given set of denominations. General routing strategies mean allowing the use of coin returns in the coin exchange problem.

Slowlier decreasing summations. We saw that a geometric series in Lemma 12 gives a linear complexity, but requires $\Theta(\log\log N)$ chords to implement. So we select a sequence that decreases slower, but still has a bounded sum; the square-harmonic series $\sum(1/i^2)$.

Assume the collection $L = \{36, 64, 256, 65536, ...\}$ of chords, where $g_{i+1} = 2^{\sqrt{g_i}}$; as $g_i = \log^2(g_{i+1})$, there is, for each d, a chord of length between $\log^2 d$ and d.

Lemma 15. *There are less than $2\log^* N$ chords in L.*

Proof. As $g_{i+2} = 2^{\sqrt{2^{\sqrt{g_i}}}} = 2^{(\sqrt{2}^{\sqrt{g_i}})} > 2^{g_i}$, the sequence $g_0, g_2, g_4, g_6, \cdots$ grows faster than $2, 2^2, 2^{2^2}, 2^{2^{2^2}}, \ldots$ and exceeds N within $\log^* N$ terms. $\qquad\square$

Lemma 16. $F(d) \leq 2 \cdot \frac{d}{\log^2 d}$.

Proof. For large d, the greedy routing algorithm first chooses a chord l larger than $\log^2 d$ and achieves

$$F(d) = 1 + F(d - l) \leq 1 + 2.\frac{d - l}{\log^2(d - l)} < 1 + 2.\frac{d - \log^2 d}{\log^2(d - \log^2 d)} < \frac{d}{\log^2 d}.$$

$$\square$$

The lower bound proof is based on a summation that decreases even slower and has unbounded sum: the harmonic series $\sum 1/i$. It is known that the first $\log n$ terms of this sequence sum to $\Theta(\log\log N)$, yet it requires $\Omega(\log^* N)$ chords to achieve it!

Lemma 17. *If, with greedy routing, $\frac{F(2^i)}{2^i} < 1/i$, then there are at least $\log^* N$ chords.*

Proof. Similar to the previous lower bound; for each i there must be a chord between i and 2^i. $\qquad\square$

Concluding: (1) $O(\log^* N)$ chords suffice to have the *convergent* square-harmonic series; (2) $\Omega(\log^* N)$ chords are required to have the *divergent* harmonic series, so any *convergent* series must have at least $\Omega(\log^* N)$ chords.

This implies that $\Theta(\log^* N)$ chords are necessary and sufficient for Attiya's algorithm to have linear complexity.

2.4 One-chord Linear Algorithm

This section presents a linear chordal ring election algorithm that needs only one chord; call the length of the single chord t and assume t is approximately $\sqrt{N}$. A chordal ring with a single chord of length close to $\sqrt{N}$ is topologically very reminiscent to a torus, and our algorithm is adapted from Peterson's [Pet85] torus algorithm.

When starting a round, an active processor attempts to find, or *see*, another active processor of the same round; a processor sees at most one other processor, but can be seen by more than one processor. There are two ways in which an active processor can be promoted to the next round.

The first is very similar to the "local maxima" promotion in Franklin's algorithm: if a processor sees a smaller one and *is seen by* a smaller processor, it can be promoted. At most half of the processors can be promoted by this rule, because if a processor is promoted, at least one smaller processor that saw it isn't.

It would be too costly to have each active processor search the network until another active processor is seen; therefore an active processor searches only a restricted subset of the network, and the search may terminate without seeing another active processor. The second promotion rule states that the searching processor is promoted to the next round in this case!

The crucial achievement of the algorithm is to design the search procedure in such a way that (i) the search area is sufficiently large to have only few processors promoted by the second rule; and (ii) the search is sufficiently efficient so as to have a good overall complexity.

Squares and boundaries, search procedure. For $g \in \mathbb{Z}_N$, define the *l-square* of g as the set $S_{g,l} = \{g + i.1 + j.t \mid 0 \leq i \leq l, 0 \leq j \leq l\}$. The set $S_{g,l}$ is the set of (at most) $(l+1)^2$ processors reachable from g by crossing at most l 1-edges and at most l t-edges. An active processor searches for other active processors in an l-square, but not by sending messages to all processors in the square because this would be too expensive.

Define the *boundary* $B_{g,l}$ as the set of points where at least one of the inequalities is an equality, i.e., $B_{g,l} = \{g+i.1, g+i.1+l.t, g+i.t, g+l.1+j.t \mid 0 \leq i \leq l\}$, and the *internal* $I_{g,l} = S_{g,l} \setminus B_{g,l}$. The boundary $B_{g,l}$ contains (at most) $4l$ processors and, if $S_{g,l}$ and $S_{h,l}$ intersect, then $B_{g,l}$ and $B_{h,l}$ intersect.

A processor in round i starts looking for other processors by sending an explorer token along the boundary of an l-square. This token attempts to make l steps in direction 1, l steps in direction t, l steps in direction -1, and l steps in direction $-t$. The length of the square depends on the round number; in round i the length is chosen as $l_i = \alpha^i$ (where α is a constant slightly larger than 1). Traversing the entire boundary takes $4l$ messages, but the traversal can be interrupted for several reasons.

If the token of p enters a processor already visited by a token of a larger round number, traversal is aborted; p will never receive its explorer back and it will never enter a next round. If the token enters for the first time a processor already visited by a (different) token (of q, say) of the same round, p "sees" q. If q is smaller then p, processor p must become aware because seeing q is essential for p in order to be promoted by rule one. If q is larger than p, p's chances of being promoted are gone, but q must be informed because being seen by p could be essential for q in order to be promoted by rule one. So, either the token goes back to p, or a chasing token is sent to q, via the boundary traversed by q's token, to inform q that it was seen by a smaller processor. Now, as it suffices for q to be informed about one smaller processor that saw it, a processor that already forwarded a chasing token to q will not forward p's chasing token anymore.

The descibed procedures for token handling imply the following local conditions for promotion of p to the next round. First, p's explorer token returns having seen a smaller processor, *and* a chasing token arrives reporting p was seen by a smaller processor. Second, p's explorer returns without having seen another processor.

Some calculations. Our algorithm is very close to Peterson's [Pet85] and the same calculations are found there also. Let A_i be the number of active processors starting round i; we have $A_0 \leq N$. We shall first bound A_i for all rounds in which the size of the squares is less than N, i.e., rounds $i \leq {}^\alpha \log \sqrt{N}$.

Lemma 18. *For the rounds $i \leq {}^\alpha \log \sqrt{N}$, we have $A_i \leq \frac{N}{\alpha^{2i}(2-\alpha^2)}$.*

Proof. We have seen that each processor promoted by the first promotion rule was seen by another processor that is not promoted. So at most half the processors that saw another processor is promoted by this rule.

Some processors may be promoted by the second rule (by not seeing another process) but we claim that if both p and q are promoted by this rule, $S_{p,l}$ and $S_{q,l}$ are disjoint. Indeed, if the squares overlap, so do the borders traversed by p's and q's token. One of the token arrives at the intersection point as the first, making it impossible for the other to complete its walk without seeing another processor. Consequently, the number of processors promoted by this rule is less than N/l_i^2.

From the above and the earlier choice of $l_i = \alpha^i$ we can conclude that

$$A_{i+1} \leq \frac{A_i + N/\alpha^{2i}}{2}.$$

Using induction on i it can be verified that this implies $A_i \leq \frac{N}{\alpha^{2i}(2-\alpha^2)}$. □

The lemma implies both a linear bound on the number of messages and a constant bound on the number of processors reaching round ${}^\alpha \log \sqrt{N}$.

Corollary 19. *In rounds 0 through ${}^\alpha \log \sqrt{N}$, less then $\frac{8\alpha}{(\alpha-1)(2-\alpha^2)} N$ messages are exchanged.*

Proof. Lemma 18 already established the number of active processors in round i. The messages are charged as follows. The explorer of an active processor p can make $4\alpha^i$ steps, charged to p. The chasing tokens routed towards p are also charged to p; as each processor visited by p's explorer forwards at most one chasing token, at most $4\alpha^i$ chasing steps are charged to p.

So, each of the $\frac{N}{\alpha^{2i}(2-\alpha^2)}$ processors in round i is charged at most $8\alpha^i$ messages, and the total number of messages in round i is bounded by $\frac{8N}{2-\alpha^2} \cdot (1/\alpha)^i$. The summation over the rounds is a geometric series with sum $\frac{8N}{2-\alpha^2} \cdot \frac{\alpha}{\alpha-1}$. □

Termination of the algorithm. Lemma 18 implies that only a constant number of processors, namely less than $1/(2 - \alpha^2)$, survives round $^\alpha \log \sqrt{N}$. To elect between these processors, the algorithm continues after that round with a second phase, organised as the Chang–Roberts algorithm [CR79]. Each processor surviving round $^\alpha \log \sqrt{N}$ sends a token along the entire ring, i.e., N steps in direction $+1$. The token is eliminated by any processor with larger identity which has also survived that round already, and aborts activity of processors in the first phase of the algorithm. This second phase ensures that only the largest processor that survives round $^\alpha \log \sqrt{N}$ receives its token back; this processor is elected.

Theorem 20. *The algorithm elects a leader using $O(N)$ messages in a chordal ring with one chord (of length $\sqrt{N}$).*

Proof. As no round in the first phase kills all active processors, at least one processor makes it to the second phase. The second phase ensures that exactly one of these processors is elected, which establishes the correctness of the algorithm.

The first phase uses $O(N)$ messages by Corollary 19, and the second phase uses only $O(N)$ messages because at most a constant number of processors initiate a token in that phase. □

Though it uses a linear number of messages and is thus asymptotically optimal, the algorithm or its analysis can probably be improved by some constant factor. A more challenging open question is how far the length of the single chord can deviate from $\sqrt{N}$ for the algorithm to be still linear.

3 Cliques and Hypercubes

Sense of direction is known to reduce the complexity of elections in cliques. Without SoD, $\Omega(N \log N)$ messages is a lower bound [KMZ84], while Attiya's algorithm achieves a linear complexity if SoD is given. It is not known if the same is true for the important class of hypercube networks, but in this section we shall present some results related to this (open) problem. The last one (Subsection 3.3) is a practical, randomized linear-message algorithm without sense of direction, leaving the question open only for deterministic algorithms.

3.1 Baseline

The algorithm of Gallager *et al.* [GHS83] does not rely on SoD and when applied to a hypercube it uses $O(N \log N)$ messages. This is the best known deterministic algorithm for hypercubes without SoD known to date, but no matching lower bound is known.

The n-dimensional hypercube with sense of direction is a network with uniform sense of direction with the n labels independent and each of order 2. For convenience we refer to the labels as $0, \ldots, n - 1$.

Consider a fixed subset L' of the generators; they generate a subgroup of size $2^{|L'|}$ and each orbit of this subgroup is called a *face* (w.r.t. L') of the cube. Given a sense of direction, the partitioning of the network in faces w.r.t. L' depends only on the link labelling. A processor can broadcast a message through a face (an L' orbit) by using Alg. 4, provided of course that the other processors agree on the set L'.

3.2 The Match-making Algorithm

The election algorithm uses the recursive structure of the hypercube graph. To elect a leader in a hypercube of dimension $d+1$, the algorithm first elects a leader in both of the faces of dimension d generated by all but the last generator, and then elects one of the two leaders. To avoid confusion between leadership at different stages of the algorithm, a node is called a *d-leader* if it has won the election in a d-dimensional face.

The base case of this algorithm, election in a face of dimension 0, is easy; the network consists of exactly one node, which becomes a 0-leader immediately.

The tournament. A node that becomes d-leader (for $d < n$) engages in a tournament with the d-leader of the adjacent face in direction d. A tournament between two nodes that can communicate directly is easily organised. Each node sends the other one a message containing its name; the node receiving a larger name than its own becomes *non-leader*, the node receiving a smaller name than its own becomes *leader*.

The tournament between the two d-leaders is organised in the same way, but with the difficulty that the nodes do not know how to reach the leader in the other (or even their own) face. As a first step, node p that becomes d-leader sends a tournament message $\langle \mathbf{tour}, p, d \rangle$, containing its name and the phase number d, through its edge in direction d; it is received by a node in the other d-dimensional face. It is the responsibility of the receiving node, called the *entry* node, to forward this message to its d-leader; see Fig. 7.

The difficulty in forwarding the message to the d-leader is that the entry node does not know the relative position of the d-leader. It is too expensive for the d-leader to announce its position to all nodes in the d-cube so that the entry node can forward the message in d steps. This announcement would cost $2^d - 1$ messages, leading to an $O(N \log N)$ overall complexity of the election. Similarly, it is too expensive to have the entry node broadcast the tournament message through the d-cube; this would also cost $2^d - 1$ messages.

Our solution uses a combination of these two basic strategies. The d-leader announces its leadership to all nodes in a $\lfloor d/2 \rfloor$-dimensional face, referred to as the leader's *row*. The entry node broadcasts the tournament message through a $\lceil d/2 \rceil$-dimensional face called its *column*. As each row intersects each column in exactly one node (as will be shown below), there is one node, called the *match node*, that receives both the announcement from the d-leader and the tournament message. The match node forwards the tournament message further to the d-leader via the spanning tree induced by the announcement messages.

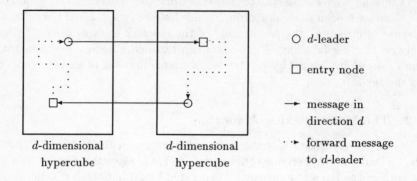

Figure 7 Message forwarding in the tournament.

Definition 21. Consider the hypercube of dimension d.
A *row* is a face w.r.t. generators 0 through $\lfloor d/2 \rfloor - 1$;
a *column* is a face w.r.t. generators $\lfloor d/2 \rfloor$ through $d - 1$.

The tournament between the two d-leaders is organised as follows.

1. A d-leader p sends a $\langle \mathbf{tour}, p, d \rangle$ message via link d.
2. A d-leader broadcasts its leadership in its row using Alg. 4. The nodes in the row store the link through which they receive the broadcast message, thus computing a spanning tree of the row. (The broadcast algorithm takes a simple form because the generators are independent, and each n_i is equal to one. The hop counter in the messages can be suppressed.)
3. An entry node (i.e., a node receiving $\langle \mathbf{tour}, p, d \rangle$ via link d) broadcasts the message through its column using Alg. 4.
4. A non-d-leader q in the row of the leader (i.e., q has received an $\langle \mathbf{ann}, d \rangle$ message) receiving a $\langle \mathbf{tour}, p, d \rangle$ message sends the message to its father.
5. A d-leader q receiving a $\langle \mathbf{tour}, p, d \rangle$ message compares p with q; if $q > p$, q becomes $(d + 1)$-leader, and q becomes non-leader otherwise.

The communication complexity. Let $T(d)$ be the number of messages exchanged in a tournament between two d-leaders and $E(n)$ the number of messages used by the election algorithm (on a hypercube of dimension n). As an election requires two elections on smaller cubes and one tournament, we find the recursion

$$E(n) = \begin{cases} 0 & \text{if } n = 0 \\ 2 \cdot E(n-1) + T(n-1) & \text{otherwise.} \end{cases}$$

In the analysis of the message complexity we need the well-known sum of the infinite geometric series (assuming $\alpha < 1$) and its (less known) derivative to α:

$$\sum_{c=0}^{\infty} \alpha^c = \frac{1}{1 - \alpha} \quad \text{and} \quad \sum_{c=0}^{\infty} c \cdot \alpha^{c-1} = \frac{1}{(1 - \alpha)^2}.$$

Counting the number of messages exchanged in each of the steps of the tournament between two d-leaders, we find:

> Step 1: 2 messages.
> Step 2: $2 \cdot (2^{\lfloor d/2 \rfloor} - 1)$ messages.
> Step 3: $2 \cdot (2^{\lceil d/2 \rceil} - 1)$ messages.
> Step 4: at most $2 \cdot \lfloor d/2 \rfloor$ messages.

Summing up, find $T(d) \leq 2 \cdot (2^{\lfloor d/2 \rfloor} + 2^{\lceil d/2 \rceil} + \lfloor d/2 \rfloor - 1)$.

For even d we have $\lfloor d/2 \rfloor = \lceil d/2 \rceil = d/2$, and for odd d we have $\lfloor d/2 \rfloor = (d/2) - \frac{1}{2}$ and $\lceil d/2 \rceil = (d/2) + \frac{1}{2}$; using this we find

$$\begin{aligned}
T(2c) &= 2 \cdot (2^c + 2^c + c - 1) &= 4 \cdot 2^c + 2c - 2 \\
T(2c + 1) &= 2 \cdot (2^c + 2^{c+1} + c - 1) = 6 \cdot 2^c + 2c - 2
\end{aligned}$$

Subsequently we write $F(n) = E(n)/2^n$, and using the recursion for E we find

$$F(n) = \begin{cases} 0 & \text{if } n = 0 \\ F(n - 1) + \dfrac{T(n - 1)}{2^n} & \text{otherwise,} \end{cases}$$

which allows to write $F(n)$ as a sum and bound it by an infinite series:

$$F(n) = \sum_{d=0}^{n-1} \frac{T(d)}{2^{d+1}} < \sum_{d=0}^{\infty} \frac{T(d)}{2^{d+1}}.$$

Next, using the expressions for T as derived above, the sum is split in its even and odd terms, which allows us to bound $F(n)$ by:

$$\begin{aligned}
\sum_{d=0}^{\infty} \frac{T(d)}{2^{d+1}} &= \sum_{c=0}^{\infty} \frac{T(2c)}{2^{2c+1}} &&+ \sum_{c=0}^{\infty} \frac{T(2c+1)}{2^{2c+2}} \\
&= \sum_{c=0}^{\infty} \frac{4 \cdot 2^c + 2c - 2}{2^{2c+1}} &&+ \sum_{c=0}^{\infty} \frac{6 \cdot 2^c + 2c - 2}{2^{2c+2}} \\
&= \sum_{c=0}^{\infty} \left(\frac{4 \cdot 2^c}{2^{2c+1}} + \frac{6 \cdot 2^c}{2^{2c+2}} \right) + \sum_{c=0}^{\infty} \left(\frac{2c}{2^{2c+1}} + \frac{2c}{2^{2c+2}} \right) - \sum_{c=0}^{\infty} \left(\frac{2}{2^{2c+1}} + \frac{2}{2^{2c+2}} \right) \\
&= 3\frac{1}{2} \cdot \left(\sum_{c=0}^{\infty} \frac{1}{2^c} \right) &&+ \frac{3}{8} \cdot \left(\sum_{c=0}^{\infty} \frac{c}{4^{c-1}} \right) &&- \frac{3}{2} \cdot \left(\sum_{c=0}^{\infty} \frac{1}{4^c} \right) \\
&= 3\frac{1}{2} \cdot 2 &&+ \frac{3}{8} \cdot \frac{16}{9} &&- \frac{3}{2} \cdot \frac{4}{3} \\
&= 7 + \frac{2}{3} - 2 &&= 5\frac{2}{3}.
\end{aligned}$$

---

cons K (∗ Safety parameter ∗)

var $state : (sleep, awake, leader)$ **init** $sleep$;
  $maxid_p$ (∗ Highest identity seen ∗)

To start an election:
  begin $i := p$; $s := 0$; $maxid_p := i$;
      if $s < K$ **then** send $\langle \textbf{walk}, i, s+1 \rangle$ through a *random* edge
          else $state_p := leader$
  end

Upon arrival of token $\langle \textbf{walk}, i, s \rangle$:
  begin if $state_p = sleep$ **then** start an election ;
      receive $\langle \textbf{walk}, i, s \rangle$; $maxid_p := \max(maxid_p, i)$;
      if $i = maxid_p$
          then if $s < K$ **then** send $\langle \textbf{walk}, i, s+1 \rangle$ through a *random* edge
              else $state_p := leader$
          else (∗ Kill token ∗) **skip**
  end

Algorithm 8 THE ELECTION ALGORITHM (FOR PROCESSOR p).

It follows that $E(n) < 5\frac{2}{3} \cdot N$. Improvements of the principle to an algorithm using $4N$ messages can be found in [Tel93, Ver94].

3.3 Verweij's Random-walk Algorithm

We now present Verweij's [VT95] randomised, Monte Carlo algorithm for the election problem; it works for any topology and does *not* use sense of direction because it is based on competing random walks.

Initially each processor is in state *sleep*. Upon becoming *awake* (this happens spontaneously or upon receipt of a message in the *sleep* state) the processor generates a token containing its identity and a hop counter. Tokens are forwarded through the network in a *random walk* and are removed from the network by a processor already visited by a token with larger identity. When a token has completed K steps without being removed, the processor holding it becomes elected; see Alg. 8.

Properties of the algorithm. The largest token initiated in some execution is not killed; consequently, this token completes K steps and causes a process to become leader; this is called a *correct* leader claim. This property implies that the algorithm can only fail by choosing multiple leaders, but *not* by choosing no leader at all.

The algorithm fails (i.e., elects more than one leader) if any non-maximal token happens to complete K steps without entering a processor already visited by a larger token. The resulting leader claim is termed a *false* one. The probability of false claims is reduced by increasing K, but because tokens can make as many as K steps, increasing K also increases the message complexity.

For $K = 0$ every generated token results in a false claim. Thus the failure probability is high (1), but the message complexity is low (0). On the other hand, if K runs to ∞ the error probability converges to 0 because no non-maximal token can make infinitely many steps and still avoid the largest processor with positive probability.

Fortunately the choice of K is not very critical for the correctness/complexity properties of the algorithm. First, even with small K, the message complexity is at least linear in N because every processor may generate a token. Second, choosing K larger than necessary for the desired reliability generates additional token steps, but (with high probability) only for the maximal token! It follows from this discussion that the asymptotic expected number of messages is not influenced by K as long as it exceeds the minimal value by a linear amount.

In the cases we have considered a linear value for K suffices for the algorithm to be correct with large probability; consequently, the asymptotic complexity cannot be improved by fine-tuning K.

Timing assumptions. The optimal value of K and the performance of the algorithm are influenced by the relative speeds of the tokens. The following discussion refers to the case where the network is a clique, i.e., each next step of the token leads to a completely random node.

On the one extreme, consider the case where the largest token is infinitely slow as compared to the second-largest one. Here the second token is killed only when entering the maximal processor, and, for example in the clique, a linear value of K would be necessary to ensure this with probability close to 1.

Considering message complexity, the worst timing arises when any token is received only when all tokens with smaller identities have been killed. Then every token is killed only by being received by a processor with larger identity, and for the $(i + 1)^{\text{th}}$ largest identity this happens

On the other hand, consider the case of synchronous cliques, where at any moment, each of the surviving tokens has made equally many steps. After $O(\sqrt{N})$ steps, the largest token has visited $O(\sqrt{N})$ processors, and after another $O(\sqrt{N})$ steps the second token enters one of these with probability close to one. Consequently $K = O(\sqrt{N})$ suffices to kill the second largest token with high probability; simulations indicate that the probability of false clams being generated by smaller tokens is then negligible.

Message complexity. Simulations [VT95] of the random walk algorithm show that the expected message complexity is linear (about $3N$ messages) in the case of clique and hypercube networks.

We have not been able to theoretically analyse the expected message complexity under the realistic timing assumption that the ratio between the speed of various tokens is bounded by a constant. Even for the case of completely synchronous operation, where each of the tokens can make one step in turn we did not succeed. The problem can be combinatorially stated as follows.

A single random walk is modelled by a random sequence of numbers taken from $1 \ldots N$, where the number i represents a visit to the ith smallest processor. The length of walk N is K, the other walks could be shorter. The simultaneous walks are then represented by N random sequences $w^{(1)}$ through $w^{(N)}$ where $w_0^{(i)} = i$ and every walk survives round 0 (because walk i starts in processor i).

With the walks generated up to round j, first extend the walks $w^{(i)}$ that are still alive by a random number $w_{j+1}^{(i)}$ from $1 \ldots N$. Next, walk $w^{(i)}$ is *killed* in round $j + 1$ if the number $w_{j+1}^{(i)}$ occurs among the numbers $w_{j'}^{(i')}$ with $i' > i$ and $j' \leq j + 1$; set $k_i = j + 1$ in this case. The random process terminates after the construction of round K.

Because there is no $i' > N$, walk $w^{(N)}$ is not killed and it lives after round K, generating a leader claim. If any other walk survives that round, it also generates a leader claim (a false one). The measure we are interested in is the expected total length of the random walks, i.e., $\sum_{i=1}^{N-1} k_i$.

4 Computing Sense of Direction

Knowing that sense of direction reduces the complexity of some tasks (election in cliques, broadcasting in tori and hypercubes), the question arises if sense of direction can be computed in networks where it is not given [Tel94b]. Risking confusion with a graph operation in which edges of the graph are directed, we call the problem of computing sense of direction *orienting* the network.

4.1 Orienting a Clique or Arbitrary Graph

The clique orientation algorithm (Alg. 9) assigns each processor a unique number in the range $0 \ldots N - 1$; each processor computes its rank in the set of all names, after receiving the name of each neighbour. The rank of each neighbour is computed similarly, and the link label is found as the difference of the neighbour's and the own rank.

Theorem 22. *Algorithm 9 computes a sense of direction in a clique, and uses* $N(N - 1)$ *messages.*

The quadratic complexity is high, but unavoidable; we have a matching lower bound; see Subsection 4.4.

Chordal sense of direction in arbitrary networks. In an arbitrary network the nodes can be numbered by a token traversing the network, for example by a Depth First Search traversal, provided that a node is distinguished as starting node. The traversal uses $2m$ messages (one message crosses each edge in each direction) and nodes will be assigned a number in the order in which they are visited. During the traversal, the processors learn their own, but also their neighbours' numbers, and are then able to compute a chordal sense of direction. (The number of nodes must be known; if this is not a priori the case, the number nodes can be counted during traversal and broadcast from the initiator using an additional $N - 1$ messages.)

```
begin for l = 1 to N − 1 do send ⟨name, p⟩ via l ;
      recₚ := 0 ;
      while recₚ < N − 1 do
         begin receive ⟨name, n⟩ via link l ;
               recₚ := recₚ + 1 ; neiₚ[l] := n
         end ;
      (* Compute node label *)
      lblₚ := #{k : neiₚ[k] < p} ;
      for l = 1 to N − 1 do
         begin (* Compute neighbour's node label and link label *)
               ll := #{k : neiₚ[k] < neiₚ[l]} ;
               if p < neiₚ[l] then ll := ll + 1 ;
               πₚ[l] := (ll − lblₚ) mod N
         end
end
```

Algorithm 9 ORIENTATION OF CLIQUES.

4.2 Hypercube: the Multi-path Flow Algorithm

We shall present an algorithm to compute sense of direction in a hypercube of dimension n. The algorithm assumes a processor is designated as initiator of the algorithm (leader) and that the links of the leader are arbitrarily labelled with numbers $0..n − 1$. The initiator's labelling uniquely defines a sense of direction as expressed in the following theorem (given here without proof).

Theorem 23. *Let w be a node and $\mathcal{P}$ a labelling of w's edges with numbers 0 through $n − 1$. There exists exactly one orientation $\mathcal{L}$ which satisfies $\mathcal{L}_w(v) = \mathcal{P}(v)$ for each neighbour of w.*

The algorithm computes exactly this orientation, and, moreover, the unique witnessing node labeling in which the leader is labelled with $(0, ..., 0)$. The algorithm uses three types of messages. The leader sends to each of its neighbours the label of the connecting link in $⟨\mathbf{dmn}, i⟩$ messages. Non–leaders send their node label to other processors in $⟨\mathbf{iam}, nla⟩$ message. Non–leaders inform their neighbours about the label of connecting links in $⟨\mathbf{labl}, i⟩$ messages.

The algorithm is given as Algorithm 10 (for the leader) and Algorithm 11 (for non–leaders). It consists of two phases, where in the first phase messages flow away from the leader, and in the second phase messages flow towards the leader. A *predecessor* of node p is a neighbour q of p for which $d(q, w) < d(p, w)$, and a *successor* of node p is a neighbour q of p for which $d(q, w) > d(p, w)$. In a hypercube node p has no neighbour q for which $d(q, w) = d(p, w)$ and a node at distance d from the leader has d predecessors and $n − d$ successors.

The leader initiates the algorithm by sending a $⟨\mathbf{dmn}, i⟩$ message over the link labelled i. When a non–leader processor p has learned its distance dis_p to the leader and has received the messages from its predecessors, p is able to compute

begin $rec_p := 0$; $dis_p := 0$; $lbl_p := (0, ..., 0)$;
      for $l = 0$ **to** $n - 1$ **do** (* Send for phase 1 *)
          begin send $\langle$ **dmn**, l $\rangle$ via link l ;
              $\pi_p[l] := l$
      end ;
      while $rec_p < n$ **do** (* Receive for phase 2 *)
          begin receive $\langle$ **labl**, l $\rangle$ (* necessarily via link l *)
              $rec_p := rec_p + 1$
      end
end .

Algorithm 10 Orientation of hypercube (Initiator).

---

its node label nla_p. Processor p forwards this label in an $\langle$ **iam**, nla_p $\rangle$ message to its successors. To show that p is indeed able to do so, first consider the case where p receives a $\langle$ **dmn**, i $\rangle$ message via link l. As the message is sent by the leader, $dis_p = 1$, and all other neighbours are successors. The node label of p has a 1 in position i, and the other bits are 0. (The label of link l becomes i in this case.) Then p forwards $\langle$ **iam**, nla_p $\rangle$ via all links $k \neq l$.

Next, consider the case where p receives an $\langle$ **iam**, $label$ $\rangle$ message. The distance d of the sender of this message to the leader is derived from the message (the number of 1's in $label$). The $\langle$ **iam**, $label$ $\rangle$ messages are sent only to successors, thus the sender is a predecessor of p and $dis_p = d + 1$. This also reveals the number of predecessors, and p waits until dis_p $\langle$ **iam**, $label$ $\rangle$ messages have been received. Then p computes its node label as the logical disjunction of the received node labels, and forwards it to the neighbours from which no $\langle$ **iam**, $label$ $\rangle$ was received, as these are the successors.

In the first phase, each non–leader processor p computes its node label. In the second phase, each non–leader processor p learns from its successors the orientation of the links to the successors, and computes the orientation of the links to the predecessors. This information is sent over the link in $\langle$ **labl**, i $\rangle$ messages. A processor sends $\langle$ **labl**, i $\rangle$ messages to its predecessors as soon as it has received these messages from all successors, and then terminates. The leader terminates when $\langle$ **labl**, i $\rangle$ messages have been received from all neighbours.

The variables for processor p are: rec_p, the number of messages already received; dis_p, the distance to the leader (computed when the first message arrives, initialised to $n + 1$); lbl_p, the node label computed by p; $nei_p[0..n-1]$, an array holding the node labels of the predecessors of p; and $\pi_p[0..n-1]$, to store the sense of direction.

Lemma 24. *The algorithm terminates in every processor.*

Proof. Using induction on d it is easily verified that all processors at distance at most d eventually send the messages for phase 1. For $d = 0$, only the leader itself has distance d to the leader and it may send the messages without receiving

```
begin recp := 0 ; disp := n + 1 ; lblp := (0, ..., 0) ;
    forall l do neip[l] := nil ;
    while recp < disp do (* Receive for phase 1 *)
        begin receive msg via link l ; recp := recp + 1 ;
            (* msg is a ⟨dmn, i⟩ or ⟨iam, nla⟩ message *)
            if msg is ⟨dmn, i⟩ then
                begin disp := 1 ;
                    neip[l] := (0, ..., 0) ; lblp[i] := 1
                    (* So now lblp = (0, .., 1, .., 0), with one 1 *)
                end
            else
                begin disp := 1 + # of 1's in nla ;
                    lblp := (lblp or nla) ;
                    neip[l] := nla
                end
        end ;
    (* Send for phase 1 *)
    forall l with neip[l] = nil do
        send ⟨iam, lblp⟩ via link l ;
    while recp < n do (* Receive for phase 2 *)
        begin receive ⟨labl, i⟩ via link l ;
            recp := recp + 1 ; πp[l] := i
        end ;
    (* Send for phase 2 *)
    forall l with neip[l] ≠ nil do
        begin πp[l] := bit in which lblp and neip[l] differ ;
            send ⟨labl, πp[l]⟩ via link l
        end
end
```

Algorithm 11 ORIENTATION OF A HYPERCUBE (NON-INITIATOR).

other messages first. Assume all processors at distance d to the leader send all messages for phase 1, and consider a processor p at distance $d+1$ from the leader. As all predecessors of p eventually send the phase 1 messages to p, p eventually receives one of these messages, and sets $dis_p := d + 1$. When p has received the phase 1 messages from all of its $d + 1$ predecessors, p sends phase 1 messages itself (to its successors).

Similarly it is shown that all processors send the messages of phase 2 and terminate. □

Lemma 25. *After termination π is an orientation. For neighbours p and q connected via link l, lbl_p and lbl_q differ exactly in bit $\pi_p[l]$ (which is equal to $\pi_q[l]$).*

Proof. According to Theorem 23 there exists exactly one orientation $\mathcal{L}$ and a witnessing node labelling $\mathcal{N}$ such that $\mathcal{L}_w(p) = \mathcal{P}_w(p)$ and $\mathcal{N}(w) = (0, .., 0)$.

In phase 1 the processors compute the node labelling $\mathcal{N}$, as is seen by using induction on the distance to the leader. Node w sets lbl_w to $(0, ..., 0)$, which is $\mathcal{N}(w)$. Neighbour p of w sets lbl_p with b_i is 1 if the link from w to p is labelled i in w, and 0 otherwise. Thus $lbl_p = \mathcal{N}(v)$.

Now assume all nodes q at distance d from w compute $lbl_q = \mathcal{N}(q)$ and consider node p at distance $d + 1$ from w. $\mathcal{N}(p)$ is a string of $d + 1$ 1's and $n - d - 1$ 0's. Node p has $d + 1$ predecessors, and $\mathcal{N}(q)$ is found for predecessor q by changing one 1 in $\mathcal{N}(p)$ into a 0. Thus the disjunction of the $d + 1$ labels $\mathcal{N}(q)$ is indeed $\mathcal{N}(p)$.

After phase 1, for predecessor q of p connected via link l, $nei_p[l] = lbl_q$. In phase 2, p computes $\pi_p[l]$ as the bit in which lbl_p and $nei_p[l]$ differ, so that lbl_p and lbl_q differ exactly in bit $\pi_p[l]$. The same label is used by q for the link, after q receives p's $\langle \mathbf{labl}, \pi_p[l] \rangle$ message. □

Concluding, Algorithm 10/11 orients a hypercube with leader, exchanging $2m$ messages. The message complexity is asymptotically optimal; see Corollary 29.

The bit complexity. As the $\langle \mathbf{iam}, label \rangle$ messages of the algorithm consist of a node label, they contain a string of n bits. It will now be shown that the algorithm can be implemented using only messages of $O(\log n)$ bits. The $\langle \mathbf{dmn}, i \rangle$ and $\langle \mathbf{labl}, i \rangle$ messages contain a number between 0 and $n - 1$ and thus contain $O(\log n)$ bits.

The algorithm does not need all information contained in the $\langle \mathbf{iam}, label \rangle$ messages; there is a lot of redundancy. It suffices to transmit the number of 1's, the smallest index at which there is a 1, and the sum modulo n of the indexes for which there is a 1. For a node label *label* define the weight, low, and index sum as $wgt(label) = \#\{i \ : \ b_i = 1\}$; $low(label) = \min\{i \ : \ b_i = 1\}$; $ixs(label) = (\sum_{b_i=1} i) \bmod n$. Finally, the *summary* is the tuple $smy(label) = (wgt(label), low(label), ixs(label))$. The summary of a node is the summary of its node label.

Lemma 26. *Let p be a node at distance $d + 1 \geq 2$ from w.*
(1) $dis_p = d + 1$ can be derived from one summary of a predecessor of p.
(2) The summary of p can be computed from the $d + 1$ summaries of p's predecessors.
(3) The node label of p can be computed from the summary of p and the $d + 1$ summaries p's predecessors.
(4) The node label of a predecessor q of p can be computed from the node label of p and the summary of q.

Proof. (1) The computation of dis_p is trivial as $wgt(\mathcal{N}(q))$ equals $d(q, w)$.

(2) Now let $d + 1$ summaries of predecessors of p be given. d of the $d + 1$ summaries have *low* equal to $low(\mathcal{N}(p))$, while one summary has a higher *low* (the predecessor whose label is found by flipping the *first* 1 in $\mathcal{N}(p)$). This gives $low(\mathcal{N}(p))$, but also identifies the index sum ixs_0 of a node label which differs

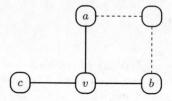

Figure 12 NEIGHBOURS OF NODE v IN THE TORUS.

from $\mathcal{N}(p)$ in position *low*. Thus $ixs(\mathcal{N}(p)) = (ixs_0 + low(\mathcal{N}(p))) \bmod n$. This completes the computation of $smy(\mathcal{N}(p)))$.

(3) The $d+1$ positions of a 1 in $\mathcal{N}(p)$ are found as $ixs(\mathcal{N}(p)) - ixs(\mathcal{N}(q)) \bmod n$ for the $d+1$ choices of q as a predecessor of p.

(4) For a predecessor q of p, $\mathcal{N}(q)$ is found by flipping the bit indexed $(ixs(\mathcal{N}(p)) - ixs(\mathcal{N}(q))) \bmod n$ from 1 to 0 in $\mathcal{N}(p)$. □

It follows from Lemma 26 that it suffices in the orientation algorithm to send the summary of node label instead of the full label, and hence the algorithm can be implemented with messages of $O(\log n)$ bits. As the messages are used to assign different labels to $\Omega(n)$ links, the information in the messages cannot be compressed below $O(\log n)$ bits.

4.3 Torus: Preorientation

In both clique and hypercube any local labelling of a leader process can be extended into a global sense of direction and this is exactly what is done in the hypercube orientation algorithm. In $n \times n$ tori (where we assume that $n > 4$) this is not the case. There are four labels (of values $(0,1)$, $(0,-1)$, $(1,0)$, and $(-1,0)$, also referred to as *north*, *south*, *east*, and *west*), which implies that there are $4! = 24$ different local labellings. However, only 8 of these can be extended to a sense of direction.

In an oriented torus the *north* and *south* neighbour of one processor are at distance 2 of each other, and there exists *one* path of length 2 between them; the same holds for the *east* and *west* neighbour. The *north* and *west* neighbours are also at distance two of each other, but are joined by two different paths of this length; see Figure 12. It follows that a labelling which assigns the labels *north* and *south* to processors forming such a pair cannot be extended to an orientation.

The first stage of the algorithm divides the four links of each processor into two pairs, with the property that the links of one pair must be assigned opposite labels.

Definition 27. A *prelabeling* $\mathcal{P}$ of the torus is an assignment in each node of labels from the set {*hori*, *verti*} to the links of that node, such that each label

---

```
begin forall links l do bag_p[l] := ∅ ;
      forall l do send ⟨one, p⟩ via l ;
      rec_p := 0 ;
      while rec_p < 16 do
         begin receive msg via link l ; rec_p := rec_p + 1 ;
               (* It is a ⟨one, n⟩ or ⟨two, n⟩ message *)
               if msg is a ⟨one, n⟩ message
                  then forall k ≠ l do send ⟨two, n⟩ via k
                  else bag_p[l] := bag_p[l] ∪ {n}
         end ;
      find l_1, l_2 such that bag_p[l_1] ∩ bag_p[l_2] = ∅ ;
      label l_1, l_2 with hori and the other links with verti
end
```

Algorithm 13 PRELABELING A TORUS.

---

is used twice.

A prelabeling $\mathcal{P}$ is *consistent* if for all nodes p and neighbours q and r of p, $\mathcal{P}_p(q) = \mathcal{P}_p(r)$ implies that there exists *exactly one* path of length 2 between q and r.

When a consistent prelabeling is available, a node may label the *verti* links with *north* and *south* and the *hori* links with *west* and *east*, and this labelling can be extended to an orientation.

Computing a consistent prelabeling. Algorithm 13 computes a consistent prelabeling using $16N$ messages. Each processor sends its name to each neighbour and each neighbour forwards the name one step further. Thus, the name of each processor is transmitted through 16 links, and each processor receives 16 messages (4 through each link). Of the 16 messages received, 8 contain names which are received only once, and 4 contain names which are received twice, but through different links, as can be seen from Figure 12. Two links via which the same name is received are perpendicular; so, when a processor has received its 16 messages a consistent prelabeling can be computed.

Orienting the torus. After the computation of a prelabeling, the processors can assign the labels *north* and *south* to the *verti* links, and *east* and *west* to the *hori* links. Each processor then has a local labelling that can be extended to a sense of direction, but the labellings of the processors are not in agreement with each other.

Our algorithm is based on the concept of *fragments*, where a fragment is a connected subset of processors for which agreement on the orientation is guaranteed. Of course we start with N fragments, each consisting of a single processor and we end with a single fragment containing all processors.

For processor v:
    send $\langle$**connect**, $\pi_v[l]\rangle$ via l ; (* to u *)
    send $\langle$ **dione**, $\pi_v[k]\,\rangle$ via one link k perpendicular to l

For processor u:
    receive $\langle$**connect**, $ll\rangle$ via l ; (* from v *)
    $\sigma[l] := oppos(ll)$; (* The opposite direction *)
    $\sigma[oppos(l)] := ll$;
    send $\langle$ **direq** $\rangle$ via the two links perpendicular to l ;
    receive $\langle$ **dians**, $kk\,\rangle$ via link k ;
    $\sigma[k] := kk$; $\sigma[oppos(k)] := oppos(kk)$
    (* Now σ is the permutation to be applied to all
            link labels in the fragment. *)

For all other processors:
    when a $\langle$ **dione**, $ll\,\rangle$ message is received via link l:
        send $\langle$ **ditwo**, $ll\,\rangle$ via the two links perpendicular to l

    when a $\langle$ **ditwo**, $ll\,\rangle$ message is received via link l
                 and a $\langle$ **direq** $\rangle$ message via link k:
        send $\langle$ **dians**, $ll\,\rangle$ via link k

Algorithm 14 FRAGMENT COMBINE PROTOCOL.

The reduction in the number of fragments is achieved by combining fragments; if the orientation of the processors in the two fragments is different, one fragment must be re-oriented by applying a permutation on the labels in all processors of the fragment. Combination of fragments occurs through one edge, connecting a processor in one fragment and a processor in the other; call these processors u and v, in fragments F, and G, respectively.

Algorithm 14 computes the permutation that must be applied to the labels in u to make it consistent with v; this permutation is broadcast in fragment G by u, so all processors can update their local labelling accordingly.

Assume node v in fragment F sends a **connect** message to node u in fragment G in order to add G to F. The combined fragment will have the name (and orientation) of fragment F. Processor v includes in the **connect** message the label of the link over which it is sent, and this defines for u the new label of the link over which the message is received, as well as the opposite link. It remains to find the correct orientation in u of the two perpendicular links. To do this (see Figure 15), v sends over one link l perpendicular to link (v, u) a message $\langle$ **dione**, $\pi_v[l]\,\rangle$, which is forwarded by the receiving node as a $\langle$ **ditwo**, $\pi_v[l]\,\rangle$ message. Processor u sends a $\langle$ **direq** $\rangle$ message via the two links perpendicular to link (u, v). A processor which receives both a $\langle$ **ditwo**, $ll\,\rangle$ and a $\langle$ **direq** $\rangle$ message, replies to the $\langle$ **direq** $\rangle$ message with a $\langle$ **dians**, $ll\,\rangle$ message. Thus u receives an answer to one of its $\langle$ **direq** $\rangle$ messages, which gives the orientation of the links perpendicular to (u, v).

We give two ways to build a complete orientation algorithm from the fragment

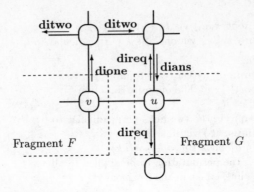

Figure 15 Extra messages in the connecting procedure.

combine protocol. If a coordinator (leader) is available, only its fragment will expand by absorbing all one-processor fragments one by one. Thus, in all join operations, fragment G contains only one node, and broadcasting of the label permutation through the fragment is not necessary. The initiator's fragment grows each time by one processor using a constant number of messages, hence the overall complexity is linear.

Another possibility is to integrate the fragment combine protocol with the Minimum Spanning Tree algorithm of Gallager, Humblet, and Spira [GHS83]. This algorithm allows all fragments to attempt fusion with neighbouring fragments simultaneously, and its overall messages complexity is $O(N \lg N + m)$ messages. Of course, no matter how fusions are organised, one needs $N - 1$ fusions to go from N fragments to a single fragment, and the combine protocol is called $N - 1$ times in the algorithm. The permutation broadcast in fragment G is combined with other activity in the fragment and adds no more messages. Consequently, the message complexity of this non-centralised variant of the fragment fusion algorithm is $O(N \lg N + m)$.

4.4 Lower Bound

In this subsection a lower bound of $\Omega(m)$ messages is shown on the message complexity of orientation algorithms, for the topologies considered in this paper.

Theorem 28. *Any orientation algorithm exchanges at least* $m - \frac{1}{2}N$ *messages in every execution.*

Proof. For a link labelling $\mathcal{P}$, let $\mathcal{P}^{u,v,w}$ (where v and w are neighbours of u) be the labelling defined by $\mathcal{P}_u^{u,v,w}(v) = \mathcal{P}_u(w)$, $\mathcal{P}_u^{u,v,w}(w) = \mathcal{P}_u(v)$, and all other labels of $\mathcal{P}^{u,v,w}$ are as in $\mathcal{P}$. ($\mathcal{P}^{u,v,w}$ is obtained by exchanging $\mathcal{P}_u(w)$ and $\mathcal{P}_u(v)$.)

If $\mathcal{L}$ is an orientation, $\mathcal{L}_u[v] = -\mathcal{L}_v[u]$ but $\mathcal{L}_u^{u,v,w}[v]$ is different, hence $\mathcal{L}^{u,v,w}$ is *not* an orientation.

Consider an execution of an orientation algorithm, with initial labelling $\mathcal{P}$, that terminates with a permutation π_v for each node (where $\mathcal{L} = \pi(\mathcal{P})$ is an orientation). Assume furthermore that in this execution some node u did not send nor receive any message to or from its two neighbours v and w. As u has not communicated with v, nor with w, the same execution is possible if the network is initially labelled with $\mathcal{P}^{u,v,w}$, and all processors terminate with the same permutation. However, $\mathcal{L}' = \pi(\mathcal{P}^{u,v,w}) = \mathcal{L}^{u,v,w}$ is *not* an orientation, and the algorithm is not correct.

It follows, that in every execution, every node must communicate with at least all its neighbours except one. □

Corollary 29. *The orientation of the N clique requires the exchange of $\Omega(N^2)$ messages. The orientation of the n–dimensional hypercube requires the exchange of $\Omega(n2^n)$ messages. The orientation of the $n \times n$ torus requires the exchange of $\Omega(n^2)$ messages.*

5 Conclusions and Open Questions

We have seen that sense of direction allows for efficient exploitation of the network topology and for more direct communication between processors. Studying the properties of sense of direction is the topic of the annual SIROCCO (Structural InfoRmatiOn and Communication COmplexity) meeting, held in 1994 (Ottawa, Canada) and 1995 (Olympia, Greece). Proceedings of the SIROCCO meeting are published by Carleton University Press.

Here are some suggestions for further research on this topic.

1. Flocchini *et al.* [FMS95] use the translations of local view as the definition rather than as a consequence of sense of direction. Is their definition equivalent to ours?
2. Prove Lemmas 14 and 17 for general routing strategies.
3. For what values of the chord length t can the one-chord algorithm (Subsection 2.4) be adapted, and still have a linear message complexity?
4. Compute the expected complexity of the random walk election algorithm (for cliques, hypercubes, and tori).
5. Does there exist a deterministic linear-message election algorithm for hypercubes without sense of direction? What is.the complexity of traversal and broadcast in this model?
6. Generalise the results in this paper for sense of direction based on non-commutative groups. Such a generalisation would be of interest, for example, wrt. the Cube Connected Cycles network, defined using a permutation group.

Acknowledgements. Hans Zantema helped me out with the calculations in Lemmas 13 through 17.

References

[ALSZ89] ATTIYA, H., LEEUWEN, J. VAN, SANTORO, N., AND ZAKS, S. Efficient elections in chordal ring networks. *Algorithmica* **4** (1989), 437–466.

[CR79] CHANG, E. J.-H. AND ROBERTS, R. An improved algorithm for decentralized extrema finding in circular arrangements of processes. *Commun. ACM* **22** (1979), 281–283.

[DKR82] DOLEV, D., KLAWE, M., AND RODEH, M. An $O(N \log N)$ unidirectional distributed algorithm for extrema-finding in a circle. *J. Algorithms* **3** (1982), 245–260.

[FMS95] FLOCCHINI, P., MANS, B., AND SANTORO, N. Sense of direction: Definitions, properties, and classes. Tech. Rep. TR-95-10, School of Computer Science, Carleton Univ., Ottawa, 1995.

[Fra82] FRANKLIN, W. R. On an improved algorithm for decentralized extrema finding in circular configurations of processors. *Commun. ACM* **25**, 5 (1982), 336–337.

[GHS83] GALLAGER, R. G., HUMBLET, P. A., AND SPIRA, P. M. A distributed algorithm for minimum weight spanning trees. *ACM Trans. Program. Lang. Syst.* **5** (1983), 67–77.

[HP93] HIGHAM, L. AND PRZYTYCKA, T. A simple, efficient algorithm for maximum finding on rings. In *Proc. 7th Int. Workshop on Distributed Algorithms* (1993), A. Schiper (ed.), vol. 725 of *Lecture Notes in Computer Science*, Springer-Verlag, pp. 249–263.

[KMZ84] KORACH, E., MORAN, S., AND ZAKS, S. Tight upper and lower bounds for some distributed algorithms for a complete network of processors. In *Proc. Symp. on Principles of Distributed Computing* (1984), pp. 199–207.

[LeL77] LELANN, G. Distributed systems: Towards a formal approach. In *Proc. Information Processing '77* (1977), B. Gilchrist (ed.), North-Holland, pp. 155–160.

[LMW86] LOUI, M. C., MATSUSHITA, T. A., AND WEST, D. B. Election in a complete network with a sense of direction. *Inf. Proc. Lett.* **22** (1986), 185–187. Addendum: *Inf. Proc. Lett.* **28** (1988), 327.

[Pet85] PETERSON, G. L. Efficient algorithms for elections in meshes and complete networks. Tech. Rep. TR 140, Dept Computer Science, University of Rochester, Rochester NY 14627, 1985.

[PKR84] PACHL, J., KORACH, E., AND ROTEM, D. Lower bounds for distributed maximum finding algorithms. *J. ACM* **31** (1984), 905–918.

[Tel93] TEL, G. Linear election in oriented hypercubes. Tech. Rep. RUU-CS-93-39, Dept Computer Science, Utrecht University, The Netherlands, 1993. To appear in Par. Proc. Lett., 1996.

[Tel94a] TEL, G. *Introduction to Distributed Algorithms.* Cambridge University Press, 1994 (xii+534 pp.).

[Tel94b] TEL, G. Network orientation. *Int. J. of Foundations of Comp. Sc.* **5**, 1 (1994), 23–57.

[Ver94] VERWEIJ, A. M. Linear-message election on hypercubes. Scriptie, Dept Computer Science, Utrecht University, The Netherlands, 1994.

[VT95] VERWEIJ, A. M. AND TEL, G. A Monte Carlo algorithm for election. In *Proc. 2nd Colloq. on Structural Information and Communication Complexity* (Olympia (GR), 1995), Carleton University Press.

Welcoming the Super Turing Theories

Hava T. Siegelmann

Faculty of Industrial Engineering and Management
Technion, Haifa 32000 Israel, iehava@ie.technion.ac.il

Abstract. This paper reasons about the need to seek for particular kinds of models of computation that imply stronger computability than the classical models. A possible such a model, constituting a chaotic dynamical system is presented. This model, which we term as the analog shift map, when viewed as a computational model has super-Turing power and is equivalent to neural networks and the class of analog machines. This map may be appropriate to describe natural physical phenomena.

1 Introduction

A straightforward method of measuring the area of a surface is by counting the number of atoms there. One may be able to develop smart algorithms to group atoms together in sets, and thus speed up the counting time. A totally different approach is by assuming continuous rather than quantized/discretized universe and calculating the relevant integral. Such a continuous algorithm should ideally be implemented on an analog machine, but it can also be approximated by a digital computer that allows for finite precision only. Although the actual hardware is discrete, the core assumption of continuity allows the development of inherently different algorithms to evaluate areas. It is possible that in the theory of computation, we are still at the stage of developing algorithms to count faster. Maybe just by assuming an analog media, we would be able to do much better for some tasks.

A more fundamental reason to look for analog computation models stems from recent advance in the field of physics. Although already in the 18th century, Poincare realized that even the orbits of simple dynamical systems may be extremely unpredictable, and even though mathematicians were dealing with this phenomenon since, it was not before 1975 and later where the Chaos was realized by physicists to be such a common behavior, occurring in many systems of scientific interest [1]. Turing machines are indeed able to simulate a large class of systems, but seem not to capture the whole picture of computation in nature, like the evolvement of many chaotic systems.

We propose an alternative model of computation, possibly realizable as well, whose computational power can surpass that of the Turing model. The proposed model builds on a particular analog chaotic system [2]; by applying the system to computer science a "Super Turing" model is developed (In this paper, the term Super Turing is meant to denote any system of computing that incorporates, but is more powerful than, the standard Turing model.).

2 Questioning the Church-Turing Thesis

In his recent book [4], Penrose has argued that the standard model of computing (Turing) is not appropriate for modeling biological intelligence. The author argues that physical processes, evolving at a quantum level, may result in computations which cannot be incorporated in Church's Thesis.

At the same year, Blum Shub and Smale [5] suggested a new type of computational model; this is the model of "computation over the real numbers." It consists of finitely many building blocks in a recurrent interconnection, where each block computes either a polynomial or a binary decision. This interesting model was originally stated in mathematical rather than computational terms; for example, in their model the input may consist of infinitely many real numbers rather than a finite binary string, and thus some power of the model may stem from the extra input knowledge.

In [3, 6], Siegelmann and Sontag introduced a particular model of super-Turing computation based on the systems of neural networks. Our Theory will be based on their model.

3 The Computational Model

In the science of computing, machines are classified according to the classes of tasks they can execute or the functions they can compute. The most popular model is the Turing Machine, but there are others that result in stronger, though non-realizable, models. "Nonuniform Turing machines" exemplify such models [7]: the machine receives on its tape, in addition to its input, another sequence w_n to assist in the computation. For all possible inputs of the same length n, the machine receives the same advice sequence w_n, but different advice is provided for input sequences of different lengths. We will later focus on the class non-uniform machines that compute in polynomial time (and use a polynomial long advice), denoted by P/poly [7]. To demonstrate, a super Turing function that appears in P/poly, is the "unary halting" function [8]: given a unary encoding of a computer program f and sequence $x \in \{1\}^*$: the function is to decide whether the program terminates when acting on the sequence x. (If both advice and time are exponentially long (i.e., $O(2^n)$), the advice can be used to indicate the desired response for each of the 2^n possible input strings of length n, and thus, compute all functions $f : \{0,1\}^* \mapsto \{0,1\}$, including non-computable ones.)

In [3, 6], Siegelmann and Sontag noticed that the non-uniform classes are indeed natural for analog computation models. They introduced the first model of computation which is uniform but yet has non-uniform super Turing capabilities; this model is the classical Analog Recurrent Neural Network (ARNN), which is popular in practice as a machine having automatic learning and adaptation capabilities [9]. The ARNN consists of a finite number of neurons. The activation of each processor is updated by the equation

$$x_i(t+1) = \sigma \left(\sum_{j=1}^{N} a_{ij} x_j(t) + \sum_{j=1}^{M} b_{ij} u_j(t) + c_i \right) , \quad i = 1, \ldots, N \qquad (1)$$

where N is the fixed number of neurons, M is the number of external input signals, x_j are the activations of the neurons, u_j are the external inputs, and a_{ij}, b_{ij}, c_i are the real coefficients, also called constants or weights (the name "analog" is due to the real rather than rational coefficients). The function σ is the simplest possible "sigmoid," namely the saturated-linear function:

$$\sigma(x) := \begin{cases} 0 & \text{if } x < 0 \\ x & \text{if } 0 \le x \le 1 \\ 1 & \text{if } x > 1 . \end{cases} \qquad (2)$$

A subset of the N neurons is singled out to communicate the output of the network to the environment. Inputs and outputs are streams of letters, and computability is defined under the convention that is sometimes used in practical communication networks: there are two binary input channels, where one is used to carry the binary input signal, and the other one indicates when the input is active. A similar convention is applied to the output.

The ARNN compute the super-Turing class P/poly in polynomial time, and all binary functions in exponential time [3]. This fact is connected to classical computability by observing that when the real weights are constrained to be rational numbers, the network has a Turing power only [10, 6]. (Follow-up generalizations appear in [11, 12, 13].)

Because the networks are defined with unbounded precision, one could think, naively, that infinite precision is required to fully describe their computation; however, we know that this is not the case. We actually have proved that "linear precision suffices; [3]; that is, up to the qth step of the computation, only the first $O(q)$ bits in both weights and activation values of the neurons influence the result.

Analogously to the Church-Turing thesis, Siegelmann and Sontag suggest their model as a basic analog computation model, stating that "any realizable analog computer will have no more power (up to polynomial time) than the analog recurrent networks." The same statement is true for the stochastic ARNN [13], as this one was proved to be computationally equivalent to the deterministic network.

3.1 About the Real Constants

The weights can be thought of modeling physical characteristics of a specific system. In a natural analog computation process, one starts from initial conditions that constitute the input, the system evolves according to the specific equations of motion to its final position, which constitutes the output. The evolution is controlled by the exact equations of motions with the exact physical constants. The analog physical system "solves" the equations of motion exactly. For example, planetary motion is used to measure time with very high precision although we know the gravitational constant G only to 2 digits. The planets, of course, evolve according to the exact value of G, irrespective of its measurement by humans! The constants do not have to be measured, their binary expansion does not have to be given, and there is no probing into their numerical features. They have their definite meaning even without being measured, just as the case with the Planck's constant, the gravitational constant, the charge of the electron, and so forth.

4 The Analog Shift Map

We present a chaotic dynamical system that computationally is as strong as the analog models; this system is called the "analog shift map". In the literature of dynamical systems, chaos is commonly exemplified by the "shift map" (such as the Baker's map [14] or the Horseshoe map [15]) over a set of bi-infinite dotted sequences: assume E is a finite alphabet. A dotted sequence over E (denoted by $\dot{E}$) is a sequence of letters where exactly one is the dot sign '.' and the rest are all in E. The dotted sequences can be finite, (one-side) infinite, or bi-infinite over E.

Let $k \in \mathbb{N}$ be an integer, the shift map

$$S^k : \dot{E} \to \dot{E} : (a)_i \mapsto (a)_{i+k}$$

shifts the dot k number of places, where negative values cause a left shift and positive ones to a right shift. For example,

$$S^3(\cdots a_{-2}\, a_{-1}\, .\, a_1\, a_2\, a_3\, a_4\, a_5 \cdots) = \cdots a_{-2}\, a_{-1}\, a_1\, a_2\, a_3\, .\, a_4\, a_5 \cdots \ .$$

The "generalized shift" map is defined by Moore [16, 17] as follows: a finite dotted substring is replaced with another dotted substring according to a function G, then this new sequence is shifted an integer number of places left or right according to a function F. Formally, the generalized shift is the function

$$\Phi : a \mapsto s^{F(a)}(a \oplus G(a)) \,, \tag{3}$$

where the function $F : \dot{E} \to \mathbb{Z}$ indicates the amount of shift (where negative values cause to shift left and positive ones to shift right), and the function $G : \dot{E} \to \dot{E}$ describes the modification of the sequence. Both F and G have a finite *domain of dependence (DoD)*, that is, F and G depend only on a finite dotted substring of the sequence on which they act. G has a finite *domain of effect (DoE)*, i.e. every sequence in the image of G consists of a finite dotted sequence, padded to both sides by infinitely many ϵ's, where ϵ is the "empty element," not contained in E. Note that the DoD and DoE of G do not need to have equal length. Finally, the operation $\oplus$ is defined by

$$(a \oplus g)_i = \begin{cases} g_i & \text{if } g_i \in E \\ a_i & \text{if } g_i = \epsilon \end{cases},$$

where ϵ is the "empty element," not contained in E.

The generalized-shift function is homeomorphic to the action of a piecewise differentiable map on a square Cantor set. Moore conjectured that such maps arise in physical systems consisting of a free particle moving between plane mirrors. Most interestingly for the present discussion, Moore proved that the generalized-shift map is computationally equivalent to a Turing Machine. This result, thus, connects chaotic dynamical systems with the classical computational model.

Here, we introduce a new chaotic dynamical system: the "analog shift map." It is similar to the generalized shift function in Equation (3), except for allowing the substituting dotted sequence (DoE) defined by G to be finite, infinite, or bi-infinite, rather than finite only. The name "analog shift map" implies the combination of the shift operation with the computational equivalence to the analog computational models (in the sense of the Siegelmann & Sontag thesis), as will be proved later.

Example 1. To illustrate, assume the analog shift defined by:

DoD	F	G
0.0	1	$\bar{\pi}$.
0.1	1	.10
1.0	0	1.0
1.1	1	.0

Here $\bar{\pi}$ denotes the left infinite string $\cdots 51413$ in base 2 rather than base 10. The table is a short description of the dynamical system, in which the next step depends upon the first letter to the right of the dot and the one to its left. If these letters (i.e. the DoD) are 0.0, then (according to the first row of the table) the left side of the dot is substituted by $\bar{\pi}$ and the dot moves one place to the right. If the DoD is instead 0.1 (as in the second row of the table), the second letter to the right of the dot becomes 0 and there is a right shift; etc.

The dynamic evolving from

$$000001.10110$$

is as follows: here the DoD is 1.1, hence (by the fourth row of the table), the letter to the right of the dot becomes 0 and the dot is shifted right:

$$1.1 : (000001.00110) \; 0000010.011$$

Now, the DoD is 0.0:

$$0.0 : (\bar{\pi}.0110) \ \bar{\pi}0.110$$
$$0.1 : (\bar{\pi}0.100) \ \bar{\pi}01.00$$
$$1.0 : (\bar{\pi}1.00) \ \bar{\pi}01.00$$

Here the DoD is 1.0 and no changes occur, this is a fixed point. □

The computation associated with the analog shift systems is the evolution of the initial dotted sequence until reaching a fixed point, from which the system does not evolve anymore. The computation does not always end; when it does, the input-output map is defined as the transformation from the initial dotted sequence to the final subsequence to the right of the dot. (In the above example, a fixed point is reached in four steps, and the computation was from "000001.10110" to "00".) To comply with computational constraints of finite input/output, attention is constrained to systems that start with finite dotted sequences and halt with either finite or left infinite dotted sequences only. Even under these finiteness constraints, the analog shift computes richer maps than the Turing Machines; this will be proved in the next section.

5   The Analog Shift Map is Super Turing

Here we prove the computational equivalence between the analog shift map and the analog recurrent neural network model. Denote by $AS(k)$ the class of functions computed by the AS map in time k, by $NN(k)$ the class of functions computed by the ARNN in time k, and by $\text{Poly}(k)$ the class of polynomials in k. The main theorem states that:

Theorem 1. *Let F be a function so that $F(n) \geq n$.*
Then, $AS(F(n)) \subseteq NN(\text{Poly}(F(n)))$, and $NN(F(n)) \subseteq AS(\text{Poly}(F(n)))$.

Proof. We assume, without loss of generality, that the finite alphabet E is binary; $E = \{0, 1\}$.

1. $AS(F(n)) \subseteq NN(\text{Poly}(F(n)))$:
    Given a bi-infinite binary sequence

    $$S = \cdots a_{-3} \, a_{-2} \, a_{-1} \, . \, a_1 \, a_2 \, a_3 \cdots \quad ,$$

    we map it into the two infinite sequences

    $$S_r = . \, a_1 \, a_2 \, a_3 \cdots \qquad S_l = . \, a_{-1} \, a_{-2} \, a_{-3} \cdots \ .$$

    A step of the AS map can be redefined in terms of the two infinite sequences S_l and S_r rather than the bi-infinite sequence S itself:

    $$\tilde{\phi}(S_l, S_r) = (S_l \oplus G_l(d_l, d_r), S_r \oplus G_r(d_l, d_r)) \ .$$

Here, $d_l = a_{-1} a_{-2} \cdots a_{-d}$ and $d_r = a_1 a_n \cdots a_d$, assuming, without loss of generality, that the DoD is of length $2d$ and is symmetric; that is $|d_l| = |d_r| = d$. The DoE of the binary sequences $G_l(d_l, d_r)$ and $G_r(d_l, d_r)$ may be unbounded.

We next prove the computational inclusion of the analog shift map in neural networks. We do so by implicitly constructing an analog recurrent net that simulates the AS map. This is done using the high level programming language NIL [18] that is associated with a compilation scheme to translate a NIL program a network which *computes exactly as the original program and requires the same computation time.*

In the following algorithm, we consider the binary sequences S_l and S_r as unbounded binary stacks ; we add two other binary stacks of bounded length, T_l and T_r, as a temporary storage. The stack operations we use are: **Top**(stack), which returns the top element of the stack; **Pop**(stack), which removes the top element of the stack; and **Push**(element,stack), which inserts an element on the top of the stack. We are now ready to describe the parts of the algorithm:

(a) Read the first d elements of both S_l and S_r into T_l and T_r, respectively, and remove them from S_l, S_r.

> **Procedure** Read;
> **Begin**
>> For $i = 1$ to d
>> Parbegin
>>> $T_l = $ Push (Top $(S_l), T_l), S_l = $ Pop (S_l) ;
>>> $T_r = $ Push (Top $(S_r), T_r), S_r = $ Pop (S_r);
>> Parend
> **End**;

The same task could be shortly written as the sequence **Push**$^d(S_l, T_l)$, **Push**$^d(S_r, T_r)$, **Pop**$^d(S_l)$, **Pop**$^d(S_r)$, where the Push and Pop operations are well defined for any finite d, to be executed d times.

(b) For each choice of the pair

$$\nu_i = (\xi_l^i, \xi_r^i) \in \{0,1\}^d \times \{0,1\}^d \quad i = 1, \ldots, 2^{2d}$$

of the DoD, there is an associated pair of substituting strings:

$$(\mu_l^i, \mu_r^i) \in \{0,1\}^{\kappa_l^i} \times \{0,1\}^{\kappa_r^i}$$

(of the DoE), where each κ_v^i $(i = 1, \ldots, 2^{2d}, v \in \{l, r\})$ is either bounded by the constant k or is ∞. We also consider μ's as stacks.

(c) Computing the $\oplus$ function.

> **Procedure** Substitute(μ_l, μ_r, S_l, S_r);
> **Begin**
>> **Parbegin**
>>> **If**$(\kappa_l > k)$ $(*\mu_l$ is Infinitely long $*)$

$$\text{then } S_l = \mu_l$$
$$\text{else } S_l = \textbf{Push}^{\kappa_l}(\mu_l, S_l);$$
$$\textbf{If}(\kappa_r > k) \quad (* \text{ The parallel case of } r \ *)$$
$$\text{then } S_r = \mu_r$$
$$\text{else } S_v = \textbf{Push}^{\kappa_r}(\mu_r, S_r);$$
Parend
End;

The following program simulates one step of the AS map:

Program AS-step();
Begin;
    Read;
    Substitute
End;

That is, there is an ARNN which computes as the AS map, and it is constructible by the methods in [18] from the algorithm above.

2. $NN(F(n)) \subseteq AS(\text{ poly }(F(n)))$:
We next show how to simulate a Turing machine with polynomial advice via an AS map. We will use the following observation. Denote the infinite string which is the concatenation of all advice by

$$w = < w_1, w_2, w_3, \ldots > ,$$

and the concatenation of the first n advises by

$$w'_n = < w_1, w_2, \ldots w_n > .$$

Constrained by polynomial computation time and polynomially long advice, it is easy to verify that a Turing Machine that receives the advice w'_n is equivalent to a Turing Machine that receives the advice w. (One side, the $< x, w >$ machine retrieves the relevant part and ignores the rest of the information; the other side, the machine $< x, w >$ cannot read more than the first polynomially many advice bits during polynomial time computation.)

We now show how to simulate a Turing Machine with a polynomial advice via an AS map; our simulation is similar to the one made by Moore, but some preprocessing is required. A configuration of the Turing Machine consists of its tape, the relative location of the read/write head in the tape, and its internal control state. Moore encoded the configuration in the bi-infinite string using the fields:

| $\bar{0}$ | tape - left | | state | tape - right | $\bar{0}$ |

That is, the string starts with infinitely many 0's $(\bar{0})$, followed by the part of the tape to the left of the read/write head, then the decimal point, the internal state of the machine, the part of the tape under the head and to its right, and again infinitely many 0's that encode the empty part of the tape. In each step of Moore's simulation, the DoD contains the state, the tape letter under the read/write head, and the two letters surrounding it. The DoE is such that the operation may simulate writing a new tape letter, entering a new control state, and moving the head one step to either right or left.

In our simulation, we allow for more flexible encoding of the Turing Machine configuration:

| garbage | left-end marker | tape - left | | state | tape - right | $\bar{0}$ |

We substitute the $\bar{0}$ string to the left of the tape with two fields: garbage and left-end marker. Here, garbage means infinitely many bits with no relevant meaning, and the left-end marker implies that there is no relevant information to its left.

We suggest the following encoding that will allow to clearly interpret the string: 10 will preset the 0 letter on the tape, 11 will present the letter 1 on the tape; 01 will present the left-end marker. The internal state of the machine will be encoded by a sequence of 0's only and will end with 1; and $\bar{0}$ still denotes the infinite sequence of 0's that represents the empty right part of the tape.

Assume the Turing Machine has the set of internal states $\{p_1, \ldots, p_Q\}$. We add the dummy states $\{q_1, \ldots, q_r\}$ for a constant r. Now the Turing Machine with a polynomial advice will act as follows:

(a) The initial bi-infinite string is

$$\boxed{\bar{0}} \quad \cdot \quad \boxed{q_1} \quad \boxed{x} \quad \boxed{\bar{0}}$$

where x is the input string. (Note that the string is describable in finite terms as required by a computational model.)

(b) In the next step the string is transferred to

$$\boxed{w} \quad \cdot \quad \boxed{q_2} \quad \boxed{x} \quad \boxed{\bar{0}}$$

where $w = < \cdots, w_3, w_2, w_1 >$. (As was previously observed, the string w adds no more advise information than the string w'_n for computations on length n input string.)

(c) In polynomially many steps, the part $< w_{n-1} \ldots w_1 >$ is removed, and the remaining part of the infinite string w is partitioned into the relevant part w_n and the garbage part $< \ldots w_{n+2} w_{n+1} >$.

| garbage | left-end marker | w_n | | q_r | x | $\bar{0}$ |

This is done by a recursive algorithm, that is linear in the length of the input string x, and thus can be executed easily by a Turing Machine, or equivalently, by a GS map. The w_n part is next transferred to the right side of the tape:

garbage	left-end marker	.	p_1	x	w_n	$\bar{0}$

where p_1 is the initial state of the Turing Machine with advice.

(d) From now on, each step of the machine is simulated as in Moore, with the only one difference that the left-end marker should be preserved to the immediate left of the relevant tape information.

■

6 The Physical Plausibility

The appeal of the analog shift map is not only as an almost classical, chaotic dynamical system that is associated with analog computation models. It is also a mathematical formulation that seems to describe idealized physical phenomena. The idealization allows for model assumptions such as any convenient scale to describe the system, noise free environment, and physics of continuous medium. Some of the physical models, previously used to simulate Turing Machines, turn out to be exactly as strong as the analog models (both to simulate and be simulated by). This assertion can be demonstrated, for example, with the system introduced by Moore [16].

The system is a "toy model," describing the motion of a particle in a three dimensional potential, such as a billiard ball or a particle bouncing among parabolic mirrors. A finite number of mirrors suffices to describe the full dynamics, one mirror for each choice of the DoD. The (x, y) coordinates of the particle when passing through a fixed, imaginary plane $[0, 1] \times [0, 1]$, simulate the dotted sequence "$x.y$". To define the computation, the particle starts in input location $\bar{0}.y$ where y is the finite input string; the output is defined in finite terms as well. The main difference between Moore's view and our is that for us, the characterizations of the few mirrors can not be fully described finitely, although we are not necessarily interested in more than some precision to some computation. On one side, analog shift can simulate this system, even with unbounded characteristics. To simulate P/poly, we note that the advice can be encoded in a uniform manner by the characterizations of the mirrors (e.g., the concatenation of all advice can be the characterization of the first mirror that is being hit, continuing with mirrors of finite characterizations, simulating the finite DoE.). The particle that starts in location $(0, y)$ first hits a particular mirror (the advice mirror) that throws it back to the plain to location (α, y), where $\frac{1}{4} < \alpha < \frac{1}{2}$ is a constant characterizing that mirror. The particle continues bouncing in the mirror system, simulating the Turing Machine operation, where it starts the "computation" at the point (α, y) rather than $(0, y)$, and is confined to the $[\alpha, 1] \times [0, 1]$ part of the plane rather than to the unit square. When reaching the halting state of the Turing machine, the particle hits a mirror that throws it to a particular observable x coordinate, there all points are fixed. The output is defined as the y coordinate when reaching this observable x. Forcing the input and output to reside in observable areas, using for example Cantor set encoding, makes the system realizable. Another possible realization may be based on the recent optical realization of the Baker's map [19].

Although it could have seemed that infinite precision was required to fully describe the associated computation, this is not the case because **linear precision suffices** for analog computation models [3]. That is, if one is interested in computing up to time q, both the mirror system and the location of the particle bouncing there, are not required to be described (or measured) with more than q bits. Digital computers are still able to approximate the model with some round-off error. This property is in accordance with the sensitivity of chaotic systems to initial conditions (here, the mirror system), suggesting that the analog shift map is indeed a natural model of chaotic (idealized) physical dynamics.

I thank Allen Ponak from the university of Calgary, Jermey Schiff from Bar-Ilan university, and Shmuel Fishman from the Technion for helpful comments.

References

1. C. Grebogi, E. Ott, and J. A. Yorke. Chaos, strange attractors, and fractal basin boundaries in ninlinear dynamics. *SCIENCE*, 238:632–637, October 1987.

2. R. L. Devaney. Dynamics of simple maps. In *Proceedings of Symposia in Applied Mathematics*, pages 1–24, 1989.

3. H. T. Siegelmann and E. D. Sontag. Analog computation via neural networks. *Theoretical Computer Science*, 131, 1994. 331-360.

4. R. Penrose. *The Emperor's New Mind*. Oxford University Press, Oxford, 1989.

5. L. Blum, M. Shub, and S. Smale. On a theory of computation and complexity over the real numbers: Np completeness, recursive functions, and universal machines. *Bull. A.M.S.*, 21:1–46, 1989.

6. H. T. Siegelmann and E. D. Sontag. On computational power of neural networks. *J. Comp. Syst. Sci*, 50(1):132–150, 1995. Previous version appeared in *Proc. Fifth ACM Workshop on Computational Learning Theory*, pages 440-449, Pittsburgh, July 1992.

7. J. L. Balcázar, J. Díaz, and J. Gabarró. *Structural Complexity*, volume I and II. Springer-Verlag EATCS Monographs, Berlin, 1988-1990.

8. J.E. Hopcroft and J.D. Ullman. *Introduction to Automata Theory, Languages, and Computation*. Addison-Wesley, 1979.

9. J. Hertz, A. Krogh, and R. Palmer. *Introduction to the Theory of Neural Computation*. Addison-Wesley, Redwood City, 1991.

10. H. T. Siegelmann and E. D. Sontag. Turing computability with neural nets. *Appl. Math. Lett.*, 4(6):77–80, 1991.

11. P. Koiran, M. Cosnard, and M. Garzon. Computability with low-dimensional dynamical systems. *Theoretical Computer Science*, 132:113–128, 1994.

12. J. L. Balcázar, R. Gavaldà, H.T. Siegelmann, and E. D. Sontag. Some structural complexity aspects of neural computation. In *IEEE Structure in Complexity Theory Conference*, pages 253–265, San Diego, CA, May 1993.

13. H. T. Siegelmann. On the computational power of probabilistic and faulty neural networks. In S. Abitebul and E. Shamir, editors, *Lecture notes in Computer Sci-*

ence, *820: Automata, Languages and Programming*, pages 23–33. Springer-Verlag, Jerusalem, 1994.

14. V. I. Arnold and A. Avez. *Ergodic Problems of Classical Mechanics*. Benjamin, New York, 1968.

15. J. Guckenheimer and P. Holmes. *Nonlinear Oscillations, Dynamical Systems, and Bifurcations of Vector Fields*. Springer, New York, 1983.

16. C. Moore. Unpredictability and undecidability in dynamical systems. *Physical Review Letters*, 64:2354–2357, 1990.

17. C. Moore. Generalized shifts: unpredictability and undecidability in dynamical systems. *Nonlinearity*, 4:199–230, 1991.

18. H. T. Siegelmann. On nil: The software constructor of neural networks. *Parallel Processing Letters*, 1995. to appear. Previous version appeared in *Proc. of the 12th AAAI conference*, Seatle, August 1994, pages: 887-882.

19. J. P. Keating Hannay, J. H. and A. M. O. Dealmeida. Optical realization of the bakers tranformation. *Nonlinearity*, 7(5):1327–1342, 1994.

What NARX Networks Can Compute

Bill G. Horne[1], Hava T. Siegelmann[2] and C. Lee Giles[1,3]

[1] NEC Research Institute, 4 Independence Way, Princeton, NJ 08540
[2] Dept. of Information Systems Eng., Faculty of Ind. Eng. and Management,
Technion (Israel Institute of Tech.), Haifa 32000, Israel
[3] UMIACS, University of Maryland, College Park, MD 20742

Abstract. We prove that a class of architectures called *NARX neural networks*, popular in control applications and other problems, are at least as powerful as fully connected recurrent neural networks. Recent results have shown that fully connected networks are Turing equivalent. Building on those results, we prove that NARX networks are also universal computation devices. NARX networks have a limited feedback which comes only from the output neuron rather than from hidden states. There is much interest in the amount and type of recurrence to be used in recurrent neural networks. Our results pose the question of what amount of feedback or recurrence is necessary for any network to be Turing equivalent and what restrictions on feedback limit computational power.

1 Introduction

1.1 Background

Much of the work on the computational capabilities of recurrent neural networks has focused on synthesis: how neuron–like elements are capable of constructing finite state machines (FSMs) [1, 11, 15, 16, 23]. All of these results assume that the nonlinearity used in the network is a hard–limiting threshold function. However, when recurrent networks are used adaptively, continuous–valued, differentiable nonlinearities are almost always used. Thus, an interesting question is how the computational complexity changes for these types of functions. For example, [18] has shown that finite state machines can be stably mapped into second order recurrent neural networks with sigmoid activation functions. More recently, recurrent networks have been shown to be at least as powerful as Turing machines, and in some cases can have super–Turing capabilities [12, 21, 22].

1.2 Summary of Results

This work extends the ideas discussed above to an important class of discrete–time nonlinear systems called *Nonlinear AutoRegressive with eXogenous inputs* (NARX) model [14]:

$$y(t) = f\left(u(t - n_u), \ldots, u(t - 1), u(t), y(t - n_y), \ldots; y(t - 1)\right), \qquad (1)$$

where $u(t)$ and $y(t)$ represent input and output of the network at time t, n_u and n_y are the input and output order, and the function f is a nonlinear function. It has been demonstrated that this particular model is well suited for modeling nonlinear systems [3, 5, 17, 19, 24]. When the function f can be approximated by a Multilayer Perceptron, the resulting system is called a *NARX network* [3, 17]. Other work [10] has shown that for the problems of grammatical inference and nonlinear system identification, gradient descent learning is more effective in NARX networks than in recurrent neural network architectures that have "hidden states." For these studies, the NARX neural net usually converges much faster and generalizes better than the other types of recurrent networks.

This work proves that NARX networks are computationally at least as strong as fully connected networks within a linear slowdown. This implies that NARX networks *with a finite number of nodes and taps* are at least as powerful as Turing machines, and thus are universal computation devices, a somewhat unexpected results given the limited nature of feedback in these networks.

These results should be contrasted with the mapping theorems of [6] which imply NARX networks should be capable of representing arbitrary systems expressible in the form of equation (1), which give no bound to the number of nodes required to achieve a good approximation. Furthermore, how such systems relate to conventional models of computation is not clear.

Finally we provide some related results concerning NARX networks with hard–limiting nonlinearities. Even though these networks are only capable of implementing a subclass of finite state machines called finite memory machines (FMMs) in real time, if given more time (a sublinear slowdown) they can simulate arbitrary FMMs.

2   Recurrent Neural Network Models

For our purposes we need consider only fully–connected and NARX recurrent neural networks. These networks will have only single–input, single–output systems, though these results easily extend to the multi–variable case.

We shall adopt the notation that x corresponds to a state variable, u to an input variable, y to an output variable, and z to a node activation value. In each of these networks we shall let N correspond to the dimension of the state space. When necessary to distinguish between variables of the two networks, those associated with the NARX network will be marked with a tilde.

2.1   Fully Connected Recurrent Neural Network

The state variables of a recurrent network are defined to be the memory elements, i.e. the set of time delay operators. In a fully connected network there is a one–to–one correspondence between node activations and state variables of the network, since each node value is stored at every time step. Specifically, the value of the N state variables at the next time step are given by $x_i(t + 1) = z_i(t)$. Each node weights and sums the external inputs to the network and the states of the network. Specifically, the activation function for each node is defined by

$$z_i(t) = \sigma \left(\sum_{j=1}^{N} a_{i,j} x_j(t) + b_i u(t) + c_i \right) , \qquad (2)$$

where $a_{i,j}$, b_i, and c_i are fixed real valued weights, and σ is a nonlinear function which will be discussed below. The output is assigned arbitrarily to be the value of the first node in the network, $y(t) = z_1(t)$.

The network is said to be fully connected because there is a weight between every pair of nodes. However, when weight $a_{i,j} = 0$ there is effectively no connection between nodes i and j. Thus, a fully connected network is very general, and can be used to represent many different kinds of architectures, including those in which only a subset of the possible connections between nodes are used.

2.2 NARX Recurrent Neural Network

A NARX network consists of a Multilayer Perceptron (MLP) which takes as input a window of past input and output values and computes the current output. Specifically, the operation of the network is defined by

$$\tilde{y}(t) = \Psi \left(\tilde{u}(t - n_u), \dots , \tilde{u}(t - 1), \tilde{u}(t), \tilde{y}(t - n_y), \dots , \tilde{y}(t - 1) \right) , \qquad (3)$$

where the function Ψ is the mapping performed by the MLP.

The states of the NARX network correspond to a set of two tapped–delay lines. One consists of n_u taps on the input values, and the other consists of n_y taps on the output values. Specifically, the state at time t corresponds to the values

$$\tilde{x}(t) = \left[\begin{array}{cccccc} \tilde{u}(t - n_u) & \dots & \tilde{u}(t - 1) & \tilde{y}(t - n_y) & \dots & \tilde{y}(t - 1) \end{array} \right] .$$

The MLP consists of a set of nodes organized into two layers. There are $\tilde{H}$ nodes in the first layer which perform the function

$$\tilde{z}_i(t) = \sigma \left(\sum_{j=1}^{\tilde{N}} \tilde{a}_{i,j} \tilde{x}_j(t) + \tilde{b}_i \tilde{u}(t) + \tilde{c}_i \right) \qquad i = 1, \dots , \tilde{H} .$$

The output layer consists of a single linear node $\tilde{y}(t) = \sum_{j=1}^{\tilde{H}} w_{i,j} \tilde{z}_j(t) + \theta_i$.

Definition 1. A function σ is said to be a *bounded, one–side saturated (BOSS) function* if it satisfies the following conditions: (i.) σ has a bounded range, i.e., $L \leq \sigma(x) \leq U$, $L \neq U$ for all $x \in \mathbb{R}$. (ii.) σ is left–side saturated, i.e. there exists a finite value s, such that $\sigma(x) = S$ for all $x \leq s$. (iii.) σ is non–constant.

Many sigmoid–like functions are BOSS functions including hard–limiting threshold functions, saturated linear functions, and "one side saturated sigmoids",

$$\sigma(x) = \begin{cases} 0 & x \leq c \\ \frac{1}{1+e^{-x}} & x > c \end{cases}$$

where $c \in \mathbb{R}$.

3   Turing Equivalence of NARX Networks

We prove that NARX networks with BOSS functions are capable of simulating fully connected networks with only a linear slowdown. Because of the universality of some types of fully connected networks with a finite number of nodes, we conclude that the associated NARX networks are Turing universal as well.

Theorem 2. *NARX networks with one hidden layer of nodes with BOSS activation functions and a linear output node can simulate fully connected recurrent networks with BOSS activation functions with a linear slowdown.*

Here we present a sketch of the proof of the theorem. The interested reader is referred to [20] for more details.

Proof. To prove the theorem we show how to construct a NARX network $\mathcal{N}$ that simulates a fully connected network $\mathcal{F}$ with N nodes, each of which uses a BOSS activation function σ. The NARX network requires $N + 1$ hidden layer nodes, a linear output node, an output shift register of order $n_y = 2N$, and no taps on the input. Without loss of generality we assume that the left saturation value of σ is $S = 0$.

The simulation suffers a linear slowdown; specifically, if $\mathcal{F}$ computes in time T, then the total computation time taken by $\mathcal{N}$ is $(N + 1)T$. At each time step, $\mathcal{N}$ will simulate the value of exactly one of the nodes in $\mathcal{F}$. The additional time step will be used to encode a sequencing signal indicating which node should be simulated next.

The output taps of $\mathcal{N}$ will be used to store the simulated states of $\mathcal{F}$; no taps on the input are required, i.e. $n_u = 0$. At any given time the tapped delay line must contain the complete set of values corresponding to all N nodes of $\mathcal{F}$ at the previous simulated time step. To accomplish this, a tapped delay line of length $n_y = 2N$ can be used which will always contain all of the values of $\mathcal{F}$ at time $t - 1$ immediately preceding a sequencing signal, μ, to indicate where these variables are in the tap.

The sequencing signal is chosen in such a way that we can define a simple function f_μ that is used to either "turn off" neurons or to yield a constant value, according to the values in the taps. Let $\mu = U + \epsilon$ for some positive constant ϵ. We define the affine function, $f_\mu(x) = x - \mu$. Then, $f_\mu(\mu) = 0$ and $f_\mu(x) \leq -\epsilon$ for all $x \in [L, U]$. It can be shown that the ith hidden layer node takes on a non–zero value only when the sequencing symbol occurs in state x_{2N-i+1} and when the values of $z_j(t-1)$ are stored in states $\tilde{x}_{N+m-i}$, $m = 1, \ldots, N$. It can be shown that the ith node in the hidden layer of $\mathcal{N}$ is updated as follows.

$$\tilde{z}_i(k+1) =$$

$$\sigma\left(\left[\sum_{m=1}^{N} a_{i,m}\tilde{x}_{N+m-i}(k) + b_i u(k) + c_i\right] + \beta_i\left[\tilde{x}_{2N-i+1}(k) - \mu\right]\right), \quad (4)$$

where the constant β_i is large enough to make the input to σ less than s when $\tilde{x}_{2N-i+1}(k) \neq \mu$ so that the whole function is zero. A similar argument is used to ensure that the final node implements the sequencing signal properly. Since only one of the hidden layer nodes is non–zero, the output node of $\mathcal{N}$ is simply a linear combination so that the output of the network is equal to the value of the currently active hidden layer node. The resulting network will simulate $\mathcal{F}$ with a linear slowdown.

It has been shown that fully connected networks with a fixed, finite number of saturated linear activation functions are universal computation devices [22]. As a result it is possible to simulate a Turing machine with the NARX network such that the slowdown is constant regardless of problem size. Thus, we conclude that

Corollary 3. *NARX networks with one hidden layer of nodes with saturated linear activation functions and linear output nodes are Turing equivalent.*

4   NARX Network with Hard–limited Neurons

Here we look at variants of the NARX networks, in which the output functions are not linear combiners but rather a hard–limiting nonlinearity.

If the inputs are binary, then recurrent neural networks are only capable of implementing Finite State Machines (FSMs), and *in real time* NARX networks are only capable of implementing a subset of FSMs called *finite memory machines (FMMs)* [13].

Intuitively, the reason why FMMs are constrained is that there is a limited amount of information that can be represented by feeding back the outputs alone. If more information could be inserted into the feedback loop, then it should be possible to simulate arbitrary FSMs in structures like NARX networks. In fact, we next show that this is the case. We will show that NARX networks with hard–limiting nonlinearities are capable of simulating fully connected networks with a slowdown proportional to the number of nodes. As a result, the NARX network will be able to simulate arbitrary FSMs.

Theorem 4. *NARX networks with hard–limiting activation functions, one hidden layer of $N+1$ nodes, and a output tapped delay line of length $4N+1$ can simulate fully connected networks with N hard–limiting activation functions with a slowdown of $2N+3$.*

Proof. See [20]. ∎

In [11] it was shown that any n–state FSM can be implemented by a four layer recurrent neural network with $O(\sqrt{n})$ hard–limiting nodes. It is trivial to show that a fully connected recurrent neural network can simulate an L–layer recurrent network with a slowdown of L. Based on the fact that a NARX network with hard–limiting output nodes is only capable of implementing FMMs, we conclude that

Corollary 5. *For every FSM $\mathcal{M}$, there exists an FMM which can simulate $\mathcal{M}$ with $O(\sqrt{n})$ nodes and $O(\sqrt{n})$ slowdown.*

5 Conclusion

We proved that NARX neural networks are capable of simulating fully connected networks within a linear slowdown, and as a result are universal dynamical systems. This theorem is somewhat surprising since the nature of feedback in this type of network is so limited, i.e. the feedback comes only from the output neuron.

The Turing equivalence of NARX neural networks implies that they are capable of representing solutions to just about any computational problem. Thus, *in theory* NARX networks can be used instead of fully recurrent neural nets without loosing any computational power.

But Turing equivalence implies that the space of possible solutions is extremely large. Searching such a large space with gradient descent learning algorithms could be quite difficult. Our experience indicates that it is difficult to learn even small finite state machines (FSMs) from example strings in either of these types of networks unless particular caution is taken in the construction of the machines [9, 4]. Often, a solution is found that classifies the training set perfectly, but the network in fact learns some complicated dynamical system which cannot necessarily be equated with any finite state machine.

NARX networks with hard–limiting nonlinearities can be shown to be capable of only implementing a subclass of finite state machines called finite memory machines. But, they can implement arbitrary finite state machines if a sublinear slowdown is allowed.

These results open several questions. What is the simplest feedback or recurrence necessary for any network to be Turing universal? Do these results have implications about the computational power of other types of architectures such as recurrent networks with local feedback [2, 7, 8]?

Acknowledgements

We would like to thank Peter Tiňo and Hanna Siegelmann for many helpful comments.

References

1. N. Alon, A.K. Dewdney, and T.J. Ott. Efficient simulation of finite automata by neural nets. *JACM*, 38(2):495–514, 1991.
2. A.D. Back and A.C. Tsoi. FIR and IIR synapses, a new neural network architecture for time series modeling. *Neural Computation*, 3(3):375–385, 1991.
3. S. Chen, S.A. Billings, and P.M. Grant. Non–linear system identification using neural networks. *Int. J. Control*, 51(6):1191–1214, 1990.
4. D.S. Clouse, C.L. Giles, B.G. Horne, and G.W. Cottrell. Learning large deBruijn automata with feed–forward neural networks. Technical Report CS94–398, CSE Dept., UCSD, La Jolla, CA, 1994.
5. J. Connor, L.E. Atlas, and D.R. Martin. Recurrent networks and NARMA modeling. In *NIPS4*, pages 301–308, 1992.
6. G. Cybenko. Approximation by superpositions of a sigmoidal function. *Math. of Control, Signals, and Sys.*, 2(4):303–314, 1989.
7. B. de Vries and J.C. Principe. The gamma model — A new neural model for temporal processing. *Neural Networks*, 5:565–576, 1992.
8. P. Frasconi, M. Gori, and G. Soda. Local feedback multilayered networks. *Neural Computation*, 4:120–130, 1992.
9. C.L. Giles, B.G. Horne, and T. Lin. Learning a class of large finite state machines with a recurrent neural network. *Neural Networks*, 1995. In press.
10. B.G. Horne and C.L. Giles. An experimental comparison of recurrent neural networks. In *NIPS7*, 1995. To appear.
11. B.G. Horne and D.R. Hush. Bounds on the complexity of recurrent neural network implementations of finite state machines. In *NIPS6*, pages 359–366, 1994.
12. J. Kilian and H.T. Siegelmann. On the power of sigmoid neural networks. In *Proc. 6th ACM Work. on Comp. Learning Theory*, pages 137–143, 1993.
13. Z. Kohavi. *Switching and finite automata theory*. McGraw–Hill, New York, NY, 2nd edition, 1978.
14. I.J. Leontaritis and S.A. Billings. Input–output parametric models for non–linear systems: Part I: deterministic non–linear systems. *Int. J. Control*, 41(2):303–328, 1985.
15. W.S. McCulloch and W.H. Pitts. A logical calculus of the ideas immanent in nervous activity. *Bull. Math. Biophysics*, 5:115–133, 1943.
16. M.L. Minsky. *Computation: Finite and infinite machines*. Prentice–Hall, Englewood Cliffs, 1967.
17. K.S. Narendra and K. Parthasarathy. Identification and control of dynamical systems using neural networks. *IEEE Trans. on Neural Networks*, 1:4–27, March 1990.
18. C.W. Omlin and C.L. Giles. Stable encoding of large finite-state automata in recurrent neural networks with sigmoid discriminants. *Neural Computation*, 1996. accepted for publication.
19. S.-Z. Qin, H.-T. Su, and T.J. McAvoy. Comparison of four neural-net learning methods for dynamic system identification. *IEEE Trans. on Neural Networks*, 3(1):122–130, 1992.
20. H.T. Siegelmann, B.G. Horne, and C.L. Giles. Computational capabilities of NARX neural networks. Technical Report UMIACS-TR-95-12 and CS-TR-3408, Institute for Advanced Computer Studies, University of Maryland, 1995.
21. H.T. Siegelmann and E.D. Sontag. Analog computation via neural networks. *Theoretical Computer Science*, 131:331–360, 1994.

22. H.T. Siegelmann and E.D. Sontag. On the computational power of neural networks. *J. Comp. and Sys. Science*, 50(1):132–150, 1995.
23. H.T. Siegelmann, E.D. Sontag, and C.L. Giles. The complexity of language recognition by neural networks. In *Algorithms, Software, Architecture (Proc. of IFIP 12th World Computer Congress)*, pages 329–335. North–Holland, 1992.
24. H.-T. Su, T.J. McAvoy, and P. Werbos. Long–term predictions of chemical processes using recurrent neural networks: A parallel training approach. *Ind. Eng. Chem. Res.*, 31:1338–1352, 1992.

Database: Introduction to Problems

Keith G. Jeffery

Systems Engineering Division, Computing and Information Systems Department
Rutherford Appleton Laboratory, Chilton, Didcot, OX11 0QX, UK
email: kgj@inf.rl.ac.uk

Abstract. Database Systems have come a long way in the 30 years or so of their existence. However, despite the relative success, there are large areas of end-user requirements that current systems just cannot address. This paper identifies key features of database technology, analyses the end-user requirement against these key features and thus highlights inadequacies. The opportunities of distribution and parallelism are discussed and the interoperation problem addressed. The major required features of future database systems are discussed and a way forward proposed.

1 Introduction

This paper is the first of a set of three related and co-ordinated invited presentations at SOFSEM '95. The topic 'database' was considered of sufficient interest to have it as a theme in SOFSEM '95, and it has been my pleasure to organise the presentations in this theme. This first paper introduces the major problems facing database technology today and indicates possible directions for their solution. These directions are taken up and discussed in detail by the authors of the two related presentations, Norman Paton and Jane Grimson.

This paper is structured as follows: in Part 2 the basic concepts of database technology are presented briefly as a reminder, bringing out in particular those aspects that will be discussed later in terms of the need for modifications, extensions or revolutionary changes. Part 3 is a discussion of data modelling and database design emphasising the richness of the real world. This leads in Part 4 to a discussion of the inadequacies of RDBMS (Relational Database Management Systems) to support this richness in an information system representation, concluding with some recent approaches to overcoming the problem. Distribution and interoperability are discussed in Part 5, particularly in the context of organisational or enterprise (real world) needs, and some recent models for solutions are presented. The final section—Part 6—looks forward to the future, and discusses recent work and directions of research to address the major problems of expressivity, representativity, tractability, interoperability, integration into user environments and ease of use concluding with a challenge and proposed direction.

2 Basic Concepts

2.1 Representation of the World of Interest

The major purpose of database technology is to store within a computer-based information system a representation of the world of interest to the enterprise or organisation. Consider an airline reservation system; booking of tickets and allocation of seats is not performed in or near the physical aircraft allocated to a particular flight, but is done in a computer system holding a representation of that aircraft (with number and layout of seats by class, smoking / non-smoking etc.). Similarly, in a large supermarket, a database system represents the stock of goods on the shelves and in the attached storeroom and is changed by information from the PoS (Point of Sale) subsystems (i.e. what goods are leaving the supermarket and paid for) and by information from the stores delivery subsystem accepting stocks of goods delivered by truck from some central warehouses to replace stock on the shelves. Of course, the database system is used to trigger orders for further stock when a certain quantity of the stock on the shelves is recorded as sold through the PoS subsystem.

The organisational consequence of the use of such technology is that management decisions are taken based on information from the database system, not from the real world. If the database system does not represent accurately the real world of interest to the enterprise or organisation then the management decisions will become progressively less relevant to the real world situation, and the direction of the organisation will be less than optimal. In the case of the airline or supermarket the consequences will be some economic penalty. Designers of database systems used by management for controlling nuclear power stations, for controlling a military aircraft, ship or tank or for controlling a toxic chemicals production plant bear a greater responsibility.

2.2 Integrity

Ensuring that the database system represents accurately the real world of interest to the enterprise or organisation is the business of integrity maintenance. This is accomplished ideally by features in the DBMS (Database Management System) which control concurrency (transactions) and data values permitted (constraints). As we shall see, facilities in present DBMSs are insufficient for many real-world problems. It is noteworthy that in most supermarkets using a database system as described above, a human check of shelf-stock is carried out periodically to validate the database system representation. Similarly on an aircraft, the cabin-crew may count the seated passengers or ask if a named person is on the plane in order to validate the database system.

2.3 Concurrency

Most databases reside on a server which is accessed by many users. Thus, there is concurrency with—at any one time—several user processes accessing the database. It is thus possible (without any controls) that while one user-program is reading and writing to the database another user-program can be doing likewise. Consider the value of a particular instance of a particular attribute in the database (variable in each program) with time—for example the stock of IBM PCs in a store:

Time	user-program A	user-program B	Data base	Real World
1	read database = 20	read database = 20	20	20
2		sale: decrement by 1 = 19		19
3	sale: decrement by 1 = 19	write to database 19	19	18
4	write to database 19		19	18

Clearly, integrity is not maintained and a mechanism is required to ensure integrity otherwise—in this case—the store will soon be selling IBM PCs it does not have in stock.

2.4 Transactions

The mechanism used in DBMSs is the transaction. The transaction is built around the concept of a unit of work—basically that amount of data processing that is atomic and which must not be interleaved with other units of work. The typical unit of work is the 'read—calculate—updatewrite' sequence. The program should lock the required area of he database before the 'read' stage and release the locks after the 'updatewrite' stage. Clearly at the stage of 'read' both the program and database reflect accurately the state of the real world. At the 'calculate' stage the state of the program is reflecting the real world but different from the database, so the database state has to be realigned with the real world as soon as possible—by the 'updatewrite' stage. The DBMS prevents interleaving of such transactions by serialising them, using the locks.

However, if the transactions involved are not updating the same areas of the database (and there are no dependencies between the two areas concerned) then the transactions can proceed in parallel. Clearly, for performance reasons, there is an advantage in transactions having as few instructions as possible and affecting as small an area of the database as possible—this allows for increased concurrency. In database systems with complex data structures and/or with complex processing requirements then the transactions have many instructions and affect large areas of the database. In this case trade-offs may be made by the designer between performance (allow concurrency) and integrity (forbid concurrency).

2.5 Constraints

Database update involves inserting new data or overwriting existing data with new values. These values should reflect the state of the real world. Much of the update / input is done by humans, and so most database systems present the user with an input screen (like a proforma) and behind which there is an associated program which checks the values input against some predefined list of acceptable values or against some algorithm, informing the user if the input value is in error. The definition of acceptable values is commonly done by expressing constraints, such as the value must be between '1' and '9' or the only acceptable values are 'M' or 'F'. In systems with complex data structures and complex processing requirements the transactions (and therefore the constraints processing within them) can become very complex; sometimes a valid database state can only be regained after a validation involving the resulting data values from several updatewrite transactions acting on different parts of the database. This is integrity maintenance; ensuring that the database represents accurately the real world of interest.

2.6 Schema and Data

Perhaps the greatest contribution made by database technology is the concept of schema and data. The schema is metadata; it describes the characteristics of the data. Typically the schema includes, for each relation (table), attribute names, type (as in programming language type) and possibly some indication if the attribute is a key or non-key attribute. Attribute constraints (such a valid range of values) may be included.

However, the real power of the schema is that application programs express their processing requirements in terms of the relation and attribute names found in the schema and not in terms of the data storage structures. This provides data independence; physical data independence where the physical storage layout of the data can be changed without affecting the programs (including optimisation of access by use of indexes) and logical data independence where additional attributes or tables may be added to the database without affecting existing programs.

The schema thus provides an insulation layer between programs and data, allowing each to change independently of the other. This is a great improvement over the pre-existing situation with files and programs in close interdependence.

There are two models or perspectives on schemas. The ANSI model [1] is topological and distinguishes:

(a) *export schema:* (possibly restricted) view of the database seen by one application;
(b) *external schema:* logical representation of the database by a schema—potentially seen by all applications;
(c) *internal schema:* physical representation of the database;

whereas the information model is based on expressivity of information and consists of:

(a) *conceptual schema:* conceptual level representation of the database—DBMS-model-independent (can implement in relational or another paradigm);

(b) *logical schema:* logical level representation of the database—DBMS-supplier-independent within one DBMS model (e.g. relational);

(c) *physical schema:* physical level representation of the database—DBMS version and target hardware/software configuration-dependent.

The (b) and (c) levels are common to the two models. However, these two perspectives on schemas become important as we shall see later.

2.7 Intension and Extension

Consider a function $y = f(a, b, c)$. A table of all possible values of y, a, b, c is the extension and the function definition itself is the intension. Similarly, the schema of a database can be regarded as an intension; there are two extensions: the tabulation of all possible values of all attributes (the possible extension) and the values of all attributes as recorded (the recorded extension). The latter—the data as opposed to the schema in a conventional database system—is a subset of the former. However, the former defines for each attribute the domain; the range of possible values an attribute in that domain can take for any instance.

Consider also an airline timetable. It may have columns (attributes) of date, time, departure airport, flight number, arrival airport, time, date. For a particular journey (say London to Paris) there will be many rows in this table for each day. This is the extension. The related intension might be a set of rules (represented in first order logic) which (in English) state that on each weekday a flight leaves London for Paris each hour at exactly 10 minutes past the hour between 0700 and 2200.

The generation of an intension from an extension is an abstraction analogous to the proposal of a scientific hypothesis from a set of observations. The generation of an extension from an intension is analogous to predicting results from a hypothesis which can then be tested by observation or experiment.

3 Data Modelling and Database Design

3.1 Representing the World of Interest

The aim of data modelling and database design is to take the world of interest—which is unbounded, continuous and dynamic—and somehow represent it within a database system that is restricted, finite and static [25]. This implies that the process (of modelling and design) loses richness of representation (representativity) in the data and richness of expression (expressivity) in the processing. Understanding these losses is important, and trying somehow to prevent the loss even more so!

3.2 Modelling

There are two major phases in the systems development process, each requiring modelling techniques. The collection, analysis and modelling of the user requirements—requirements engineering—leads to the production of a conceptual model of the system expressed more formally in a conceptual schema. This conceptual schema forms the starting point for the second phase—design engineering—which transforms the model represented by the conceptual schema progressively to an implemented system.

3.3 Requirements Engineering

Requirements engineering records the user requirements (utterances), analyses them, resolves inconsistencies and ambiguities and produces a conceptual schema representing a conceptual model of the system. Importantly, this conceptual model is validated by the end-user(s) through a series of technique such as rapid prototyping, natural language explanation, comparison with similar system models and system diagnosis. The requirements can be divided into FRs (functional requirements) and NFRs (non-functional requirements); FRs concern the organisational purpose whereas NFRs concern properties required of the final system such as performance, security, standards conformance.

3.4 Design Engineering

Design engineering takes the conceptual model from requirements engineering, represented by the conceptual schema, and transforms it progressively to an implemented system. The progression is from the conceptual model, through a logical model to the physical model. This recalls the information (as opposed to topological) perspective on schemas described above. The conceptual model is realised typically as an E-R model for data and a dataflow model for process. The logical model is realised as a relational schema and process specifications. The physical model is the implemented system.

3.5 Systems Engineering

This information system modelling, giving the level of schema conceptual, logical physical, is extended in systems engineering to include the enterprise model—a representation of the organisation or enterprise within which the information system will operate. This model use the same tools and constructs as the information systems model at conceptual level, but the tools and techniques are applied to the enterprise, not the information system.

4 RDBMS Inadequacies

4.1 Introduction

The relational model of data [7]—which provided a firm theoretical basis for database design (metadata and data) and an associated algebra and calculus for data manipulation—is perhaps the most important advance in information systems to date. It stimulated in addition the discipline of conceptual modelling, now part of data modelling and database design. However, with the known limitations at the time of its first publication, and more than 20 years experience of it use in real-world applications, it is now possible to enumerate its limitations and to follow what efforts have been made to understand and address those limitations. The major limitations concern the inability to express sufficiently the richness expressed by requirement engineering in a design engineering phase with a target implementation in a RDBMS.

4.2 Data Structure Representation

An appropriate data structure representation is very important from the point of view of the end-user both for understanding of data interrelationships and for correctly expressed data manipulation. The relational model at once makes it both easy and difficult for the end-user; simple data structures are represented simply (single table) but more complex data structures require careful structuring into relations which—to an end-user—is unnatural. There are associated problems of integrity maintenance (especially referential integrity), data locality (related tuples in different tables are physically scattered in storage, efficiency (because of multiple joins) and difficulty of expressing the data manipulation or processing requirement (SQL becomes inelegant and unwieldy).

4.3 Computational Completeness

Computational completeness is very important for the end-user to express in one environment both data manipulation operations (e.g. retrieval or update) and data processing operations (e.g. arithmetic). The relational model provides an algebra that is relationally complete but not computationally complete. Computational completeness is achieved by embedding the data manipulation directives in a traditional third generation programming language as procedure calls. One effect of this is the so-called *impedance mismatch*; the programming language environment works one tuple at a time whereas the data manipulation (relational algebra) environment works on sets of tuples. Thus here is a need for cursors top keep track of the current tuple for computation within the set.

4.4 Constraints

Constraints are important because they ensure that the internal representation of the world of interest (the database) is consistent with the external (real) world. Relational constraint handling is limited; usually primary key uniqueness and referential integrity are supported, together with type and range checking for validation of data. There is no support for more complex constraints, although inter-attribute constraints may be supported by a 4GL environment associated with the RDBMS. There is no support for semantic constraints which should be grammatically correct, semantically correct and internally self-consistent [13].

4.5 Temporal

Many applications require expression of temporal features; the travel and tourism domain, the banking domain and the medical domain are examples. There is a need to express concepts such as 'now', 'before', 'after', 'until', 'during' and relational theory does not provide for this. There have been attempts to use the data structures of RDBMS for temporal data but always additional processing capability has been needed and the data manipulation language and data definition language have been subject to extension beyond their natural expressive powers. Perhaps the best example is TEMPORA [37] which approached the problem from the conceptual modelling perspective, but there have been many other attempts based on logic.

4.6 Roles

Roles are important because they express data / process relationships, possibly through constraints and possibly temporally bounded. For example, consider the roles 'student' of person and 'father' of person—both are constrained subentities of person and (usually) temporally bounded. In a RDBMS roles are usually expressed as separate relations, but this means the user has to control the validity of processing—with the poor constraint handling facilities available in a RDBMS.

4.7 Long transactions

Certain applications have a requirement for long transactions. The usual data processing system has very short, atomic transactions (e.g. to update stock in a supermarket, or to allocate a seat on an aircraft). However, applications in CAD (computer-aided design), office systems, CASE (computer assisted software (or systems) engineering) and others have instances of (usually complex) entities 'open' for long periods of time while changes are being made. This raises questions of serialising versus concurrency and how to recover work done during transactions in the event of a system crash. Clearly RDBMSs do not support this functionality.

4.8 Versions

Associated with long transactions is the concept of versions. In many design applications it is required to store several versions of instances of each subentity of each entity. A particular entity instance can be assembled dynamically from different instance versions of different sub-entities. Versions also imply the need of temporal expression and may require specialised constraints. RDBMSs do not support this.

5 Distribution and Interoperation

5.1 Introduction

There has been a long history of R&D in distributed database systems. The adoption of the client-server model, while not in itself providing a distributed system, did provide the tools, interface definitions and architectural insights to make the construction of distributed database systems realistic.

5.2 Client Server Architecture

Client-server architecture involves splitting an overall application into a client part and a server part. In database terms, the interface was defined as the SQL language (with associated protocols for passing the query and returning the answer as a relation or table). This led to the idea that one client could access several different RDBMS servers, using a protocol such as ODBC. However, it should be noted that the end-user at the client workstation has to know and understand the schemas of the target databases, and the results are not integrated; the table of tuples from each accessed is returned separately.

Modern thinking splits an application into more components, namely

(a) the user interface including GUI, running on a device with screen, keyboard and mouse (or possibly touch-screen for kiosk applications);
(b) application dialogue control and local constraint handling;
(c) the application itself
(d) the persistent store (database)

In the classical client-server architecture, at runtime, only (d) is on the server, the rest on the client. In modern thinking the client is itself partitioned into the (a) and (b) components, where (b) may be shared between several (a) components. (c) may reside on the server, or on yet another architectural component, shared by several (b) components.

5.3 Distributed Database Systems

True distributed database systems can be classified using the scheme of [5]. Homogeneous distributed systems, with central authoritative control of schema and transactions have been built for applications requiring either:

(a) complex queries where a 'divide and conquer' strategy can be utilised—so exploiting server parallelism or
(b) where the data placement can be optimised geographically for application loads.

Heterogeneous distributed systems arise either because of the same reasons for homogeneous, or because a new requirement has arisen to access together (and integrate the results from) disparate DBMSs; the requirement commonly arising from a company take-over or strategic information sharing decision (e.g. for environmental protection or medical care).

The issues in classifying such systems—or choosing an appropriate architecture for an application requirement—concern autonomy. The real question is 'can an individual site location change its database schema, and change it transaction strategy or not'? Clearly there is a tension between the local site requirement to evolve with local application needs and the requirement of the federation to ensure a consistent end-user image across all databases in the distributed system.

In the Object-Oriented environment, interoperability has been demonstrated by all participating DBSs adopting CORBA (Common Object Request Broker Architecture). However, while this may be realistic for newly designed applications, the cost of retro-fitting CORBA routine to an existing application is large—and if the application is not object-oriented probably prohibitive.

As indicated above, the real problem concerns legacy systems [6]. These are pre-existing applications almost always involving a persistent store which are business-critical yet are required to interwork with other systems of different architectures.

The problem from the database perspective is heterogeneous distributed database design with pre-existing components. The engineering problem is how to provide the end-user with a consistent view (for both query and returned information) over this heterogeneity, without the user needing to have detailed knowledge of the syntax and semantics of the different schemas. Solutions require the utilisation of other, but related, technologies and is a very active research area, and so are discussed under 'Future' later.

5.4 Distributed and Parallel Systems

It has been indicated above that one motivation for distributed database systems is the increased potential performance from a 'divide and conquer' strategy so that multiple servers are used, each receiving a query fragment and retrieving part of the answer to the overall query. This is coarse-grained or processor parallelism, and is more-or-less indistinguishable from distribution in distributed database systems. Fine-grained or instruction parallelism has been attempted for some applications but generally has been rather unsuccessful.

5.5 Models for Interoperating Distributed Database Systems

A model for interoperating distributed database systems was proposed by [34]. This extends the ANSI/SPARC 3-layer model to 5 layers, and is topological, describing the schemas at any one site. External and Federal layers are added above (between the federation and the local site schema layers) the export, component (matches external) and local (matches internal) layers or schemas of the ANSI/SPARC model.

Sheth and Larsen 1990	ANSI/SPARC 1971
Federal	
Export	Export
Component	External
Local	Internal

The External layer (or schema) presents to the federation the export schema in federation terms; the federal layer providing this translation from the export schema (the restriction) and the external schema (the logical description of the database). As the author themselves admit, it does little to aid integration of the distributed components, leaving syntactic and semantic integration to the database administrator constructing the schemas. Their mis-use of pre-existing terms is also unhelpful.

A model using the information richness layers (based on the 3-layer model of physical, logical, conceptual used widely in the data analysis and design methods) has been produced with 5 layers [19]; a semantic layer is added above conceptual to capture information lost in the reduction from rich end-user requirement language to a conceptual model, and an intensional layer inserted between logical and conceptual to capture the design information lost in the reduction from conceptual to logical design in classical methods.

Jeffery et al 1994	Classical Model
Semantic	
Conceptual	Conceptual
Intensional	
Logical	Logical
Physical	Physical

This model has been developed for, and used successfully in, the extremely complex heterogeneous distributed hyperlinked multimedia system MIPS. It has been validated independently on a problem in airport engineering [10].

6 Future

6.1 Introduction

In its (approximately) 30 year history, database technology has achieved much. Without it, the banking and finance systems of the world would stop. Without it retail trade would function much less efficiently. The lack of database technology would ground the airlines and halt other transport systems. Database technology has contributed significantly to better medical care, safer drugs, targeted investment for famine relief aid and social funding. It has become an essential tool for space science and particle physics research; it has helped greatly in the understanding of meteorology, climate and the environment. At a mundane level, millions of people use the technology for domestic finances or to catalogue collections of photographs or music recordings. There is some evidence to support the statement from some R&D strategists that 'the database problem is solved'. However, this paper contends that we have solved the easy problem; the real work starts here.

Consider a query of the form: *where can I buy inexpensive coffee downtown?* Thousands of people ask themselves such a question every day. As we shall see, it is not so easy for a database system to handle it. The 'where' implies geolocation; 'buy' implies the target location is a retail store; 'downtown' is a geo-area. Immediately there is a need for the system to solicit more precise information from the end-user—'what do you mean by downtown? Please supply the geo-coordinates of the South-West and North-East corners of a bounding rectangle'.

'Coffee' is also poorly defined and further query refinement is required to discover the form (beans, ground, granules, powder), type (from which country, area), whether it is decaffeinated or not, what quantity (by weight), what storage medium (jar, tinor sold as loose beans)...the refinement is quite lengthy. Finally, there is 'inexpensive'. This is relative term, a function of average income, individual income and coffee price (at its simplest!). Of course, the price of the coffee should also include some fraction of the cost of getting to the retail store (cheaper coffee at the far end of downtown may be more expensive overall than more expensive coffee closer to the home (or intended travel route) of the end-user).

Clearly, SQL does not even approach this kind of end-user query requirement. It lacks expressivity. The information requires much more complex structuring than can be represented using a relational database to be a model of the world of interest—it lacks representativity. Furthermore, the typical tabular listing of tuples as an answer is hardly sufficient—a map showing locations with symbols sized to represent price might be more helpful—this is integration into the end-user environment. All this, and we have only considered a query on one database; in practice to answer such a query access to many heterogeneous distributed databases would be necessary, with all the problems of different schemas—this is interoperability. Finally, there is the economic question—can the query be satisfied with economically justifiable resources (or for certain applications within a given time as well)—this is tractability. The 'coffee query' is relatively simple; just imagine the effort to answer: *give me in order the optimal 5 locations for my new production plant in Europe.*

The real problem facing database technology is to handle the requirements for expressivity, representativity, interoperability, tractability, integration into end-user environments and ease of use highlighted by examples such as the those above.

6.2 Expressivity

This concerns the ability of the DBS to transport to its data server(s) from the client end-user query interface sufficient richness of expression to reflect accurately the user's requirement. The current standard is SQL. As demonstrated above, this is clearly insufficient to represent the 'coffee query'. Modern GUIs with graphical query interfaces are pioneering the communication between the end-user and the client part of the DBS; however, no such richer interface between client and server(s) exists at present. There exist several possible directions:

(a) build much intelligence into the system to interact with the user to refine the high-level query to SQL; this may be performed on the client or (more usually) using both client and server;
(b) build much intelligence into the system to refine automatically the end-user high-level query to SQL; this may be performed on the client or (more usually) using both client and server;
(c) pass the high-level query in a richer-than-SQL form to the server and resolve it there using built-in intelligence.

It is likely that all three techniques in judicious combination should be used. This leads to the requirement for an internal representation language between the processing elements; the most successful experiments to date have used extended first order logic.

6.3 Representativity

One of the key features in effective end-user utilisation of information is understanding the data structure—the inter-relationships between entities. Such understanding leads to more precise queries and optimal output report requests. Visual presentation of the data structures is a promising line of development. However, this requires a representation in the database suitable for rendering visually. Clearly, the relational structure—with high-level entities being split as sub-entities across multiple relations, linked by primary / foreign keys, is not readily understandable by the end-user.

Object-Orientation, with the concept of encapsulated objects, provides a much more natural representation of real-world entitites, although there is some danger of application-specific entity views losing the canonical representation advantage of relational systems. There remains the requirement to represent the temporal duration of state, the maintenance of temporally-bound versions and integrity constraints related to the data. The addition of logic or active features allows the object state to be changed by declared conditions; a much more accurate representation of the real world than third generation language programs updating relational data tables through embedded SQL calls. This technique can also be used for temporal representation—although there is also an implication on the expressivity issue—and for constraints [9].

6.4   Interoperability

Perhaps the greatest challenge to Information Technology today is interoperability. When starting from a green-field situation, the use of OODBSs and CORBA technology can provide interoperation. However, more usually interoperation is required to access pre-existing information and systems—the legacy problem.

The phenomenal growth of WWW demonstrates the end-user demand—even when the end-user has to first determine relevant information sources (via catalogues and sometimes exhaustive search), secondly access each information source individually to retrieve the information required and thirdly to integrate this retrieved information into something like an answer.

The systems engineering problem involves not only the expressivity and representativity issues, but also the need to equivalence the schemas of relevant information sources. There are several techniques for this which apply equally to strategies for data or information exchange [23], and data or information access [17]:

(a) impose a global schema with equivalences mapped (by hand) to attributes in each participating schema;

(b) analyse participating schemas, identify common attributes (at least semantically if not syntactically) and then produce a global schema (this is the technique used by [34];

(c) analyse participating schemas, reverse engineer to a higher-information-representation model (e.g. conceptual level), equivalence entities based on conceptual semantics, forward engineer a federated schema to each participating schema to allow local equivalencing between the local syntax / semantics and the local projected federated schema [29];

(d) as in (c) but using object-oriented conceptual level representation [31];

(e) enhancing each participating schema with knowledge from a knowledge-based system to a higher higher-information-representation model (usually the layers of the 5-layer model [19]) and fragment the query so that query terms match knowledge-enhanced attribute ontologies related to each participating database schema [26];

(f) use of mediators, with knowledge, to mediate between different schemas to reach a consensus schema [4]. This research is beginning to yield some results and an ambitious project using this technology for medical applications is just starting—led by Carole Goble who spoke on medical informatics at a SOFSEM '93 [12].

Clearly, the promising line of development here is to utilise advanced knowledge-based systems to mediate the schema equivalencing, either by the use of mediators or knowledge-based systems embedded within the interoperating system.

6.5   Tractability

The requirement for more representative data structures introduces complexity. Transitive closures of large structures, or handling recursive structures can use a lot of computing resource. If logic constructs are added, there is further danger; simple negation or update of the rules can cause unsafe execution which is potentially non-terminating. If the requirements for expressivity are added to this, again utilising logic, there is clearly a problem in satisfying the user request with an economically justifiable use of resources, or within an acceptable time-limit (if the answer is time-critical). If the information is on interoperating distributed servers, the problem is even more complex because of the resources required for some form of schema reconciliation.

Fortunately, with interoperability comes distribution and therefore potential coarse-grained parallelism with independent query fragments executing concurrently on different servers.

6.6 Integration into end-user environments

The end-user requires the answer to the query to be in an appropriate form. This implies a document integrated into the office or desktop environment of the end-user. The document should be able to accommodate hyperlinked multimedia, and for co-operative working environments should include workflow information off the active / eager type.

6.7 Ease of Use

However expressive the query environment, however rich the media capability of the answer document the system as seen by the end-user is of little help unless it is easy to use. Basically, if the benefit of using the system is perceived to be less than the effort threshold of the user the system will not be utilised.

6.8 The Challenge and Direction

The challenge to systems engineers is to produce DBSs that produce:

(a) the relevant information (no more, no less);
(b) at the right time (when needed);
(c) at the right place (where the end-user is, even if travelling);
(d) in the appropriate form (including hyperlinked multimedia where 33 required);

at an economically acceptable cost.
Here is a R&D agenda for many years yet.

References

1. ANSI/XS/SPARC: Interim Report from the Study Group on Database Management Systems. in Bull ACM SIGMOD 7,2 1975
2. Arens, Y., Chee, C. Y., Hsu, C., Knoblock, C., A.: Retrieving and Integrating Data from Multiple Information Sources. University of Southern California Information Sciences Institute Internal report ISI-RR-93-308, April 1993

118

3. Batini, C., Lenzerini, M., Navathe, S., B.: A Comparative analysis of methodologies for database schema integration. ACM Computing Surveys, 15, 1986
4. Barsalou, T., Wiederhold, G., Knowledge-directed mediation between Application Objects and Base data. in Data and Knowledge Base Integration, Ed. S. M. Deen, 1993
5. Bell, D., Grimson, J.: Distributed Database Systems. Addison-Wesley, Wokingham, England, (1992)
6. Brodie, M., L.: The Promise of Distributed Computing and the Challenges of Legacy Systems. Proceedings BNCOD10, Aberdeen. LNCS 618, Springer-Verlag, (1992)
7. Codd, E., F: Relational Model for Large Shared Databanks. CACM **13** 6 (1970) 377–387
8. Cooper, R., Qin, Z: A Graphical Modelling Program with Constraint Specification and Management. Proceedings BNCOD10, LNCS 618, Springer-Verlag (1992) 192–208
9. Das, S., K., Williams, M., H: Integrity Checking Methods in deductive Databases: A Comparitive Evaluation. Proceedings BNCOD7, Cambridge University Press (1989) 85–116
10. Dixon, M., Kalmus, J., Jeffery, K., G.: A Five-Layered Information Expressivity Model Applied to Sermantic Heterogeneity in a Decentralisd Organisation. Proceedings ERCIM Database Research Group Workshop 8 Trondheim, Norway, August 1995, ERCIM Office, INRIA, Paris.
11. Fonkham, M., M., Gray, W., A.: Employing Integrity Constraints for Query Modification and Intensional Answer Generation in Multi-Database Systems. Proceedings BNCOD10, Aberdeen. LNCS 618, Springer-Verlag (1992)
12. Goble, C.: Medical Informatics. Proceedings SOFSEM'93 Conference, Ed. M. Bartošek, Masaryk University Brno, Czech Republic
13. Goble, C., A., Glowinski, A., Jeffery, K.,G: Semantic Constraints in a Medical Information System. Proceedings BNCOD11 Keele, LNCS 696, Springer-Verlag (1993)
14. Gradwell, D., J., L: The Arrival of the IRDS Standards. Proceedings BNCOD8, York, Pitman Publishing (1990)
15. Hayne, S., Ram, S.: Multi-User View Integration System (MUVIS): An Expert System for View Integration. Proc 6th International Conference on Data Engineering (1986)
16. Howells, D., I., Fiddian, N., J., Graw, W., A.: A Source-to-Source Meta-Translation System for Relational Query Languages. Proceedings VLDB13, Brighton (1987)
17. Jeffery, K., G.: Database Integration. Proceedings SOFSEM'92 Conference, Ed. M. Bartošek, Masaryk University Brno, Czech Republic
18. Jeffery, K., G., Extended Transition Networks for Systems Development. Proceedings SOFSEM'93 Conference, Ed. M. Bartošek, Masaryk University Brno, Czech Republic
19. Jeffery, K., G., Hutchinson, E., K., Kalmus, J., R., Wilson, M., D., Behrendt W., Macnee, C., A.: A Model for Heterogeneous Distributed Databases. Proceedings BNCOD12, LNCS 826, Springer-Verlag (1994) 221–234
20. Jeffery, K. G., Lay, J. O., Curtis, T.: A Logic-Based System for Data Validation. Proceedings BNCOD7, Cambridge University Press (1989) 71–84
21. Jeffery, K., G., Lay, J., O., Miquel, J., F., Zardan, S., Naldi, F., Vannini Parenti, I.: IDEAS: A System for International Data Exchange and Access for Science. Information Processing and management **25**,6 (1989) 703–711

22. Kim, W., Ballou, N., Garza, J., F., Woelk, D.: A Distributed Object Oriented Database System supporting Shared and Private Databases. ACM Trans on Information Systems **9**,1 (1991)

23. Kohoutková, J., Jeffery, K., G: Intelligent Hypermedia Access: The Universal Information-Space Guide. Proceedings SOFSEM '94, Conference, Milovy, Czech Republic, November 1994, Ed. M. Bartošek, Masaryk University, Brno

24. Litwin, W., Mark, L., Roussopoulos, N.: Interoperability of Multiple Autonomous Databases. ACM Computing Surveys **22**,3 1990

25. Loucopoulos, P., Zicari, R.: Conceptual Modeling, Databases and CASE. Wiley, (1992)

26. Macnee, C., A., Behrendt, W., Wilson, M., D., Jeffery, K., G., Kalmus, J., R., Hutchinson, E., K.: Presenting Dynamically Expandable Hypermedia. Information and Software Technology **37**, 7 (1995) 339–350

27. Manola, F., Heiler, S., Georgakopoulos, D.: Distributed Object Management. International Journal of Intelligent and Cooperative Information Systems **1**, 1 (1992)

28. Naldi, F., Jeffery, K., G., Bordogna, G., Lay, J., O., Vannini Parenti, I.: A Distributed Architecture to Provide Uniform Access to Pre-Existing, Independent, Heterogeneous Information Systems. RAL Report 92–003. (1992)

29. Omololu, A., O., Fiddian, N., J., Gray, W., A.: Confederated Database Management Systems. Proceedings BNCOD7, Heriot-Watt University, Edinburgh, Cambridge University Press (1989)

30. Papazoglou, M., P., Laufmann, S., C., Selis, T., K.: An Organizational Framework for Cooperative Intelligent Information Systems. International Journal of Intelligent and Cooperative Information Systems **1**,1 1992

31. Qutaishat, M., A., Fiddian, M., J., Gray, W., A: Association Merging in a Schema Meta-Integration System for a Heterogeneous Object-Oriented Environment. Proceedings BNCOD10, Aberdeen. LNCS 618, Springer-Verlag (1992)

32. Ramfos, A., Fiddian, N., J., Gray, W., A.: A Meta-translation System for Object-Oriented to relational Schema Translations. Proceedings BNCOD9 Wolverhampton, Butterworth-Heinemann, 1991

33. Saltor, F., Castalanos, M., Garcia-Solaco, M.: Suitability of data models as canonical models for federated databas. SIGMOD Record **20**,4 (1991)

34. Sheth, A., P., Larson, J.: Federated Databae Systems for managing heterogeneous, distributed and autonomous databases. ACM Computing Surveys **22**,3 (1992)

35. Siegel, M., Madnick, S., E.: A Metadata Approach to resolving Semantic Conflicts. Proc 17th VLDB, Barcelona (1991)

36. Spacciapetra, S., Parent, C., Dupont, Y.: Model Independent Assertions or Integration of Heterogeneous Schemes. VLDB Journal **1** (1992)

37. Theodoulidis, C., Wangler, B., Loucopoulos, P.: The Entity-Relationship-Time Model. in [25]

38. Wilson, M., D., Falzon, P.: Multimedia and Multimodal Systems: Architectures for Cooperative Dialogue. Proceedings ERCIM Workshop on Multimedia. Lisbon (1991)

39. Woo, C., Lochovsky, F.: Knowledge Communication in Intelligent Information Systems. International Journal of Intelligent & Cooperative Information Systems **1**,1 (1992)

40. Yu, C., Sun, W., Dao, S.: Determining Relationships among names in heterogneous Databases. SIGMOD Record **20**,4 (1991)

Distributed Information Systems

Jane Grimson *

Department of Computer Science,Trinity College, Dublin, Ireland

Abstract. The Information Systems of the future will be distributed, heterogeneous and open. They will require the integration of five key technologies - databases, multimedia, object orientation, artificial intelligence and telecommunications. This paper explains the contribution of these technologies to the vision of the future and how they can be integrated. Key technical challenges and open research issues will be discussed. A detailed case study from the healthcare domain is presented which demonstrates interoperability of databases, knowledge based techniques and telecommunications in an open, object-based distributed information system.

1 Introduction

The information systems of the future will be distributed, heterogeneous and open. Distributed computing has become the norm in virtually all organisations ranging from small enterprises with a handful of employees in a single location, to multinational conglomerates employing thousands of people across the world. The movement away from centralised computing, which was initially triggered by the technological developments of the PC revolution of the 1980s, coupled with the availability of reliable data communications networks, has been given a significant impetus by the organisational desire to make much more efficient and cost-effective use of computing resources. This movement seeks to address, in a small way, the all too familiar situation in which the typical IT project comes in late, is vastly over budget, and does not meet the expectations of management [17],[19].

Distributed computing offers the possibility of "right-sizing" by allowing organisations to replace large, costly and monolithic central processors with smaller, vastly cheaper and more flexible PCs and workstations. In such a distributed environment, heterogeneity at both the hardware and software levels is inevitable. Heterogeneity at the hardware level, and even at the operating systems level, poses few problems today. The software applications level, on the other hand, is typified by a bewildering array of systems including mission- critical legacy systems left over from the days of centralised computing. Thus, while it is accepted that a user can purchase a PC or a UNIX workstation from whatever vendor they choose and connect it into their network, the same kind of "plug-and-play" interface is not yet available for software systems. It is this problem

---

* email: jane.grimson@tcd.ie

which those involved in the development of open systems are seeking to address. Therefore, openness, distribution and heterogeneity are each a consequence of the other and all form part of the same problem.

The enabling technologies - open distributed processing, distributed/federated databases, object orientation, artificial intelligence, multimedia and telecommunications - required to achieve the distributed, heterogeneous and open information systems of the future are well understood but need to be merged and integrated into an interoperable framework as shown in Figure 1.

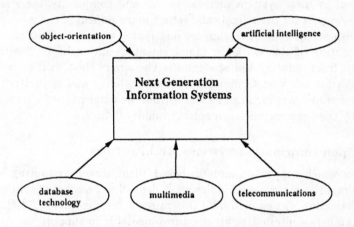

Fig. 1. The enabling technologies for the next generation of information systems

In this paper, the contribution of these technologies to the next generation of information systems will be examined. Key technical challenges and open research issues will be discussed. A case study from the healthcare domain will be presented which demonstrates the interoperability of databases, knowledge based techniques and telecommunications in an open, object-based distributed information system.

2 Open Distributed Processing

2.1 Client/server Computing

The key to achieving open systems is the use of standards to which the interfaces between components must adhere. As indicated above, agreement on standards at the hardware and telecommunications levels tends to be easier to achieve than standards at the software level.

Open Distributed Systems (ODP) are generally based on the client/server paradigm, which allows clients (application programs) to use the services offered by a server without either having to know the details of the inner workings of the other. Communication between client and server is via a standard, published interface, the Application Programming Interface (API). The client/server approach provides a standardised, flexible, modular and evolvable approach to building information systems. It brings computing power to the desktop, which, as the PC revolution has shown, is crucial to the productivity of workers [33]. Like all technological breakthroughs in computing, it was seen as the universal panacea for all information technology problems. However, experience in many organisations has shown that migration from a centralised approach to computing to a client/server approach is painful, costly and time-consuming. There is an urgent need for methodologies and tools to support the migration process. Moreover, as these systems increase in size and complexity, there is a need to provide support for the reliable and secure management of client/server systems often with a requirement to support distributed workflow. This has resulted in the formation of the Workflow Management Coalition in 1993 with over 100 members from industry and academia [2]. The aim of the Coalition is to promote standards for software terminology, interoperability and connectivity between workflow products. Much can be learnt from the extensive work on management issues by the network management community [34].

2.2 Open Information Systems Architectures

Software which supports standards-based client/server computing is generally termed middleware, where middleware is defined as "any set of routines or functions that allow(s) two dissimilar programs to interoperate" [20]. Today, there are a number of alternative architectures available to support one or a number of aspects of distributed processing based on the client/server paradigm. Although, most of them are not as yet fully interoperable, it is only a matter of time before this happens. It would be beyond the scope of this paper to go into these architectures in any detail. Instead a brief overview of three representative approaches is given, all of which are relevant to the need to support interfaces to databases:

- SQL Access Group (SAG)
- CORBA from OMG and OLE from Microsoft
- transaction monitors

2.3 SQL Access Group

The SQL Access Group (SAG) was formed in 1989 and includes most of the major database and tool vendors. One of its main roles was to define a standard client/server interface to relational (SQL) databases. Two competing standards emerged - Open Database Connectivity (ODBC) from Microsoft and the Integrated Database Application Programming Interface (IDAPI) from a consortium including Borland, IBM, Novell and Wordperfect. ODBC specifies a standard interface through which Windows applications can access SQL databases and drivers have been developed for most of the major database engines. The aims of IDAPI are similar but are not confined to Windows platforms.

---

[2] Further information about the Coalition can be found on http://www.aiai.ed.ac.uk/WfMC/

2.4 CORBA and OLE

The Common Object Request Broker Architecture, CORBA, [26] specification was developed by the Object Management Group (OMG), an international trade association consisting of approximately 250 information system corporations. The goal of the group is to maximise reusability, portability and interoperability of software. The first OMG specification describes an Object Request Broker (ORB) which specifies the interfaces to object services and an API for common services. There are now several commercial ORBs available from a number of different vendors on a wide range of computing platforms. CORBA is being developed to provide general-purpose distributed computing and it is planned to support distributed data via a distributed data management (attached) service which is not part of the core architecture.

OLE (Object Linking and Embedding) is Microsoft's approach to providing support for distributed computing in a Windows environment. Already several strategic alliances are being formed with a view to achieving interoperability between the two approaches.

2.5 Transaction monitors

Transaction monitors, such as CICS (Customer Information and Control System from IBM) were originally designed to provide support for distributed applications rather than distributed data. However, the arrival of client/server computing has meant that modern transaction monitors, such as Tuxedo from AT&T [38] and Encina from IBM [39], can be used to access a variety of remote databases and services. The case study presented below in Section 8 shows how Tuxedo was successfully used in this way. Support for distributed transactions in the CORBA world will be provided through an attached service. Such a service is already offered by at least one of the ORB vendors, namely Iona Technologies, whose ORB implementation, Orbix, interoperates with Tuxedo.

3 Distributed/federated Database Systems

3.1 Homogeneous Distributed Database Systems

The history behind the development of distributed database technology is interesting in that the early distributed database management systems (DDBMS) developed at the beginning of the 1980's were described by some as "solutions in search of problems" [4]. In other words, they offered an interesting technical solution to a problem which did not actually exist in the real world. These early DDBMSs were homogeneous; it was assumed that every site in the system ran the same database software as shown in Figure 2.

Distributed databases (DDBs) were designed top-down in that a global conceptual schema was defined and then mapped onto the local conceptual schema at each of the sites. Global relations (these systems were almost all relational) were thus partitioned into fragments which were then allocated to the various

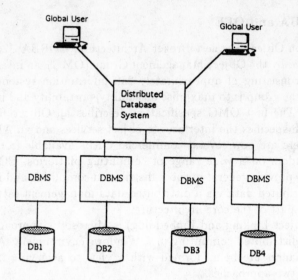

Fig. 2. Homogeneous DDBMS

sites (with or without replication) in order to optimise performance. These systems triggered much research into topics such as data distribution, concurrency control and query optimisation. However, the systems made very little impact on the market and indeed many of the prototypes never made the transition into full commercial products.

The reason for the lack of acceptance of this "pure" DDBMS technology are complex but undoubtedly one of the main problems was that they did not address the issue of allowing legacy systems to avail of the latest database technology. The development of DDBMS technology coincided with the widespread the emergence onto the market of several major relational database management systems (RDBMS), which subsequently became the *de facto* standard for databases. Thus many organisations were much more interested in finding ways to migrate their legacy, non-relational systems towards relational, or at the very least, to support an SQL interface to them. They therefore had enough problems moving to centralised relational technology without the added complication of distributed relational technology. Indeed it is really only in the past few years that distributed RDBMS technology has taken off and this had been largely spurred on by the development of client/server database environments and gateway technology (see Section 3.3).

3.2 Heterogeneous Distributed Database Systems

What organisations were seeking in the early 1980's was a means of integrating the data in their legacy systems with the newer relational technology. This need is still acutely felt today, where businesses themselves have become increasingly decentralised leading to a corresponding need for decentralised information systems to support business operations. Moreover there is still a huge investment tied up in business-critical legacy systems [6], [8]. These systems are massive (10^7 lines of code) and are practically impossible to rewrite [?]. Thus there is a fundamental need for a cooperative solution based on distribution and interoperability. In other words, the requirement is for heterogeneous DDBMS technology or multidatabase (MDB) technology. In an MDB, the individual local DBMSs operate as autonomous units with their own set of users. They function totally independently of the global users as shown in Figure 3.

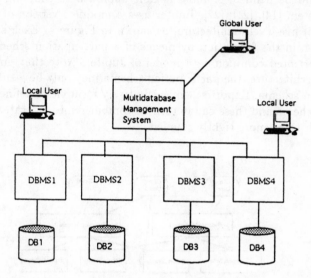

Fig. 3. Multidatabase system

An MDB is thus "designed" from the bottom-up. The pre-existing local conceptual schemas (or portions of them) are integrated into a single global conceptual schema. This integration process is very complex since it involves not only mapping the local data model into a common conceptual model, i.e. syntactic integration, but also semantic integration. Since the local DBs are pre-existing and autonomous, there may well be inconsistent duplication of data. There will also be problems of homonyms and synonyms, as well as different coding schemes, units (miles and kilometres) and so on. Detecting this type of heterogeneity is very difficult. The problem is that DB schemas generally do not provide enough semantics to interpret data consistently. Data model (hierarchical, network, relational, object-oriented) differences exacerbate the difficulty of locating and resolving semantic heterogeneity as there is a strong coupling of heterogeneities due to differences in DBMSs and those relating to semantics.

There are many different ways of classifying distributed information systems, although consensus is emerging in which the taxonomy is based initially on the degree of coupling between the individual sites/components of the overall distributed system e.g. [4],[35]. Thus for example, the early homogeneous DDBMS described above would be classified as examples of tightly coupled systems, whereas a multidatabase federation of autonomous DBMSs with no centralised control would be representative of the class of loosely coupled systems. Obviously, there are many systems which lie between these two extremes. However, one issue in this classification which is of particular significance is whether or not a single global conceptual schema (representing the union of all the data from the individual sites) is developed. Early MDBMSs, such as SDD-1 [30] and R* [41] relied on a single integrated conceptual schema against which global user views could be defined. A more flexible approach to coupling is used in the Jupiter system [14], [21], [22]. Jupiter uses a modified version of the Sheth and Larson [35] five-level architecture, as shown in Figure 4. Each site defines its participation in the federation by means of a participation schema defined in the object-oriented common data model of Jupiter. Note that unlike Sheth and Larson's architecture, the participation schema may only be a subset of the local conceptual schema. Export schemas effectively form views defined over the participation schema and these can in turn be combined into federated schemas, when sites wish to be more tightly coupled.

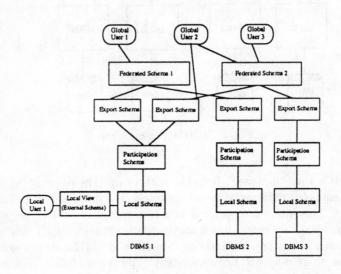

Fig. 4. Schema architecture of Jupiter

Each local site therefore has two DBs - the first the local DB under the control of the local DBMS and the second, the Jupiter/MDD (Multidatabase Data Dictionary) under the control of Jupiter. The kernel of Jupiter is a dictionary system and multidatabase language, JIL, to provide end-users with what is effectively a single consistent view of the enterprise data resource as a uniform, distributed object-oriented database system. Syntactic and semantic conflicts are resolved so that users can access the underlying data resources using a single uniform database language.

Using the Jupiter Interoperator Language, JIL, individual sites will specify which data they will share with other users via export schemas. Global users can browse the export schemas and construct a number of federation schemas from them. Users can request direct access to a data resource or opt to use a quasi-copy i.e. a nearly up-to-date copy. Quasi-copies provide a means of increasing availability of data across the network while at the same time ensuring that the replica does not drift too far from the original. An important advantage of this protocol is that it allows the information provider, i.e. the publisher of an export schema, to automatically decide whether or not to share information with an information requester.

3.3 Gateways

While significant progress has been made in the development of heterogeneous DDB technology, many problems remain. Hence a number of organisations are adopting *ad hoc* solutions which allow their systems to interoperate, albeit often only in a limited way. This has been greatly assisted by the commercial development of gateways by a number of major DBMS vendors, as illustrated in Figure 5.

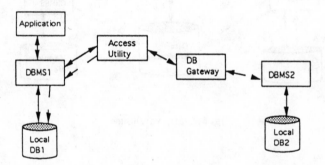

Fig. 5. Gateway

These gateways range from those which simply support the extraction of data from the legacy system to those which support distribution transactions across the gateway [33]. Gateways are a useful tool in allowing organisations to move towards client/server systems. They are an absolutely essential part of the migration strategy for legacy systems [8]. However, they are difficult to build and operate. They require highly skilled designers and implementors and can place virtually all the burden of resolving semantic conflicts on the application programmers. It is difficult to envisage the development of generic gateway technology which encapsulates databases, interfaces, communications, etc. Examples of the more powerful gateway products include Ingres/Star and Sybase [37]. They provide access to several standard relational DB engines as well as more widely used file systems such as RMS and VSAM.

3.4 Data Warehouses

Loosely coupled federated DBMS undoubtedly offer the most powerful and flexible tool for the development of distributed information systems. Gateways provide an interim solution and, as they become more powerful and offer increased functionality and in particular allow the incorporation of business rules, the distinction between the two - in terms of functionality - may become less clear. A third approach which has generated considerable interest in the business world is the data warehouse [18]. Typically, data in legacy systems is extracted and uploaded on a periodic basis to a centralised (relational) database, the data warehouse, where it is stored in summary form as shown in Figure 6. The warehouse then supports high level strategic planning in Executive Information Systems (EIS).

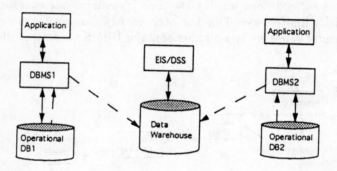

Fig. 6. Data warehouse

Warehouses provide EIS with integrated uniform access to most of the corporate data and there are a number of success stories. The major drawback of the data warehouse is to do with data integrity since data, albeit in summarised form, is replicated in the warehouse and hence can get out of step with the primary source. Moreover, in large organisations these warehouses can become very large indeed and therefore difficult and costly to manage.

However, data warehouses are not databases. They are designed to support high-level decision-making within an organisation not routine business processes and transactions. The main characteristics of warehouses are that they are subject-oriented, integrating subject-related data from one or more operational databases, and are non-volatile i.e. they do not support updates. This means that there is an important time dimension to data in a warehouse.

4 Object Orientation

Just as databases were seen in the 1970's as the universal panacea for all information processing problems, so object orientation (OO) is seen by some as the golden bullet which will wipe out all other methods of programming and information modelling. On the programming side, OO offers the potential of code re-use through extensive class libraries, while on the modelling side, OO is said to provide a more faithful representation of real world objects. Certainly, the fact that the relations in a relational database must be normalised leads to unnecessary fragmentation of data across several relations, which may then need to be de-normalised at the physical level in order to ensure adequate performance. Moreover, the inability of the current generation of relational systems to support multimedia data items - images, unstructured text, video clips, etc. - is potentially very restrictive. Object oriented DBMS (OODBMS) do indeed offer a solution to these problems but as yet the technology has not received widespread acceptance in the world of business data processing.

It seems very unlikely that OODBMSs will replace RDBMSs in all application areas [4]. RDBMS and SQL are now an accepted industry DB standard and many organisations have invested vast resources in this technology to support complex applications, the legacy systems of the future. Moreover, for many organisations, the relational approach meets all their needs. They do not need complex objects, long lived transactions or abstract data types, so there is no incentive whatever for them to change. It is probable therefore that OODBMS will co-exist with extended or next generation relations systems as industry moves towards the SQL-3 standard, where support for abstract data types etc. are provided [3]. The big advantage of this approach is that each new version of SQL represents an evolution from the previous version and is backwards compatible. Hence, applications built using ANSI-SQL will continue to run under SQL-3.

Thus, while OODBMS are unlikely to capture the whole information systems market, object-oriented technology is becoming increasingly widely used at the programming and lower levels of distributed processing. Thus C++ is gradually replacing C as the preferred application programming language in many organisations and object-based middleware, such as CORBA and OLE are increasingly seen as a means of supporting distributed application programming.

From the point of view of the information systems of the future, there is no doubt that object orientation will play an important role at the application programming level and as middleware, but will only gradually be introduced at the persistent data storage level as the relational systems are extended further such that the distinction, for all practical purposes, between OODBMSs and extended relational systems disappears.

An example of how OO middleware, specifically the CORBA ORB, can help to support distribution transparency in distributed information systems can be found in Jupiter system [21], [22], [23]. As was indicated above in Section 3.2, central to Jupiter is the distributed data dictionary, which describes all the data in the federation. This data dictionary actually consists of a set of dictionaries, Jupiter/MDDs, distributed across the sites in the multidatabase. Together they can be represented naturally as a set of distributed, possibly replicated, objects managed by an implementation of CORBA, Orbix [28]. Orbix provides platform-independent transparent access to the distributed dictionary objects. This Jupiter provides a layer of services to support interoperability between heterogeneous database systems on top of CORBA, as shown in Figure 7.

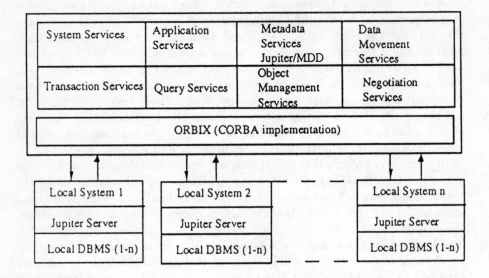

Fig. 7. The architecture of Jupiter

5 Artificial Intelligence

The field of artificial intelligence (AI) is very broad and covers a wide range of disciplines including psychology, philosophy, linguistics and sociology, as well as computer science itself. There are probably many different ways in which AI techniques will be incorporated into the distributed information systems of the future. However, it is possible to identify two major contributions which AI is already making and which will certainly grow further:

(a) intelligent filtering of data to avoid information overload
(b) natural language interfaces

5.1 Intelligent filtering

The volume of information in the world is growing at an ever-increasing rate. It is becoming increasingly difficult for a user to locate the information of interest. This is nowhere more apparent than on the world wide web (WWW) where ever more sophisticated search engines are being developed to help surfers. While information overload may be a time-consuming irritant to users of WWW, for users in mission critical applications such as healthcare, for example, it can become life threatening. The case study presented in Section 8 of this paper shows how supporting interoperability between knowledge-based systems and databases can tackle the problem.

5.2 Natural language interfaces

It is now taken for granted that a database system will, among other interfaces, offer an icon-based Graphical User Interface (GUI) to users. GUIs allow the development of forms-based interfaces so that entering data into the database is almost as simple as filling out a form by hand. However, while forms-based query languages are very user-friendly, they are designed to support a particular task, registering a student, discharging a patient, placing an order, etc. If a user wishes to pose an un-anticipated *ad hoc* query for which no form has been designed, they must resort to a language based interface such as SQL. Such interfaces are too complex for end-users. The DB community therefore has long expressed an interest in the development of query interfaces based on natural language (NL). Indeed, such interfaces were one of the first applications of NL processing. It soon became apparent that a general purpose NL interface, which could cope with all the semantic richness and ambiguity of NL, was not feasible in the short term. However, NL interfaces can work fairly well in restricted domains. For example, in the MIPS project [7], [2], NL has been used to assist the user in refining his/her query. The MIPS, Multimedia Information Presentation System, Project is a 3-year Esprit project which is nearing completion. Its aim is to develop platform-independent tools to retrieve and display multimedia data from heterogeneous sources in a consistent and integrated manner. MIPS uses a template-based approach for retrieving data. A template is similar in some respects to the form-based interfaces described above, although by allowing the user to enter NL phrases, it is more flexible. The choice of templates in MIPS is motivated by the fact that users who are searching for information have a particular task in mind e.g. to arrange transport to Dublin, to book a two-week holiday in the sun. Thus once the desired task has been identified it is possible for the system to focus in on a narrow domain of discourse. This makes it realistic to engage in a heavily-constrained, but very user-friendly NL-based dialogue with the user to further refine his/her query [12].

6 Multimedia

Relational databases are very good at handling conventional numeric and character based data. Many now provide support for bit-mapped images and large sections of unstructured text, although both are generally treated as single un-differentiated objects. There is, however, a growing demand to be able to access and zoom in on small sections of an individual image or to be able to search text for given keywords, for example. In addition, there is an increasing need to be able to store video and audio clips in databases.

The only technology available today which goes partially towards the goal of integrated management of multimedia data is the OODBMS. However, it seems likely that MDB technology could also have an important role to play, whereby the participant DBs in the MDB could be specialised systems for storing and managing the different media types. Other open research issues relate to the vast increase in data volume involved and the consequent pressures on secondary storage devices. For example, 1 second of full screen 24-bit colour video can require up to 1 Mbyte of storage. Optical discs are increasingly being used to store multimedia data; their mode of operation is different from the conventional magnetic disc and will require new indexing techniques and data placement strategies. The design of multimedia databases, both physical and logical, will be fundamentally different from conventional databases. User interfaces will also change to meet a much wider variety of access mechanisms including voice and touch.

7   Telecommunications

The availability of reliable telecommunication facilities at ever-increasing speeds and wider bandwidths is taken for granted today. Virtually all computers in the workplace today, from the basic PC up to the largest mainframe, are connected to a network. These networks range from Novel networks, connecting together a few PCs to the Internet which it is estimated today links well over a 2 million computers and has over 20 million users. The monthly traffic on the NSF Internet backbone alone was 10 terabytes in 1994 [15].

Distributed information systems are built on top of these networks and while issues such as the reliability and security of the network are important, the actual details of the communication protocols themselves are not normally of great concern. Indeed it is a sign that networks are now so generally reliable that they can be taken for granted.

Of course, the speed and bandwidth of a network is an important issue for the transmission of multimedia data. Thus, for example, Integrated Services Digital Network, ISDN, typically offers 64 - 128 kbits/s today which is sufficient for many applications. However, the transmission of real-time TV-quality video across digital transmission lines requires the sort of capability offered by the emerging Asynchronous Transfer Mode, ATM, networks which support speeds of 2 Gbits/s.

8   A Distributed Information System Case Study

8.1   Introduction

In this section, a case study of a distributed information system which brings together some of the technologies discussed here in a practical and successful way. A full specification according to the 5 Open Distributed Processing (ODP) Viewpoints - enterprise, information, computational, engineering and technology - has been developed [25].

This case study describes a generic user-driven solution to interoperability of both databases, knowledge bases and legacy systems in a limited domain, namely hospital computing and, more specifically, clinical laboratory information systems. The approach has been applied to the development of an Advanced Laboratory Information System, OpenLIS, for use in clinical laboratories in hospitals. A prototype, in limited form, is currently in operation in a large general hospital.

The OpenLabs Project was a three-year project which began in 1992 and was funded under the Advanced Informatics in Medicine Programme (AIM) of the European Commission [13]. OpenLabs involves pre-competitive research between 28 different organisations representing 4 major sectors: commercial developers of medical software, leading hospital laboratory instrument manufactures, research institutes and a number of hospital laboratories representing end-users of the technology being developed in OpenLabs.

The modern clinical laboratory is a complex, heterogeneous environment, typically with a mix of autonomous and partially interworking applications running on a range of hardware (PCs, micros, minis). It is generally one of the first areas in a hospital to become computerised mainly because of the large volume of data involved. OpenLabs therefore has to interwork with a variety of existing legacy systems, extending these to support advanced functionalities based on the application of knowledge bases (KBs), databases and telecommunications. Typically, the existing systems have been developed in a very piecemeal fashion. One of the most important and novel features of OpenLabs has been the development and implementation of an open architecture for the hospital laboratory which enables a variety of new and existing sub-systems to co-operate together in an efficient and flexible manner. The ultimate aim of OpenLabs is to improve the quality of patient care by ensuring that the results of laboratory tests ordered for patients are supplied to the medical staff quickly, accurately and clearly.

To meet this objective, OpenLabs has developed advanced application modules using innovative techniques from DB and KB technologies, including, for example, temporal DBs and reasoning strategies, neural networks, case-based reasoning and co-operative Knowledge-based systems (KBSs). The novelty of the work undertaken in OpenLabs arises not only from these innovative applications which provide the advanced functionalities, but also, and more importantly in the context of this paper, from the fact that it has provided an infrastructure whereby all the disparate systems can interopérate.

8.2 Laboratory medicine

Laboratory medicine is concerned with the analysis of blood, tissue etc. As will be explained, the domain is complex and in order to appreciate the issues involved in supporting interoperability in such an environment, it is necessary to give a reasonably comprehensive account of the clinical laboratory and the way it functions. The modern hospital laboratory today is a complex and highly auto-mated environment with dozens of different instruments. Modern multi-channel analysers are capable of processing up to 1000 samples per hour, performing up to 30 measurements of different analytes for each sample. A medium to large laboratory will generate approximately 5-10 MBytes of new data per day, all of which must be kept on-line for several months or even years, depending on the discipline. This data consists of test requests, test results, quality control information and so on. Hence it is now almost a necessity for laboratories to be computerised even if only to implement quality assurance/control on this ever-increasing volume of data. This has led to the development of specialised database systems, known as Laboratory Information Systems (LIS). These range in complexity from simple systems which support test reporting, to increasingly sophisticated software which supports a very diverse range of applications, ef-fectively controlling virtually all aspects of the clinical laboratory.

This rapid technological progress in the Clinical Laboratory has been accom-panied by an increasing dependence by doctors on a whole range of diagnostic services for patient management. Workloads are increasing by 5-10% annually, but the expertise required to interpret these highly specialised tests is often not available. This is particularly true of the growing number of "less expert" users such as General Practitioners (primary care physicians), who are often required to use laboratories, as delivery of health services moves increasingly away from the hospital towards ambulatory or primary care.

At the same time, there has been increased refinement in the interpretation of test results. The normal or "reference" range for each variable (numbering over 1000 today) includes factors such as age, gender, ethnic origin, method of analysis, accuracy and precision of analysis, specimen timing, collection and handling techniques, and drugs which the patient may be taking which may interfere with the analysis. Thus the interpretation of even a single data item may be quite complex.

One of the detrimental results of this expanding complexity has been mount-ing evidence of information overload or data intoxication amongst clinicians who are faced with masses of data, which can lead to abnormal results being overlooked or normal results being misinterpreted [9]. Furthermore, it has been estimated that 20-60% of tests performed are actually unnecessary and several studies have shown that less than 10% of the laboratory data produced actually influence the medical decision [27]. Many techniques have been tried to help overcome these problems and the most promising to date has been the use of knowledge based systems (KBS) [16].

On the hospital management side, the need for increased effectiveness and efficiency is gradually leading to the provision of departmental computer sys-tems for the collection of relevant clinical information which will be available as part of hospital wide integrated information systems (HIS). This combination of relevant clinical information with laboratory data has already proved to be one of the most useful and effective KBS applications in existence [5]. Medicine represents an ideal domain for the development of knowledge-based Decision

Support Systems (DSS) and it is no coincidence that early expert systems such as MYCIN [32] tackled problems in the medical domain. Medicine comes neatly packaged into pre-defined, highly compartmentalised specialities which appear to be perfectly suited to expert system techniques. However, although it is true that medicine provided early researchers in Artificial Intelligence with a good application domain in which to develop prototypes to test their ideas, there really is genuine need in medicine for the technology and this is nowhere more apparent than in the field of laboratory medicine. With increased automation of the laboratory, the conditions now appear to be opportune for the development and integration of laboratory KBS with clinical information systems.

8.3   Application of information technology in the laboratory

Figure 8 shows the structure of and workflows in a typical clinical laboratory.

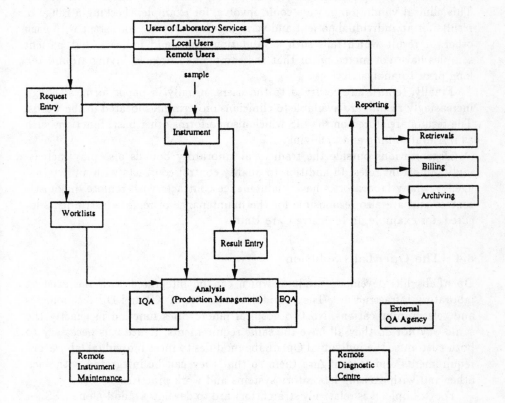

Fig. 8. Laboratory Structure

The users of laboratory services (e.g. local users in the hospital or remote users locate in GP surgeries etc.) initiate a request for laboratory services. The request and sample arrive in the Laboratory, are entered on a worklist and then sent to an instrument. The instrument performs analyses under the overall control of the production management modules of the LIS. Quality control samples are analysed in addition to patient samples. Typically this would involve inserting a control specimen, for which the result is known, every tenth sample, checking the result obtained against pre-set reference ranges and adjusting the results where necessary. If, for example, the result for the control for a particular analyte, is high, but still within acceptable limits, the results for patients samples for that analyte will be adjusted to produce a corrected result. Where the result for the control sample is outside the acceptable range, corrective maintenance will be carried out. In addition, provision is made for both Internal Quality Assurance (IQA) and External Quality Assurance (EQA) for monitoring the performance of the laboratory.

After analysis, results are reported back after a manual validation procedure. Quality control as outlined above, is concerned with verifying that the instrument is performing correctly, but results must also be checked for clinical believability. This clinical validation process could involve, for example, checking a range of results for an individual patient and verifying that they are consistent with each other. A result which fails such a validation test could indicate that patient samples have got mixed up or that the sample has been left lying around too long prior to analysis.

Finally, reports are returned to the users, usually in paper form, although increasingly results are available to clinicians on terminals located in the wards. The results are stored on the LIS which also performs other basic functions such as retrieval, billing and archiving.

Organisations outside the traditional laboratory bounds also play increasingly important roles. In addition to quality control contracts with an external agency, many laboratories have maintenance contracts with remote diagnostic centres and are also responsible for the maintenance of remote instruments located, for example, in Intensive Care Units.

8.4   The OpenLabs Solution

OpenLabs has developed modules which can be integrated with the existing laboratory infrastructure. These modules make use of KB and DB technologies and telecommunications. No two hospital laboratories function in exactly the same way nor do they all have the same requirements. Hence it is necessary to both customise the individual OpenLabs modules to meet individual laboratory requirements and to configure them so that they can be integrated with each other and with existing laboratory systems and work practices.

For example, it is relatively straightforward to develop a stand-alone DSS for a particular domain, but it is much more complex to integrate it with an existing information system. This lack of integration is one of the main reasons why, of the hundreds of medical ESs/DSSs developed over the years, so few are actually routinely used. They remain confined to the research laboratory as interesting experiments providing source material for lots of research papers! Central to OpenLabs is the specification and prototype implementation and evaluation of an open architecture which will specify an environment for intelligent interoperability in the Clinical Laboratory based on existing and emerging standards. The idea is to be able to integrate new and existing modules on a mix-and-match basis into any laboratory with a variety of existing legacy LISs.

Not only must tools be provided to facilitate integration of OpenLabs modules into a laboratory, but also to customise those modules to meet the clinical needs and work methods. It is well known, for example, that a diagnostic DSS/ES developed for a patient population spanning all ages from 0 to 100, will not necessary be equally applicable if the patient population consists exclusively of children or elderly people. Many diseases, for example, are very rare or even unknown in children and the inferencing strategy of the KBS needs to take such considerations into account. Furthermore, most DSSs/ESs in the clinical laboratory are centered around certain tests, but not all laboratories perform all tests. At the very least, it must therefore be possible to allow for customisation of individual KBs, to alter probability thresholds where appropriate, to change standard reference ranges for test results, to include/exclude certain tests and so on.

8.5 OpenLabs Architecture

The OpenLabs platform architecture [40] had to achieve two important goals, namely

(i) the provision of an environment for facilitating the integration of modules implementing the advanced OpenLabs functionalities and

(ii) the provision of an open solution by which these modules could be developed in a vendor-independent way (i.e. provide portability and interoperability) in a distributed computing environment.

The architecture had to be capable of supporting a mix of hardware (e.g. workstations, minicomputers, PCs) and software (e.g. MS-DOS, UNIX) in an open distributed environment. A standard client/server approach with an OpenLabs Application Programming Interface (API) was adopted, which is illustrated in Figure 9[10]. Both clients and servers can have local data- and knowledge bases as well as access to databases on the servers.

The architecture supports transparent access to local and remote clients and servers via a product-independent communications handler. Standard communication protocols were used across the networks. For the Local Area Networks (LANs), TCP/IP was chosen as the protocol for network access with X400 across Wide Area Networks (WAN). NFS was used to provide the sharing of file systems across the LAN with FTP to transmit files across the network. Host operating systems on which OpenLabs servers and clients were developed included UNIX and PC/DOS based systems.

Rather than develop a private OpenLabs Communication handler, several appropriate products were considered for the prototype and TUXEDO [38] was chosen. However, to ensure portability, a Generic Communication Interface (GCI)

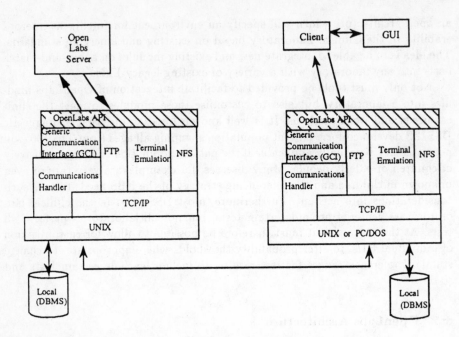

Fig. 9. The OpenLabs Architecture

was developed to insulate OpenLabs servers and clients and, above all, the APIs, from the actual TUXEDO software running below it. The GCI is a layer of software, developed in the 'C' programming language, for the Demonstrator which hides the low-level details of the TUXEDO product. This was considered very important as it was a strong requirement that the architecture could be implemented using other communication handlers as they become available on the market. Tuxedo has been successfully replaced by both CORBA and RPC.

8.6 System Design

The design of a distributed information system is a difficult task even when the design process itself is centralised. OpenLabs was a pan-European project with 28 geographically dispersed partners working independently. It was therefore necessary to develop a methodology which would be appropriate to such a working environment, and which would ultimately arrive at a coherent and unified view of OpenLabs. Since OpenLabs is all about the provision of advanced laboratory functionalities, the obvious starting point was to agree a common set of OpenLabs services which would implement these functionalities. The services themselves could then be implemented independently and clients would be free to use those services in any way they wish.

OpenLabs API Given that it had been decided to use a client/server approach, it was necessary to define a standard OpenLabs API, or, more correctly, a set of APIs, which specify the functions offered by all of the OpenLabs servers. The progress from the Information viewpoint to the Computational viewpoint, in Ansaware terms [1], involved a detailed examination of interprocess transactions and a choice of processes as either client or server processes. The service API's were thus identified and defined. Guidelines were developed to ensure consistent API specification throughout the OpenLabs environment [24].

To facilitate this design process, it was decided that all application developers would use a PC-based CASE Tool, System Architect [31], to define their process and data models. In addition, tables defining the characteristics of the data involved in the data flows were devised. At first these tables were kept separate from the data and process models, but they were subsequently integrated into the process models by means of data flow descriptions. A number of meetings were held at which the process and data models were integrated to yield a unified and harmonised OpenLabs model. Services were then identified and grouped to form Servers, with API's specified in accordance with the OpenLabs API Guidelines.

Regarding the data model the OpenLabs modules have a particular view of the service which it expects to be provided by an existing Laboratory Information System. This "OpenLabs" LIS is referred to as the OpenLIS. This integration work resulted in the identification of all the entities and attributes which comprise the OpenLIS and the CASE tool was used to store these in a data dictionary, the OpenLabs Data Dictionary (ODD).

Interfacing to legacy systems There is a wide range of LISs available today, ranging from those implemented on networked PCs catering for laboratories which process up to a few hundred patient samples per day, to those which require the processing power of a mini- or mainframe computer with a throughput of thousands of samples per day. Traditionally, LISs operate in a closed environment with the only external link being provided by an ASCII download of data to external applications. Not only do the implementations of LISs vary, but so also do the data models on which they are built. Indeed many, except for the most recent, which tend to be relational, use highly non-standard data models. Even in the case of the relational LIS, there is no common conceptual model and hence there will be a mismatch between the OpenLIS and the existing LIS. In addition, information content varies considerably from LIS to LIS and from laboratory to laboratory. Finally, many LISs already operate at full capacity and performance limitations would require that no further load be placed on them by the additional functionality provided through the OpenLabs modules. Indeed there may well be a strong argument in favour of off-loading some of the processing elsewhere. For example, it is well known that even simple DSS technology in the laboratory can be beneficial in reducing information overload and many existing LISs provide facilities for incorporating simple rules to monitor results [29]. However, if every result has to be examined in this way, response time will inevitably deteriorate and hence these facilities may not in fact be used in the LIS itself. The OpenLabs approach to interoperability with the existing LIS allows for such functions to be off-loaded onto a supplementary LIS, in addition to providing support for OpenLabs modules themselves, as explained below.

The process of designing the OpenLIS, i.e. the OpenLabs view of a Laboratory Information System, began with the ODD described above. Using the information contained in the ODD, the global conceptual schema for the Open-LIS was produced and defined in the relational model. An individual laboratory will probably only require a subset of this global schema since it will only install a subset of all the OpenLabs modules. Moreover, of the subset it requires, some of those entities and attributes will already be stored in its existing LIS. Hence what is required is a mechanism which will allow the construction of an auxiliary LIS for the entities and attributes required which are not in the current LIS. The OpenLabs subset of the existing LIS and the auxiliary LIS together comprise the OpenLIS.

This work involved the construction of a limited form of multidatabase system [36]. The design of an MDB (see Section 3.2) normally proceeds in a bottom-up fashion by integrating the local schemas to form a global schema. In the case of OpenLabs, this would mean integrating the conceptual schema of the auxiliary LIS, S_{AUX}, with the subset of the existing LIS, S_{LIS} to produce the global OpenLabs schema, GS_{OL} i.e.

$$GS_{OL} = S_{AUX} \cup S_{LIS}$$

However, in the case of OpenLabs, the global schema, GS_{OL} and the LIS schema, S_{LIS}, are known, hence the schema integration process in OpenLabs meant solving the above "equation" for S_{AUX}; in other words the aim was to identify the data which must be stored in the auxiliary LIS to make up the deficiencies in the legacy LIS.

While it is true that early MDBMSs had only limited success using the relational model as the canonical model and subsequent efforts have focused on object-oriented models, it was felt that the relational model would be adequate to meet the needs of OpenLabs. Semantically richer models are required in conventional MDBMSs to support generic schema integration, whereas in OpenLabs the global schema is fixed and known. Furthermore, the semantics are well understood in such a highly specialised and limited domain. Also, even though many of the existing LISs in use today are based on non-standard, highly proprietary data models, vendors are increasingly offering read-only SQL interfaces (gateways) which are particularly advantageous for OpenLabs and open systems in general.

Just as it is not possible to produce a global conceptual schema for a conventional MDB automatically without any human intervention, so it will not be possible to automate the process of interfacing to the legacy LIS in OpenLabs.

For example, the relational schema for the OpenLabs subset of the LIS will have to be manually produced and a method of resolving any coding anomalies dealt with. All OpenLabs modules use a standard coding scheme, Euclides [11][3] throughout, whereas individual laboratories may use their own private coding schemes. A Euclides bridge has been developed in OpenLabs which allows individual laboratories to map their coding scheme in an unambiguous way to the OpenLabs codes. This bridge was then integrated with the gateway software to the existing LIS.

Requests for data from OpenLabs clients to the OpenLIS server via the standard API, are in the form of SQL queries, which are decomposed, by the Query Processor, into individual queries against the existing LIS via a gateway and the auxiliary LIS, as appropriate, as shown in Figure 10. The query processor is driven by the OpenLabs Catalogue, which effectively functions as an active Data Dictionary/Directory System.

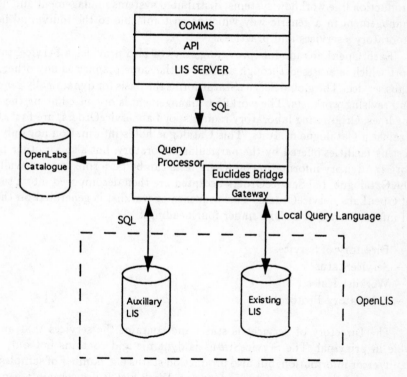

Fig. 10. The OpenLabs Laboratory Information System (OpenLIS)

This approach can be extended to encompass other clinical information systems within the hospital such as a department-based Intensive Care System or

---

[3] The Euclides coding scheme has been proposed to the Comitié Européen de Normalization (CEN) as the European standard for hospital laboratories

a Hospital Information System. In this way the OpenLabs federation can be extended to include additional systems.

Workflow in the laboratory The management of the hospital laboratory today is either done manually or is supported by production management software within the LIS. As samples arrive in the laboratory, they are entered onto work sheets and routed to the appropriate instruments, results are then authorised following appropriate quality control and sent to the requesting physician. In the centralised LIS of today, such an approach to workflow management is perfectly possible. However, the distributed environment envisaged by OpenLabs requires a more complex approach. A mechanism is required for recording the status of all the various services in the laboratory i.e. whether or not they are available, and of monitoring the flow of samples through the laboratory automatically. This involves the application of a blend of various technologies including conventional production line workflow systems, distributed systems management and network management in a generic way which is customisable to the individual hospital laboratory's services and practices.

Each OpenLabs module providing services also provides a ServiceStatusReport which is accessed through an API in the same manner as any other OpenLabs service. The global ServiceStatus forms the basis for dynamically generating and revising worklists. The workflow management is organised along the following lines. Originating laboratory requests, or LabServiceOrders, are first checked against a Catalogue of Tests. This Catalogue holds information not only about testing facilities offered by the particular Laboratory, but also for other Laboratories. Advisory information on where tests can be performed is also available in the Catalogue. LabServiceOrders accepted are then decomposed into a sequence of OpenLabs ServiceOrders. This sequence or worklist is generated on the basis of information held in DBs under four headings:

- Directory of Services
- ServiceStatus
- Worklist Rules
- Laboratory Protocols

The Directory of Services is static and contains the services that are available in principal. The ServiceStatus is dynamic and contains not only service fault/error information, but also production status e.g. number of samples awaiting processing on a particular instrument. Work List Rules contain a generic set of worklist rules conforming to the OpenLabs environment and general laboratory practice. Specific Laboratory Protocols are also used to meet the requirements of a particular laboratory. The worklist thus generated is worked through using a ServiceOrder Dispatcher and returning ServiceReports are logged. Data in these ServiceReports is used to form part of the information necessary to dispatch subsequent ServiceOrders. The execution of the last item on the worklist terminates the process. The worklist once generated is not necessarily static; to accommodate a changing ServiceStatus, a mechanism is provided by which the Dispatcher can request a revised worklist.

9 Conclusions

OpenLabs demonstrates the integration of open systems, distributed database technology (including legacy systems), artificial intelligence through the knowledge-based components, object-based technology and telecommunications. Full integration of objected-orientation will come with the use of CORBA instead of TUXEDO. Thus all the technologies, with the exception of multimedia, which will form the basis for the next generation of Distributed Information Systems have been included. The present OpenLabs demonstrator does not need to support multimedia data since it has focused largely on the domain of clinical biochemistry where data is generally numeric or character-based. Such data can be easily and efficiently handled by RDBMSs. However, work is underway to incorporate other laboratory specialities, in particular histopathology and haematology where there is a need to support images. This will undoubtedly have implications for the communications architecture. At the applications' level, there is is also a need for multimedia data entry via touchscreen and voice.

The OpenLabs case study has deliberately been presented in considerable detail in order to illustrate clearly the requirements of the environment in which the Distributed Information System is being built. Such systems are not going into "green fields" sites, but rather often have to integrate a complex mix of existing applications and systems. This implies the need for a thorough understanding and comprehensive modelling of the existing system and the target integrated Distributed Information Systems. The biggest obstacle to achieving this goal is undoubtedly the almost total absence of methodologies and tools to assist in this migration strategy. Brodie and Stonebraker [8] have put forward an incremental strategy which goes some way towards assisting in the process. Above all, it covers all the main issues which must be addressed and emphasises the need to proceed in a logical step-wise fashion rather than adopting the big-bang approach. The Jupiter systen [21], [22], [23] envisages the construction of a formal model of the legacy system(s) on the basis that it is only when the legacy system is fully understood that it can be meaningfully integrated with other systems. Typically, the details of the inner workings - even the original data model - of the legacy system have long since been lost.

In summary, no one technology can possibly meet all the expectations of users for the next generation of information systems. PC users take for granted that they can purchase shrink-wrapped software from whatever vendor they chose, install it with the minimum of fuss and be able to cut and paste objects between different applications such as word processors, graphics packages and spreadsheets. They are demanding the same "plug-and-play" capability in the context of corporate information systems. Perhaps then, at least some major Information Technology projects will deliver their promise on time and within budget - and without giving the users enough time to change their minds!

Acknowledgements The author would like to acknowledge the contributions of all the partners in the OpenLabs Project, in particular Bill Grimson and the members of the Dublin Demonstrator Team; Ray McGuigan and Mark Riordan from MIPS and John Murphy from Jupiter.

References

1. Architecture Projects Management Ltd.: The overview of ANSAware 4.0. March 1992.
2. Austin, W.J., Hutchison, E.K., Kalmus, J. R., McKinnon, L.M, Jeffery, K. J., Marwick, D. H., Williams, M.H. and Wilson, M.D.: Processing travel queries in a multimedia information system. Proceedings of Information and Communication Technologies in Tourism, W. Schertler et al (eds), Springer-Verlag, 64-71, 1994.
3. Beech, D.: Collections of objects in SQL. Procs. VLDB 93, Dublin, Ireland, Morgan-Kaufmann 1993, 244-255
4. Bell, D.A. and Grimson, J.B.: Distributed Database Systems. Addison-Wesley, 1992.
5. Bradshaw, K.E., Gardiner, R.M. and Pryor, T.A.: Development of a computerised laboratory alerting system. Computers in Biomedical Research, 22, 1989.
6. Brodie, M.: The promise of distributed computing and the challenges of legacy information systems. Procs. of IFIP DS5 Semantics of Interoperable Database Systems, Lorne, Victoria, Australia, November 1992, 1-25.
7. Bruffaerts, A.: The role of HyTIME in the MIPS System. SGML Congress '94 - SGML Users Group, Holland, Amsterdam, November 1994.
8. Brodie, M. and Stonebraker, M.: Migrating Legacy Systems. Morgan Kaufman, 1995.
9. Connelly, D.P. and Bennet, S.T.: Expert systems and clinical laboratory information systems. Clinical Laboratory Medicine, 11, 1991, 135-151.
10. Coulouris, G.F. and Dollimore, J.: Distributed Systems Concepts and Design. Addison-Wesley, 2nd edition, 1994
11. De Moor, G.: Telestroika in healthcare informatics: a challenge for standardisation in Europe. Medical Informatics, 1993.
12. Dunphy, L.: HOLLY: A domain independent query interface with natural language feedback. MSc thesis, Trinity College Dublin, 1995.
13. Grimson, W., Grimson, J., Groth, T., O'Moore, R., Wade, V.: The OpenLabs approach to clinical laboratory computing. Procs. MEDINFO 1995, Vancouver, Canada, IMIA 1995, 372-376.
14. Grimson, J. and Murphy, J.: The Jupiter approach to interoperability with healthcare legacy systems. Procs. MEDINFO 1995, Vancouver, Canada, IMIA 1995, 367-371.
15. Goodman, S.E., Press L.I., Ruth S.R., Rutkowşki A.M.: The global diffusion of the internet: patterns and problems. CACM 37:8, August 1994, 27-31.
16. Grimson, J.B.: Integrating knowledge bases and databases. Clinica Chimica Acta, 222, 1993, 101-115.
17. Hochstrasser, B., Griffiths, C.: Controlling IT Investment Strategy and Management. Chapman and Hall 1991.
18. Inmon, W.H.: Using the Data Warehouse. Wiley-QED Publishing, 1994.
19. Khosrowpour, M. and Yaverbaum G.J.: Information Technology Resources Utilisation and Management. Ida Group Publishing 1990.

20. Louderback. J.: Making sense of middleware. Procs. June 1993 DCI Database World, Vol II, E26-11.

21. Murphy, J. and Grimson, J.: The Jupiter system: an environment for multidatabase interoperability. Journal of Information Science, 1994, 20:2, 120-136.

22. Murphy, J. and Grimson, J.: Multidatabase interoperability in healthcare legacy applications: research and experience. Second International Conference on Cooperative Information Systems (COOPIS-94), Toronto, Canada, 1994, 166-176.

23. Murphy, J. and Grimson, J.: A CORBA based architecture for multidatabase interoperability. International Conference on Data and Knowledge Systems for Manufacturing and Engineering, Hong Kong, May 1994, IEEE 1994, 630-635.

24. Guidelines for the Definition of OpenLabs Application Programming Interfaces (APIs). OpenLabs Project Internal Document ARCH-TF/DOC3, 1993.

25. J. Brender at al (eds): Specfication of the architecture for an open clinical laboratory information system environment. Available from W.Grimson, Dublin Institute of Technology, Kevin Street, Dublin 8, Ireland.

26. The Object Management Group: The OMG Object Model. OMG 1992.

27. O'Moore, R.R.: Decision support based on laboratory data. Methods of Information in Medicine, 27 (1988) 187-190.

28. Iona Technologies Ltd.: Programmers Guide to Orbix. Iona Technologies, 1993.

29. Pryor. T.A., Gardner, R.M., Clayton, P.D. and Warner H.R.: The HELP System. In Information Systems in Patient Care, B Blum (ed), Springer, New York, 1984, 109-128.

30. Rothnie, J.B., Bernstein, P., Fox, S. et al: Introduction to a system for distributed database systems (SDD-1). ACM TODS, 5:1, March 1980, 1-17.

31. Popkin Software and Systems Inc.: System Architect. 1993.

32. Shortcliffe, E.H.: MYCIN: computer based medical consultation. American Elsevier (1976).

33. Simon, A.R.: Strategic Database Technology Management for the year 2000. Morgan Kaufmann, 1995.

34. Sloman, M.: Network and distributed systems management. Addison-Wesley, 1994.

35. Sheth, A.P. and Larson, J.A.: Federated database systems for managing distributed, heterogeneous, and autonomous database systems. ACM Computing Surveys, 22(3), 1990, 183-236.

36. Stevenson, D.: A multidatabase approach to open laboratory information systems. MSc thesis, University of Dublin 1995.

37. Thomas, G., Thompson, G., et al: Heterogeneous distributed database systems for production use. ACM Computing Surveys 22:3, 1990, 237-266.

38. Unix System Laboratories: On-line Transaction Processing in Open Systems. April 1992.

39. UNIX International: Distributed Transaction Processing Environment: a competitive analysis of UNIX System Laboratories' TUXEDO and Transarc Encina. April 1992.

40. Wade, V., Grimson, J., Grimson, W. and O'Moore, R.: The OpenLabs architecture for advanced Laboratory Information Systems. Procs. MIE 94, May 1994, Lisbon, Portugal.

41. Williams, R. et al: R*: an overview of the architecture. Procs. International Conference on Database Systems, Jerusalem, Israel, 1982, Also available as IBM Research Report RJ3325, December 1981.

Extending Database Technology

Norman W. Paton

Department of Computer Science
University of Manchester, Oxford Road, Manchester, UK
email: norm@cs.man.ac.uk

Abstract. Throughout the 1980s and 1990s, a significant proportion of database research activity has been directed towards extending the modelling and programming facilities supported by database systems. This paper looks into the motivation for such activity, characterises and summarises representative proposals for extensions, and presents a concrete example of a database system incorporating a range of advanced features.

1 Introduction

The development of database management systems can be considered as belonging to a number of generations [6] thus:

1. The *first generation*, which consists of navigational database systems such as CODASYL and IMS.
2. The *second generation*, which consists of relational database systems, as supported by a range of vendors.
3. The *third generation*, which consists of advanced database systems that extend the applicability of database technologies towards new application areas.

It can be seen that the third generation is less well defined than the first two, and indeed it remains to be seen which category (or categories) of database system will rise to prominence from those investigated by researchers during the last fifteen years. It is clear, however, that many future database products will offer more powerful data modelling and processing facilities than first or second generation systems, as it is perceived that new application areas require such extensions.

The relationship between a database system and the application functionality that it must support is depicted in figure 1. As a database system provides a finite range of facilities for modelling the concepts in a domain, these concepts must be mapped onto the modelling facilities of the database system for implementation. For some application concepts, this mapping may be quite straightforward, but for other concepts the mapping may be rather complex, leading to complicated and potentially inefficient processing for storage, retrieval and analysis of database data.

This has led to the situation depicted in figure 2 in many advanced application domains. Rather than perform complex mappings from application concepts

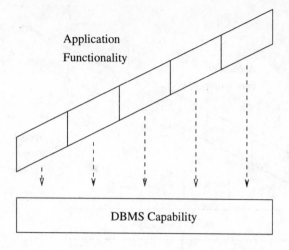

Fig. 1. Representation gap for advanced application

to generic data modelling facilities, the database is used to store only part of the data from the application domain, and some special purpose subsystem(s) are used to represent other parts of the application. As an example of such an architecture, a leading Geographic Information System, ARC/INFO [29], uses a relational database (INFO) to store aspatial aspects of a domain, and a spatial data manager (ARC) for storing explicitly spatial data. This multi-component approach does avoid certain of the mapping problems of figure 1, but is not without drawbacks of its own, as illustrated in figure 3. Specific problems for the programmer of the application include the following:

1. It is necessary to understand the call interfaces of the DBMS and of every special purpose system (e.g. spatial data handler, graphics package, expert system shell, etc) used by the application.
2. The data types and structures used by the different subsystems are often overlapping but incompatible, so transformations must be carried out between different data formats within the application.
3. The complete system can only be readily ported to new platforms which support identical versions of the DBMS and the different subsystems.

These problems manifest themselves in low programmer productivity and poor system performance. It is with a view to simplifying this environment, by providing more direct support within the database system for application concepts, that many extensions to databases are being developed. Thus the aim is to overcome the representation gap as illustrated in figure 4.

The remainder of this paper provides an overview of proposed extensions to database technologies, some of which are becoming well established in products,

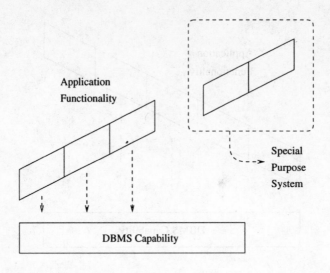

Fig. 2. Avoiding the representation gap by partitioning

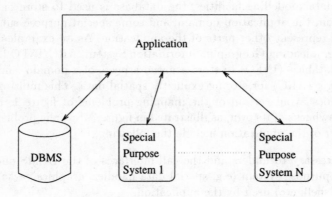

Fig. 3. Multi-component architecture

and some of which are the subject of ongoing research. Section 2 provides a classification of different kinds of extension; section 3 outlines how the data structuring facilities of database systems can be extended; section 4 introduces a range of behavioural extensions to database systems; section 5 considers how extensions can be introduced into database systems without making such systems unnecessarily cumbersome; section 6 makes some of the previous considerations more concrete in the context of a specific system; and section 7 presents some conclusions.

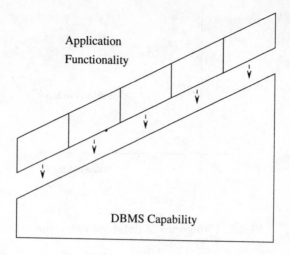

Fig. 4. Overcoming the representation gap by extending the database

2 Categorising Database Extensions

This section considers what is meant by an extension to a database system, and thus clarifies the scope of the following sections. Figure 5 presents three dimensions of functionality along which a database system can be extended. These dimensions are not strictly orthogonal, but many proposals for extensions to database systems can be considered as lying along one or more of these dimensions:

- *Data model* extensions increase the range of data modelling concepts supported by the database system (e.g. object-oriented data models support inheritance, while the relational model does not).
- *Primitive type* extensions increase the range of built in types within the database system (e.g. a spatial database system supports spatial modelling using concepts such as points, lines and polygons). Any increase in the primitive types supported by a database system implies an increase in the primitive operations supported, to allow creation and manipulation of these types.
- *Behaviour* extensions provide greater power or variety in the language(s) available for describing user defined operations over the data stored in the database (e.g. if a relational query language is extended with constructs for defining recursive functions, this increases the number of tasks that can be performed within the database system).

It is clearly the case that database systems can be extended in ways that are not covered by these dimensions. For example, the ability to distribute a

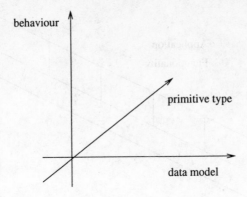

Fig. 5. Categories of database extension.

database over multiple sites is clearly an extension to the functionality of the database. The focus in this paper, however, is upon extending the modelling and programming facilities of database systems, without reference to how or where such activities are carried out.

The dimensions from figure 5 are considered further in the following two sections, which look at structural (data model and primitive type) and behavioural extensions to database systems.

3 Structural Extensions

Relational database systems are characterised by the simplicity of their underlying data model. The basic relational model has the following facilities:

- *Data model:* A single compound type, *relation*, which corresponds to a *set* of *tuples*.
- *Primitive types:* A limited collection of primitive types, which typically include *string, integer, real* and *date*.

The following subsections indicate how these facilities can be extended to provide more direct representations of application concepts.

3.1 Data Model Extensions

Increasing the range of modelling facilities in a database system allows the database to be more precise about the structural characteristics of the data which is to be stored. The most straightforward way to extend a data model is to increase the number of type constructors, for example, to include:

- *Tuple:* a new type which is constructed from a fixed number of potentially distinct component types (e.g. an *address* can be built from three components representing the *number* of the property in a given *street* in a specific *town*).
- *Set:* a new type which is constructed from an unordered, duplicate-free homogeneous collection of data items from an existing type (e.g. the set of *phone numbers* at which an individual may be contactable).
- *List:* a new type which is constructed from an ordered, homogeneous collection of data items from an existing type (e.g. the ordered collection of *point* tuples that make up the boundary of a *polygon*).
- *Bag:* a new type which is constructed from an unordered, homogeneous collection of data items from an existing type, which may contain duplicates (e.g. the collection of *weights* of fish caught by an angler in a fishing competition).
- *Subtype:* a new type which shares the characteristics of an existing type, but adds some additional features of its own (e.g. an *office_location* is a subtype of *address* which also has a *room_number* and a *floor_number*).

A data model with these type constructors subsumes the modelling facilities of the relational model, and thus is likely to provide a more direct representation of the structural features of application concepts.

An increased range of type constructors can be found in a wide range of different types of database system, such as the following:

- *Extended Relational:* the basic data model is relational, but the type constructors may be extended to allow nested relations [39], inheritance [41], or identification of data items using an internal identifier rather than a scalar key [11, 45].
- *Semantic Data Model:* a range of modelling constructs are provided, normally along with a drawing notation, for use in the design [26, 34] or implementation [20, 22] of data intensive applications.
- *Database Programming Language:* the modelling constructs are used as the type system of a programming language [3, 32]; further details of this approach are given in section 4.1.
- *Object-Oriented Databases:* the modelling facilities, which must include inheritance and object identity [28] are used as the basis of a database system which may in turn be classifiable as one of the three categories of system mentioned above.

It is normal for proposals for third generation database systems to include modelling constructs which are significantly more comprehensive than those of the relational model. It is worth noting, however, that this does lead to an increase in the complexity of the resulting system, and can mean that systems provide less comprehensive support for data independence than the relational model. Thus more is not always better; the pragmatics of overall system design are considered in section 5.

3.2 Primitive Type Extensions

The identification of primitive type extensions as a separate category of database extension would not be universally accepted as appropriate, as certain database systems allow user-defined abstract data types that are indistinguishable from the primitive types supplied with the system. It is clear, however, that several proposals for extended database systems can be considered to belong to this category, and seem to fit less well into the framework of subsection 3.1.

Facilities that can be supported using primitive type extensions include:

- *Spatial Data:* built in support for spatial data types (such as *points, lines* and *polygons*) and operations (such as *distance, overlaps* and *inside*). Where spatial concepts are supported within database systems, it is often as a result of modifications to the primitive types supported (e.g. GRAL [23] or GEO-SAL [42]).
- *Graphical Data:* built in support for primitive graphics concepts, which may be built upon to provide more comprehensive display facilities [31].

The motivation for extending the primitive types of a database system rather than using some alternative approach, which would normally involve a layering of the new facilities on top of the generic data modelling and manipulation facilities of the database, include: the seamlessness of built-in extensions to the type system; increased performance resulting from kernel support for the new concepts; and the ability of the query optimiser to perform type-specific transformations when looking for efficient evaluation strategies.

4 Behavioural Extensions

Section 3 has indicated how the data structuring facilities of a database system can be extended, to make them more comprehensive than those supported by the relational model. However, the limited structure modelling facilities are not the only weakness of the relational model, which has also been criticised for the limited computational power of its associated query languages, such as SQL [13].

The fact that SQL lacks programming facilities required for many applications has led to its use in an embedded form, along with conventional programming languages such as C. This has given rise to the *impedance mismatch* problem, which has the following aspects:

- *Type system mismatch:* the types of the programming language cannot be stored directly in the database, and vice versa. This means that a mapping must be performed between the types stored in the database (e.g. relation) and the types used within the programming language (e.g. record, array). This results in cumbersome programming and poor type checking across the database/programming language interface.
- *Evaluation strategy mismatch:* the computational engines of the database system and the programming language operate at different granularities. For example, the relational data model operates on *sets* of tuples, whereas

C lacks the data type *set*, and can store only a single tuple in a record. This means that *cursors* must be used to allow an imperative program to step through the results of a query evaluated by the database. This results in cumbersome programming and poor system performance.

There are thus a number of motivations for the development of languages for use with databases that differ from those associated with the relational model:

- Relational languages are not computationally complete.
- Relational programming is characterised by impedance mismatch problems.
- The programming paradigm associated with relational languages may be considered inappropriate for certain tasks.

A number of proposals have been made for approaches which seek to overcome some of these weaknesses, as outlined in the following subsections.

4.1 Database Programming Languages

A database programming language (DBPL) can be considered as a programming language with integrated database capabilities, or a database system with integrated programming language facilities. An important notion is that of *orthogonal persistence*, which indicates that the length of time that a data item can be stored is independent of its type. It is noteworthy that in an embedded SQL system, only a limited number of types (relations and their attributes) can be stored in the database, whereas in a system supporting orthogonal persistence, every type that can be used to declare short term or long term persistent data.

An example of a DBPL which supports orthogonal persistence is Napier88 [30], in which every data item stored in a persistent environment, or which is reachable from such a data item, persists. For example, the following program creates a persistent environment ps and stores in it the integer variable i with an initial value of 0:

```
let ps = PS()
in ps let i := 0
```

This variable can then be accessed and manipulated by other programs which access the environment ps, such as the following program, which increments the persistent variable i:

```
let ps = PS()
use ps with i : int in i := i + 1
```

While these examples stored a variable of a simple scalar type, it is also possible to store arrays, lists, trees, etc, without introducing additional constructs for manipulating persistent data explicitly.

The notion of orthogonal persistence has been applied (to a greater or lesser extent) to the development of DBPLs based upon a range of programming paradigms [32]:

- *Imperative:* examples include PS-algol [3] and Napier88 [30].
- *Functional:* examples include FDL [36] and PFL [37].
- *Object-Oriented:* examples include Gemstone [7] and Galileo [2].
- *Deductive:* examples include CORAL [38] and Glue-Nail [35].

4.2 Active Databases

The presence or absence of active capabilities in a database systems is largely
independent of the underlying data model or programming paradigm. In essence,
active mechanisms allow a database system to respond automatically to specific
situations that have been identified as being of interest. Active behaviour is
normally described using rules with three components:

- An *event* which describes a specific occurrence (e.g. an update to the database,
  a particular time of day) to which some reaction may be required.
- A *condition* which examines the database to ascertain the context within
  which the event has taken place.
- An *action* which describes the response which should be made to the event
  if the condition is true.

The characteristics of an active database system depend upon two principal
aspects: the *knowledge model*, which specifies the languages used to describe
events, conditions and actions; and the *execution model*, which specifies how and
when different aspects of rule processing will take place.

Active rule systems have been proposed that are associated with different
categories of database system, including:

- *Relational:* examples include Starburst [43] and POSTGRES [40].
- *Object-Oriented:* examples include HiPac [14], Adam [16] and Samos [21].

Simple active rule mechanisms are now supported by a number of commercial
relational databases, and are likely to be included in the SQL-3 standard.

5 Coherence and Extensions

Extensions to database systems, such as those presented in previous sections can
be seen as 'a good thing', in that they help to overcome certain of the problems
with earlier database systems identified in section 1. However, there is then the
important question as to *which* extensions should be included into specific systems, and *how* different extensions are blended together. It is clearly the case that
an ad hoc coupling together of different concepts is likely to lead to complex and
unwieldy database systems. Different approaches to the integration of different
extensions can be identified, as summarised in the following subsections.

5.1 Extensible Database Systems

The idea behind extensible database systems is the provision of a core set of facilities that can be extended readily with additional features as required for specific applications. There have been different approaches to the provision of extensibility:

- *Primitive type extensibility:* the provision of a fixed data model, with hooks into the kernel that allow new primitive types to be supported which can be queried and manipulated as if they were built in [41].
- *Data model extensibility:* the provision of an inherently extensible data model, which can be revised to support additional modelling constructs [33].
- *Toolkit extensibility:* the provision of a collection of database programming facilities that can be used together for the development of new database systems [12, 8].

Of these, primitive type extensibility is beginning to be supported with commercial relational databases, and toolkit extensibility has been exploited in the development of a number of commercial object-oriented databases.

5.2 Model Based Systems

The development of a collection of database facilities around an enhanced data model was poineered commercially by O_2 [15], where a formally defined data model was used as the starting point for the development of a number of programming languages, query interfaces, and tools. A similar approach has been adopted in the ODMG-93 standard [9], in which a data model is associated with a standard query language and a number of language bindings. As the model has been developed with an eye to language integration, the impedance mismatch manifests itself less in the language bindings of [9] than in embedded SQL systems.

5.3 Summary

The coherent integration of different extensions is not always a straightforward task. For example, there is work ongoing on the integration of deductive and object-oriented capabilities [18], on the integration of deductive and active rules [25, 44], and on developing expert database systems [27]. Certain of the extensions proposed seem more complementary or more compatible than others, although all seem to have merits in specific contexts. Thus future systems will include most if not all of the functionalities mentioned in the previous sections, although not necessarily at the same time. The following section presents a specific example of an advanced database system which combines a number of the features mentioned in previous sections, with a view to providing a concrete example of an advanced database system.

6   Example Database Extension: ROCK & ROLL

This section presents an example of an advanced database system, specifically the deductive object-oriented database (DOOD) system ROCK & ROLL [4].

6.1   Motivation

The general motivation behind the development of DOODs is that the strengths of deductive and of object-oriented database systems are in different areas. Indeed, an effective DOOD system should be able to use the strengths of one paradigm to overcome the weaknesses of the other. The strengths and weaknesses of deductive systems can be summarised as:

- *Strengths:* formal foundation in 1st order logic, declarative query/constraint expression, well understood optimisation facilities.
- *Weaknesses:* limited data modelling capabilities, cumbersome update and IO facilities, lack of application demand.

The strengths and weaknesses of object-oriented databases (OODBs) can be summarised as:

- *Strengths:* comprehensive modelling facilities, powerful data manipulation languages, considerable application demand.
- *Weaknesses:* sporadic availability of formal definitions, rarely effective support for both programming and querying.

The approach that has been adopted in ROCK & ROLL involves the derivation and subsequent integration of two languages, one a logic query language (ROLL), and the other an imperative programming language (ROCK), from a single object-oriented data model (OM). The architecture is presented in figure 6.

The two languages can be combined seamlessly because they have been derived from a single underlying data model, which means that neither type system nor evaluation strategy impedance mismatches occur when either language calls the other [5]. The following sections present the individual components and their integration.

6.2   OM

The OM data model was the first part of ROCK & ROLL to be designed; it supports a range of modelling constructs, including most of those mentioned in section 3.1. To illustrate some of the features of OM, the example trains application from [32] will be used, part of the schema of which is given in figure 7. In this figure:

- **visit** is an object type with three attributes that record the **station** that is being visited, the **Time** that the visit is being made, and the **train** that is making the visit.

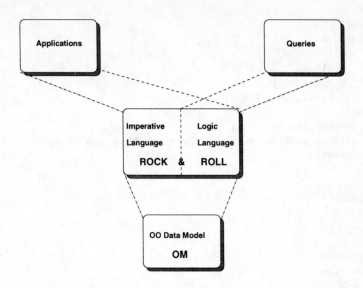

Fig. 6. Relationship between the principal components of ROCK & ROLL.

- **visits** is an object type that is declared to be constructed from a list (denoted using [...]) of **visits**.
- **station** is an object type with a single attribute that records its **name**.
- **train** is an object type with four attributes that record the **number** of the train, the **source** and **destination** stations that it connects, and the **visits** that are made on route.

Figure 7 also provides declarations for operations associated with these types under the headings **ROCK** and **ROLL**. Definitions for the operations associated with a type are provided on a classwith the same name as the type; some example operation definitions are presented in subsequent subsections. Facilities that are not illustrated in this schema fragment, but which are supported by OM, include inheritance and a *set* data type.

OM can be considered to be a conventional object-oriented data model, with a significant amount in common with semantic data models [26, 34] or the ODMG-93 standard [9], in that an attempt is made to provide facilities that can be used to describe the structural characteristics of application concepts in a direct manner.

6.3 ROCK

ROCK is an imperative object-oriented database database programming language based upon OM (i.e. OM describes the structural characteristics of objects that can be created and manipulated by ROCK). As such, ROCK can be used to

```
type visit:
    properties:
        public:
            place:       station,
            visit_time: Time,
            visit_train:train;
    ROCK:
        new(the_station: station, the_time: Time),
        new(the_station: station, the_time: Time, the_train: train),
        print();
end-type

type visits:
    public [ visit ];
end-type

type station:
    properties:
        public:
            name: string;
    ROCK:
        new (nam: string),
        find_routes(end_station: station),
        get_visits(the_visit: visit): { visit }
        print(),
    ROLL:
        is_station_in_visits(visits);
end-type

type train:
    properties:
        public:
            number: int,
            source: station,
            destination: station,
            route: visits;
    ROCK:
        get_stations_ahead(the_station: station): visits,
        show_routes(end_station: station, visited: visits),
        print();
end-type
```

Fig. 7. OM type declarations for trains application.

6.5 ROCK & ROLL

The languages ROCK and ROLL can be used together in the development of a single program. The following facilities are available for their combined use:

- ROLL queries can be embedded in ROCK programs. For example, the example query from the previous section can be embedded in ROCK thus:

```
var ss := [{St} | get_place@Visit == St,
                  get_visit_train@Visit == Tr,
                  get_number@Tr == 101];

foreach s in ss do print()@s;
```

The type of the ROCK variable ss is inferred by the type inference system from the type of the logic variable St. ROLL queries can also access ROCK variables, which are named in ROLL with the prefix !.
- ROCK methods can be invoked from ROLL queries and rules, although with the restriction that the ROCK method must not have any side-effects. The check for side-effects is carried out at compile time.

It is argued in [5] that the integration of ROCK with ROLL is seamless, as it has the following characteristics:

- *Evaluation strategy compatibility* – no copying is required when passing objects between the two languages.
- *Type system uniformity* – the types which can be processed are the same in both languages.
- *Type checker capability* – static type checking is carried out even when both languages are used in a single program.
- *Syntactic consistency* – similar tasks are described using similar syntaxes.
- *Bidirectionality* – each language can call the other.

It is perhaps worth noting that none of these characteristics are exhibited by an embedded SQL system.

6.6 Summary

This section has introduced the ROCK & ROLL deductive database system, which is available freely over the WWW from http://www.cee.hw.ac.uk/Databases. ROCK & ROLL brings together a number of extensions to database technology in a single system, so that the complementary facilities they represent can be employed together in data intensive applications. ROCK & ROLL can be seen, as a representative of an extended database system, to improve upon the relational model in the following respects:

1. Richer data modelling facilities are supported through the OM data model, which has many more modelling constructs than relational systems.

2. Integrated programming facilities are provided through the ROCK DBPL, which avoids impedance mismatch problems by providing direct access to database data for ROCK programmers.

3. Deductive inference capabilities are made available through ROLL, thereby providing a rule-based programming style, which is complementary to the imperative facilities offered by ROCK.

ROCK & ROLL is also being used as a testbed for further extensions:

- *Active Extensions* are being provided by supporting ECA-rules within ROCK & ROLL. In this extension, ROLL is used as the condition language, and ROCK as the action language. Event specification is supported by a language which is syntactically similar to ROLL, but which essentially queries a history of events which are being monitored by the system. The ROLL optimiser is being extended to support efficient evaluation of sets of active rule conditions that have to be evaluated at the same time.
- *Spatial Extensions* are being provided by extending the set of primitive types supported within ROCK & ROLL to include those of the ROSE spatial algebra [24]. The integration process involves extending the syntax of both ROCK and ROLL to accommodate the new spatial types, and the kernel of the database is being revised to support storage of spatial concepts and optimisation of spatial queries. The use of ROCK & ROLL for spatial data handling is described in [1].

7 Summary

This paper has reviewed various aspects of extensions to database technologies. The extensions presented are broadly motivated by the increasing representation and manipulation requirements of application domains which have previously been less than comprehensively supported by database systems.

Certain of the extensions that have been presented can be considered to be complementary and compatible; others may seem to be complementary but not obviously compatible; some will be seen as alternatives. Which individual or collections of extensions will come to be most widely used in future database systems is not yet clear, but emerging standards for extended relational databases and for object-oriented databases are incorporating a range of functionalities based upon those described in this paper, thereby providing access for user communities to the research results of recent years.

Acknowledgements: The development of ROCK & ROLL was a collaborative effort involving Alia Abdelmoty, Marisa Barja, Andrew Dinn, Alvaro Fernandes and Howard Williams, and is continuing to be supported by the UK Engineering and Physical Sciences Research Council (grants GR/H43847 and GR/J99360), and the EU HC&M Network ACT-NET. The trains application used in section 6 was implemented in ROCK & ROLL by Andrew Dinn.

References

1. A.I. Abdelmoty, N.W. Paton, M.H. Williams, A.A.A. Fernandes, M.L. Barja, and A. Dinn. Geographic Data Handling in a Deductive Object-Oriented Database. In D. Karagiannis, editor, *Proc. 5th Int. Conf. on Databases and Expert Systems Applications (DEXA)*, pages 445–454. Springer-Verlag, 1994.

2. A. Albano, G. Ghelli, and R. Orsini. Objects for a Database Programming Language. In Paris Kanellakis and Joachim Schmidt, editors, *Proceedings of the Third International Workshop on Database Programming Languages - Bulk Types and Persistent Data*, pages 236–253, San Mateo, CA 94403, August 1991. Morgan Kaufman Publishers, Inc. ISBN 1-55860-242-9.

3. M.P. Atkinson and O.P. Buneman. Types and Persistence in Database Programming Languages. *ACM Computing Surveys*, 19(1):105–190, 1987.

4. M.L. Barja, A.A.A. Fernandes, N.W. Paton, M.H. Williams, A. Dinn, and A.I. Abdelmoty. Design and Implementation of ROCK & ROLL: A Deductive Object-Oriented Database System. *Information Systems*, 20:185–211, 1995.

5. M.L. Barja, N.W. Paton, A.A.A. Fernandes, M.H. Williams, and A. Dinn. An Effective Deductive Object-Oriented Database Through Language Integration. In J. Bocca, M. Jarke, and C. Zaniolo, editors, *Proc. 20th Int. Conf. on Very Large Data Bases (VLDB)*, pages 463–474. Morgan-Kaufmann, 1994.

6. D. Beech, P. Bernstein, M. Brodie, M. Carey, B. Lindsay, L. Rowe, and M. Stonebraker. Third-generation data base system manifesto. In W.Kent R.A. Meersman and S. Khosla, editors, *Object-Oriented Databases: Analysis, Design and Construction (DS-4)*. North-Holland, 1991.

7. R. Bretl, D. Maier, A.Otis, J. Panney, B. Schuchardt, J. Stein, E.H. Williams, and M. Williams. The Gemstone Data Management System. In Won Kim and Frederick H. Lochovsky, editors, *Object-Oriented Concepts, Databases and Applications*, pages 283–308. ACM Press/Addison-Wesley(Frontier Series), New York, NY, 1989. ISBN 0-201-14410-7.

8. M. Carey, D. DeWitt, G. Graefe, D. Haight, J. Richardson, D. Schuh, E. Shekita, and S. Vandenberg. The EXODUS Extensible DBMS Project: An Overview. In S. Zdonik and D. Maier, editors, *Readings in Object-Oriented Databases*, CA 94303-9953, 1990. Morgan Kaufman Publishers, Inc.

9. R.G.G. Cattell. *The Object Database Standard: ODMG-93*. Morgan Kaufmann, 1993.

10. S. Ceri, G. Gottlob, and L. Tanca. *Logic Programming and Databases*. Springer-Verlag, Berlin, 1990.

11. E.F. Codd. Extending the database relational model to capture more meaning. *ACM TODS*, 4(4):397–434, 1979.

12. R. Cooper, M. Atkinson, A. Dearle, and D. Abderrahmane. Constructing database systems in a persistent environment. In W. Kent P. Stocker, editor, *13rd. Intl. Conf on Very Large Data Bases*, pages 117–126. Morgan Kaufmann, 1987.

13. C.J. Date. *Introduction to Database Systems, Volume 1 (5th Edition)*. Addison-Wesley, 1990.

14. U. Dayal, A.P. Buchmann, and D.R. McCarthy. Rules are objects too: A knowledge model for an active object oriented database system. In K.R. Dittrich, editor, *Proc. 2nd Intl. Workshop on OODBS*, volume 334, pages 129–143. Springer-Verlag, 1988. Lecture Notes in Computer Science.

15. O. Deux and et al. The Story of O_2. *IEEE Transactions on Knowledge and Data Engineering*, 2(1), March 1990.

16. O. Diaz, N. Paton, and P.M.D. Gray. Rule management in object oriented databases: a uniform approach. In G.M. Lohman, A. Sernadas, and R. Camps, editors, *17th Intl. Conf. on Very Large Data Bases, Barcelona*, pages 317–326. Morgan Kaufmann, 1991.

17. A. Dinn, N.W. Paton, M.H. Williams, A.A.A. Fernandes, and M.L. Barja. The Implementation of a Deductive Query Language Over an Object-Oriented Database. In *Proc. 4st Intl. Conf. on Deductive Object-Oriented Databases*. Springer-Verlag, 1995. to be published.

18. A. A. A. Fernandes, N. W. Paton, M. H. Williams, and A. Bowles. Approaches to Deductive Object-Oriented Databases. *Information and Software Technology*, 34(12):787–803, December 1992.

19. A.A.A. Fernandes, M.H. Williams, and N.W. Paton. A Logical Query Language for an Object-Oriented Data Model. In N.W. Paton and M.H. Williams, editors, *Proceedings of First International Workshop on Rules in Database Systems*, pages 234–250. Springer-Verlag, 1994.

20. D.H. Fishman, D. Beech, H.P. Cate, E.C. Chow, T. Connors, J.W. Davis, N. Derrett, C.G. Hoch, W. Kent, P. Lyngbaek, B. Mahbod, M.A. Neimat, T.A. Ryan, and M.C. Shan. Iris: An Object-Oriented Database Management System. *ACM Transactions on Office Information Systems*, 5(1):48–69, November 1987.

21. S. Gatziu, A. Geppert, and K. Dittrich. Integrating active concepts into an object-oriented database system. In P. Kanellakis and J.W. Schmidt, editors, *Proc. 3rd Workshop on Database Programming Languages*. Morgan-Kaufmann, 1991.

22. P.M.D. Gray, K.G. Kulkarni, and N.W. Paton. *Object-Oriented Databases: A Semantic Data Model Approach*. Prentice-Hall International(UK), 1992.

23. R.H. Guting. Geo-Relational Algebra: A Model and Query Language for Geometric Database Systems. In J.W. Schmidt, S. Ceri, and M. Missikoff, editors, *Advances in Database Systems (Proc EDBT)*, pages 506–527. Springer-Verlag, 1988.

24. R.H. Guting and M. Schneider. Realm-Based Spatial Data Types: The ROSE Algebra. *VLDB J.*, 4(2):243–286, 1995.

25. J.V. Harrison and S.W. Dietrich. Integrating active and deductive rules. In N.W. Paton and M.H. Williams, editors, *Proc. 1st Int. Workshop on Rules In Database Systems*, pages 288–305. Springer-Verlag, 1994.

26. Richard Hull and Roger King. Semantic Database Modelling: Survey, Applications, and Research Issues. *ACM Computing Surveys*, 19(3):202–260, September 1987.

27. K.G. Jeffery. *Expert Database Systems*. Academic Press, 1992.

28. Setrag N. Khoshafian and George P. Copeland. Object Identity. In *OOPSLA '86 Conference Proceedings Object-Oriented Programming: Systems, Languages and Applications*, pages 406–416, Portland,OR, September 1986. ACM Press. Also in [46], pages 37-46.

29. S. Morehouse. ARC/INFO: A Geo-Relational Model for Spatial Information. In *Proceedings of 7th Int. Symposium on Computer Assisted Cartography*, pages 388–398, Washington, DC, 1986.

30. R. Morrison, A.L. Brown, R.C.H. Conner, Q.I. Cutts, A. Dearle, G.N.C. Kirby, and D.S. Munro. *The Napier88 Reference Manual (Release 2.0)*. FIDE Technical Report FIDE/94/104, University of Glasgow, 1994.

31. R. Morrison, A. Dearle, A. L. Brown, and M. P. Atkinson. An Integrated Graphics Programming Environment. *Computer Graphics Forum 5(2)*, pages 147–157, 1986.

32. N.W. Paton, R.L. Cooper, M.H. Williams, and P. Trinder. *Database Programming Languages*. Prentice-Hall, 1995.

33. N.W. Paton, O. Diaz, and M.L. Barja. Combining active rules and metaclasses for enhanced extensibility in object-oriented systems. *Data and Knowledge Engineering*, 10:45–63, 1993.

34. J. Peckham and F. Maryanski. Semantic Data Models. *ACM Computing Surveys*, 20(3):153–189, September 1988.

35. G. Phipps, M.A. Derr, and K.A. Ross. Glue-Nail: A Deductive Database System. In James Clifford and Roger King, editors, *Proc. ACM SIGMOD International Conference on the Management of Data*, pages 308–317. ACM Press, 1991.

36. A. Poulovassilis and P.J.H. King. Extending The Functional Data Model to Computational Completeness. In F. Bancilhon, C. Thanos, and D. Tsichritzis, editors, *Proceedings of Extending Database Technology Conf.*, pages 75–91. Springer-Verlag, 1990.

37. A. Poulovassilis and C. Small. A Functional Programming Approach to Deductive Databases. In G.M. Lohman, A. Sernadis, and R. Camps, editors, *Proceedings of Very Large Data Bases Conf.*, pages 491–500. Morgan Kaufmann, 1991.

38. R. Ramakrishnan, D. Srivastava, and S. Sudarshan. CORAL-Control, Relations and Logic. In Li-Yan Yuan, editor, *Proceedings of the 18th International Conference on Very Large Databases*, pages 239–250. Morgan Kaufman, 1992.

39. Hans-Joerg Schek and M. H. Scholl. The Relational Model with Relation-valued Attributes. *Information Systems*, 11(2):137–147, 1986.

40. M. Stonebraker, A. Jhingran, J. Goh, and S. Potamianos. On rules, procedures, caching and views in database systems. In *Proc. ACM SIGMOD*, pages 281–290, 1990.

41. M. Stonebraker and G. Kemnitz. The POSTGRES Next-generation Database Management System. *Communications of the ACM*, 34(10):78–92, October 1991.

42. P. Svensson and H. Zhexue. Geo-SAL: A Query Language for Spatial Data Analysis. In O. Gunther and H.J. Scheck, editors, *Advances in Spatial Databases, 2nd Symposium, SSD'91*, Lecture Notes in Computer Science, 525, pages 119–142, Zurich, Switzerland., 1991. Springer-Verlag.

43. J. Widom and S.J. Finkelstein. Set-Oriented Production Rules in Relational Database Systems. In *Proceedings of the ACM SIGMOD International Conference on Management of Data*, pages 259–270, 1990.

44. C. Zaniolo. A unified semantics for active and deductive databases. In N.W. Paton and M.H. Williams, editors, *Rules in Database Systems*. Springer-Verlag, 1994.

45. Carlo Zaniolo. The Database Language GEM. In *Proceedings of the 1983 ACM SIGMOD International Conference on the Management of Data*. ACM Press, 1983. Also in [46], pages 449-460.

46. S.B. Zdonik and D. Maier, editors. *Readings in Object-Oriented Database Systems*. Morgan Kaufmann, San Mateo, CA, 1990. ISSN 1046-1698, ISBN 1-55860-000-0.

Introducing SSADM4+ and PRINCE

A. J. G. Betts

CCTA, Rosebery Court, St Andrews Business Park, Norwich NR7 0HS, UK
email: abetts@ccta.gov.uk

Abstract. This paper describes some of the major changes in information systems (IS) requirements in the 90s and compares them with recent and planned changes to SSADM and PRINCE (for IS development and IS project management respectively). Background is provided describing CCTA's role in UK government and its rationale in developing public domain methods.

Delivering business solutions, delivering them quickly and cost-effectively, and getting return on investment in legacy systems are the dominant concerns in IS development. They have to be addressed in an environment of rapidly-developing technology, a changing role for central IT in organisations (eg more development based in business groups, outsourcing), and a move from individual to group IS support.

IS need to become integral parts of the business systems they support. Generally, IS development still has a stronger focus on technology solutions than business requirements.

SSADM4+ is becoming part of a family of complementary methodologies for IS development—addressing business process engineering, work flow, reuse and re-engineering of legacy systems, communication-oriented technology (such as email and groupware) as well as the analysis and design of database and transaction processing systems.

Most of the paper considers the technical aspects of IS development focusing on the role of application architecture in providing flexibility and speed of delivery.

1   CCTA's Role

CCTA is the UK Government Centre for Information Systems and is part of the Office of Public Service. We help UK central government departments to use information systems (IS) in support of their policy objectives and improved services to the public. Departments spend more than £ 2 billion a year on IS services. These services are tested in the market-place to ensure they are provided in the most cost-effective way.

The planning, procurement and management of computer-based IS cannot be done successfully unless the appropriate IT skills are available. We help organisations make the best use of these resources by spreading best practice and standards. Our products and services help organisations to adopt a strategic approach to the use of IS. We help them to specify the IS services they need and enable them to get best value for money when they acquire IS. Our guidance also helps them to run their IS within the framework of national, European and international law.

Since IS services are increasingly provided by the private sector it is important that these services and therefore our guidance should reflect national, European and international best practice. We therefore work closely with bodies such as the IS Examination Board, British Computer Society and the European Commission as well as user and supplier organisations to ensure that our advice reflects best practice and meets customer needs in the most effective way.

1.1 CCTA's Guidance

The private sector is now a major user of CCTA guidance. Foreign governments are increasingly using it. We are prepared to stand by what we say when customers follow our advice.

Our guidance covers the issues which concern managers, users of IS and IS professionals within organisations of all sizes. It includes: strategic planning, standards, telecommunications, methods, and advanced technology.

Our guidance is targeted at a number of levels, including top managers and business managers. We also provide more detailed guidance for IS practitioners including standard methods and supporting libraries of associated guidance.

All the methods and guidance are legally owned by CCTA but are made available publicly in support of one of our major objectives: to create an 'open market' in CCTA products supported by a wide variety of sources of supply. CCTA has recently applied for trade marks for all its methods to help ensure that service providers deliver a quality service to users.

1.2 Partnerships with other Organisations

As its methods, products and guidance attain maturity, it is CCTA's intention to establish partnerships with commercial and professional organisations to oversee the day-to-day development, publication and marketing of the products. The combination of commercial expertise and CCTA's continued commitment to open, public domain products is intended to provide user organisations with current best practice, at low cost, without requiring them to commit to a particular service provider.

A Management Board comprising representatives of CCTA, NCCBlackwell (the SSADM Management and Marketing Organisation) and the International SSADM Users Group has already been established for SSADM and the Information System Engineering (now renamed System Development) Library. Management Boards are also being established for:

- PRINCE, CCTA's project management method, the Programme and Project Management Library, and the Risk Management Library
- The IT Infrastructure Management Library and Data Management Library.

2   What is SSADM?

SSADM (Structured Systems Analysis and Design Method) is a systematic approach to the analysis and design of IT applications. SSADM is defined in the form of a structured set of procedural, technical and documentation standards. SSADM is a product-oriented specification of what IS practitioners need to do. It defines a process, which users can tailor to suit project needs, for capturing requirements and transforming them into a detailed system specification.

In recent years, SSADM has become a de facto standard in the UK and elsewhere, in both the private and public sectors. It is now the most widely used method of analysis and design in the UK. It is supported by an infrastructure of accredited training organisations, consultants, proficient practitioners and automated tools. Over 120 companies have registered to use the SSADM Trade Marks as part of the provision of SSADM services. Over 5000 people have taken the ISEB examination.

The International SSADM Users Group has members in many counties around the world including Canada, South Africa, the far East and Eastern Europe. Affiliate membership is available for non-UK groups. Affiliate groups are being established in Hungary, Switzerland and Ireland.

3   What is PRINCE?

PRINCE (PRojects IN Controlled Environment) is a fully documented structured method for project management, covering the planning, progress, quality and organisation of IS projects. It provides a framework within which Business, User and Technical concerns are addressed in order to deliver quality products on time and to budget. Like SSADM, it is backed by a substantial private sector infrastructure providing training, consultancy and support and an independent User Group.

4   But are CCTA's Methods Relevant in the 90s?

Through the 1970s and 1980s, there has been extensive take-on of computer technology by end-user organisations. This take-on created pressure on suppliers of IT products and services who responded by developing newer and more advanced technology that effectively began to drive end-user organisations' needs.

The users of IT needed to harness and control the extensive technology now available to them. Throughout the 80s and 90s, we have seen a tremendous take-up of structured methods, productivity tools and IS development techniques, all intended to improve the effectiveness of delivering applications to support business requirements. The need to control this continually evolving technology continues to be prevalent as we move through the 90s. However, users still want to benefit from new technology developments. Controlled exploitation of IT is now the underlying theme for organisations in both the public and private sectors. SSADM4+ and PRINCE are key parts of CCTA's strategy to give its customers controlled exploitation of IT.

5 What are the key IS Activities?

Changes in the business environment are leading to changes in the way that systems are developed and operated. Businesses have to be far more responsive and far more flexible.

There are four very different activities which are key to understanding the role of IS:

- identifying business requirements
- setting a strategy and maintaining an 'architecture' for both systems and information
- developing and maintaining systems
- running the computers and the telecommunications networks to provide operational IT services.

Businesses need to enhance their ability to define requirements. As systems focus on innovation rather than just replacing past procedures, there is a much greater requirement for insight and imagination. This activity requires real business understanding. Users therefore play an increasingly important role. But they also need to understand the technological possibilities.

The business must also maintain its capability to guard the business's system infrastructure and information architecture. Cheaper technology does not solve the problem. In many cases it has added to it as IT buying decisions are dispersed around the business. The ability to devise new systems—perhaps whole new processes—can give the business a genuine competitive edge. Having a systems architecture allows such systems to be introduced rapidly, in a coherent fashion. An inappropriate architecture will constrain flexibility, an appropriate one will provide flexibility. Effective design requires real insight into the nature of the business.

Application architectures are being developed in many organisations to provide a framework for adopting and exploiting new technologies. Unfortunately, most architectures are driven from the bottom up by the constraints of existing technologies. As the enabling technologies are replaced at increasingly frequent intervals, the enormous investment in the logical layer of the architecture needs to remain intact. Organisations must be able to justify new investment in technology and in applications through more direct analysis of the support of critical business requirements. Within the application architecture, business objectives should drive technology, instead of technology determining the capabilities of the business.

If the need to specify business requirements and to define an application architecture are becoming more important for business effectiveness, the abilities of writing programs and operating computers are being highlighted from a cost-efficiency perspective. They can have a major impact on reliability and require a high degree of technical proficiency but they involve little real knowledge of the business.

There are increasing arguments, therefore, for treating the third and fourth activities as commodities—buying them externally where sensible—whilst treating the first two as capabilities to be preserved or enhanced.

External service providers are increasingly offering highly competitive services. The customer organisation will not want to be locked into the services of a particular provider and should therefore seek commitment to a proven method of working supported by a range of service providers. Within the customer organisation, there remains a need for individuals who are aware of what the technology can do and who are skilled in high-level analysis and design. Many prudent customers will also want to have their own project manager ensuring that applications are being developed effectively.

The application development department is under increasing pressure to keep costs down and to provide more effective support for the business. At the same time, users are increasingly computer-literate and are much more accustomed to introducing new IT systems. As a consequence, the line between central IS and decentralised Business Units is breaking down. This is now an unstoppable trend. The IS department needs to provide effective, professional skills (project management, knowledge of tools etc) to help the BU. Otherwise the power and availability of end-user tools threatens to dismantle any centrally-designed architecture or infrastructure which will lead to chaos and considerable expense for the business.

IS strategy (including standards) and IS methods must allow both rapid development of BU-focused projects as well as the extension of these projects into larger, more complex, enterprise applications that make extensive reuse of development products. Time to deliver business functionality is an increasingly important factor in virtually all new applications under development. This imperative will apply irrespective of whether the applications are developed with an architected, model-driven approach or an implementation-focused one. Organisations will therefore need to carefully identify which core functional components will bring competitive advantage. These should be developed internally, while other components can be bought. Reusable functionality will come in the form of application packages, off-the-shelf component and object libraries and internally developed components and objects.

Packaged software vendors are likely to sell frameworks, objects and assembly services for different industries. Business users evaluating externally available functionality must carefully compare the benefits with the risk of inheriting potentially rigid, non-compliant architectures. Further, architectures and infrastructures must be developed for flexibility to maximise the likelihood of success in assimilating third-party-developed functionality. The business must understand where the key integration interfaces will need to be, and then design their technical architectures around those interfaces.

Object-oriented (OO) tools and techniques are increasingly significant in providing reuse but are still deficient in supporting the development of complex business systems. Standards, procedures and metrics are immature, as are object cataloguing and management tools. There are some encouraging signs that OO methods are coming together. Whether or not 'pure' OO methods are used for application development, the principles of encapsulation and messages are very important for architecture design. Many of the barriers to reuse are not technical but relate to application development culture and management.

6 How do we Handle Legacy?

Although business systems need to be far more responsive, existing systems cannot be changed quickly. How do we ensure legacy systems can evolve with the business?

Legacy systems need to be extended and enhanced with new application architectures. Most systems are likely to be moved to some form of client/server configuration. Application functionality consists of: user interface, data access routines, business logic and specific implementation code. Organisations need to decouple these components. It is then possible to consider how they might migrate. This might involve providing frontware, partial rewrites, salvage, or complete replacement. They could convert external user interfaces into graphical format. They might reuse data access logic to integrate a legacy data store eg IMS into a desktop client/server architecture. Redevelopment can include restructuring code to better locate business logic that can be 'wrapped' in a client/server application. It can also include data standardisation and rationalisation in support of data warehousing or the implementation of common business logic ie data routines.

The goal of legacy to client/server transitions is to locate business logic, data and data-oriented code on the appropriate platform—all viewed via graphical user interface from the desktop.

7 Rapid Application Development

There are, broadly, three approaches for rapid development:

- desktop database systems
- 'thin client' systems
- new technology and hybrid systems

7.1 Desktop Database Systems

Desktop database systems are used by individuals or small workgroups. They usually have simple file structures, with no replication or partitioning of data, and little or no business logic built into the data structure. Update transactions are usually simple and short. Business rules are either in the heads of the users, or in tools like macros in spreadsheets that use the stored data.

Most desktop database systems are not scalable; the technologies that make them quick and cheap to develop will not support large numbers of users at multiple locations, or high throughput. There may be many copies of a desktop database system in use, but generally there would be no requirement to synchronise updates of any replicated data.

7.2 'Thin Client' Systems

There is a general move towards 'thin client' applications, supported by client/server and object-oriented technology. The concept is to have an architected, model-driven base, which contains the essential business logic and acts as a server to many applications.

Business objects in the base have stable, extensible behaviour—they will continue to support existing applications, while being extended to support new ones—but should change more slowly than the applications. The base is typically supported by both purpose-built databases and legacy systems (often with wrappers to present consistent behaviour).

Applications have a presentation layer sitting above minimal application logic to invoke business objects. There is a widely-held view in the industry that 'thin' applications will eventually become scripts invoking user interface objects and business objects.

Note that the 'thin client' concept is not a physical architecture, it is a design and implementation approach. For performance, some business objects can be replicated and distributed. The important point is that they are designed and implemented only once, and are not fused into the application logic.

7.3   New Technology and Hybrid Systems

Systems can often be developed faster with communication-oriented technologies such as groupware, email and workflow than with database and transaction processing, and hence deliver business benefits earlier. Such systems may be integrated with database systems to form hybrids (they can be one style of 'thin client') and the technologies are expected to converge over the next two to three years.

Current development techniques are mainly fairly informal. This is manageable for small workgroups, or for cellular networks of small workgroups (where most of the interaction is within groups). It often means that systems are inflexible and difficult to maintain over long periods, but these disadvantages are traded against rapid development and early return on investment.

But the informal approaches do not scale up. For larger systems, more sophisticated than the basic shared-document model eg for large, dispersed workgroups requiring:

- replicated documents with multi-source updating
- documents that appear in multiple threads of interaction
- integration with shared databases.

Disciplines for managing consistency are needed, similar to those for database systems. Implementation tools are becoming more complex and difficult to use—supporting database access, programmable user interfaces, dynamic object linking between documents.

8   Business Requirements

I have focused on the design of application architecture but business requirements are also very important. Information systems must become an integral part of business systems. Generally, IS development still has a stronger focus on technology solutions than on business requirements. This situation is improving:

- as techniques for business process modelling and engineering, requirements engineering and workflow design evolve and are interfaced with IS development techniques,
- with the growth of IT, such as groupware, email, and desktop services, that is more embedded in users' work practice than are database and transaction processing IT services, and the integration of these two strands of IT into hybrid systems, but there is quite a way to go. A significant problem is the failure of many business process modelling approaches to separate the essential business process from the organisational structure and work practice.

9   What has Happened to SSADM since 1990?

Since SSADM version 4 was launched in 1990, CCTA has developed a range of guidance supporting SSADM covering client/server, distributed systems, use of application packages, re-use and object-oriented ideas, rapid development, application integration, customising SSADM and many other issues. These guides have now been published as part of the ISE Library (published by HMSO).

Interfaces with complementary methodologies have been defined including the Soft Systems Methodology and the Booch TM OO methodology ('SSADM has a sound approach to the design of database-centred systems, very compatible with the Booch Method' Grady Booch, November 1994).

In total the guidance provides a useful insight into how SSADM might be extended to focus on application architectural design and business requirements capture. But the work needed to be consolidated. A major step was taken in late 1994, when the core of SSADM was updated to include:

- business modelling interface to extend the front-end of SSADM and to allow integration with non-IT business requirements and process improvement issues
- work practice modelling and job design
- technique extensions and enhancements to improve the applicability of SSADM techniques and deliverables
- guidance on SSADM customisation to provide a framework for the adaptation of SSADM to support different project environments
- the System Development Template to re-position SSADM within an overall framework for application development and to reduce emphasis on a single Structural Model
- the 3-Schema Specification Architecture to separate the elements of application development (between conceptual modelling, external design and internal design) to enable a flexible and portable specification of the required application
- consolidation of the results of Euromethod and European Modelling Language collaborations.

The updated version of SSADM was published in May 1995. It provides better integration with other CCTA published guidance on IS best practice and enables future incremental development of key areas. The new release builds on and extends the guidance defined in SSADM Version 4. To reflect the new emphasis and coverage, the core method together with related Information System Engineering guidance is called SSADM4+, and the first release of the method under SSADM4+ is version 4.2.

10 What are the Major Elements of SSADM 4.2?

10.1 The Business Focus

The business focus of SSADM is based on a Business Activity Model and a Work Practice Model. In earlier versions of SSADM, business processing and user work practice were expected to be defined outside the scope of SSADM. In practice, this often did not work well. In SSADM 4.2, a Business Activity Model and a Work Practice Model are project products.

The Business Activity Model addresses four of Kipling's 'six honest serving men':

Why — the rationale of the business;
What — the business activities and the dependencies between them;
When — business events and the activities they trigger;
How — the rules for carrying out business processes.

The Work Practice Model deals with the Who and Where. It is a mapping of the Business Activity Model to a user organisation—management structure, user roles, geography. SSADM 4.2 does not mandate how these models are to be produced. The Reference Manual defines their content and the User Guide gives some examples of how they can be developed but practitioners may use other techniques.

The scope of an IT system is defined by the information support needed by the business.

In SSADM, the provision of information support is specified by:

- developing a Logical Data Model (LDM) from the entities and relationships within the scope of the business activities. Eventually, the LDM is turned into a database that simulates the behaviour of those entities and relationships
- testing the LDM for its capability of providing information support, producing access paths that document how the required outputs can be extracted from the LDM.

We can build up the attributes of the LDM entities as a result of this validation, informally (by asking for each entity as we develop access paths, 'what attributes would be needed to support this output') or formally, using Relational Data Analysis on the output specification—usually both, in practice.

For the LDM to provide useful information support, it must be kept up-to-date. We need to identify the changes in the business that have to be simulated in the LDM.

If we know what has to be in the LDM (to provide the outputs needed to support the business activities) we can find out what inputs are needed to keep it up-to-date. These inputs will be related to business events in the business activity model, but not necessarily in one-to-one correspondence. Some business events will not affect the stored data; some may be modelled in simplified form.

We can identify inputs by analysing LDM entities, attributes and relationships to identify what events are needed We can relate the information model to the business by ensuring that input is available for every type of event identified, and find out which business activity provides it.

10.2 SSADM's 'Architecture'

SSADM is positioned in an overall framework, the Systems Development Template (SDT). Within the SDT, the Conceptual Model, External Design and Internal Design directly map onto components of an application and define the 3-schema specification architecture.

The part of the system description described so far—LDM, enquiry processes and update processes—we call the Conceptual Model. It defines the services that have to be provided by the IT system, regardless of:

- what DBMSs the data will be stored in
- what kinds of workstations or styles of dialogues may be provided to users
- what combinations of services any given user may be permitted to use.

The Conceptual Model specifies the Logical Data Model and the services needed to support the Business Activity Model; these include data update and enquiry processes and automated business activities (fig. 1). In Physical Design, Conceptual Model Processes map naturally to servers (although some may be moved to clients for performance).

External Design specifies how IS services will be packaged into functions, and to whom and where they will be delivered. If the user organisation and responsibilities change, the Work Practice Model and External Design will change correspondingly—the Business Activity Model and Conceptual Model should not. In Physical Design, External Design processes map naturally to dialogues and client processes.

The Internal Design is the Physical Design of the data and the data access facilities. It isolates the physical data management, including the location and replication of data, from the server processes (fig. 2).

The Internal Design is a mapping of the LDM onto a data storage and retrieval technology. The physically-stored data is hidden from the update and enquiry process by a process-data interface (PDI), which could be a simple SQL interface to a relational database, or could deal with, for example, data distribution, data replication, data held on a mixture of new databases and legacy systems. The PDI can also insulate the database processes from migration of data between storage technologies (fig. 3).

The Internal Design (and External Design) is developed by design rather than discovery; there could be more than one internal design for the same conceptual model. There are many DBMS technologies available to implement a conceptual model, and many ways to use their facilities to meet the design objectives. In a distributed system, the same data model (or submodel) could be

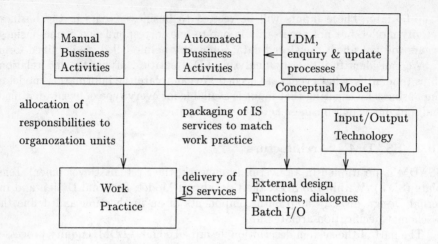

Fig. 1. Conceptual Model

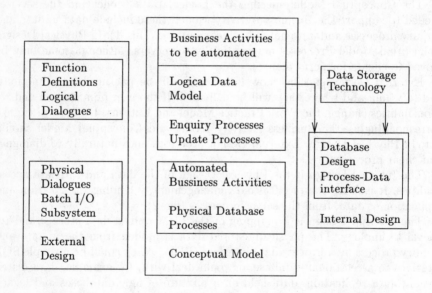

Fig. 2. Internal Design is a mapping to data storage technology

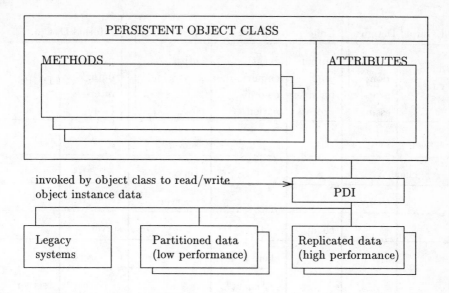

Fig. 3. Process-data interface

implemented (with replicated or partitioned instance data) at different locations, using different DBMSs (fig. 4).

Note that all the schema are implemented. One SSADM user is currently developing an architecture where:

- External Design is generally to be implemented in SmallTalk
- Conceptual Model is generally to be implemented in C or C++
- the PDI will be a mixture of simple SQL and 'wrappers' for legacy databases.

10.3 Customisation Guidance

SSADM Version 4 has a structural model that defines project stages, steps and activities, when products are produced; and where techniques are used.

The SSADM customisation guide was published in 1994. It recognised that a structural model is important for planning, scheduling, work allocation and so forth but also that a single structural model will work only for a narrow range of projects, meeting a set of explicit assumptions. The guide uses a Systems Development Template (fig. 5) rather than a network diagram as the basis for a project structure and describes how to customise SSADM for projects that do not meet the assumptions of the default (version 4) model. This guidance has been incorporated into SSADM4+.

SSADM4+ Version 4.2 defines a minimum set of elements (the data model, the event concept and the 3-Schema Specification Architecture) without which a customisation would not be considered to constitute SSADM. It is expected that

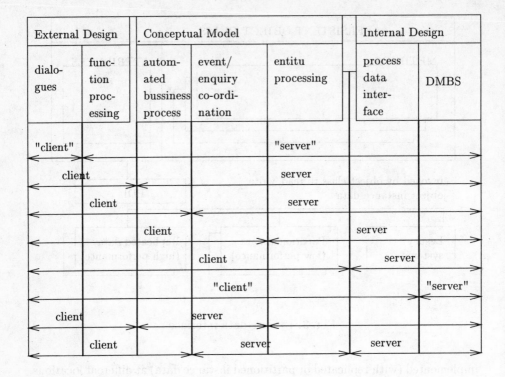

External Design		Conceptual Model			Internal Design	
dialo-gues	func-tion proc-essing	autom-ated bussiness process	event/ enquiry co-ordi-nation	entitu processing	process data inter-face	DMBS
"client"				"server"		
client				server		
	client			server		
		client			server	
			client		server	
			"client"			"server"
client			server			
	client			server		server

Fig. 4. A 'generic client/server architecture' that can map to many implementation architecture

each project will start from this SSADM baseline (using the Reference Manual and User Guide, or guidance provided in the ISE Library) and the customiser will then justify and document changes.

Specification in the System Development Template is based on the 3-schema architecture—supporting a generic client/server style of specification (which can also be mapped onto a non-client/server technical architecture).

11 Incremental Change to SSADM4+

SSADM 4.2 is the first step in an incremental approach to maintaining SSADM in line with application development best practice and changes in technology. It is planned to provide further increments (4.3, 4.4 etc) on approximately an annual basis. At the time of writing, the content and delivery date of SSADM 4.3 were undecided. The most likely date is March 1996. Ongoing development within the SSADM community includes: further OO guidance (including tighter co-ordination of SSADM4+ with Booch/Rumbaugh Design); distributed client/ server; further guidance on RAD; extending the Business Activity Model into

Decision structure	Investigation	User organization	Policies and procedures
Selection of options - strategy - feasibility - business - technical	Business activity model requirements definition investigation of current IS		User culture Project management
	Specification	User rules Work practice model	Architecture: - technical - application - corporate data
	Internal design		
	Conceptual model		Procurement Specialist skills
	External design		Style guides Tools & libraries
	Construction		

Fig. 5. Systems Development Template

business process re-engineering; extending the Work Practice Model into job design and workflow methods.

It has been proposed that SSADM4+ should develop in the following way over the next two years:

- addressing weak spots in Version 4.2
- use of Soft Systems Methodology (used in COMPACT, CCTA's small office system method) as the recommended business process modelling approach
- development of guidance on work practice modelling, including use case, workflow, prototyping and job design
- development of guidance on automating business activities—procedural implementation, rule interpreters, knowledge-based and expert systems
- increasing the emphasis on business-driven requirements definition
- updating COMPACT to address new communication-oriented technologies, such as groupware, workflow, email via external services such as Internet
- extending guidance on customisation of SSADM, to address a wider range of project types and technical environments, and bridging to other methods (eg Booch/OMT)
- enabling compatibility with wider standards—EDIFACT, DCE, CORBA

- guidance on technical and distribution architectures
- upgrading COMPACT to address larger-scale systems, by adapting SSADM guidance for distribution, consistency management
- integrating SSADM and COMPACT as the corresponding technologies converge, to provide common analysis and specification techniques, with different design transformations and technology mappings
- enhancing the SSADM metamodel, supporting more formality in end-product descriptions—to improve tools and increase automated support.

12 PRINCE

Many of the problems of IS development from a customer perspective are well-known, for example striking the balance between vague requirements and over-engineered requirements. In spite of the rise in outsourcing of IS services, the customer cannot transfer the risk that it will not get the IS support it needs.

PRINCE is no magic answer but it does provide a framework for managing IS which helps to reduce risk. With PRINCE the customer has to say what the project is to deliver and the quality criteria the deliverables must meet so that they will know whether and when the project has produced what they asked for.

Roles and responsibilities are assigned and documented. It is impossible to run a PRINCE project without knowing for whom the project is being run and who the owner or user of the new system will be.

A PRINCE project is always directed by a Project Board representing business, user and IT interests. The Project Board needs to have authority to decide direction, allocates resources and takes decisions. Project plans are based on what is to be delivered. Projects are broken down into stages each of which ends with the sign-off by the Project Board of one of more deliverables.

The Project Manager is empowered to run the project without out-of-course reference to the Project Board so long as the project does not exceed its timetable or budget by more than tolerances set by the Project Board. When things go wrong, the Project Board has the right to alter the project plans or even to cancel the project. Even if the project has been outsourced, these controls, by the in-house Project Board, still apply—subject of course to the terms and conditions of the contract.

PRINCE is a very successful product. It is widely used in countries as far afield as Hong Kong, the Czech and Slovak Republics and South Africa.

On conservative estimates, use of PRINCE has saved the UK government tens of millions of pounds and a good deal of political embarrassment. PRINCE (and SSADM) ideas have been fed into the CEC Euromethod project to develop a standard European framework for IS development.

One of the ironies from CCTA's perspective is that we do not know who is using PRINCE (and SSADM). Sometimes organisations themselves do not know they are using PRINCE concepts, because they have tailored it to suit their needs, given it a new name and forgotten where it came from!

Feedback from users received during 1991 to 1993 persuaded CCTA to invest in a new version of PRINCE. The version 2 project started in the summer of 1994 and PRINCE version 2 is due to be launched in April 1996.

13 Changes in PRINCE Version 2

Why change such a successful product? One of the biggest changes since the advent of PRINCE version 1 has been the explosive growth in outsourcing. While PRINCE can be used in outsourcing projects, many users and CCTA itself felt that it should be changed to handle the customer-supplier relationship more naturally and more clearly.

The concept of programme management has assumed greater prominence in the last 2 to 3 years as organisations get to grips with an environment of continual, and often large-scale and complex, change. CCTA in 1993/94 published the only public domain guidance that we know of on programme management.

Whereas projects tend to be narrowly focused on the delivery of something specific, programmes have a wider focus on the realisation of business benefits. Programme management typically assumes that there will be 'moving goalposts' with the Programme Board fully expecting, for example, to change direction, reprioritise projects or never reach the original destination. PRINCE has to be able to work for projects in a programme management environment.

Other important aspects of PRINCE that users wanted to see improved were:

- coverage of risk (CCTA's recent Project Risk guidance is much more comprehensive than PRINCE 1)
- its tailorability (PRINCE 1 does not explain how)
- its applicability to small projects.

There is considerable demand for PRINCE to be easily applicable to non-IT projects, to enable organisations to use a standard approach across projects of all types

14 Conclusion

The range of problems to be solved and the range of technologies to deploy has grown dramatically in the 90s. There are, as always, a range of panaceas being promoted in the market place. Although the technologies are improving and there is emerging agreement on some of the techniques necessary to improve IS, it still requires considerable skill to understand the problem to solve and to select the right tools for the job.

There is an ongoing debate about the role of methods. Some argue that RAD or OO are likely to sweep away structured methods which are characterised as inflexible or out-of-date. But none of the methods available today is appropriate under all circumstances. SSADM is based on 15 years experience (object-orientation has been around for a long-time as well—and there are many similarities, such as with SSADM's behaviour model). There is a place for implementation driven development and for architected, model-driven development. The developer needs to understand the different benefits by looking at the problem situation.

Increasingly, SSADM is becoming a framework for describing system development within which a wide range of techniques and complementary methods can be chosen including architected and implementation driven approaches. This will require considerable investment. For example, the 3-Schema Specification Architecture is the central structure of SSADM4+. It is a client/server architecture and will support the move to 'thin client', but it is generic. Projects will need a target architecture for implementation. This will require additional guidance. As technology continues to advance, this will be an ongoing requirement. Methods and techniques for reusing and re-engineering legacy systems are beginning to emerge. SSADM4+ will need to accommodate them. CCTA has put a great deal

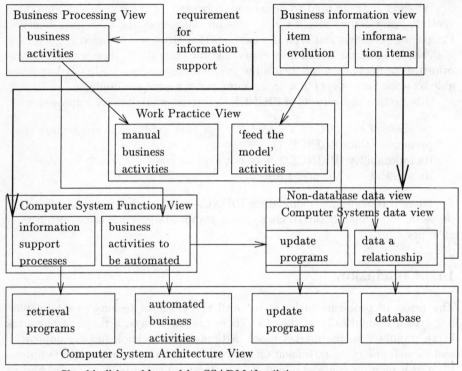

Fig. 6. Standard European framework for IS development

of effort into helping the CEC Euromethod project to develop a standard European framework for IS development (fig. 6). So far, there has been no detailed results. SSADM4+ will cover all of the framework defined by Euromethod and, although different techniques are required, will attempt to cover new and hybrid technologies as well as the more traditional transaction processing IS. We will retain consistency between our methods and Euromethod.

For Further Information:

On the Official SSADM4+ Version 4.2 Reference Set new System Development Library including: Euromethod in Practice—using Version 0 with TAP, PRINCE and SSADM (ISBN 1 85554 707 4)
The RECAST Method for Reverse Engineering (ISBN 0 11 330619 9)

PRINCE Reference Set: Anne Kitson, NCC Blackwell, 108 Cowley Road, Oxford, OX4 1JF Tel: 01865 791100, Fax: 01865 798210, email: akitson@blackwellpublishers.co.uk

On the ISE Library: Applying Soft Systems Methodology to an SSADM Feasibility Study (ISBN 0 11 330601)
Distributed Systems: Application Development (ISBN 0 11 330623 7)
SSADM and Client/Server Applications (ISBN 0 11 3306245)
Managing Reuse (ISBN 0 11 330616 4)
HMSO Publications Centre, PO Box 276, London, SW8 5DT or
HMSO bookshops

For general information about SSADM: Pippa Newman, International SSADM Users Group, 21 Windsor Forest Court, Mill Ride, Ascot, Berkshire, SL5 8LT

For general information about CCTA publications CCTA, Rosebery Court, Thorpe St Andrews Business Park Norwich, NR7 0HS, Tel: 01603 704704, Fax: 01603 704817

For an Introduction to SSADM4+ presented to Data Management '95 at Worcester College, Oxford, 6 April 95 John Hall, Model Systems, 1 Wendle Court, 135 Wandsworth Road London, SW6 2LY, UK

For information about Euromethod: Euromethod Information Office, Excelsiorlaan 48/50 1930 Zaventem, Belgium
Object-oriented analysis and design, Grady Booch, Benjamin/Cummings, (2nd edition, 1994), ISBN 0-80532-5340-2

Formal Methods in Practice:
A Comparison of Two Support Systems for Proof

Juan C. Bicarregui
Brian M. Matthews

Systems Engineering Division
Rutherford Appleton Laboratory

Abstract. This paper discusses the use of formal methods in the light of experience gained from two industrial projects using the B Abstract Machine Notation. An simple example is presented which demonstrates the use of formal specification, refinement and proof in the B-Method, and this is compared with a similar development in VDM. The role of fully formal proof is considered and, in particular, the construction of application specific theories for balancing automation and interaction in the verification of designs is explored.

1 Introduction

This paper relates experiences gained from the use of formal methods in two projects using the B-Method [1] The first project comprised a number of case studies in the use of B. The second Project developed part of a high-integrity system by applying formal techniques to all phases of development using VDM [14] and B for different stages.

For reasons of brevity, only the briefest discription of the projects will be given here. The features of the languages used, and the experiences gained from the developments are more easily conveyed when transposed into a simpler setting free from the clutter of the actual examples.

The rest of this section introduces the B-Method and gives a brief description of the two projects. Section 2 discusses the role of proof in software development. Section 3 describes the B Notation and support for proof through a simple example and Section 4 considers the same example in VDM. Lastly, Section 5 draws on the experience of the two proof systems to give some general principles for the design of proof support tools.

1.1 The B Method, Abstract Machine Notation and Toolkit

The B method[1] is a "model-oriented" formal method providing a unified notation and support tool for many of the activities in the software develop-

---

[1] The "B-Tool" and "Abstract Machine Notation" were originally developed by Jean-Raymond Abrial in conjunction with the Programming Research Group at Oxford University. More recently, support for the B method is being developed by several organisations: our study was based upon the B-Toolkit developed originally at British Petroleum PLC and subsequently by B-Core (UK) Ltd. [2]

ment lifecycle. Modularity is central to the B method and this is achieved by structuring specifications and developments into "Abstract Machines".

Machines are essentially abstract data types with state. The state is defined by the construction of a set theoretic model. Similar constructors to those of other model-oriented notations are available, although, in practice, one tends to use a number of variables each of simple type, rather than building more complex, user-defined, types as encouraged by VDM[14] or Z[20]. State initialisation and invariant conditions are given explicitly.

The invariant and other predicates are given in first order predicate calculus and set theory. The underlying logic is untyped and typing constraints appear as set memberships in the invariant along with the usual relationships between variables. The foundations are based on Zermelo set theory with an axiom of choice, an axiom of infinity, and an axiomatic definition of Cartesian product.

Operations are defined as "Generalised Substitutions". This departure from the before-after predicates of VDM and Z, yields the same expressive power whilst giving the language a more programmatic feel and thus making it more accessible to those with programming, rather than mathematical, experience. For example, a number of constructs are available which mimic the usual notation for assignment, $x := y$ for x becomes equal to y, to give loose specifications such as $x :\in S$ for x becomes any member of S. As in Morgan's Refinement Calculus[18], the semantics of operations are given via weakest preconditions.

The overall specification is structured by using machine composition. Specifications can be built incrementally by using the "sees" and "includes" mechanisms which respectively allow a read-only and read-write extension of a machine by new variables and operations. Data reification is provided by "refinements" and compositional development by "imports". Low-level machines, "implementations", can be written in an executable subset of the language and a library of "base" machines which can be automatically translated into C code.

Validation is supported by an animation facility which allows the developer to interactively "execute" a specification by providing input to simplify non-executable constructs or to resolve non-determinism. Verification is supported through the generation and discharge of proof obligations which ensure the consistency of specifications and the correctness of refinements.

The emphasis on modularity is also applied to proof. The motivation here is that the overall proof task should, as far as possible, be decomposed into proofs concerning individual machines. Once a machine has been proven consistent and correct, those proofs should be valid in any context in which this machine is used as part of a more complex specification. Indeed, it is this aim that has determined the structuring mechanisms available for machines. Thus, a highly compositional method is provided for proof so that, although numerous, proof obligations are mostly simple and the majority can be discharged automatically.

Two proof tools are provided: the "autoprover" is used to automatically discharge the majority of proof obligations using a "rulebase" of built-in rules and tactics; and the "interprover" which is used to interactively explore the failed proof attempt and extend the rulebase with user defined "theories" which provide problem specific rules and tactics.

1.2   B User Trials

"B User Trials" was a collaborative project[2] assessing the effectiveness of the B method in industrial applications. The project encompassed a number case studies which exposed the method and tools to a range of technical problems drawn from both industrial and research sources. It also developed training courses in B, as well as evolving the existing support in the light of requirements drawn from the case studies.

RAL's participation involved two case studies and investigations into the methodology employed in the construction of proofs. The first case study involved the comparison of the B and VDM notations [8] and the second compared B with some aspects of Z [19]. The investigations into proof construction focused on the use of theory structuring to facilitate the proof process [9]. An overview of the project as a whole can be found in [3].

1.3   MaFMeth

The MaFMeth project[3] involved the development of a component of a distributed transaction processing monitor deployed in financially critical banking environments. This software allows applications running on heterogeneous platforms to coordinate their transactional activities via message passing. The monitor provides message storage and transformation services. The development method employed was designed to use formal techniques for as many lifecycle stages as possible, from requirements to implementation.

The toolkit "VDM through Pictures"[10] was used to create an initial abstract specification. With this technique, the specification structures are initially described in a diagrammatic form which is then used to generate a skeletal VDM-SL specification to which further detail is added. The VDM specification was then translated into the B Abstract Machine notation and the B Toolkit used to refine the design towards code. The B to C code generation facilities available in the toolkit were used to generate code from the refined specification. For further descriptions of the system developed, the techniques used and for qualitative and quantitative descriptions of the problems encountered see [23], [24], [4] and [5].

---

[2] The partners in B User Trials were: Lloyds Register of Shipping, Program Validation Limited, the Royal Military College of Science and the Rutherford Appleton Laboratory (RAL). It was part-funded jointly by the U.K. Department of Trade and Industry and the Science and Engineering Research Council (IED4/1/2182).

[3] MaFMeth was a collaboration between the Bull development centre (Hemel Hempstead), Bull S.A. (Paris), B-Core Limited (Oxford) and RAL. It was an "application experiment" funded under the European Strategic Software Initiative (ESSI).

2   The role of proof in software development

The above two developments are perhaps unusual in that they made use of formal proof as well as formal specification and refinement. Generally, proof is perceived as an expensive and highly specialised task which is justifiable only in the most safety-critical applications. If the full benefit of the formal approach is to be reaped by the software engineering industry at large, the development of viable methods to support proof production is essential.

Arguably, the great effort required to produce proofs could be ameliorated by the correct blend of automatic and interactive support for the proof process. If the power of mechanical support to accurately perform symbolic manipulations could be effectively guided by the developers understanding of the application domain then it is reasonable to expect that the vast majority of the proofs that arise in the software engineering context could be constructed with relatively little expense. The effective cost of proof could also be reduced by increasing the degree of reuse in proof production.

This section addresses these two issues in the context of a state-of-the-art in proof support where there is an apparent schism between support facilities for proof which are either highly automatic or highly interactive. It contends that the schism between interactive and automatic systems arises from a failure to realise some basic requirements. A clear exposition of these different principles leads to a framework in which the most appropriate support can be discussed.

This exposition is given by considering the theorem proving support of two systems: the B-Toolkit [2], supporting the B method [1], which takes an semi-automated approach and Mural [15], in its instantiation for VDM [6], a highly interactive support tool for VDM. The two systems are similar in that both support the 'posit and prove' approach, separating the activities of the development of specifications, the generation of proof obligations and the construction of proofs of those obligations. Both also make use of extensive 'base theories' of proof rules supplied with the system and allow for the development of 'user theories' on top of these. However, the two systems differ considerably in their mechanisms for constructing proofs. The B-Toolkit aims for a highly automated approach with user intervention when necessary: in Mural the basic mode of proof is highly user-driven with only minimal automation available.

In order to present the two approaches, we here describe the application of each to a simple example development and from this propose directions to be explored to realise more effective proof support. Whilst concentrating on these two systems, the authors acknowledge the influence of other systems supporting proof within software development. Other systems which have been studied include the RAISE Justification Editor[12], which provides an extensive rule base with rapid search facilities supporting an interactive style of proof; the HOL system[13] which while providing a flat domain of theories, builds rules definitionally thus maintaining a minimal set of primitive assumptions; the Z support tool ProofPower [16], which uses HOL as its basic mechanism and builds theories of Z in a hierarchical store; the W system [22] which provides an alternative proof theory for Z, which has been implemented in [17]; and the Larch Prover

[11] which uses the rewriting paradigm to generate proofs with a high degree of automation.

3 Proof in the B Toolkit

As stated above, the B Abstract Machine Notation is a model-oriented specification language which encourages the use of a highly structured, modular specifications. The structuring mechanisms are such that the overall proof task is decomposed in a compositional way into many smaller proof tasks. Verification of a development is based on the generation and discharge of a number of proof obligations which together ensure consistency and correctness of design. Support for the process is provided by the B-Toolkit.

In practice, many proof obligations are discharged automatically by the "autoprover" leaving others to be tackled interactively with the "interprover". Automated proof is based upon a large *rulebase* of built-in rules and associated control tactics. If the built-in rules and tactics do not automatically discharge the obligations, interactive proof is undertaken in order to develop *user theories* which are then integrated into the automatic process in order that future attempts to autoprove will be successful. The built-in rulebase is not normally visible to the user, but rather a number of 'hooks' are provided whereby user theories for forward and backward proof are called from the automatic process. For the purposes of this discussion, the internal structure of the built-in rulebase has been investigated in greater depth than is normally required by the users of the Toolkit[4].

Within the rule base, rules are organised in a collection of theories arranged to facilitate the automatic discharge of proof obligations. Each theory is a linear collection of rules. Each rule can include a tactic call which directs the prover in the proof search. These included tactic calls encode the dependencies between rule sets. Thus the *theories* are not logical theories in the usual sense, rather they provide a hierarchy of control for guiding the automatic proof. The rule base is in effect a program interpreted by the B-Tool which underlies the B-Toolkit. The logic in the form of rules, and control in the form of special functions, tactics and the theories themselves are all embedded in the language it interprets. The structure of the rule base is dictated by the automation of control in order that the whole should form an efficient program for proving theorems.

To illustrate some of the points made above and to give a flavour for the style of proof in the B-Toolkit, we give a brief description of an example development.

3.1 The Specification

The specification is of a simple operation to remove an element from a set of elements, returning that element. (The example is based on one used in §11.4 of [6].) The specification is given by the AMN machine in figure 1. The state is a

---

[4] The source of the rulebase was made available courtesy of B-Core (UK) Ltd.

single variable which is a set of elements. The initialisation and operations are given by "generalised substitutions" which relate before and after states. Generalised substitutions provide an alternative to the more familiar precondition and postcondition predicates retaining the same potential for abstraction whilst allowing a programmatic style. Here, the initialisation "chooses" an arbitrary set of elements for the state and the operation, *pull*, removes an arbitrary element from the state and returns that element as result. The two substitutions in the body of *pull* are composed with a pseudo-parallelism operator, '||', which is modelled as simultaneous assignment. For more explanation of the notation see [1] or for a comparison with VDM see [8].

The typical B-Toolkit development process generates proof obligations automatically using predefined criteria; for this specification only one proof obligation is generated, namely that the operation maintains the invariant and that is immediately discharged by the autoprover with the built-in rules.

3.2 The Refinement

A refinement of this machine is also given in figure 1. The refinement of the state is by a non-repeating sequence and an index defining the next item to be pulled from the sequence. It is straightforward to define non-repeating sequences in AMN by using the constructor for injective lists, iseq.

The specification and the refinement are related via a coupling relation which is given in the last conjunct of the refinement's invariant. This refinement uses an auxiliary function *remove*, which deletes an element at a particular index from a sequence. *remove* is a constant of the machine defined via a characteristic property in terms of initial and final segments of the sequence.

3.3 Proof Obligations

To prove that this refinement is valid, the B-Toolkit generates sixteen proof obligations: five concern the initialisation; ten concern the operation *pull*; and the other concerns the satisfiability of the property defining *remove*.

Here the autoprover is less successful. Using only the base theories it discharges just three obligations. To proceed further we need to develop some user theories. Let us consider the proof of one obligation. The interprover displays the following:

MACHINE

   pull0 (ELEMS)

VARIABLES

   ss

INVARIANT

   $ss \in \mathbb{P} (ELEMS)$

INITIALISATION

   ANY   *ss1*   WHERE
     $ss1 \in \mathbb{P} (ELEMS)$
   THEN
     $ss := ss1$
   END

OPERATIONS

   $ee \longleftarrow pull \;\; \widehat{=}$
     PRE $ss \neq \varnothing$
     THEN
        ANY   *xx*   WHERE
          $xx \in ss$
        THEN
          $ss := ss - \{ xx \} \;\|$
          $ee := xx$
        END
     END

END

REFINEMENT

   pull1

REFINES

   pull0

CONSTANTS

   remove

PROPERTIES

   $remove \in seq(ELEMS) \times \mathbb{N} \twoheadrightarrow seq(ELEMS)$
   $\wedge$
   $\forall s1 . (s1 \in seq(ELEMS) \Rightarrow$
     $\forall i1 . (i1 \in dom(s1) \Rightarrow$
       $remove(s1 , i1) =$
         $s1 \uparrow (i1 - 1) \frown (s1 \downarrow i1)))$

VARIABLES

   ll , ii

INVARIANT

   $ll \in iseq (ELEMS) \wedge$
   $ii \in \mathbb{N} \wedge$
   $ll = [ ] \Leftrightarrow (ii = 0) \wedge$
   $(ll \neq [ ] \Rightarrow ii \in dom (ll)) \wedge$
   $ss = ran (ll)$

INITIALISATION

   ANY   *ll1*   WHERE
     $ll1 \in iseq (ELEMS)$
   THEN
     $ll := ll1 \;\|$
     IF $ll1 = [ ]$ THEN $ii := 0$
     ELSE $ii :\in dom (ll1)$
     END
   END

OPERATIONS

   $ee \longleftarrow pull \;\; \widehat{=}$
     PRE $ii \neq 0$
     THEN
       $ee := ll (ii) \;\|$
       $ll := remove (ll , ii) \;\|$
       IF $remove (ll , ii) = [ ]$
         THEN $ii := 0$
       ELSE $ii :\in dom(remove(ll,ii))$
       END
     END

Fig. 1. The Specification and Refinement in the B notation.

Current Goal

```
cst(pull$1) &
ctx(pull$1) &
asn(pull$1) &
inv(pull$1) &
pre(pull)
=>
    not(remove(ll$1,ii$1) = <>) &
    iix: dom(remove(ll$1,ii$1))
    =>
        ss-{ll$1(ii$1)} = ran(remove(ll$1,ii$1))
```

This proof obligation states that in the appropriate context (that is the constants, *cst*, context, *ctx*, assertions, *asn*, invariant, *inv* and precondition, *pre*), in the case when the state after the operation in not empty, the coupling relation is maintained by the operation.

Using the Interprover, the failed proof search is explored. The machine hypothesises a succession potential lemmas which would discharge the obligation and the user selects one such suggestion which is believed to be valid. In this case, it is simply the same goal after some antecedants of the final implication are moved into the hypostheses (an application of the deduction theorem)

```
Lemmas - unproved:
 1 ...
 =>
    ss-{ll$1(ii$1)} = ran(remove(ll$1,ii$1))
```

The responsibility for discharging this lemma by defining new rules in a User Theory is deferred for consideration at a later stage and the obligation is discharged.

In attempting to discharge the lemma the interprover displays the point at which the proof fails

```
Library failed to prove:
    ss-{ll$1(ii$1)} = ran(remove(ll$1,ii$1))

Failed to prove lemma
```

It is clear that the prover is unable to break down the right hand side of the equality so the following rewrite rule is added to the user theory

```
THEORY UsersTheory IS

    binhyp(s:iseq(e))  => (ran(remove(s,i))) == (ran(s) - {s(i)})

END
```

This rule instructs the prover to rewrite the expression `ran(remove(s,i))` as `ran(s) - {s(i)}` provided that there is currently a hypothesis of the form `s:iseq(e)`. Note the use of *binhyp* (B-in hypotheses) which not only restricts when the rule is applied, but also enables the metavariable e to be instantiated. Since e does not appear in the matched part of the expression, the prover would not otherwise know how to instantiate it.

When applied in conjunction with the built-in rules, the prover now discharges the lemma:

```
Applying UsersTheory.1 to:
   ran(remove(ll$1,ii$1)) == ran(ll$1)-{ll$1(ii$1)}
```

```
Lemma discharged
```

Future invocations of the autoprover will now make use of the new rule in the proof of this obligation which will therefore now be discharged automatically.

The proof process is therefore a cycle between automatic and interactive proof involving the generation and discharge of "lemmas". Each iteration introduces a new 'level' of user theory thus allowing the addition of only those rules which are necessary to prove the obligations to hand. On the other hand, this style of adding user rules to distinct theories does not encourage their reuse as these theories are not then available for future proofs in another context. There may also be some doubt as to the validity of the new rule which has in effect been added as an axiom of the logic. The rest of this section describes some means by which resuse can be improved and confidence in consistency increased. The next section describes how the same example would be tackled in VDM using Mural.

3.4   Reuse of User Theories

A mechanism using the `#include` facility of the B-Toolkit can be utilised to enhance reuse. User theories are constructed independently in various files and imported into top-level user theories as required. For our example, the following top-level user theory was developed for this example.

```
PROOFMETHOD

  pull1.ref.1

IS
   USETAC
    (UsersSeq~ ; RemoveTheory~; UsersISeq~ ; UserFOLTheory~)~ ,
    (FwdRemoveTheory~;FwdUsersISeq~;FEQL~)~
   END
#include examples/UserLib/userFOL.bck    &
#include examples/UserLib/userISeq.fwd   &
#include examples/UserLib/userISeq.bck   &
#include examples/UserLib/remove.bck
END
```

When control is passed to this theory, it will call the tactic as defined in the USETAC clause which uses other theories defined separately. In this case these theories are imported from other files via #includes.

To prove the obligations several small theories were developed, with both backward and forward rules and rewrite rules. The rules developed fell into three categories.

The first category were rules with logical content equivalent to other rules already in the base theories but which steer the control of the proof in a particular direction not otherwise explored by the existing rulebase. A simple example of this was a variant of the law of contraposition which uses *binhyp* as a control strategy to ensure the rule is only applied when the implication is already in the knowns

```
(((binhyp(p => q)) & not(q)) => not(p))
```

The second class of rules gave properties of language constructs that were not otherwise exploited in the proof. For example, a sequence with non-empty range is non-empty

```
THEORY FwdUsersSeq IS

    ((s : seq(e)) & ({} /= ran(s))) => s /= <>

END
```

In particular a number of rules had to be added involving the type constructor for injective sequences, *iseq*. They included the following

```
THEORY UsersISeq IS
    s:seq(e) & (card(ran(s)) = size(s)) => s:iseq(e)
    . . .

THEORY FwdUsersISeq IS
    ((s : iseq(e)) => (s : seq(e)))
    . . .
```

iseq is a defined construct in AMN but, presumably because it is little used, it is not well covered by the built-in rule base. However, injective sequences are also sequences and so we should expect that the rules used for sequences should also be applied to injective sequences. This is partly expressed by the first forward rule above which derives from a hypothesis that an expression is an injective sequence, the weaker hypothesis that it is an arbitrary sequence, and thus allows the general sequence rules to apply.

The third class of rules are those which concern the specific operators and functions of the specification. For example rules concerning the function *remove* include

```
THEORY RemoveTheory IS

  binhyp(s:seq(e)) & i:dom(s) => remove(s,i) == s/|\(i-1)^(s\|/i)

  binhyp(s:seq(e)) & i:dom(s) => ran(remove(s,i))==ran(s)-{s(i)}

THEORY FwdRemoveTheory IS

  (remove(s,i) = <>) & (i : dom(s)) => (size(s) = 1)

  (s:seq(e)) & (i:dom(s)) => (remove(s,i)) == (s/|\(i-1)^(s\|/i))
```

These domain-specific rules are qualitatively different to the first two categories in that they would have little applicability to proofs of other machines. Note that the rewrite rule which unwinds the definition of *remove* is a reiteration of the properties clause and could be considered to be its definition, whereas the other rules concerning *remove* could probably be derived from it. However, no facility for this kind of layering of definitions and proofs is easily available in the B-Toolkit.

3.5 Proving Lemmas

We have seen that in order to discharge proof obligations we add rules to the user theory. For example, in trying prove an obligation with conclusion of the form

```
remove(ll,ii): iseq(ELEMS)
```

and knowing that `remove(ll,ii)` will be rewritten in terms of initial and final seqments as `(ll/|\(ii-1))^(ll\|/ii)` by the rewrite rule given above, we may wish to add a rule such as the following which will further break down the goal

```
s:iseq(e) & r:iseq(e) & ran(s) /\ ran(r) = {} => (s^r):iseq(e)
```

However, we might feel uncomfortable about adding this rule as an axiom since it is reasonably complex, relying on properties of *iseq* and of various operators on sequences. By adding rules in effect as axioms, one can easily introduce an inconsistency to the rule base or simply restate an obligation as a rule and discharge it immediately without doing any "meaningful" reasoning. It would be preferable to add this rule as a lemma and give a separate proof to verify it. However, currently, the only lemmas which can be conjectured and proven with the toolkit are those generated by the system in the specific circumstances described above.

In order to synthesise the proof of lemmas it is possible to fabricate a rule similar to the desired lemma in such a way that will be proved each time it is applied. This is done by embedding the rule in itself as a hypothesis. For the above example we restate the lemma as

```
(s:iseq(e)) & (r:iseq(e)) & (ran(s) /\ ran(r) = {}) &
!(S,R,E).((S:iseq(E)) & (R:iseq(E)) & (ran(S) /\ ran(R) = {})
            => (S^R):iseq(E))
=> (s^r):iseq(e)
```

This has the same three initial antecedents, but the fourth is a restatement of the whole rule with new variables bound by a universal quantifier ('!' in the ascii syntax). When this rule is called, and the other antecedents are satisfied, the rule itself becomes the next goal to be proved, perhaps by the addition of other, 'simpler' rules to the theory.

In this way lemmas can be hierarchically nested and proven, although clearly, the technique is rather contrived.

4   Proof in VDM with Mural

In many ways the basis of support for proof in the VDM instantiation of Mural [15] [7] is very similar to that described above. Like the B-Toolkit, Mural supports the development of specifications and refinements, the generation of proof obligations and the construction of proofs to discharge them. However, the approach taken to the creation of proofs is quite different. Whilst the emphasis with the B-Toolkit is primarily on automatic proof with user intervention upon failure, the Mural approach is primarily interactive.

The underlying philosophy behind Mural's interactive approach is that by providing a sophisticated user-interface, users are able to maintain their intuition of the problem domain and easily guide the proof in the right direction, whilst the tireless symbolic manipulation of the machine maintains the integrity of the proof. Furthermore, the increased input required on the part of the user in pursuing this interactive approach can be lessened by the construction of a logical hierarchy in the structure of the rule base, which enables the development of application-oriented theories and hence raises the level of reasoning in order to lessen the proof burden. Rules are collected into theories where declarations and axioms are structured along with derived rules and their proofs. Theories are organised in a hierarchical store where each theory inherits from and extends its parents.

In order to facilitate the interactive style of proof, it is crucial to allow the user as much flexibility as possible in the proof process. For example, little prescription is imposed on the order of proof construction. Rules can be used in proofs of other rules before they themselves are proven and so partial proofs can be constructed and viewed as desired. Mechanical support is provided for dependency checking which can be used to ascertain all the assumptions upon which a proof depends, which can then be subjected to inspection or further proof. Thus, unlike the B-Toolkit, there is no prescribed proof cycle in Mural.

A proof consists of a series of lines and boxes: a line consists of a statement together with a justification and a box is a "local proof", which introduces some local assumptions. The proof process is the construction of a "bridge" between hypotheses and conclusion. An incomplete proof can be thought of as having two frontiers: the set of lines that are valid consequences of the hypotheses (the *knowns*), and the set of unjustified lines upon which justification of the conclusion depends (the *goals*). Proof construction can proceed by forward reasoning, backward reasoning or a mixture of the two. Within this user-directed approach to proof construction, machine assistance is provided for the problem of finding suitable rules and definitions to apply. This is done by marking some knowns and goals, and also by selecting part of the logical hierarchy to search. The search will reveal those rules which match and, depending on which rule the user selects, will then make new goals from any other hypotheses in the rule. Lines of reasoning can be temporarily abandoned whilst alternative approaches are attempted, and lemmas conjectured and proved on the fly. Mechanical support will prevent construction of circular arguments, either within a single proof, or the mutual proof of two or more rules. By not prescribing the order in which a proof is constructed, it is possible explore the interesting parts of the proof, where perhaps there is doubt as to the validity of the conjecture, before tackling the more obvious parts.

As in the B-Toolkit, the basic theory store is provided with the system which is augmented as necessary for the application domain. The base theories provide the necessary rules to reason about the basic language constructs, the user theories provide for application-specific rules. A typical Mural Theory store is illustrate in Figure 2. The base theories beginning with propositional logic, incrementally introduce the constructs of the language until the whole of VDM's logic and data is covered. Upon this base, the domain specific theories of the user's specifications and reifications are built. The base theories make no claim to be a complete collection of rules, but just a large number of useful rules covering the language. However, unlike the B-Toolkit approach, in keeping with the logic-oriented structure of the store in Mural, should it be necessary to derive a new rule about one of the basic constructs, the user is encouraged to place that result in its appropriate base theory.

Thus both base and user theories are open to the user for browsing, extension and modification. The possibility of changing the underlying rulebase has, of course, serious repercussions on the maintenance of soundness and consistency. It now becomes necessary to trace dependencies of rules in proofs, to recheck proofs to ensure that they have not become invalid through a change in the rules, and to update them as necessary. In a development situation where specifications are constantly being modified, this form of configuration management can be tedious to do by hand; however, because of the formal nature of the dependencies involved it is easily mechanised. Of course, as in B, ensuring that no inconsistencies are introduced is ultimately the responsibility of the user.

Although primarily interactive in nature, Mural does provide some facilities for the automation of the proof processes by the development of tactics. A simple

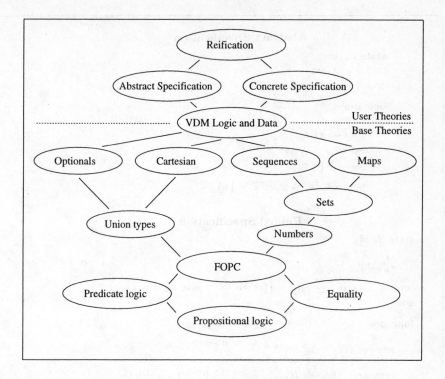

Fig. 2. The Structure of the Mural Theory Store.

tactic language is available whereby common proof strategies can be encoded and rerun in new situation. Tactics are non-destructive as applying them in a given situation can only add new lines to a proof. The application of a tactic may well complete a proof, if not the tactic may still give an extension to the proof which is of use to the user. Typically, the use of a tactic will leave a lot of 'debris' in the form of failed branches in the proof tree. When a proof is complete these can be cleaned up automatically, leaving only those branches that form the 'bridge'. The use of tactics in Mural is explored at length in [21].

4.1 The Example Revisited in Mural

In order to 'reify' the above description of Múral, we describe how one might use it to tackle the example of Section 3. The example is restated in VDM in Figure 3. The abstract specification, refined specification, and retrieve function are given. For brevity, we do not describe how one would use Mural to construct the specification and proof obligations. This can be found in [7].

One of the proof obligations generated in this development is given by the (unproven) rule:

Abstract Specification

state S_a of
$\qquad s \,:\, X\text{-set}$
end

operations

$\quad PULL_a \;() \; x{:}X$
$\quad$ ext wr $s \;:\; X\text{-set}$
$\quad$ pre $s \neq \{\,\}$
$\quad$ post $x \in \overleftarrow{s} \;\wedge\; s = \overleftarrow{s} - \{x\}$

Reified Specification

state S_c of
$\quad l \;:\; X^*$
$\quad i \;:\; \mathbb{N}$
inv $mk\text{-}S_c(l,i) \;\;\triangle\;\;$ if $l = [\,]$ then $i = 0$ else $i \in \text{inds}\, l$
end

functions

$\quad remove : \mathbb{N}_1 \times X^+ \to X^*$

$\quad remove(i,l) \;\;\triangle\;\; l(1,\ldots,i-1) \frown l(i+1,\ldots,\text{len}\, l)$

$\quad$ pre $i \in \text{inds}\, l$

operations

$\quad PULL_c \;() \; x{:}X$
$\quad$ ext wr $l \;:\; X^*$
$\qquad$ wr $i \;:\; \mathbb{N}$
$\quad$ pre $i \neq 0$
$\quad$ post $x = \overleftarrow{l}\,(\,\overleftarrow{i}\,) \;\wedge\; l = remove(\,\overleftarrow{i}\,,\,\overleftarrow{l}\,)$

Retrieve Function

$\quad retr : S_c \to S_a$

$\quad retr(mk\text{-}S_c(l,i)) \;\;\triangle\;\; mk\text{-}S_a(\text{elems}\, l)$

Fig. 3. The *Pull* example in VDM

$$x : X$$
$$mk\text{-}S_a(s) : S_a; \quad mk\text{-}S_c(l, i) : S_c$$
$$mk\text{-}S_a(\overleftarrow{s}) : S_a; \quad mk\text{-}S_c(\overleftarrow{l}, \overleftarrow{i}) : S_c$$
$$mk\text{-}S_a(s) = retr(mk\text{-}S_c(l, i))$$
$$mk\text{-}S_a(\overleftarrow{s}) = retr(mk\text{-}S_c(\overleftarrow{l}, \overleftarrow{i}))$$
$$\overleftarrow{s} \neq \{\}$$

$$PULL\text{-res-obl} \quad \frac{x = \overleftarrow{l}(\overleftarrow{i}) \wedge l = remove(\overleftarrow{i}, \overleftarrow{l})}{x \in \overleftarrow{s} \wedge s = \overleftarrow{s} - \{x\}}$$

This obligation states that the element removed from the concrete state was
an element of the abstract pre-state, but is not an element of the abstract post-
state. Although perhaps a little daunting, the first five lines of hypotheses simply
give the context of the proof and can readily be ignored in the first instance[5].
The system automatically provides a proof template upon which proof proceeds.
It is not appropriate in this paper to give a detailed description of how the proof
progresses, but after some steps of reasoning we may arrive at the partial proof
in figure 4. This partial proof has been generated by working backwards from
the conclusion generating new goals from the hypotheses of each rule applied.
On the right hand side of each line is the name of the rule which justifies it. If
a line has yet to be completed, it is marked by the 'blank' ⟨?? justify ??⟩ and
ellipses are inserted above it as markers for the missing proof steps.

The three rules used thus far in this proof have been found in the base theories
provided with the system. They are

$$=\text{-subs-left}(a) \quad \frac{a : A; \quad a = b; \quad P(b)}{P(a)}$$

$$\wedge\text{-I} \quad \frac{e_1; \quad e_2}{e_1 \wedge e_2}$$

$$\wedge\text{-E-left} \quad \frac{e_1 \wedge e_2}{e_2}$$

However, the equality in line 8 might be justified by the lemma:

$$S_a\text{-}S_c\text{-reif-lemma} \quad \frac{mk\text{-}S_a(s) : S_a; \quad mk\text{-}S_c(l, i) : S_c \quad mk\text{-}S_a(s) = retr(mk\text{-}S_c(l, i))}{s = \mathsf{elems}\, l}$$

which, since it involves operators specific to the specification and reification,
one would expect to have to define and prove in the theory of the reification.
Similarly for line 26, we would require the following lemma which may not be in
the theory store:

---

[5] Note that the appearance of numerous typing assertions throughout the VDM treatment is a consequence of the strong typing and the three-valued logic upon which the
formal system is built. In the untyped logic of B, the corresponding type constraints
appear as proof obligations.

from $x: X$
$\qquad mk\text{-}S_a(s): S_a; \quad mk\text{-}S_c(l, i): S_c$
$\qquad mk\text{-}S_a(\overleftarrow{s}): S_a; \quad mk\text{-}S_c(\overleftarrow{l}, \overleftarrow{i}): S_c$
$\qquad mk\text{-}S_a(s) = retr(mk\text{-}S_c(l, i))$
$\qquad mk\text{-}S_a(\overleftarrow{s}) = retr(mk\text{-}S_c(\overleftarrow{l}, \overleftarrow{i}))$
$\qquad \overleftarrow{s} \neq \{\}$
$\qquad x = \overleftarrow{l}(\overleftarrow{i}) \wedge l = remove(\overleftarrow{i}, \overleftarrow{l})$
$\qquad \cdots$

2	$\overleftarrow{s}: X\text{-set}$	$\langle ??\ \text{justify}\ ?? \rangle$
	$\cdots$	
8	$\overleftarrow{s} = \text{elems}\ \overleftarrow{l}$	$\langle ??\ \text{justify}\ ?? \rangle$
	$\cdots$	
22	$x = \overleftarrow{l}(\overleftarrow{i})$	$\wedge\text{-E-left(h9)}$
	$\cdots$	
24	$s = \text{elems}\ \overleftarrow{l} - \{x\}$	$\langle ??\ \text{justify}\ ?? \rangle$
25	$s = \overleftarrow{s} - \{x\}$	$=\text{-subs-left(a)(2,8,24)}$
	$\cdots$	
26	$\overleftarrow{l}(\overleftarrow{i}) \in \text{elems}\ \overleftarrow{l}$	$\langle ??\ \text{justify}\ ?? \rangle$
27	$x \in \text{elems}\ \overleftarrow{l}$	$=\text{-subs-left(a)(h1,22,26)}$
28	$x \in \overleftarrow{s}$	$=\text{-subs-left(a)(2,8,27)}$
	infer $x \in \overleftarrow{s} \wedge s = \overleftarrow{s} - \{x\}$	$\wedge\text{-I (28,25)}$

Fig. 4. Partial Proof from the VDM Mural System.

$$\boxed{\in\text{-elems-lemma}} \quad \frac{l: A^+; \quad i: \mathbb{N}; \quad i \in \text{inds}\ l}{l(i) \in \text{elems}\ l}$$

In the style encouraged by Mural, one would wish to place this in the appropriate base theory, possibly that for sequences, in order that it should be available for reuse in future proofs. Applying this rule to line 26 adds the following unjustified line to the proof

$$14 \quad \overleftarrow{i} \in \text{inds}\ \overleftarrow{l} \qquad\qquad \langle ??\ \text{justify}\ ?? \rangle$$

and justifying this will in turn require the definition of the following rule in the theory of the concrete specification

$$S_c\text{-theory-lemma} \quad \dfrac{mk\text{-}S_c(l,i)\colon S_c;\quad l \neq [\,]}{i \in \mathsf{inds}\ l}$$

Thus we see that lemmas required to complete the proof are conjectured and justified throughout the store. The proofs of these lemmas may well spawn further lemmas as appropriate.

In this interactive proof style, the user is in control at all times reinforcing his or her intuition. Typically, there are many applications of equality or typing rules which are trivial but tiresome, thus, completing the proof is a rather tedious exercise to undertake by hand. The completed proof and lemmas used therein can be found in the readers notes to [6].

5 Discussion: Balancing Automation and Interaction in Proof of Software Development

Drawing on experience of the two systems described, we now discuss some principles for the design of the proof support tools in general.

As stated above, the logical mechanisms employed by the two systems are similar. Even though the details of the logics used differ, both manage stores of axioms, lemmas, specifications and refinements, derive proof obligations, and build and store proofs; both use a matching mechanism to construct proofs and a searching mechanism to find candidate rules. Both systems distinguish between base theories which define the basic constructs of the logic and language, and users theories which handle constructs specific to particular specifications. All of these features are beneficial.

On the other hand the methodologies used for the proof process are radically different. The B-Toolkit emphasises an automatic approach with user intervention when this process fails as part of a strict proof development cycle; conversely the Mural approach is primarily user driven with some possibility for automation. These complementary styles may to some extent arise from a different focus in the formal tasks supported by the notations; the aspects of VDM supported by Mural place an emphasis on high-level design in particular data reification, while the B-Toolkit is primarily concerned with low-level operation decomposition with a view to code generation. However, to maximise utility and hence lessen the expense of proof, and to make proof acessible to a wider community of practitioners, a means to combine the strengths of each system should be found.

This section discusses requirements for proof support from the two points of view: firstly from the interactive and then the automatic perspective. It then discusses what aspects should be considered in their combination.

5.1 Structures for User Control

User viewing. Perhaps the most salient features required to facilitate user directed proof are *clarity* and *openness*. Only by having a clear view of the goal to be proven and of the logical system available for its proof, can the user effectively guide the proof process. Furthermore, in order to establish confidence in the proof system itself, its logical content must be available to inspection and analysis.

In practice, there is a need to browse the rules in order to find those which are relevant to goal at hand and in order to enable the manipulation of that goal into a form where existing rules can be applied. Equally, when adding new rules to the store, it is necessary to be able to compare the proposed addition with any similar rules which may already exist in order not to reproduce variants of rules already in the base. This form of browsing and comparison is basically an informal activity and is best left under the control of the user.

Clearly, in order to avoid overwhelming the user by presenting a large number of rules as a homogeneous mass, the rules need to be stored in a structure which the user can navigate in an intuitive fashion. One aspect of a rule that is immediately obvious is the logical constructs it manipulates. Thus this would seem to be a sensible basis for a structuring mechanism designed to aid user viewing.

Reuse. Another motivation for the organisation of the theory store in a transparent, hierarchical structure is to facilitate the reuse of rules. There is a clear temptation when presented with unproven obligations to develop their proofs by whatever means may may come to mind. For example, one might introduce rules into a user theory which involve the specific application constants and object variables used in the specification. Such rules will not be applicable to other similar constructs. Clearly, where possible, it is a sound investment to prove the results in a more general form, perhaps by replacing some specification constants by logical metavariables, and to place them in the global theory store in such a way that they can be reused in future proofs. If these rules are to play their full role in the development of future proofs, some mechanism must be provided for them to take their place in the structures of the store so that they are later incorporated into both interactive and automatic proof.

5.2   Structures for Automatic Control

Efficient and Accurate Search. When control is passed to the machine, the important criteria for structuring the theory store relate to the search for matching rules and selection of those rules which give the maximum possibility of successful proof. The machine has no intuition for which construct needs to be manipulated, but rather requires efficient mechanisms to find rules which may have similar applicability. For example, in backward proof it may be useful to group rules according to the top symbol in the consequent expression, whereas in rewriting it is the structure of the left hand sides which are of interest.

It is also possible to develop *oracles* for sub-theories such as propositional logic or arithmetic, or canonical sets of rewrite rules which can be embedded into a program which exploits some efficient decision procedure. However, such mechanisms will need to access rules which are distributed throughout the store. For instance, typing rules which might be found distributed among the theories of the individual operators, will all need to be available to a type checking oracle which would act on all types of expressions.

Managing Change. For both interactive and automatic proof there is a need for the machine to recognise dependencies between the formal objects in order to maintain the integrity of the system as a whole. In a development environment where specifications are continually evolving, it is particularly important to minimise the degree of user participation in the re-establishment of this integrity under change. When a modification occurs, the system should to a large extent be able to re-establish the consistency of proofs without intensive user involvement. Where user intervention is necessary a flexible mechanism to support reproof is required.

5.3 The User/Machine Interaction

It is clear that for an efficient and comprehensible proof methodology, a balance of control is required between user and machine. Control of the proof process must therefore be able to pass smoothly between the user and machine in both directions.

Graceful Failure. When a machine proof fails and control is returned to the user, it is necessary to present the current state of the proof in such a form which will facilitate understanding of why the failure has occurred and how best to proceed. In practice this may mean that the expressions involved at the 'frontiers' of the proof will need to be in a form as close as possible to their presentation in the original statement. Many systems, notably where rewriting has been used, present the current state in a normal form which is far removed from the original expressions and often unintelligible. It is worthwhile for the machine to devote some effort to *failing gracefully.* This will involve presenting the proof state in a user-friendly form and providing some mechanism for exploring the search that has been undertaken in order to find the best point for the user to take over control of the proof process.

Aiding the Autoprover. On the other hand, in moving from interactive to automatic proof, it is important that progress made by the user should then be exploitable by the mechanism. To achieve this, for example, new rules may need to be annotated in some way in order that they are incorporated appropriately into the automated aspects of the system.

6   Conclusion: an Architecture for Proof Engineering

This paper has described the use of the B-Method and the tools for proof available in the B-Toolkit, and has compared them to the support for proof available for VDM in Mural. It has drawn out requirements for proof support that arise from the needs of proof.

Although these two approaches to proof place contrary requirements on the design of the theory store, there is no reason why suitable architecture should not accommodate both by providing complementary structuring mechanisms on the same logical content. One possible basis for such a system could be in the use established database technology as a platform providing multiple views on the same formal entities. The increase in effectiveness that an effective synthesis between automation and interaction could bring would encourage the widespread utilisation of formal proof as a viable industrial technology.

7 Acknowledgements

I would like to thank my collegues also involved in projects described here. In particular, Jeremy Dick and Eoin Woods were central to the MaFMeth project, and Brian Ritchie and Brian Matthews in B User Trials.

References

1. J-R Abrial. *Deriving Programs from Meaning.* Prentice Hall International, 1995. To appear.
2. B-Core (UK) Ltd. *B-Toolkit User's Manual,* release version 2.0 edition, 1994. A full release of the B Toolkit is now available. For details, contact Ib Sorensen, B Core (UK) Ltd, Magdalen Centre, Robert Robinson Avenue, The Oxford Science Park, Oxford OX4 4GA. Tel: +44 865 784520. E-mail: Ib.Sorensen@comlab.ox.ac.uk.
3. J.C. Bicarregui, et al. Formal Methods into Practice: case studies in the application of the B-Method, B User Trials Deliverable, D 18, Rutherford Appleton Laboratory. Submitted to the Software Engineering Journal.
4. J.C. Bicarregui, J. Dick and E. Woods, Supporting the length of formal development: from diagrams to VDM to B to C Proceedings, 7th International Conference on: Putting into practice method and tools for information system design", Nantes (France), October '95, IUT de Nantes, H. Habrias (Editor) 1995.
5. J.C. Bicarregui, J. Dick and E. Woods, Qualitative analysis of an application of formal methods. Submitted to FME'96, Springer-Verlag.
6. J C Bicarregui, J S Fitzgerald, P A Lindsay, R Moore, and B Ritchie. *Proof in VDM: A Practitioner's Guide.* Springer-Verlag, 1994.
7. J C Bicarregui and B Ritchie. Reasoning about VDM developments using the VDM support tool in Mural. In *Proc. of VDM'91: Formal Software Development Methods,* volume 552 of *Lecture Notes in Computer Science.* Springer-Verlag, 1991.
8. J C Bicarregui and B Ritchie. Invariants, frames and postconditions: a comparison of the VDM and B notations. In J C P Woodcock and P G Larsen, editors, *Proc. of Formal Methods Europe'93: Industrial Strength Formal Methods,* volume 670 of *Lecture Notes in Computer Science,* pages 162–182. Springer-Verlag, 1993.
9. D. Clutterbuck, J.C. Bicarregui and B. Matthews. Experiences with Proof in Formal Development. Submitted to FME'96, Springer-Verlag.
10. Jeremy Dick and Jerome Loubersac. *A Visual Approach to VDM: Entity-Structure Diagrams.* Technical Report DE/DRPA/91001, Bull, 68, Route de Versailles, 78430 Louveciennes (France), January 1991.

11. Stephen J Garland and John V Guttag. An overview of LP, the Larch Prover. In N Dershowitz, editor, *Proc. 3rd Conference on Rewriting Techniques and Applications.*, volume 355 of *Lecture Notes in Computer Science*, pages 137–151. Springer-Verlag, 1989.

12. Chris George and Søren Prehn. The RAISE Justification Handbook. Draft Manual, 1993.

13. M J C Gordon and T F Melham. *Introduction to HOL.* Cambridge University Press, 1993.

14. C B Jones. *Systematic Softare Development using VDM.* Prentice Hall International, 2nd edition, 1990.

15. C B Jones, K.D. Jones, P.A.Lindsay, R.Moore. Mural; A formal Development Support Environment. IBSN 3-540-19651-X, Springer Verlag, 1991.

16. R B Jones. Methods and tools for the verification of critical properties. In R Shaw, editor, *Proc. of 5th BSC-FACS Refinement Workshop.* Springer-Verlag, 1992.

17. Andrew Martin. Encoding W: A Logic for Z in 2OBJ. In J C P Woodcock and P G Larsen, editors, *Proc. of Formal Methods Europe'93: Industrial Strength Formal Methods*, volume 670 of *Lecture Notes in Computer Science*, pages 462–481. Springer-Verlag, 1993.

18. C. Morgan. *Programming From Specifications.* Prentice Hall, 1990.

19. B. Ritchie, J. Bicarregui, and H. Haughton. Experiences in Using the Abstract machine Notation in a GKS Case Study. In *Proc. of FME'94*, volume 873 of *Lecture Notes in Computer Science.* Springer-Verlag, 1994.

20. J.M. Spivey. *The Z Notaion (Second Edition).* Prentice Hall, 1993.

21. Sunil Vadera. *Heuristics for Proofs.* PhD thesis, University of Manchester, Manchester M13 9PL, UK, 1992.

22. J C P Woodcock and S Brien. W: a Logic for Z. In *Procs of the 6th Z User Group Meeting.* Springer-Verlag, 1992.

23. E. Woods. M.Sc. Thesis. University of Manchester, 1995.

24. E. Woods and J. Dick. Lessons Learned Applying Formal Methods to Systems Software Development. IEE Software, to appear.

Development of Safety-Critical Real-Time Systems[*]

Hans Rischel[1], Jorge Cuellar[2], Simon Mørk[1],
Anders P. Ravn[1], Isolde Wildgruber[2]

[1] Dept. of Computer Science, Technical University of Denmark, Lyngby
e-mail: `sm,apr,hr@id.dtu.dk`
[2] Siemens Corporate Research and Development, ZFE T SE 11, Munich,
e-mail: `Jorge.Cuellar, Isolde.Wildgruber@zfe.siemens.de`

Abstract. This paper presents an approach to the development of safety-critical real-time systems linking from the Requirements Language developed in the ESPRIT Project ProCoS to the Temporal Language of Transitions (TLT) specification language developed at Siemens Corporate Research. A system is defined by a conventional mathematical model for a dynamic system where application specific states denote functions of time. Requirements are constraints on the system states, and they are given by formulas in duration calculus (DC), a real-time interval logic. A functional design is a distributed system consisting of sensors, actuators, and a program which communicate through shared states. The sensors and actuators are specified in DC while the program is specified in TLT. The design as a whole is linked together semantically by using a DC semantics for TLT. Verification is a deduction showing that a design implies requirements. The TLT specification is the basis for developing the control program. The method is illustrated by a steam-boiler example.

1 Introduction

A developer of software for a complex control application faces a number of difficult tasks: first, the application must be understood in sufficient detail to formulate the essential requirements; then one must find an appropriate architecture that gives a modular structure to the overall system; and finally descriptions must be written for components that are assumed given, while design specifications are written for software components.

When such a system is safety-critical, there are strict demands for traceability and visibility throughout the development, i.e., the development path must be well documented. To some software developers the word documentation brings memories of endless mountains of prose, diagrams, etc. – only vaguely connected to the actual system developed. The development technique presented here, tries

---

[*] Supported by the CEC under the ESPRIT BRA Project No. 7071: **ProCoS II**, by the Danish Technical Research Council under the **Codesign** Project, and by the german BMFT project **KORSYS**.

to combat these syndromes by selecting a few succinct notations suited for particular tasks in the development, and linking them together through an underlying mathematical theory.

The application domain of complex control systems is closely associated with control engineering, because this will be applied in the design of the control object – the *plant*. The first notation selected is thus the conventional model language for dynamic systems: states as functions of time. In order to get a precise interface to control engineering, our specification language must include concepts of analysis like differential or integral calculus. A complex system is, however, characterized by having discrete changes in operation, caused by operator interventions, failing components, or changing environments. Therefore, the specification language must also be able to specify discrete state changes over time. The notation that we have selected is therefore Duration Calculus (DC), a real-time interval logic, which incorporates integral calculus into reasoning about patterns of consecutive state changes. This language is highly expressive, and well suited to document requirements including assumptions about the plant.

For purpose of design, one must consider further aspects like a module notation and a program specification notation. The module notation used is based on Z schemas because the logical operators on such schemas correspond well with a logic based specification language like DC.

The program design notation TLT [4, 9, 11, 12, 13, 14, 15] is basically a program logic like TLA [27, 1] or Unity [10] and is selected because it maps conveniently to programs, and links in a simple manner to temporal logics like DC.

In summary, the main points of this paper is to illustrate a mathematically coherent development path for complex control systems. We think that the languages selected are well suited for their specific purposes, but freely admit that other choices could be made with a similar rationale as the one given above, cf. the proceedings [16, 25].

Overview. The remaining sections of this paper are organized as follows: Section 2 introduces the system model and Duration Calculus illustrated by the running example of the steam boiler. Section 3 introduces the controller architecture and Temporal Logic of Transitions. Sensor, actuators and control program for a high level design of the steam boiler are specified. In section 4 it is proved that the design implements the requirements under certain assumptions which are made explicit by the proofs. The proofs combine reasoning from both notations. Section 5 contains the complete specification of the program covering also the failure supervision and reporting which where abstracted from in section 3. Section 6 describe the translation of the program specification to a C program, and the validation using a simulator of the steam boiler.

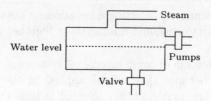

Fig. 1. Steam boiler system

2 System Model and Requirements

We illustrate our approach through a running example: the computer controlled steam-boiler problem from the Dagstuhl Seminar, June 1995 (cf. [2] and [3]). The problem is to control the level of water in a steam-boiler. It is important that the system works correctly because the quantity of water present when the steam-boiler is working has to be neither too low nor to high; otherwise the steam-boiler or the turbine sitting in front of it might be seriously affected. The physical system comprises the following units as depicted in figure 1:

– The steam-boiler.
– A device to measure the quantity of water in the steam-boiler.
– Pumps to provide the steam-boiler with water.
– A device to measure the quantity of steam which comes out of the steam-boiler.
– A valve for evacuation of water from the steam-boiler. It serves only to empty the steam boiler in its initial phase.

It should be noted that the *heating* of the boiler is *not* controlled by the system, so the only way of coping with variations in the water level is by opening or closing the pumps.

2.1 System Identification

The first step in formalizing requirements to a system is a *system identification* (cf. [28]) where control engineers build a mathematical model of the system. This is done by use of the well-known *time-domain model* (cf. [30]) where a system is described by a collection of states (often called state variables) that are functions of *time*, modeled by the set of non-negative real numbers

$$Time \stackrel{def}{=} \{x : \mathbf{R} \mid x \geq 0\}$$

For the steam boiler system we use the states shown in the following schema in the Z style

```
┌─ BoilerStates ──────────────────────────────────────
│ BoilerParams
│ q : Time → [0, C]   (Water level (liters))
│ v : Time → [0, W]   (Quantity of steam (liters/sec))
│ p : Time → [0, P]   (Total throughput of pumps (liters/sec))
│ d : Time → [0, D]   (Throughput of valve (liters/sec))
└─────────────────────────────────────────────────────
```

where $[a, b]$ denote a closed interval, $[a, b] \overset{\text{def}}{=} \{x : \mathbf{R} \mid a \leq x \wedge x \leq b\}$, and where the parameters C, W, etc. are specified in the schema

```
┌─ BoilerParams ────────────────────────────────────────
│   C : R          (Max water level)
│   W : R          (Max quantity of steam)
│   P : R          (Max total throughput of pumps)
│   D : R          (Max throughput of valve)
│   U₁, U₂ : R     (Limits for steam gradient)
│ ─────────────────────────────────────────────────────
│   C > 0 ∧ W > 0 ∧ P > 0 ∧ D > 0 ∧ U₁ > 0 ∧ U₂ > 0
└───────────────────────────────────────────────────────
```

$BoilerParams$
$C : \mathbf{R}$ (Max water level)
$W : \mathbf{R}$ (Max quantity of steam)
$P : \mathbf{R}$ (Max total throughput of pumps)
$D : \mathbf{R}$ (Max throughput of valve)
$U_1, U_2 : \mathbf{R}$ (Limits for steam gradient)

$C > 0 \wedge W > 0 \wedge P > 0 \wedge D > 0 \wedge U_1 > 0 \wedge U_2 > 0$

This schema contains a set of constraints expressing that the parameters should be positive numbers.

The data types in the schema $BoilerStates$ express some constraints on the range of values for the states, for instance that the water level is bounded by 0 and C, i.e. $0 \leq q(t) \leq C$ for $t \in Time$. Further properties of the system are preservation of mass, i.e. the change in the water level is equal to the throughput of the pumps minus the quantity of steam and minus the throughput of the valve

$$\forall t : Time \bullet q(t) = p(t) - v(t) - d(t)$$

and ranges for the change in the quantity of steam

$$\forall t : Time \bullet -U_2 \leq \dot{v}(t) \leq U_1$$

It turns out that these formulas are more useful in forms where we integrate over an arbitrary time interval $[b, e]$ with $0 \leq b \leq e$. For the first formula we get

$$Mass \overset{\text{def}}{=} \forall b, e : Time \bullet q(e) - q(b) = \int_b^e p(t)\,dt - \int_b^e v(t)\,dt - \int_b^e d(t)\,dt$$

For the second formula we get

$$\forall b, e : Time \bullet v(e) - v(b) \in [-(e - b)U_2, (e - b)U_1]$$

and by a further integration in e

$$\forall b, e : Time \bullet \int_b^e v(t)\,dt - (e - b)v(b) \in [-\tfrac{1}{2}(e - b)^2 U_2, \tfrac{1}{2}(e - b)^2 U_1]$$

If we have an estimate of $v(b)$, say $v(b) \in [v_1, v_2]$, then these formulas can be used to give estimates of $v(e)$ and $\int_b^e v(t)\,dt$ in terms of $e - b$ and $[v_1, v_2]$

$$Steam_1 \overset{\text{def}}{=} \forall b, e : Time, V : Interval \bullet v(b) \in V \Rightarrow v(e) \in G(V, e - b)$$
$$Steam_2 \overset{\text{def}}{=} \forall b, e : Time, V : Interval \bullet v(b) \in V \Rightarrow \int_b^e v(t)\,dt \in F(V, e - b)$$

where $Interval$ denotes the set of closed subintervals of the real numbers

$$Interval \overset{\text{def}}{=} \{X \mid \exists a, b : \mathbf{R} \bullet a \leq b \wedge X = \{x : \mathbf{R} \mid a \leq x \wedge x \leq b\}\}$$

and where $F : Interval \times \mathbf{R} \to Interval$ and $G : Interval \times \mathbf{R} \to Interval$ denote the functions

$$G([v_1, v_2], y) \overset{\text{def}}{=} [v_1 - yU_2 , v_2 + yU_1]$$
$$F([v_1, v_2], y) \overset{\text{def}}{=} [y\,v_1 - \tfrac{1}{2}y^2 U_2 , y\,v_2 + \tfrac{1}{2}y^2 U_1]$$

2.2 Duration Calculus

As illustrated above it is possible to formalize properties of systems using predicate logic and mathematical analysis. However, formal reasoning is rather cumbersome when all formulas contain several quantifiers. This is the rationale for having a temporal logic: it will implicitly quantify over the time domain.

Syntax. The syntax of Duration Calculus distinguishes (*duration*) *terms*, each one associated with a certain type, and (*duration*) *formulas*. Terms are built from names of elementary states like q or v, *rigid variables* representing time independent logical variables and are closed under arithmetic and propositional operators. Examples of terms are $p = P$ and $d \neq 0$ of Boolean type and $p - d$ of real type.

Terms of type real are also called *state expressions* and terms of Boolean type are called *state assertions*. We use f for a typical state expression and P for a typical state assertion.

Duration terms are built from $\mathbf{b}.f$ and $\mathbf{e}.f$ denoting the *initial* and *final value* of f in a given interval, and $\int f$ denoting the *integral* of f in a given interval. For a state assertion P, the integral $\int P$ is called the *duration* because it measures the time P holds in the given interval.

Duration formulas are built from duration terms of Boolean type and closed under propositional connectives, the chop connective, and quantification over rigid variables and variables of duration terms. We use D for a typical duration formula.

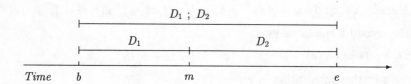

Fig. 2. Timing diagram for chop.

Semantics. The semantics of Duration Calculus is based on an *interpretation* $\mathcal{I}$ that assigns a fixed meaning to each state name, type and operator symbol of the language, and a time interval $[b, e]$. For given $\mathcal{I}$ and $[b, e]$ the semantics defines what domain values duration terms and what truth values duration formulas denote. For example, $\int f$ denotes the integral $\int_b^e f(t)\,dt$, $\mathbf{b}.f$ denotes the limit from the right in b, and $\mathbf{e}.f$ denotes the limit from the left in e.

A duration formula D *holds* in $\mathcal{I}$ and $[b, e]$, abbreviated $\mathcal{I}, [b, e] \models D$, if it denotes the truth value *true* for $\mathcal{I}$ and $[b, e]$. D is *true* in $\mathcal{I}$, abbreviated $\mathcal{I} \models D$, if $\mathcal{I}, [0, t] \models D$ for every $t \in$ *Time*. A *model* of D is an interpretation $\mathcal{I}$ which makes D true, i.e. with $\mathcal{I} \models D$. The formula D is *satisfiable* if there exists an interpretation $\mathcal{I}$ with $\mathcal{I} \models D$.

Examples. The modalities $\diamond$ (on some subinterval) and $\square$ (on any subinterval) are defined by

$$\diamond D \stackrel{\text{def}}{=} true \; ; \; D \; ; \; true$$
$$\square D \stackrel{\text{def}}{=} \neg \diamond (\neg D)$$

so $\diamond D$ denotes *true* on an interval if the interval can be chopped into three subintervals such that D denotes *true* on the middle interval, i.e. if there is *some subinterval* where D denotes *true*. A similar argument shows that $\square D$ denotes *true* on an interval if D denotes *true* on *any subinterval*.

The above equations for preservation of mass and for the range of steam gradient can be expressed in DC formulas: using the definition of **b.**, **e.** and duration $\int$ we find that the formula under the quantifier in the *Mass* formula correspond to the DC formula

$$\mathbf{e}.q - \mathbf{b}.q = \int p - \int v - \int d$$

This formula should hold on *any* time interval $[b, e]$, i.e. for any subinterval of any interval $[0, t]$

$$Mass \stackrel{\text{def}}{=} \square(\mathbf{e}.q - \mathbf{b}.q = \int p - \int v - \int d)$$

The length of the interval is the duration $\int 1$ of the constant function 1. This duration is used so often, so it is abbreviated ℓ, pronounced "the length". The terms $e - b$ in the above *Steam$_1$* and *Steam$_2$* formulas denotes the length so the formulas become

$$Steam_1 \stackrel{\text{def}}{=} \square(\forall V : Interval \bullet \mathbf{b}.v \in V \Rightarrow \mathbf{e}.v \in G(V, \ell))$$
$$Steam_2 \stackrel{\text{def}}{=} \square(\forall V : Interval \bullet \mathbf{b}.v \in V \Rightarrow \int v \in F(V, \ell))$$

We collect the system identification of the boiler in the schema

---
Boiler

BoilerStates
BoilerParams

$Mass \wedge Steam_1 \wedge Steam_2$

2.3 Requirements

The controller operates in two phases: an initial phase *not ready* with no production of steam and with the goal of operating the pumps and the valve such that the water level q gets inside the limit interval $M = [M_1, M_2]$, and a normal phase *ready* with production of steam and with the goal of operating the pumps such that the water level is kept inside the limit interval while the valve is kept closed.

In the Dagstuhl problem text [2] these basic goals are intertwined with failure detection, failure reporting, and fault tolerant operation. These further features depends on a particular selection of components for a specific design of a steam boiler system. We are, however, able to state the basic requirements to the system without presenting a design by proceeding as follows

- Requirements are stated in the form: *Assumption* $\Rightarrow$ *Commitment* where *Commitment* is written down but where *Assumption* is left open for a later stage.
- Further requirements concerning the equipment (e.g. failure detection and failure reporting) may be added at a later stage.

Abstraction means under-specification – only essential safety and operational features are considered here. Further design detail are given in the program.

The controller extends the physical system with an extra state *ready* (program ready) and various parameters

---
Controller

ready : *Time* $\rightarrow$ **Bool**	
M : *Interval*	(Limit interval for water level)
T : **R**	(Max $\neg$*ready* time)
ε : **R**	(Max inaccuracy on water level)

As mentioned above we do only state the commitments $Commit_i$ of the requirements

$$Req_i \stackrel{\text{def}}{=} Assumpt_i \Rightarrow Commit_i \quad i = 1, \ldots 5$$

The assumptions $Assumpt_i$ are later derived when the design is verified.

The first commitment states that the controller should start in the $\neg ready$ phase, i.e. that $\neg ready$ is *true* in an initial time interval.

For an arbitrary assertion P, it is obvious that it is *true* in an interval, just when the duration $\int P$ is equal to the length of the interval. Recalling that ℓ denotes the length of the interval, the property that P is *true* is thus given by the formula $\int P = \ell$. This holds trivially for a point interval, so we consider proper intervals of positive length. These two properties are combined in the abbreviation

$$\lceil P \rceil \stackrel{\text{def}}{=} \int P = \ell \wedge \ell > 0$$

We use the formula $\lceil \rceil$ to denote a point interval

$$\lceil \rceil \stackrel{\text{def}}{=} \ell = 0$$

The first commitment for the controller can now be expressed in the formula

$$Commit_1 \stackrel{\text{def}}{=} \lceil \rceil \vee \lceil \neg ready \rceil ; \ true$$

It expresses that any time interval $[0, t]$ is either a point or can be chopped into two parts such that $\neg ready$ is *true* on the first part. (Note, that the chop operator has higher priority than disjunction.)

The second commitment states that the controller stays in the phase *ready* once it has been reached. In order to assure this it suffices to know that whenever *ready* is *true* in a time interval $[b, e]$ then it will also be *true* in some succeeding interval $[e, e+\delta]$.

We introduce the abbreviation $D \longrightarrow \lceil P \rceil$ for this property for arbitrary duration formula D and assertion P. Using this the second commitment is

$$Commit_2 \overset{\text{def}}{=} \lceil ready \rceil \longrightarrow \lceil ready \rceil$$

Note, that a violation of the property $D \longrightarrow \lceil P \rceil$ would be the existence of an interval with D followed by $\neg P$, i.e.

$$D \longrightarrow \lceil P \rceil \;\Leftrightarrow\; \neg \Diamond (D ; \lceil \neg P \rceil)$$

The third commitment states that the controller will proceed to phase *ready* within time T. This is expressed in the formula

$$\lceil \neg ready \rceil \wedge \ell = T \longrightarrow \lceil ready \rceil$$

which is written

$$\lceil \neg ready \rceil \overset{T}{\longrightarrow} \lceil ready \rceil$$

Commitment 4 states that the valve is kept closed in phase *ready*

$$Commit_4 \overset{\text{def}}{=} \lceil ready \rceil \longrightarrow \lceil d = 0 \rceil$$

and commitment 5 that the water level is kept inside the interval M in phase *ready*

$$Commit_5 \overset{\text{def}}{=} \lceil ready \rceil \longrightarrow \lceil q \in M \rceil$$

We collect the requirements in the schema

```
┌─ Requirements ──────────────────────────────────
│  Boiler
│  Controller
├─────────────────
│  Req₁ ∧ Req₂ ∧ Req₃ ∧ Req₄ ∧ Req₅
└─────────────────────────────────────────────────
```

$Req_1 \wedge Req_2 \wedge Req_3 \wedge Req_4 \wedge Req_5$

3   Controller Architecture

A controller consists of sensors and actuators, and a control program. The control program reads values from the sensors and computes values which are output to the actuators. For the steam boiler we define a top level controller with "intelligent" sensors and actuators for water level, pumps, valve and ready indicator, and a clock as shown in Figure 3. We have abstracted from the reporting of errors and error modes, but this can be added later as an extension of the specification. Also at this stage we do not describe the internal structure of the

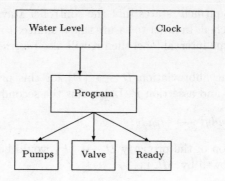

Fig. 3. Top level architecture for the steam boiler.

intelligent sensors and actuators, but this can be done as an refinement of the specifications.

The exchange of data between the components takes place when the program is active. Each activation of the program comprises

1. reading values from sensors
2. computing of new values
3. writing values to actuators

upon which the program awaits the next activation. We will assume that the time spend during each program activation is ignorable compared to other reaction times in the system, so that the reading, computing and writing in each activation of the program can be considered to all take place at the same time instant.

3.1 Program Variables

Variables
Read	*#a:*	Nat
Read	*adj(1):*	Interval
Private	*pRd:*	Bool
Private	*pCmd, vCmd:*	Bool

Fig. 4. Program variable declarations in TLT.

Program variables are used for the communication between program and sensors or actuators, and for communication internally in programs. A set of TLT declarations of program variables is shown in Figure 4. It declares a set

$$Vars \stackrel{\text{def}}{=} \{\#a, adj(1), pRd, pCmd, vCmd\}$$

of variable names with associated types and indicates a division of the variables into read, private and local variables (the example has no local variables).

The program variables define states

```
ProgramVars
```
$\#a$:	$Time \to \mathbf{N}$	(Activation signal from clock)
$adj(1)$:	$Time \to Interval$	(Value interval from water level sensor)
pRd :	$Time \to \mathbf{Bool}$	(Program ready signal to actuator)
$pCmd$:	$Time \to \mathbf{Bool}$	(Command to pump actuator)
$vCmd$:	$Time \to \mathbf{Bool}$	(Command to valve actuator)

where the *read* and *private* variables give the *interface* between the program and the other components while the *local* variables are internal to the program.

3.2 Synchronization of Components

The steam boiler is a *sampled* system where all components are activated simultaneously for exchange of information. Other systems may be *event driven* where individual components can be activated at different points of time by events from the environment or from other components.

The periodic activation of components is implemented by means of an *activation clock* which performs "ticks" with period τ. We model the ticks by the increments of the *activation counter* $\#a$

1. The value of $\#a$ is changing only by increments

$$AC_1 \stackrel{\text{def}}{=} \lceil \#a = n \rceil \longrightarrow \lceil \#a = n \vee \#a = n + 1 \rceil$$

2. The value of $\#a$ will change after at most time τ

$$AC_2 \stackrel{\text{def}}{=} \lceil \#a = n \rceil \stackrel{\tau}{\longrightarrow} \lceil \#a \neq n \rceil$$

3. The value of $\#a$ is stable for time τ after each increment

$$AC_3 \stackrel{\text{def}}{=} \lceil \#a \neq n \rceil \; ; \; \lceil \#a = n \rceil \stackrel{\leq \tau}{\longrightarrow} \lceil \#a = n \rceil$$

where $D \stackrel{\leq \tau}{\longrightarrow} \lceil P \rceil$ means $D \wedge \ell < \tau \longrightarrow \lceil P \rceil$.

4. The state $\#a$ has initially value 0 for time τ

$$AC_4 \stackrel{\text{def}}{=} \lceil \rceil \vee (\lceil \#a = 0 \rceil \wedge \ell < \tau) \vee ((\lceil \#a = 0 \rceil \wedge \ell = \tau) \; ; \; true)$$

which are collected in the schema

```
ActivationClock
ProgramVars
```

$$AC_1 \wedge AC_2 \wedge AC_3 \wedge AC_4$$

The exchange of information in the sampled system takes place at the point in time where $\#a$ is incremented. This is modeled by having each program variable x stable except at the points in time where $\#a$ is incremented as expressed in the following *synchronization* formula

$$Sync \overset{\text{def}}{=} \forall x : Vars \bullet \lceil \#a = n \wedge x = x_0 \rceil \longrightarrow \lceil \#a \neq n \vee x = x_0 \rceil$$

The synchronization is specified in the schema

```
┌─ Sync ────────────────────────────────────
│  Program Vars
│  ─────────────────────────────────────────
│  Sync
└───────────────────────────────────────────
```

3.3 Sensors

The design proposed in the description of the steam boiler [2, 3] uses a *fault tolerant* control algorithm where sensor readings of the water level and steam are replaced by estimated values if the sensors are failing. The calculations are based on the formulas in the system identification (cf. schema *Boiler*) and use measurements of water level and steam, plus information from the pump controller. The calculations are also used for supervision of sensor failures.

An implementation of these ideas will result in a subsystem comprising A/D converters for water level and steam, and a program. In this section we will abstract from details in the design of such a subsystem, and simply consider it an "intelligent" water level sensor which provides the program with an interval $adj(1)$ containing the water level. When the sensor is working correctly the interval $adj(1)$ is a small interval (to describe the imprecise measurement). In case of failure in the reading of the water level the interval $adj(1)$ gives computed upper and lower bounds on the water level. The most pessimistic value for $adj(1)$ is the whole interval $[0, C]$.

Recall that $adj(1)$ is synchronized with the activation clock, cf. formula *Sync*, thus it is stable except when the clock $\#a$ ticks. The change at the ticks gives a new interval for the current water level

$$WLS_1 \overset{\text{def}}{=} \lceil \#a = n \rceil \wedge \mathbf{e}.q = q_0 \longrightarrow \lceil \#a = n \vee q_0 \in adj(1) \rceil$$

This formula can be placed in a schema

```
┌─ WLS ─────────────────────────────────────
│  Plant
│  Program Vars
│  ─────────────────────────────────────────
│  WLS_1
└───────────────────────────────────────────
```

3.4 Actuators

The *pump actuator* controls the pumps. It switches the pumps on and off as a reaction on the commands indicated by the control program through the variable *pCmd* which is a joint boolean set-point value for all pumps. The pump controller should start all pumps when *pCmd* has been *true* for at least time τ

$$PA_1 \stackrel{\text{def}}{=} \lceil pCmd \rceil \stackrel{\tau}{\longrightarrow} \lceil p = P \rceil$$

and it should stop all pumps when *pCmd* has been *false* for at least time τ

$$PA_2 \stackrel{\text{def}}{=} \lceil \neg pCmd \rceil \stackrel{\tau}{\longrightarrow} \lceil p = 0 \rceil$$

These formulas are collected in the schema

```
┌─ PA ─────────────────────────────────────────
│ Plant
│ ProgramVars
│ ─────────────────
│ PA₁ ∧ PA₂
```
$$
\begin{array}{|l}
\hline
\mathit{PA} \\
\hline
\mathit{Plant} \\
\mathit{ProgramVars} \\
\hline
PA_1 \wedge PA_2 \\
\hline
\end{array}
$$

The *valve actuator* should open the valve when *vCmd* has been *true* for at least time τ and close the valve when *vCmd* has been *false* for at least time τ. These requirements are expressed in the formulas

$$VA_1 \stackrel{\text{def}}{=} \lceil vCmd \rceil \stackrel{\tau}{\longrightarrow} \lceil d = D \rceil$$
$$VA_2 \stackrel{\text{def}}{=} \lceil \neg vCmd \rceil \stackrel{\tau}{\longrightarrow} \lceil d = 0 \rceil$$

which are collected in the schema

$$
\begin{array}{|l}
\hline
\mathit{VA} \\
\hline
\mathit{Plant} \\
\mathit{ProgramVars} \\
\hline
VA_1 \wedge VA_2 \\
\hline
\end{array}
$$

The *program ready actuator* controls the *ready* signal to the environment based on *pRd*. We will assume that this is done without any time delay

$$RdyA_1 \stackrel{\text{def}}{=} \Box \left(\lceil \, \rceil \vee \lceil ready = pRd \rceil \right)$$

The schema for the actuator is

$$
\begin{array}{|l}
\hline
\mathit{RdyA} \\
\hline
\mathit{Plant} \\
\mathit{ProgramVars} \\
\hline
RdyA_1 \\
\hline
\end{array}
$$

Variables
   Read $\#a$:   Nat INIT *0*
   Read $adj(1)$:   Interval INIT *[0, C]*
   Private pRd: Bool INIT *0*
   Private $pCmd, vCmd$:   Bool INIT *0*
Always *(* Contol *)*

$\|\ \#a\!\uparrow\ \wedge\ \neg pRd\ \wedge\ \neg vCmd\ \wedge\ \neg pCmd\ \wedge\ (adj'(1) \succ N)\ \Rightarrow\ vCmd'$

$\|\ \#a\!\uparrow\ \wedge\ \neg pRd\ \wedge\ (adj'(1) \subseteq NN)\ \Rightarrow\ \neg vCmd'\ \wedge\ \neg pCmd'$

$\|\ \#a\!\uparrow\ \wedge\ \neg pRd\ \wedge\ \neg vCmd\ \wedge\ \neg pCmd\ \wedge\ (adj'(1) \subseteq N)\ \Rightarrow\ pRd'$

$\|\ \#a\!\uparrow\ \wedge\ \neg vCmd\ \wedge\ \neg pCmd\ \wedge\ (adj'(1) \prec N)\ \Rightarrow\ pCmd'$

$\|\ \#a\!\uparrow\ \wedge\ pRd\ \wedge\ (adj'(1) \succ N)\ \Rightarrow\ \neg pCmd'$

Fig. 5. Program specification in TLT.

3.5 Semantics of Program Specification

A *program state* is a mapping associating a value of the proper type to each program variable name (we use the word *program state* to avoid confusion with states which are functions of time). The set of program states is denoted by Σ.

The specification of the control program for the steam boiler is given in figure 5. Beside the declarations of variables this specification defines a predicate $\mathcal{I}$ and a binary relation $\mathcal{R}$ on program states

$$\mathcal{I} : \Sigma \rightarrow \textbf{Bool}$$
$$\mathcal{R} : \Sigma \times \Sigma \rightarrow \textbf{Bool}$$

The *initialization predicate* $\mathcal{I}$ is given by the "INIT" part of the variable declarations. The *state transition relation* $\mathcal{R}(\sigma_1, \sigma_2)$ is given by the formulas in the "Always" part of the specification. An "unprimed" variable name (like pRd) denote the value for the variable in the first state σ_1 while a "primed" name (like $pCmd'$) denote the value in the second state σ_2. The logical connective are used with their usual meaning. The operator " $\Rightarrow$ " means implication, but with the extra role, that private and local variables appearing in primed form on the right hand side of " $\Rightarrow$ " are considered to be "constrained" by the specification. The operator "$\|$" denotes *conjunction* with *framing* of constrained variables, so that e.g. the constraint $pCmd' = pCmd$ is implied in situations where the formulas do not explicitly constrain $pCmd'$. The expression $\#a\!\uparrow$ is short for $\#a' > \#a$. The symbols $\prec$ and $\succ$ are explained below.

In order to define the DC semantics of a TLT specification we collect the states (cf. schema *ProgramVars*) corresponding to the program variables in a single "grand" state giving the program state as function of time

$$\sigma : Time \rightarrow \Sigma$$

where

$$\sigma(t)(x) = x(t) \quad \text{for any } t \in Time \text{ and } x \in Vars$$

(Note that the symbol x on the left hand side of the equality sign denotes the *variable name* which is a character string, while the same symbol on the right hand side denotes the corresponding *state* which is a function of time).

Using the state σ the semantics can be expressed as follows: the initialization predicate $\mathcal{I}$ should hold initially and any pair of consecutive program states should satisfy the state transition relation $\mathcal{R}$

$$Sem_1 \overset{\text{def}}{=} \lceil\,\rceil \vee \lceil \mathcal{I}(\sigma) \rceil \; ; \; true$$

$$Sem_2 \overset{\text{def}}{=} \square \left(\lceil \sigma = \sigma_1 \rceil \; ; \; \lceil \sigma = \sigma_2 \rceil \Rightarrow \mathcal{R}(\sigma_1, \sigma_2) \right)$$

Remarks: It follows from the specification AC_1, AC_2, AC_3, AC_4 and *Sync* that the program state σ is *piecewise constant*, so any non-empty time interval has an initial and final subinterval where σ is constant

$$FinVar(\sigma) \overset{\text{def}}{=} \square \left(\ell > 0 \Rightarrow (\exists \sigma_1 \bullet \lceil \sigma = \sigma_1 \rceil \; ; \; true) \wedge (\exists \sigma_2 \bullet true \; ; \; \lceil \sigma = \sigma_2 \rceil) \right)$$

When the semantics of TLT is expressed in Lamports TLA (cf. [27]) an execution of the program is represented by an infinite sequence of states

$$\sigma_1, \sigma_2, \ldots, \sigma_k, \sigma_{k+1}, \ldots$$

such that the initial state satisfied $\mathcal{I}$ and such that each step from a state σ_k to the next state σ_{k+1} satisfies $\mathcal{R}$

$$\mathcal{I}(\sigma_1) \wedge \forall k \bullet \mathcal{R}(\sigma_k, \sigma_{k+1})$$

For the DC semantics we have that any non point finite prefix of a behavior σ can be decomposed into a finite sequence of program states

$$\ell > 0 \Rightarrow \exists k : \mathbf{N}, \sigma_1, \ldots, \sigma_k : \Sigma \bullet \lceil \sigma = \sigma_1 \rceil \; ; \; \lceil \sigma = \sigma_2 \rceil \; ; \; \ldots \; ; \; \lceil \sigma = \sigma_k \rceil$$

The finite program state sequences $\sigma_1, \ldots, \sigma_k$ obtained in this way are precisely the prefixes of the infinite program state sequences in the TLA semantics.

3.6 The Control Program

This section gives a brief, informal description of the control strategy in the *ready* phase (the $\neg ready$ phase is more involved).

The symbols $\prec$ and $\succ$ denote partial ordering for intervals

$$[x_1, x_2] \prec [y_1, y_2] \overset{\text{def}}{=} x_1 \leq y_1 \wedge x_2 \leq y_2$$

$$[x_1, x_2] \succ [y_1, y_2] \overset{\text{def}}{=} x_1 \geq y_1 \wedge x_2 \geq y_2$$

The control program uses two intervals $N = [N_1, N_2]$ and $NN = [NN_1, NN_2]$ with $NN \subset N \subset M$. The N interval is used in computing the pumps on/off commands in the *ready* phase, while the NN interval is used in the $\neg ready$ phase to ensure that the water level is inside N when the phase is changed to *ready*.

Comparison of intervals give three cases in the *ready* phase, assuming that the water level interval $adj(\mathbf{l})$ is shorter than the interval N

– If $adj(1) \succ N$ a stop command is sent to the pumps:

$$\| \quad \#a{\uparrow} \ \wedge \ pRd \wedge (adj'(1) \succ N) \Rightarrow \neg pCmd'$$

The width of the interval $[N_2, M_2]$ ensures that the pumps will be turned off before the water level reaches the "fatal" limit M_2.

– If $adj(1) \prec N$ a start command is sent to the pumps:

$$\| \quad \#a{\uparrow} \ \wedge \ \neg vCmd \wedge \neg pCmd \wedge (adj'(1) \prec N) \Rightarrow pCmd'$$

The width of the interval $[M_1, N_1]$ ensures that the pumps will be turned on before the water level reaches the "fatal" limit M_1.

– In case $adj(1) \subseteq N$ the commands to the pumps are left unchanged by the framing.

4 Verification

In order to verify that the controller design satisfies the system requirements, we combine reasoning from both notations: Duration Calculus for temporal reasoning about sensors, actuators and the physical environment, and TLT for reasoning about the program.

As the requirements are stated in DC, the proofs must be performed in this notation at the top level. Formulas proved in TLT can be used directly in DC proofs as non-temporal "mathematical" formulas. A program invariant $Inv : \Sigma \longrightarrow \mathbf{Bool}$ proved in TLT (using first order logic) give rise to a temporal DC formula by use of the following "lifting" rule:

If we can prove the formulas $\mathcal{I}(\sigma) \Rightarrow Inv(\sigma)$ and $\mathcal{R}(\sigma_1, \sigma_2) \wedge Inv(\sigma_1) \Rightarrow Inv(\sigma_2)$ in TLT, then $\square (\lceil \rceil \vee \lceil Inv(\sigma) \rceil)$ will hold in DC.

For a program variable v of type $\mathbf{Bool} = \{0, 1\}$ we "abuse the notation" by using $\sigma_1(v)$ as short for $\sigma_1(v) = 1$, i.e. to denote that v has the value 1 in the state σ_1. Similarly we will use $\neg \sigma_1(v)$ as short for $\sigma_1(v) = 0$.

The sections below contain proofs for the requirements Req_1, Req_2, Req_4 and Req_5. All proofs are made by contradiction. The contradiction is derived by identifying two consecutive observations of the state σ, $\lceil \sigma = \sigma_1 \rceil$; $\lceil \sigma = \sigma_2 \rceil$ which are in conflict with the transition relation, i.e. where $\neg \mathcal{R}(\sigma_1, \sigma_2)$.

The proofs are made assuming the following relations between the intervals M, N and NN:

$$
\begin{aligned}
M_2 - N_2 \quad &> 2\tau \cdot max(P, D) + 2\epsilon \\
N_2 - NN_2 \quad &> \tau \cdot max(P, D) + 2\epsilon \\
NN_2 - NN_1 \quad &> \tau \cdot max(P, D) + 4\epsilon \\
NN_1 - N_1 \quad &> \tau \cdot max(P, D) + 2\epsilon \\
N_1 - M_1 \quad &> 2\tau \cdot max(P, D, W) + 2\epsilon
\end{aligned}
$$

In some of the proofs below, requirements proved earlier will be used.

4.1 Proving the Requirements

Proof for Req_1 Without additional assumptions (i.e. with $Assumpt_1 = true$) $Commit_1$ is proved by contradiction using $TLTLem_{1,1}$. Assume $\neg Commit_1$, i.e. that:

$$\lceil ready \rceil \; ; \; true$$
$$\Rightarrow \{ FinVar, \; RdyA_1 \}$$
$$\exists \sigma_1 \bullet \lceil \sigma = \sigma_1 \rceil \; ; \; true \wedge \sigma_1(pRd)$$
$$\Rightarrow \{ Sem_1 \}$$
$$\exists \sigma_1 \bullet \mathcal{I}(\sigma_1) \wedge \sigma_1(pRd)$$
$$\Rightarrow \{ TLTLem_{1,1} \}$$
$$\exists \sigma_1 \bullet \sigma_1(pRd) \wedge \neg \sigma_1(pRd)$$
$$\Rightarrow \{\}$$
$$false$$

Thus, the requirement $Req_1 \stackrel{\text{def}}{=} \lceil \rceil \vee \lceil \neg ready \rceil \; ; \; true$ has been proved.

Proof for Req_2 Without additional assumptions, $Commit_2$ is proved by contradiction using $TLTLem_{2,1}$. Assume $\neg Commit_2$, i.e. that:

$$true \; ; \; \lceil ready \rceil \; ; \; \lceil \neg ready \rceil \; ; \; true$$
$$\Rightarrow \{ RdyA_1 \}$$
$$\exists \sigma_1, \sigma_2 \bullet true \; ; \; \lceil \sigma = \sigma_1 \rceil \; ; \; \lceil \sigma = \sigma_2 \rceil \; ; \; true \wedge \sigma_1(pRd) \wedge \neg \sigma_2(pRd)$$
$$\Rightarrow \{ TLTLem_{2,1}, \; Sem_2 \}$$
$$\exists \sigma_2 \bullet \neg \sigma_2(pRd) \wedge \sigma_2(pRd)$$
$$\Rightarrow \{\}$$
$$false$$

Thus, the requirement $Req_2 \stackrel{\text{def}}{=} \lceil ready \rceil \longrightarrow \lceil ready \rceil$ has been proved.

Proof for Req_3 This proof is extensive and has been left out. In order to prove the commitment $Commit_3 \stackrel{\text{def}}{=} \lceil \neg ready \rceil \stackrel{T}{\longrightarrow} \lceil ready \rceil$, it is necessary to make the assumption

$$Assumpt_3 \stackrel{\text{def}}{=} WLSTol(\epsilon)$$

where

$$WLSTol(\epsilon) \stackrel{\text{def}}{=} \square (\lceil \rceil \vee \lceil | \; adj(1) \; | < 2\epsilon \rceil)$$

We have made the proof of Req_3 for $T = 3\tau + max(\frac{C - NN_2 + 2\epsilon}{D}, \frac{NN_1 + 2\epsilon}{P})$.

Proof for Req_4 Without any additional assumptions, $Commit_4$ is proved by contradiction using the lemmas $Lem_{4,1}$ and $TLTLem_{4,2}$. Moreover, Req_2 is used (but this has been proven earlier). Assume $Commit_4$ to be invalid, i.e. that:

$$true \; ; \; \lceil ready \rceil \; ; \; \lceil d \neq 0 \rceil \; ; \; true$$
$$\Rightarrow \{Req_2, RdyA_1\}$$
$$true \; ; \; \lceil pRd \wedge d \neq 0 \rceil \; ; \; true$$
$$\Rightarrow \{d \text{ is either } 0 \text{ or } D \text{ when phase } pRd \text{ is entered}\}$$
$$(true \; ; \; \lceil \neg pRd \rceil \; ; \; \lceil pRd \wedge d \neq 0 \rceil \; ; \; true)$$
$$\vee \; (true \; ; \; (\lceil pRd \rceil \wedge \lceil d = 0 \rceil \; ; \; \lceil d \neq 0 \rceil) \; ; \; true)$$
$$\Rightarrow \{Lem_{4,1}, Sync\}$$
$$false \vee (true \; ; \; (\lceil pRd \rceil \wedge \lceil d = 0 \rceil \; ; \; \lceil d \neq 0 \rceil) \; ; \; true)$$
$$\Rightarrow \{Req_1\}$$
$$true \; ; \; (\lceil pRd \rceil \wedge \ell = \tau) \; ; \; \lceil d \neq 0 \rceil \; ; \; true$$
$$\Rightarrow \{\text{Lifting rule on } TLTLem_{4,2}\}$$
$$true \; ; \; (\lceil \neg vCmd \rceil \wedge \ell = \tau) \; ; \; \lceil d \neq 0 \rceil \; ; \; true$$
$$\Rightarrow \{\}$$
$$true \; ; \; (\lceil \neg vCmd \rceil \wedge \ell = \tau) \; ; \; \lceil d \neq 0 \rceil \; ; \; true$$
$$\Rightarrow \{VA_2\}$$
$$false$$

Thus, the requirement $Req_4 \stackrel{\text{def}}{=} \lceil ready \rceil \longrightarrow \lceil d = 0 \rceil$ has been proved.

Proof for Req_5 Under the assumption $Assumpt_5 \stackrel{\text{def}}{=} WLSTol(\epsilon)$, the commitment $Commit_5$ is proved by contradiction using the lemmas $Lem_{5,1}$ and $Lem_{5,2}$.

In order to prove the commitment by contradiction, we assume $Commit_5$ to be false, i.e. that one of the two formulas $\Diamond \lceil ready \wedge q > M_2 \rceil$ and $\Diamond \lceil ready \wedge q < M_1 \rceil$ are satisfied.

Since the proofs corresponding to each of these formulas are very similar, we will show only the proof for the first:

$$true \; ; \; \lceil ready \rceil \; ; \; \lceil q > M \rceil \; ; \; true$$
$$\Rightarrow \{Req_2, RdyA_1\}$$
$$true \; ; \; \lceil pRd \wedge q > M \rceil \; ; \; true$$
$$\Rightarrow \{Req_1, \; Req_2\}$$
$$\lceil \neg pRd \rceil \; ; \; \lceil pRd \rceil \; ; \; \lceil q > M_2 \wedge pRd \rceil \; ; \; true$$
$$\Rightarrow \{[\lceil \rceil \vee \Diamond \lceil q > M_2 \rceil \vee \Box \lceil q \leq M_2 \rceil], \; Lem_{5,1}\}$$
$$\lceil \neg pRd \rceil \; ; \; \lceil pRd \wedge q \leq M_2 \rceil \; ; \; \lceil pRd \wedge q > M_2 \rceil \; ; \; true$$
$$\Rightarrow \{Lem_{5,1}, \; \text{continuity of } q\}$$
$$\lceil \neg pRd \rceil \; ; \; (\lceil pRd \wedge q \leq M_2 \rceil \wedge \mathbf{b}.q \leq N_2 + 2\epsilon \wedge \mathbf{e}.q = M_2)$$
$$; \; \lceil pRd \wedge q > M_2 \rceil \; ; \; true$$
$$\Rightarrow \{Mass, \quad M_2 - (N_2 + 2\epsilon) > 2\tau P\}$$
$$true \; ; \; (\lceil pRd \wedge N_2 + 2\epsilon < q \leq M_2 \rceil \wedge \ell \geq 2\tau) \; ; \; \lceil q > M_2 \rceil \; ; \; true$$
$$\Rightarrow \{\text{continuity of } q, \; Lem_{5,2}\}$$
$$true \; ; \; (\mathbf{b}.q = M_2 \wedge \mathbf{e}.q > M_2 \wedge \lceil p = 0 \rceil) \; ; \; true$$
$$\Rightarrow \{Mass\}$$
$$false$$

Thus, the requirement $Req_5 \overset{\text{def}}{=} WLSTol(\epsilon) \Rightarrow (\lceil ready \rceil \longrightarrow \lceil q \in M \rceil)$ has been proved. In order to make the other half of the proof, one has to use the assumption that the pumps can supply enough water to match the steam, i.e. that $P \geq W$.

4.2 Lemmas

The lemmas used for proving the requirements of the previous section, are listed here:

$$Lem_{4,1} \overset{\text{def}}{=} \lceil \neg pRd \rceil \longrightarrow \lceil \neg pRd \vee d = 0 \rceil$$
$$Lem_{5,1} \overset{\text{def}}{=} \lceil \neg pRd \rceil \longrightarrow \lceil \neg pRd \vee q \in [N_1 - 2\epsilon, N_2 + 2\epsilon] \rceil$$
$$Lem_{5,2} \overset{\text{def}}{=} \lceil pRd \wedge N_2 + 2\epsilon < q \rceil \overset{\tau}{\longrightarrow} \lceil p = 0 \rceil$$

and they will be proved in the following sections.

Proof for $Lem_{4,1}$ Assume $Lem_{4,1}$ to be false, i.e.:

$$true \; ; \; \lceil \neg pRd \rceil \; ; \; \lceil pRd \wedge d \neq 0 \rceil \; ; \; true$$
$$\Rightarrow \{ Req_1, \, Sync, \, AC_3 \}$$
$$true \; ; \; (\lceil \neg pRd \rceil \wedge \ell = \tau) \; ; \; \lceil pRd \wedge d \neq 0 \rceil \; ; \; true$$
$$\Rightarrow \{\}$$
$$\exists \sigma_1, \sigma_2 \bullet true \; ; \; (\lceil \sigma = \sigma_1 \rceil \wedge \ell = \tau) \; ; \; \lceil \sigma = \sigma_2 \wedge d \neq 0 \rceil \; ; \; true$$
$$\wedge \; \neg \sigma_1(pRd) \wedge \sigma_2(pRd)$$
$$\Rightarrow \{ TLTLem_{4,1} \}$$
$$\exists \sigma_1 \bullet true \; ; \; (\lceil \sigma = \sigma_1 \rceil \wedge \ell = \tau) \; ; \; \lceil d \neq 0 \rceil \; ; \; true \wedge \neg \sigma_1(vCmd)$$
$$\Rightarrow \{\}$$
$$true \; ; \; (\lceil \neg vCmd \rceil \wedge \ell = \tau) \; ; \; \lceil d \neq 0 \rceil \; ; \; true$$
$$\Rightarrow \{ VA_2 \}$$
$$false$$

Proof for $Lem_{5,1}$ Under the assumption $Assumpt_5$[3], $Lem_{5,1}$ is proved by contradiction using the TLT lemma $TLTLem_{5,1}$.

---

[3] We are allowed to make the assumption since $Lem_{5,1}$ is used to prove the commitment $Commit_5$, assuming exactly this.

$$true \; ; \; \lceil \neg pRd \rceil \; ; \; \lceil pRd \wedge q > N_2 + 2\epsilon \rceil \; ; \; true$$
$$\Rightarrow \{Sync, \; \text{continuity of } q\}$$
$$true \; ; \; (\lceil \neg pRd \wedge \#a = a_0 \rceil \wedge \mathbf{e}.q \geq N_2 + 2\epsilon)$$
$$; \; \lceil pRd \wedge \#a \neq a_0 \rceil \; ; \; true$$
$$\Rightarrow \{WLS, \; WLSok(\epsilon)\}$$
$$true \; ; \; \lceil \neg pRd \rceil \; ; \; \lceil pRd \wedge adj(1)_2 > N_2 \rceil \; ; \; true$$
$$\Rightarrow \{\}$$
$$\exists \sigma_1, \sigma_2 \bullet true \; ; \; \lceil \sigma = \sigma_1 \rceil \; ; \; \lceil \sigma = \sigma_2 \rceil \; ; \; true$$
$$\wedge \; \neg\sigma_1(pRd) \wedge \sigma_2(pRd) \wedge (\sigma_2(adj(1)_2) > \sigma_2(N_2))$$
$$\Rightarrow \{TLTLem_{5,1}, \; Sem_2\}$$
$$false$$

Proof for $Lem_{5,2}$

$$true \; ; \; (\lceil pRd \wedge N_2 + 2\epsilon < q \rceil \wedge \ell = \tau) \; ; \; \lceil p \neq 0 \rceil \; ; \; true$$
$$\Rightarrow \{Sync, \; Req_1\}$$
$$true \; ; \; \lceil \#a = a_0 \rceil \wedge \mathbf{e}.q \leq N_2 + 2\epsilon) \; ; \; (\lceil pRd \wedge \#a = a_0 + 1 \rceil \wedge \ell = \tau)$$
$$; \; \lceil \#a = a_0 + 2 \wedge p \neq 0 \rceil \; ; \; true$$
$$\Rightarrow \{\}$$
$$\exists \sigma_1 \bullet true \; ; \; (\lceil \sigma = \sigma_1 \rceil \wedge \ell = \tau) \; ; \; \lceil p \neq 0 \rceil \; ; \; true \wedge \neg\sigma_1(pCmd)$$
$$\Rightarrow \{PA_2\}$$
$$true \; ; \; \lceil p = 0 \wedge p \neq 0 \rceil \; ; \; true$$
$$\Rightarrow \{\}$$
$$false$$

4.3   TLT-lemmas

The TLT lemmas needed for the above proofs are listed here:

$$TLTLem_{1,1} = \mathcal{I}(\sigma_0) \Rightarrow \neg\sigma_0(pRd)$$
$$TLTLem_{2,1} = \mathcal{R}(\sigma_1, \sigma_2) \wedge \sigma_1(pRd) \Rightarrow \sigma_2(pRd)$$
$$TLTLem_{4,1} = \mathcal{R}(\sigma_1, \sigma_2) \wedge \neg\sigma_1(pRd) \wedge \sigma_2(pRd) \Rightarrow \neg\sigma_1(vCmd)$$
$$TLTLem_{4,2} = \mathcal{I}(\sigma_0) \Rightarrow (\sigma_0(pRd) \Rightarrow \neg\sigma_0(vCmd))$$
$$\wedge \begin{pmatrix} \mathcal{R}(\sigma_1, \sigma_2) \wedge (\sigma_1(pRd) \Rightarrow \neg\sigma_1(vCmd)) \\ \Rightarrow (\sigma_2(pRd) \Rightarrow \neg\sigma_2(vCmd)) \end{pmatrix}$$
$$TLTLem_{5,1} = \mathcal{R}(\sigma_1, \sigma_2) \wedge \sigma_2(pRd) \wedge (\sigma_2(adj(1))_2 > N_2)$$
$$\Rightarrow \sigma_1(pRd)$$

In the following sections some of these lemmas are proved.

Proof for $TLTLem_{2,1}$ We show that $\mathcal{R} \wedge pRd \Rightarrow pRd'$:

Observe that the only constraint for pRd is

$$\|\; \#a\!\uparrow \;\wedge\; \neg pRd \wedge\; \neg vCmd \wedge \neg pCmd \wedge (adj'(1) \subseteq N) \Rightarrow\; pRd'$$

Therefore the corresponding frame equation is

$$pRd \neq pRd' \Rightarrow \#a\!\uparrow \;\wedge \neg pRd \wedge\; \neg vCmd \wedge \neg pCmd \wedge (adj'(1) \subseteq N)$$

Since $\mathcal{R}$ implies both the constraint and the frame, it follows that

$$\mathcal{R} \Rightarrow (pRd \neq pRd' \Rightarrow pRd')$$

and from this we obtain the conclusion.

Proof for $TLTLem_{4,2}$ The fact that

$$\mathcal{I} \Rightarrow (pRd \Rightarrow \neg \sigma_0(vCmd))$$

is trivial since $\mathcal{I} \Rightarrow \neg pRd$.

By propositional logic $\mathcal{R} \wedge (pRd \Rightarrow \neg vCmd) \Rightarrow (pRd' \Rightarrow \neg vCmd')$ follows from

$$\mathcal{R} \wedge \neg pRd \wedge pRd' \Rightarrow \neg vCmd' \quad (*)$$
$$\mathcal{R} \wedge \neg vCmd \wedge vCmd' \Rightarrow \neg pRd' \,(**)$$

The first claim $(*)$ follows from the frames of pRd and $vCmd$:

$$
\begin{aligned}
\mathcal{R} \wedge \neg pRd \wedge pRd' &\Rightarrow \neg vCmd \wedge (adj'(1) \subseteq N) \\
&\Rightarrow \neg vCmd \wedge (adj'(1) \not\subseteq N) \\
&\Rightarrow \neg vCmd \wedge (vCmd' = vCmd) \\
&\Rightarrow \neg vCmd'
\end{aligned}
$$

The proof of the proposition $(**)$ is similar.

5 Program

In this section we refine our program to include all components: two communication components (the modules "*Input_Actions*" and "*Output_Actions*"), two modules for abbreviations and time stamps, a module "*Counter*" to collect STOP messages from the operator and count them, three modules to implement the intelligent sensors, a "*Mode*" module and the "*Control*" module that is already discussed. We give an overview of the complete program, whose architecture is shown in figure 6, and explain the modules in some detail.

To avoid confusions, we will call the 7 boxes of figure 6 the *software components* of the program, while the TLT program itself is divided into 11 *TLT sections* or *TLT modules*. These modules correspond exactly to the software components of figure 6, except for the two connectors *Input_Actions* and *Output_Actions*

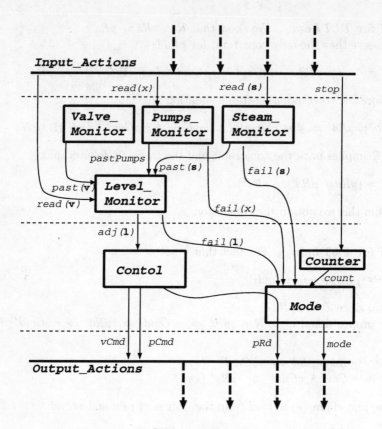

Fig. 6. The architecture of the complete program.

(which are drawn as lines in the figure: they just translate from messages to variables and vice-versa) and the modules *Abbreviations* and *Time_Stamps*, which do not appear in the figure, but may be found to be implemented in existing components. Also, the TLT Program contains the declarations of actions. TLT has different types of sections, to express assumptions over the environment, or spontaneous instruction (not triggered by external events), etc., but in this program we use only "Always" sections. Each TLT section corresponds to a logical module of the program, in the sense that each one can be translated to a transition relation or transition predicate independently of the others (since they contain disjoint sets of variables), while the global transition relation is exactly the conjunction of the relations for the individual modules. From the point of view of the whole program, all variables are local variables (since they may not be seen by the environment) but from the perspective of each module, the variables that the module is constraining are private variables.

5.1 Input Actions

In the previous sections, we have only considered submodules of the program. They communicate with other submodules via shared variables. For the purpose of inter-process communication, we use actions. Actions may be understood with the intuitive meaning of messages, but we now briefly give the semantic link from this TLT notion of actions to DC. A declaration of an action like

In $A : Typ_A$

defines a *trace* state

$TR_A : Time \rightarrow Typ_A^*$

with value a list of values of type Typ_A. The trace is initially empty, and it changes over time by appending values of type Typ_A

$$Tr_1 \stackrel{\text{def}}{=} \lceil \rceil \vee \lceil TR_A =<> \rceil$$
$$Tr_2 \stackrel{\text{def}}{=} \Box (\lceil TR_A = s_1 \rceil \; ; \; \lceil TR_A = s_2 \rceil \Rightarrow \exists v : Typ_A \bullet s_2 = s_1 \frown < v >)$$

In this semantics an A action with value v occurs when the value v is appended to the state TR_A.

The first module (*Input_Actions*) collects the incoming messages from the simulation, (or from the console, for instance, STOP, FAILURE_ACK, etc., and from the physical units, i.e., the sampled values of the water level, READLEVEL, or of the steam READSTEAM) and stores this information in some (local) variables. The incoming messages are declared in TLT as:

Actions
In   PHYSICAL_UNITS_READY: ()
In   STOP: ()
In $\|_{x:\text{PhU}}$ FAILURE_ACK(x), REPAIRED(x): ()
In $\|_{x:\text{PhU}}$ READ(x): Real

We use PhU to denote the set of physical units, PhU = { l, v, s } $\cup$ P $\cup$ PC where P denotes the set of pumps and PC the set of pump controllers. We also use a map $Pump\_Contr : P \rightarrow PC$ which maps a pump to the corresponding pump controller, and $NoPumps$ denotes the number of pumps.

An action A of type Typ_A may have a value x of Typ_A on a given transition (we say that the transition satisfies $A(x)$) or it has no value (we say that in the transition $\neg A$ holds). Thus, as transition predicates, $A \Leftrightarrow \exists_x A(x)$ holds. An action A of type () (Unit Type) can only "happen" or not (without values): $A \vee \neg A$. In our example, there are $2 + 3 \mid$ PhU $\mid$ different actions. The notation $\|_{x:Typ_A} A(x):$ () expresses that for each x in the domain of Typ_A there is an action $A(x)$ of Unit type. This is almost the same as $\|A: Typ_A$. The only difference is that in the second case $\forall_{x,y} A(x) \wedge A(y) \Rightarrow x = y$. Intuitively, if A is *one* action, then in one transition it may have at most one value (if any). This is not true if $A(x)$ and $A(y)$ are *two* different actions.

The corresponding variables to the Input actions and the constraints that change their values are:

Variables

Local	#a:	Nat INIT 0
Local	physURd:	Bool INIT 0
Local	stop:	Bool INIT 0
Local	#ack, #reps:	PhU → Nat INIT 0
Local	read:	PhU → Real

Always (* Input Actions *)

‖ PHYSICAL_UNITS_READY ∨ STOP ∨ FAILURE_ACK
  ∨ REPAIRED ∨ READ $\Rightarrow$ $\#a' = \#a + 1$
‖ PHYSICAL_UNITS_READY $\Rightarrow$ $physURd'$
‖ STOP $\Rightarrow$ $stop'$
‖ $\#a\uparrow$ ∧ ¬STOP $\Rightarrow$ $\neg stop'$
‖$_{x:\text{PhU}}$ FAILURE_ACK(x) $\Rightarrow$ $\#ack'(x) = \#ack(x) + 1$
‖$_{x:\text{PhU}}$ REPAIRED(x) $\Rightarrow$ $\#reps'(x) = \#reps(x) + 1$
‖$_{x:\text{PhU},val:\text{Real}}$ READ$(x)(val)$ $\Rightarrow$ $read'(x) = val$

The module *Input_Actions* receives one or several messages at a time and
increments (on each transmission) the variable $\#a$ (number of activations). If
the message PHYSICAL_UNITS_READY is present in the transmission, then the
variable *physURd* is set to one. (TLT uses the convention that a boolean variable may be used syntactically as a predicate, denoting that the variable is 1).
Each time a STOP message is received, the variable *stop* is set to true, but if in
any incoming transmission, the message STOP is missing, *stop* is reset to 0. If
FAILURE_ACK(x) is received, for x of type PhU, then $\#fails(x)$ is incremented
by one. (Similarly for the repair messages).

5.2 Output Actions

The module *Output_Actions* tries to control the steam boiler only if the program
is not in (and it is not entering) emergency mode. The structure is dual to the
Input_Actions module: if the value of a certain local variable changes, then the
output action is triggered. These variables and their corresponding actions are
now declared:

Variables

Local	pRd:	Bool INIT 0
Local	#fails:	PhU → Nat INIT 0
Local	pCmd, vCmd:	Bool INIT 0
Local	mode:	{init, normal, rescue, degraded, emstop} INIT init

Actions

Out PROGRAM_READY: ()
Out ‖$_{x:\text{PhU}}$ FAILURE_DETECTED(x), REPAIRED_ACK(x): ()
Out OPEN_PUMPS, CLOSE_PUMPS: ()
Out VALVE: ()
Out MODE: Mode_Type

The event REPAIRED(x) is triggered by $\#reps{\uparrow}(x)$. Therefore, REPAIRED(x) $\Rightarrow$ REPAIRED_ACK(x). Observe that the command VALVE is used both for opening and closing the valve. (This is the way the simulation works).

Always *(* Output_Actions *)*
pRd'	$\wedge$ $\neg emergency'$		$\Rightarrow$ PROGRAM_READY
$\|_{x:\text{PhU}}$ $\#fails(x){\uparrow}$	$\wedge$ $\neg emergency'$	$\Rightarrow$ FAILURE_DETECTED(x)
$\|_{x:\text{PhU}}$ $\#reps(x){\uparrow}$	$\wedge$ $\neg emergency'$	$\Rightarrow$ REPAIRED_ACK(x)
$pCmd{\uparrow}$	$\wedge$ $\neg emergency'$	$\Rightarrow$ OPEN_PUMPS
$pCmd{\downarrow}$	$\wedge$ $\neg emergency'$	$\Rightarrow$ CLOSE_PUMPS
$pCmd{\updownarrow}$	$\wedge$ $\neg emergency'$	$\Rightarrow$ VALVE
$\#a{\uparrow}$		$\Rightarrow$ MODE*(mode')*

5.3   Local Variables and Failure Management

We need some local variables:

Variables
   Local   *past:* $\{\mathbf{v}, \mathbf{s}\} \cup P \rightarrow$ Intervals
   Local   *calc, adj:* $\{\mathbf{l}, \mathbf{s}\} \rightarrow$ Intervals
Always *(* Abbreviations *)*
$\|_{x:\text{PhU}}$ $fail(x) :\Leftrightarrow \#fails(x) > \#reps(x)$
$\|$ $risk :\Leftrightarrow (adj(\mathbf{l}) \ominus F(adj(\mathbf{s}), \tau) \oplus P \times [0,1] \times \tau) \not\subseteq M$
$\|_{x:\text{PhU}}$ $repaired(x) :\Leftrightarrow \#reps'(x) = \#fails(x)$
Always *(* Time_Stamps *)*
$\|_{k:\text{Nat}}$ $pCmd{\uparrow} \wedge \#a' = k \Rightarrow \#a'_{pCmd{\uparrow}} = k$
$\|_{k:\text{Nat}}$ $vCmd{\downarrow} \wedge \#a' = k \Rightarrow \#a'_{vCmd{\downarrow}} = k$

The module *Abbreviations*, may be seen as an introduction of "macros" which, whenever used in other modules, can be replaced by their definitions. The next module introduces two time stamps that will be needed later: it will be necessary to know when pumps were opened and when the valve was closed, in order to estimate how much water could have flown in or out in the previous cycle.

If you wish, the abbreviations *fail(x)* and *risk* may be seen as variables or as (state) predicates. But *repaired(x)* is not a variable: it is a transition predicate.

This is also a convenient place to explain the failure management. In the "normal case", $\#fails = \#ack = \#reps$. (Initially they are all 0). If the program detects a failure in the physical unit x, then it increments $\#fails(x)$ and therefore, in this transition $\#fails'(x) = \#reps'(x) + 1$ and thus *fail'(x)* is true. Also, since $\#fails(x){\uparrow}$, the message FAILURE_DETECTED(x) is sent. In any of the subsequent transitions the failure may be acknowledged with FAILURE_ACK(x), increasing $\#ack(x)$. In the same transition, or later, the failure may be repaired with REPAIRED(x), increasing $\#reps(x)$. Whenever this happens, the predicate *repaired(x)* is true and remains true until the *next* transition after $\#fails(x)$ is incremented again. Notice, that it is still possible that in the same transition a new failure is detected. (For instance, because the repaired unit broke immediately again). In this case, in the same transition $fail(x)$ and $repaired(x)$ will be true.

5.4 The operator console: the stop counter

The operator may issue a STOP command (message) at the console. If this message arrives three consecutive times, then the variable $stop$ is true in three consecutive $\#a\uparrow$ events. This implies that counter will increment to 3. This is one of the conditions (in $Mode$) to enter emergency mode.

Always *(* Counter *)*
$\parallel$ $\#a\uparrow$ $\wedge$ $stop$ $\Rightarrow$ $count' = count + 1$
$\parallel$ $\#a\uparrow$ $\wedge$ $\neg stop$ $\Rightarrow$ $count' = 0$

5.5 The Intelligent Sensors: Monitors

The 4 monitors implement the intelligent sensors for the corresponding physical units. Generally speaking, the main purpose of these monitor modules is to estimate the accumulated changes of the physical variables on the last interval (we call them $past(x)$) and to determine if a failure has occurred in the physical unit x.

Always *(* Valve_Monitor *)*
$\parallel$ $\#a\uparrow$ $\wedge$ $vCmd$ $\vee$ $(\#a' - \#a_{vCmd\downarrow}) = 1$ $\Rightarrow$ $past'(\mathbf{v}) = [0, Vv] \times \tau$
$\parallel$ $\#a\uparrow$ $\wedge$ $\neg vCmd$ $\wedge$ $(\#a' - \#a_{vCmd\downarrow}) > 1$ $\Rightarrow$ $past'(\mathbf{v}) = [0,0]$
Always *(* Pumps_Monitor *)*
$\parallel_{x:P}$ $\#a\uparrow$ $\wedge$ $repaired(x)$ $\wedge$ $read(x)' \neq pCmd$
$\qquad\qquad \Rightarrow \#fails'(x) = \#fails(x) + 1$
$\parallel_{x:PC}$ $\#a\uparrow$ $\wedge$ $repaired(x)$ $\wedge$ $[$ $(read(x)'$ $\wedge$ $\neg pCmd)$
$\qquad\qquad \vee$ $(\neg read(x)'$ $\wedge$ $pCmd$ $\wedge$ $(\#a' - \#a_{pCmd\uparrow}) > 1)$ $]$
$\qquad\qquad \Rightarrow \#fails'(x) = \#fails(x) + 1$
$\parallel_{x:P}$ $\#a\uparrow$ $\wedge$ $(read(x)' \neq read(x)$ $\vee$ $fail(x)$ $\vee$ $fail'(x)$
$\qquad\qquad \vee$ $fail(Pump\_Contr(x))$ $\vee$ $fail'(Pump\_Contr(x))$ $)$
$\qquad\qquad \Rightarrow past'(x) = [0,1] \times \tau$
$\parallel_{x:P}$ $\#a\uparrow$ $\wedge$ $(read(x)' = read(x)$ $\wedge$ $\neg fail(x)$ $\wedge$ $\neg fail'(x)$
$\qquad\qquad \wedge$ $\neg fail(Pump\_Contr(x))$ $\wedge$ $\neg fail'(Pump\_Contr(x))$ $)$
$\qquad\qquad \Rightarrow past'(x) = [read(x), read(x)] \times \tau$
$\parallel$ $\qquad pastPumps' = P \times \sum_{x:P} past'(x)/NoPumps$
Always *(* Steam_Monitor *)*
$\parallel$ $\#a\uparrow$ $\Rightarrow past'(\mathbf{s}) = F(adj(\mathbf{s}), \tau)$
$\parallel$ $\#a\uparrow$ $\Rightarrow calc'(\mathbf{s}) = G(adj(\mathbf{s}), \tau)$
$\parallel$ $\#a\uparrow$ $\wedge$ $read(\mathbf{s})' \not\subseteq calc'(\mathbf{s})$ $\wedge$ $repaired(\mathbf{s})$ $\Rightarrow \#fails'(\mathbf{s}) = \#fails(\mathbf{s}) + 1$
$\parallel$ $\#a\uparrow$ $\wedge$ $fail'(\mathbf{s})$ $\Rightarrow adj'(\mathbf{s}) = calc'(\mathbf{s})$
$\parallel$ $\#a\uparrow$ $\wedge$ $\neg fail'(\mathbf{s})$ $\Rightarrow adj'(\mathbf{s}) = (read(\mathbf{s})' \oplus [-\epsilon, \epsilon]) \cap [0, W]$

Always *(* Level_Monitor *)*

  ‖ $\#a\uparrow \;\Rightarrow\; calc'(\mathbf{l}) = [0,C] \cap (adj(\mathbf{l}) \ominus past'(\mathbf{s}) \oplus pastPumps' \ominus past'(\mathbf{v}))$

  ‖ $\#a\uparrow \;\wedge\; read(\mathbf{l})' \notin calc'(\mathbf{l}) \;\wedge\; repaired(\mathbf{l}) \;\Rightarrow\; \#fails'(\mathbf{l}) = \#fails(\mathbf{l}) + 1$

  ‖ $\#a\uparrow \;\wedge\; fail'(\mathbf{l}) \;\Rightarrow\; adj'(\mathbf{l}) = calc'(\mathbf{l})$

  ‖ $\#a\uparrow \;\wedge\; \neg fail'(\mathbf{l}) \;\Rightarrow\; adj'(\mathbf{l}) = (read(\mathbf{l})' \oplus [-\epsilon,\epsilon]) \cap [0,C]$

To illustrate the monitors, let us consider the *Steam_Monitor*: recall from section 2.1 that if the steam v is in an interval I, then after a time t it is in the interval $G(I,t)$, and the amount of exited steam is included in $F(I,t)$. If the interval $adj(\mathbf{s})$ contains v on a certain activation, then at the next one (after time τ) v will be in $G(adj(\mathbf{s}), \tau)$. This is the calculated value for the steam, $calc'(\mathbf{s})$. During the same cycle, the amount of exiting steam was contained in $past'(\mathbf{s}) = F(adj(\mathbf{s}), \tau)$. If the read value of steam is not in $calc'(\mathbf{s})$, then an error must have occurred. The program will attribute this error to the steam sensor: $\#fails'(\mathbf{s}) = \#fails(\mathbf{s}) + 1$. If steam has no error, the read value is taken as the next adjusted value (plus or minus ϵ), else, the value of $calc'(\mathbf{s})$ is used.

5.6 Mode

The module "*Mode*" checks if there is an emergency condition and sets the value of *mode* correspondingly. We have not explained the requirements for this, but for the sake of completeness, we include the TLT specifications:

Always *(* Mode *)*

  ‖ $\#a\uparrow \;\wedge\; [\; count' \geq 3 \;\vee\; \exists_{x:\mathsf{PhU}} \; \#reps'(x) > \#ack'(x)$

         $\vee \; \exists_{x:\mathsf{PhU}} \; \#ack'(x) > \#fails(x)$

         $\vee \; (\neg pRd \;\wedge\; adj'(\mathbf{s})_2 > \epsilon)$

         $\vee \; (physURd' \;\wedge\; \neg pRd)$

         $\vee \; (\neg physURd' \;\wedge\; (fail'(\mathbf{l}) \;\vee\; fail'(\mathbf{s})))$

         $\vee \; (pRd \;\wedge\; risk')$

         $\vee \; (\; fail'(\mathbf{l}) \;\wedge\; \exists_{x:\mathsf{PhU}} \; (x \neq \mathbf{l}) \;\wedge\; fail'(x)) \;]$

     $\Rightarrow emergency'$

  ‖ $\#a\uparrow \;\wedge\; \forall_{x:\mathsf{PhU}} \; \neg fail'(x) \;\wedge\; physURd' \;\wedge\; \neg emergency' \;\Rightarrow\; mode' = \textbf{normal}$

  ‖ $\#a\uparrow \;\wedge\; physURd' \;\wedge\; \neg emergency'$

       $\wedge \; fail'(\mathbf{l}) \;\wedge\; \forall_{x:\mathsf{PhU}} \; (x \neq \mathbf{l} \Rightarrow \neg fail'(x)) \;\Rightarrow\; mode' = \textbf{rescue}$

  ‖ $\#a\uparrow \;\wedge\; physURd' \;\wedge\; \neg emergency'$

       $\wedge \; \neg fail'(\mathbf{l}) \;\wedge\; \exists_{x:\mathsf{PhU}} \; (x \neq \mathbf{l} \;\wedge\; fail'(x)) \;\Rightarrow\; mode' = \textbf{degraded}$

  ‖ $\#a\uparrow \;\wedge\; emergency' \;\Rightarrow\; mode' = \textbf{emstop}$

The module "*Control*", as discussed already in section 3.6, opens and closes the pumps and the valve and sets the variable pRd, terminating the initial phase.

6 Implementation and Validation

Now, we describe how the TLT-program was implemented in a machine executable version. As target language we choose the programming language C.

This program uses some syntactical constructs that the existing TLT-compiler does not yet support. Therefore, the C-code given below has been written by hand. The running object code runs against a simulation of the process, written at FZI, [29]. This simulator is written in tcl/tk and the interconnection between it and the C-program (equivalent to actions) is performed via unix pipes. Failures (e.g. steam failure) can be triggered in the simulation by pressing a button of a failure panel on the simulator display. Each five seconds the simulator sends the values from the measuring units. Then, the controller checks these values and produces the corresponding outputs (e.g. OPEN_PUMPS) which are given back to the simulator through actors. The simulator accepts inputs at any time.

6.1 Compilation Strategy

To obtain the C code, first a data flow analysis is necessary to obtain the order in which the sections have to be processed. If a section reads primed variables constrained by another section, then they have to be processed in the correct order.

The implementation works like this: first it saves the "pre-images" of the variables that it will need in the future. This is necessary since some modules will later refer to both a non-primed and a primed version of a variable or to a non-primed variable after it has been updated. For instance, there are two instances of the variable *adj* and *adjpr*. The flow analysis gives the set of variables that for which a pre-image will be (probably) necessary.

After saving the values of the pre-images, the implementation collects the incoming messages in corresponding variables, processes the transitions in a sequential way where the sequence is given mostly by the data-flow graph and returns the output messages to the environment.

Now we will look at how the module *Control*, described in section 3.6 (Figure 5) was implemented. At first, we need some constant and type definitions in C, to accommodate the TLT type Bool and Intervals for the variables used in that section:

```
#define N1  <... some value ...>
#define N2  <... some value greater than N1 ...>
#define NN1 <... some value greater than N1 and smaller than N2...>
#define NN2 <... some value greater than NN1 and smaller than N2 ...>
#define LEVEL 0
#define STEAM 1

typedef enum {FALSE, TRUE} bool;

struct floatIntervalStruct { float low;
                             float high;
                           };
typedef struct floatIntervalStruct levStIntervalType[2];
```

and define the variable in the following way:

```
bool progReady = 0;
bool vCommand = 0;
bool pCommand = 0;
struct floatIntervalStruct N;
struct floatIntervalStruct NN;
levStIntervalType adj;
```

whereby the variables *N*, *NN* and *adj* has to be initialized:

```
N.low = N1; N.high = N2;
NN.low = NN1; NN.high = NN2;
adj[LEVEL].low = 0; adj[LEVEL].high = 0;
adj[STEAM].low = 0; adj[STEAM].high = 0;
```

The functions $\subseteq$ and $\prec$ on Intervals are implemented like this:

```
bool contains(in1, in2)
  struct floatIntervalStruct in1;
  struct floatIntervalStruct in2;
{
    if ((in1.low >= in2.low) &&  (in1.high <= in2.high))
        return(TRUE);
    return(FALSE);
}

bool precedes(in1, in2)
  struct floatIntervalStruct in1;
  struct floatIntervalStruct in2;
{
    if ((in1.low < in2.low) &&  (in1.high < in2.high))
        return(TRUE);
    return(FALSE);
}
```

Now the translation of the module *Control* to C code is quite straight-forward:

```
if (!progReady && !vCommand && !pCommand && precedes(N,adjpr[LEVEL]))
                    vCommandpr;                   /* open valve */
if (!progReady && contains(adjpr[LEVEL], NN))
           {!vCommandpr; !pCommandpr}; /* close valve and pumps */
if (!progReady && !vCommand && !pCommand && contains(adjpr[LEVEL], N))
                    progReadypr;        /* send PROGRAM_READY */
if (!vCommand && !pCommand && precedes(adjpr[LEVEL], N))
                    pCommandpr;                   /* open pumps */
if (progReady && precedes(N, adjpr[LEVEL]))
                    !pCommandpr;               /* close pumps */
```

References

1. M. Abadi, L. Lamport. *An Old-Fashioned Recipe for Real Time*. Research Report 91, Digital Equipment Corporation System Research Center 1992.
2. J.-R. Abrial: *Steam-boiler control specification problem*, August 10, 1994.
3. J,-R. Abrial, E. Börger, H. Langmaack: *Additional Information Concerning the Physical Behaviour of the Steam Boiler*, note send to the participants in the Dagstuhl seminar, 1995.
4. Dieter Barnard, and Simon Crosby. A Tutorial Introduction to TLT. Part III: Case Study - an ATM signalling protocol. In Proc. of PSTV'95, 1995
5. Dines Bjørner, H. Langmaack, C.A.R. Hoare (eds): *ProCoS I Final Deliverable*, ProCoS Technical Report ID/DTH DB 13, 1993.
6. J.P. Bowen et.al.: A ProCoS II Project Description, ESPRIT BRA 7071, *EATCS Bull.*, No. 50, pp. 128-137, 1993.
7. J.P. Bowen et.al.: A ProCoS-WG Working Group Description, ESPRIT BRA 8694, to appear in: *EATCS Bull.*, No. 94, 1994.
8. J.P. Bowen, M. Fränzle, E.-R. Olderog, A.P. Ravn: Developing Correct Systems, *Proc 5'th EuroMicro Workshop on Real-Time Systems*, pp. 176 - 187, IEEE Press, 1993.
9. Holger Busch. First-order automation for higher-order-logic theorem proving. In *HOL 1994 - 7th International Conference on Higher Order Logic Theorem Proving and its Applications*. Springer-Verlag, LNCS 859, September 1994.
10. K.M. Chandy, J. Mishra. *Parallel Program Design. A Foundation*, Addison-Wesley, 1988.
11. J. Cuéllar, D. Barnard, and M. Huber. Concurrency and Synchronization in TLT. In Prof. R. Gotzhein, editor, *Proc. of GI-Fachgespräch on Formal Description Techniques*, Kaiserslautern, June 1995. GI.
12. J. Cuéllar, D. Barnard, and M. Huber. TLT Basics. Technical report, ZFE T SE 1, Siemens AG, D-81370 Munich, Germany, July 1995.
13. J. R. Cuéllar, I. Wildgruber, and D. Barnard. Combining the Design of Industrial Systems with Effective Verification Techniques. In M. Naftalin, T. Denvir, and M. Betran, editors, *Proc. of FME'94*, volume 873 of *LNCS*, pages 639–658, Barcelona, Spain, October 1994. Springer-Verlag.
14. Jorge Cuéllar and Dieter Barnard. A Tutorial Introduction to TLT. Part I: The Design of Distributed Systems. Internal report, Siemens Corporate Research and Development, ZFE T SE 1, D-81730 Munich, Germany, 1994.
15. Jorge Cuéllar, Dieter Barnard, and Martin Huber. A Tutorial Introduction to TLT. Part II: The Verification of Distributed Systems. Internal report, Siemens Corporate Research and Development, ZFE T SE 1, D-81730 Munich, Germany, 1994.
16. R.L. Grossman, A. Nerode, A.P. Ravn, H. Rischel (Eds.): *Hybrid Systems, LNCS* 736, Springer Verlag, 1993.
17. M.R. Hansen, Zhou Chaochen: Semantics and Completeness of Duration Calculus. *Real-Time: Theory in Practice, REX Workshop. Mook, The Netherlands*, June 1991. Proceedings, *LNCS* 600, pp. 209-225, 1992.
18. C.A.R. Hoare: *Communicating Sequential Processes*, Prentice-Hall, 1985.
19. J. Hooman. Correctness of real time systems by construction. In *Symposium FTRTFT'94 (Formal Techniques in Real Time and Fault Tolerant Systems)*, LNCS, vol. 863, 1994.

20. J. Hooman. Extending Hoare logic to real-time. *Formal Aspects of Computing*, to appear, 1994.

21. F. Jahanian and A. K-L. Mok. Safety analysis of timing properties in real-time systems. *IEEE Trans. Software Eng.*, 12(9):890–904, September 1986.

22. M.S. Jaffe, N.G. Leveson, M.P.E. Heimdahl and B.E. Melhart: Software Requirements Analysis for Real-Time Process-Control Systems, *IEEE Trans. Software Eng.*, vol. SE-17, 3, pp. 241-258, 1991.

23. M. Joseph, editor. *Proceedings Symp. on Formal Techniques in Real-Time and Fault-Tolerant Systems*, volume 331 of *LNCS*. Springer-Verlag, 1988.

24. R. Koymans. Specifying real-time properties with metric temporal logic. *Real-Time Systems*, 2(4):255–299, November 1990.

25. H. Langmaack, W.-P. de Roever, J. Vytopil (Eds.): *Symposium FTRTFT'94 (Formal Techniques in Real Time and Fault Tolerant Systems)*, *LNCS*, vol. 863, 1994.

26. N.G. Leveson, M.P.E. Heimdahl, H. Hildreth, J.D. Reese: *Requirements Specification for Process-Control Systems*, *IEEE Trans. Software Eng.*, vol. 12, pp. 684-707, 1994.

27. L. Lamport. *The Temporal Logic of Actions*. Research Report 79, Digital Equipment Corporation System Research Center 1991.

28. L. Ljung: *System Identification. Theory for the User*, Prentice-Hall, 1987.

29. A. Lötzbeyer *Simulator for the Dagstuhl Seminar 1995: "Steam-Boiler Control Specification Problem"* Implementation and Documentation (README and inline) at FZI (Forschungszentrum für Informatik) Karlsruhe, 1995.

30. D.G. Luenberger: *Introduction to Dynamic Systems. Theory, Models & Applications*, Wiley, 1979.

31. Z. Manna and A. Pnueli. Verifying hybrid systems, pp. 4-35 in [16].

32. B. Moszkowski. A temporal logic for multi-level reasoning about hardware. *IEEE Computer*, 18(2):10–19, 1985.

33. B. Moszkowski. *Executing Temporal Logic Programs*. Cambridge University Press, 1986.

34. J. S. Ostroff. *Temporal Logic for Real-time Systems*. Advanced Software Development Series. Wiley, 1989.

35. A.P. Ravn, H. Rischel, K.M. Hansen: Specifying and Verifying Requirements of Real-Time Systems, *IEEE Trans. Software Eng.*, vol. 19, pp. 41-55, 1993

36. A.P. Ravn. *Design of Embedded Real-time Computing Systems*, Manuscript, Department of Computer Science, Technical University of Denmark, September 1994.

37. R. L. Schwartz, P. M. Melliar-Smith, and F. H. Vogt. An interval logic for higher-level temporal reasoning. In *Proceedings of the 2nd. Annual ACM Symposium on Principles of Distributed Computing*, pages 173–186, 1983.

38. J. Vytopil, editor. *Proceedings Symp. on Formal Techniques in Real-Time and Fault-Tolerant Systems*, volume 571 of *LNCS*. Springer-Verlag, 1991.

39. Zhou Chaochen, C.A.R. Hoare, A.P. Ravn: A Calculus of Durations, *Information Processing Letters*, vol. 40, 5, pp. 269-276, 1991.

40. Zhou Chaochen, M.R. Hansen, A.P. Ravn, H. Rischel: Duration Specifications for Shared Processors, pp. 21-32 in [38].

41. Zhou Chaochen, A.P. Ravn, M.R. Hansen. Extended Duration Calculus for Hybrid Real-Time Systems, pp. 36–59 in [16].

Why Use Evolving Algebras for Hardware and Software Engineering?

Egon Börger

Università di Pisa, Dipartimento di Informatica, Corso Italia 40,
I-56125 Pisa, Italy

Abstract. In this paper I answer the question how evolving algebras can be used for the design and analysis of complex hardware and software systems. I present the salient features of this new method and illustrate them through several examples from my work on specification and verification of programming languages, compilers, protocols and architectures. The definition of a mathematical model for Hennessy and Patterson's RISC architecture DLX serves as a running example; this model is used in [24] to prove the correctness of instruction pipelining. I will point out the yet unexplored potential of the evolving algebra method for large-scale industrial applications.

> *Ich habe oft bemerkt, dass wir uns durch allzuvieles Symbolisieren*
> *die Sprache für die Wirklichkeit untüchtig machen.*
> Christian Morgenstern[1]

It needs some courage to come after three decades of intensive research in the area of formal methods and to advocate yet another general method for software and hardware design. However the huge gap between much of academic theory and the prevailing software and hardware practice is still with us, as is a wide-spread scepticism about the industrial benefit of formal methods (see the discussion in the literature about what are the right methods and criteria [33, 68, 69, 47, 78, 31, 32]) for software engineering to become a "mature engineering discipline"[54]. I accept with pleasure the invitation to explain to this audience how the new evolving algebra approach contributes to bridging this gap. I will try to convince you that it offers a mathematically well founded and rigorous but nevertheless simple discipline practical and scalable to industrial applications.

The notion of *evolving algebra* has been discovered by Gurevich in an attempt to sharpen Turing's thesis by considerations from complexity theory (see [39]) where the notion has led to important new developments [6]. At that time I was trying to develop a mathematical model for the programming language Prolog; this led me to the idea to use the notion of evolving algebras for defining transparent and simple specifications of complex dynamic systems at various levels of abstraction and to relate such specifications through hierarchies of provably correct stepwise refinements. I understood that using this notion one can

---

[1] Translation: I have often observed that by over-symbolizing we make the language inefficient to use in the real world.

develop a powerful and elegant specification method which a) supports the way programmers work and and b) provides a rigorous basis for it. Through numerous real-world case studies this idea has been confirmed.

I will illustrate the main features of this new approach through examples from evolving algebra specifications and verifications of real-life programming languages, compilers, protocols and architectures (see [11] for an annotated bibliography complete up to 1994). The running technical example is an abstract mathematical definition of the well known RISC architecture DLX [49]. For DLX the notion of sequential evolving algebra suffices; note however that in [41] this notion has been extended to that of distributed evolving algebras which turned out to be natural and powerful for modeling distributed systems. I start from scratch without presupposing any knowledge of DLX. It is not the worst argument for a specification method that for this architecture one can define a clear mathematical model which is easy to manipulate; the model has been used in [24] in a correctness proof of current instruction pipelining techniques.

The discussion leads also to the question what constitutes a *proof* and what is the role of *ground models* when we *apply* our mathematical notions and methods to the physical and technical world.

More precisely I will explain in sections 1–9 the following 9 features of the evolving algebra approach to the specification and verification of complex computer systems:

1. *freedom of abstraction* by which evolving algebras offer hierarchical structuring combined with systematic use of stepwise refinement and by which they support the software life-cycle phases from initial specifications to executable code,
2. powerful but simple mechanism for *information hiding* and defining *precise interfaces* which makes evolving algebra models easily adaptable,
3. *locality principle for dynamics*,
4. *separating specifications from verifications*,
5. *avoiding the "formal system straitjacket"*,
6. satisfactory links to application domains by *appropriate ground models*,
7. *support of abstract operational views*,
8. *scalability* to large complex systems including hardware/software co-design,
9. *easy learning by the practitioner* without presupposing any previous theoretical training, although the method has a *rigorous mathematical foundation*.

Other formal methods (VDM, Z, RAISE, B, ... [2]) share some of these features, but to my knowledge only evolving algebras combine them all.

1 Freedom of Abstraction

It is well known that general abstraction principles are needed to cope with the complexity of large systems. Whereas the algebraic specification theory [79]

---

[2] This is not the place for the interesting task to compare evolving algebras to other formal methods in the literature.

shows a way to deal with abstract data types and the action semantics approach [64] proposes a scheme for constructing complex operations out of basic components, evolving algebras offer the possibility to choose both, the data and the basic actions, at any level of abstraction and independently of each other. The way this is done is simple and corresponds to common practice in systems engineering: when specifying a software or hardware system one has to define its basic *objects* and the elementary *operations* which the system uses for its actions (dynamical behaviour). In other words one has to define the basic domains and functions of a system. This leads in a natural way to the mathematical notion of *structures* as formalization of system *states*, as I am going to explain now.

1.1 Universes

Each system S deals with certain basic *objects* which might be classified into different categories. This is reflected in an evolving algebra model of S by corresponding *sets* (also called universes or domains), one for each category of objects. These sets can be completely abstract—this is the case if no restriction is imposed on the corresponding category of objects. In case that the objects are assumed to have certain properties or to be in certain relations with other objects, we formalize these properties and relations by corresponding conditions (integrity constraints) which the objects in those sets are required to satisfy. The evolving algebra approach accepts any precise formulation of such conditions, in whatever language or framework they are given. The domains might also be equipped with certain functions providing some basic structure which can be used in the operations to be performed by the system.

In the remaining part of this subsection I illustrate this data abstraction principle by a discussion of basic DLX domains. I will try to show that the evolving algebra approach allows one to make well known ideas rigorous following simple patterns of reasoning every programmer is familiar with.

DLX is a general purpose register machine,.i.e. the operands of the basic operations are stored internally in CPU registers. Thus registers are basic objects of the architecture and are formalized as elements of a set REG. The content of registers is represented abstractly by a function $reg : REG \to WORD$ where $WORD$ is not furthermore specified at this stage but is intended to be implemented by a set of words. One use of registers in DLX is to contain addresses for memory access. This can be reflected abstractly by a set $ADDR$ satisfying $ADDR \subset WORD$ and coming with a function $mem : ADDR \to WORD$ which yields the content of the memory at the given address. We will see below that various interesting features of DLX can be described appropriately and succinctly on the basis of such an abstract notion of memory.

DLX is a load–store machine, i.e. the operands of ALU–instructions are not memory addresses but are taken from registers or from the instruction itself. This design decision for the location of operands can be reflected by an abstract set $INSTR$ of instructions on which functions are defined which provide the operands. The design decision for DLX that no instruction can have more than two operands and that some instructions have a so called immediate value as (part of) an operand is reflected by the fact that we can formalize by three abstract functions how the machine gets its operands from an instruction, namely $fst\_op, scd\_op : INSTR \rightarrow REG$ and $ival : INSTR \rightarrow VALUE$. These functions are partial because the R–type instructions have two register operands whereas the I–type instructions take only one operand from a register and have the other one directly encoded into the instruction as immediate value and the J–type instructions (J for jumps) have only an immediate operand. We can use once more an abstract function $iop :\, INSTR \rightarrow BOOL$ to formalize the mode of addressing operands without imposing any details for the instruction format. In accordance with this view we also use an abstract function

$$opcode : INSTR \rightarrow ALU\_SET \cup TRANSFER \cup CONTROL$$

to split the instructions into three disjoint sets which have the obvious intended interpretation as set of arithmetical and logical, data transfer or jump instructions. At a certain abstraction level we will define these sets explicitly following [49, p.165]. For example ALU_SET is split into ALU and SET where ALU contains the usual arithmetical, logical and shift instructions and SET contains the usual operations for zero-test and $\leq, \geq$ etc. tests (in R–type and in I–type form), i.e.

$$ALU = \{ADD, SUB, \ldots, AND, OR, \ldots, SLL, SRL, \ldots, ADDI, \ldots\}.$$

Similarly TRANSFER is split into sets LOAD, STORE, INTERRUPT and CONTROL into JUMP and BRANCH. The principles of pipelining in DLX can be described without further specification of the instruction format. This means that we also do not formulate here any conditions which assure that no instruction needs both to calculate an address and to perform an operation on data. This feature will become apparent from the formalization of the instruction interpretation below; it is this feature which allows us in the pipelined version of the architecture to combine the execution step proper with the effective address calculation for memory access and jump instructions.

The above mentioned universes are static—i.e. they do not change; in general, the evolving algebra framework permits universes also to be dynamic. Since the main intention of the concept of evolving algebras is to reflect the dynamical system behaviour in a direct and simple way, there is a construct for growing of universes, namely **extend** A **by** $x_1, \ldots, x_n$ **with** — **endextend** where '—' is used to define certain properties or functions for (some of) the new objects x_i of the universe A. We use it in our Prolog model [27] which reflects the underlying resolution tree. Upon calling a user-defined activator the system creates as many new children nodes to start alternative computations as there are candidate clauses in the procedure definition of the activator in the user's database db. The child relation is needed for the backtracking behaviour of the system and is formalized using a function $father$. To each new node t_i the corresponding clause occurrence c_i in the program db is associated using a function cll and the current node records the candidates to be selected as possible alternatives to continue the current computation. This is formalized by the following Call Rule of Prolog:

$$\textbf{if } is\_user\_defined(act) \wedge mode = Call$$
$$\textbf{then extend } NODE \textbf{ by } t_1, \ldots, t_n \textbf{ with}$$
$$father(t_i) := currnode$$
$$cands(currnode) := [t_1, \ldots, t_n]$$
$$cll(t_i) := c_i$$
$$\textbf{endextend}$$
$$mode := Select$$
$$\textbf{where } [c_1, \ldots, c_n] = procdef(act, db)$$

By the way domain extension and deletion of elements can be reduced to function updates [41].

1.2 Dynamic Functions

Once it has become clear what are the basic objects of a system S, one has to think about what are the elementary operations which are performed on those objects in S. Typically, a basic operation consists of setting a certain value, given the values of certain parameters. The most general framework of such operations is the following *function update*:

$$f(t_1, \ldots, t_n) := t$$

where f is an arbitrary n–ary function and $t_1, \ldots, t_n$ represent the parameters at which the value of the function is set to t. Evolving algebras allow function updates with arbitrary functions f and expressions t_i, t of any complexity or level of abstraction. Functions whose values can change are called *dynamic* in contrast to *static* functions which do not change.

Function updates provide the basic notion of *destructive assignment at any level of abstraction*. The above Call Rule for Prolog updates the dynamic functions *father, cands, cll, currnode, mode*. The last two functions have arity 0 and thus correspond to (global) variables in programming which can be updated dynamically and at different moments can assume different values. Also the typical fetch–execution mechanism in an architecture can be described in terms of two 0–ary functions, say $IR, PC \in REG$ for the instruction register (containing the currently executed instruction) and the program counter (containing the address of the next instruction to be fetched). The updating of the program counter is expressed by the function update $reg(PC) := next(reg(PC))$ where the function $next : INSTR\_ADDR \rightarrow INSTR\_ADDR \subset ADDR$ determines for a given instruction address (in PC) the next instruction address (to be stored in PC). The fetching of the next instruction to be executed is described by the function update $reg(IR) := mem(reg(PC))$. Clearly we rely here upon the obvious integrity constraint that the range of the restriction of *mem* to INSTR_ADDR is a subset of INSTR.

Function updates are the mechanism by which the dynamics of arbitrary systems can be described in an explicit way. In accordance with usual practice the execution of updates in evolving algebras can be conditioned by guards, giving rise to *transition rules* of the form **if** *Cond* **then** *Updates*. *Cond* is an arbitrary boolean valued expression (first–order logic formula) and *Updates* a finite set of updates. If *Cond* is true the rule can be executed by simultaneously executing each update in the set *Updates*. (The simultaneous execution of more than one update helps to avoid an explicit description of intermediate storage, see for example the updates $a := b, b := a$.)

The above Call Rule for Prolog is a typical example of an evolving algebra transition rule. This type of rules suffices to describe the sequential control of DLX following elementary ideas familiar to every programmer; see section 1.4.

1.3 States as Static Algebras

To speak about a system means to talk about its objects in terms of functions and relations defined on them. Domains, functions, and relations constitute what in mathematics is called a *structure*. Structures without relations are traditionally called *algebras*. Since relations (and in particular sets) can be represented by their characteristic functions, for simplicity we deal only with algebras.

A sequential *evolving algebra* can be defined as a finite set of transition rules **if** *Cond* **then** *Updates*. The effect of a transition rule R when applied to an algebra $\mathcal{A}$ is to produce another algebra $\mathcal{A}'$ which differs from $\mathcal{A}$ by the new values for those functions at those arguments where the values are updated by the rule R.

The *consistency* of updates is the responsibility of the programmer who may use special tools for the purpose. For the simple evolving algebra model for the sequential control of DLX defined in the next subsection it is obvious from the form of the rules that they are consistent.

Note that no rule changes the type of the functions; only the incarnation (the concrete interpretation) of a function changes by changing some of its values. We speak therefore of algebras also as *static* algebras, to distinguish them from evolving algebras. Evolving algebras are transition systems which transform static algebras.

Thus, the abstraction principle which is built into the notion of evolving algebra can be summarized as follows: (static) algebras as "states" and guarded destructive assignments for abstract functions as basic dynamic operations. This is the most general notion of state and of dynamic changes of states modern mathematics offer. As a consequence evolving algebras are the most general notion of a (discrete) dynamic system. A priori no restriction is imposed on the abstraction level where one might want to place an evolving algebra description of a system.

This freedom explains the success of the simple and transparent evolving algebra models for the semantics and the implementation of numerous complex programming languages like Prolog [7, 8, 27, 28], C [43], VHDL [20, 21], Occam [17, 16], for protocols [22, 55], architectures [14, 13, 24], real–time algorithms [45, 46], etc. which have been developed in a relatively short time by a relatively small number of persons who used only evolving algebras as tool. It is also the

feature of evolving algebras which assure *extensibility* and *reusability*; see the ease
with which the Prolog model in [7, 8, 27] could be modified to provide models for
various well known extensions of Prolog by parallelism [25], constraints [30, 29],
types [2], functional [23] or object–oriented features (see [9] for a detailed survey).

The importance of the freedom of abstraction is also confirmed by a common
experience in the design of algorithms. Namely, the need to model phenomena
of the real world, which are given a priori, leads the designer of programs to use
'abstract structures', as has been well expressed a long time ago by N. Wirth:
*"... Data in the first instance represent abstractions of real phenomena and are
preferably formulated as abstract structures not necessarily realized in common
programming languages."* [80, p.10]

The reciprocal dependency of algorithms and data structures makes it important for the designer not to be hindered by inappropriate restrictions of the
framework; in Wirth's words: *"It is clear that decisions about structuring data
cannot be made without knowledge of the algorithms applied to the data and
that, vice versa, the structure and choice of algorithms often depend strongly on
the structure of the underlying data. In short, the subjects of program composition and data structures are inseparably intertwined."* [80, p.9]

By their power of abstraction evolving algebras offer the freedom the designer
needs to 'tailor' his models to the given level of abstraction and to express his
ideas without introducing any extraneous formal overhead. This allows one to
build an arbitrarily complex system as a hierarchy of appropriate simpler evolving algebras , making systematic use of stepwise refinement. As a consequence
the evolving algebra method supports all the software life-cycle phases from
initial specifications to executable code; see for example [3, 28, 16].

1.4   The Sequential Control for DLX

The sequential control of DLX is formalized as in Prolog's Call rule by the values
of *mode* for the different execution phases. In mode OPERAND the operands
of the previously fetched instruction are decoded by putting them into the two
register file exits (0–ary functions) A, B from where they are taken as input by
the ALU. The next value of *mode* is determined by the result *opcode*(IR) of
decoding the operation code.

For ALU or SET instructions the ALU computes the value of the function
$opcode(IR)'$ for the given operands and outputs it to the register file entry C
from where this result is written in mode WRITE_BACK into the corresponding
destination register *dest(IR)* in the register file.[3]

For LOAD or STORE instructions first—i.e. in mode MEM_ADDR—the
Memory Address Register MAR is used for the result of the MEM_ADDR calculation (which involves the immediate value and the value in A); for STORE
instructions also the value to be transfered to the memory is passed from B to

---

[3] For the sequential model of DLX an additional register TEMP appears in [49] which
   temporarily stores the right second operand (namely $fst\_op(IR)$ or $ival(IR)$, depending on the type of the instruction); this call for an intermediate mode ALU'.

the Memory Data Register MDR. Then—i.e. in mode MEM_ACC—the memory is accessed for the transfer of data between MDR and the calculated memory position. In case of LOADing the data are then—i.e. in mode WRITE_BACK— written from MDR into the destination register in the register file.[4]

The special interrupt address register IAR is accessed only by instructions in INTERRUPT = {MOVS2I, MOVI2S} (for moving the interrupt information from or to IAR) or by the system jump TRAP (for moving PC into IAR).

The set JUMP splits into PLAINJ, LINKJ and {TRAP}. The characteristic difference of LINKJ instructions is that they record the current value of PC in the destination register.

These explanations should suffice for an understanding of the following evolving algebra rules which formalize the diagrams in [49] for the sequential control of DLX; the model is complete except for the floating point related DLX instructions which are left out for reasons of space.

For notational succinctness the function *reg* is systematically suppressed and the abbreviation $\alpha \leftarrow \beta \equiv \alpha' := \beta'$ is used where γ' is obtained from γ by substituting $reg(R)$ for R. For the same reason the standard argument IR for the static decoding functions is dropped and an abbreviation *new_mode* is used with *AS* standing for $ALU \cup SET$, *M* for $LOAD \cup STORE$, *I* for INTERRUPT, *J* for $JUMP \cup BRANCH$.

if *mode* = ⎡FETCH⎤
then $IR \leftarrow mem\ (PC)$
  $PC \leftarrow next\ (PC)$
  $mode := OPERAND$

if *mode* = ⎡OPERAND⎤
then $A \leftarrow fst\_op$
  $B \leftarrow scd\_op$
  $mode := new\_mode$

if *mode* = ⎡ALU⎤
then if $iop(opcode)$
  then $TEMP \leftarrow ival$
  else $TEMP \leftarrow B$
  $mode := ALU'$

$new\_mode =$
$\begin{cases} ALU & \textbf{if}\ opcode \in AS \\ MEM\_ADDR & \textbf{if}\ opcode \in M \\ IAR & \textbf{if}\ opcode \in I \\ JUMPS & \textbf{if}\ opcode \in J \end{cases}$

if *mode* = ⎡ALU'⎤
then $C \leftarrow opcode'(A, TEMP)$
  $mode := WRITE\_BACK$

if *mode* = ⎡WRITE_BACK⎤
then $dest \leftarrow C$
  $mode := FETCH$

if *mode* = ⎡MEM_ADDR⎤
then $MAR \leftarrow A + ival$
  if $opcode \in STORE$
  then $mode := pass\_B\_to\_MDR$
  else $mode := MEM\_ACC$

if *mode* = ⎡pass_B_to_MDR⎤
then $MDR \leftarrow B$
  $mode := MEM\_ACC$

---

[4] Note that in DLX it is supposed that depending on the operation code only a subword of what has been loaded from the memory to MDR is copied into the destination register; this calls for an intermediate mode SUBWORD.

if $mode = \boxed{\text{MEM\_ACC}}$
  $\wedge \; opcode \in STORE$
then $mem(MAR) \leftarrow MDR$
    $mode := FETCH$

if $mode = \boxed{\text{MEM\_ACC}}$
  $\wedge \; opcode \in LOAD$
then $MDR \leftarrow mem(MAR)$
    $mode := SUBWORD$

if $mode = \boxed{\text{SUBWORD}}$
then $C \leftarrow opcode'(MDR)$
    $mode := WRITE\_BACK$

if $mode = \boxed{\text{IAR}}$
then if $opcode = MOVS2I$
    then $C \leftarrow IAR$
       $mode := WRITE\_BACK$
    if $opcode = MOVI2S$
    then $IAR \leftarrow A$
       $mode := FETCH$

if $opcode \in \boxed{\text{BRANCH}}$
  $\& mode = JUMPS$
then if $opcode'(A)$
    then $PC \leftarrow PC + ival$
    $mode := FETCH$

if $mode = \boxed{\text{JUMPS}}$
then if $opcode = TRAP$ **then** $IAR \leftarrow PC$
          $PC \leftarrow ival$
    if $opcode \in PLAINJ \cup LINKJ$
    then if $iop(opcode)$ **then** $PC \leftarrow ival + PC$
          else $PC \leftarrow A$
    if $opcode \in \{TRAP\} \cup PLAINJ$ **then** $mode := FETCH$
    if $opcode \in LINKJ$ **then** $C \leftarrow PC$
          $mode := WRITE\_BACK$

2 Information Hiding and Interfaces

Information hiding, introduced by D. Parnas [67], calls for modular structuring of systems. In a practical specification method, information hiding has to go hand in hand with a good discipline to handle interfaces. The evolving algebra approach offers both in a most general way through the concepts of *oracle functions* and *externally alterable functions*.

Let f be a function of an evolving algebra $\mathcal{A}$. If f has no updates of the form $f(t_1, \ldots, t_n) := t$ in any transition rule of $\mathcal{A}$, it is called an *oracle function* of $\mathcal{A}$; if f does appear in an update $f(t_1, \ldots, t_n) := t$ of a transition rule of $\mathcal{A}$ it is called *internally updatable* or internally alterable. Dynamic functions whose values can be affected by the environment are called *externally alterable*.

Oracle functions are completely determined by the environment. They can be static or dynamic; if they are dynamic they are externally but not internally alterable. For the description of distributed systems it is convenient that in the evolving algebra framework one can speak about functions which are both externally and internally alterable; for such functions it depends on the system which discipline is imposed to avoid conflicts between external and internal changes of the function.

Usually the rules of A give some crucial information on the dynamical behaviour of internally updatable functions f of A . In contrast the rules of A give no information on how an oracle function f of A operates; such a function cannot be modified ('written') by A, but it can be used ('read') in the rules of A to determine arguments at which an internally updatable function is changed dynamically or to determine the new value in such updates. Oracle functions and externally alterable functions f are used to represent influences of the environment in which the given evolving algebra is intended to work. It is the task of the system designer to provide the information on f which he wants the programmer to know and to use. In the evolving algebra approach this interface information can range from nothing at all—this is the case of a function for which only the number and the types of its arguments and values are known—to a full specification by some axioms or by a set of equations or by another evolving algebra (module), etc. Note that due to the abstraction principle explained in the previous section the evolving algebra approach imposes no restriction at all on the choice of externally alterable or oracle functions and the way they are described. The use of evolving algebras does not trivialize the difficult task of "designer control of the distribution of information" ([67]:p. 344), but at least it does not hinder this task by extraneous overhead of formalities and offers a flexible and open framework to guarantee information hiding and the definition of precise abstract interfaces.

As a consequence, the evolving algebra approach helps to ensure that programs, once developed, can be extended, maintained and reused as components of larger systems in a systematic and reliable way. Also it integrates well into existing development environments without requiring a complete revision of the latter. Another pragmatically important feature in this context is that through skilful introduction of the appropriate abstractions high–level evolving algebra specifications allow one often to produce precise definitions of modules which are considerably shorter than implementations of those modules in a programming language.

In the following subsection I explain some examples showing the power of abstraction which is offered through the introduction of externally alterable or oracle functions in evolving algebra descriptions of complex systems.

Examples of Externally Alterable and Oracle Functions. The code related functions *fst_op, scd_op, iop, ival, opcode* and *next* in DLX are static, determined by an initialization (not given here) which contains the given program to be executed. The four simple rules [27] which define the complete behaviour of Prolog for user–defined predicates make crucial use of two oracle functions *procdef* and *unify.*

The function *procdef* is supposed to provide for given literal l and program db the clauses in db which are relevant for l, in the order in which they have to be applied. The whole backtracking behaviour of Prolog (including optimizations like determinacy detection) can be described on the basis of this abstract function *procdef.* If one considers Prolog without program modifying operations like *assert, retract*, then *procdef* is a static oracle function. If one wants to model also Prolog's program modification features then *procdef* becomes a dynamic and internally updatable function (see [15, 26]). Through the refinement process by which the Prolog model of [27] is linked in a provably correct way to the WAM implementation model in [28] *procdef* receives an explicit definition.

unify is supposed in [7, 8, 27] to provide for each pair of literals either a unifying substitution or the information that there is no such unification. The function describes the abstract behaviour of unification without being bound to any concrete unification algorithm. It also hides from the programmer the details about the representation of terms which appear in the refined WAM models of [28]. As a result the abstract PROLOG model of [27] and its refinement to the WAM model of [28] could easily be extended to constraint logic programming languages with or without types where unifiability appears as a particular case of constraints (see the evolving algebra definitions of PROLOG III [30], Protos–L [2], and CLP(R) [29]).

The oracle function *find-catcher* for which a recursive definition is given in [27] leads to a concise formalization of the error–handling predicates *catch* and *throw* of Prolog.

In the evolving algebra model [20, 21] for the IEEE VHDL Standard we have obtained a simple and uniform rule set for signal assignments by introducing for the inertial delay an oracle function *reject* for which we give a natural and easily understandable recursive definition. Similarly, a transparent description is obtained for the propagation of signal values by introducing oracle functions for the so–called driving and effective values; the former is determined by a recursion on the signal sources, the latter by a recursion on port association elements from ports to signals. In both cases the recursive definitions replace rather complex algorithmic characterizations in the VHDL'93 language reference manual [56].

In the abstract evolving algebra models of Occam (see [17]) which are the starting point for the correctness proof of a compilation scheme into Transputer instructions in [16] we have taken great advantage of the usual flowchart layout of programs; we define it by oracle functions which in the later refinement steps are replaced by recursive definitions of the compiling function. Considerable simplifications for both the specifications and the proofs have also been obtained there by leaving the evaluation and compilation of expressions and the implementation of values abstract, realized by appropriately restricted oracle functions.

For Lamport's mutual exclusion protocol, known as the Bakery Algorithm, a considerable simplification of the correctness proofs in the literature has been achieved in [22] by introducing two externally alterable functions, namely *Ticket* and *Go*, on which three natural conditions and an induction principle are imposed which imply the correctness of the protocol.

The widely used parallel virtual machine PVM realizes a distributed computation model which is characterized by the *reactive behaviour* of concurrently operating PVM daemon processes, each residing on one of several host computers. The daemons are triggered by the environment; they carry out the PVM instructions of the local tasks they have to manage and interact with each other through asynchronous message–passing communication. No daemon can influence when, from where and which request or message will reach him, rather he has to wait for the next such event to come whenever he is idle. We have modelled this intuition faithfully by introducing an externally alterable oracle function *event* which for a given daemon might yield a PVM instruction or a message as value. If *event(pvmd)* is defined and has the value *instr/mssg*, then the daemon *pvmd* is going to execute/read *instr/mssg*. This is formalized in our PVM model [18, 19] by a rule of form

$$\textbf{if } event(pvmd) = instr/mssg \textbf{ then } execute\_instr/read\_mssg$$

for each individual PVM instruction *instr* or PVM message *mssg*, where *execute_instr/read_mssg* represents the corresponding updates. An integrity constraint on the function *event* is that a defined value of *event(pvmd)* remains stable until the PVM daemon pvmd has evaluated the function. However, we assume 'destructive reading' such that *event(pvmd)* is reset to *undef* or indicates the next event as soon as the pvmd has read the current value. The dynamic oracle function *event* thus directly reflects the way in which tasks interact with their local PVM daemon when they want PVM routines to be invoked. Using the dynamic oracle function *event* we abstract from the specific way how the daemon's walk through his sequence of instructions/messages is determined by the activities of his tasks.

In all these cases the externally alterable or static functions allowed us to define a precise interface with respect to which the model under discussion works in a simple and transparent way. If for such an abstract model one wants to prove general properties about the behaviour of the system where externally updatable or oracle functions play a role, one has to state and assume the properties which are used. In order to guarantee an unchanged interface behaviour these properties have to be proved to be satisfied when those functions are defined explicitly or implemented in later refinement steps or modified by changing requirements.

The most general *concept of modularity* which is present through the notions of externally alterable and oracle functions is deliberately kept open in the definition of evolving algebras. The resulting flexibility in using and dealing with different module structures is an advantage for real–life specification endeavors. Nothing prevents us from restricting this notion to specific and even syntactic concepts of compositionality where the need arises; an example where it turned out to be useful to stick to a simple and well known automaton–theoretic concept of composition of evolving algebras through sequencing, juxtaposition, and feedback can be found in [13].

3 Locality Principle for Dynamics

It is typical for large systems that their overall behaviour is determined by the actions of their components, i.e. by *local* changes. Even for the dynamic performance of large *sequential* systems it is characteristic that at each moment and in a given context only a few things do change whereas the rest remains unchanged.

The complexity of the behaviour of a large system is due to the overall effect of a lot of small local changes. Often descriptions which build upon the locality phenomenon are considerably simpler and more natural than global descriptions which try not to refer to single computation steps. Exploiting a locality property can lead often to a modular design. In contrast to a widely held view not only the description of the system behaviour, but also the mathematical reasoning about it can become considerably simpler if the locality principle is used. It allows one to concentrate on the parameters which *do* change and not to have to worry about the other state components which *do not* change under the considered transition.

The evolving algebra method allows one to reflect this characteristic interplay between global and local dynamic system behaviour in a direct and faithful way by viewing (global) system states as static algebras and by providing the possibility to express local updates $f(t_1, \ldots, t_n) := t$ in a uniform way *at any level of abstraction*. We have used the locality principle with advantage for modelling parallel or distributed systems. See for example the succinct formalization given in [19] for the PVM message–passing interface. Another example is the parallel version DLX^p of DLX which we have defined as starting point for several further refinement steps leading to the pipelined version of DLX and a mathematical proof of its correctness [24].

3.1   The Basic Parallel Control for DLX with Pipelining

The refinement of DLX to a parallel model DLX^p in this section is taken from [24]. It resolves structural pipelining hazards and serves as link between DLX and its further refinements to the fully pipelined model in which also data and control hazards are resolved by the architecture.

The intuitive idea of pipelining is simple. The execution of an instruction is done in *DLX* in five stages, namely Instruction Fetch (IF), Instruction Decode which includes reading the operands (ID), EXecution proper for ALU operations which include (data or branch) address calculations using the ALU (EX), MEMory access (MEM) and Writing the computed result Back into the final register-file destination (WB). Since at each stage different actions are taken, ideally one can pipeline *DLX* by letting the processor execute during each clock cycle simultaneously one different *pipe stage* for each of five instructions. Roughly this can be described by eliminating the sequential control and by replacing where necessary the *mode* guards by *opcode(I)* guards which correspond to the pipe stage of the instruction *I* in question. The resulting rule system should then be interpreted under the *lock-step parallelism* semantics of evolving algebras; under this semantics at each moment each rule whose guard is true is applied.

Special care has to be taken however to avoid conflicts resulting from dependencies between instructions which can occur when some of their execution stages overlap. Structural hazards arise when during one clock cycle two instructions compete for resources, each functional architectural unit of *DLX* being available at each step only once. For example fetching a new instruction on each clock cycle would create a *mem* access conflict with load/store instructions. This can be avoided by increasing the memory bandwidth. We introduce therefore an additional memory access function mem_{instr} which is used only for fetching instructions and which is supposed to be a subfunction of mem; in this way we abstract from any particular implementation feature related to using separate instruction and data caches.

Similarly one avoids to use the ALU for incrementing the program counter PC by providing a separate PC-incrementer. This is reflected by the constraint that our abstract function $next$ has to be implemented without using the ALU. Note that the ALU is also not needed for the zero test in BRANCH–instructions because this test can be done using the standard exit of registers.

Some of the values which appear during the execution of an instruction at a certain pipe stage are needed also at later pipe stages and therefore should not be overwritten by the corresponding values of a subsequent instruction occurring in the pipeline. An example is the immediate value $ival(IR)$ which is used by jump instructions in their EX stage. For reasons of simplicity we abstract from possible optimizations and provide three additional 0–ary functions (latches) $IR1, IR2, IR3$ to keep full copies of a fetched instruction through the three pipe stages EX, MEM, WB. Similarly two latches $PC1$ and $C1$ are used to save the values of PC and C respectively for one pipe stage; $PC1$ provides at pipe stage EX of an instruction I a copy of the value of PC after the FETCH stage of I (serving in case I is a jump instruction the execution of which triggers a transfer or an update of that PC–value); $C1$ provides at pipe stage WB of an instruction I a copy of the ALU output value C computed in the pipe stage EX of I (which is the case for instructions with ALU/SET–operations, for $LINKJ$ instructions and for the interrupt instruction $MOVS2I$).

In DLX the register MDR is the only interface between the register-file and the memory and serves for both loading and storing to the memory. In the pipelined version for DLX however a load instruction I which in the pipeline immediately precedes a store instruction I' would compete with I' for writing into MDR in its pipe stage MEM (when consequently I' in its pipe stage EX wants to write B into MDR). This resource conflict is resolved by doubling MDR into two registers $LMDR$ and $SMDR$ and by refining the DLX–rules correspondingly. (Note that the refined rule $pass\_B\_to\_MDR$ requires a new direct link from the exit of B to the entry of $SMDR$ in order to avoid the use of the ALU for this data transfer.)

Since all pipe stages proceed simultaneously and the time which is needed for moving an instruction one step down the pipeline is a machine cycle, the length of the latter is determined by the time required for the slowest pipe stage. In order to balance the length of the pipeline stages the two ALU–rules of DLX are combined into one DLX^p–rule. Similarly the SUBWORD–rule (which selects and outputs to C the required portion of the word just loaded from the memory) is incorporated into the WRITE_BACK–rule under the guard that the value to be written comes through a loading instruction from the memory, i.e. has not been computed by executing an $ALU/SET, LINKJ, MOVS2I$ instruction in which case the value comes from $C1$. This is done at the expense of linking the exit of *LMDR* directly (without passing through *C1*) to the entry of the register-file and adding to the latter a selector for choosing among *C1* and (the required portion of) *LMDR*.

Note also that transferring a subword of *LMDR* into a destination register can be realized without using the ALU by relying upon the usual register shift functions.

We prove in [24] that the evolving algebra DLX^p obtained from DLX as described above resolves structural conflicts and therefore is a correct implementation of DLX under the assumption that the compiler takes care about avoiding data and control hazards. (In the further refinement steps we show how this assumption can be dismissed by additional architectural changes.)

The **IF stage** is described by the following $\boxed{\text{FETCH}}$ updates:

$$IR \leftarrow mem_{instr}(PC) \quad \textbf{if } \neg jumps \textbf{ then } PC \leftarrow next(PC)$$

where the condition $jumps \equiv$ opcode(IR1) $\in$ JUMP or (opcode (IR1) $\in$ BRANCH and opcode(IR1)'(A)) prevents the inconsistency with updates of PC in the EX stage of jump instructions (see the JUMP rule below).

The **ID stage** is described by the following $\boxed{\text{OPERAND}}$ and latch updates:

$$A \leftarrow fst\_op(IR) \quad B \leftarrow scd\_op(IR) \quad PC1 \leftarrow PC$$
$$IR1 \leftarrow IR \qquad\quad IR2 \leftarrow IR1 \qquad\quad IR3 \leftarrow IR2$$

The **EX stage** is described by the following nine rules:

$\boxed{\text{ALU}}$ **if** $opcode(IR1) \in ALU \cup SET$
then if $iop(opcode(IR1))$
      then $C \leftarrow opcode(IR1)'(A, ival(IR1))$
      else $C \leftarrow opcode(IR1)'(A, B)$

$\boxed{\text{MEM\_ADDR}}$
if $opcode(IR1) \in LOAD \cup STORE$
then $MAR \leftarrow A + ival(IR1)$

$\boxed{\text{pass\_B\_to\_MDR}}$
if $opcode(IR1) \in STORE$
then $SMDR \leftarrow B$

$\boxed{\text{INTERRUPTS2I}}$
if $opcode(IR1) = MOV S2I$
then $C \leftarrow IAR$

$\boxed{\text{INTERRUPTI2S}}$
if $opcode(IR1) = MOV I2S$
then $IAR \leftarrow A$

$\boxed{\text{TRAP}}$
if $opcode(IR1) = TRAP$
then $IAR \leftarrow PC1$
    $PC \leftarrow ival(IR1)$

$\boxed{\text{JUMP}}$
if $opcode(IR1) \in PLAINJ \cup LINKJ$
then if $iop (opcode (IR1))$
    then $PC \leftarrow ival(IR1) + PC1$
    else $PC \leftarrow A$

$\boxed{\text{LINKJ}}$
if $opcode(IR1) \in LINKJ$
then $C \leftarrow PC1$

$\boxed{\text{BRANCH}}$
if $opcode(IR1) \in BRANCH$
then if $opcode(IR1)'(A)$
    then $PC \leftarrow PC1 + ival(IR1)$

The **MEM stage** is described by the following three rules:

STORE	LOAD	$C1 \leftarrow C$
if $opcode(IR2) \in STORE$	**if** $opcode(IR2) \in LOAD$	
then $mem(MAR) \leftarrow SMDR$	**then** $LMDR \leftarrow mem(MAR)$	

The **WB stage** is described by the following WRITE_BACK rules:

$$\textbf{if } opcode(IR3) \in ALU \cup SET \cup \{MOVS2I\} \cup LINKJ$$
$$\textbf{then } dest(IR3) \leftarrow C1$$
$$\textbf{if } opcode(IR3) \in LOAD$$
$$\textbf{then } dest(IR3) \leftarrow opcode'(IR3)(LMDR)$$

4 Separating Specifications from Verifications

The use of evolving algebra allows one to tune specifications to a given application domain without having to care about the peculiarities of an a priori given verification system.

To many this feature of the evolving algebra approach will appear as either trivial or not desirable at all. They will insist that a good specification system has to come together with specific proof and implementation principles and techniques. Surprisingly one finds here representatives from both proof theory and software engineering. Many proof–theoretically inclined researchers tend to identify a semantic definition of a computing system with a (deductive system for a) logic and the reasoning on the so defined objects with proving theorems within that system of logic. But one finds here also software engineers who are looking for specifications produced using some general design calculus which leads to (mechanically verified) transformations into executable code. Let us look at two well-known witnesses.

Dijkstra's calculus for program design is a representative example of such a program development method. In [10] I have given my arguments why such a method, even if applied not to system development in the large but only to programming in the small, limits in an unacceptable way our ability to turn mathematical insight into good programs. Another example is the program synthesis approach which is based on the so–called formulae–as–types interpretation. It advocates the construction of provably correct programs by building proofs in a calculus for which it has been shown that the programs which are extracted from those proofs are correct with respect to formal specifications in the language of the system. Systems like NUPRL, COQ, ALF, LEGO have been implemented to support this researchwise productive approach [50] which encounters however great difficulties where it attempts to synthesize complex real–life programs. The method relies on intuitionistic logic and does not work for classical logic. Furthermore the proofs have to be constructed within a fixed formal system which does not support the use of simplifying heuristics coming from concrete application domains. Thereby the user is forced into a rigid corset in the same way as the programmer is who has to write code in an *a priori* fixed programming language and in a representation which is determined by an underlying machine architecture. Such restrictions can hinder the free exploration of corners of the design space which are difficult to reach and where interesting efficient solutions may be waiting for being discovered.

How important it is for a general design method to separate the concerns of specification and verification can be seen also from the impact this distinction has on building verification tools. Each particular specification language and tool relies upon a certain number of built-in assumptions and design decisions. Therefore one has to be careful to use it only for applications which share those assumptions. For example Lamport's TLA is based on a fixed notion of equivalence. If the system is used for proving equivalence concerning an application with a coarser notion of equivalence, one is forced to prove more than required; if the application has a finer notion of equivalence, one has to identify items which one really wants to distinguish (see [44]). Evolving algebras can be used in connection with *any* notion of equivalence.

Another illustration comes from the success obtained by tools for program development and verification which have been tailored to particular application domains. As outstanding recent examples one can cite here D. Smith's method for synthesis of high–performance transportation scheduling programs [77, 76] and Clarke and Dill's machinery for the verification of programs which can conveniently be mapped to finite state transition systems of manageable size and can be dealt with by automated model checking. Another remarkable example is Russinoff's [73] functional definition of an important subset of VHDL—the IEEE standard for a hardware description language; it comes together with related procedures for deriving and verifying behavioral specifications of combinatorial and sequential devices which can be formally encoded in Boyer–Moore Computational Logic for mechanical proof checking.

In such situations it is the precise knowledge of a well defined application domain which provides the insight into how to tune the design and verification— or analysis and synthesis—principles to each other and to the given application domain. Our experience shows that evolving algebras make it possible to take advantage from the separation of concerns: they assure the highest degree of flexibility in adapting the means of description to the specific features of any application domain and they allow one to incorporate into the proof methods all the knowledge which is available in the application. Indeed in complex design situations drastic simplifications can be obtained if one *first* circumscribes the conceptual constituents of a specification and only then starts to look for possible means of proof. But more importantly the evolving algebra approach allows one to use the brain where the muscles of even the strongest mechanized proof system ("brawn methods") cannot really help any more.

This claim is supported by our experience in working with evolving algebras for proving run-time properties of complex systems. For example during our work on the correctness proofs for the compilation of Prolog and Occam compilers [28, 17, 16], at various occasions we avoided getting stuck only because the evolving algebra framework allowed us to invent intermediate models which had not been expected at the beginning. By introducing these intermediate specification levels we could reduce the complexity of each single refinement step in such a way that we were enabled to formulate and prove the relevant correctness statements. There is a trade–off between the abstraction difference of two specification levels and the difficulties one encounters when trying to prove properties which relate specifications at those levels. My guiding principle for breaking complex statements into simpler ones has been to stop only where the proofs become routine inductions and case distinctions which can be carried out by an automatic or interactive theorem proving system. Indeed at present two research groups at the universities of Karlsruhe and Munich are using their theorem proving systems KIV and ISABELLE respectively to provide a machine verification of our mathematical WAM correctness proof.

The flexibility of evolving algebras has also the effect that their use can easily be integrated into existing development systems—a vital feature for a practical design method. Such an integration might easily turn out to be impossible for a fixed formal system which could require, by its rigidity, to completely change the entire already existing development system—a pragmatically speaking unrealistic request.

It is still unclear to what degree complex systems can be satisfactorily let alone completely verified. The evolving algebra approach allows one to give *relative* correctness proofs, i.e. proofs that specific system parts function well under precisely stated assumptions on a well behaving environment. Such environmental parameters and their properties enter the specification and the proof as abstract interface, technically speaking as externally alterable or as oracle functions. Since evolving algebras can be appropriately tailored to any desired interface they permit to satisfactorily solve the design and analysis problems of an embedded system *modulo the context* into which this system is embedded.[5] For solutions of practical problems in our real word we cannot expect more from a scientific method as Popper explains with a good picture [71]:

> Die Wissenschaft baut nicht auf Felsengrund. Es ist eher ein Sumpfland, über dem sich die kühne Konstruktion ihrer Theorien erhebt; sie ist ein Pfeilerbau, dessen Pfeiler sich von oben her in den Sumpf senken— aber nicht bis zu einem natürlichen, 'gegebenen' Grund. Denn nicht deshalb hört man auf, die Pfeiler tiefer hineinzutreiben, weil man auf eine feste Schicht gestossen ist; wenn man hofft, dass sie das Gebäude tragen werden, beschliesst man, sich vorläufig mit der Festigkeit der Pfeiler zu begnügen.

---

[5] I am far from saying that this tailoring of a model to a desired interface is trivial: "The trickiest part is in explicitly stating the assumptions about the environment in which each critical piece is placed." [78, p. 13] Evolving algebras allow one to make such assumptions explicit in a direct way, without creating additional overhead which deals only with the formalism and not with the reality to be modeled. If there are problems in the subject matter, they are not solved by using evolving algebras; but use of the latter avoids the introduction of additional problems.

No formal method can guarantee the absolute correctness and safety of computer systems. The best one can obtain is relative correctness. Evolving algebras allow us to push the frontier of this effort much beyond what is widely believed—in particular in engineering and industrial circles—to be an inherent limitation of mathematical methods.

5   Avoiding the Formal System Straitjacket

Instead of building upon just one particular formal system the evolving algebra approach is an open framework into which a variety of systems can be incorporated. Evolving algebras assure the greatest possible *freedom of language* and *freedom of proof*.

Freedom of language. The freedom to choose how to represent the basic objects and operations of the system under consideration is crucial in two respects, namely for constructing satisfactory ground models and for building hierarchies of system levels. Related to this is the need to distinguish between concepts (*mathematical modelling*) and notation (*formalization*) and to remain flexible enough to be able to "choose the right notation".

A special "correctness" problem arises in those cases where the original requirement specification is given informally. This problem is a case of the general problem about the applicability of scientific methods to the real world and is relevant for the design of computer systems. I will explain in the section on *ground models* that using evolving algebras one can satisfactorily settle this problem thanks to the possibility to *tailor a description to the given application domain*.

The methods of *abstraction* and of *stepwise refinement* have been rightly recommended as a way to cope with complexity by *building and crossing hierarchies of system levels*. The two methods are intimately connected: only a specification framework which allows one to freely choose the appropriate abstractions for a given problem can provide the full freedom of refining abstract descriptions to intended lower level implementations. How else can we freely move among different language levels in computer design? This is well illustrated by an example suggested by Simon Read [72]: the industrial hardware design process at present uses separate languages for specification (behavioural VHDL), for design (Register Transfer Level VHDL), for implementation (cells), for verification (BDD's) and for mathematical reasoning (Boolean algebras). The example shows that any a priori restriction of the language by a fixed formal framework either results in restrictions of the application domain or forces you to work on encodings which are extraneous to the problems under investigation and usually are responsible for the well known combinatorial explosion encountered so often when specification frameworks are applied to real systems.

The freedom of language offered by evolving algebras assures that they can be integrated into arbitrary contexts at arbitrary system level without encountering any compatibility problems. Technically speaking this is based upon the choice of the language of mathematics (i.e. classical logic) as the underlying language.

This does not represent an a priori restriction of the specification language because the language of logic is as broad as a precise algorithmic language can be; as explained above there is no more basic algorithmic device than a transition rule system with guarded abstract function updates. The language of evolving algebras is flexible enough to deal with any practical algorithmic language of the working computer scientist. The choice of the language of mathematics guarantees that in the evolving algebra framework one can adapt the formalization of a model or a mathematical concept to the need of what has to be modelled. There is no special notation one has to learn; no peculiar syntax is imposed on the designer.

Freedom of proof. The evolving algebra approach offers the necessary freedom for the choice of the proof techniques used to establish properties of computer systems. This has to do with the fundamental *distinction between formal and rigorous* descriptions (or proofs), and more generally between various *degrees of precision*.

Traditional mathematical proofs aim at understanding by humans, at revealing structure which guides the comprehension; as a result they typically lead to further investigations. The essential ingredient of this process is creativity in *finding* proofs; creativity is the heart of mathematical progress. Formalized proofs provide *verifications* within a particular proof system. They belong to what Gurevich [40] proposed to call *Pedantics*, a respectful and badly needed scientific discipline of validating mathematical proofs. It is here that we will find machine checked proofs providing all the details which are suppressed in traditional mathematical proofs. Machine checked proofs can contribute to the pragmatic acceptance of theorems. Progress in pedantics will provide more freedom for writing less formal creative proofs. The role of interactive proof checkers is to couple in a practically fruitful manner the checking abilities of automated theorem provers with the user's creativity in finding proofs.

In connection with the need to develop correct programs for safety-critical applications, Pedantics has a still more important and (with respect to traditional mathematics) new role. Professional deontology obliges the mathematician to check the proof of any theorem he is going to use. This obligation was sufficient until the middle of this century to guarantee for mathematical results a very high (although not absolute) degree of reliability. The slow pace of this proof checking process by the mathematical community, a process which involved generations, was in equilibrium with the pace of discovery and of applications of new theorems. This has changed radically in the second half of this century. Statistics show us that nowadays on average there are only 2.5 readers per publication in mathematics. This fits the often quoted anecdotal claim that about one third of the published mathematical papers contain serious errors. But such statements say more about the refereeing process than about the inherent unreliability of mathematical proofs. Often despite errors in the proof, the theorem is correct and the proof can be corrected; a good mathematical proof creates the right images in the reader which allow him to fill the details and to repair the flaws.

The discipline of pedantics has to provide the laboratory conditions in which the traditional and slow proof checking process by humans is if not replaced then at least enhanced and speeded up by machine assisted interactive proof checking procedures; see the interesting report [66]. This is a rationale for programs like Beta testing. Pedantics has to create appropriate methods and criteria which an applied computer scientists can use when they need to decide whether and to what degree a proposed proof is reliable.

The notion of proof is not absolute. There is a hierarchy of notions of proof, each level having its own degree of precision. There are not only classical, intuitionistic, constructive proofs, but also flat and deeply structured ones. Mathematical proofs are always to be understood within a context of concepts, methods, groups of experts, background of previously developed theories. Their role, as analyzed by Plato who made the fundamental discovery of the underlying notion of universally valid law, is to establish *valid arguments*. Aristotle made this concept operational by inventing specific proof principles, even a proof format which has deeply influenced the occidental culture until it was again revolutionized by Frege and Hilbert. It is well known that the progress in mathematics is intimately related to the discovery of new notions and proof principles. Gödel's incompleteness theorem shows that this is not a historical accident but that it is necessarily so when we codify mathematical knowledge in concrete and well delimited formal frameworks.

The same holds for mechanical proofs. They are surely useful but also not absolute; their reliability depends on the correctness of the environment where they are executed and on the adequacy of the formalization. Fully formalized proofs are certainly less convincing for humans than well checked traditional mathematical proofs (see the discussion in [42]). It is for a reason that theorem proving researchers try hard to make machine produced proofs readable to humans.

Thus we have to accept that the notion of mathematical proof has a pragmatic component and thereby is limited by the progress of mathematics and pedantics.[6] On the other side one can say that the mathematical rigour has the highest degree of reliability which has been reached in occidental culture. I do not want to enter here into the discussion whether it is good to identify "formal" with "mathematical". We may be well advised to equate formal with other forms of rigour, as encountered in natural or engineering sciences or in jurisprudence. But in any case, a mathematical verification method has better chances to prove interesting theorems for real systems if it is not restricted to a fixed deductive system but can make use of all what mathematics has to of-

---

[6] To recognize the limitation of knowledge acquisition by mankind does not imply "that, in the end, it is a social process that determines whether mathematicians feel confident about a theorem", as has been claimed in [36, p. 271]. Here is not the place to enter the philosophical discussion on the status of objectivity of mathematical knowledge, a dispute which is with us since the ancient Greeks. One should keep in mind that a rigorous foundation of science must and can be *self-evident* in the Aristotelian sense, neither psychological nor social, see [1].

fer. This includes deductive systems, the discipline of Pedantics and the use of crisp and powerful mathematical techniques for the stepwise development and verification of complex software and hardware systems. The freedom to choose proof methods freely is a key to the success of the evolving algebra approach in proving non–trivial run–time properties.

6   Appropriate Ground Models

Ground models[7] play a crucial role in attempts to face the general problem of applicability of mathematical concepts and methods to the physical world. In this section I illustrate the notion of ground models in relation to computer science and explain the extraordinary potential of the evolving algebra approach to build satisfactory ground models.

The fundamental question is about the relation between our mind and the in-exact real–world phenomena. How can we relate our theoretical scientific models to the reality of our world? Typically what is given is a system S of problems in the real world for which I want to find a scientific solution. In computer science the solutions we are looking for are algorithms (in the general sense of the term, including interpreters for programming languages, protocols, architectures, etc.).

6.1   The foundational problem.

In the realm of our models we have mathematical methods to solve precisely defined classes of problems. The given system S itself is not a formal one but incorporates our intuitions about the basic objects and the basic operations which are the constituents of the given problem. What we have to relate to them in our mathematical models are definitions of concepts and of functions. We orient ourselves in the real world by the expertise in the application area to which S belongs. In the world of scientific methods we have instead formal manipulations of models, say sequences $S_0 \to \ldots \to S_n$ of models S_i where typically the final element of such a chain is an executable version of the proposed problem solution and where—at least ideally—the transformations $\to$ which lead from S_i to S_{i+1} are provably correct. Aristotle pointed out that such a chain of provably correct stepwise refined specifications has to start somewhere and has to be finite. The whole specification chain will remain an intellectual exercise if we do not "know" that S_0 is "correct".

How can one establish the *correctness* of such a first model S_0 in a specification chain? The question is how we can relate the non–formal system S to the formal model S_0. By definition there is no provable relation between the mathematical object S_0 and the loosely given informal system S. Therefore the only thing we can hope for is a pragmatic foundation: we have to grasp the

---

[7] In [9, 27] I had called them primary models. This was to stress that these models are not unique but are naturally thought of as those models from which others are derived by formal transformations. Ground models in this sense should not be confused with the notion of ground models as it is used in logic programming.

correctness of S_0 with respect to S *by inspection*. To say it in computer science terms: we have to understand the semantics of S through the model S_0.[8] Or to say it from the software engineering perspective (see [48, p. 346]): "a specification must be validated against the intuitive understanding". In order to make such a pragmatic foundation safe, the *ground model* S_0 (which formalizes the basic intuitions, concepts and operations of S) has to satisfy a certain number of requirements.

Before describing these requirements I want to stress once more that this correctness problem is part of the general problem how to relate rigorous scientific methods to the real world. Since building satisfactory ground models is the working computer scientist's daily bread the correctness problem cannot be solved once and for all for the whole body of the current basic concepts of the discipline. The computer scientist has to solve an instance of this problem each time he has to implement a system which satisfies a given requirement specification. In classical engineering disciplines, the experience accumulated through one hundred years of work has produced a body of "right" modelling concepts and methods which in general permit the satisfactory resolution of the issue of finding good ground models. There is no such well established body of engineering knowledge in computer science yet. Remember that as we know from statistics, 80% of the errors in system programming do occur at the level of requirement specifications, i.e. at the place where we have to relate the given system S to a ground model S_0 for it.

6.2 Properties of ground models.

There are at least three requirements which must be satisfied by ground models in order to serve as safe basis for a specification chain which provides a correct implementation of a given application system S. Namely ground models must be *precise*, *abstract* and must have a *rigorous foundation*.

Precision. A ground model must be precise in order to become subject to mathematical analysis at all. In connection with the distinction to be made between *rigorous* and *formal* (see above) it has to be required that despite of its precision, a ground model has to be *flexible, simple, concise* and *falsifiable*.

The **flexibility** requirement wants to make sure that ground models are adaptable to the characteristics of different application domains. Flexibility has also to permit ground models to meet the important software engineering principle which asks the models to be easily modifiable and in particular extendable. Extensibility is necessary for ground models to serve as prototypes and also to become reusable in the design process.

---

[8] This is the typical situation of a standardization effort for a programming language: S is what the standardization wants to abstract from the existing descriptions and implementations of the language. Once the standard is defined— ideally by a ground model—it should be possible to understand the behaviour of a proposed implementation through that model. For Prolog I have developed an evolving algebra ground model, see [7, 12, 27]; it defines the semantics of the ISO Prolog standard. An IEEE VHDL'93 Standard evolving algebra ground model appears in [21].

The condition of **simplicity** and **conciseness** wants to make sure that ground models are understandable by the user. This is crucial from the software engineering point of view (see [48, p. 346]): "To be useful in industrial practice, specifications must be comprehensible". I am not saying that say aircraft specifications should be comprehensible by the future passenger or by the Airline executive who buys them; they must be comprehensible to the engineer who understands the application. [9]

The user typically is not a computer science specialist but an expert in the given application area. He is the one who has to check by inspection that the ground model S_0 faithfully reflects the application system S of problems formalized by S_0. That is why the model S_0 must be as close as possible to the reality it is going to formalize, i.e. its elementary objects and functions must represent directly, without encoding, the basic concepts and operations which appear in the application system S. "A significant engineering project begins with a specification describing *as directly as possible*[10] the observable properties and behaviour of the desired product"[53, p. 4]. This formalization task "... is not simple: it requires a careful choice of those aspects of the real world to be described in the formal language and an understanding of both the detailed practical problems of the application and of the formal language. Errors would likely be introduced during this process ..."[59, p. 41]. Therefore the ground model must reflect the user's domain expert knowledge, it must capture the domain intrinsics and go hand in hand with the requirements capture in the software cycle (see [5]).

The ground model represents the precise interface where the discussion between the user and the designer of the system has to take place and where the contract between the customer and the implementor is formulated. All the furthermore refined models $S_i (i > 0)$ belong to the world of the designer, not to the world of the client. The ground model S_0 has to express what the system

---

[9] From my work for the ISO Prolog standardization I can cite an interesting example which might serve as illustration here. In the ISO Prolog standardization working group (ISO/IEC JTC1 SC22 WG17) it has been discussed for years whether the semantics of the language should be defined by executable stratified control-free Prolog code proposed for this purpose by Deransart [37]. The alleged advantage was that whenever a question comes up about what the standard requires, it can be answered in a definite way by running the program which defines the standard. But one has to be conscious about the difference between explaining and executing a program. What if we have difficulties in understanding the program? Then running the code to decide a question is like querying an oracle and just believing the answer and behaving accordingly, even if the answer is cryptic. As a matter of fact Deransart's program is a rather large one (of "about 500 clauses" [37, p. 30]) which has two crucial problems: a) it is written in a sublanguage of Prolog whose semantics and therefore implementation depends upon subtle problems having to do with the non classical treatment of negation in Prolog (see [7, section 4] for a detailed discussion of this problem); b) "it is not very easy to understand by anyone unfamiliar with their (viz. the authors') methods and notations"[60, p. 1]—a reason why it had to be accompanied by an extra "Explanation of the Formal Definition" [60]. This confirms the need of a comprehensible ground model for a standardization effort.

[10] My italics.

is supposed to do, the refined models $S_i(i > 0)$ define how this behaviour is achieved. Clearly the *what* has to precede the *how*. The practical software engineering importance of the simplicity and the comprehensibility of the language for ground models comes out clearly also from statistical evidence: two thirds of the development time is spent for communication between user and designer and one quarter of the failures of software projects are due to communication problems between user and designer.

The ground model S_0 must satisfy the Popperian criterion of being *falsifiable*. This means that a) the ground model must assure the possibility to make statements about the design that are either verifiable or falsifiable and that b) the user must have the possibility to test the appropriateness of the model by experiments with reproducible results, using S_0 or executable prototypes[11]. In [54] these consequences of the Popperian falsifiability criterion are postulated as quality standard for any verification method.

The falsifiability request for *ground* models does not contradict but complements the role of the use of formal methods during the—ideally provably correct—development of the *refined* formal models $S_i(i > 0)$. Thus it is natural that in the GEC Alsthom project of software development for speed– and switching control of the French railways, the entire design is based upon Abrial's formal method B, but nevertheless also functional tests are done. Fernando Mejia who directs this formal development project indicates two reasons which illustrate my analysis (see [38, p. 77]): "First, programmers do occasionally make mistakes in proofs." As explained above the discipline of *pedantics* creates the laboratory conditions which have to enhance or to replace the traditional form of the mathematical proof checking process. "Secondly, formal methods can guarantee only that software meets its specification, not that it can handle the surprises of the real world". This expresses the fundamental distinction between the pragmatic scientific foundation of ground models and the mathematical justification of refined models.

Abstractness. Ground models must be abstract. They have to reflect the intrinsic functionalities which are constituents of what appears in the non–formal problem formulation and therefore will be needed for an algorithmic solution of S, but they should not contain any irrelevant representation or optimization features. The latter will have to be considered only in the specification chain which leads from the ground model to an implementation. Being abstract has to go together with being *complete*. Completeness means that the semantically relevant parameters of S must be present in S_0 although they might appear there only as interface relating to a possibly abstract environment.

Ground models with the right abstractions satisfy the postulates in [54, p. 36] for a mature engineering discipline, namely that one is *"able to make explicit formal statements about the correctness requirements for a new design that are independent of the design itself"*, that one can *"discriminate between requirements and implementations"*, that one can predict the essential characteristics

---

[11] Simple and easily implementable ground models are also important for simulation purposes; they allow one to test performance criteria at an early development stage.

of a product before it is built and that one is *"able to build an abstraction of the behaviour ... which is susceptible to formal analysis"*. The last mentioned postulate is in accordance with the view explained below that practical (in particular ground) models better support the process-oriented understanding of a dynamic system.

Rigorous foundation. The necessity of the third requirement for ground models, namely to have a rigorous foundation, is obvious. But note that this requirement does not only satisfy an academic intellectual desire. It also corresponds to a practical need when it comes to build reliable tools which help for design and transformation of ground models in connection with prototyping. In [54, p. 36] a sound formal framework for capturing prototypes is even considered as the first quality standard for any verification method.

Also through this requirement one can see how fundamental the notion of evolving algebra is: the foundation of evolving algebras [41] is in first order logic, the most general and simplest basis occidental culture knows for mathematics. Paraphrasing a famous slogan I am tempted to comment this by saying that *Simplicity is our business.*

7 Support of Abstract Operational Views

Evolving algebra specifications directly support the process-oriented understanding of the behaviour of dynamic systems and they allow one to build operational models at arbitrarily high or low levels of abstractions. If for given dynamic features one looks for mathematical descriptions which are simple and concise, easy to understand and manipulate (whether by humans or by machines), one is well advised to try to express dynamic changes *directly* by dynamic concepts. As explained above, the notion of evolving algebra incorporates directly the most basic dynamic concept we know in computer science, namely destructive assignment, and it does it in the most abstract form one can conceive. By supporting such abstract operational views evolving algebras allow one to deal in an explicit and transparent way with non–trivial run–time properties.

For example the analysis of the dynamic properties of Prolog database operations in [15, 26] is based upon a simple but precise model of the backtracking behaviour of Prolog for user–defined predicates which abstracts away from irrelevant features by working with abstract interfaces for terms, goals, clauses, procedure definitions, substitution and unification. Whereas the analysis in [15] is at the user's level of observation, the model in [26] covers the behaviour of pseudo–compiled Prolog code which reflects all the features of the database related WAM instructions. In our evolving algebra specification of the Warren Abstract Machine [28] we develop various abstract models for different WAM layers (predicate structure, clause structure, term structure, etc.) in order to state and prove the intended correctness theorem for compilation of Prolog programs. These models make a mathematical (implementation independent) study of WAM-related execution or implementation issues possible. Also the evolving algebra definition of Prolog [27] yields several modules around the simple Prolog nutshell for user-defined predicates, each for a different group of built-in predicates. These modules provide the mathematical basis to extend abstract analysis from Horn clauses to real Prolog programs which contain built-in predicates formalized in those modules.

The claims about abstract operational specifications will surprise those who share the widely believed view that *operational* and *abstract* are conflicting properties of formal methods, that they exclude each other. For a long time it has been a common place in theoretical computer science that in comparison to the equational or axiomatic approaches, the operational approach to semantics is scientifically not so respectable. It is considered to be of lower level of abstraction which may be good for producing implementations but not for defining succinct high–level descriptions of desired functionalities of a system. It is supposed to deal with dirty control features or efficiency considerations which belong to code execution but should be hidden from the system designer.

Only Plotkin's structural operational semantics SOS [70] is sometimes considered as an acceptable style of defining the meaning of programs. In that approach, the program constructs guide the formulation of axioms and rules which define the meaning of programs and serve for proof schemes. Indeed SOS has been useful. The formal definition of Standard ML makes crucial use of Kahn's *Natural Semantics* [58]—a version of structural operational semantics. The semantic rules are used to answer questions about the meaning of program constructs. Theorems justify particular design decisions and are typically proved by induction on the programs, see [61, 62].

In the communities of functional and logic programming and of artificial intelligence it is still rather common to identify *abstract* with *equational* or *declarative* as opposed to *operational*. Surprisingly enough not only among theoreticians but even among researchers in system design and analysis one encounters such an attitude. For example to my surprise this view was held by a distinguished VHDL specialist in a panel discussion on the use of formal methods at the 1994 *European Design Automation Conference* in Grenoble. Also some advocates of "pure" programming styles have contributed to discrediting operational (imperative) methods as "impure" by banning "side effects".

I explain in the rest of this section why I believe it to be misleading to look at *operational* concepts as being in conflict with the method of *abstraction*.
Abstract versus operational. Let me start by recalling that when the attractive and fruitful concept of denotational semantics was discovered, its pioneers explicitly aimed at providing mathematical models and tools to deal in a precise and safe way with real languages and systems. In [75, p. 40] we read:

> An essential topic will be the discussion of the relation between the mathematical semantics for a language and the implementation of the language. What we claim the mathematics will have provided is the standard against which to judge an implementation.

Only later it has been claimed that for defining the semantics of a program one should forget the notion of *state* and the notion of *individual computation step*.

Both notions have been relegated to the world of implementations as not abstract enough. Also in the stateless process algebra we can observe the high price paid for abstracting from states; for example, the proposed general refinement theory does not capture many refinements that are crucial for the analysis of complex real systems which do refer to state constituents; see e.g. the refinements in the evolving-algebra-based correctness proofs in [27, 17, 16, 55, 43, 22].

Purely functional (equational) definitions of the semantics of programs have been advocated which are global and do not refer to single computation steps. By now it is acknowledged by many [63, p. 626] that such semantics has problems in coping with data abstraction mechanisms in programming languages (descriptive inadequacy) and with reactive programs. The notions of state and single computation step, which such pure approaches want to avoid, need not to reflect irrelevant details of execution but serve as the basis for the important *principle of locality* discussed above. The vast literature on models of logic programming languages offers an interesting illustration of the difference between "local" and "global" specifications. Compare the evolving algebra definition of the full programming language Prolog in [27] with various equational, or abstract algebraic, or axiomatic, or "pure" logic specifications for the sublanguage of definite Horn clauses extended by some control elements (see [65] and more references in the introduction to [27]).

In a sense fixed point based descriptions of programming languages reintroduce both the 1–step computation and the state notion; but they do this in an implicit and technically more involved way. Single computation steps reappear in the form of successive approximations to the fixed points for the given equations. The relevant state components reappear in the form of continuations. Again an example is provided by some denotational definitions of the semantics of Prolog programs in the literature. For each abstract domain which appears in the evolving algebra definition of the core of Prolog for user–defined predicates [27], the denotational descriptions in [57, 34, 35] introduce a continuation: for terms, goals, (occurrences of) clauses, programs, substitutions, etc. The difficulty is that the denotational Prolog models have to deal with these continuations explicitly—as constituents of the global "object" which encodes the "state"—via complicated and numerous equations which describe the effect of the Prolog computation. In the evolving algebra description of Prolog [27], the corresponding elements of abstract domains appear without any encoding; no overhead is needed for their representation, they occur directly in the four simple rules which define the complete Prolog machine for user–defined predicates. These abstract elements are subject to further refinement at the moment when their implementation becomes the issue, e.g. in the WAM [28].

Models versus Syntax. It is true that in the theoretical computer science community serious attempts are made to overcome the practical problems of purely denotational approaches to semantics.[12] The development of *Action Semantics*

---

[12] I do not want to throw doubt on the many achievements which have been obtained in the area of denotational semantics. The development of denotational semantics has brought us a good understanding of types and higher–order functions (in particular

[64] is an example. In general, during the last years there seems to be a trend in theoretical computer science to make semantics more operational. The interest in full abstraction and observational equivalences is a related phenomenon.

It is my belief that people put too much emphasis on syntax. In Plotkin's Structural Operational Semantics, the proof rules for actions are directly derived from the syntactical structure of the programs. Such semantics is compositional which allows one to establish many useful properties, but there is a price. Not all programming constructs lend themselves to such treatment which limits the applicability of the method. Similar restrictions apply to abstract interpretations of run–time investigations. In this connection compare the following:

1. According to Hoare, it should be the case that "all the properties of a program and all the consequences of executing it can, in principle, be found out from the text of the program itself by means of purely deductive reasoning" [51, p. 576].

2. Von Henke, one of the fathers of the successful PVS system [66], points out that most tools which have been developed up to now "in dealing primarily with syntactic and structural aspects of software ... fail to address major issues of software quality having to do with *semantic* aspects of software" [48, p.345].

The evolving algebra approach allows one to model and analyze the run–time program behaviour at the desired level of abstraction. What is considered as one step in a computation depends on the level of abstraction at which we want to build the computation model. Evolving algebras overcome the presumed insufficient abstractness of operational semantics by allowing one to have as 1–step computation an arbitrary (intendedly finite) number of conditional updates of functions of arbitrary level of abstraction. The use of guarded function updates for local transformations of structures provides a tool to build precise yet simple, abstract yet operational models for complex real-life systems which support the intuitive process-oriented understanding of the system. It gives the notions of state and state transformation a mathematical status which allows one to use powerful mathematical techniques for characterizing the dynamic behaviour of complex real systems.

Evolving algebras utilize all the traditional means for the description of static features. For example the initial states from which evolving algebra computations start can be often described adequately by algebraic (purely equational or axiomatic) specifications. Evolving algebras take advantage of abstract data types. The explicit dynamic behaviour is defined on top of all that.

The evolving algebra approach to program design and analysis is semantical. It allows one to study in precise and abstract mathematical terms the *effect* of

---

of recursive and polymorphic types) for functional programming, especially for the λ–calculus which plays the role of the underlying canonical computation model. I am discussing only whether these results gave as much to practical applications as the pioneers intended. Who does still remember the goal stated in [74, p. 2] that the mathematical definition of a language should enable one to determine whether a proposed implementation is *correct*? I certainly do not deny that in particular contexts denotational definitions can be both elegant and useful. I have mentioned already Russinoff's work on VHDL [73] as an example. Another instructive example is Björner's application domain model for the Chinese railway computing system [4].

programs; it permits one to concentrate on those *behavioral* features for which the program has been or is to be developed. There is no limitation imposed by, say, viewing programs as logical formulae or viewing programming as carrying out proofs (or normalizations of proofs) within a fixed deductive system. However a proof theoretical analysis is *also* possible[13].

8 Scalability

I have often heard the statement that formal methods had their chance and failed. It cannot be denied indeed that several traditional formal methods are not scalable. They work well for small examples, often invented to illustrate the method. But when it comes to real–life large systems many of them face the well known combinatorial explosion or simply fail. *Developing techniques for crossing abstraction levels* [52] represents one of the challenging goals of current computer science research and is of vital importance for the development of reliable safety critical systems (see the title *Developing abstraction for coping with complexity* of a section on safety in the IFIP 1994 World Computer Congress, op.cit.). The use of evolving algebras allows one to cope with the complexity of real systems by building hierarchies of system levels.

I have mentioned already several real-world case studies through which I wanted to test whether they support the preceding claim. One is the mathematical definition [27] of the semantics of the real programming language Prolog which went into the ISO standard (see [12]) and has been refined by a hierarchy of intermediate models to a definition—coming with a correctness proof—of its implementation on the Warren Abstract Machine. Another example is the recently finished project of a formal definition of Occam at the level of the user [17] which has been refined through a hierarchy of intermediate models to the Transputer level [16], again coming with a mathematical correctness proof for the compilation of Occam programs into Transputer code. A recent example is the reverse engineering project [13] where evolving algebras have been used for a mathematical specification (leading to only four pages of abstract parallel code) of the VLSI implemented microprocessor which controls the successful dedicated massively parallel architecture APE100.

The experience gained in those projects gives me the conviction that the evolving algebra method scales up to complex systems. I believe that it can play a particular role in hardware/software co-design. Through the freedom of abstraction together with the information hiding and interface mechanism evolving algebras can serve as tool to develop and analyze a design without committing to a particular technology for realizing the design; by the flexibility to formally represent all the system parts as evolving algebras one can postpone to a late design stage the decision about which parts to realize in hardware and which ones in software. I am seriously interested in finding a challenging industrial size problem where these convictions could be proved.

---

[13] Indeed there are attempts to analyze evolving algebras as systems of rewrite rules or a form of Horn clause programs.

9 Easy Learning

It is easy for the practitioner to learn to use evolving algebras in his daily design and analysis work. Evolving algebras use only standard mathematical notation; one can work with them using any knowledge or technique from existing practice and avoiding the straitjacket of any particular formal system. As a consequence the use of special application domain knowledge or design expertise is supported and provides the possibility to decompose complex systems by *familiar* techniques into simpler subsystems in such a way that this decomposition is formalized in a rigorously controllable manner.

During the last years I have experienced with numerous programmers, implementors and hardware designers that evolving algebra models—i.e. abstract assembler-like code— can be understood by the working computer scientist without any formal training in theory. It needs not more than a day or two of explanation, through simple examples, to convey to a hardware or software engineer the idea and a precise definition of evolving algebras in such a way that he can start to produce his own well defined evolving algebra models. Look at the two evolving algebra models for DLX. It is true that this RISC architecture is simple by itself, but nevertheless the example illustrates I hope how one can formalize or construct a real system following a natural path of explanation and using standard mathematical notation in such a way that the resulting evolving algebra model becomes simple and transparent and easy to read, to understand and to manipulate.

This refutes, for the evolving algebra approach, an objection which is often put forward against large scale industrial use of formal methods. It is said that the average programmer has not enough mathematical skill to be able to apply a formal method which needs a PhD to be understood. I cannot judge whether this claim is true, but for sure no PhD is needed to understand and to correctly use evolving algebra models; just experience with algorithmic (programming) phenomena is sufficient. If "mathematical abilities" are needed for the system development process, this is due to the fact that the development of any algorithm aimed at solving a given problem constitutes among others also a mathematical (combinatorial) achievement and includes a formalization (representation) task. The question therefore is not whether "mathematics" is needed or not, but how the intrinsically mathematical part of the programming activity is supported by a method, be it "formal" or not. This is expressed also by Wing [78, p. 10]: *"Programs, however, are formal objects, susceptible to formal manipulation ... Thus, programmers cannot escape from formal methods. The question is whether they work with informal requirements and formal programs, or whether they use additional formalism to assist them during requirements specification."*

Evolving algebras support the system development activity ideally because they give a chance also to the non-theoretically drilled programmer to express the system features appropriately at the desired level of abstraction. This feature can also be put to use for writing informative manuals. As a side effect of a stepwise refined system development (ideally coming with proofs which relate the different levels) one gets a systematic documentation of the system for free.

Thus the use of evolving algebras can not only make the system design process more reliable, but it can also speed up the whole process and thereby make it less expensive. This is good news which however has still to be understood by industrial circles.

The ease with which the working computer scientist can build simple and clean evolving algebra models is one of the reasons why evolving algebra models can be delivered, not only promised or built "in principle"; this holds even under industrial constraints.[14] I would be very much surprised indeed should this potential of the evolving algebra method not influence the fate of Industrial-strength Formal specification Techniques[15].

10   Conclusions

I have illustrated some important features of the evolving algebra method to design and analysis of complex computer systems. I have shown that this method satisfies the conditions which are widely required for a "mature engineering discipline" ([54, p. 36]). After having finished this text I became acquainted with [31]; I must confess that the evolving algebra method seems to be an orthodox one: it obeys all the *Ten Commandments* of [31]. I hope to have revealed its practicality for the working computer scientist and also its potential to become a viable mathematical method especially under industrial constraints.

At this point the reader might wonder what are the limitations of the evolving algebra approach. In principal they seem to coincide with the limitations of the human capabilities of mathematical formalization and structuring. I do *not* advocate the reformulation in terms of evolving algebras of all the successful techniques which have been developed by the use of other approaches, especially not for the description and analysis of static phenomena. I want to suggest however that wherever dynamic behaviour is at stake, evolving algebras will be helpful and are there at their best.

Important future achievements will be a) to marry the concept of evolving algebra with control theory and b) to develop the "Pedantics" and the tool side of the approach. I hope that some readers will feel challenged to contribute to this work.

Acknowledgment. I am grateful to the following colleagues for stimulating conversations on the subject, for valuable criticism and last but not least for helpful comments on previous versions of this paper: Dines Björner, Jonathan Bowen, Uwe Glässer, Yuri Gurevich, Nils Klarlund, Leslie Lamport, Jim Lipton, Erich Marschner, Peter Mosses, Alan Mycroft, Peter Päppinghaus, Lutz Plümer,

---

[14] For example the four simple rules which constitute my evolving algebra model in [7, 8, 27] for the Prolog kernel for user-defined predicates have been implemented in two leading Prolog companies, one in the US and one in Europe. Such implementations can be used as running prototypes for industrial experiments with new developments.

[15] WIFT is the acronym for the Workshop on Industrial-Strength Formal Specification Techniques which is sponsored by the IEEE Technical Committee on Software Engineering.

Simon Read, David Russinoff, Britta Schinzel, Peter Schmitt, Kirsten Winter. A few paragraphs in this paper are direct quotations from [19]. Thanks to Franz Rammig for the occasion offered to discuss some of the ideas presented here to the panel on *Formal Semantics: Practical Need or Academic Pleasure?* at the annual *European Design Automation Conference with EURO-VHDL* in Grenoble (19.–23.9.1994). Last but not least my thanks go to BRICS at the University of Aarhus for the invitation to an intensive and pleasant summer month which allowed me also to finish this paper.

References

1. D. Barnocchi. L'"Evidenza" nell'assiomatica aristotelica. *Proteus*, II,5 (1971), pp. 133–144.
2. Ch. Beierle and E. Börger. A WAM extension for type-constraint logic programming: Specification and correctness proof. Research report IWBS 200, IBM Germany Science Center, Heidelberg, December 1991.
3. Ch. Beierle, E. Börger, I. Đurđanović U. Glässer, and E. Riccobene. An evolving algebra solution to the steam-boiler control specification problem. Seminar on *Methods for Specification and Semantics* (Dagstuhl, June 1995), Report, 1995.
4. D. Björner. A Formal Model of the Railway Application Domain System. UNU/IIST PRaCoSy Document no. SP/5/3, January 7, 1994, pages 1–19.
5. D. Björner. Domain Analysis, a Prerequisite for Requirements Capture. UNU/IIST Document, 1995.
6. A. Blass and Y. Gurevich. *Evolving Algebras and Linear Time Hierarchy*. In B. Pehrson and I. Simon, editors, *Proc. of the IFIP 13th World Computer Congress 1994, Vol. I*, pp. 383–390. Elsevier, 1994.
7. E. Börger. A logical operational semantics for full Prolog. Part I: Selection core and control. *CSL'89*. Springer LNCS 440, 1990, 36–64.
8. E. Börger. A logical operational semantics for full Prolog. Part II: Built-in predicates for database manipulations. *MFCS'90. Mathematical Foundations of Computer Science* (B. Rovan, Ed.). Springer LNCS 452, 1990, 1–14.
9. E. Börger. Logic Programming: The Evolving Algebra Approach. In B. Pehrson and I. Simon (Eds.) *IFIP 13th World Computer Congress 1994, Volume I: Technology and Foundations*, Elsevier, Amsterdam, 391–395.
10. E. Börger. Review of: E.W. Dijkstra & C.S. Scholten: *Predicate Calculus and Program Semantics*. Springer-Verlag, 1989. *Science of Computer Programming* 23 (1994) 1–11 and *The Journal of Symbolic Logic* 59 (1994) 673–678
11. E. Börger. Annotated bibliography on evolving algebras. In E. Börger, editor, *Specification and Validation Methods*. Oxford University Press, 1995.
12. E. Börger and K. Dässler. Prolog: DIN papers for discussion. ISO/IEC JTCI SC22 WG17 Prolog standardization document no. 58, NPl, Middlesex, 1990, pp. 92–114.
13. E. Börger and G. Del Castillo. A formal method for provably correct composition of a real-life processor out of basic components (The APE100 reverse engineering project). In *Proc. of the First IEEE International Conference on Engineering of Complex Computer Systems (ICECCS'95)*. See also BRICS NS-95-4, pp. 195–222, University of Aarhus, 1995.
14. E. Börger, G. Del Castillo, P. Glavan and D. Rosenzweig. Towards a mathematical specification of the APE100 architecture: The APESE model. In B. Pehrson and

I. Simon, editors, *Proc. of the IFIP 13th World Computer Congress 1994, Vol. I*, pp. 396–401. Elsevier, 1994.

15. E. Börger and B. Demoen. A framework to specify database update views for Prolog. In M. J. Maluszynski, editor, *PLILP'91*. LNCS 528, 1991, 147–158.

16. E. Börger and I. Đurđanović. Correctness of compiling Occam to Transputer code. BRICS NS-95-4, pp. 153–194 , University of Aarhus, 1995.

17. E. Börger, I. Đurđanović, and D. Rosenzweig. Occam: Specification and compiler correctness. Part I: The primary model. In E.-R. Olderog, editor, *Proc. of PRO-COMET'94 (IFIP Working Conference on Programming Concepts, Methods and Calculi)*, pages 489–508. North-Holland, 1994.

18. E. Börger and U.Glässer. A formal specification of the PVM architecture. In B. Pehrson and I. Simon (Eds.) *IFIP 13th World Computer Congress 1994*, Volume I: *Technology and Foundations*, Elsevier, Amsterdam, 402–409.

19. E. Börger and U.Glässer. Modelling and analysis of distributed and reactive systems using evolving algebras. BRICS NS–95–4, pp. 128–153, University of Aarhus.

20. E. Börger, U. Glässer and W. Mueller, The Semantics of Behavioral VHDL'93 Descriptions. In: *EURO-DAC'94 European Design Automation Conference with EURO-VHDL'94*. Proc. IEEE CS Press, Los Alamitos/CA, 1994, 500-505.

21. E. Börger, U. Glässer and W. Mueller. Formal definition of an abstract VHDL'93 simulator by EA–machines. In C. Delgado Kloos and Peter T. Breuer, editors, *Semantics of VHDL*. Kluwer, 1995.

22. E. Börger, Y. Gurevich and D. Rosenzweig. The bakery algorithm: Yet another specification and verification. In E. Börger, editor, *Specification and Validation Methods*. Oxford University Press, 1995.

23. E. Börger, F.J. Lopez-Fraguas and M. Rodrigues-Artalejo. A Model for Mathematical Analysis of Functional Logic Programs and their Implementations. in: B. Pehrson and I. Simon (Eds.) *IFIP 13th World Computer Congress 1994*, Vol. I, pp. 410-415, 1994, Elsevier. See the full version *Towards a Mathematical Specification of Narrowing Machines*, Report DIA 94/5, Dep. Informática y Automática, Universidad Complutense, Madrid, March 1994, pp.30.

24. E. Börger and S. Mazzanti. A correctness proof for pipelining in RISC architectures. Manuscript, 1995.

25. E. Börger and E. Riccobene. A Formal Specification of Parlog. In: *Semantics of Programming Languages and Model Theory* (M. Droste, Y. Gurevich, Eds.), Gordon and Breach, 1993, pp.1-42.

26. E. Börger and D. Rosenzweig. An analysis of Prolog database views and their uniform implementation. *Prolog. Paris Papers-2*. ISO/IEC JTC1 SC22 WG17 Prolog Standardization Report no.80, July 1991, pp. 87-130.

27. E. Börger and D. Rosenzweig. A mathematical definition of full Prolog. *Science of Computer Programming*, 1995.

28. E. Börger and D. Rosenzweig. The WAM – definition and compiler correctness. In L. C. Beierle and L. Plümer, editors, *Logic Programming: Formal Methods and Practical Applications*. Elsevier Science B.V./North–Holland, 1995.

29. E. Börger and R. Salamone. CLAM specification for provably correct compilation of CLP($\mathcal{R}$) programs. In E. Börger, editor, *Specification and Validation Methods*. Oxford University Press, 1995.

30. E. Börger and P. Schmitt. A formal operational semantics for languages of type Prolog III. Springer LNCS 533, 1991, 67–79.

31. F.P. Bowen and M.G. Hinchey. Ten Commandments of Formal Methods. *IEEE Computer* 28(4):56–63, April 1995.

32. F.P. Bowen and M.G. Hinchey. Seven More Myths of Formal Methods. *IEEE Software* 12(4):34–41, July 1995.

33. F. P. Brooks, No Silver Bullet—Essence and Accidents of Software Engineering. *IEEE Computer* 20, 1987, 10–19.

34. S.K. Debray and P. Mishra, Denotational and Operational Semantics for Prolog. In: *Journal of Logic Programming* 5, 1988, 61–91

35. A. de Bruin and E. P. de Vink, Continuation semantics for Prolog with cut. In: *Theory and practice of software engineering*, Springer LNCS 351, 1989, 178–192.

36. R. DeMillo, R. Lipton and A. Perlis, A social process and proofs of theorems and programs. In: *Comm. ACM* 22 (5), 271–280, 1979.

37. P. Deransart and G. Ferrand, An operational formal definition of Prolog.INRIA RR 763. See *Proc. 4th. Symposium on Logic Programming*, San Francisco 1987, 162—172 and *New Generation Computing*, 10.2, 1992, 121–171.

38. W.W. Gibbs, Software's Chronic Crisis, *Scientific American*, Sept 1994, 72–81.

39. Y. Gurevich. Logic and the challenge of computer science. In E. Börger, editor, *Current Trends in Theoretical Computer Science*, pp. 1–57. CS Press, 1988.

40. Y. Gurevich. Logic Activities in Europe. in: ACM SIGACT NEWS, 1994.

41. Yuri Gurevich. Evolving Algebra 1993: Lipari Guide. In E. Börger, editor, *Specification and Validation Methods*. Oxford University Press, 1995.

42. Yuri Gurevich. Platonism, Constructivism, and Computer Proofs vs. Proofs by Hand. In Bulletin of the EATCS, October 1995.

43. Y. Gurevich and J. Huggins. The semantics of the C programming language. Springer LNCS 702, 1993, 274–308 and LNCS 832, 1994, 334–336.

44. Y. Gurevich and J. Huggins. Equivalence is in the eye of the beholder. CSE TR 240-95, University of Michigan at Ann Arbor.

45. Y. Gurevich, J. Huggins and R. Mani. The Generalized Railroad Crossing Problem: An Evolving Algebra Based Solution. CSE-TR-230-95, University of Michigan.

46. Y. Gurevich and R. Mani. Group Membership Protocol: Specification and Verification. In E. Börger, editor, *Specification and Validation Methods*. Oxford University Press, 1995.

47. D. Harel, Biting the Silver Bullet. *IEEE Computer* 25, 1992, 8—20.

48. F.W. von Henke, Putting Software Technology to Work, In: K. Duncan and K. Krueger (Eds.) *IFIP 13th World Computer Congress 1994*, Vol. III, pp.345-350, 1994, Elsevier, Amsterdam.

49. J. Hennessy and D.A. Patterson. Computer Architecture: a Quantitative Approach. Morgan Kaufman Publisher, 1990.

50. H. Herbelin. Types for Proofs and Programs. Note on the ESPRIT Basic Research Action 6453 in: *Bulletin of the EATCS* vol.54, 1994, 105–116.

51. C.A.R. Hoare. An axiomatic basis for computer programming. In: *Comm. ACM* 12, pp. 576–580 and 583, 1969.

52. C.A.R. Hoare, ProCoS Working Group Meeting, Gentofte/DK 18.-20.1.1994.

53. C.A.R. Hoare, *Mathematical Models for Computing Science*. Manuscript, August 1994, 65 pp.

54. G.J. Holzmann, The Theory and Practice of a Formal Method: NewCoRe, in: B. Pehrson and I. Simon (Eds.), *Proc. of the IFIP 13th World Computer Congress 1994*, Vol.I, pp. 35–44, Elsevier, Amsterdam.

55. J. Huggins. Kermit: Specification and verification. In E. Börger, editor, *Specification and Validation Methods*. Oxford University Press, 1995.

56. *IEEE Standard VHDL Language Reference Manual—IEEE Std 1076-1993*, The Institute of Electrical and Electronics Engineering. New York, NY, USA, 1994.

57. N.D. Jones and A. Mycroft, Stepwise development of operational and denotational semantics for Prolog. In: *Proc. Int. Symp. on Logic Programming* 2/84, Atlantic City, IEEE, 289–298

58. G. Kahn, *Natural Semantics*, INRIA Rapport de Recherche No. 601, Février 1987.

59. B. Littlewood, L. Strigini, The Risks of Software, in: *Scientific American*. November 1992, p.38-43.

60. A. J. Mansfield, An Explanation of the Formal Definition of Prolog. NPL Report DITC 149/89, Teddington, 1989, p. 1–9.

61. R. Milner and M. Tofte, and R. Harper. *The definition of Standard ML*. Cambridge, Mass.: MIT Press, 1990.

62. R. Milner, M. Tofte, *Commentary on Standard ML*. MIT Press, 1990.

63. Peter D. Mosses. Denotational Semantics. In: Jan van Leeuwen (Ed.), *Handbook of TCS*. Elsevier 1990.

64. Peter D. Mosses. *Action Semantics*. Cambridge University Press, 1992.

65. N.North, A denotational definition of Prolog. NPL, Teddington, TR DITC 106/88.

66. S. Owre, J. Rushby, N. Shankar and F. von Henke, Formal Verification for Fault-tolerant Architectures: Prolegomena to the Design of PVS. In: *IEEE Transactions on Software Engineering*, vol. 21, no. 2, February 1995, pp.107–125.

67. D. L. Parnas. Information distribution aspects of design methodology. In C. V. Freiman, editor, *Proc. of IFIP Congress 1971, Volume 1: Foundations and Systems*, pp. 339–344. North-Holland, 1972.

68. D. L. Parnas, Software Aspects of Strategic Defense Systems. In: *Comm. ACM*, 28 (12), 1985, 1.326–1.335.

69. D. L. Parnas, Education for Computer Professionals. In: *IEEE Computer* 23, 1990, 17—22.

70. G. Plotkin, A structural approach to operational semantics, Internal Report, CS Department, Aarhus University, DAIMI FN-19

71. K. Popper, *Logik der Forschung*.1935.

72. S. Read, e-mail 25 Oct 1994, Compass Design Automation, Columbia/MD.

73. D. M. Russinoff, Specification and verification of gate-level VHDL models of synchronous and asynchronous circuits. In: *Specification and Validation Methods*, Ed. E. Börger, Oxford University Press, 1995, pp. 411–459.

74. D. Scott, Outline of a Mathematical Theory of Computation, PRG-2, November 1970, Oxford Univ. Comp. Lab., Progr. Res. Group, pp.1–24

75. D. Scott, C. Strachey, Toward a Mathematical Semantics for Computer Languages. Proc. 21st Symp. Computers and Automata, Polyt.Inst. of Brooklyn, 1971, 19–46.

76. D.R. Smith, Classification Approach to Design, TR KES.U.93.4, Kestrel Institute, Palo Alto, CA, November 1993, pp.24

77. D.R. Smith and E.A. Parra, Transformational Approach to Transportation Scheduling, in: *Proc of the Eighth Knowledge-Based Software Engineering Conference*, IEEE Computer Society Press, September 1993, 60–68.

78. J. M. Wing, A Specifier's Introduction to Formal Methods. In: *IEEE Computer*, 23 (9), 1990, 8–24.

79. M. Wirsing. Handbook of Algebraic Specifications. In J. van Leeuwen, editor, *Handbook of Theoretical Computer Science B*, pages 675–788, Elsevier, 1990.

80. N. Wirth. Algorithms & Data Structures. Prentice-Hall, 1975.

Experience with Chorus

Christian Bac, Guy Bernard, Denis Conan,
Quang Hong Nguyen, Chantal Taconet

Institut National des Télécommunications
9 rue Charles Fourier, 91011 EVRY Cedex, France

Abstract. This paper summarizes works done at I.N.T. with Chorus [1] Operating System. It briefly describes Chorus' concepts and abstractions useful to understand our work.

Then it focuses on Chorus micro-kernel capabilities and explains how these capabilities have been used to make an experiment allowing the cohabitation between the Chorus micro-kernel and the Macintosh Operating system.

Then, it describes how a new subsystem can be built over the micro-kernel. As an example, it shows how a subsystem which emulates the Macintosh Operating System has been built.

Then, it explains how new capabilities can be integrated into an existing subsystem. To illustrate this point, it gives two examples of work we are currently doing on Chorus/MiX running on PCs. The first project adds "Quality of Service" support for distributed multimedia applications; the second one allows "Fault Tolerant" aspects to be taken into account in distributed applications.

Finally, we discuss some limitations of Chorus, especially in supporting large networks, and how the system should be extended to address this new feature.

1 Introduction

The "distributed operating system" research group of INT has been working with the Chorus Operating System, since 1989. The first experience was the port of a Chorus simulator in the A/UX [2] environment. The Chorus simulator is composed of a UNIX process and a library that can be used to program and test Chorus applications in a UNIX environment. This port was done to gain experience in the Chorus area. The simulator was later used to develop graphical applications using the distributed IPC of the Chorus system in an attempt to anticipate future research. Then we ported a Chorus kernel to Macintosh hardware, and we made the two operating systems (Chorus and MacOS) cohabit and cooperate [Bac93].

After this we built a new subsystem [Bac94] that encapsulated the Macintosh Operating System and allowed Chorus active entities (called actors) to use the MacOS operating system interface. The resulting subsystem is composed of two

---

[1] Chorus is a registered trademark of Chorus Systèmes.

[2] A/UX is a version of UNIX for Macintosh hardware.

actors: a Supervisor actor and a Server which executes at the user level. The supervisor actor handles MacOS system calls and interrupts.

Presently, we are working in three different directions with Chorus:

- the first adds support for quality of service [Nguy95] to handle multimedia communications;
- the second addresses the problem of fault tolerant distributed computing in networks of workstations [Bern94];
- the third focuses on some limitations in the localization service [Taco94].

This paper is organized as follows:

- Section 2 briefly describes Chorus' concepts and abstractions, as well as notions about subsystems.
- Section 3 focuses on some Chorus micro-kernel capabilities and explains how these capabilities have been used to allow the cohabitation between the Chorus micro-kernel and the Macintosh Operating system.
- Section 4 shows how a subsystem which emulates the Macintosh Operating System has been built over the Chorus micro-kernel.
- Section 5 explains how we can integrate new capabilities in an existing subsystem. In this part we explain how quality of services and fault tolerance may be added to a Chorus/MiX subsystem.
- Finally, in section 6, we discuss some limitations of Chorus, especially in supporting large networks.

2   Chorus

A Chorus System is composed of a small-sized Nucleus and of possibly several System Servers that cooperate in the context of subsystems to provide a coherent set of services and user interface. The interfaces [Walp92] to the subsystem and to the kernel are described in Figure 1.

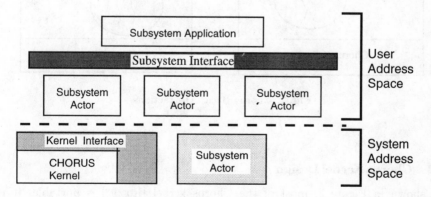

Fig. 1. Chorus Subsystem Interfaces

A Chorus domain consists of a set of Chorus sites. Each site hosts the Chorus Kernel and some actors. A detailed description of the Chorus system and of the Chorus/MiX UNIX subsystem can be found in [Rozi88].

2.1 Basic Abstractions

The Chorus kernel provides the following basic abstractions (see Figure 2):

- The actor defines an address space that can be either in user space or in supervisor space. In the latter case, the actor has access to the privileged execution mode of the hardware. User actors have a protected address space.
- One or more threads can run simultaneously within the same actor. They can communicate using the memory space they share.
- Threads from different actors communicate through the Chorus IPC that enables them to exchange messages through ports named by global unique identifiers.
- The Chorus IPC provides the ability for one thread to communicate transparently with another thread, regardless of the nature or location of the two threads.
- Multi cast is achieved through group communications. Ports can be inserted into "port groups". On the sender behalf, messages that are sent to a port group can reach all the ports, one "random" port, or one port targeted to a machine.

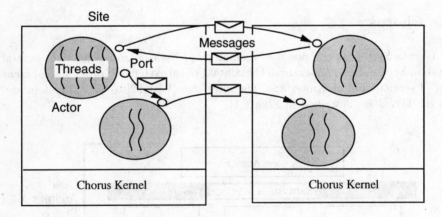

Fig. 2. Chorus Basic Abstractions

2.2 Chorus Kernel Design

As shown in Figure 3, most of the Chorus kernel [Rozi93] is portable. It is composed of four independent elements:

- The supervisor dispatches the interrupts, traps and exceptions delivered by the hardware.
- The real-time executive controls the allocation of the processor.
- The virtual memory manager is responsible for manipulating virtual memory hardware and local memory resources.
- The inter-process communication manager provides message passing facilities.

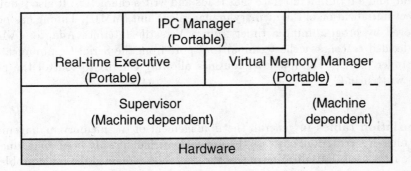

Fig. 3. Chorus Kernel Architecture

2.3 Kernel Services to Subsystems

Chorus kernel allows user or system threads to take control of exceptional events within an actor.

For supervisor actors, the kernel provides facilities to connect hardware interrupts to interrupt handlers within the actors. When an interrupt occurs, the kernel sequentially calls a prioritized sequence of user routines associated with the given interrupt. Any of the individual routines may initiate a break in the sequence if necessary.

The supervisor supports a similar facility, through which actor routines may be associated with hardware traps or exceptions. This facility allows subsystem managers to provide efficient and protected subsystem interfaces.

3 Chorus micro-kernel capabilities

This section tries to explore some of the technologies that allow the Chorus Kernel to be adapted to new configurations. The first part deals with some aspects of porting Chorus to new hardware and the second deals with features like interrupt relays in the kernel.

3.1 Some aspects of Porting Chorus to new Hardware

The target machine was a Macintosh [3] II CX. It is based on a MC68030. We used the Chorus sources for the MC680X0 0. In this area our work was simpler than the one usually done to port a kernel to new hardware.

Chorus hardware requirements Chorus hardware requirements are small. In order to run, the kernel needs a timer that performs an interrupt every 1/100th second, and a terminal interface that reads and writes characters. It also requires correct initialization of the memory management unit (MMU). Timing has been achieved by programming a timer from a Versatile Interface Adaptor (VIA). We decided to connect the terminal to a port from the Serial Communication Controller (SCC). The low level routines allowing Chorus to control the port were written in C.

Translation tables In general, the management of the memory management unit must be written; in our case the greater part had already been done, due to the sources used. Initialization of translation tables remained the main problem.

Chorus on MC68030 uses a virtual address space composed of 4 K Bytes memory pages and four levels of memory index (called levels A to D). Translation tables are set up at boot time. When Chorus is running, the first level A entry describes the actor in user space, and the second level A entry describes the Chorus kernel space. This space includes actors running in supervisor mode.

In the Mac version, the other level A entries are reserved for the kernel and map the physical address space allowing the kernel to have access to the I/O space and extension bus.

Conclusions on Porting Chorus The use of the Macintosh hardware by Chorus was limited to SCC and VIA. SCC was used to transmit and receive characters. VIA was programmed to emit clock ticks. Despite complexity of the Macintosh hardware (which is beyond the scope of this paper), Chorus has proved to be easily portable on it.

3.2 Features used to make Chorus and MacOS Cohabit

To allow Chorus and MacOS cohabitation, we changed the way Chorus managed the hardware to keep the MacOS system able to run. Conversely, we modified the boot phase so as to present Chorus as an application to MacOS. The modifications allow the two systems to share the memory space and to manage the interrupts.

---

[3] Macintosh, MacOS, and A/UX are a registered trademarks of Apple Computers, Inc.

Sharing memory space As the MacOS operating system needs the lower and the higher part of.the physical memory, Chorus kernel access to memory is restricted to 6MB from address 0x80000. This is possible because Chorus can behave as if memory does not begin at physical address 0, and also because the kernel gets the memory size from the boot program.

The boot program asks MacOS for a 6.5MB fixed block of memory. There are small amounts of memory which are 8 in this process but this allows changes in both versions of system.

In this way, the physical memory is separated in three areas (see Figure 4 above):

- the memory reserved for the MacOS system (composed of two parts),
- the memory reserved for the Chorus system (for the kernel and actors),
- and a third area that first allowed a correct alignment of memory space and that was later used to go from one system to the other. This space is called "No Man's Land".

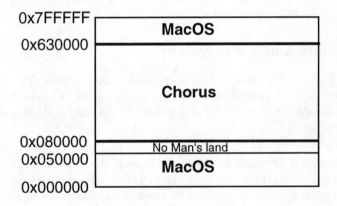

Fig. 4. Sharing memory space

In this configuration, the MacOS system is still able to run, and Chorus can stop and return back to MacOS as if Chorus was a Mac application.

Sharing system events In order to let MacOS control some types of interrupt, low level functions were added. These functions enable the CPU to commute from Chorus system to MacOS, so that Macintosh can run either system. These functions change the MMU setting and the value of the interrupt base register.

As Chorus can connect an interrupt to multiple tasks, interrupts can be connected to a handler in Chorus, a handler in MacOS or a handler in both. To call a MacOS handler, there is a standard function in the "No man's land" that creates an interrupt frame on MacOS stack. This jump into MacOS allows it to acknowledge the interrupts correctly.

Events in MacOS For preserving the MacOS feeling, the preboot program (MacOS space) has been modified so as it can perform some events every 1/50s.
This allows MacOS back to perform many operations:

- mouse moving is detected and mouse pointer is displayed on the screen,
- accessories like Clock and Super Clock display correct time,
- mouse position can be read from the program,
- and keyboard events are recognized.

At this point, the two systems are present in memory and they can share system events like interrupts.

3.3 Experience

Chorus kernel contains features that helped making it cohabit with MacOS. In our last version, both systems co-operate so that Chorus uses MacOS to read from the keyboard and write to the screen. To achieve this co-operation, the boot program in MacOS system space acts on behalf of the Chorus system. A part of the "No Man's land" is used as a buffer to exchange characters between Chorus and the boot application.

4 Building a new Subsystem

In this section, we try to show how a subsystem can be built. To illustrate our purpose, we take the Macintosh Operating System as an example. In this example, the subsystem reuses the MacOS software providing a Macintosh interface to Chorus actors.

Chorus Toolbox Design As shown in Figure 5, the Chorus Toolbox is a small subsystem consisting in two actors. As in every subsystem, there is an actor running in supervisor mode that handles system calls and interrupts. This actor is called **ChorusTbxSup** (later called Supervisor) and relays MacOS system calls as well as hardware interrupts. It provides a MacOS interface to user level actors.

In complex subsystems as shown in Figure 1, there are specialized actors that handle parts of the subsystem work. For example in Chorus/MiX [Rozi88], the Process Manager manages processes, the Object Manager manages the file systems, and the Stream Manager handles communications.

In the MacOS subsystem, there is only one actor that acts as a server. It is called **ChorusTbxServer** (later called Server) and runs at the user level. It calls the MacOS routines in RAM or in ROM.

The Supervisor and the Server actors communicate by means of the Chorus IPC. Exceptions resulting from MacOS system calls are caught by the Supervisor. The Supervisor builds a message and sends it to the Server.

There is an initial negotiation between the Supervisor and the application. This negotiation is used to map the application memory space into the server address space allowing a greater flexibility to exchange parameters and results.

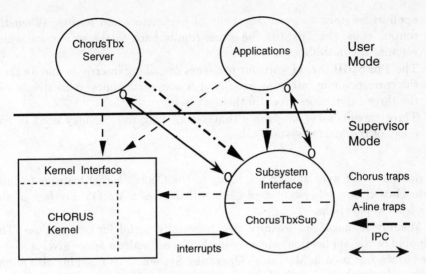

Fig. 5. ChorusToolbox subsystem

Supervisor Design This actor executes at the supervisor level. It handles the low level part of the MacOS system calls and the interrupts. It contains the following threads:

- The main thread initializes the subsystem when it starts. It connects exceptions and interrupts handlers. Then it waits for an application to start a MacOS session. When the application asks for MacOS operation, it sets the server memory mapping so that the server can use the memory segments of the application directly.
- The other thread is called **TbxSupIt**: it relays the interrupt handlers messages to the server. To avoid deadlocks, interrupt handlers are not allowed to use IPC. They must use a restricted form named mini-messages. Mini-messages are allocated in the actor memory and can be sent to a thread in the same actor. So interrupt handlers send mini-messages to TbxSupIt and TbxSupIt sends a message to the Server to service the interrupt.

Server Design This actor executes at the user level. It handles requests to Macintosh Operating System. It also encapsulates the MacOS interrupt handlers into separated threads. It contains the following threads:

- The **TbxServerInit** executes once when the Server starts its execution. It creates the communication ports, sends identifiers to the Supervisor actor allowing it to modify the Server address space and to send messages to the Server ports. It then launches the other threads (described below), and finally ends allowing them to execute.
- The **TbxStdAline** thread waits for messages describing system calls. It analyzes the system calls and launches a thread executing at the address of the MacOS routine. As will be explained later, this new thread uses the

application stack to avoid any copy of parameters and results. When the routine ends, the TbxStdAline sends results back to the supervisor which resumes the initiating thread.

- The **TbxStdIt** thread waits for messages describing interrupts and awakens the corresponding interrupt handler. For some interrupts, it creates one of the three threads described in the next item.
- Three threads serve interrupts that take a long time or may need to call many of the MacOS system calls.

Experience We were able to use many of the Chorus kernel features to integrate MacOS in a subsystem over Chorus that gives a MacOS interface at the user level applications.

Memory management features were especially useful for our purpose. The mapping of the application' memory in the Server address space gives a vision close to the one used in Macintosh Operating System. This mapping also allows quick and efficient exchange of data between the application and the Server.

Interrupt and exception handlers were also easy to add to the system. In order to allow MacOS interrupt handlers to execute at the user level, the subsystem catches the privilege violations and emulates the corresponding instructions.

5 Adding Services

In this section, we show how new capabilities, such as support for Quality of Service and Fault Tolerance, can be added to Chorus/MiX.

5.1 Quality of Service

We present an Object Manager (OM) able to support Quality of Services as described in [Nguy95].

Access Time Problems of OM OM is an independent system server of the Chorus/MiX [Rozi88]. It acts both as a *swap device* for virtual memory management and as a file server. The other system managers communicate with it exclusively by message exchanges in order to access data segments.

OM implements a UNIX System V file system semantic [Bach86]. It uses the same data structures and algorithms as in the standard UNIX System V File System.

In data structures and algorithms used by OM, we identify the three following reasons that make the I/O time for a data block indeterminate [4] (and unbounded):

---

[4] we only consider the block data reading case.

1. The *layout* of UNIX file data blocks makes the time to read a data block not homogeneous. UNIX file data blocks are organized into levels using indirect blocks that content pointers to next level indirect blocks or to real data blocks. As there are 3 indirection levels, the file system may read 1 to 4 disc blocks for a data block.

2. The *cache management policy* does not allow an estimation of the reading delay upper bound. The server manages a pool of cache buffers, and allocates a buffer from the cache before transferring a data block. It must wait if either the selected buffer is found in the pool but is busy, or if it isn't found but the free buffer list is empty.

3. The *strategy algorithm* used by the driver can delay the queuing time for block reading in order to optimize the magnetic head movement. This means that the handling order of block read requests at the disk driver is not the same as the arrival order. Due to *strategy* the queuing time at the disk driver is indeterminate.

Therefore, the standard UNIX system file is not suitable to support QoS requirements of multimedia applications. However, we have identified the sources of non-determinism in the file management. We will now show how to overcome this non-determinism.

QoSOM design We propose modifications of algorithms and data structures used by OM so that the resulting OM, called QoSOM, will have a deterministic behavior behind standard UNIX system file characteristics. Our first version only considers the *continuous reading* of multimedia streams which are stored as UNIX files.

The QoSOM can run in normal or QoS mode. In normal mode, it uses standard algorithms and data structures. When being switched in QoS mode, it uses new algorithms and abstractions as follows:

We define the *trace* of a file being read as the path composed of 0 to 3 indirect block(s) that leads to the current data block. In standard UNIX, the algorithm called *bmap* is used to do the mapping between the logical and physical block numbers of the current data block. This algorithm finds the *trace* leading to the current data block in order to extract the physical block number of this later. As the indirect block(s) are freed after use, then next mapping may have to read them again.

We propose an enhanced algorithm for *bmap*, called *cbmap* (standing for *continuous bmap*), that keeps the *trace* during a *continuous reading*. Using this algorithm, it is necessary to get indirect blocks only when the *trace* must change. The number of indirect blocs to read and the moment when they must be fetched from disk can be computed.

QoSOM applies a *FIFO strategy* in QoS mode. As QoSOM is an independent server and as all data requests go through a specific *port*, the processing order of I/O requests is easy to control. *FIFO strategy* means that the server handles one request at a time. Although this strategy penalizes the overall performance, it allows to determine the time needed to process a read request. This strategy also excludes the cache buffer race problem that occurs in the standard strategy.

In QosOM, we use a new abstraction, namely *partial_read*. A partial read is a read request associated to a *quota*. The *quota* describes the number of disk blocks that the server can fetch during the request. *Partial_read* and *Trace conservation* allow to split the reading of an application buffer into steps. This is useful for the *QoS Manager* to schedule the reading of multiple continuous media as described below.

QoSOM System Model The interaction scheme between the applications, the QoS Manager (QoSMgr) and the QoSOM is shown in Figure 6. The QoSMgr negotiates with the applications in order to set up QoS contracts. It controls the QoSOM function mode. The QoSOM handles two sources of requests: the non-QoS I/O queue, and the QoS scheduled requests stack. When QoSOM is in QoS mode, it serves the QoS stack first, and it serves standard requests only if there is "time" quotas remaining.

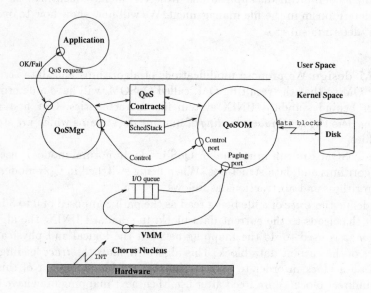

Fig. 6. QoSOM System Model

The QoSMgr achieves the *admission control* on the basis of *resource capacity*. Capacity for disk controllers is expressed by the number of blocks that the controller can fetch per second. Based on the application QoS specifications (rate, buffer size), the QoSMgr computes the *application required capacity*. It grants or denies access to the application, and before granting access, the QoSMgr reserves the necessary cache buffers.

The QoSMgr controls the correct execution of contracts on the basis of *rounds*. A *round* is the time interval that is equal to the smallest common multiplier of all contracted stream periods. A new stream can only be started at the beginning of next round. Before each round, the QoSMgr computes the read scheduling for this round and pushes it onto the *SchedStack*. The QoSOM pops scheduled QoS requests from *SchedStack* and executes them.

The QoSMgr computes the scheduling stack using the *partial_read* abstraction. The algorithm, namely *StmSched*, for this computing is relatively simple. However, two interesting results are deduced from it: *(i)* all application data buffers are available before their deadline, and *(ii)* each stream needs two buffers for continuous reading (i.e. one in use by the application and the other in use by QoSOM – this is the minimum buffer number).

Conclusion on QoS We are now achieving the implementation of an experimental version of the QoSOM and the QoSMgr under Chorus/MiX v4 and Chorus Kernel v3 r4.2. The modularity in Chorus/MiX makes it easier to implement new servers and to modify existing ones.

5.2 Fault Tolerance

We address the problem of fault tolerant distributed computing in networks of workstations, where distributed applications consist in several processes running on several workstations in parallel, with communication links between them. Several methods can be used to provide fault tolerance in distributed systems. Using a specialized hardware may be efficient, but such a component cannot be easily added to existing systems. Application-specific methods and atomic transactions require the use of a particular programming model. Active replication is well suited for real time systems but require the use of extra processors. We propose to handle machine failures using checkpointing, message logging and rollback-recovery [Stro85, Borg89, John89, Elno93]. When a machine failure is detected, a replacement machine is found in the network. Practically, a checkpointing algorithm registers from time to time the state of the distributed application, a message logging algorithm saves the history of the execution in stable memory and a recovery algorithm restarts the distributed application from a previous state in case of a machine failure.

UNIX version A fault tolerance fully portable software has been implemented on a network of SUN workstations and demonstrates the intrinsic limitations of monolithic operating systems [Bern94]. The functionalities where implemented in a daemon process running in user space. This daemon acts as an intermediary between the processes for the distributed applications for their communication. When an application process has a message to send to another application process, the message is first passed to the daemon process that performs the appropriate tasks related to fault tolerance (logging, checkpointing, recovery). On the receiving side, messages are buffered by the daemon until being requested by application process. Primitives for communication between remote part of the distributed application are implemented in a library that is to be linked with programmer's source modules. As could be expected, fault tolerance is expensive because of communication operations. So, we decided to move the whole software in the Chorus UNIX subsystem, i.e. Chorus/MiX. In the following, we study fault tolerance enablers of the Chorus micro-kernel and present the overall architecture of the software.

Prerequisites We found six prerequisites to define what could be a good support for designing and implementing a rollback recovery mechanism. For each of them, we compare the standard (Berkeley) UNIX system - here, called UNIX - with the Chorus micro-kernel. The four first elements are common to migration mechanisms [Alar92].

1. A location-transparent inter-process communication service
   In UNIX, whereas an elementary form of naming service (binding between service names and process ports) is provided, the binding scope is only local to a machine. In Chorus, port' names are global but when a machine failure occurs the localization service broadcasts a request in order to find the new locations of the ports. Because this mechanism is too expensive, we need the concept of reliable ports [Gold90].
2. A global naming scheme for every object handled by the system
   In UNIX and Chorus, most external and internal names are local, particularly process identifiers. Some of these names are very important for interactive and real time applications. Thus, we don't support those applications in a first step.
3. An implementation of services via system server processes remotely accessible
   In UNIX, system calls are procedure calls (without message passing) and local by definition. In Chorus, client processes (either user processes or system processes) can communicate with system server processes via messages on the network.
4. The state of processes easily accessible and grouped in a single place
   In UNIX, the state of processes is disseminated in several parts of the kernel space and most of the information is only relevant to the local machine. In Chorus/MiX, the Process Manager contains the whole state of processes.
5. A reliable and ordered communication service
   The UNIX reliable and ordered communication service is TCP. TCP is also available with Chorus/MiX.
6. A multi-cast communication service
   In UNIX, there is no group functionality, i.e. there are only broadcast messages. The Chorus micro-kernel offers group communication primitives with several addressing mode through the concept of port group.

Therefore, Chorus is a good candidate for the support of a rollback recovery mechanism.

Architecture Now, we present the overall architecture and next show which of the Chorus functionalities are the most useful for the design of each part of the rollback recovery mechanism.

As shown in Figure 7, the fault tolerance software is implemented as a server - the Fault Tolerance Manager, FTM - added to Chorus/MiX. All FTMs have the same role, except one called the controller, which has a complete view of the distributed applications. The controller maintains port groups. Each distributed application is associated to two port groups: the first group is composed of FTMs ports corresponding to the sites where the application is spread, the second group is composed of the control ports of the processes.

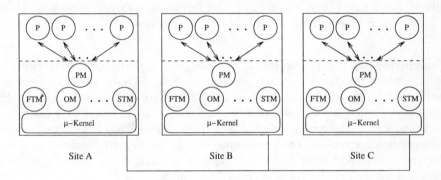

Fig. 7. FTM in Chorus/MiX

As FTMs are parts of the UNIX subsystem, the associated ports are default ports. Groups help in controlling checkpointing, logging and recovery of the distributed applications.

Since processes data structures are managed by the PM, it must checkpoint these structures. Checkpointing is very similar to the one described in [Phil95]. PM transmits the data structures to the FTM, which must end the checkpoint, by saving the process virtual memory and data structures in stable memory. Indeed, inhibition of PM due to checkpointing must be as short as possible, because the PM has to trap every process system calls. Saving of the virtual memory is straightforward because the micro-kernel implements copy-on-write [Abro89] operations. So, we only have to stagger in time the checkpoints by the FTM in order to minimize the storage overhead.

At the beginning of its execution, a process establishes connections with other processes. The STM informs the local FTM, the local FTM constructs a reliable port and transmits it to the controller which saves it in stable memory. The contents of inter-process messages are logged in the volatile memory at the sender site. Stamps (sender identifier + sending sequence number + receiver's identifier + receiving sequence number) are logged in volatile memory at the receiver site, and then regularly transmitted to the controller. Finally, the controller is responsible for saving the stamps in stable memory. The STM captures the message to be sent and transmits a copy of the message to the local FTM that replies by giving the sending sequence number. At the receiving side, the STM notifies the new arrival to the FTM, the FTM stamps the message and later transmits the stamp to the controller. Therefore, the only modification we add in Chorus/MiX is a dialogue between the FTM and the STM on the sending s and receiving of inter-process messages.

When the STM detects a communication fault, it informs the local FTM, the local FTM informs the controller and the controller broadcasts a warning to all other FTMs. The controller takes the control of the distributed application and is responsible for the recovery. It asks FTMs to reinstall the state of failed processes, then to reconnect failed processes and reconfigure fault-free ones according to reliable ports saved in stable memory, and finally to restart all processes. Thus, FTMs cooperate with PMs and STMs for the recovery.

Conclusion on FT In conclusion, the design of a rollback recovery requires six functionalities. Chorus already implements four of them : system servers remotely accessible via message passing, processes' state grouped in a single place, reliable ordered communication service and multi-cast communication service. To those, we add the concept of reliable ports. More work has to be done in order to support more realistic processes using signals, file and terminal connections. For instance, in [O'Co94], the authors wrote a terminal server to buffer all data sent between actors and their associated terminals.

6   Limitations and Extensions

Chorus offers distributed system developers key tools for distribution (modularity of global systems, performing communications, transparent localization of entities), but so far these capabilities have been limited to local area networks.

Capabilities of large scale networks will undoubtly increase significantly in the next years. High speed, up to now reserved for local area networks, will soon be available in wide area networks. A lot of applications which could be used in the context of local area networks only will be usable in wide area networks. These observations lead us to think that microkernel systems must be modified to fit to large scale networks.

In order to make Chorus work upon a large scale network, we propose a localization mechanism which would operate over large scale networks.

We first describe the current localization mechanism in the Chorus microkernel, and then present an extended localization service, and its implementation in Chorus.

6.1   Current Localization Mechanism in Chorus

Each Chorus resource (port, ports group, site, actor) is identified by a Unique Identifier (UI). An UI is made up with *(i)* the resource's creation site address, *(ii)* an identifier of the type of resource, *(iii)* and a unique stamp provided by the creation site's micro-kernel. Some stamps are well known stamps which may be used by any site.

Chorus sites are grouped into domains. IPC (Chorus Inter Process Communication) are implemented above network protocols which provide a broadcast facility. A Chorus domain is typically a local area network, or a multiprocessor computer. Protocols used by Chorus are organized in an oriented graph. The micro-kernel chooses dynamically a way in this graph for each message.

The current localization mechanism of Chorus resources can be broken down into several stages [Syst95a]: given an UI, *(i)* the micro-kernel looks for a resource identified by that UI on the local site, *(ii)* the micro-kernel looks for a localization information in its localization cache where the last localizations it found are stored, *(iii)* the micro-kernel uses some hint such as finding a port on its creation site, *(iiii)* if the hint does not work, the microkernel sends a broadcast message on the domain in order to find the entity.

Localization does not go any further than the limits of the domain.

6.2 An Extended Localization Service

We propose a method for propagating localization searches over a large scale network.

The large scale network is broken down into **domains**. The domains composing the large scale network may be bound by point to point links, or through several Internet routers. All the domains are organized in a **neighborhood graph**. The number of neighbors of each domain and the maximum diameter of the graph have to be limited. The search is propagated step to step into the graph. If the search in the local domain fails, in the next step the domains which are immediate neighbors of the first one take part in the search, next step neighbors of the neighbors are involved – and so on. We estimate the **distance** between two domains by half of the round time trip of a message between them.

Every application fixes freely the scope of its localization searches. For some applications, it is preferable to stay in the local area network because an extended search would be too costly; for other ones, a solution is needed within the limit of a maximum response time; for yet others, only some domains need to be consulted as they know where to find the solution.

Every actor decides on the **visibility** of its ports. A server may restrict its services to sites in its domain, or to sites in specific domains. Other servers may be public, namely they may be used by any domain in the graph. Thus, every server chooses which domains are enabled to use it, by setting the visibility of its ports.

In order to reduce response time, the result of an extended localization search is memorized in a cache. A local cache (present on every site) keeps the information used by local actors. For the domain a **global cache** keeps all the information gathered from outside of the domain. These caches will be managed with a Least Recently Used policy.

When the microkernel of some site is unable to find itself the localization information it needs, it asks an **Extended Localization Server** (*ELS* in the following) for it. There is one ELS on every domain.

A site converses with the ELS of the domain on several occasions : to modify the visibility of its ports, to migrate a port outside of the domain, to invalidate a localization information provided by the ELS, and to initiate an extended localization search.

For an extended search, when the ELS does not find a convenient solution in its global cache, it assigns a **request identifier** to the search, and begins a dialog with other domain ELSs. The waiting site receives the request identifier, and is able to follow the evolution of the search on request.

The dialog between ELSs vary according to the type of search (ports or port groups), and to the scope of the search (list of domains, maximum distance). For ports, the ELS polls directly the creation domain of the port, which is informed in case of migration. For port group with a list of domains, the ELS polls all domains in parallel. For port group with a maximum distance search, the search is propagated step to step, first to immediate neighbors, then possibly to the neighbors of the neighbors, and so on. This search will be stopped on the occurrence of one of three events: *(i)* when enough solutions have been found, or *(ii)* when maximum distance is overrun, or *(iii)* when a domain has already dealt with the same request.

A maximum distance search may become costly in time and in message number when a near solution cannot be found. This drawback may be minimized with a sizable cache which keeps information for a long time, and with efficient stopping tests such as limiting maximum distance.

6.3   Integration of the ELS in Chorus

To integrate the Extended Localization Service into Chorus we need : *(i)* an Extended Localization Library (ELL), which will be linked with applications with extended communications, and *(ii)* the Extended Localization Server (ELS) (see figure 8 an example of extended communication between domain A and domain B).

1. **Application – Library Interface**
   The large majority of communications will be inside a domain. In order to not degrade the performance of local communications, we put extended localization routines in a separate library (outside of the microkernel). Interfaces to extended communications routines will be nearly the same as local ones.
   The Extended library includes other routines in order to : *(i)* modify the visibility of applications ports, *(ii)* modify the limits of a search, *(iii)* anticipate a localization search, and *(iv)* follow the result of an extended search. A localization search is automatically started when a message is sent, but for extended localization it could be interesting to anticipate this search, and to follow the result of the search in order to keep the user waiting.

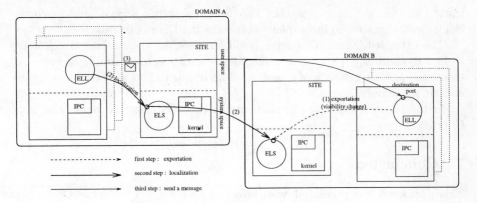

Fig. 8. ELS Architecture

2. ELS Implementation

The heart of the localization service is the ELS. We present here its tasks, and the broad lines of its implementation. The ELS of a domain will be implemented as a **supervisor actor** on one site of this domain. Other sites will contact it through a well known port group. This actor will be made up of several threads corresponding to the different tasks it has to perform.

(a) Tasks to be performed by ELSs

An ELS has *(i)* to be kept informed of which ports of the domain can be seen from the outside, *(ii)* to localize out of domain entities, *(iii)* to answer other domain requests, *(iv)* to register the ports born in the domain which have migrated outside of it, *(v)* to record the use of the server, to detect occasional anomalies and other servers failures.

(b) Memory Resident Information

The server needs to maintain a lot of data areas in order to perform its tasks: a global localization cache for the domain, the last requests processed for each domain, the ports visible out of the domain, the ports that have migrated out of the domain, and lastly its neighbors with their current distances. All these table areas should be stored in main memory in order to provide low response times. They must also be saved in permanent memory in order to keep information even if the ELS fails, thus ensuring normal response times just after recovery.

3. Changes needed in the microkernel

The graph of protocols which is implemented in the microkernel will have to be modified in order to cope with messages destinated to other domains: two protocols will be needed *(i)* a router protocol, *(ii)* an intergateway transport protocol [Syst95b].

6.4 Conclusion on Limitations

This study leads us to the conclusion that microkernels should be adapted to operate over large scale networks. This adaptation involves an extended localization service. We have presented the design of such a service, and given an implementation scheme for implementation in the Chorus microkernel.

The extended localization service will be useful to applications which need to find dynamically a server in a large scale network, for example in order to locate the nearest instance of a replicated server, or to find a server knowing its domain name only.

In the future we plan to implement the extended localization service into Chorus.

7 Conclusion

This document has presented work done at INT with the Chorus Operating System since 1989. It has listed benefits and limits in using the micro-kernel and subsystem technologies.

The main benefits in using these technologies are the followings:

- As shown by the port on Macintosh and the cohabitation with MacOS, the system allows a great flexibility in using the memory management.
- As shown by the cohabitation version and by the MacOS subsystem, interrupt management can be very versatile too.
- Our research works on Fault Tolerance and Quality of Service, show that it is easier to add services in a subsystem than in a traditional kernel.
- Multiplexing servers is also very easy due to threads of control known at the system level. This is useful to build new subsystem as well as to create new applications.
- IPC mechanism and mini-messages are a good base to build distributed multi threaded servers.

Although there are limits to Chorus, many of which are common to other micro-kernels [Amsa95], these limits have never prevented us from building new applications or adding services to the system. Moreover, the modular design of the micro-kernel allows modifications to the internal mechanisms. In particular, we are adapting Chorus so as it can operate over large scale networks.

We now know much about these technologies and will continue to use them as a basis to experiment our research work.

References

[Abro89] V. Abrossimov and M. Rozier. Generic Virtual Memory Management for Operating System Kernels. In *Proc. 12th ACM Symposium on Operating Systems Principles*, Litchfield Park(USA), December 1989.

[Alar92] E. Alard and G. Bernard. Preemptive Process Migration in Networks of UNIX Workstations. In *Proc. 7th International Symposium on Computer and Information Sciences*, Antalya (Turkey), November 1992.

[Amsa95] L. Amsaleg, G. Muller, I. Puaut, and X. Rousset de Pina. Experience with Building Distributed Systems on top of the Mach Microkernel. In *Broadcast, Esprit Research Project 6360, Third Year Report*, July 1995.

[Bac93]   C. Bac and E. Garnier. Cohabitation and Cooperation of Chorus and Ma-
          cOS. In Proc. USENIX Symposium on Micro-Kernels and Other Kernel
          Architectures, San Diego (USA), September 1993.

[Bac94]   C. Bac and H.Q. Nguyen. ChorusToolbox : MacOS running on top of Chorus.
          In Proc. SUUG '94 Conference, Moscou (Russie), April 1994.

[Bach86] M. J. Bach. The Design of the UNIX Operating System. Prentice-Hall Soft-
          ware Series, Englewood Cliff, New Jersey (USA), 1986

[Bern94] G. Bernard and D. Conan. Flexible Checkpointing and Efficient Rollback-
          Recovery for Distributed Computing. In Proc. SUUG '94 Conference,
          Moscou (Russie), April 1994.

[Borg89] A. Borg, W. Blau, W. Graetsch, F. Herrmann, and W. Oberle. Fault Toler-
          ance Under UNIX. ACM Transactions on Computer Systems, 7(1), February
          1989.

[Elno93] E.N. Elnozahy. Manetho: Fault Tolerance in Distributed Systems Using
          Rollback-Recovery and Process Replication. PhD thesis, Rice University
          (USA), October 1993.

[Gold90] A.P. Goldberg, A. Gopal, K. Li, R. Strom, and D.F. Bacon. Transparent
          Recovery of Mach Applications. In Proc. 1st USENIX Mach Symposium,
          1990.

[John89] D.B. Johnson. Distributed System Fault Tolerance Using Message Logging
          and Checkpointing. PhD thesis, Rice University (USA), December 1989.

[Nguy95] H.Q. Nguyen, G. Bernard, and D. Belaid. System Support for Distributed
          Multimedia Applications with Guaranteed Quality of Service. In Proc.
          HPN'95, 6th IFIP International Conference on High Performance Network-
          ing, Palma de Mallorca, Balearic Islands (Spain), September 1995.

[O'Co94] M. O'Connor, B. Tangney, V. Cahill, and N. Harris. Micro-kernel Support
          for Migration. Distributed Systems Engineering Journal, 1(4), June 1994.

[Phil95] L. Philippe and G.-R. Perrin. Migration de processus dans Chorus/MiX. Re-
          vue Électronique sur les Réseaux et l'Informatique Répartie, (1), Avril 1995.

[Rozi88] M. Rozier, V. Abrossimov, F. Armand, I. Boule, M. Gien, M. Guillemont,
          F. Herrmann, C. Kaiser, S. Langlois, P. Léonard, and W. Neuhauser. Chorus
          Distributed Operating Systems. Computing Systems Journal, The USENIX
          Association, 1(4), December 1988.

[Rozi93] M. Rozier. Chorus Kernel v3r4.2 Programmers Reference Manual. Tech-
          nical Report CS/TR-92-26.1, Chorus Systèmes, Saint-Quentin-en-Yvelines
          (France), March 1993.

[Stro85] R.E. Strom and S.A. Yemini. Optimistic Recovery in Distributed Systems.
          ACM Transactions on Computer Systems, 3(3), August 1985.

[Syst95a] Chorus Systèmes. Chorus Kernel v3r5 : Implementation Guide. Technical
          report, Chorus Systèmes, March 1995.

[Syst95b] Chorus Systèmes. Chorus Kernel v3r5 : Network Artchitecture. Technical
          report, Chorus Systèmes, March 1995.

[Taco94] C. Taconet and G. Bernard. A Localization Service for Large Scale Dis-
          tributed Systems based on Microkernel Technology. In Proc. ROSE'94 Tech-
          nical Sessions, Bucharest (Romania), November 1994.

[Walp92] J. Walpole, J. Inouye, and R. Konuru. Modularity and Interfaces in Micro-
          Kernel Design and Implementation: a Case Study of Chorus on the HP PA-
          RISC. In Proc. USENIX Workshop on Micro-Kernels and Other Kernel
          Architectures, Seattle (USA), April 1992.

High-Level Languages for Parallel Scientific Computing *

Barbara Chapman[a] Piyush Mehrotra[b] Hans Zima[a]

[a]Institute for Software Technology and Parallel Systems,
University of Vienna, Liechtensteinstr. 22, A-1090 Vienna, Austria
E-Mail: {barbara,zima}@par.univie.ac.at

[b]ICASE, MS 132C, NASA Langley Research Center,
Hampton VA 23681 USA
E-Mail: pm@icase.edu

Abstract. Highly parallel scalable multiprocessing systems are power-ful tools for solving large-scale scientific and engineering problems. Lan-guages such as Vienna Fortran and High Performance Fortran (HPF) have been introduced to allow the programming of these machines at a relatively high level of abstraction, based on the data-parallel Single-Program-Multiple-Data (SPMD) model. Their main features focus on the distribution of data across the processors of a machine. In this pa-per, we outline the state-of-the-art in this area and provide a detailed description of HPF. A significant weakness of current HPF is its lack of support for many advanced applications, which require irregular data distributions, dynamic load balancing, or task parallelism. We introduce HPF+, an extension of HPF based on Vienna Fortran, that addresses these problems and provides the required functionality.

1 Introduction

The continued demand for increased computing power has led to the develop-ment of **highly parallel scalable multiprocessing systems (HMPs)**, which are now offered by all major vendors and have rapidly gained user acceptance. These machines are relatively inexpensive to build, and are potentially scalable to large numbers of processors. However, they are difficult to program: most of the architectures exhibit non-uniformity of memory access which implies that the locality of algorithms must be exploited in order to achieve high performance, and the management of data becomes of paramount importance.

Traditionally, HMPs have been programmed using a standard sequential pro-gramming language (Fortran or C), augmented with message passing constructs.

* The work described in this paper was partially supported by the Austrian Research Foundation (FWF Grant P8989-PHY) and by the Austrian Ministry for Science and Research (BMWF Grant GZ 308.9281- IV/3/93). This research was also supported by the National Aeronautics and Space Administration under NASA Contract No. NAS1-18605, while the authors were in residence at ICASE, NASA Langley Research Center, Hampton, VA 23681.

In this paradigm, the user is forced to deal with all aspects of the distribution of data and work to the processors, and to control the program's execution by explicitly inserting message passing operations. The resulting programming style can be compared to assembly language programming for a sequential machine; it has led to slow software development cycles and high costs for software production. Moreover, although MPI is evolving as a standard for message passing, the portability of MPI-based programs is limited since the characteristics of the target architectures may require extensive restructuring of the code.

As a consequence, much research and development activity has been concentrated in recent years on providing higher-level programming paradigms for HMPs. Vienna Fortran, building upon the KALI programming language [12] and experiences from the SUPERB parallelization system [22], was the first fully specified data-parallel language for HMPs. It provides language features for the high-level specification of data distribution and alignment, as well as explicitly parallel loops. High Performance Fortran (HPF) [9], a de-facto standard developed by a consortium including participants from industry, academia, and research laboratories, is based on concepts of CM Fortran [21], Vienna Fortran, and Fortran D [8]. It provides support for regular applications, alleviating the task of the programmer for a certain segment of applications. However, it is generally agreed that the current version of the language, *HPF-1*, is not adequate to handle many advanced applications, such as multiblock codes, unstructured meshes, adaptive grid codes, or sparse matrix computations, without incurring significant overheads with respect to memory or execution time.

This paper is structured as follows. In Section 2, we provide a detailed description of HPF-1. We then identify some of the weaknesses of the language by considering requirements posed by irregular algorithms and dynamic load balancing. This study leads to the discussion of an HPF extension, **"HPF+"**, which, based upon Vienna Fortran, addresses many of these problems and thus contributes to the present effort of the HPF Forum for defining a suitable successor to HPF-1 (Section 3). The paper conludes with Section 4.

2   High Performance Fortran (HPF-1)

Recently an international group of researchers from academia, industry and government laboratories formed the High Performance Fortran Forum aimed at providing an approach in which the user and the compiler share responsibility for exploiting parallelism. The main goal of the group has been to design a high-level set of standard extensions to Fortran called, High Performance Fortran (HPF), intended to exploit a wide variety of parallel architectures [9]

The HPF extensions allow the user to carefully control the distribution of data across the memories of the target machine. However, the computation code is written using a global name space with no explicit message passing statements. It is then the compiler's responsibility to analyze the distribution annotations and generate parallel code inserting communication statements where required by the computation. Thus, using this approach the programmer can focus on high-level algorithmic and performance critical issues such as load balance while allowing the compiler system to deal with the complex low-level machine specific details.

Earlier efforts The HPF effort is based on research done by several groups, some of which are described below. The language IVTRAN [13], for the SIMD machine ILLIAC IV, was one of the first languages to allow users to control the data layout. The user could indicate the array dimensions to be spread across the processors and those which were to be local in a processor. Combinations resulting in physically skewed data were also allowed.

In the context of MIMD machines, Kali (and its predecessor BLAZE) [11, 12] was the first language to introduce user-specified distribution directives. The language allows the dimensions of an array to be mapped onto an explicitly declared processor array using simple regular distributions such as *block, cyclic* and *block-cyclic* and more complex distributions such as *irregular* in which the address of each element is explicitly specified. Simple forms of user-defined distribution are also permitted. Kali also introduced the idea of dynamic distributions which allow the user to change the distribution of an array at runtime. The parallel computation is specified using *forall* loops within a global name space. The language also introduced the concept of an *on clause* which allows the users to control the distribution of loop iterations across the processors.

The Fortran D project [8] follows a slightly different approach to specifying distributions. The distribution of data is specified by first aligning data arrays to virtual arrays knows as decompositions. The decompositions are then distributed across an implicit set of processors using relative weights for the different dimensions. The language allows an extensive set of alignments along with simple regular and irregular distributions. All mapping statements are considered executable statements, thus blurring the distinction between static and dynamic distributions.

Vienna Fortran [3, 23] is the first language to provide a complete specification of distribution constructs in the context of Fortran. Based largely on the Kali model, Vienna Fortran allows arrays to be aligned to other arrays, which are then distributed across an explicit processor array. In addition to the simple regular and irregular distributions, Vienna Fortran defines a generalized block distribution which allows unequal sized contiguous segments of the data to be mapped the processors. Users can define their own distribution and alignment functions which can then be used to provide a precise mapping of data to the underlying processors. The language maintains a clear distinction between distributions that remain static during the execution of a procedure and those which can change dynamically, allowing compilers to optimize code for these different situations. It defines multiple methods of passing distributed data across procedure boundaries including inheriting the distribution of the actual arguments. Distribution inquiry functions facilitate the writing of library functions which are optimal for multiple incoming distributions.

High Performance Fortran effort has been based on the above and other related projects [1, 15, 10, 14, 16, 17, 18]. In the next few sub-sections we provide an introduction to HPF concentrating on the features which are critical to parallel performance.

2.1   HPF Overview

High Performance Fortran[2] is a set of extensions for Fortran 90 designed to allow specification of data parallel algorithms. The programmer annotates the program with distribution directives to specify the desired layout of data. The underlying programming model provides a global name space and a single thread of control. Explicitly parallel constructs allow the expression of fairly controlled forms of parallelism, in particular data parallelism. Thus, the code is specified in a high level portable manner with no explicit tasking or communication statements. The goal is to allow architecture specific compilers to generate efficient code for a wide variety of HMPs including SIMD, MIMD shared and distributed memory machines.

Fortran 90 was used a base for HPF for two reasons. First, a large percentage of scientific codes are still written in Fortran (in particular Fortran 77), providing programmers using HPF with a familiar base. Second, the array operations as defined for Fortran 90 make it eminently suitable for data parallel algorithms.

Most of the HPF extensions are in the form of directives or structured comments which assert facts about the program or suggest implementation strategies such as data layout. Since these are directives they do not change the semantics of the program but may have a profound effect on the efficiency of the generated code. The syntax used for these directives is such that if HPF extensions are at some later date accepted as part of the language only the prefix, **!HPF$**, needs to be removed to retain a correct HPF program. HPF also introduces some new language syntax in the form of data parallel execution statements and a few new intrinsics.

Features of High Performance Fortran   In this subsection we provide a brief overview of the new features defined by HPF. In the next few subsections we will provide a more detailed view of some of these features.

- *Data mapping directives:* HPF provides a set of directives to specify the distribution and alignment of arrays.
- *Data parallel execution features:* The **FORALL** statement and construct and the **INDEPENDENT** directive can be used to specify data parallel code. The concept of *pure* procedures callable from parallel constructs has also been defined.

---

[2] This section is partially based on the HPF Language Specification document [9] which has been jointly written by several of the participants of the HPF Forum.

- *New intrinsic and library functions:* HPF provides a set of new intrinsic functions including system functions to inquire about the underlying hardware, mapping inquiry functions to inquire about the distribution of the data structures and a few computational intrinsic functions. A set of new library routines have also been defined so as to provide a standard interface for highly useful parallel operations such as reduction functions, combining scatter functions, prefix and suffix functions, and sorting functions.
- *Extrinsic procedures:* In order to accommodate programming paradigms other than the data parallel paradigm, HPF provides *extrinsic* procedures. These define an explicit interface and allow codes expressed using a different paradigm, such as an explicit message passing routine, to be called from an HPF program.
- *Sequence and storage association:* The Fortran concepts of sequence and storage association[3] assume an underlying linearly addressable memory. Such assumptions create a problem in architectures which have a fragmented address space and are not compatible with the data distribution features of HPF. Thus, HPF places restrictions on the use of storage and sequence association for distributed arrays. For example, arrays that have been distributed can not be passed as actual arguments associated with dummy arguments which have a different rank or shape. Similarly, arrays that have been storage associated with other arrays can be distributed only in special situations. The reader is referred to the HPF Language specification document [9] for full details of these restrictions and other HPF features.

2.2 Data Mapping Directives

A major part of the HPF extensions are aimed at specifying the alignment and distribution of the data elements. The underlying intuition for such mapping of data is as follows. If the computations on different elements of a data structure are independent, then distributing the data structure will allow the computation to be executed in parallel. Similarly, if elements of two data structures are used in the same computation, then they should be aligned so that they reside in the same processor memory. Obviously, the two factors may be in conflict across computations, giving rise to situations where data needed in a computation resides on some other processor. This data dependence is then satisfied by communicating the data from one processor to another. Thus, the main of goal of mapping data onto processor memories is to increase parallelism while minimizing communication such that the workload across the processors is balanced.

HPF uses a two level mapping of data objects to abstract processors as shown in Figure 1. First, data objects are aligned to other objects and then groups of objects are distributed on a rectilinear arrangement of abstract processors.

---

[3] Informally, sequence association refers to the Fortran assumption that the elements of an array are in particular order (column-major) and hence allows redimensioning of arrays across procedure boundaries. Storage association allows COMMON and EQUIVALENCE statements to constrain and align data items relative to each other.

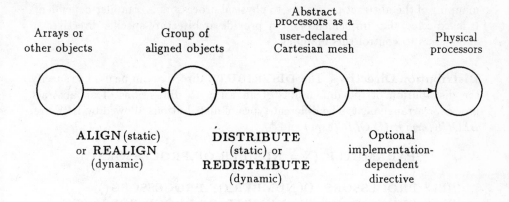

Fig. 1. HPF data distribution model

Each array is created with some mapping of its elements to abstract processors either on entry to a program unit or at the time of allocation for allocatable arrays. This mapping may be specified by the user through the **ALIGN** and **DISTRIBUTE** directives or in the case where complete specifications are not provided may be chosen by the compiler.

Processors Directive The **PROCESSORS** directive can be used to declare one or more rectilinear arrangements of processors in the specification part of a program unit. If two processor arrangements have the same shape, then corresponding elements of the two arrangements are mapped onto the same physical processor thus ensuring that objects mapped to these abstract processors will reside on the same physical processor.

The intrinsics **NUMBER_OF_PROCESSORS** and **PROCESSOR_SHAPE** can be used to determine the actual number of physical processors being used to execute the program. This information can then be used in declaring the abstract processor arrangement.

```
!HPF$ PROCESSORS  P(N)
!HPF$ PROCESSORS  Q( NUMBER_OF_PROCESSORS ())
!HPF$ PROCESSORS  R(8, NUMBER_OF_PROCESSORS ()/8)
!HPF$ PROCESSORS  SCALARPROC
```

Here, P is a processor arrangement of size N, the size of Q (and the shape of R) is dependent upon the number of physical processors executing the program while $SCALARPROC$ is conceptually treated as a scalar processor.

A compiler must accept any processor declaration which is either scalar or whose total number of elements match the number of physical processors. The mapping of the abstract processors to physical processors is compiler-dependent. It is expected that implementors may provide architecture-specific directives to allow users to control this mapping.

Distribution Directives The **DISTRIBUTE** directive can be used to specify the distribution of the dimensions of an array to dimensions of an abstract processor arrangement. The different types of distributions allowed by HPF are: *BLOCK(expr), CYCLIC(expr)* and *.

```
            PARAMETER (N = NUMBER_OF_PROCESSORS())

!HPF$  PROCESSORS   Q( NUMBER_OF_PROCESSORS())
!HPF$  PROCESSORS   R(8, NUMBER_OF_PROCESSORS()/8)

       REAL A(100), B(200), C(100,200), D(100, 200)

!HPF$  DISTRIBUTE   A( BLOCK ) ONTO Q
!HPF$  DISTRIBUTE   B( CYCLIC (5))
!HPF$  DISTRIBUTE   C( BLOCK , CYCLIC ) ONTO R
!HPF$  DISTRIBUTE   D( BLOCK (10), *) ONTO Q
```

In the above examples, A is divided into N contiguous blocks of elements which are then mapped onto successive processors of the arrangement Q. The elements of array B are first divided into blocks of 5, which are then mapped in a wrapped manner across the processors of the arrangement Q. The two dimensions of array C are individually mapped to the two dimensions of the processor arrangement R. The rows of C are blocked while the columns are cyclically mapped. The one-dimensional array D is distributed across the one-dimensional processor arrangement Q such that the second axis is not distributed. That is each row of the array is mapped as a single object. To determine the distribution of the dimension, the rows are first blocked into groups of 10 and these groups are then mapped to successive processors of Q. In this case, N must be at least 10 to accommodate the rows of D. Note, that in the case of array B, the compiler chooses the abstract processor arrangement for the distribution.

The **REDISTRIBUTE** directive is syntactically similar to the **DISTRIBUTE** directive but may appear only in the execution part of a program unit. It is used for dynamically changing the distribution of an array and may only be used for arrays that have been declared as **DYNAMIC**. The only difference between **DISTRIBUTE** and **REDISTRIBUTE** directives is that the former can use only specification expressions while the latter can use any expression including values computed at runtime.

```
       REAL A(100)
!HPF$  DISTRIBUTE ( BLOCK ),  DYNAMIC :: A
       k = ...
!HPF$  REDISTRIBUTE A( CYCLIC (k))
```

Here, A starts with a block distribution and is dynamically remapped to a cyclic distribution whose block size is computed at runtime.

When an array is redistributed, arrays that are *ultimately aligned* to it (see below) are also remapped to maintain the alignment relationship.

Alignment Directives The **ALIGN** directive is used to indirectly specify the mapping of an array (the alignee) by specifying its relative position with respect to another object (the align-target) which is ultimately distributed. HPF provides a variety of alignments including identity alignment, offsets, axis collapse, axis transposition, and replication using dummy arguments which range over the entire index range of the alignee. Only linear expressions are allowed in the specification of the align-target with the restriction that a align dummy can appear only in one expression in an **ALIGN** directive. The alignment function must be such that alignee is not allowed to "wrap around" or "extend past the edges" of the align-target.

```
!HPF$ ALIGN A(:,:)  WITH B(:,:)     ! identity alignment
!HPF$ ALIGN C(I)    WITH D(I-5)     ! offset
!HPF$ ALIGN E(I,*)  WITH F(I)       ! collapse
!HPF$ ALIGN G(I)    WITH H(I,*)     ! replication
!HPF$ ALIGN R(I,J)  WITH S(J,I)     ! transposition
```

If A is aligned to B which is in turn aligned with C then A is considered to be *immediately aligned* to B but *ultimately aligned* to C. Note, that intermediate alignments are useful only to provide the "ultimate" alignment since only the root of the alignment tree can be distributed.

The **REALIGN** directive is syntactically similar to the **ALIGN** directive but may appear only in the execution part of a program unit. It is used for dynamically changing the alignment of an array and may only be used for arrays that have been declared as **DYNAMIC**. As in the case of **REDISTRIBUTE**, the **REALIGN** directive can use computed values in its expression. Note that only an object which is not the root of an alignment tree can be explicitly realigned and that such a realignment does not affect the mapping of any other array.

Template Directive In certain codes, we may want to align arrays to an index space which is larger than any of the data arrays declared in the program. HPF introduces the concept of *template* as an abstract index space. Declaration of templates uses the keyword **TEMPLATE** and a syntax similar to that of regular data arrays. The distinction is that templates do not take any storage.

Consider the situation where two arrays of size $N \times (N+1)$ and $(N+1) \times N$ have to be aligned such that bottom right corner elements are mapped to the same processor. This can be done as follows:

```
!HPF$ TEMPLATE T(N+1,N+1)

!HPF$ REAL A(N,N+1), B(N+1,N)
!HPF$ ALIGN A(I,J) WITH T(I+1,J)
!HPF$ ALIGN B(I,J) WITH T(I,J+1)
!HPF$ DISTRIBUTE  T( BLOCK , BLOCK )
```

As seen above, templates can be used as align-targets and may be distributed using a **DISTRIBUTE** (or **REDISTRIBUTE**) directives but may not be an alignee.

Procedure Boundaries HPF allows distributed arrays to be passed as actual arguments to procedures. As noted before, HPF places restrictions on sequence association, therefore the rank and shape of the actual arguments must match with those of the corresponding dummy arguments. HPF provides a wide variety of options to specify the distribution of the dummy argument. The user can specify that the distribution of the actual argument be inherited by the dummy argument. In other cases, the user can provide a specific mapping for the dummy and actual argument may need to remapped to satisfy this mapping. If the actual is remapped on entry, then the original mapping is restored on exit from the procedure. The user can also demand that the actual argument be already mapped as specified for the dummy argument. In this case, it is incumbent upon the callee to explicitly remap before the call to the procedure. In the presence of interface blocks such a remap may be implicitly provided by the compiler.

HPF also provides a **INHERIT** directive which specifies that the template of the actual argument be copied and used as the template for the dummy argument. This makes a difference when only a subsection of an array is passed as an actual argument. Without the **INHERIT** directive, the template of the dummy argument is implicitly assumed to be the same shape as the dummy and the dummy is aligned to the template using the identity mapping.

2.3   Data Parallel Constructs

Fortran 90 has syntax to express data parallel operations on full arrays. For example, the statement $A = B + C$ indicates that the two arrays B and C should be added element by element (in any order) to produce the array A. The two main reasons for introducing these features is the conciseness of the expressions (note the absence of explicit loops) and the possibility of exploiting the undefined order of elemental operations for vector and parallel machines. HPF extends Fortran 90 with several new features to explicitly specify data parallelism. The **FORALL** statement and construct generalize the Fortran 90 array operations to allow not only more complicated array sections but also the calling of *pure* procedures on the elements of arrays. The · **INDEPENDENT** directive can be used to specify parallel iterations.

Forall Statement The **FORALL** statement extends the Fortran 90 array operations by making the index used to range over the elements explicit. Thus, this statement can be used to make an array assignment to array elements or sections of arrays, possibly masked with a scalar logical expression. The general form the **FORALL** statement is as follows:

> **FORALL** (*triplet, ...* [, *scalar-mask*])
>   *assignment*

where, a *triplet* has the form:

> *subscript = lower: upper* [: *stride*]

Here, the **FORALL** header may have multiple triplets and *assignment* is a arithmetic or pointer assignment. First the lower bound, upper bound and the optional stride of each triplet are evaluated (in any order). The cartesian product of the result provides the valid set of subscript values over which the mask is then evaluated. This gives rise to the active combinations. The right hand side of the assignment is then evaluated for all the active combinations before any assignment to corresponding elements on the left hand side.

> **FORALL** (I=1,N, J=2,N)
>   A(I,J) = A(I,J-1)*B(I)

In the above example, the new values of the array A are determined by the old values of A in the columns on the right and the array B.

Forall Construct The **FORALL** construct is a generalization of the **FORALL** statement allowing multiple statements to be associated with the same forall header. The only kind of statements allowed are assignment, the **WHERE** statement and another **FORALL** statement or construct.

> **FORALL** (*triplet, ...* [, *scalar-mask*])
>   *statement*
>   . . .
>
> **END FORALL**

Here, the header is evaluated as before and the execution of one statement is completed for all active combination before proceeding to the next statement. Thus, conceptually in a **FORALL** construct, there is a synchronization before the assignment to the left hand side and between any two statements. Obviously, some of these synchronization may not be needed and can be optimized away.

Pure procedures HPF has introduced a new attribute for procedures called **PURE** which allows users to declare that the given procedure has no side effects. That is the only effects of the procedure are either the value returned by the function or possible changes in the values of **INTENT(OUT)** or **INTENT(INOUT)** arguments. HPF defines a set of syntactic constraints that must be followed in order for a procedure to be pure. This allows the compiler to easily check the validity of the declaration. Note, that a procedure can only call other pure procedures to remain pure.

Only pure functions can be called from a **FORALL** statement or construct. Since pure functions have no side-effects other than the value returned, the function can be called for the active set of index combinations in any order.

Independent Directive The **INDEPENDENT** directive can be used with a **DO** loop or a **FORALL** statement or construct to indicate that there are no cross-iteration data dependences. Thus, for a **DO** loop the directive asserts that the iterations of the loop can be executed in any order without changing the final result. Similarly when used with a **FORALL** construct or statement, the directive asserts that there is no synchronization required between the executions of the different values of the active combination set.

With a **DO** loop, the **INDEPENDENT** directive can be augmented with a list of variables which can be treated as private variables for the purposes of the iterations.

```
!HPF$ INDEPENDENT, NEW (X)
      DO I = 1,N
         X = B(I)
         ...
         A(f(I)) = X
      END DO I = 1,N
```

Here, the **INDEPENDENT** directive is asserting that the function $f(I)$ returns a permutation of the index set, i.e., no two iterations are going to assign to the same element of A. Similarly, the *new clause* asserts that the loop carried dependence due to the variable X is spurious and the compiler can execute the loops by (conceptually) allocating a *new X* variable for each iteration.

2.4 Examples of HPF Codes

In this section we provide two code fragments using some of the HPF features described above. The first is the Jacobi iterative algorithm and the second is the Modified Gram-Schmidt algorithm discussed earlier.

The HPF version of the Jacobi iterative procedure which may be used to approximate the solution of a partial differential equation discretized on a grid, is given below.

```
!HPF$  PROCESSORS  p( NUMBER_OF_PROCESSORS ())
         REAL. u(1:n,1:n), f(1:n,1:n)
!HPF$  ALIGN u :: f
!HPF$  DISTRIBUTE u (*, BLOCK)
         FORALL  (i=2:n-1, j = 2:n-1)
            u(i,j) = 0.25 * (f(i,j) + u(i-1, j) + u(i+1, j) +
                             u(i, j-1) + u(i, j+1)
         END FORALL
```

At each step, it updates the current approximation at a grid point, represented by the array u, by computing a weighted average of the values at the neighboring grid points and the value of the right hand side function represented by the array f.

The array f is aligned with the array u using the identity alignment. The columns of u (and thus those of f indirectly) are then distributed across the processors executing the program. The computation is expressed using a **FORALL** statement, where all the right hand sides are evaluated using the old values of u before assignment to the left hand side.

To reiterate, the computation is specified using a global index space and does not contain any explicit data motion constructs. Given that the underlying arrays are distributed by columns, the edge columns will have to be communicated to neighboring processors. It is the compiler's responsibility to analyze the code and generate parallel code with appropriate communication statements inserted to satisfy the data requirements.

The HPF version of the Modified Gram-Schmidt algorithm is given below.[4].

```
         REAL  v(n,n)
!HPF$  DISTRIBUTE v (*, BLOCK)
         DO i = 1,n
           tmp = 0.0
           DO k = 1,n
             tmp = tmp + v(k,i)*v(k,i)
           END DO
           xnorm = 1.0 / sqrt(tmp)
           DO k = 1,n
             v(k,i) = v(k,i) * xnorm
           END DO
!HPF$  INDEPENDENT, NEW(tmp)
           DO j = i+1,n
             tmp = 0.0
             DO k = 1,n
               tmp = tmp + v(k,i)*v(k,j)
             END DO
```

---

[4] A Fortran 90 version of the code fragment, not shown here, would have used array constructs for the k loops. This would make the parallelism in the inner loops explicit.

```
DO k = 1,n
  v(k,j) = v(k,j) - tmp*v(k,i)
END DO
END DO
END DO
```

The first directive declares that the columns of the array v are to be distributed by block across the memories of the underlying processor set. The outer loop is sequential and is thus executed by all processors. Given the column distribution, in the ith iteration of the outer loop, the first two k loops would be executed by the processor owning the ith column.

The second directive declares the j loop to be *independent* and *tmp* to be a *new* variable. Thus the iterations of the j loop can be executed in parallel, i.e., each processor updates the columns that it owns in parallel. Since the ith column is used for this update, it will have to be broadcast to all processors.

The distribution of the columns by contiguous blocks implies that processors will become idle as the computation progresses. A *cyclic* distribution of the columns would eliminate this problem. This can be achieved by replacing the distribution directive with the following:

!HPF$ **DISTRIBUTE** v (*, **CYCLIC**)

This declares the columns to distributed cyclically across the processors, and thus forces the inner j loop to be strip-mined in a cyclic rather than in a block fashion. Thus, all processors are busy until the tail end of the computation.

The above distributions only exploit parallelism in one dimension, whereas the inner k loops can also run in parallel. This can be achieved by distributing both the dimensions of v as follows:

!HPF$ **DISTRIBUTE** v (**BLOCK**, **CYCLIC**)

Here, the processors are presumed to be arranged in a two-dimensional mesh and the array is distributed such that the elements of a column of the array are distributed by block across a column of processors whereas the columns as a whole are distributed cyclically. Thus, the first k loop becomes a parallel reduction of the ith column across the set of processors owning the ith column. Similarly, the second k loop can be turned into a **FORALL** statement which is executed in parallel by the column of processors which owns the ith column. The second set of k loops, inside the j loop, can be similarly parallelized.

Overall, it is clear, that using the approach advocated by HPF allows the user to focus on the performance critical issues at a very high level. Thus, it is easy for the user to experiment with a different distribution, by just changing the distribute directives. The new code is then recompiled before running on the target machine. In contrast, the effort required to change the program if it was written using low-level communication primitives would be much more.

3   HPF+

In this section, we will discuss a number of advanced applications which require irregular data distributions, dynamic load balancing, and task parallelism. Although HPF-1 is a good language for expressing data parallel problems with regular behavior, its use for advanced applications exposes several weaknesses related to limitations in expressivity, functionality, and performance.

We will discuss extensions to HPF-1 that are needed to address these problems. The discussion informally introduces an HPF extension, called "**HPF+**", using an ad-hoc HPF-like syntax. The extensions to HPF-1 incorporated into HPF+ are of two sorts: first, a generalization of the data distribution mechanisms, and, secondly, control facilities providing coarse-grain task parallelism integrated with the data-parallel HPF computation model.

3.1   Distribution to Processor Subsets and Subobject Distribution

The HPF-1 **DISTRIBUTE** directive specifies the distribution of data to a processor array which has been declared by the user. It does not permit distribution to a part of the processor array. Also, HPF-1 allows only the distribution of top-level objects – components of a derived type cannot be distributed. Here, we show that multiblock problems need both features, and describe simple extensions to HPF-1 which provide these functionalities. This will be illustrated by a program skeleton creating a corresponding grid structure.

Scientific and engineering codes from diverse application areas may use multiple grids to model the underlying problem domain. These grids may be structured, unstructured or a mixture of both types, individually chosen to match the underlying physical structure and allocate the computational resources efficently with high node densities in selected areas. A typical application may use anywhere from 10 to 100 grids of widely varying sizes and shapes. Each sweep over the domain involves computation on the individual grids before data is exchanged between them. Thus, these types of applications exhibit at least two levels of parallelism. At the outer level, there is coarse grain parallelism, since the computation can be performed on each grid simultaneously. The internal computation on each grid, on the other hand, exhibits the typical loosely synchronous data parallelism of structured grid codes.

Distributing the array of grids to the processors so that each grid is mapped to exactly one processor offers limited parallelism since it only exploits the outer level, the number of grids may be to small to allow the use of all processors, and the grids may vary significantly in size resulting in an uneven workload. Another strategy is to distribute each grid independently to all processors, enabling the parallelism within a grid to be exploited. This will lead to a more even workload; however, the grids may not all be large enough for this to be a reasonable solution.

Both of the above distribution strategies are likely to be·inefficient, particularly on machines with a large number of processors. A flexible alternative is to permit grids to be separately distributed to a suitably sized subset of the available processors. This approach allows both levels of parallelism to be exploited while providing the opportunity to balance the workload.

HPF-1 does not, however, permit data arrays to be distributed directly to subsets of processors. In HPF-1 this can be expressed indirectly by using templates and alignment, but these solutions are difficult to achieve and will generally require a priori precise knowledge of the size of both the grid and the processor array, and must be reimplemented for each modification of the problem. A simpler solution is to adopt a direct approach, which permits a processor subsection to be the target of a distribution. An example of this is shown in Figure 2.

Consider the case of a multiblock problem where the number of grids and their sizes are not known until runtime. Each grid can be declared as a pointer within a derived type and the set of all grids can be an allocatable array, where each element is a grid. HPF-1 allows us to distribute the array of grids to the processors. However, we may not distribute the individual grids across processors, since these are subobjects and their distribution is explicitly prohibited. This is necessary for exploiting the parallelism present within the individual grids. The algorithm in Figure 2 illustrates a solution for this problem, by providing a notation for the distribution of subobjects. We assume that at most one level in a nested structure can be distributed in this way.

3.2   General Block Distributions

Dimensions of data arrays or templates can be mapped in HPF-1 by specifying either block or cyclic distributions. There are a number of problems for which these regular mappings do not result in an adequate balance of the workload across the processors of the target machine, but which can be handled by **general block distributions**, a relatively simple extension of HPF-1's regular block distributions.

General block distributions were initially implemented in SUPERB and Vienna Fortran. They are similar to the regular block distributions of HPF-1 in that the index domain of an array dimension is partitioned into contiguous blocks which are mapped to the processors; however, the blocks are not required to be of the same size. Thus, general block distributions provide more generality than regular blocks while retaining the contiguity property, which plays an important role in achieving target code efficiency.

Consider a one-dimensional array A, declared as **REAL** $A[l : u]$, and assume that there are N processors $p_i, 1 \leq i \leq N$. If we distribute A using a general block distribution $GENERAL\_BLOCK(B)$, where B is a one-dimensional integer array with N elements, and $B(i) = s_i$ (with $s_i > 0$ for all i) denotes the size of the i-th block, then processor p_1 owns the local segment $A[l : l+s_1-1]$, p_2 owns $A[l+s_1 : l + s_1 + s_2 - 1]$ and so on. B, together with the index domain of A, completely determines the distribution of A and provides all the information required to

```
!HPF$ PROCESSORS R(NPR)
TYPE subgrid
   INTEGER xsize, ysize
   REAL, DIMENSION (:,:), POINTER ::grid
!HPF+$ DYNAMIC ::grid
   ...
END subgrid

TYPE (subgrid), DIMENSION (:), ALLOCATABLE :: grid_structure
   ...
READ (*,*) no_of_grids
ALLOCATE (grid_structure(no_of_grids))
DO i = 1, no_of_grids
   READ (*,*) ix, iy
   grid_structure(i)%xsize = ix
   grid_structure(i)%ysize = iy
ENDDO
!  Compute processor array section for each grid: low(i), high(i)
DO i = 1, no_of_grids
ALLOCATE (grid_structure(i)%grid(grid_structure(i)%xsize,
grid_structure(i)%ysize))
!HPF+$ REDISTRIBUTE ,(BLOCK,*) ONTO R(low(i):high(i))
ENDDO
```

Fig. 2. Creation of the grid structure for a multiblock code

handle accesses to A, including the organization of the required communication. The above scheme can be readily generalized to multi-dimensional arrays, each dimension of which is distributed by regular or general block.

The following code fragment illustrates an array A, whose rows are distributed in blocks of sizes 400,400,200,100,100,100,500, and 800.

```
!HPF$ PROCESSORS R(8)
INTEGER :: B(8) = (/400,400,200,100,100,100,500,800/)
REAL A(2600,100)
!HPF+$ DISTRIBUTE (GENERAL_BLOCK(B),*)::A
```

Although the representation of general block distribution requires on the order of the number of processors to describe the entire distribution, optimization often permits a local description of the distribution to be limited to just a few processors, with which there will be communication. Also, the space overhead due to this representation is not large in general, since most problems do not require a large number of distinct general block distributions.

Arrays distributed in this way can also be efficiently managed at runtime, allowing the use of the *overlap* [25] concept to optimize communication related to regular accesses. Finally, codes can be easily parameterized with such distributions: for example, a procedure with a transcriptive formal argument[5] that is supplied with differently distributed actual arguments can be efficiently compiled if the representation of the argument's distribution is passed along as a set of additional implicit arguments created by the compiler.

3.3 Irregular Distributions

General block distributions provide enough flexibility to meet the demands of some irregular computations: if, for instance, the nodes of a simple unstructured mesh are partitioned prior to execution and then appropriately renumbered, the resulting distribution can be described in this manner. This renumbering process is similar to domain decomposition and can be a complex and computationally demanding task. However, this approach is not appropriate for all irregular problems. A general block distribution, even with two or three dimensions, may not be able to provide an equal workload per processor. Also, block distributions are always constrained by the adjacency of data. The single workspaces typically used in Fortran programs cannot necessarily be renumbered in such a way as to produce a sequential group of regions. Irregular distributions offer the ability to express totally unstructured or irregular data structures but at some cost in terms of the code the compiler must generate.

We will here introduce two different mechanisms to handle general data distributions. We begin with *indirect distribution functions*, which allow the specification of a distribution via a mapping array and continue with *user-defined distribution functions*.

Indirect Distributions **Indirect distribution functions** can express *any* distribution of an array dimension that does not involve replication. Consider the following program fragment in HPF+:

```
!HPF$ PROCESSORS R(M)
REAL A(N)
INTEGER MAP(N)
   ...
!HPF$ DYNAMIC, DISTRIBUTE(BLOCK)::A
!HPF$ DISTRIBUTE (BLOCK)::MAP
   ...
! Compute a new distribution for A and save it in the mapping array MAP: the
! j-th element of A is mapped to the processor whose number is stored in MAP(j)
```

---

[5] If such an argument is passed by reference, the distribution is left intact, and thus no movement of data will be necessary.

CALL PARTITIONER(MAP, A,...)

! *Redistribute* A *as specified by* MAP

!HPF+$ **REDISTRIBUTE** A(INDIRECT(MAP))

Array A is dynamic and initially distributed by block. MAP is a statically distributed integer array that is of the same size as A and used as a **mapping array** for A; we specify a reference to an indirect distribution function in the form $INDIRECT(MAP)$. When the reference is evaluated, all elements of MAP must be defined and represent valid indices for the one-dimensional processor array R, i.e., they must be numbers in the range between 1 and M. A is then distributed such that for each $j, 1 \leq j \leq N$, $A(j)$ is mapped to $R(MAP(j))$. In this example, MAP is defined by a *partitioner*, which will compute a new distribution for A and assign values to the elements of MAP accordingly. (This distribution will often be used for a number of arrays in the program).

Indirectly distributed arrays must be supported by a runtime system which manages the internal representation of the mapping array and handles accesses to the indirectly distributed array. The mapping array is used to construct a *translation table*, recording the owner of each datum and its local index. Note that this representation has $\mathbf{O}(N)$ elements, on the same order as the size of the array; however, most codes require only a very small number of distinct indirect mappings. The PARTI routines developed by J. Saltz and collaborators [19] represent a runtime library which directly supports indirect distribution functions, in connection with irregular array accesses.

User-Defined Distribution Functions Indirect distribution functions incur a considerable overhead both at compile time and at runtime. A difficulty with this approach is that when a distribution is described by means of a mapping array, any regularity or structure that may have existed in the distribution is lost. Thus the compiler cannot optimize the code based on this complex but possibly regular distribution. **User-defined distribution functions (UDDFs)** provide a facility for extending the set of intrinsic mappings defined in the language in a structured way. The specification of a UDDF establishes a mapping from (data) arrays to processor arrays, using a syntax similar to Fortran functions. UDDFs have two implicit formal arguments, representing the data array to be distributed and the processor array to which the distribution is targeted. Specification statements for these arguments can be given using the keywords **TARGET_ARRAY** and **PROCESSOR_ARRAY**, respectively. UDDFs may contain local data structures and executable statements along with at least one *distribution mapping statement* which maps the elements of the target array to the processors.

UDDFs constitute the most general mechanism for specifying distributions: any arbitrary mapping between array indices and processors can be expressed, including partial or total replication. We illustrate their use by an example, representing indirect distributions. For simplicity we assume here that A and MAP have the same shape.

```
!HPF+$ DFUNCTION INDIRECT(MAP)
!HPF+$ TARGET_ARRAY A(*)
!HPF+$ PROCESSOR_ARRAY R(:)
!HPF+$ INTEGER MAP(*)

!HPF+$ DO I=1,SIZE(A)
!HPF+$   A(I) DISTRIBUTE TO R(MAP(I))
!HPF+$ ENDDO
!HPF+$ END DFUNCTION INDIRECT
```

3.4 Extensions of the INDEPENDENT Loop Concept

Whenever a do loop contains an assignment to an array involving an indirect access, the compiler will not be able to determine whether the iterations of the loop may be executed in parallel. Since such loops are common in irregular problems, and may contain the bulk of the computation, the user must assert the independence of its iterations.

For this purpose, HPF-1 provides the **INDEPENDENT** directive, which asserts that a subsequent do loop does not contain any loop-carried dependences, allowing the loop iterations to be executed in parallel.

There are two problems with this feature:

- There is no language support to specify the **work distribution** for the loop, i.e., the mapping of iterations to processors. This decision is left to the compiler/runtime system.
- **Reductions**, which perform global operations across a set of iterations, and assign the result to a scalar variable, violate the restriction on dependences and cannot be used in the loop. [6]

The first problem can be solved by extending the **INDEPENDENT** directive with an **ON** clause that specifies the mapping, either by naming a processor explicitly or referring to the *owner* of an element. The second problem can be solved by extending the language with a **REDUCTION** directive – which is to be permitted within independent loops – and imposing suitable constraints on the statement which immediately follows it. It could be augmented by a directive specifying the order in which values are to be accumulated. Note that simple reductions could be detected by most compilers.

For more detailed discussion of these features and their application to an unstructured mesh code see [6].

---

[6] Note however that HPF-1 and Fortran 90 provide intrinsics·for some important reductions.

3.5 Data Distribution and Alignment – Other Issues

There are a number of other issues with the specification of data distribution and alignment in HPF-1 which we have not discussed here. These include processor views, control of dynamic data distributions, library interfaces, and the procedure boundary; they are discussed in [6].

3.6 Integration of Task With Data Parallelism

With the rapidly growing computing power of parallel architectures, the complexity of simulations developed by scientists and engineers is increasing fast. Many advanced applications are of a multidisciplinary and heterogeneous nature and thus do not fit into the data-parallel paradigm.

Multidisciplinary programs are formed by pasting together modules from a variety of related scientific disciplines. For example, the design of a modern aircraft involves a variety of interacting disciplines such as aerodynamics, structural analysis and design, propulsion, and control. These disciplines, each of which is initially represented by a separate program, must be interconnected to form a single multidisciplinary model subsuming the original models and their interactions. For task parallelism to be useful, the parallelism both within and between the discipline models needs to be exposed and effectively exploited.

In this section, we propose language features that address this issue. These extensions provide a software layer on top of data-parallel languages, designed to address the "programming in the large" issues as well as the parallel performance issues arising in complex multidisciplinary applications. A program executes as a system of *tasks* which interact by sharing access to a set of **Shared Data Abstractions (SDAs)**. SDAs generalize Fortran 90 modules by including features from object-oriented data bases and monitors in shared-memory languages. They can be used to create persistent shared "objects" for communication and synchronization between coarse-grained parallel tasks, at a much higher level than simple communication channels transferring bytes between tasks.

A task is *spawned* by activating a subroutine with a list of arguments all of which must be of intent IN. Tasks are asynchronously executing autonomous activities to which *resources* of the system may be allocated. For example, the physical machine on which a task is to be executed, along with additional requirements pertaining to this machine, may be specified at the time a task is created.

Tasks may embody nested parallelism, for example by executing a data-parallel HPF program, or by coordinating a set of threads performing different functions on a shared data set.

An SDA consists of a set of data structures along with the methods (procedures) which manipulate this data. A set of tasks may share data by creating an SDA instance of appropriate type, and making it accessible to all tasks in the set. Tasks may then asynchronously call the methods of the SDA, with each call providing exclusive access. Condition clauses associated with methods and synchronization facilities embodied in the methods allow the formulation of a range of coordination strategies for tasks. The state of an SDA can be saved on external storage for later reuse. This facility can be seen as providing an I/O capability for SDAs, where in contrast to conventional byte-oriented I/O the structure of the object is preserved.

ORCA [2] is a language that allows the implementation of parallel applications on loosely coupled distributed systems. It provides a virtual layer that allows processes on different machines to share data, and thus pursues a similar approach as OPUS. However, it does not address the problem of integrating task with data parallelism.

Other Fortran-based approaches to the problem of combining task with data parallelism include the programming languages Fortran M [7], which provides a message-passing facility in the context of a discipline enforcing determinism, and Fx [20], which allows the creation of parallel tasks that can communicate at the time of task creation and task termination by sharing arguments. These approaches address a small grain of parallelism.

4 Conclusion

In the first part of this paper, we provided a detailed description of HPF. After an analysis of weaknesses of HPF-1 in the context of advanced algorithms, we proposed an extension, HPF+, based on Vienna Fortran, that addresses these problems. HPF+ can be seen as a contribution to the work of the HPF Forum towards the standardization of parallel languages for scalable High Performance architectures.

References

1. F.André,J.-L.Pazat and H. Thomas. PANDORE: A System to Manage Data Distribution. In: International Conference on Supercomputing (ICS'90), pp.380-388, June 1990.
2. H.E.Bal,M.F.Kaashoek, and A.S.Tanenbaum. Orca: A Language For Parallel Programming of Distributed Systems. *IEEE Transactions on Software Engineering* 18 (3):190-205, March 1992.
3. B. Chapman, P. Mehrotra, and H. Zima. Programming in Vienna Fortran. *Scientific Programming* 1(1):31-50, Fall 1992.
4. B. Chapman, P. Mehrotra, and H. Zima. High Performance Fortran Without Templates: A New Model for Data Distribution and Alignment. Proc. Fourth ACM SIGPLAN Symposium on Principles and Practice of Parallel Programming, San Diego (May 19-22, 1993), ACM SIGPLAN Notices Vol.28, No.7, pp.92-101, July 1993.
5. B.Chapman,P.Mehrotra,J.Van Rosendale,and H.Zima. A Software Architecture for Multidisciplinary Applications: Integrating Task and Data Parallelism. Proc.

CONPAR'94, Linz, Austria, September 1994. Also: Technical Report TR 94-1, Institute for Software Technology and Parallel Systems, University of Vienna, Austria, March 1994 and Technical Report 94-18, ICASE, NASA Langley Research Center, Hampton VA 23681.

6. B. Chapman, P. Mehrotra, and H. Zima. Extending HPF for Advanced Data-Parallel Applications. *IEEE Parallel & Distributed Technology* 2(3):59-70, Fall 1994.

7. I. T. Foster and K. M. Chandy. Fortran M: A Language for Modular Parallel Programming. Technical Report MCS-P327-0992 Revision 1. Mathematics and Computer Science Division, Argonne National Laboratory, June 1993.

8. G. Fox, S. Hiranandani, K. Kennedy, C. Koelbel, U. Kremer, C. Tseng, and M. Wu. Fortran D language specification. Department of Computer Science Rice COMP TR90079, Rice University, March 1991.

9. High Performance Fortran Forum. High Performance Fortran Language Specification Version 1.0. Technical Report, Rice University, Houston, TX, May 3, 1993. Also available as Scientific Programming 2(1-2):1-170, Spring and Summer 1993.

10. J.Li and M.Chen. Index Domain Alignment: Minimizing Cost of Cross-Referencing Between Distributed Arrays. Technical Report YALEU/DCS/TR-725, Yale University, November 1989.

11. P.Mehrotra. Programming Parallel Architectures: The BLAZE Family of Languages. In: Proc.Third SIAM Conference on Parallel Processing for Scientific Computing, Los Angeles, CA, pp.289-299, December 1988.

12. P. Mehrotra and J. Van Rosendale. Programming distributed memory architectures using Kali. In A. Nicolau, D. Gelernter, T. Gross, and D. Padua, editors, *Advances in Languages and Compilers for Parallel Processing*, pp. 364–384. Pitman/MIT-Press, 1991.

13. R.E.Millstein. Control Structures in ILLIAC IV Fortran. *Communications of the ACM* 16(10):621-627, October 1973.

14. MIMDizer User's Guide, Version 7.02. Pacific Sierra Research Corporation, Placerville, CA.,1991.

15. P.Hatcher,A. Lapadula,R.Jones,M.Quinn, and J.Anderson. A Production quality C* Compiler for Hypercube Machines. In: Proc.3rd ACM SIGPLAN Symposium on Principles and Practice of Parallel Programming", pp.73-82, April 1991.

16. A.P.Reeves and C.M.Chase. The Paragon Programming Paradigm and Distributed Memory Multicomputers. : In: (J.Saltz,P.Mehrotra,Eds.) Compilers and Runtime Software for Scalable Multiprocessors. Elsevier,Amsterdam,The Netherlands, 1991.

17. A.Rogers and K. Pingali. Process Decomposition Through Locality of Reference. In: Proc.ACM SIGPLAN Conference on Programming Language Design and Implementation, June 1989

18. M.Rosing,R.W.Schnabel and R.P.Weaver. Expressing Complex Parallel Algorithms in DINO. In: Proc.4th Conference on Hypercubes, Concurrent Computers, and Applications, pp.553-560, 1989.

19. J. Saltz, K. Crowley, R. Mirchandaney, and H. Berryman. Run-time scheduling and execution of loops on message passing machines. *Journal of Parallel and Distributed Computing*, 8(2):303–312, 1990.

20. J. Subhlok, J. Stichnoth, D. O'Hallaron, and T. Gross. Exploiting Task and Data Parallelism on a Multicomputer. Proc. Fourth ACM SIGPLAN Symposium on Principles and Practice of Parallel Programming, San Diego (May 19-22, 1993), ACM SIGPLAN Notices Vol.28, No.7, July 1993.

21. Thinking Machines Corporation. CM Fortran Reference Manual, Version 5.2. Thinking Machines Corporation, Cambridge, MA, September 1989.
22. H. Zima, H. Bast, and M. Gerndt. Superb: A tool for semi-automatic MIMD/SIMD parallelization. *Parallel Computing*, 6:1–18, 1988.
23. H. Zima, P. Brezany, B. Chapman, P. Mehrotra, and A. Schwald. Vienna Fortran – a language specification. ICASE Internal Report 21, ICASE, Hampton, VA, 1992.
24. H. Zima and B. Chapman. *Supercompilers for Parallel and Vector Computers*. ACM Press Frontier Series, Addison-Wesley, 1990.
25. H. Zima and B. Chapman. Compiling for Distributed Memory Systems. *Proceedings of the IEEE*, Special Section on Languages and Compilers for Parallel Machines, pp. 264-287, February 1993. Also: Technical Report ACPC/TR 92-16, Austrian Center for Parallel Computation, November 1992.

On Some New Aspects of Networked Multimedia Systems

Hermann Maurer

Institute for Information Processing and
Computer Supported New Media,
Graz University of Technology, Graz/Austria
email: hmaurer@iicm.tu-graz.ac.at

Abstract. Internet is continuing to spread like wildfire and is used more and more for networked multimedia systems, often called hypermedia systems. In this paper we analyze some aspects of modern hypermedia systems, concentrate on what are often called "second generation tools" and discuss electronic publishing as one of their applications in some detail.

1 Introduction

In this paper we discuss aspects of multimedia and hypermedia systems. We first show that "multimedia" is more than the combination of traditional media in digital form and that hypermedia is more than "multimedia with links". We then explain why hypermedia systems are starting to play such a prominent role on the Internet and continue by showing that "first generation" hypermedia systems should (and seamlessly can) be replaced by "second generation" systems such as Hyper-G. We compare features of WWW and Hyper-G superficially, but two concepts (links and collections) in more detail. We then report on how such second generation systems can be used for electronic publishing. In a brief chapter on the future of hypermedia we caution against too much euphoria particularly concerning the combination of Internet and hypermedia, and conclude this paper with a list of references.

2 Multimedia and Hypermedia

Multimedia is often defined as the combination of established "media" such as text, graphics, pictures, maps and audio- and movie clips in computerized (digitized) form. This is not wrong, but only half the truth. I want to emphasize this point explicitly since most multimedia productions you see today fit above description. However, by not offering more they do not exploit the real possibilities of multimedia as they are emerging [Lennon et al 1994c].

Real computer-based multimedia means applying the power of the computer to achieve interactivity beyond just being able to choose, from time to time, from a number of alternatives presented. Such real interactivity includes e.g.:

- viewing a section of a map (or a technical drawing, or whatever) and having the capability to move the section (regularly shaped window) smoothly around in all directions to explore the underlying large document, and to be able to zoom in and out as desired [Hoelzel 1994];
- being able to manipulate a 3D object like a statue, a carving, a piece of mineral or whatever by turning it in any direction, by zooming in and out, maybe by even changing light-sources or other parameters;
- having the possibility to maneuver around ("fly-through") the 3D model of a building, a city, a model of some engine or part of the human body, or some computer generated "virtual word". Note that the new Virtual Reality Modelling Language (VRML) has become an important component of modern multi- and hypermedia systems [Pichler et al 95];
- activating ("clicking at") any "word of interest" on the screen to obtain (multimedia) information on that item.

Two observations seem appropriate at this point:

(a) Due to the speed/cost limitations of the Internet some of the more advanced multimedia applications will first be available on a CD basis, rather than via Internet (publications such as "From Alice to Ocean" or sophisticated games like "Myst", "The 7th Guest" or "Space Quest V" are typical examples.

(b) When I say "CD based" I either mean CD-I or CD-ROM. A word of caution is necessary concerning CD-I: CD-I is a technology standardized in 1986 and hence is now fairly obsolete; its remaining (slim) chance is that CD-I players are audio-CD compatible (some CD-ROM drives are not) and easier to use than computers and CD-ROM. However, the very much higher functionality of CD-ROM will, I believe, allow CD-I at most a small survival-niche. To be fair, this opinion is shared by most but not all multimedia experts, so take it with a grain of salt!

Let us now turn our attention to the difference between multimedia and networked multimedia, i.e., hypermedia, a concept rapidly growing in importance. The best way to describe hypermedia is to define it as linked multimedia, where linked refers to three aspects: linking data, computers and people.

Linking data refers to the fact already alluded to earlier: if information is presented on the screen the user should be able to obtain more information by activating words, parts of a picture, etc. Sometimes this is called "following a hyerlink" and is compared with the kind of "associative thinking" we are used to, see e.g., [Nelson 1987]. Linking computers means that users are not restricted to access just one computer, but can (via e.g., Internet) easily also access data in potentially far remote locations. And linking people means that not only can data be "passively" received, but that user-feedback and user-to-user or user-to-information provider electronic communication is possible. It is clear that all three kinds of links are of significant value: the first provides convenient cross-referencing to other material; the second allows world-wide distribution of material developed; and the third adds an important new dimension of information exchange.

For background information on hypermedia see [Nelson 1987], [Conklin 1987], [Tomek et al 1991], [Koegel-Buford 1994]. For a survey of hypermedia applications in general see [Lennon et al 1994c], to teaching [Lennon et al 1994b] to large cultural application [Maurer 1994b], for more unorthodox applications [Foresta et al 1993], [Maurer 1995], [Jayasinha et al 1995] and [Qualthrough et al 1994]. For hypermedia applications to electronic publishing see Chapter 6.

3   Internet and Hypermedia

Before starting to discuss Internet and its relation to hypermedia publishing I want to make one all-important remark: if you plan to publish on Internet make sure that the same material can also be published, with little effort, on CD-ROM and vice-versa. Using the right tools such as e.g., the PC-Library (used by BI, Duden, Langenscheidt, Oxford University Press, Brockhaus, Meyer and Springer publishing companies (to mention just the "pioneers"), or HM-Card (see FTP server iicm.tu-graz.ac.at., directory pub/hmcard or [Maurer et al 1996]), and particularly Hyper-G (to be discussed in more detail later; see [Maurer 1996] or FTP server iicm.tu-graz.ac.at, directory pub/Hyper-G or http://www.iicm.tu-graz.ac.at if you happen to be a WWW fan and the references to Hyper-G at the end of Chapter 5) this is quite feasable and provides two ways of offering basically the same information at almost no additional cost, maximising distribution and hence potential profit. All of the above mentioned products have been developed at the author's institute, hence this list is likely to be biased. However, if you find better products both serving the Internet and CD-ROM let me know: I then want to learn of them. Anyway, aside from mentioning some of the products I am responsible for, the important message is: don't let anyone talk you into preparing a CD-ROM whose contents you can't easily use on the Internet and conversely! As you will see later systems like Hyper-G, to be dealt with below, allow to offer information on the Internet yet allow to press it on CD's with almost no extra effort.

Now let us turn our attention to the Internet. With currently 5 million computers and 50 million users (numbers vary a bit in different sources) and a continued growth rate of 80 % annually Internet is not only a phenomenon, it offers right now a sizeable number of users, particularly scientists. By the time you have finished your first Internet projects (that is: if you have not started yet) the user population is likely to exceed 100 million ...

Thus, is Internet the "Information Highway" or "Infobahn" of the future we so often hear about (too often ... we are all really getting tired of hearing the same stuff all over again, aren't we?)

The answer to this is a resounding "No"! Internet right now is good for (a) distribution of text, graphics, and medium quality images and can be used for all kinds of communicational facilities, or offering special services like educational packages, certain types of games, etc and (b) it caters for mainly "computer literate" users. It is less suited for the run-of-the-mill household and also possibly too expensive for such applications, and it is too slow and too expensive for high-quality pictures, sound-recordings and videos. "Video on Demand", "Videophony", "Videoconferences", "Virtual Reality Experiences", etc. will become more and more feasable via the Internet as time goes by, but it will take more than a couple of years before such applications can be widespread.

Internet has other problems on top of the speed/cost issue addressed: there is no good billing mechanism available, privacy, authenticity and security are not satisfactorily resolved, etc.

Nevertheless, Internet is very useful for many applications, e.g., for "emails", "file transfers" (FTP), various types of presentations for typically PR reasons and, increasingly, for electronic publications. However, to make full use of Internet efficient tools have to be employed. One such tool that has obtained wide-spread recognition is the hypermedia system WWW (the World Wide Web or W3). However, it is important to understand that WWW is not the end of a development, but the beginning: if WWW is considered a "first generation system" then we have to start looking at "second generation systems" as discussed in the next section.

4   The Need for Second Generation Hypermedia Systems

In this chapter we show that the navigational and structural tools currently available on the Internet are not sufficient to fully exploit the tremendous power of the largest information and communication ressource mankind has ever had. Current hypermedia systems and its most prominent specimen WWW do not have enough functionality to provide the power that is needed.

The steady growth of the Internet [Fenn et al 1994] has made resource discovery and structuring tools increasingly important. Historically first was the introduction of various dictionary servers, Archie [Deutsch 1992] being probably the first and most prominent. As an alternative to having servers that need constant updating, WAIS [Kahle et al 1992] introduced a powerful search engine permitting full-text searches of large databases and returning a ranked list, the ranking based on a heuristic approach. Although directory servers like Archie (to locate a database) and search engines like WAIS (to locate a desired item in that database) alleviated the problem of finding information in the Internet somewhat, it soon became apparent that other techniques would also be necessary.

The most important such technique is to emphasise the a-priori organisation of information, rather than try to search for information in a universe of completely different databases. Two efforts in this direction have proved particulalry successful: Gopher, originally developed at the University of Minnesota [Alberti et al 1992] and the World-Wide Web (WWW, W3, or "The Web" for short) originally developed at CERN in Geneva [Berners-Lee et al 1992 and 1994].

In both cases information is stored in a simple structured fashion on servers, and can be accessed via clients, with clients available for most major hardware platforms. Thousands of Gopher and WWW servers are currently reachable in the Interent, albeit most of them with little more than a token presentation of the institution running the server. There are some very notable exceptions, however. Examples of substantial Gopher and WWW databases include the EARN ("European Academic & Research Network") Gopher server (gopher.earn.net), the ACM Siggraph Gopher server (siggraph.org), the CERN WWW Server - the birthplace of WWW (http://www.cern.ch), MUSE - a Hypermedia Journal from the Johns Hopkins University (http://muse.mse.jhu.edu), Nando ("News and Observer") News net (http://www.nando.net), and The Canadian Internet Handbook WWW Server (http://www.csi.nb.ca/handbook/handbook.html).

Information in Gopher is structured in a hierarchical fashion using menus, an access technique which, though simple to use, has many well-known weaknesses. Information in WWW is structured in documents; documents are linked together according to the hypertext-paradigm (see [Conklin 1987], [Tomek et al 1991] and [Koegel-Buford 1994] for a general and thorough discussion of hypertext and hypermedia). "Anchors" within documents are associated with "links" leading to other documents. Although many stand-alone systems using the hypertext-metaphor have emerged since the introduction of HyperCard on the Mac in 1987, WWW can claim to be the first wide-spread hypertext system whose component servers are accessible via the Internet. Indeed, WWW is not just a hypertext system but a hypermedia system, i.e., documents can comprise text, image, and audio and film clips.

WWW servers are easy to install and clients are available on all major platforms. All software is free and sources are available. The node-link technique for navigating and finding information is quite appealing at least for small to medium amounts of data, and the mix of media makes the use of WWW aesthetically pleasing. All this has contributed to the proliferation of WWW, recently overtaking Gopher in terms of number of installed servers. Indeed there is no doubt that WWW is not only the first widespread hypermedia system available through the Internet, but that WWW has actually replaced some earlier more traditional information systems. The success of WWW, the number of WWW proponents and freaks, and its publicity even in non-scientific publications like Time magazine may create the impression that WWW is the solution for most information needs and will remain the dominating system for the forseeable future.

The reality is different, however. Whilst WWW is undoubtedly a big step forward compared to pre-WWW times, experience shows that much functionality required for sizeable applications is missing from WWW. In this sense, WWW should be considered a first generation networked hypermedia system. More advanced "second generation" hypermedia systems are required to cope with the problems currently being encountered on the Web. Just to give one example, while pure node-link navigation is satisfactory in small systems it tends to lead to confusion and disorientation, if not chaos, when applied to large amounts of data [Conklin 1987]. For substantial applications, some additional structuring and searching facilities are clearly required. That links may actually be more harmful than useful has been already pointed out in [Van Dam 1988] and elaborated in [Maurer et al 1994a]. Similarly, the necessity to keep links separate from rather than embedded in documents as is the case in WWW has already been demonstrated in the pioneering work on Intermedia at Brown University [Haan et al 1992].

In what follows, we concentrate on features we find desirable in second generation hypermedia information systems. We compare the features found in the first generation hypermedia system WWW with those found in what might be the first second generation hypermedia system, Hyper-G. This is not to belittle WWW or to glorify Hyper-G, but rather to clarify why certain facilities are needed. We also briefly look at communicational and cooperational features that will have to be integrated in hypermedia systems if they are to be successful: such features are currently scarcely supported by any hypermedia system. They are often dealt with in the context of computer supported cooperative work, rather than hypermedia. Although we look in a little more detail at Hyper-G in this chapter as it allows a smooth transition from WWW and hence from the first generation to the second, yielding increased functionality supporting a range of new applications we look at two of the most important aspects of Hyper-G separately in the next Chapter 5.

Information in a hypermedia system is usually stored in "chunks". Chunks consist of individual documents which may themselves consist of various types of "media". Typically, a document may be a piece of text containing a picture. Each document may contain links leading to (parts of) other documents in the same or in different chunks. Typical hypertext navigation through the information space is based on these links: the user follows a sequence of links until all relevant information has hopefully been encountered.

In WWW, a chunk consists of a single document. Documents consist of textual information and may include pictures and the (source) anchors of links. Pictures and links are an integral part of the document. Pictures are thus placed in fixed locations within the text ("inline images"). Anchors can be attached to textual information and inline images, but not to parts of images. Links may lead to audio or video clips which can be activated. The textual component of a document is stored in so-called HTML format, a derivative of SGML.

In Hyper-G the setting is considerably more general: chunks, called "clusters" in Hyper-G terminology consist of a number of documents. A typical cluster may, for example, consist of five documents: a piece of text (potentially with inline images), a second piece of text (for example in another language, or a different version of the same text, or an entirley different text), a third piece of text (the same text in a third language perhaps), an image and a film clip. Anchors can be attached to textual information, to parts of images, and even to regions in a film clip. Links are not part of the document but are stored in a separate database. They are both typed and bidirectional: they can be followed forward (as in WWW) but also backwards.

The support for multiple pieces of text within a cluster allows Hyper-G to handle multiple languages in a very natural way. It also elegantly handles the case where a document comes in two versions: a more technical (or advanced) one and one more suitable for the novice reader. As indicated, pictures can be treated as inline images or as separate documents. Often, inline images are convenient, since the "author" can define where the user will find a picture in relation to the text. On the other hand, with screen resolution varying tremenduously, the rescaling of inline images may pose a problem: if a picture is treated as separate document, however, it appears in a separate window, can be manipulated (shifted, put in the background, kept on-screen while continuing with other information, etc.) independent of the textual portion (which in itself can be manipulated by for example narrowing or widening its window).

Thus, the potential to deal with textual and pictorial information separately provides more flexibility when required. Text can be stored in Hyper-G in a variety of formats. The use of PostScript with high-quality PostScript viewers built into the native Hyper-G clients Amadeus and Harmony (for MS-Windows and X Windows respectively), gives Hyper-G the necessary professionalism for high quality electronic publishing of journals, books, and manuals. We return to this aspect in Chapter 5.

In addition to the "usual" types of documents found in any modern hypermedia system, Hyper- G also supports 3D objects and scenes [Pichler et al 95]. The native X Windows client for Hyper-G (Harmony) provides four different ways to navigate within such 3D models. Finally, Hyper-G allows the use of documents of a "generic" type. This permits future extensions and the encapsulation of documents otherwise incompatible with Hyper-G.

One of the most crucial differences between WWW and Hyper-G is the treatment of links. In WWW links are unidirectional, have no type and are embedded in documents. In Hyper-G they are bidirectional, can have types and are stored in a link datebase separate from the actual documents. This difference is very significant, hence we dedicate a good part of a separate chapter (Chapter 5) to it.

Navigation in WWW is performed solely using the hypertext paradigm of anchors and links. It has become a well accepted fact that structuring large amounts of data using only hyperlinks in a way that users don't get "lost in hyperspace" is difficult to say the least. WWW databases are large, flat networks of chunks of data and resemble more an impenetrable maze than well- structured information. Indeed every WWW database acknowledges this fact tacitly, by preparing pages that look like menus in a hierarchically structured database: items are listed in an orderly fashion, each with an anchor leading to a subchapter (subdirectory). If links in WWW had types, such links could be distiguished from others. But as it is, all links look the same: whether they are "continue" links, "hierarchical" links, "referential" links, "footnote links", or whatever else.

In Hyper-G not only can have links a type, links are by no means the only way to access information. Clusters of documents can be grouped into collections, and collections again into collections in a pseudo-hierachical fashion. We use the term "pseudo-hierarchical" since, technically speaking, the collection structure is not a tree, but a DAG. I.e., one collection can have more than one parent: an impressionist picture X may belong to the collection "Impressionist Art", as well as to the collection "Pictures by Manet", as well as to the collection "Museum of Modern Art". The collection "hierarchy" is a powerful way of introducing structure into the database. Indeed many links can be avoided this way [Maurer et al 1994a], making the system much more transparent for the user and allowing a more modular approach to systems creation and maintainance. Collections, clusters and documents have titles and attributes. These may be used in Boolean queries to find documents of current interest. Finally, Hyper-G provides sophisticated full-text search facilities. Most importantly, the scope of any of such searches can be defined to be the union of arbitrary collections, even if the collections reside on different servers. We will return to this important aspect of Hyper-G as a distributed database below. The concept of collections has one other very significant advantage: it allows insertion and deletion of documents into a Hyper-G database without any link adjustment, a luxury unknown in WWW. We return to this aspect in the second half of Chapter 5.

Note that some WWW applications also permit full-text searches. However, no full-text search engine is built into WWW. Thus, the functionality of full text search is bolted "on top" of WWW: adding functionality on top of WWW leads to the "Balkanisation", the fragmentation of WWW, since different sites will implement missing functionality in different ways. Thus, to stick to the example of the full text search engine, the fuzzy search employed by organisation X may yield entirley different results from the fuzzy search employed by organisation Y, much to the bewilderment of users. Actually, the situation concerning searches in WWW is even more serious: since documents in WWW do not have attributes, no search is possible on such attributes; even if such a search or a full text search is artificially implemented, it is not possible to allow users to define the scope for the search, due to the lack of structure in the WWW database. Hence full-text searches in WWW always work in a fixed, designated part of the WWW database residing on one particular server.

Hyper-G provides various types of access rights and the definition of arbitrarily overlapping user groups. Hyper-G is also a genuine distributed database: servers (independent of geographical location) can be grouped into collections, with the hyperroot at the very "top". Thus, users can define the scope of searches by defining arbitrary sets of collections on arbitary servers. Different groups can work with the same server without fear of interfering with someone else's data.

First generation hypermedia systems like WWW have traditionally been seen mainly as (simple) information systems. Most applications currently visible support this view: very often WWW servers offer some pleasantly designed general information on the server-institution, but only rarely does the information go much deeper. If it does, usually a "hybrid" system is used, WWW with some add-ons using the scripting interface of WWW.

It is our belief that hypermedia systems acting as simple information systems, where someone inputs information to be read by other users, do not offer much potential: they will disappear into obscurity sooner rather than later. To ensure the success of a hypermedia system, it must allow users also to act as authors, allow them to change the database, create new entries for themselves or other users, create a personal view of the database as they need it, and, above all, allow the system to be used also for communication and cooperation.

First generation hypermedia systems like WWW almost entirely lack support for such features. Emerging second generation hypermedia systems are bound to incorporate more and more features of the kind mentioned; Hyper-G provides a start.

The native Hyper-G clients Amadeus and Harmony are designed to allow the easy import of data into the server. They are also designed to allow point-and-click link generation: select the source anchor location with a mouse-click, select the destination anchor with a mouse-click and confirm that a link should be created. Similarly, powerful "gardening functions" to support changes in the hierarchy ("tree") of collections are available.

Hyper-G supports annotations (with user-definable access rights): in contrast to some WWW clients which also allow annotations which are then kept locally, Hyper-G annotations become part of the database, i.e., are also available when working with other clients, or from another user account or machine. Annotations can themselves be annotated; the network of annotations can be graphically displayed using the local map function of Harmony. Thus, the annotation mechanism can be used as the basis of (asynchronuous) computer-conferencing, and has been sucessfully employed in this fashion. The client-server protocol in WWW is "static" in the sense that the server can only react to requests by the client, but cannot become active itself. In Hyper-G the client-server protocol is "active" in the sense that the server can contact the client: this can be used for example to send update notification to a client, and provides the first (rudimentary) possibilities for client-client communication for synchronuous communication, conferencing and cooperation.

We believe that many of the features discussed in the area of computer supported cooperative work [Dewan 1993] will eventually be incorporated into second generation hypermedia systems. This approach is also planned for Hyper-G, but will not be fully supported for some time yet.

As has become clear from the above discussion, first generation hypermedia systems such as WWW do not have enough functionality to serve as a solid and unified basis for substantial multi-user information systems with a strong communicational component.

Hyper-G is a first attempt to offer much more basic functionality, yet to continue the path started by WWW and remain fully interoperable with WWW: every WWW client can be used to access every Hyper-G server, albeit occasionally with some loss in functionality; a Hyper-G client may, through a Hyper-G server, access WWW, Gopher, and WAIS servers without any loss of functionality, indeed providing "free" caching as a by-product.

The compatibility of Hyper-G with WWW and Gopher actually goes much further: tools to import complete WWW and Gopher databases into Hyper-G without manual intervention are in preparation. Thus, users of WWW can migrate up to an environment allowing all kinds of searches, access control, etc., without being forced to abandon their current database or their favourite WWW client.

5 Two Crucial Concepts of Hyper-G

Hyper-G differs in its design significantly from WWW by adding for both users and information providers better and more convenient facilities.

In this chapter we discuss two important points in a bit more detail: the link concept and the notion of collections.

As has been mentioned earlier, WWW uses unidirectional links that are embedded in the documents and cannot be typed. In Hyper-G links are bi-directional, can have a type and attributes and are handled not as part of the document but in a separate database. These extensions of the link concept have far-reaching consequences. We mention a few of the most important ones in what follows.

When viewing a document it is clearly always necessary to know which other documents can be reached from it: this is after all what links are all about, and such "out-links" are of course supported in both WWW and Hyper-G. However, it is equally important to also know which documents are pointing to the current one, i.e., to know the "in-links"; this is what bidirectional links are all about. There are many reasons why also the knowledge of "in-links" is important:

First, it gives users (and information providers) the valuable information who is pointing to a particular document for "information only" reason: the context of the document becomes clearer, its "popularity" can be determined, etc. To be specific, suppose you are interested in impressionist art and you have located a picture in the (virtual) gallery of the Museum of Modern Art in Vienna; by examining all "in-links" you are bound to find valuable information about the painting that would have escaped your attention otherwise.

Second, having bidirectional links allows to generate a graphic representation of the "local surroundings" of the current document (the "local map" of Harmony, see [Fenn et al 1994]).

This local map will show you an iconized version of your current document, plus all those that (via one or more steps) lead to it or can be reached from it: this is a very powerful support for navigation and helps to avoid the "lost in hyperspace" syndrome mentioned earlier.

Third, and still more important, it is the only way towards better link maintenance to avoid "dangling links", a phenomenon that is a problem on all large WWW servers. Again, to be specific, suppose an important document X is pointed to by documents $A_1, A_2, \ldots, A_n$. If X is removed and only unidirectional links are used there is no way to know that $A_1, A_2, \ldots, A_n$ point to X, particularly if the A_i's reside on different servers. Hence the links in all A_i's when activated by users will all yield the very frustrating message "document cannot be found" or such, a phenonmenon well-known to every WWW user. However, if bidirectional links are used then the removal of X can at least result in notifying the owners of the documents $A_1, A_2, \ldots, A_n$ that X has disappeared so that the links in the A_i's can be adjusted. Indeed, if the links in $A_1, A_2, \ldots, A_n$ are not embedded within the A_i's rather than just notifying the A_i's the links in the A_i's leading to X can be deactivated automatically.

This, then, is a first step towards automatic link maintenance, a feature imperative for large systems and addressed in Hyper-G for the first time: to be able to carry it out it is necessary to have bidirectional, not-embedded links and to be able to assign rights and attributes to links that differ from those assigned to the document at issue. Typically, you may permit automatic link deletion of a link to X in a document A_i you have authored although you are unlikely to permit any change of the **contents** of A_i. This is one reason why keeping links separate from the documents is very important! Automatic link maintenance does not stop at deleting links that are no longer valid, it can also be used to automatically generate links. Suppose you have a contribution about St. Stephen's Cathedral in Vienna and you have activated automatic link generation for documents of type picture. Then, in a properly working hypermedia system, when a picture of St. Stephen's Cathedral is inserted with "Title: St. Stephen's Cathedral; Type: Picture" an automatic link can be generated from your essay about the cathedral to that picture ... again, of course, only if non-embedded links are available.

Links are usually attached to pieces of text or to pictures. However, one may also want to attach them to parts of a picture, to a moving object in a movie, a 3D object in a 3D scene, etc. In all such cases it is clearly impossible to embed the link information in the document (how would you embed such information in an MPEG film without destroying the MPEG coding?). I.e., links in "unorthodox documents" are only feasable if non-embedded links are used.

Another reason why it is of paramount importance to keep links and documents separate and to be able to differentiate between the rights of links and documents and to add attributes to the links ("typed links") is that only in this way can hypermedia systems be "personalized" and "customized". Suppose teachers want to prepare multimedia presentations based on existing material for a particular class without (e.g., for copyright reasons) being allowed to copy the material. The teachers can connect various bits and pieces of information using links with the name of the class at issue as attribute. Students of the class are identified as such when they log-in and hence only the links generated for that class become visible. Thus, the concept of being allowed to add "private" links to arbitrary documents combined with link filtering based on some link attribute allows to customize a hypermedia system arbitrarily without copying any information. This is basically the original "transclusion" idea of Ted Nelson, see [Nelson 1987], and see [Maurer et al 1995] for applications to teaching support.

To be able to type links offers a tremenduqus additional potential: it is possible to display different links differently (indicating that one is a footnote, the other one a reference, the next one a link back to a table of contents), to filter out links (e.g., to only show links created by certain authors within a certain time period), or to perform even more complex computations based on the link types.

Hyper-G allows **annotations**, another feature that requires non-embedded, typed links: an arbitrary document can be attached as annotation to another one by you (even if you have no editing priviledges for either of the two documents) and the link to the document attached is shown as annotation. This can be generalised to computer conferencing where link types can be used to show that for a particular thesis a certain number of counterexamples, supporting arguments, generalisations, etc. have been proposed.

Typed links are also convenient tools for version control! Summarizing, the original link concept of WWW works well for small amounts of data (say 50 documents) but just does not support larger amounts of data, multi-person cooperation, customization and other desirable features: more powerful additional features as available in Hyper-G are essential.

There is still another twist to links: without additional structure, using links in a large system becomes very confusing, much like "spaghetti-programming" in first generation high level programming languages such as Fortran or Basic. It is desirable to organise and structure information in a way going beyond having a "flat database with myriads of links". In Hyper-G one crucial concept in this direction is the notion of **collection** mentioned earlier. Documents are gathered into collections, collections may belong to other collections, etc. with a DAG-like structure.

Not only does this allow to structure material better so that it is easier to find; not only does it allow to define the scope for searches, or for the material to be packaged on a CD-ROM, or printed out, or whatever. It is also a powerful tool to replace links to some extent. To be specific, suppose we have defined a collection "pictures of Graz". Once this has been done adding a picture to this collection does not require the creation of any links (nor would the removal of a picture necessitate adjustment of links): when the collection is accessed the title of all pictures are shown and the relevant ones can be selected. If the collection has the attribute sequence one can automatically step forwards and backwards in the sequence of pictures, again requiring no links at all.

It may be worth mentioning that this concept is used particularly extensively in HM-Card [Maurer et al 1996] and makes administration of large amounts of material much easier. To quote Dieter Fellner form the University of Bonn, Germany: "The collection concept alone is enough reason to choose Hyper-G as WWW server".

In this chapter we have just mentioned two of the important "second generation" concepts of Hyper-G, features that go beyond WWW.

It is our contention that WWW and HTML should be seen as "thin interface layers" (and this is how Hyper-G treats them) but that more powerful tools must be used as further underpinning (and this is what Hyper-G does). For detailed information see the forthcoming book [Maurer 1996]. A preliminary electronic version of this book is available under http://www.iicm.tu-graz.ac.at/Celectronic_library. Additional information on Hyper-G can also be found in [Andrews at al 1995], [Kappe et al 1993a,b and 1994 a,b].

6 Electronic Publishing and J.UCS

In this chapter we concentrate on electronic journal publishing via the Internet, although many of the remarks are also valid for other materials, for other nets, and for CD-ROM publishing. Remember in particular that I have made a strong "pitch" to consider Internet and CD-ROM publishing as activities to be pursued simultaneously, anyway.

To be useful for Internet publishing it is necessary to have workable charging mechanisms. Today, the following three alternatives are realistic:

(a) subscription (based on passwords of users with mechanisms assuring that passwords are not circulated to non-paying persons);
(b) permitting organisations to copy some data into their local area network and charging on the basis of "maximum number of simultaneouos user's";
(c) collecting page-charges.

Of above alternatives, (b) is the most desirable one from the publisher's point of view (since licenses bought by large organisations can be substantial) but customers will be reluctant to use this approach unless the local infrastructure is easy to maintain and the cost for the software necessary is bundled with the general licensing fee; (a) is acceptable for publishers but unacceptable for the occasional reader; and (c) is doubtful (unless prepaid techniques are used!) for two reasons: invoicing for small amounts is exorbitantly expensive; and paying per page is psychologically similar to renting a car with a charge to be paid per kilometer driven: most people prefer "unlimited" mileage.

Obvious charging techniques (like via credit cards) are currently not easily usable due to the low level of security on the Internet. (Hackers could easily find out credit-card numbers and PIN; this can be avoided using sophisticated cryptographic protocols that are starting to emerge).

Note that the subscription based approach (a) requires a mechnism to avoid that subscribers pass on their password to an arbitrarily large number of friends. A technique that has been used sucessfully e.g., for the Internet version of the ED-MEDIA'95 proceedings (http://www.iicm.tu-graz.ac.at/Celectronic_library) is to allow each subscriber to access each document only a certain number of times (e.g., 3 times).

Before going into a more technical discussion let me make a few general points:

(a) Some 500 "journals" are already available on the Internet. However, most are free, not or poorly refereed, hence of mediocre quality, and none has been a real commercial success, sofar. The main reasons are given in [Maurer et al 1994b]. In a nut-shell, poor quality of both contents and technical implementation, lack of prestige, plus a user-base that only now is becoming sizeable are the decisive factors;
(b) Printed journals and libraries as we know them today are going to be eventually replaced to a very large extent by electronic versions. See e.g., [Marchionini et al 1995], [Maurer et al 1995], or the eloquent paper [Odlyzko

1995] in which the demise of printed journals in certain technical areas is seen as an impending paradigm shift that will happen very rapidly.

(c) It is the last part of point (b) that deserves special attention: printed specialist journals in areas where the computer saturation among those specialists is very high are, of course, those journals whose printed version will loose importance first. Thus, computer science, mathematics and physics journals on a research level are prime targets.

(d) The reason why Internet publishing of journals is attractive for users (if done the right way!) is not only the resulting universal availability of the material ("anytime, everywhere") but also the increased functionality like searches (full-text or others), pointers (links) to more recent results, etc.

Let us now look at the two main alternatives for journal publishing on the Internet, the "generic" and the "online" approach.

In the generic approach papers are stored in a database with a simple table of contents (typically, in a so-called FTP archive). They can be "downloaded" by subscribers for print-out. In its pure form the generic approach replaces (at best) the distribution of journals in printed form by ordinary mail by electronic distribution.

Attempts to offer traditional journals this way have met with little success, even if the electronic version was offered to subscribers at no additional cost as additional service(!). The main reason for this is probably a logistic one: technical journals are usually (over 95%) sold by subscription to libraries; in the experiments known to the author the electronic version was only available to subscribers. But why should a librarian download a journal and print it out if a printed version is available, anyway? In other words, electronic distribution only makes sense if either no printed version is available (reducing the "prestige" of the journal!) or if the electronic version is available to the ender-user, not the librarian!

The generic approach is working to some extent for free (usually unrefereed) publications, much along the lines that "departmental reprint or report series" have been and are still used. However, the generic approach in its pure form does not provide strong incentives and is hence augmented by a variety of techniques such as e.g.:

- subscribers can submit "profiles" and are notified by email if a paper fitting their profile is "published";
- information on papers is made available in an on-line database that can be searched to locate contributions of interest;
- titles and abstracts of papers are available in a system such as Gopher, WWW or Hyper-G to permit a first evaluation of what is offered.

Overall, the generic approach even with some of the extensions mentioned has not achieved a real break-through, but improved versions might offer viable solutions in the future.

In the "on-line" approach journals are kept in an on-line database. This database can be accessed using various techniques (including e.g., full-text search).

Once a paper is found it can be read on-screen or printed out, if desired. A typical instance for this approach is J.UCS, the Journal of Universal Computer Science.

J.UCS is called "universal" since it is supposed to cover all areas of computer science (following ACM's Computing Review classification), and is available on-line everywhere at any time.

Submission is done electronically, and papers are reviewed by at least three referees determined by a prominent editorial board whose chief editors are C. Calude (Auckland), A. Salomaa,(Finland), and myself. See [Calude et al 1994] and [Maurer et al 1994b] for details.

J.UCS is published in twelve yearly issues, each new issue appearing on the 28th of each month. For a pilot issue 0 and the first ten issues see http://www.iicm.tu-graz.ac.at/Cjucs_root.

Papers in J.UCS can be read using any Gopher, WWW or Hyper-G viewer. J.UCS is sponsored by Springer and will be free of charge 95-96, but will cost $ 100,– per subscription as of 1997. A subscription allows to install J.UCS in a local sever for arbitrary many users, but for only one user at a time. If n users want to read J.UCS, n x $ 100,– have to be paid as subscription fee as of 1997.

J.UCS has a number of unusual features that make it a possible prototype for other similar undertakings:

(a) Submissions to J.UCS are possible in the form of LaTeX or PostScript files. Since virtually all word-processing systems provide a PostScript file for printer-output, most word-processing systems can be used to produce J.UCS contributions;

(b) Each J.UCS paper is available in hypertext format (for casual perusal even on very simple machinery); and in PostScript form for high-resolution screens and for a professionally looking print-out.

(c) J.UCS is published in printed form and as CD-ROM (in addition to its Internet form) for archival purposes and to profit from the prestige still associated with printed publications.

(d) J.UCS is not just available on one server (making acess slow and creating bottlenecks) but is "mirrored" on many servers world-wide. Since the server software, Hyper-G, is free of charge for non-profit organisations all organi-sations interested in J.UCS are well advised to install their own server: this allows speedy access to J.UCS independent of occasional Internet problems.

(e) J.UCS, being based on Hyper-G, is fully searchable: by date, author, title, category, keywords, words in the body of the text, etc. Thus, using J.UCS, e.g., all papers "published since 1995 in the category operating systems con-taining the word synchronis. as prefix" can be located immediately.

(f) J.UCS is free during the pilot trial, i.e., during 95-96, but the billing-scheme used for J.UCS and described earlier makes it easy to subscribe J.UCS for an arbitrarily large local area network for $ 100,– for "one user at a time"; this can be changed to, say, "five users at at time" as the demand increases.

(g) J.UCS contributions can be hyperlinked and "annotated". In particular, if at some stage an error in a J.UCS publication is discovered, or a better technique appears, the original publication in J.UCS cannot be modified (a major credo!), but the new aspect can be pointed out using this annotation mechanism.

The process used for converting J.UCS submissions from PostScript to hypertext format that also allows full-text searches and links in PostScript files has received much attention and is indeed similar, but independent, of Adobe Acrobat's PDF format. Indeed, if PDF is as successful as Adobe wants to make it, J.UCS (and Hyper-G) will support PDF from 1996 onward.

To obtain more information on J.UCS use the URL mentioned earlier, or send an email to jucs@iicm.tu-graz.ac.at with subject [info].

The techniques used for J.UCS are based on Hyper-G: They are starting to become known as "J.UCS technology" and will be employed far beyond J.UCS for further undertakings.

Altogether, Hyper-G and J.UCS technology offer an attractive alternative to electronic Internet publishing and should be kept in mind as alternative whenever contemplating such undertakings. Observe that the wide-spread WWW-technology does not suffice for high quality electronic publishing unless augmented by much additional programming and that CD-ROM production of Hyper-G material can be automated due to the collection concept.

7   The Future of Hypermedia

The enormous growth of the first generation hypermedia system WWW has lead to an euphoric attitude towards the potential of such systems. In particular, they are seen by some as the universal information systems of the future that nobody will be able to live without in the very near future.

Although it must be emphasized that Internet has become an important tool for some applications the current fairly myopic view of what one can do with systems such as WWW is unjustified:

Internet cannot succeed merely based on large amounts of information presented on WWW servers for a variety of reasons:

(1) WWW technology (both from an information provider and user point of view) is not geared towards handling large quantities of data. New tools such as Hyper-G and beyond will be necessary to exploit the richness of information available;

(2) Users do not want hundreds of thousands of information providers with small amounts of data, and data whose reliabilty and completeness is doubtful: they need "information hubs" (electronic publishers) that filter and "package" information for the needs of different groups of users, much as after the invention of the printing press publishing houses, journalists, editors, etc. had to emerge to prepare information in the form of books or journals suitable for the taste of a variety of readers;

(3) Electronic publishing should not be seen as an activity as such, but as part of a larger attempt: an attempt to build significant digital libraries e.g., for teaching and learning support [Lennon et al 1994b], [Marchionini al 1995];

(4) Hypermedia systems are more than just large information systems: they offer a variety of applications [Lennon et al 1994c] and will only be successful if the communicational, cooperational and transactional capabilities will be fully exploited;

(5) World wide hypermedia systems will have to stick to some code of honor to avoid violating local laws and hence being curtailed by anti-Internet laws: organisations like the Web Society (http://info.websoc.org) are trying to propose ideas and techniques that are compromises between unwanted censorship and unacceptable total freedom of offensive information;

(6) Internet is not the only net that allows networked multimedia systems: others like Videotex, CompuServe, Prodigy and the just emerging MSN are providing much of the services one would want to find on the Internet in a much more organized and user-friendly form. Thus, unless hypermedia systems will soon offer a similar quality of services Internet may well revert to what it has been up to 1994: a valuable tool for a certain restricted community of users;

(7) Internet has grown to an extent that the network capacities have not kept up with the volume of traffic resulting in a system that is often sluggish at best; higher bandwidth is urgently needed unless MAN like two-way cable TV become much more attractive alternatives;

(8) The security aspect is still not entirely resovled in Internet based systems; yet security is very much needed for certain transactions.

Summarizing, networked multimedia systems will play a dominant role, both in LAN's, MAN's, and WAN's. Whether purely Internet based varieties will be successful on the scale often described remains to be seen, however. We should hope for such a success since despite all weaknesses of the Internet this is the most democratic and free net that has ever been available: it is up to all of us to make it successful, by working for the efficient and disciplined use of it, the motto of the Web Society (http://info.websoc.org).

Acknowledgements.

Much of the material in Chapter 4 has been compiled together with K. Andrews, F. Kappe, and K. Schmaranz and versions thereof have appeared elsewhere before.

References

[Alberti et al 1992] Alberti, B., Anklesaria, F., Lindner, P., McCahill, M., Torrey, D.: Internet Gopher Protocol:A Distributed Document Search and Retrieval Protocol; FTP from boombox.micro.umn.edu, directory pub/gopher/gopher_protocol.

[Andrews et al 1995] Andrews, K., Kappe, F., Maurer, H., Schmaranz, K.: On Second Generation Hypermedia Systems; Proc.ED-MEDIA'95, Graz (June 1995), 75-80. See also J.UCS 0,0 (1994), 127–136 at http:///www.iicm.tu-graz.ac.at /Cjucs_root.

[Berners-Lee et al 1992] Berners-Lee, T., Cailliau, R., Groff, J., Pollermann, B.: World-WideWeb: The Information Universe; Electronic Networking: Research, Applications and Policy 1,2 (1992), 52–58.

[Berners-Lee et al 1994] Berners-Lee, T., Cailliau, R., Luotonen, A., Nielsen, H.F. and Secret, A. (1994). The World-Wide Web; CACM 37 (8), 76–82.

[Calude et al 1994] Calude, C., Maurer, H., Salomaa, A.: J. UCS: The Journal of Universal Computer Science; J.UCS 0,0 (1994) 109–117 at http://www.iicm.tu-graz.ac.at/Cjucs_root.

[Conklin 1987] Conklin, E.J.: Hypertext: an Introduction and Survey; IEEE Computer 20 (1987), 17–41.

[Deutsch 1992] Deutsch, P.: Resource Discovery in an Internet Environment-the Archie Approach; Electronic Networking: Research, Applications and Policy 1, 2 (1992), 45–51.

[Dewan 1993] Dewan, P.: A Survey of Applications of CSCW Including Some in Educational Settings; Proc. ED-MEDIA'93, Orlando (1993), 147–152.

[Fenn et all 1994] Fenn, B., Maurer, H.: Harmony on an Expanding Net; ACM Interactions 1,3 (1994), 26–38.

[Foresta et al 1993] Foresta, D., Goetschl, J., Maurer, H., Schinagl, W.: Interactive Information Center; Proc. ED-MEDIA'93, Orlando (June 1993), 197–202.

[Haan et al 1992] Haan, B.J., Kahn, P., Riley, V.A., Coombs, J.H., Meyrowitz, N.K.: IRIS Hypermedia Services; Communications of the ACM 35,1 (1992), 36–51.

[Hoelzel 1994] Hoelzel Pub. Co.: Geothek – the Interactive World Atlas; CD-ROM Vienna (1994).

[Jayasinha et al 1995] Jayasinha, C., Lennon, J., Maurer, H.: Interactive and Annotated Movies; Proc. ED-MEDIA'95, Graz (June 1995), 366–371.

[Kahle et al 1992] Kahle, B., Morris, H., Davis, F., Tiene, K., Hart, C., Palmer, R.: Wide Area Information Servers: An Executive Inforamtion System for Unstructured Files; Electronic Networking: Research, Applications and Policy 1,2 (1992), 59–68.

[Kappe et al 1993a] Kappe, F., Maurer, H., Scherbakov, N.: Hyper-G – a Universal Hypermedia System; Journal of Educational Multimedia and Hypermedia 2,1 (1993), 39–66.

[Kappe et al 1993b] Kappe, F., Maurer, H.: Hyper-G: A Large Universal Hypermedia System and Some Spin-offs; IIG Report 364, Graz, Austria (1993); also appeared as electronic version, anonymous FTP siggraph.org, in publications/May-93-online/Kappe.Maurer.

[Kappe et al 1994a] Kappe, F., Maurer, H.: From Hypertext to Active Communication/Information Systems; J.MCA 17,4 (1994), 333–344.

[Kappe et al 1994b] Kappe, F., Andrews, K., Faschingbauer, J., Gaisbauer, M., Maurer, H., Pichler, M., Schipflinger, J.: Hyper-G: A New Tool for Distributed Multimedia; Proc. Conf. on Open Hypermedia Systems, Honolulu (1994), 209–214.

[Koegel-Buford 1994] Koegel-Buford, J.: Multimedia Systems; ACM Press, SIGGRAPH Series (1994).

[Lennon et al 1994a] Lennon, J., Maurer, H.: Hypermedia in the Making; Datamation (October 1994), 84–85.

[Lennon et al 1994b] Lennon, J., Maurer, H.: Lecturing Technology: A Future With Hypermedia; Educational Technology 34, 4 (1994), 5–14.

[Lennon et al 1994c] Lennon, J., Maurer, H.: Applications and Impact of Hypermedia Systems: An Overview; J. UCS 0,0 (1994), 54-108 at http://www.iicm.tu-graz.ac.at/Cjucs_root.

[Marchionini et al 1995] Marchionini, G., Maurer, H.: The Role of Digital Libraries in Teaching and Learning; Communications of the ACM 38,4 (April 1995), 67–75.

[Maurer 1995] Maurer, H.: Hypermedia in a Gambling Casino Setting; Proc. HIM , Konstanz (April 1995), 233–241.

[Maurer 1996] Maurer, H. (1996). Power to the Web! The Official Guide to Hyper-G. Addison Wesley Pub. Co., UK (1996).

[Maurer et al 1994a] Maurer, H., Philpott, A, Scherbakov, N.: Hypermedia Systems Without Links; Journal of Microcomputer Applications 17, 4 (1994), 321–332.

[Maurer et al 1994b] Maurer, H., Schmaranz, K.: J. UCS – The Next Generation in Electronic Journal Publishing; Proc. Electronic Publ. Conference, London (November 1994), in: Computer Networks for Research in Europe 26, Supplement 2-3 (1994), 63–69.

[Maurer et al 1995] Maurer, H., Lennon, J.: Digital Libraries as Learning and Teaching Support; Proc. ICCE'95, Singapore (December 1995).

[Maurer et al 1996] Maurer, H., & Scherbakov, N. (1996). Multimedia Authoring for Presentation and Education: The Official Guide to HM-Card. Addison Wesley Pub. Co. Germany (1996).

[Nelson 1987] Nelson, T.H.: Literary machines; Edition 87.1, 702 South Michigan, South Bend, IN 46618, USA (1987)

[Odlyzko 1994] Odlyzko, A.M.: Tragic Loss or Good Riddance? The Impending Demise of Traditional Scholarly Journals; to appear in: Electronic Publishing Confronts Academia: The Agenda for the Year 2000; (Peek., R.P., Newby, G.B., eds.) MIT Press (1995); see also J. UCS 0,0 (1994), 3–53 at http://www.iicm.tu-graz.ac.at/Cjucs_root.

[Qualthrough et al 1994] Qualthrough, P., Schneider, A.: Let's See What is Happening in Auckland; University of Auckland, Department of Computer Science, TR 100 (1994).

[Pichler et al 1995] Pichler, M., Orasche, G., Andrews, K., Grossmann, E., McCahill, M.: VRweb: A Multi-System VRML Viewer; Proc. VRML 95, San Diego, CA (December 1995).

[Tomek et al 1991] Tomek, I., Khan, S., Muldner, T., Nassar, M., Navak, G., Proszynski, P.: Hypermedia- Introduction and Survey, Journal for Microcomputer Applications 14, 2 (1991), 63–100.

[Van Dam 1998] Van Dam, A.: Hypertext'87 Keynote Address; Communications of the ACM 31, 7 (1988), 887–895.

Quo Vadis GIS:
From GIS to GIMS and Open GIS

Aleš Limpouch and Karel Charvát

Help Service – Mapping,
Brdičkova 1916, 155 00 Praha 5, Czech Republic

Abstract. Modern Geographic Information Systems should provide powerful user-oriented information systems for maintenance and analyses of spatially referenced data. The first part of the paper gives a gentle introduction into the area of GIS, their applications and provides a short overview of fundamental features in traditional GIS. Problems and deficiencies in the traditional point of view on GIS are indicated. The second part shows an impact of new computer technologies on future GIS and the use of GIS in future environments. Some important problems for future research are suggested. Fundamental features of future GIS are discussed and the concept of object-oriented data model and Geographic Information Management Systems are introduced. Exciting world of Open user-oriented GIS is proposed.

1   GIS overview

Geographic information system (GIS) is a special information system designed to work with spatially referenced data. With the introduction of low-cost personal computers and evolution of information oriented society, the use and application of GIS increased rapidly during past fifteen years. This section gives a gentle introduction into the exciting world of GIS. The notion of GIS is briefly introduced. Fundamental concepts are briefly described. Short overview of GIS applications shows the impact of GIS technologies on human activities.

1.1   What is GIS?

More than thirty years have passed since GIS was first invented in the early 1960s. Many applications, components and systems with mark "GIS" were developed during this time and we can found big differences in their functionality, look and feel and architecture. For that reason, it is very difficult to find uniform and clear definition of the term GIS.

In the most situations, the term GIS is used for a system which enable users to join information with spatially referenced data. Then GIS is a tool for modelling real world in form of geographical data. In other words, a GIS is both a database system with specific capabilities for spatially referenced data, as well as a set of operations with that data. GIS systems provide functions for the capture, storage, maintenance, manipulation, integration, retrieval, analyses and presentation of spatially referenced data.

But in a widest sense of the term, GIS could be considered to be complete technology for the creation, maintenance, analyses and presentation of spatially referenced data. In this case, the term GIS includes special hardware (computers as well as special devices), software (GIS system), data (digital maps, non-spatial databases) and know-how (data manipulation methods and procedures). It is important to note, that data are the key and most expensive part of the whole technology. Similarly to other information systems, GIS does not have sense without data. But large divergence in stored data creates the main difference from usual information systems.

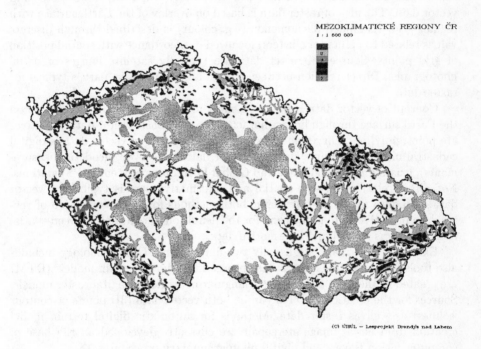

MEZOKLIMATICKÉ REGIONY ČR
1 : 1 600 000

(C) ÚHÚL – Lesprojekt Brandýs nad Labem

Fig. 1. Map of mesoclimatic regions in the Czech Republic.

Large extent of GIS and the use of many data sources form the base for wide interdisciplinary cooperation. The use of research results and technologies from various fields of human activities is necessary. GIS includes, of course, many different computer-oriented domains, such as computer graphics, image processing, computer vision, database systems and human-computer interaction. GIS technology uses methods and results from survey, cartography, aerial photography, remote sensing, photogrammetry, and various geosciences. In certain extent, GIS is also influenced with special procedures and methods used within GIS application fields.

1.2   Fundamental concepts of GIS

Data are one of the most important parts of GIS technology. Current GIS theory divides GIS data into spatial and non-spatial data. Spatial data are typically graphical data, such as geometrical entities. Non-spatial data are usually numeric or textual attributes stored in databases. In some cases, GIS system are able to process temporal data. Temporal data form another dimension of GIS data and are not completely covered within above given data categories. GIS data model defines usually special data structures for spatial data primitives and data organization.

We can distinguish two main types of spatial (graphical) data: raster and vector data. The idea of raster data is based on overlay of the Earth surface with regular grid. Examined phenomenon (e.g. colour) is described through discrete values related to points (or clusters) localized in accordance with spatial position of grid points. Sources of raster data are typically satellite images or aerial photographs. Direct relation between spatial and informative part is typical for raster data.

Concept of vector data is based on effort to express geometric attributes on the Earth surface through linear characteristic. The basic vector data primitives are point, polylines, curves and areas. Typical example of vector data is digital cadastral map. The main sources of vector data are survey (geodetic measurements), existing maps and plans and Global Positioning System (GPS) stations. Non-direct relation between spatial and informative part is typical for vector data. GIS data model have to define both methods for the organization of vector data primitives into groups and for the definition of relations between spatial data as well as spatial and informative data.

Existing paper maps are usually two-dimensional. GIS technology includes also tools for three-dimensional data processing. Digital terrain models (DTM) are created in the form of irregular triangular networks or digital raster models. Sources for the creation of DTM can be both vector data (3D points or contour isolines) as well as raster data. Methods for automatic digital terrain model creation from aerial image stereopair are currently developed on the base of computer vision theory and digital photogrammetry procedures.

The main role of GIS systems is the creation, maintenance, analyses and presentation of spatially referenced data. Emphasis on GIS functionality is given by users and their field of interest. In very simplified way, two main groups of users in GIS can be distinguished. First group is interested in creation and maintenance of GIS data. Classical way of mapping and cartography are continuously replaced by digital mapping methods. These users are usually well-educated in mapping, cartography or related fields. They are interested especially in data capture, conversions and manipulations as well as precise data output.

Second and larger group of users are interested in data retrieval, analyses and presentation. These users are usually experts in their fields and GIS systems are tools for their activities. Data analyses is especially important functionality for them. In fact, it has been the real aim for GIS introduction. Within data analyses GIS system should be able to give answers on following questions about object state (what?), location (where?), evolution trends (when?) and modelling changes (what if?):

- What is at this place?
- Where are particular objects?
- How are particular objects related?
- Which objects satisfy a particular relation?
- Which trend is going for a particular factor?
- Which changes occurred?
- What happens if a particular action occur?

The given list of questions is not exhaustive, but it is provides good overview of analysis functionality which can be supported within GIS. Functionality for the presentation of analysis results is also emphasized.

1.3 GIS applications

During past fifteen years, the use of GIS systems spread into many different fields of human activities. GIS systems are currently used in governmental bodies, industry, agriculture, forestry and services for various tasks starting from simple applications for simplified plan display to complex systems for policy decision-making with the help of spatial data analyses. Well-arranged GIS applications can help people to find necessary information, analyse specific situation, verify strategic decisions as well as control complex systems.

GIS systems are currently used in various organizations, for example, in government, ministries, district and municipal councils, project offices, surveying services, technical network administration, large factories, transport enterprises, army, ecologic institutions, agriculture farms, forest district offices, business organizations, banks, insurance companies, universities, museums and information centres.

Environmental analyses and nature protection were probably the first fields for GIS applications. The use of GIS enables people to monitor, evaluate and model the mutual influence of human activities and nature factors (industry, agriculture, settlements, rains, wind, etc.) on our environment. For example, data from air pollution monitoring systems are transferred into GIS systems for the evaluation of pollution changes within time. Then analyses results serve as the source of information for decision-making in regional management and strategic planning for a particular locality.

GIS systems are widely used in *governmental bodies* (such as ministries and district councils), especially for policy decision-making, control strategic activities and monitoring spatially referenced aspects of their field. GIS provides a tool for presentation of global information overview. For example, districts with high unemployment ratio are demonstrated through color highlighting or diagrams in map more naturally than in table form. Of course, GIS systems are used in Land Registry offices for maintenance of cadastre and at district councils for *land management*.

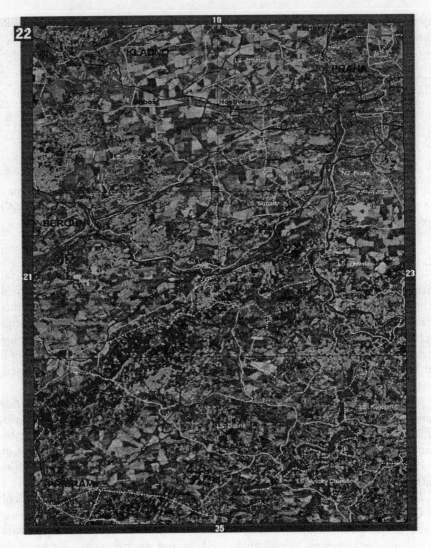

Fig. 2. Atlas of forests in the Czech Republic (one map).

In the similar manner, but with detailed maps, GIS is used within *municipal information systems*. In this situation technical and cadastral maps and street plans are included into such a system. In addition to decision-making and control, GIS system is also used to retrieve spatially referenced data and to discover spatial relations between objects in various registers (e.g. register of unmovable properties).

GIS systems can really help in administration of large *technical networks*. Suppliers of power, gas, water and other resources use these systems as large information bases with the possibility of quick retrieval of necessary data for particular objects. They can be used also for break-down solutions, economic management, maintenance plan creation, network designs as well as flow control. We can notice the similar use of GIS in *transportation*. Rail, coach, underground and other enterprises can use these systems for transport management as well as line design and maintenance.

More effective *agriculture* production management can be achieved with the use of GIS. GPS controlled cultivation and harvest data acquisition forms detailed information base for plant production management. After creation of detailed cost-effective production scheme, plant management systems control cultivation mechanisms with the use of GPS station tracking.

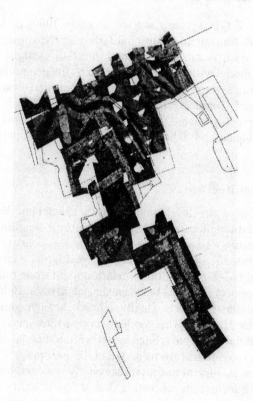

Fig. 3. Documentation of an archaeological site in GIS.

Forestry is another field of GIS applications. GIS systems are used for the processing of forest management data and the preparation of forest management plans. These plans forms fundamental base for accurate forest planting, cultivation, exploitation and afforestation. Remote-sensing analysis software is used for satellite image classifications to create an inventory of forest resources and to demonstrate forest vitality and damages.

We should also mention GIS applications in *army, police, security and rescue services*. For example, some GIS systems support on-line GPS station tracking to display position of security car or truck with dangerous freight. GIS applications are also used in *education and research* from primary schools to universities. GIS systems are also used for the presentation of *market analyses* and the creation of future business plans. Proper location for new shop within city, district or state can be found with the help of GIS. The wide range of GIS applications can be demonstrated with their use for *archaeology*. GIS system makes rescue excavations less expensive and increases information value of data about discovered site.

2 State of the art in GIS

The development of GIS systems started at early 1960s in Canada and USA. From this time the concept of traditional GIS oriented towards geometrical objects and spatial data matured. Current large GIS systems are based on the topographic data model with the concentration to the geometrical and geographical view at the expense of non-spatial information and descriptive part. This section gives a short technical overview of traditional GIS. It shows fundamental features of current systems from the point of view of computer science and technologies. Problems and deficiencies in the traditional point of view on GIS are indicated.

2.1 System architecture

From the beginning of the development of GIS, special emphases were layed on the geometrical data structures and spatial relations handling. Architecture of these systems is usually based on two monolithic components. Main component is spatial engine intended to spatial data processing. The latter is built on top of database kernel based on traditional relational database management system. Spatial engine supports relations between spatial objects. Relation between spatial and non-spatial attributes is usually defined through some unique identifier or set of attributes. However, this mechanism provides very vague link between spatial engine and database part. Such systems should be labelled "Gis' but they are considered in most literature to be true GIS systems.

On the other side, several information systems was extended with some possibility of spatial information processing. Usual functionality of these systems is limited to display spatial data, select relation between spatial and non-spatial data an highlight selected data. They does not support relations between spatial objects. Such systems should be marked "gIS" and in most literature they are not included into GIS domain.

2.2 Data model and structures

The architecture of traditional GIS is fully reflected in traditional data model. Spatial data are stored separately from non-spatial data. Raster data for each phenomenon are typically stored in separate files composed from values for each point (or facet) within spatially referenced grid. Vector data are stored in special graphical databases in binary form, which has unique design for each system. Non-spatial textual and numeric data are stored within relational databases. For large non-spatial data (sound, video), informative part contain only necessary reference. Relational database management system proved to be unusable for graphical data storage.

Fig. 4. Photoplan of Prague 4 (detail).

Vector data organization is based on group of objects for which the term *layer* is used. Layer consist of several homogeneous collections of graphical objects (i.e. point collection, polyline collection etc.). One database of non-spatial data is assigned to each collection. Classification of objects and class separation have to be done through attributes within non-spatial data. Relation between spatial and non-spatial attributes is usually defined through some unique identifier or set of attributes. This model is usually considered to be traditional relational model within GIS domain.

Topographic data model has one important feature which is not covered by relational model. Relations between spatial objects within one layer are included in graphical database. Topographic relations and topology are handled automatically. Some important graphical attributes (such object position, length or area) are communicated through link from spatial engine to database kernel.

This model is used in most large GIS systems and does not fully support the object-oriented view of real world.

2.3 Functional model

Traditional common GIS systems support usually wide range of functionality for the manipulation of vector and raster data as well as for analyses of descriptive information attached to data in databases. This functionality provides only common procedures for data manipulation, access and analyses, which are necessary for users to achieve their goals. Functional orientation of traditional systems provide users with limited support for task-oriented technologies.

Common users would like to use GIS systems as the tool to find answers for their spatially oriented questions. It requires usually data retrieval and analyses. This means to follow several steps available through functions oriented and labelled towards data model. It is necessary to be well-trained to accomplish such a task. This is the main reason for the common consideration that GIS is specific professional tool which is hard to use. This problem should be solve through user-oriented applications based on common object-oriented GIS technology.

3 New technologies for future GIS

New fascinating technologies such as world-wide computer networks, object-oriented environments, multimedia and object-oriented database systems were introduced within last years. Human society also constantly changes to information oriented community. GIS must comply with the rapid changes in both society and computer technologies.

Future GIS systems should adopt such technologies and use their advantages for increase of their potentials. On the other side GIS should be more adopted in future environments. This section outline the impact of new computer technologies on future GIS and some trends in the use of GIS for future environments. The role of object-oriented architecture and databases, multimedia and hyperinformation system on future GIS is outlined. Some important problems for future research are suggested.

3.1 Object-oriented design and architecture

Increased use of multitasking environments and computer networks emphasized the role of information exchange and system communications. Data exchange and communication between future systems (both GIS and other applications) is real must. The wide-spread use of large computer networks and the possibility to access data within this extent impose various requirements on proper GIS design. Object-oriented design and architecture should provide help in this situation. Their advantages should be especially highlighted in GIS, which is object-oriented in its nature.

Future GIS systems should also adopt object-oriented features in their architecture and new object-oriented data model should be properly designed. Client-server model in GIS environment should be clearly defined and used. Data inheritance and encapsulation will support data integration and extension. Notion of object services should be incorporated within future GIS. In this way, the most important deficiency of traditional GIS could be solved. The definition of common virtual geodata model and proper decomposition of GIS systems into service-oriented client-server frameworks are the most difficult problems for GIS design and development.

3.2 Object-oriented database management systems

Deficiencies of current relational database system and object-oriented nature of GIS will lead naturally to the use of object-oriented database management system (OODBMS) for GIS in future. This task raise following important questions:

- Are OODBMS mature enough for the use (especially in commercial GIS)?
- Is the current model of OODBMS sufficient for the use in GIS?

Proper definition of object-oriented GIS data model is necessary to answer these questions. But some requirements for OODBMS are well-known. For example, scalability and low-cost systems are necessary to create GIS applications with accurate extent according to user needs.

Data access and analyses based on spatial relations rank among the most important functionality of GIS systems. Then spatial-oriented query languages form topical research problem within current GIS. From this point of view, object-oriented query languages might provide necessary flexibility and extensions to achieve such a task. But they does not mature enough so that necessary extensions cannot be estimated. But it is clear that a concept of object-oriented quey language for spatial analyses as well as methods for spatial indexing within OODBMS must be developed.

3.3 Human-computer interaction and multimedia

From the point of view of computer technologies the last decade of this century can be considered like the era of graphical user interfaces (GUI) and multimedia. Special hardware, windows and multimedia systems spread into all computer environments and applications. New GUI and multimedia technologies can be easily adopted into GIS systems. Fifteen years experience with the use of current GIS should be reflected within new user environments. The most important problem of current sophisticated technologies is lack of proper metaphors for their use.

New hardware techniques, such as pen-based systems and touch screens, will also have their application within GIS. Routine non-spatial data acquisition and data checking could be done with pen-based system directly at particular place during survey. Touch screens could be used for quick data retrieval and will provide extremely easy-to-use environment for positional queries. Current popular user interface items, such as icons, notebook tabs, forms etc., will make GIS data more accessible and GIS environment more clearly arranged. Results of spatial cognition research should be also adopted within the design and development of future GIS environments.

The use of multimedia currently ranges from encyclopedia publishing, education and entertainment to production process monitoring and control. Multimedia technologies could be easily (and in some cases are) adopted into GIS systems. But the most important problem of current sophisticated multimedia technologies is lack of proper metaphors for their use.

Future GIS systems should solve two main task: adoption of multimedia for the use in GIS applications as well as supply of GIS services for other multimedia applications. But the solution of these problems need not be limited to technological part, but it should be concentrated on questions:

- Why use multimedia in GIS?
- How should be multimedia used in GIS?
- Which metaphors are proper to use within GIS environment?
- Which media should be used within GIS as well as for digital maps?
- How should be digital map used in other multimedia applications?

It is quite clear that new media (photographs, sound, video, etc.) can increase information value of GIS data. These media are in many cases the most natural way of communicating information. Multimedia enable people to accept various information (e.g. music, actions) in its natural state and in familiar manner. But large amount of information increase potential danger for mind and perception overloading.

Multimedia information in GIS systems should be structured and presented very carefully with the help of user-oriented and thematically-oriented data organization. Methods for the presentation of data changes and temporal relations within GIS could be prepared with the help of multimedia. But proper media should be chosen in that situation. For example, proper method for alarm communicating should be found for on-line tracking of objects (e.g. security cars), when forbidden or dangerous situation raise.

On the other side, adoption of digital maps like new media in common multimedia applications can increase their quality and potential. It is quite clear that people are used to describe positional relations on the Earth by maps and in this way maps represents natural media for communication positional information. We can found maps incorporated in many current multimedia applications (such as encyclopedia).

For example, they provides information about states which include statistical data as well as simple maps. These maps are usually closed into such an application and cannot be linked with data in other systems. Creation of new links to personal data outside of application (e.g. economic or environmental databases) and methods for data exchange are important tasks which should be solved in future GIS systems.

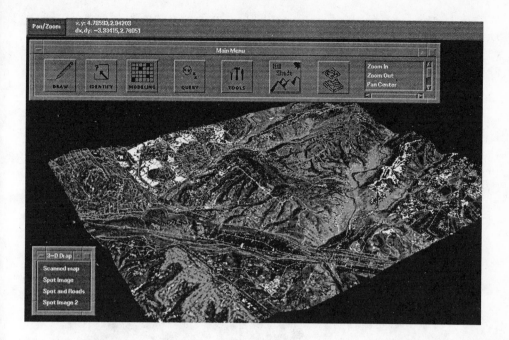

Fig. 5. Three-dimensional model of countryside.

3.4 Hyperdocuments and hyperinformation

The current era of information technologies has also introduced notion of hypertext and hyperlinked information within large data structures. World Wide Web
(WWW) represents the real hit in computer network environment. It provides
easy-to-use access to large information databases and big amount of information, data, software and media resources within world-wide Internet network
system. This technology bring unconceivable amount of information to screens
of computer users. But new methods for information access, search and queries
should be introduced to improve these environments, as mind and perception
overloading is imminent.

This technology allows to incorporate images (such as maps) into documents.
It also includes simple methods for definition of links within picture, which enable
hypertext document developer to create "sensitive map". These mechanisms are
very limited and are not appointed for true relations between GIS data. WWW
does not provide any spatial query mechanism for the creation of hyperlinked
documents. It seems to be helpful for some hyperlink databases to incorporate
basic GIS technology to provide more sophisticated spatial-oriented data access.

On the other side, it should be useful to provide some methods for the creation
of hyperenvironment within GIS systems and applications. For example, the
most simple solution provides data link between reference areas and groups of

layers. From our experience, this method provides quite effective tool for access within larger collection of data layers which can be easily divided according to spatial position. The notion of true hypermap environment will be introduced in following sections.

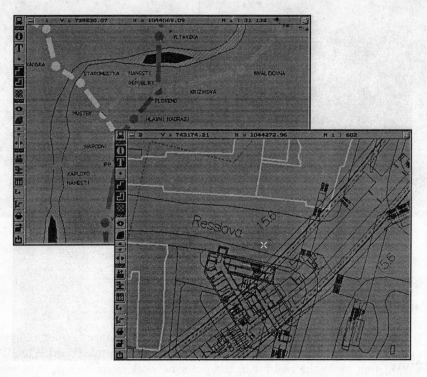

Fig. 6. Graphical documentation of Prague underground is organized into simple hyperenvironment according to stations and their connections.

4 Future of GIS

At present, we can see the first efforts to shift the view of GIS systems from traditional common to user-oriented systems. Modern GIS should provide powerful user-oriented information systems for maintenance and analyses of spatially referenced data. Open user-oriented GIS systems should help users with management and control of the society and environment in the future. This section gives our view of future modern user-oriented GIS. The concept of Open GIS, object-oriented data model and Geographic Information Management Systems are introduced.

4.1 Open user-oriented GIS

Future GIS system should provide users with functionality for processing georeferenced information in user-oriented manner. Information should be accessed in easy-to-use framework which enable users to navigate within increasing amount of information and to find answers to their questions. Modern GIS systems should address user needs more clearly and provide tools for easier adoption of extensions to achieve user goals. Future GIS systems should also support new methods of data organization and data access which enable users to maintain their data in the same way independently of their graphical representation and location in computer networks.

Sophisticated GIS systems will provide an open object-oriented environment for the development of particular GIS applications and information system for geographical data processing within distributed heterogeneous computer networks. Advanced GIS systems will allow to combine vector and raster data and handle these data in combined analyses. A quite new kind of user interface will make full use of the object-oriented data model truly possible. Powerful visual programming languages will give users the possibility to customize the system to their needs.

Correct data exchange and communication with other systems (such as office software) is also necessary. For this reason open data and communication standard are created. The development of standard for GIS system architecture and virtual geodata model is currently done within the Open GIS project. Common standards for data exchange and program communications are developed in computer industry. The most important project seems to be effort of the Object Management Group in the project for access to object data and services within Common Object Request Broker Architecture (CORBA) framework.

4.2 Object-oriented GIS data model

Future data organization will shift from traditional view based on geometrical objects and layers to user-oriented view based on thematic objects and geographical blocks. Thematic objects encapsulate a complete entity, which contains information attributes, executable methods as well as set of spatially referenced geometrical elements in both vector and raster form. Encapsulated pictures, sound and video clips introduce new media to form sophisticated multimedia GIS systems. These objects provide users with access to essential information to complete their tasks and achieve necessary results.

This information era creates unlimited amount of information data and future developments should create tools for management and access of these data. Spatial catalogues and hypermaps might be solutions for future organization of georeferenced data. Future GIS systems will provide tools for registration of data in spatial catalogues. This catalogues provide users with easier access to large data sources based on their spatial locations.

Live true links between thematic objects, geographical.blocks and spatial catalogues create unique notion of hypermap environment. It creates structured framework for data retrieval and will make future access to necessary details of information easier and more extensive. Efficient data query tools should be developed for simplification of data access. Development of spatial indexing methods and spatially oriented query languages is necessary.

Data exchange within large network environments should be also facilitated with GIS data definition language and format description. These tools should ensure data compatibility for future data access and provide easy way for extension adoption during the future developments. Canadian standard SAIF is the first attempt to create object-oriented data standard with data description language. This standard has also influenced developments within Open GIS project.

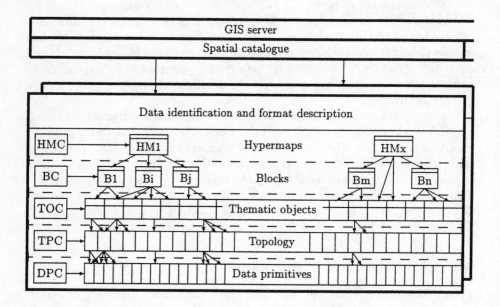

Fig. 7. Simplified model of future data organization.

4.3 Geographic Information Management System

Architecture of modern GIS systems will based on client-server architecture. Main GIS server module will provide basic functionality for data access and handling including data registration database. Special server modules will add more sophisticated functionality for data transformation, processing, management, analyses, modelling and output. All modules are registered within GIS server and provides so-called "service" to GIS environment. Registration mechanism gives the base for flexibility and future extension. Such a kernel creates generic **Geographical Information Management Systems (GIMS)**, which will form future generation of GIS systems.

This framework should be treated as construction kit which will facilitate the development of customized user-oriented GIS clients (i.e. GIS applications). Object-oriented data model, client-server architecture and effective development environments enable developers to supply GIS applications (clients) in optimal structure and extent. These applications will have user interface tuned for particular study field, technologies and data. Object-oriented extensible data organization and open development environment for the creation of GIS applications based on client-server architecture provide the required base for the effective development of user-oriented GIS applications.

References

1. Beran, V., Míka, D., Kučera, L.: GIS - Geoinformation Systems (in Czech). Klub Zeleného telefonu, Praha, 1991.
2. Bouille, F.: Towards 2000: The actual main trends in future GIS. Proceedings of the conference Europe in Transition: The Context of GIS, Brno, 1994, K-13–K-27.
3. Charvát, K., Limpouch, A.: TopoL GIS System. Proceedings of the conference Europe in Transition: The Context of GIS, Brno, 1994, II-51–II-63.
4. Kroha, P.: Objects and Databases. McGraw-Hill, London, 1993.
5. Kubo, S.: GIS for the Twenty-One Century. Proceedings of the conference Europe in Transition: The Context of GIS, Brno, 1994, K-2–K-5.
6. Kuhn, W.: Object-orientation and Geographic Information Systems. Workshop on the conference Europe in Transition: The Context of GIS, Brno, 1994.
7. Limpouch, A.: Architecture for Interactive Systems with Highly Graphical User Interfaces. Proceedings of the conference SOFSEM '94. Contributed talks, Masaryk University, Brno, 1994, 63–68.
8. Limpouch, A.: GIS for the Next Century. Proceedings of the 17th International Cartographic Conference. Barcelona, 1995 (to appear).
9. The Open Geodata Interoperability Specification. Draft base Document – OGIS Project Document 94-0251R1, OGIS Ltd., Wayland, USA, 1994.
10. Šmíd, O., Beneš, T.: LIS TopoL: the new tool of remote sensing utilization in the Czech Republic. Proceedings of the 13th EARSeL Symposium Remote Sensing – From Research to Operational Applications in the New Europe. Springer, Budapest, 1994, 165–171.
11. Spatial Archive Interchange Format: Formal Definition. Release 3.1, April 1994, Surveys and Resource Mapping Branch, Ministry of Environment, Lands and Parks, Province of British Columbia, Canada.
12. Understanding GIS. ESRI, 1990.
13. Worboys, M.F.: Object-oriented Approaches to Geo-Referenced Information. Int. Journal of GIS 8 (1994) 385–399.

WWW — The World Wide Web

Victoria A Marshall

Advanced Hypermedia Systems Group, Computing and Information Systems Department
Rutherford Appleton Laboratory, Chilton, DIDCOT, UK OX11 0QX

v.a.marshall@rl.ac.uk
http://www.cis.rl.ac.uk/people/vam.html

Abstract. Over the last few years there has been a phenomenal growth in the use of *WWW (World Wide Web)* for a wide variety of purposes from advertising and publicity, to collaborative work and teaching.

Because it is so easy to set up a server, there are almost as many web philosophies, uses and page designs as there are web pages. Of course some of these are better than others and within CISD we believe that our corporate-wide style and practices are particularly effective.

This talk will give a brief history of WWW, and then go on to describe the philosophy and technical theory of the design and structure of the CISD web, and explain how it fits into the CCLRC corporate web and philosophy. It will also touch on more advanced uses of the web.

1   The History of WWW

The *World Wide Web* (also known as *the Web* or *WWW* in one of those rare cases in which the acronym is longer than the original name!) has been called many things including *"A map to the buried treasures of the Information Age"* (John Markoff in the New York Times), *"the Global Village"* and *"seriously addictive"* (almost anybody on the Internet, anywhere).

WWW is a term used to refer to the concept of a networked information discovery and retrieval tool which allows anyone with Internet access to browse any information that anyone anywhere in the world has chosen to make available about themselves, their company, their institute, their products, or indeed anything else that they think might be of interest to someone, somewhere.

WWW was originally developed at CERN in March 1989 to allow information dissemination and sharing within collaborative High Energy Physics groups across the world. At the time, the information was available by anonymous FTP using a simple line mode browser. In January 1993 Marc Andreessen released the alpha version of the XMosaic browser, which made access to WWW information much easier. Since then, WWW has spread to many other disciplines and is now the most advanced information system on the Internet. In March 1993, 0.1% of NSF backbone traffic was due to WWW; by October 1993 there were over 500 known HTTP servers. Today, use of the Internet is estimated to be expanding at a rate of 100,000% per annum, the number of WWW servers is estimated in the tens of thousands, and the number of users in the millions.

Anybody with the necessary hardware and software can create pages and establish their presence on the web. Although originally developed at CERN, WWW has no central administration point. Rather, it operates a self-regulating "progression by mutual consent" policy whereby anybody can contribute to WWW; ideas and tools are adopted or rejected by common consent within the WWW community. WWW development is however guided by *W3C* (the *World Wide Web Consortium*) currently based between INRIA in France and MIT in the USA. W3C consists of a membership of interested research institutes and commercial companies. Current membership is approximately 70 of mostly American companies and institutes; RAL joined W3C early in 1995.

2   The Architecture of WWW

The architecture of WWW can be viewed from two points of view — that of the user, and that of the system. From the user point of view there are HTML (the *HyperText Markup Language*) [1] and client-side browsers enabling users to create and view web pages; from the system point of view there are HTTP (the *HyperText Transfer Protocol*) [2] (and associated protocols) and the architecture of a web server giving access to the pages. The following sections describe some of these aspects very briefly.

2.1   Architecture from the User Point of View

From the user point of view, WWW consists of *pages*, and uses hypertext as the method of presentation. Pages need not be just textual — they can also include graphics, icons, photographic images, film clips, animations and sound, so they are more hypermedia rather than merely hypertext documents.

Pages can contain links to other pages (or parts of pages) either locally or anywhere else in the world. The interface for the user is extremely simple — to follow a link, click on it with the mouse. Links are specified using a *URL (Uniform Resource Locator)* such as *http://www.cis.rl.ac.uk/people/vam.html* which indicates the protocol to be used (*HTTP*), the full name of the machine to be accessed (*www.cis.rl.ac.uk*), and the directory path and name of the file to be retrieved (*people/vam.html*). Pages are created using HTML (see Figure 1) and is described by Dave Raggett as:

> *"...a simple mark-up language used to create hypertext documents*
> *that are portable from one platform to another. HTML documents*
> *are SGML documents with generic semantics that are appropriate*
> *for representing information from a wide range of applications..."*

```
<HTML>
<HEAD>
<TITLE>CISD</TITLE>
</HEAD>
<BODY>
<P>
<A HREF="/mission.html"><IMG SRC="/img/cisd-logo.gif"></A>
<H1>
<A HREF="/mission.html">Computing and Information Systems Department</A>
</H1>
Welcome to the Computing and Information Systems Department (CISD) of Rutherford
Appleton Laboratory, part of CCLRC (Council for the Central Laboratory of the Research
Councils). CISD provides high quality computational facilities, specialist and research
services, and high value IT solutions for customers.
<HR>
<P>
<A HREF="/struct.html"><IMG ALIGN=BOTTOM SRC="/img/struct.gif"> Structure</A>
<P>
<A HREF="/people.html"><IMG ALIGN=BOTTOM SRC="/img/people.gif"> People</A>
<P>
<A HREF="/proj.html"><IMG ALIGN=BOTTOM SRC="/img/proj.gif"> Projects</A>
<HR>
<P>
<A HREF="http://www.ccl.ac.uk/"><IMG ALIGN=MIDDLE SRC="/img/org.gif"></A>
<P>
Please send any comments to the Web Manager
<A HREF="mailto:web@inf.rl.ac.uk">web@inf.rl.ac.uk</A>.
</BODY>
</HTML>
```

Figure 1. HTML for (part of) the CISD home page [3]

Note that each HTML tag is enclosed in angled brackets < and >, and that many tags consist of a pair of start and end parts — *<HTML>* and *</HTML>* for example. Icons are included using the *<IMG>* tag, specifying the *SRC* (source) filename of the icon. Links are enclosed between *<A HREF>* and *</A>* tags; any text or icons between these tags will become "hot", and if clicked on will take the user to the page specified as the source. Further information about HTML markup is available on the web [4].

The disadvantage of the current version of HTML is that it is a structural, not presentational, markup language. Thus it provides authors with only a small number of text processing capabilities such as logical heading levels, logical font styles, lists and some foreign language characters, but not tables, equations, text flow control, physical font styles and so on. The advantages of HTML are that it is very easy to learn, can be written using a flat text editor, and can be used to include in-line images and vocative links to other destinations and a wide variety of media formats.

Although no version of HTML has yet been formally approved by the standards bodies, the most commonly implemented version is HTML-2 which provides fairly simple formatting capabilities. HTML-3 is currently an Internet draft; its main features additional to those of HTML-2 will probably be the inclusion of tables, style sheets and text flow around images.

More people-friendly *wysiwyg* editors are being developed. Perhaps the newest and best of these so far is Microsoft's *Internet Assistant* [5] which allows the user to create HTML documents via MS-Word 6.0 (although some Word features which do not translate to HTML are made unavailable). Internet Assistant is primarily intended as an editor, but can also be used to browse the web.

Web pages can be read using a variety of browsers. Until recently, the most common was NCSA's *Mosaic* [6], but this has now been largely superseded by Netscape Communications Corporation's *Netscape* [7] browser. The main advantage of Netscape over Mosaic is that it fetches and displays the text of an HTML page before fetching the inline images; on many machines, Mosaic fetches all elements of a page before displaying it. Thus the reader can start to read a Netscape page sooner. The disadvantage of Netscape however is that it has introduced a number of proprietary extensions to the HTML language which do not conform to the standards work (although Netscape have stated that they are committed to the standards and will modify their product as and when a standard is ratified). The future licensing of Netscape is also unclear. Another browser is CERN's *Arena* [8] which checks HTML and flags any pages which do not meet the specification.

Common features of browsers are that they should be tolerant of non-conforming HTML, and simply ignore any tags which are not understood. Browsers also generally use some form of *History List* to provide a distinction between links which the user has already followed and links which have not been followed; the resulting tree of followed links can be traversed by repeatedly clicking the *Back* and *Forward* buttons. (Note that this is not necessarily a strictly historical traversal.) Most browsers also provide the user with a *Hotlist* or *Bookmarks* which can be used to save the URL of chosen pages.

Other, more specialised browsers are being developed. Sun's *HotJava* [9] browser uses an object-oriented language known as Java which enables clients to execute self-contained objects; thus HotJava provides facilities for interactive documents and on-page animation of graphics. Silicon Graphics Incorporated's browser uses *VRML* (the *Virtual Reality Modelling Language*) [10] based on SGI's Inventor standard, and allows an efficient transfer of virtual reality models across the web for clients to manipulate.

2.2 Architecture from the System Point of View

WWW is implemented using HTTP. This is described as:

> *"HTTP is an application-level protocol with the lightness and speed necessary for distributed, collaborative, hypermedia information systems. It is a generic, stateless, object-oriented protocol which can be used for many tasks such as name servers and distributed object management systems, through extension of its request methods (commands). A feature of HTTP is the typing and negotiation of data representation, allowing systems to be built independently of the data being transferred."*.

The current version of HTTP is *HTTP/1.0*, and on the Internet usually operates over a TCP/IP connection to a default port number 80.

The HTTP protocol is client/server based. The requesting application (the *client*) establishes a connection with the receiving application (the *server*) and sends its request. This request consists of several parts: the required method, the identifier of the resource, protocol version, and a MIME-type body of key-value pairs giving request modifiers, client information, a blank line and any appropriate text. The method is usually *GET* to retrieve the entity (usually an HTML page) specified. (See Figure 2.) Other methods are possible including *HEAD* which returns only the metainformation of the requested entity.

```
GET /people/vam.html HTTP/1.0
Date: Wed, 16 Aug 1995 17:36:35 GMT
Accept: text/*, image/gif
From: v.a.marshall@rl.ac.uk
```

Figure 2. A simple HTTP request from client to server

The server responds with a status line giving its protocol version and a success/error code, and a MIME-type body giving server details, entity metainformation, a blank line and any appropriate text (usually an HTML page). (See Figure 3.)

The success code is 200; other common codes are used to indicate that that the client does not have access to the entity (403), the entity has not been found (404), that the request has timed-out (408), and so on.

3 The Design of a Web

There are many ways in which to design a web depending on the information to be presented and the needs of the anticipated audience. This section discusses some of the issues involved in the design process.

```
HTTP/1.0 200
Date: Wed, 16 Aug 1995 17:36:41 GMT
Allow: GET, HEAD
Content-Language: en, de
Content-Type: text/html
Last-Modified: Mon, 14 Aug 1995 09:05:59 GMT

<HTML>
<HEAD>
<TITLE>Simple page</TITLE>
</HEAD>
<BODY>
<H1>This is a simple HTML page.</H1>
</BODY>
</HTML>
```

Figure 3. A simple HTTP response from server to client

3.1 Structure of a Web

Several different types of web structure have been used. A *sequence* of pages can be used easily by the majority of users because of its similarities with a conventional paper book. Such a structure is however very restrictive for the reader, and offers little expressivity for the author. At the opposite extreme, a full *network* of pages is a highly expressive structure, but one which will almost certainly confuse, and lose, the reader. The structure adopted for the majority of webs therefore is a hierarchical *tree*. Such structures are relatively rich for authors, and also fairly easily followed by their readers.

One of the key features of a tree-structured web is its root page, which can be used for a variety of functions including that of a *Welcome Page* and a *Home Page*. These pages typically give an overview of the information contained in that web which is usually organised by concept, one concept for each branch of the tree.

When CISD initially set up its web in July 1994 there was much debate on the structure to be used. Some members of the department thought that a purely departmental organisational view should be used; projects within each group should be described within leaf nodes. Other members of the department suggested several branches including departmental structure, projects within the department, people within the department, and so on. After much discussion, the latter design was implemented as it seemed the most appropriate for a research institute such as RAL since the majority of our readers are also researchers who are interested in the work we do. A subsequent analysis of the server logs has shown that the People branch of the CISD web is consistently the most popular (accounting for 40% of all pages looked at), followed by Projects (12% of all the pages); the Departmental Structure branch often falls outside the list of top five branches within the web.

3.2   Icons and the Structure of a Web

One common problem with many non-trivial webs is that it is easy for the reader to get lost within them. As the number of levels of hierarchy within the web increases, so too does the reader's disorientation, leading to general dissatisfaction and frustration. Another problem with large repository-type webs which are pointed-to from a number of locations is that the reader is linked to a specific page within that web, but does not necessarily have any means of navigating back up the hierarchy if the information found is too specific for their needs. In this case, the browser's Back button is useless as it will take the reader back through pages already seen, rather than back up the current hierarchy.

Within the CISD web a scheme of icons is used to try and alleviate these problems. At the bottom of the first-level page (the Department's home page at the root of the web hierarchy) is the CCLRC corporate icon linking to the corporate web. Second-level pages (such as the list of projects within the Department) include not only the corporate icon and link, but also the Department's icon and link. Third-level pages (such as the overview of a particular project) include the corporate icon and link, the Department's icon and link, and another to the relevant list page (in this case, the list of projects). Fourth-level pages (such as a specific section within a project description) include the corporate, Departmental, list and project overview icons and links. (See Figure 4.)

Thus readers know, for example, that clicking on the Projects icon will always take them to the Projects page. The icons do not have to be strictly representational, but they should be individualistic and identifiable with the section in which they are used.

Such an icon schema has several disadvantages and also advantages. The disadvantages are that even small in-line images take time to down-load, and of course that icons and logos require design work! The main advantages are that icons make the web visually attractive (an important consideration for a web that is intended as the Department's primary publicity tool), the number and type of icons used at the bottom of each page gives the reader a sense of how deep they are within the web and in which branch, and (when used in conjunction with larger-sized logos) give each branch of the web and items within it an individual identity or *persICONality*.

Finally, it is worth mentioning the use of icons within weblets. Some sections (such as the various Community Clubs) of the CISD web are designed to be read *in situ*, and indeed are advertised as webs in their own right. These sections of the web, or *weblets*, generally consist of the Community Club Welcome Page, and extend several levels downwards. The Club's Welcome Page includes icons and links to the corporate, Departmental and list of Community Clubs pages, but pages below the Club's Welcome Page include only one icon and link — that of the appropriate Club. Thus readers are not confused by too many icons, and yet have a reliable method of getting back to the Club's Welcome Page. This is an important point as it enables logical weblets to be organised and presented distinct from the main web, and yet remain an integral and coordinated part of it.

357

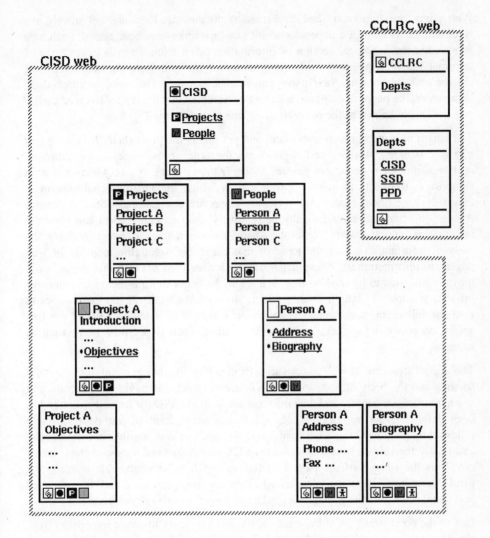

Figure 4. Navigation icon structure within the CISD web

This approach is also used within the CCLRC corporate web [11]. Top-level pages contain publicity text plus pointers to further, technical information at deep levels of the relevant department's web. CCLRC web pages *per se* are navigable in the usual way, but the departmental pages include links within that web, and to the welcome page of the corporate web.

3.3 Design of Web Pages

Not only is the overall design of a web important, so too is the design of information included on its pages. This section discusses some of these issues.

Web pages are hypertext (and hypermedia) documents; they are not merely the electronic equivalent of a paper document to which links have been added. Each web page represents a logical section of information taken from a much larger body of information. Web pages should relate to each other and have the same sense of closure and cohesion as their paper equivalents, but they also need to stand-alone because, unlike paper documents, it cannot be assumed that the reader has read earlier pages. (This is known as the *paradox of on-line text chunking*.)

The length of a web page is important, and yet this is the proverbial *"How long is a piece of string?"* problem and depends on the type of the page — *navigational*, *informational*, or a document *per se*. A *navigational page* is one which acts as a signpost to the sections within a web and in which the informational content is relatively low; (most Home and Welcome pages are navigational). Such pages are referred-to often and should ideally be relatively short so that readers can view the information without having to scroll. An *informational page* is one containing the body of information about the topic of that particular page; (the majority of web pages are informational). These pages can be longer than navigational pages but if they are intended to be read on-line then it may be better to limit them to a couple of browser windows in length so that readers do not have to scroll too many times to read the full text. A document page is one which is intended to be read (on-line and/or on paper) as a document in its own right. Such pages may be as long as necessary.

The overall structure of web pages varies from site to site, but generally consists of a heading and the body of text, and, at the bottom of the page, navigational icons, and any author and/or contact and date information. Within CISD the overall structure has been defined as an appropriate logo (if this is some form of introductory page) followed by page heading, a horizontal rule, the body of text, another horizontal rule, and finally the relevant meta-information such as navigational icons, contact details etc. Thus the subject of the page is given an "up front" recognisable identity, the meta-information is visually separated from the body of text, and the matched horizontal rules give the page a more balanced look than one rule only.

One of the great strengths of hypertext is that it is very easy to create hyperlinks from almost everything to anything else. Such *hyperactive hypertext* is however also one of the great problems of hypertext — if the text contains an undisciplined number of links then the likelihood is increased of accidentally creating a self-referential set of pages. If a reader then tries to follow this cyclic chain they can easily get lost and disorientated in webspace. The undisciplined use of links also causes problems for web managers if, for example, the name is changed of the destination of a frequently used link. (This happened within RAL when the corporate name was changed!) Each web page then has to be inspected and deprecated links modified. Within the CISD web, most of the upwards links within the text of web pages have been removed, but the hierarchy is still navigable via the icons. This makes the whole web structure much more stable; hot links take the reader down the hierarchy or sideways to another branch of it, while the navigation icons take the reader up the hierarchy.

3.4 Webiquette

In addition to technical aspects, there are also many niceties of web and page design. This section describes aspects of this "web etiquette" or *webiquette*.

Certain words and phrases are inappropriate on web pages because they assume device and/or medium independence. For example, *Click here* assumes that the reader is using a mouse rather than some line browser, and also that the reader is reading the page in its electronic form rather than on paper when "click" becomes meaningless. (If you owned a shop you would have *Welcome* on the door, not *Open this door to enter* [12].)

Although the majority of browsers now is use can handle images and pages in formats other than HTML, it is nevertheless considered webiquette to give readers warning of items which may take a considerable time to download because they are large, because they contain a large number of images, or one very large image. In the latter case, it is usual to use an in-line "thumbnail" version of the image as a vocative link which can be clicked to display the full-sized version. For example:

```
<A HREF="/docs/report.ps">Introduction</A> (PostScript, 68K)
<A HREF="/ral/site.html">RAL in pictures</A>
<A HREF="/photos/view.jpg"><IMG SRC="/thumbn/view.gif"></A>
```

For pages which are still in the process of being prepared, readers should be warned that the link may lead to an empty page. For example:

```
<A HREF="/news/latest.html">Latest news</A> (in preparation)
```

(Of course, it might be better still not to put the link in at all until the pages was ready!)

4 Advanced uses of WWW

What of the future and more advanced uses of WWW? CISD's research work and on-going interests as a member of W3C covers various aspects. Some of these are described briefly in the next sections.

4.1 Semantic Mark-Up

WWW technologies are designed to deliver information to a human reader, but do not as yet provide much support for machine-manipulable presentations of information. This makes tasks such as cross-server searching and document re-structuring more difficult: examples of this are the problems of users sharing complex information across servers and generating paper copies of a hypertext documents.

The WWW research team within CISD have been investigating making WWW more amenable to automatic processing by importing ideas from the database world directly into HTML [13]. A small extension to HTML is proposed which "publishes" the information structure of a set of pages as a database conceptual model. Elements of pages may be identified directly with entities and attributes from this underlying model, and relationships between entities may be described independently of the hypertext structure of the pages. Relationships are constructed using full URLs, so related entities may reside on different machines. Information may then be retrieved from this *"lightweight database"* using database-like queries, or create a more sophisticated index of pages than would be possible with simple keyword searching.

Collaborative work often involves the creation and update of information structures by people in different locations. For many tasks this information will have substantial structure with complex inter-dependencies. A database management system may be used to ensure the consistency of this information, but few DBMSs can cope with information distributed across a wide user population. A lightweight database may be used to create, maintain and verify links in the information base in a simple and browsable form, across server boundaries, without excessive database support.

As an example, CISD is involved in many international scientific collaborations, performing experiments in high-energy physics and space science. These involve different groups of researchers publishing (to each other) the results of their parts of the experiments. A lightweight database may be used to facilitate the scientists' access to these results. Firstly, a data model is defined for the information using the usual entity-attribute-relationship approach. The important results from the experimental reports (in HTML) are then marked-up to correspond to this model. The reports may contain extra information — formatting, hyper-structuring and so on. The ATSR project for Earth observation uses reports which include attributes defining the satellite, its position and sets of observation data. (See Figure 5.)

This data may be linked to other observations by making a relationship to the appropriate entities using primary keys. (See Figure 6.)

It is then possible to pose queries to the database such as "Find the co-ordinates of all ATSR-2 images of category 15 phenomena in July 1995", and have a suitable engine extract the necessary elements directly from the web. Relationships may be added as appropriate by members of the group to connect the observations.

4.2 Mobile Code

WWW currently transfers data, not programs. Despite the security implications, there are several reasons for wanting to be able to transfer executables between systems, including sending complex queries (such as SQL) to a server, off-loading compute-intensive functions from the server to the client requesting the data so as to maintain the performance of the server, and enabling *active documents* by including actions (such as checking the user's input to a text box within a form) within HTML.

WWW may transfer data of any MIME type [14] so such mobile code would be easy in principle. There are however many technical issues which need to be taken into consideration. Amongst these is the issue of security in defining a suitable set of library calls; should the access model be that of a *Padded Cell* (where functions which the client does not explicitly allow are forbidden) or that of a *Sea of Objects* (where all functions are available but many remain unadvertised on the client).

```
<PRE>
<H1>Observation .of ....</H1>
<ENT class="observation" key="atsr950724">
<ATTR name="satellite">ATSR-2</ATTR>
observed a snow-shower over the England today,
<ATTR name="date">24-7-95</ATTR>
at
<ATTR name="time">1027GMT</ATTR>
<P>
Coordinates:
<ATTR name="coord">xxx-yyyW, zzz-fffN</ATTR>
<P>
Category:
<ATTR name="category">15</ATTR>
(climatic change) Channel 1 image.
<P>
<ATTR name="channel-1"><IMG SRC="950724.gif"></ATTR>
</ENT>
</PRE>
```

Figure 5. A sample of lightweight database HTML mark-up

```
<PRE>
<P>
This is like the shower we saw the other week in
<REL class="observation" name="supporting" key="940601"
href="http://www.sat.fr/sat/i7680.html">France</REL>
</PRE>
```

Figure 6. A sample lightweight database relationship

It is clear that there will never be a single web mobile code scripting language to satisfy the needs of all the users all of the time. However, two current front-runners would seem to be *Safe-Tcl* and *Java* [15].

5 Afterword

This paper has not attempted to cover in detail all technical, design and social aspects associated with WWW, but rather to mention some of them as a pointer to further and more complete information elsewhere. It is clear that over the last few years there has been a phenomenal growth in the use of the web which is likely to continue into the future. Hopefully growth of the web will be towards a sensible and powerful set of standards without stifling the creative aspects of this tool for the Global Village.

The author would like to thank all her WWW colleagues for their help and support in writing this paper, especially Prof Keith Jeffery and Dr Simon Dobson who helped spark within CISD many of the ideas described here.

References

1. Raggett, D.: HyperText Markup Language Specification Version 3.0. Internet draft standard *ftp://ds.internic.net/internet-drafts/draft-ieft-html-specv3-00.txt* March 1995.

2. WWW Organisation: HyperText Transfer Protocol. *http://www.w3.org/member/WWW/Protocols/Overview.html* page available as of August 1995.

3. *http://www.cis.rl.ac.uk/* page available as of August 1995.

4. NCSA: A Beginner's Guide to HTML. *http://www.ncsa.uiuc.edu/General/Internet/WWW/HTMLPrimer.html* page available as of July 1995.

5. Microsoft: Internet Assistant for Word. *http://www.microsoft.com/MSWord/ia/default.htm* page available as of July 1995.

6. NCSA: Mosaic for the X Window System. *http://www.ncsa.uiuc.edu/SGD/Software/XMosaic/* page available as of August 1995.

7. Netscape Communications Corporation: Netscape. *http://home.netscape.com/* page available as of August 1995.

8. CERN: Arena — W3C's HTML3 browser. *http://www.w3.org/hypertext/WWW/Arena/* page available as of August 1995.

9. Sun: Java *http://java.sun.com/* page available as of August 1995.

10. Silicon Graphics Inc: Virtual Reality Modelling Language. *http://vrml.wired.com/* page available as of July 1995.

11. *http://www.cclrc.ac.uk/* page available as of August 1995.

12. White, B.: HTML and the art of authoring for the World Wide Web. Notes from a tutorial given at RAL, March 1995.

13. Dobson, S., Burrill, V.: Lightweight databases. Computer Networks and ISDN Systems **27**(3) pp. 1009-1015. Proceedings of the Third International World Wide Web Conference, Darmstadt, April 1995.

14. Borenstein, N., Freed, N.. MIME (Multipurpose Internet Mail Extensions) Part One: Mechanisms for specifying and describing the format of Internet message bodies. RFC 1521, 1993.

15. Connolly, D.: Mobile Code. *http://www.w3.org/hypertext/WWW/MobileCode/* Preparatory notes, W3C Workshop, July 1995, page available as of August 1995.

Implementation of higher-order unification based on calculus of explicit substitution

Peter Borovanský *

CRIN & INRIA-Lorraine, B.P. 239,
F 54506 Vandoeuvre lès Nancy Cedex, France,
E-mail: borovan@loria.fr

Abstract. In this paper, we present several improvements of an algorithm for a higher-order unification based on the calculus of explicit substitutions. The main difference between our algorithm and the already known version is, that we try to postpone normalisation of $\lambda\sigma$-terms as long as possible, i.e. until some information of these $\lambda\sigma$-terms is necessary for the next step of the unification algorithm.

1 Introduction

In this paper, we describe an improved version of a higher-order unification algorithm, which was presented in [DHK95]. The main idea of this algorithm is based on a calculus of explicit substitutions in a simply typed λ-theory (for definitions and details, see [ACCL90]), which integrates substitutions in the framework of the first-order formalism. In this calculus, substitutions are treated as the first-order objects, i.e. all basic operations over substitutions, like an application, a composition and a concatenation are defined in the first-order theory (their semantic is described by a small set of rewriting rules). As a result of this, the higher-order unification algorithm can be formulated in this formalism, which is the principal result of the paper [DHK95]. We have implemented the original version of described algorithm as it was presented in [DHK95], and it can be seen as a good programming exercise. However, we have also implemented a refined version of that algorithm, which we would like to illustrated in this paper. The speed-up that we have obtained is about 2.5. Thus, this paper can be viewed also as an extension of the already mentioned fundamental paper. Both versions of the algorithm (original and improved) were implemented in ELAN [KKV95].

2 Decorations and $\lambda\sigma$-calculus

It is not difficult to show how a unification problem formulated in λ-calculus can be transformed into $\lambda\sigma$-calculus with de Bruijn notation. In [DHK95] is also shown how all solutions of this new problem can be transformed back into λ-calculus. Thus, let us concentrate to problems formulated in $\lambda\sigma$-calculus.

---

* author's current address is Institute of Informatics, Comenius University, Bratislava

The computation (i.e. normalisation by the set of semantic rules) in the simply typed $\lambda\sigma$-calculus preserves types and contexts of sub-expressions. Moreover, from the analysis of the higher-order unification algorithm in [DHK95] it is clear, that it is necessary to know both types and contexts of all sub-expressions during unification. The general idea for solving this problem is based on assigning types and contexts to all sub-expressions at the beginning of unification. For this purpose, we will introduce a notion of decorations and a decoration algorithm.

Definition 1 Let a be a $\lambda\sigma$-term. Term a is a *decorated* if each sub-term b of a is associated with a context Γ^b and type A^b such that $\Gamma^b \vdash b : A^b$ (well-typed), and each substitution s of a is associated with a context Γ_1^s and type Γ_2^s such that $\Gamma_1^s \vdash s \triangleright \Gamma_2^s$ (means that s is well-typed in the contexts Γ_1 and Γ_2).

For the representation of decorations[2], we have to extend syntax of $\lambda\sigma$-terms[3]:

$$a_{dec-\lambda\sigma} ::= n_A^\Gamma \mid X_A^\Gamma \mid (a_A^{\Gamma_1} b_B^{\Gamma_2})_C^{\Gamma_3} \mid (\lambda C.a_A^{\Gamma_1})_B^{\Gamma_2} \mid a_A^{\Gamma_1}[s_B^{\Gamma_2}]_C^{\Gamma_3}$$

$$s_{dec-\lambda\sigma} ::= id_{\Gamma_2}^{\Gamma_1} \mid \uparrow_{\Gamma_2}^{\Gamma_1} \mid (a_A^{\Gamma_1}.s_{\Gamma_3}^{\Gamma_2})_{\Gamma_5}^{\Gamma_4} \mid (s_{\Gamma_2}^{\Gamma_1} \circ t_{\Gamma_4}^{\Gamma_3})_{\Gamma_6}^{\Gamma_5}$$

Decorated versions of typing and semantic rules for $\lambda\sigma$-calculus are straightforward extensions of the corresponding rules for traditional $\lambda\sigma$-calculus. In the next, we show an efficient algorithm for computation of decorations[4]. More precisely, we are going to solve the following problem:

For the given $\lambda\sigma$-term a (substitution s) and the context Γ_1 find a corresponding decorated $\lambda\sigma$-term a' (s') such that the context of a' (s') is Γ_1, if it exists.

The main idea of the solution presented here is based on the propagation of contexts and types through the term. This propagation is performed by a set of rewriting rules applied to a 'partially decorated' term (substitution). We extend definitions of $\lambda\sigma$-types, and contexts by the symbol $\bot$, which corresponds to an unknown type or context.

- we translate $\lambda\sigma$-term a in the decorated syntax such that all contexts and types are set to $\bot$,
- we replace the context of the top-most decoration in the type-checked term by the context Γ_1, in which we want to find decorations of the initial term,
- we apply the following set of rules until a non-reducible term is obtained,
- if the type (resp. context) of the whole term (substitution) is known (not $\bot$), then the term a (substitution s) is well-typed in the context Γ_1, and the type (context) in the top-most decoration is its type (context). Otherwise, the term a (substitution s) is ill-formed in the context Γ_1.

---

[2] Decoration is the most appropriate expression for the role of these components, because they are not crucial for the description of the algorithm - they can be recomputed each time - but they significantly improve the performance of the higher-order unification algorithm

[3] Instead of using the traditional notation $\Gamma \vdash a : A$ for the well-typed $\lambda\sigma$-term, we introduce more compact notation a_A^Γ, which we will not use only in a relational sense, but also for attaching the type A and the context Γ to the term a. Similarly, we will use more compact notation $s_{\Gamma_2}^{\Gamma_1}$ instead of $\Gamma_1 \vdash s \triangleright \Gamma_2$.

[4] Several modifications of this problem are solved in [Bor95].

(var)	$1_\perp^{A.\Gamma}$	$\Rightarrow 1_A^{A.\Gamma}$	(id)	$id_\perp^\Gamma \qquad \Rightarrow id_\Gamma^\Gamma$
$(\lambda \Downarrow)$	$(\lambda A.a_\perp^\perp)_\perp^\Gamma$	$\Rightarrow (\lambda A.a_\perp^{A.\Gamma})_\perp^\Gamma$	$(shift)$	$\uparrow_\perp^{A.\Gamma} \qquad \Rightarrow \uparrow_\Gamma^{A.\Gamma}$
$(\lambda \Uparrow)$	$(\lambda A.a_B^{A.\Gamma})_\perp^\Gamma$	$\Rightarrow (\lambda A.a_B^{A.\Gamma})_{A\to B}^\Gamma$	$(cons \Downarrow)$	$(a_\perp^\perp.s_\perp^\perp)_\perp^\Gamma \Rightarrow (a_\perp^\Gamma.s_\perp^\Gamma)_\perp^\Gamma$
$(app \Downarrow)$	$(a_\perp^\perp b_\perp^\perp)_\perp^\Gamma$	$\Rightarrow (a_\perp^\Gamma b_\perp^\Gamma)_\perp^\Gamma$	$(cons \Uparrow)$	$(a_A^\Gamma.s_{\Gamma_1}^\Gamma)_\perp^\Gamma \Rightarrow (a_A^\Gamma.s_{\Gamma_1}^\Gamma)_{A.\Gamma_1}^\Gamma$
$(app \Uparrow)$	$(a_{A\to B}^\Gamma b_A^\Gamma)_\perp^\Gamma$	$\Rightarrow (a_{A\to B}^\Gamma b_A^\Gamma)_B^\Gamma$	$(comp \Downarrow)$	$(s_\perp^\perp \circ t_\perp^\perp)_\perp^\Gamma \Rightarrow (s_\perp^\perp \circ t_\perp^\Gamma)_\perp^\Gamma$
$(clos \Downarrow)$	$a_\perp^\perp[s_\perp^\perp]_\perp^\Gamma$	$\Rightarrow a_\perp^\perp[s_\perp^\Gamma]_\perp^\Gamma$	$(comp \Leftarrow)$	$(s_\perp^\perp \circ t_{\Gamma_1}^\Gamma)_\perp^\Gamma \Rightarrow (s_\perp^{\Gamma_1} \circ t_{\Gamma_1}^\Gamma)_\perp^\Gamma$
$(clos \Leftarrow)$	$a_\perp^\perp[s_{\Gamma_1}^\Gamma]_\perp^\Gamma$	$\Rightarrow a_\perp^{\Gamma_1}[s_{\Gamma_1}^\Gamma]_\perp^\Gamma$	$(comp \Uparrow)$	$(s_{\Gamma_2}^{\Gamma_1} \circ t_{\Gamma_1}^\Gamma)_\perp^\Gamma \Rightarrow (s_{\Gamma_2}^{\Gamma_1} \circ t_{\Gamma_1}^\Gamma)_{\Gamma_2}^\Gamma$
$(clos \Uparrow)$	$a_A^{\Gamma_1}[s_{\Gamma_1}^\Gamma]_\perp^\Gamma$	$\Rightarrow a_A^{\Gamma_1}[s_{\Gamma_1}^\Gamma]_A^\Gamma$	$(comp \Uparrow)$	$(s_{\Gamma_2}^{\Gamma_1} \circ t_{\Gamma_1}^\Gamma)_\perp^\Gamma \Rightarrow (s_{\Gamma_2}^{\Gamma_1} \circ t_{\Gamma_1}^\Gamma)_{\Gamma_2}^\Gamma$
$(meta)$	$X_\perp^\Gamma$	$\Rightarrow X_A^\Gamma$	if $\Gamma = context(X)$ and $A = type(X)$	

We can see that decorating rules of this algorithm correspond to the type-checking rules of $\lambda\sigma$-calculus. For better understanding, we have attached additional symbols to the label rules: $\Downarrow$ – for a propagation of a context from top to down in a decorated term, $\Uparrow$ for a propagation of a type from down to up and $\Leftarrow$ for a propagation a type or a context on the same level of the decorated term. This algorithm can be efficiently implemented with linear complexity on the size of the input decorated term.

3 Higher-order unification in $\lambda\sigma$-calculus

A computation of the higher-order unification algorithm presented in [DHK95] uses the notion of η-long normal form [Río93]. In this section, we define a *weak η-long normal form*, which combines two important features of *weak head normal form* [ACCL90] and *η-long normal form* [DHK95][5]. Then, we will be able to present an improved version of the higher-order unification algorithm, which simplifies an equational system on decorated $\lambda\sigma$-terms in weak η-long normal form to its solved form. For better understanding of what we are going to do, we recall these definitions.

Definition 2 Let a be a term of type $A_1 \to A_2 \to \ldots \to A_n \to B$, in the context Γ in $\lambda\sigma$-normal form. The *η-long normal* form, written $\eta lnf[a]$, is defined by:

- if $a = \lambda A_1.b$ then $\eta lnf[a] = \lambda A_1.\eta lnf[b]$,
- else if $a = (\ldots(m\ b_1)\ \ldots\ b_p)$ and $c_i = \eta lnf[b_i[\uparrow^n]]$ then
  $\eta lnf[a] = \lambda A_1.\cdots.\lambda A_n.(\ldots((\ldots(m+n\ c_1)\ldots c_p)\ n)\ldots 1)$,
- else if $a = (\ldots(X[s]\ b_1)\ \ldots\ b_p)$ and $c_i = \eta lnf[b_i[\uparrow^n]]$, $s = d_1.\ \cdots\ .d_q.\uparrow^k$
  then $\eta lnf[a] = \lambda A_1.\cdots.\lambda A_n.(\ldots(X[t]\ c_1)\ldots c_p)\ n)\ldots 1)$,
  where $t = e_1.\ \cdots\ .e_q.\uparrow^{k+n}$ and $e_i = \eta lnf[d_i[\uparrow^n]]$.

---

[5] The efficient computation of weak η-long normal form is illustrated in [Bor95]

Definition 3 The *weak head normal form*[6] of a $\lambda\sigma$-term, written $whnf[a]$, is:

- $(\ldots((n\ a_1)\ a_2)\ \ldots\ a_p)$, where $n > 0$ and $p \geq 0$,
- $(\ldots((X[s]\ a_1)\ a_2)\ \ldots\ a_p)$, where $p \geq 0$,
- $(\lambda\ A.a)[s]$.

Definition 4 Let a be a $\lambda\sigma$-term of type $A \to B$ in the context Γ in weak head normal form. The *weak η-long normal form* of a, written $w\eta lnf[a]$, is defined by:

- if $a = (\lambda\ A.b)[s]$ then $w\eta lnf[a] = a$,
- else if $a = (\ldots(n\ a_1)\ \ldots\ a_p)$ then $w\eta lnf[a] = \lambda A.((n{+}1\ a_1[\uparrow])\ \ldots\ a_p[\uparrow])\ 1)$,
- else $a = (\ldots(X[s]\ a_1)\ \ldots\ a_p)$ then $w\eta lnf[a] = \lambda A.((X[s{\circ}\uparrow]\ a_1[\uparrow])\ \ldots\ a_p[\uparrow])\ 1)$

If a is of an atomic type, then $w\eta lnf[a] = a$.

The higher-order unification algorithm presented in [DHK95] works on equational systems, which consist of a disjunction of existentially quantified conjunctions. Each conjunct is an equation of two $\lambda\sigma$-terms, which are eagerly normalised by this unification algorithm into a η-normal form. The main reason for this is the fact that the symbol λ is a constructor, i.e. a $\lambda\sigma$-term $\lambda\ A.a$ can be reduced (unified) only to (with) some term of the form $\lambda\ A.b$. The second constructor is a $\lambda\sigma$-term of the form $(\ldots(n\ a_1)\ \ldots\ a_p)$, because it is also unifiable only with a $\lambda\sigma$-term of the form $(\ldots(m\ b_1)\ \ldots\ b_r)$, where $n = m$, $p = r$ and the system $\bigwedge_{i=1}^{p} a_i = b_i$ is unifiable.

The main idea of our improvements is the following:

We compute the weak η-long normal form, and only when it is necessary. We have removed the normalisation rule from the original algorithm, and instead of this, we normalise the equational system only when something has been changed. We do not compute η-long normal form deeply, i.e. do not compute η-long normal forms for the sub-terms b_i, c_i and the substitution s. The computation of their η-long normal forms can be postponed until they become of the top of the term.

Using the notion of weak η-long normal form we can also (slightly) improve a replacement, which is the crucial operation in the higher-order unification algorithm. The problem is to replace a variable X by a term a in a term b, where both a and b are in weak η-long normal form, and obtain a term $\{X \mapsto a\}b$ in weak η-long normal form. A case, in which we can perform replacement without the re-computation of weak and η-long normal forms, is the following:

if $b = (\ldots(c[s]\ a_1)\ \ldots\ a_p)$ and $X \notin c$ then $\{X \mapsto a\}b = (\ldots(c[t]\ b_1)\ \ldots\ b_p)$ where $t := \{X \mapsto a\}s$ and $b_i := \{X \mapsto a\}a_i$

Unification rules: In this subsection, we present a modified set of rules for higher-order unification. These rules simplify a system of equations of decorated $\lambda\sigma$-terms in weak η-long normal form[7]. Therefore, after the transformation of the

---

[6] The weak head normal form can be efficiently computed by Krivine's weak head normalisation machine [ACCL90].

[7] This system of transformation rules is presented in 'non-decorated' version (just for improving readability), however its decorated version is implemented

initial problem from λ-calculus into $\lambda\sigma$-calculus, we have to normalise our initial equation to its weak η-long normal form. Then, we can apply the following set of rules until we obtain a solved form of this system. The variables P and P' represent conjunctions of equations. The notation (a data structure). $\langle a, s, b_1 \ldots b_p \rangle$ that we will use in the description of unification rules, encodes the $\lambda\sigma$-term $(\ldots(a[s]\ b_1)\cdots b_p)$. Using this notation we can encode all kinds of $\lambda\sigma$-terms in weak η-long normal form: $\langle(\lambda A.a), s, \epsilon\rangle, \langle n, id, b_1 \ldots b_p\rangle$ and $\langle X, s, b_1 \ldots b_p\rangle$. Rules are enumerated (for the referencing in the subsequent example). The unification strategy for the application these rules is the same as in [DHK95].

$(1.dec - \lambda)$ $P \wedge \langle(\lambda\ A.a), s, \epsilon\rangle = \langle(\lambda\ A.b), t, \epsilon\rangle \Rightarrow$

$\qquad P \wedge w\eta lnf[whnf[\langle a, (1.(s \circ \uparrow)), \epsilon\rangle]] = w\eta lnf[whnf[\langle b, (1.(t \circ \uparrow)), \epsilon\rangle]]$

$(2.decapp_1)$ $P \wedge \langle n, id, a_1 \ldots a_p\rangle = \langle n, id, b_1 \ldots b_p\rangle \Rightarrow$

$\qquad P \wedge \bigwedge_{i=1}^{p} w\eta lnf[whnf[\langle a_i, id, \epsilon\rangle]] = w\eta lnf[whnf[\langle b_i, id, \epsilon\rangle]]$

$(3.decapp_2)$ $P \wedge \langle n, id, a_1 \ldots a_p\rangle = \langle m, id, b_1 \ldots b_p\rangle \Rightarrow fail \qquad if \quad n \neq m$

$(4.replace)$ $P \wedge \langle X, id, \epsilon\rangle = \langle a, s, b_1 \ldots b_p\rangle \Rightarrow P' \wedge \langle X, id, \epsilon\rangle = \langle a, s, b_1 \ldots b_p\rangle$

$\qquad where\ P' := \{X \mapsto a\}P, X \in \mathcal{T}Var(P)\ and\ X \notin \mathcal{T}Var(a),\ and$

$\qquad if\ a \in \mathcal{X}\ then\ a \in \mathcal{T}Var(P)$

$(5.exp - \lambda)$ $P \Rightarrow P \wedge \langle X, id, \epsilon\rangle = \langle(\lambda\ A.Y), id, \epsilon\rangle$

$\qquad if\ X \in P, Y \notin P,\ X\ is\ not\ solved\ and\ type(X) = A \to B\ then$

$\qquad type(Y) := B\ and\ context(Y) := A.context(X)$

$(6.expapp)$ $P \wedge \langle X, s, \epsilon\rangle = \langle m, id, b_1 \ldots b_p\rangle \Rightarrow P \wedge \langle X, s, \epsilon\rangle = \langle m, id, b_1 \ldots b_p\rangle \wedge$

$\qquad \left(\bigvee_{r \in \{1, \ldots, p\} \cup R} \langle X,\ id, \epsilon\rangle = (\ldots (r\ H_{1,r}) \ldots H_{k,r}) \right),$

$\qquad where\ a_1 \cdots a_p . \uparrow^n\ is\ the\ \lambda\sigma - normal\ form\ of\ s,$

$\qquad R := if\ m \geq n + 1\ then\ \{m - n + p\}\ else\ \emptyset,$

$\qquad C_r = B_{1,r} \to \ldots \to B_{k,r} \to A = r - th\ type\ of\ the\ context(X),$

$\qquad and\ H_{i,r}\ are\ new\ distict\ variables\ not\ occuring\ in\ P,$

$\qquad such\ that\ context(H_{i,r}) := context(X)\ and\ type(H_{i,r}) := B_{i,r}$

Small example:
We would like to finish with a very small example of a problem solved by this unification. Let us start with an equation: $(X\ (f\ a)) = (f\ (X\ a))$, where signatures of symbols are defined $f : A \to A, X : A \to A$ and $a : A$. This problem translated into decorated $\lambda\sigma$-calculus with de Bruijn notation looks like:

$(X_{A \to A}^{A \to A.A} (1_{A \to A}^{A \to A.A}\ 2_A^{A \to A.A})_A^{A \to A.A}) = (1_{A \to A}^{A \to A.A} (X_{A \to A}^{A \to A.A}\ 2_A^{A \to A.A})_A^{A \to A.A}).$

Our algorithm starts with an equation $\langle X, id, (1\ 2)\rangle = \langle 1, id, (X\ 2)\rangle$. Using $exp - \lambda$ rule we obtain $\langle X, id, (1\ 2)\rangle = \langle 1, id, (X\ 2)\rangle \wedge \langle X, id, \epsilon\rangle = \langle(\lambda A.Y), id, \epsilon\rangle$. Then by *replace* rule $\langle Y, (1\ 2).id, \epsilon \rangle = \langle 1, id, ((\lambda A.Y)\ 2) \rangle \wedge \langle X, id, \epsilon \rangle = \langle (\lambda A.Y), id, \epsilon \rangle$. Then by *expapp* rule we obtain a disjunction of two conjunctions, and we continue with one of them: $\langle Y, (1\ 2).id, \epsilon \rangle = \langle 1, id, ((\lambda\ A.Y)\ 2) \rangle \wedge \langle X, id, \epsilon \rangle = \langle (\lambda\ A.Y), id, \epsilon \rangle \wedge \langle Y, id, \epsilon \rangle = \langle 1, id, \epsilon \rangle$ by *replace* rule and, finally, we obtain a solved form: $\langle X, id, \epsilon \rangle = \langle (\lambda\ A.1), id, \epsilon \rangle \wedge \langle Y, id, \epsilon \rangle = \langle 1, id, \epsilon \rangle$, which corresponds to the solution $(\lambda\ x.x)$.

The following table shows some of the infinite set of solutions and sequences of applications of unification rules:

$X = (\lambda\ A.(2\ (2\ (2\ 1))))$ $X = (\lambda\ x.(f\ (f\ (f\ x))))$ 5464264264264

$X = (\lambda\ A.(2\ (2\ 1)))$ $X = (\lambda\ x.(f\ (f\ x)))$ 5464264264

$X = (\lambda\ A.(2\ 1))$ $X = (\lambda\ x.(f\ x))$ 5464264

$X = (\lambda\ A.1)$ $X = (\lambda\ x.x)$ 5464

4 Conclusion

We have shown some basic ideas and improvements, which are necessary for the implementation of the higher-order unification algorithm in ELAN (more of them are in [Bor95]). We plan to continue in this approach towards an implementation of a prototype of λ-Prolog.

We have also proved that ELAN is powerful enough for prototyping such non-trivial applications. But, we think that for obtaining a more efficient version, we would have to change the implementation environment and introduce a lot of low-level optimisation tricks.

Acknowledgements

I would like to thank to Hélène and Claude Kirchner for valuable remarks and careful reading of this paper. This work has been supported by the ESPRIT basic research project, working group 6028 CCL.

References

[ACCL90] M. Abadi, L. Cardelli, P.-L. Curien, and J.-J. Lévy. Explicit substitutions. Technical Report 54, Digital Systems Research Center, February 1990.

[Bor95] P. Borovanský. Implementation of higher-order unification based on calculus of explicit substitutions. Technical report (in preparation), CRIN & INRIA-Lorraine, France, 1995.

[DHK95] Gilles Dowek, Thérèse Hardin, and Claude Kirchner. Higher-order unification via explicit substitutions, extended abstract. In Dexter Kozen, editor, *Proceedings of LICS'95*, San Diego, June. 1995.

[KKV95] Claude Kirchner, Hélène Kirchner, and M. Vittek. Designing constraint logic programming languages using computational systems. In P. Van Hentenryck and V. Saraswat, editors, *Principles and Practice of Constraint Programming. The Newport Papers.*, pages 131–158. 1995.

[Río93] A. Ríos. *Contributions à l'étude des λ-calculs avec des substitutions explicites*. PhD thesis, U. Paris VII, 1993.

A Modular History-Oriented Access Structure for Bitemporal Relational Databases

Alessandro Cappelli and Cristina De Castro and Maria Rita Scalas

C.I.O.C.–C.N.R. and Dipartimento di Elettronica, Informatica e Sistemistica
Università di Bologna, Viale Risorgimento 2, I-40136 Bologna, Italy
Tel. + 39 (51) 644.3542, Fax: +39 (51) 644.3540, E-mail: cdecastro@deis.unibo.it

Abstract. Two time dimensions are usually considered in temporal databases: *transaction-time*, which tells when an event is recorded in a database, and *valid-time*, which tells when an event occurs, occurred or is expected to occur in the real world. Transaction-time is defined by the system and can only grow, since it records the time of successive transactions. This peculiarity makes it difficult to adapt traditional access structures for non-temporal data, such as indices or grid files, since transaction-time unbalances such structures. The maintenance of access structures for temporal data can thus be very expensive, also due to the large amount of data contained in temporal relations. In this paper, we propose a variant of an index composed by as many sub-indices as the number of objects. The main feature of this structure is to localize the unbalancements and thus, whenever a sub-index needs reorganization, not to burden the whole structure.

Keywords: *Transaction-time, Valid-time, Temporal Database, History*

1   Introduction

Two distinct and independent time dimensions were defined in literature for temporal databases: *transaction-time*, which tells when an event is recorded in a database, and *valid-time*, which tells when an event occurs, occurred or is expected to occur in the real world [6, 5]. According to the temporal dimensions they support, temporal databases can be classified as *monotemporal* (transaction- or valid-time), *bitemporal* or *snapshot* [3]. Transaction-time DBs record all the versions of data inserted, deleted or updated in successive transactions (current and non current versions). Valid time DBs maintain the most recently inserted (*current*) versions of data, each relative to a distinct valid-time interval (current versions only). Bitemporal DBs support both transaction and valid-time and thus maintain all the valid-time versions recorded in successive transactions (current and non current versions). Snapshot DBs do not support time: they maintain only the most recently inserted (current) version.

In relational databases, time can be represented by the addition of the valid-time interval $\mathcal{T}_v$ (whose endpoints are FROM, TO) and the transaction-time interval $\mathcal{T}_t$ (endpoints: IN, OUT).

The definition of suitable access structures for temporal databases is quite a hard problem to solve, due at least to the following problems: first, with respect to non-temporal relations, the temporal ones store a much higher volume of data.

Second, the presence of transaction-time causes traditional access structures to evolve in a very unbalanced way, since transaction-time can only grow. Smart solutions for accessing temporal data were proposed, among which the *Time Index* for valid-time relations [1] and the *Time Split B-tree* for transaction-time relations [4]. The Time Index is based on the choice of a *totally ordered* subset of valid-time values out of the endpoints of the valid-time intervals of tuples, in order to make it possible to use a B^+-tree. The Time Split B-tree reorganizes data according to splits of the 2-dimensional space (key, IN). A split can be effected on the key or on the time.

A possible idea for the management of access structures reorganization in temporal databases can be based on the definition of a multi-level structure, composed by as many sub-indices as the number of object identifiers. Such sub-indices being independent allows to make "local" reorganization and, thus, not to involve the whole structure. This idea is at the basis of the structure we propose, which is described in Section 2.

Notation: The symbol T_{now} denotes the current value of transaction-time, the symbol T_∞ as second endpoint (OUT) of transaction-time means that the tuple has not been updated yet. FROM $= t_\infty$ in small letters refers to valid-time and means that a tuple is considered indefinitely valid.

2 Description of the Access Structure

In the following, after giving some preliminary definitions, we describe the three levels of the index and then show how the insertion of new versions is managed.

2.1 Histories and T-sections

Let us denote by *history* the collection of all the versions of the same object within a relation [2]. For instance, assuming the key EMP in Tab. 1 is a time-invariant identifier, the history of Mr. Verdi contains all and only the tuples whose key value is Verdi.

Given an object O and a transaction-time instant T^*, the *T-section* of O at time $T = T^*$ is defined as the subset of tuples in the history of O whose transaction-time intervals contain T^*. In other words, the T-section of O at time T^* contains all the valid-time versions of O *which were current at transaction-time T^**.

Note that it can be either $T^* < T_{now}$ (eg.: $T^* = 1988$) or $T^* \geq T_{now}$ (eg.: $T^* = 1995$). If $T^* \geq T_{now}$, the T*-section of O contains all and only the current versions of O along valid-time. If $T^* < T_{now}$, the T*-section of O can contain both archived and current versions of O along valid-time. As a matter of fact, a version that was current in a past transaction-time can be still current, if it has not yet been updated.

Note that, for instance, the T-section of Mr. Verdi at IN $= 1988$ contains the three tuples in Tab. 2, one of which is still current. The T-section of Mr. Verdi at IN $= 1995$ (T_{now} section) contains the four tuples in Tab. 3, which are all current.

TID	EMP	SALARY	$\mathcal{T}_v$	$\mathcal{T}_t$
1	Rossi	1000	$\{1985\ldots t_\infty\}$	$\{1985\ldots 1987\}$
2	Verdi	NULL	$\{1985\ldots 1988\}$	$\{1987\ldots T_\infty\}$
3	Verdi	1300	$\{1988\ldots t_\infty\}$	$\{1987\ldots 1988\}$
4	Rossi	1000	$\{1985\ldots 1988\}$	$\{1987\ldots T_\infty\}$
5	Rossi	NULL	$\{1988\ldots t_\infty\}$	$\{1987\ldots 1989\}$
6	Verdi	1400	$\{1988\ldots 1989\}$	$\{1988\ldots 1991\}$
7	Verdi	1500	$\{1989\ldots t_\infty\}$	$\{1988\ldots 1989\}$
8	Rossi	NULL	$\{1988\ldots 1989\}$	$\{1989\ldots T_\infty\}$
9	Rossi	1200	$\{1989\ldots 1991\}$	$\{1989\ldots 1990\}$
10	Rossi	1500	$\{1991\ldots t_\infty\}$	$\{1989\ldots 1990\}$
11	Verdi	1500	$\{1989\ldots 1991\}$	$\{1989\ldots 1991\}$
12	Verdi	1600	$\{1991\ldots t_\infty\}$	$\{1989\ldots 1991\}$
13	Rossi	1200	$\{1989\ldots 1990\}$	$\{1990\ldots T_\infty\}$
14	Rossi	1500	$\{1990..\, t_\infty\}$	$\{1990\ldots T_\infty\}$
15	Verdi	1500	$\{1988\ldots 1989\}$	$\{1995\ldots T_\infty\}$
16	Verdi	1600	$\{1989\ldots 1994\}$	$\{1995\ldots T_\infty\}$
17	Verdi	2000	$\{1994\ldots t_\infty\}$	$\{1995\ldots T_\infty\}$

Table 1. Bitemporal relation Salary

TID	EMP	SALARY	$\mathcal{T}_v$	$\mathcal{T}_t$
2	Verdi	NULL	$\{1985\ldots 1988\}$	$\{1987\ldots T_\infty\}$
6	Verdi	1400	$\{1988\ldots 1989\}$	$\{1988\ldots 1991\}$
7	Verdi	1500	$\{1989\ldots t_\infty\}$	$\{1988\ldots 1989\}$

Table 2. T-section at IN = 1988 of Mr. Verdi

TID	EMP	SALARY	$\mathcal{T}_v$	$\mathcal{T}_t$
2	Verdi	NULL	$\{1985\ldots 1988\}$	$\{1987\ldots T_\infty\}$
15	Verdi	1500	$\{1988\ldots 1989\}$	$\{1995\ldots T_\infty\}$
16	Verdi	1600	$\{1989\ldots 1994\}$	$\{1995\ldots T_\infty\}$
17	Verdi	2000	$\{1994\ldots t_\infty\}$	$\{1995\ldots T_\infty\}$

Table 3. T-section at IN = 1995 of Mr. Verdi

2.2 Description of the Three-Level Temporal Index

The logical structure of the index is shown in Fig. 1 and is organized in three distinct levels. The first level is a traditional index on the object identifier OID. For the sake of simplicity, only two objects, Mr. Rossi and Mr. Verdi, are considered. The second level contains as many sub-indices as the number of object identifiers. Each of them is a traditional index on the registration time IN and is separate and independent of the others. In the example, the second level contains two sub-indices, one for Mr.Rossi and one for Mr. Verdi. Each value IN $= T^*$ in a sub-index of the second level addresses a cluster in the third level. Such cluster is composed by pairs of the type (TID, $\mathcal{T}_v$). The pairs in each cluster identify the tuples of the T-section of the OID at time IN $= T^*$. For instance, the value IN = 1988 in the sub-index of Mr. Verdi, addresses a cluster whose pairs contain the set of TIDS $\{2, 6, 7\}$. Such TIDS are the tuple identifiers of the T-section of Mr. Verdi at IN = 1988 (cfr. Tab. 2). In the same sub-index, the value IN = 1995 addresses a cluster whose pairs contain the TIDS $\{2, 15, 16, 17\}$, which identify the T_{now}-section of Mr. Verdi (cfr. Tab. 3).

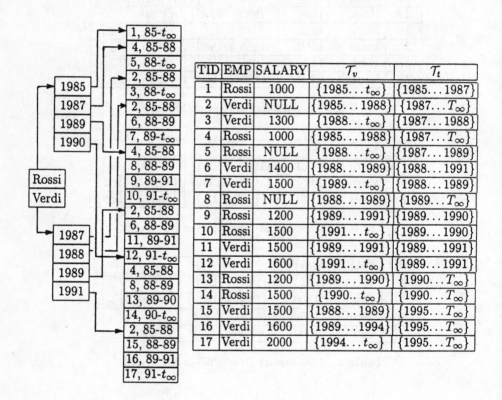

TID	EMP	SALARY	$\mathcal{T}_v$	$\mathcal{T}_t$
1	Rossi	1000	$\{1985\ldots t_\infty\}$	$\{1985\ldots 1987\}$
2	Verdi	NULL	$\{1985\ldots 1988\}$	$\{1987\ldots T_\infty\}$
3	Verdi	1300	$\{1988\ldots t_\infty\}$	$\{1987\ldots 1988\}$
4	Rossi	1000	$\{1985\ldots 1988\}$	$\{1987\ldots T_\infty\}$
5	Rossi	NULL	$\{1988\ldots t_\infty\}$	$\{1987\ldots 1989\}$
6	Verdi	1400	$\{1988\ldots 1989\}$	$\{1988\ldots 1991\}$
7	Verdi	1500	$\{1989\ldots t_\infty\}$	$\{1988\ldots 1989\}$
8	Rossi	NULL	$\{1988\ldots 1989\}$	$\{1989\ldots T_\infty\}$
9	Rossi	1200	$\{1989\ldots 1991\}$	$\{1989\ldots 1990\}$
10	Rossi	1500	$\{1991\ldots t_\infty\}$	$\{1989\ldots 1990\}$
11	Verdi	1500	$\{1989\ldots 1991\}$	$\{1989\ldots 1991\}$
12	Verdi	1600	$\{1991\ldots t_\infty\}$	$\{1989\ldots 1991\}$
13	Rossi	1200	$\{1989\ldots 1990\}$	$\{1990\ldots T_\infty\}$
14	Rossi	1500	$\{1990.. t_\infty\}$	$\{1990\ldots T_\infty\}$
15	Verdi	1500	$\{1988\ldots 1989\}$	$\{1995\ldots T_\infty\}$
16	Verdi	1600	$\{1989\ldots 1994\}$	$\{1995\ldots T_\infty\}$
17	Verdi	2000	$\{1994\ldots t_\infty\}$	$\{1995\ldots T_\infty\}$

Fig. 1. Three Level Temporal Index

2.3 Duplication in the Index

As follows from the observations in Section 2.1, a T-section with $T = T^*$ addressed by a value in a sub-index of the second level can contain both versions inserted at $IN = T^*$ and versions inserted before and still current. Therefere, whenever a new cluster is created in the third level, not only must it contain all the pairs of the new versions, but also a copy of the pairs of still current versions. For instance, the tuple $(2, \text{Verdi}, \text{NULL}, \{1985 \ldots 1988\}, \{1987 \ldots T_\infty\})$ was recorded in 1987 and never updated, so the pair $(2, 85\text{-}88)$ is contained in all the four clusters addressed by the second-level sub-index of Mr. Verdi. The tuple $(6, \text{Verdi}, 1400, \{1988 \ldots 1989\}, \{1988 \ldots 1991\})$ was recorded in 1988 and updated in 1991. The second-level sub-index of Mr. Verdi contains the IN values $\{1987, 1988, 1989, 1991\}$, so the tuple belongs to the two T-sections defined by $IN = 1988$ and $IN = 1989$. Thus there are two copies of the pair $(6, 88\text{-}89)$, one in its "original" cluster, addressed by $IN = 1988$ and one in the cluster addressed by $IN = 1989$.

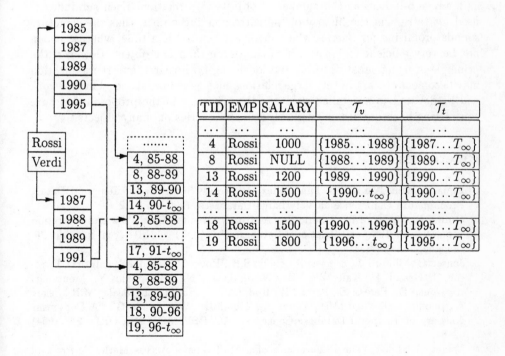

Fig. 2. Index Update

2.4 Index Update

Suppose that at $T_{now} = 1995$, a new transaction records that Mr.Rossi will earn 1800 from 1996 on. As a consequence, tuple 14 Tab. 1 is archived by setting to 1995 the second endpoint of its transaction-time pertinence; the portion with validity $\{1990\ldots1996\}$ of such tuple is restored and the new data recorded, by appending the two following tuples to Tab. 1: $(18, Rossi, 1500, \{1990\ldots1996\}, \{1995\ldots T_\infty\})$ and $(18, Rossi, 1800, \{1996\ldots t_\infty\}, \{1995\ldots T_\infty\})$. The index is updated as shown in Fig. 2: the new IN value is recorded in the second-level sub-index of Mr. Rossi and such value addresses a new cluster. In this case, all the pairs of the previous cluster must be duplicated, but $(14, 90\text{-}t_\infty)$, since the corresponding tuples have not been archived and two new pairs are also included. For the sake of simplicity, in Fig. 2 only the portion of interest is reported.

3 Conclusions

In this paper we proposed an index for bitemporal data which is composed by as many sub-indices as the number of objects in a relation. Each sub-index is used for retrieving the history of the corresponding object, thus the structure sounds promising for queries which involve a history at a time, whereas it can not be very efficient for queries involving more than one object. However, the principle of using substructrures and localizing both search and reorganization may become necessary in very large relations such as temporal ones. Further work will be devoted to a detailed study on the efficiency of the proposed structure considering both queries on single objects and queries on many objects.

References

1. Elmasri, Wuu, Kim: "The Time Index: An Access Structure for Temporal Data", Proc. of 16th Conference on Very Large Databases, 1990, pp 1–12.
2. Grandi F., Scalas M.R., Tiberio P., "A History Oriented Data View and Operation Semantics for Temporal Relational Databases," C.I.O.C.–C.N.R. Tech. Rep. No. 76, Bologna, Jan. 1991.
3. Jensen C., Clifford J., Elmasri R., Gadia S.K., Hayes P., Jajodia S. (editors), Dyreson C., Grandi F., Kafer W., Kline N., Lorentzos N., Mitsopoulos Y., Montanari A., Nonen D., Peressi E., Pernici B., Roddick J.F., Sarda N.L., Scalas M.R., Segev A., Snodgrass R., Soo M.D., Tansel A., Tiberio P., Wiederhold G.: "A Consensus Glossary of Temporal Database Concepts", ACM SIGMOD RECORD, **23** (1994) 52–64.
4. Lomet, Salzberg: "The Performance of a Multiversion Access Method", Proc. of ACM SIGMOD Conf. on the Management of Data, 1990, pp 353–363.
5. Tansel A., Clifford J., Gadia V., Jajodia S., Segev A., Snodgrass R.T. (eds.), *Temporal Databases: Theory, Design and Implementation*, The Benjamin/Cummings Publishing Company, Redwood City, 1993.
6. Soo M., "Bibliography on Temporal Databases", ACM SIGMOD Record, **20**, No. 1, Mar. 1991, pp 14–23.

Software Engineering meets Human-Computer Interaction: Integrating User Interface Design in an Object-Oriented Methodology

Hans-W. Gellersen

University of Karlsruhe, Telecooperation Office,
Vincenz-Prießnitz-Str. 1, 76131 Karlsruhe, Germany,
Ph. [+49] (721) 6902-49, hwg@teco.uni-karlsruhe.de

Abstract. User interface design is a complex task within the development of interactive software, and not sufficiently supported in general software development. We present MEMFIS, a method laid out for development of software with non-trivial human-computer interaction. MEMFIS integrates structured user interface design into the object-oriented methodology OMT, defining three phases: *analysis* for modeling of problem domain and conceptual user interface; *interaction design* for modeling of user interface artifacts in abstraction of software concepts; and *software design* for mapping problem domain model and user interface model to software concepts.

1   Introduction

With the advent of graphical interaction a decade ago design of the interactive parts of an application became a complex problem no longer solvable by an application developer's intuition. Rapid advances in interaction technologies (multimedia, multimodality) and an increased demand for highly customized user interfaces (for different user communities and usage environments) add to the complexity. In recognition of this problem, the field of human-computer interaction (HCI) investigates methods for systematic user interface design. Alas, as to yet the adoption of HCI methods into general software design is minimal.

In this paper we present MEMFIS[1], a method for development of interactive software currently covering the life cycle from analysis to software design. MEMFIS is firmly based on object-oriented software engineering but tightly integrates explicit support for design of the interactive parts of a software system. MEMFIS is a general methodology for design of systems that include non-trivial human-computer interaction. The major goals underlying the development of MEMFIS are:

- Maximizing use of an established software engineering methodology rather than defining a new method from scratch. This supports reuse of available experience and increases acceptability of the approach in the software engineering community.

- General user interface design support independent of particular interaction technologies, aiming at protection of investment in view of technological advances.

- Support of abstractions in user interface design to increase flexibility and reusability, based on the assumption that interactive applications increasingly will have to be developed for heterogeneous interaction platforms (e.g. in adaptation to available technologies or special needs of individual users).

---

1. *Methodology for Engineering Multimodal Flexible Interactive Software*

2 Related Work

Several process models have been proposed for interactive software. Mayhew, for example, decomposes each phase of the traditional software life cycle into user interface related activities and general development activities, thereby defining two largely independent processes [6]. She specifies temporal constraints among activities but does not specify how activities of the two processes are linked. Similarly, Bass/Coutaz describe a separate process for user interface design carried out in parallel to the design of the so-called application core. Most notably, their user interface design process covers only the analysis and design phases in the traditional life cycle, based on the assumption that later life cycle phases do not differ for user interface software and other software [1][2]. Again, links between the two design processes are not defined by Bass/Coutaz. A more elaborate description of an integrated process model was described by Hix/Hartson [5]. Although admitting that the user interface domain and application domain cannot be separated cleanly, they still suggest a development process consisting of separate tracks for each domain (fig. 1). Note, that in Hix/Hartson's model the user interface development process contains an additional phase between analysis and software design. This is to separate specification of interaction concepts from specification of software concepts. The separation of development processes found in all these approaches forms is also reflected in the proposed IFIP reference model for interactive software engineering environments [2].

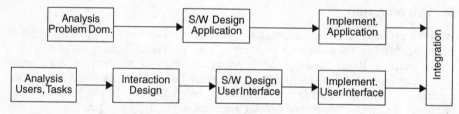

Fig. 1. Process model for development of interactive software[3]

Apart from integrated process models, work on integration of user interface design with object-oriented analysis has been reported (e.g. [3]). In general, these approaches aim at deriving standardized user interface designs from application data models. These approaches are bound to particular technologies (currently, graphical user interfaces) and do not provide general support for user interface design. The same accounts for the many model-based user interface management systems (UIMS) which also fail to integrate with established software engineering methodologies.

3 MEMFIS: A Methodology for Design of Interactive Software

3.1 General Concepts

Object-orientation. Over the last years, a number of object-oriented methods (OOM) have evolved in software engineering. In particular with respect to interactive software, OOM have a number of virtues. First, object-oriented analysis models concepts

---

2. We do not fully agree, e.g. the test phases would differ, but currently support the same phases as Bass/Coutaz.

3. For sake of simplicity, recurrent links have been omitted in figures 1 and 2. By no means we want to imply non-iterative development!

of the problem domain in a software-independent way. Such a specification is suitable as conceptual model for user interface design. Secondly, object-orientation supports abstraction by means of generalization and reuse of abstractions by means of inheritance. These features are particularly useful for support of abstractions in user interface design, one of the key goals of MEMFIS. Thirdly, OOM are characterized by a seamless development process. This eases iteration over development phases, a feature particularly important for user interface design, as user interface related decisions are very susceptible to potential changes.

Separation of conceptual/functional interface and interaction modalities. We advocate strict separation of the conceptual and functional interface model from interaction modalities. The conceptual/functional interface model captures all interaction decisions driven by the application logic, describing *what* a user can do with an interactive system. This description has to comprise all application concepts the end user needs to know about and all functions exported to the end user, fully specified with their parameters and pre- and postconditions. On the other hand it should not contain any decisions that depend on any interaction technology and define an interaction modality. An interaction modality defines *how* the user can interact with an interactive system. The same conceptual/functional interface can be realized using different interaction modalities[4].

Separation of interaction design and design of user interface software. Interaction design is concerned with specification of interaction objects and dialog control to meet the requirements of a conceptual/functional interface model. User interface software design is based on interaction design and concerned with software concepts for realization of an interaction design. In state-of-the-art design of interactive system, interaction design decisions and software design decisions are usually coupled, which leads to interaction designs driven by software concerns rather than human factors concerns.

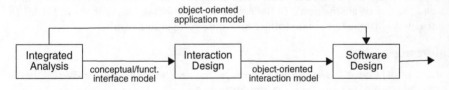

Fig. 2. MEMFIS phase model

3.2 Phase Model

MEMFIS structures design of interactive software into three phases. The integrated analysis phase and the software design phase are based on analysis and design phases of OMT (Object Modeling Technique [7]), which we found to be the most suited among currently available OOM. The interaction design phase has been included to encapsulate all decisions related to interaction modality. With respect to the interactive parts of a system, analysis captures *what a user can do*, interaction design *how it should be done*, and software design *how it should be implemented*.

Analysis in OMT comprises object modeling, dynamic modeling and functional mode-

---

4. Note the difference between interaction modes and interaction modalities: in a system with multiple modes, the same interaction can yield different results. In a systems with multiple modalities, different interactions can yield the same result.

ling. In MEMFIS, we have added task modeling to drive functional modeling, an HCI technique for ensuring task-oriented functionality in an interactive system. The task model is also used to capture temporal constraints for dialog control, and for identification of required data and control flow between user and system. The MEMFIS analysis yields to specifications: an application model for software design consisting of the three OMT models, and a conceptual/functional interface model for interaction design. This model can be derived partly from the OMT models (thereby ensuring consistency) and partly from the additional task model. In interaction design, interaction objects and dialog control are specified to meet the requirements of the conceptual/functional model. The design methodology is based on a set of generic technology-independent interaction objects which are refined step by step into concrete interaction objects. This approach aims at increased reusability and flexibility [4]. The resulting interaction model together with the OMT models form the external design of an interactive system. In the software design phase, the external design has to be mapped to software concepts, yielding an internal design. MEMFIS provides a generic architecture, reusable components and a mapping method for this phase.

4 Conclusion

MEMFIS gives user interface design a clearly defined place in software design. Moreover, user interface related decisions are cleanly structured into technology-dependent and technology-independent phases. The whole approach makes maximal use of an established and successful OOM. As to yet, MEMFIS has only been evaluated in a lab environment, where the methodology was applied to several smaller applications. The methodology proved to be easy to learn for persons familiar with OOM. The integration of task analysis in object-oriented analysis was found to be a major improvement for determination of software functionality. The designs yielded were found to be easier to adapt to different interaction technologies as designs of interactive software developed with plain OMT, due to effective encapsulation of interaction related decisions and the use of abstractions. In the next evaluation phase, we will apply MEMFIS to a real-world project to obtain further and more comparable results.

References

1. Bass, L. and Coutaz, J. *Developing Software for the User Interface*, Addison-Wesley, 1991.
2. Bass, L., Cockton, G. and Unger, C. IFIP Working Group 2.7 User Interface Engineering: A Reference Model for Interactive System Construction. In Larson, J. and Unger, C. (Eds.), Proc. of the IFIP TC 2/WG 2.7 Working Conference, Ellivuori, Finland, Aug 10-14, 1992, North-Holland, p. 1-12.
3. Beck, A., Janssen, C., Weisbecker, A. and Ziegler, J. Integrating Object-Oriented Analysis and Graphical User Interface Design. In *R. Taylor, J. Coutaz (Eds.): Software Engineering and Human-Computer Interaction*, LNCS 896, Springer-Verlag, 1995, p. 127-140.
4. Gellersen, H.-W. Toward Engineering for Multimodal Interactive Systems. In *Proc. of First International Workshop on Intelligence and Multimodality in Multimedia Interfaces (IMMI-1)*, Edinburgh, July 13-14, 1995.
5. Hix, D. and Hartson, R. *Developing User Interfaces. Ensuring Usability Through Product & Process*. Wiley, 1993.
6. Mayhew, D. *Principles and Guidelines in Software User Interface Design*, Prentice Hall, 1992.
7. Rumbaugh, J., Blaha, M., Premerlani, W., Eddy, F. and Lorensen, W. Object-Oriented Modeling and Design, Prentice-Hall, 1991.

Parsing of Free-word-order Languages [*]

Tomáš Holan[1], Vladislav Kuboň[2], Martin Plátek[3]

[1] Department of Software and Computer Science Education
[2] Institute of Formal and Applied Linguistics
[3] Department of Theoretical Computer Science
Faculty of Mathematics and Physics
Charles University, Prague
Czech Republic
holan@ksvi.ms.mff.cuni.cz
vk@ufal.ms.mff.cuni.cz
platek@kki.ms.mff.cuni.cz

Abstract. This paper introduces a new type of grammars, suitable for parsing of free-word-order (natural) languages. It shows CYK-like algorithms based on such grammars for parsing and introduces a natural restriction on it, to achieve an essential speed-up, and a more adequad parsing for natural languages.

1 Introduction

There is still absence of tools describing adequatelly syntax of free-word-order (natural) languages in the literature. The CF grammars can not describe some typical constructions in Czech, containing relations between non-neighbouring symbols. In the framework of the dependency theory these constructions are called non-projective constructions. We introduce a class of formal grammars capable to describe these syntactic constructions in a dependencies-stressed shape.

2 Definition of NCFDG

Definition 1. Non-projective context-free dependency grammar (NCFDG) *is a quadruple*
(N, T, S, P), *where* N, T *are sets of nonterminals and terminals,* $S \in N$ *is a starting symbol and* P *is a set of rewriting rules of the form* $A \to_L BC$ *or* $A \to_R BC$, $A \in N$, $B, C \in V$ *where* $V = N \cup T$.
   The relation of immediate derivation $\Rightarrow$ *is defined as:*
   $rAst \Rightarrow rBsCt$, *if* $(A \to_L BC) \in P$
   $rsAt \Rightarrow rBsCt$, *if* $(A \to_R BC) \in P$,

[*] The work on this paper is a part of the joint research project PECO 2824 "Language Technologies for Slavic Languages" supported by EC and of the project "Automatic checking of grammatical errors in Czech" supported by a grant of the Grant Agency of the Czech Republic No.0475/94.

where

$$A \in N, B, C \in V, r, s, t \in V^*$$

The relation of derivation is the transitive and reflexive closure of the relation $\Rightarrow$.

NCFD grammar G *defines language* $L(G)$ *as a set of all words* $t \in T^*$ *that can be derived from the starting symbol* S. *We say that* $L(G)$ *is recognized (generated) by* G.

Remark 2. *We can impose certain limitations on the defined language by minor changes of the definition of the relation* $\Rightarrow$. *For example, the condition* $s = EmptyString$ *reduces the relation* $\Rightarrow$ *to derivation without nonprojectivities — i.e. the same as in the standard CFGs.*

Remark 3. *If we allow to specify that conditions for each rule individually, as limitations of usability, we obtain class of grammars with improved generative power.*

Definition 4. *A Tree of a word* $a_1 a_2 \ldots a_n \in T^*$ *dominated by the symbol* $X \in V$, *created by NCFDG* G *is a binary branching tree* Tr *fullfilling the following conditions*

a) *a node of* Tr *is a triad* $[A, i, j]$, *where* $A \in V$ *and* $i, j \in 1 \ldots = n$. *The number* i *is the horizontal index of the node and* j *is the vertical index.*
b) *a node* $[A, i, m]$ *of* Tr *has daughters* $[B, j, p]$, $[C, k, r]$ *only if*
   1) $j < k$, $m = p + 1$, $j = i$ *and* $(A \rightarrow_L BC) \in P$ *or*
   2) $j < k$, $m = r + 1$, $k = i$ *and* $(A \rightarrow_R BC) \in P$
c) *a root of* Tr *is such a node of* Tr *which has no mother.*
   We can see that the root has a form $[X, i, m]$ *for some* $i, m \in 1 \ldots n$.
d) *leaves of* Tr *are exactly all nodes* $[a_i, i, 1], i \in 1 \ldots n$.

Remark 5. *For the sake of simplicity we are going to use in the following text the simple term* $Tree$ *instead of the term* $Tree$ *dominated by the symbol* S *(where* S *is a starting symbol).*

There are two differences between $Tree$ and a standard parsing (derivation) tree of CFG. The first one is that a (complete) subtree of $Tree$ may cover non-continuous subset of the input sentence. Second difference is that $Trees$ contain enough information for building dependency trees. The basic type of the output of our parser is the dependency tree. Some constraints for our grammar-checker are introduced with the help of trees.

Definition 6. *Let* Tr *be a Tree of a word* $a_1 a_2 \ldots a_n \in T^*$ *created by a NCFDG* G. *The* dependency tree $Dep(Tr)$ *to* Tr *is defined as follows: The set of nodes of* $Dep(Tr)$ *is the set*

$$\{[a, i]; \text{ there is a leaf of } Tr \text{ of the form } [a, i, 1]\}.$$

The set of edges of Dep(Tr) is the set of pairs

$$([a,i],[b,j]),$$

so that $[a,i,1]$, $[b,j,1]$ *are two differrent leaves of Tr and there is an edge* $([A,i,p],[B,j,r])$ *of Tr for some* A,B,p,r.

Observation 7. *The language*

$L = \{w \in (a,b,c)^+; \text{the number of the symbols } a,b,c \text{ contained in } w \text{ is equal}\}$

may be recognized by a NCFDG G_1 *and is not context-free.* $G_1 = (N,T,S,P)$, $T = \{a,b,c\}$, $N = \{T,S\}$, $P = \{S \to_L aT|Ta|SS, T \to_L bc|cb\}$

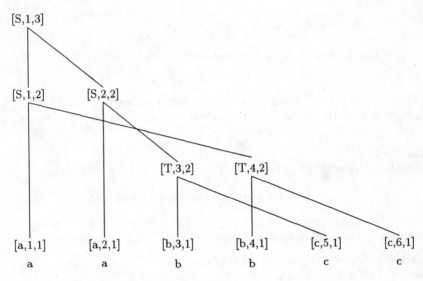

Fig. 1. A tree generated by the grammar G_1

3 Parsing Algorithms

The task of parsing is to compute for given words $a_1 a_2 \ldots a_n$ all *Trees* constructed according to a given NCFDG G.

The algorithm described in the following paragraph is based on a similar process of construction of items as for the Cocke–Younger–Kasami (CYK) algorithm (see [5]). The items are represented by six-tuples containing enough information necessary for both the reconstruction of the parsing process and for the creation of *Tree* (or dependency tree) representing the structure of the parsed sentence.

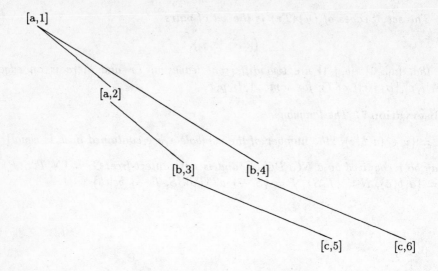

382

Fig. 2. Dependency tree corresponding to the tree from Fig 1.

The decision which information will be taken into account by the algorithm is then influenced by the fact whether we are trying to do only the recognition or a full parsing of a particular sentence.

Algorithm 1 (parsing). This algorithm works with a list D of items

$$D_i = [symbol, position, coverage, ls, rs, rule]$$

where every item corresponds to a root of some $Tree$ of a word $a_{i_1} a_{i_2} \ldots a_{i_m}$ dominated by the symbol $symbol$, where $\{i_1, i_2, \ldots, i_m\} = coverage$.

$symbol$ represents the root symbol of the $Tree$
$position$ is its horizontal index,
$coverage$ represents the set of horizontal indices of its leaves (yield),
ls, rs are indices of items D_{ls}, D_{rs} coreponding to the left and right daughter of the root of the $Tree$
$rule$ means the serial number of the rule according to which the item was created.

The basic idea of the algorithm is to repeatedly add new items to the list as long as possible.

The list D is initialized so that for each word a_i (the word from the input sentence) we create an item

$$[a_i, i, \{i\}, 0, 0, 0]$$

Let $|D|$ be the leghth of the list D, $D[i]$ denotes the i-th item of D.
The derivation is then performed by gradual comparison of all pairs i, j, $1 <= i, j <= |D|$ and by investigating whether it would be possible to apply

some rule $A \to_X BC$ (x is either L or R), which would derive the left-hand side from the right-hand side. If this is possible, a new item is created, which inherits the position either from $D[i]$ or from $D[j]$, according to whether X was L or R. The new coverage is a union of both coverages.

Two items may create a third one only if their coverages are disjoint. The difference between this algorithm and CYK is in the way how the coverage is handled by both algorithms. In CYK, the coverage is a continuous interval from-to and since the new, derived item also has to have a continuous coverage, the rule is applied only in case that j's "from" follows i's "to".

Our approach, which allows to deal with non-projective constructions, replaces this constraint by the constraint on the disjointness of both coverages. The coverage of the result is the same in both cases — the union of original individual coverages.

Algorithm 2 (recognition). This algorithm is the same as Algorithm 1 with only one difference: the adding of a derivated item to the list D is limited only to those cases, in which D does not yet contain an item equal to the new item in the fields $[symbol, -, coverage, -, -, -, -]$.

Upper estimation of the complexity of both parsing and recognition by Algorithm 1 according to a general NCFDG is exponential. That leads us to the following restriction.

3.1   One Gap

The algorithm described above has, despite of its similarity to CYK, greater computational complexity because it is extended to non-projective constructions. We introduce a constraint which may be imposed on non-projectivity and therefore may improve the complexity of the algorithm.

We say that a relation $\Rightarrow$ is *derivation with one gap* if for every item *Item* derived by $\Rightarrow$ there are some

$$i, j, k, l \in 1 \ldots n, i \leq i \leq j \leq k \leq l \leq n$$

so that

$$Item.coverage = \{i \ldots j\} \cup \{k \ldots l\}$$

The recognition with one gap is polynomial in the length of the sentence both with respect to time and space complexity. The complexity to the size of the grammar is polynomial, too. Moreover from our observations follows that the parsing with one gap is much more adequate for Czeck than the general one.

In our grammar-checker of Czech we implemented the recognition/parsing with one gap (see [6]).

Upper bound for complexity of parsing with one gap theoretically still remains exponential because the number of *Trees* can be exponential.

This leads to the idea to divide parsing into two parts. First part counts items by the algorithm for recognition with one gap. Next part takes the items from the first task and repeatedly in every step gives one new *Tree* (dependency tree).

We can see, that the upper bound for the time and space complexity of the first part (recognition with one gap) is polynomial, and the complexity of every step of the second task is also polynomial.

4 Conclusion

It can be imposed some further restriction on the algorithm to be improved the computational complexity, and the adequatness of the natural language parsing. A promising one seems to be the restriction on the size of the 'one gap'. The effort to formulate some adequat general restrictions on the used algorithm, instead of allowing to write some complicated rules in grammars, is very important from the ingeneering point of view. It allows to keep the grammars relatively small and transparent.

References

1. M. A. Harrison : Introduction to Formal Language Theory, Addison - Wesley, 1978
2. V. Kuboň, M. Plátek : Robust Parsing and Grammar Checking of free Word Order Languages, in Natural Language Parsing: Methods and Formalism eds. K. Sikkel, A. Nijholt, TWLT 6, December 1993, pp. 157 - 161
3. V. Kuboň, M. Plátek : A Grammar Based Approach to Grammar Checking of Free Word Order Languages, In: Proceedings COLING 94, Vol.II, Kyoto, August, 1994, pp. 906 - 910
4. M. Plátek : The Architecture of a Grammar Checker, In: Proceedings SOFSEM '94, Milovy, 1994, pp. 85 - 90
5. N. Sikkel: Parsing Schemata, Proefschrift, Enschede,ISBN 90-9006688-8, 1993
6. T. Holan, V. Kuboň, M. Plátek: An implementation of a syntactic analysis of Czech, Technical Report No 113. of KKI MFF UK Prague

Distributed Algorithm for Finding a Core of a Tree Network

Esther Jennings

Division of Computer Science, Luleå University, S-971 87, Luleå, Sweden

Abstract. A *core* of a graph $G = (V, E)$ is a path P in G which minimizes $d(P) = \sum_{v \in V} d(v, P)$ where $d(v, P)$ is the distance of vertex v from P. Finding a core of a network is essential in locating the best sites to set up service facilities. Here we present the first distributed algorithm which finds a core of a tree network in $O(D)$ time using $O(n)$ messages, where D and n are the diameter and the number of vertices of G respectively.

Keywords: tree, location problem, core, distributed algorithm.

1 Introduction

Network facility location concerns the optimal location of point sites in a network. Two extensively studied optimality criteria are the *minimax* and the *minisum* criteria. The *minimax* criteria minimizes the maximum distance between the site and any other vertex in the network, i.e., finding the network *centers*. The *minisum* criteria minimizes the total distance from the site to all other vertices in the network, i.e., finding the network *medians*.

The concept of center and median can be generalized to locate a set of p vertices S_p which form a multi-center (p-center) or a multi-median (p-median) [3, 8]. Another generalization is made by Morgan and Slater to locate a central path in a graph [6, 9]. They define a *core* as a path in a graph G which minimizes the sum of distances from the vertices of G to the path.

In [6], a sequential algorithm is given for the computation of a core of a tree network. Recently, optimal parallel algorithms for the computation of a core of a tree network have been presented in [1, 7] using $O(n/\log n)$ processors in $O(\log n)$ time on the EREW PRAM. To our knowledge, there is no distributed algorithm for the computation of a core in a tree network yet, although several distributed algorithms for the computation or approximation of network centers and medians do exist [2, 4].

Finding the core of a network is useful in practical situations where special services may need to be set up along a path. A particularly nice application is the setup of a pipeline which services the network vertices [9].

The network is modeled by a connected graph $G = (V, E)$ where every edge has unit length. The distance $d(u, v)$ between two vertices u and v is the minimum number of edges in a u to v path in G. The distance $d(u, S)$ between a

---

* This research is partially supported by the Swedish Council for Engineering Sciences.

vertex u and a set S of vertices is defined as the smallest of the distances from u to the vertices of S, i.e., $d(u, S) = min\{d(u, w)|w \in S\}$.

In this paper, we present a distributed algorithm which finds a core in a tree network. Our algorithm is based on the observation that an end-point v of a core can be identified by finding a *rooted core*, a path in G which passes through a prespecified root vertex, and which minimizes the sum of distances from the vertices of G to the path. A rooted core is not necessarily a core. However, a core can be found by extending a path P from the end-point v while minimizing the sum of distances from all $w \in V$ to P. The algorithm is decentralized and may be started by one or more initiators. At the end of the algorithm, every vertex knows whether it is on the computed core P and which of its incident edges are in P. The algorithm can be easily modified to find a core in a tree network where edges have arbitrary positive lengths (weights).

2 Model

Given an asynchronous network G of n vertices, we assume that each vertex has a unique identity representable in $O(\log n)$ bits. A vertex has only local knowledge of the network topology and exchanges information by point-to-point message passing. We assume message length of $O(\log n)$ bits. For the sake of time complexity analysis, we assume the message delay to be arbitrary but takes at most one unit time. However, the correctness of the algorithm does not rely on this message delay assumption.

3 Preliminaries

Let P be a path in G, then the distance from a vertex v to P is $d(v, P) = min_{w \in P} d(v, w)$.

Definition 1. A core (or path median) of a graph $G = (V, E)$ is a path P of minimum total distance $d(P) = \sum_{v \in V} d(v, P)$. A path P in G is a core if $d(P) \leq d(P')$ for any path P' in G.

A *path center*, unlike a *core*, is a path which minimizes the maximum distance of any vertex from the path (a minimax criteria). The path center of a tree G passes through the center of G. However, a core is not necessarily unique and does not necessarily pass through the median of G [6]. Therefore, we cannot simply extend a path from a median to obtain a core.

Let T_u be the maximal subtree of G rooted at u and $\delta(u)$ be the degree of u, we observe the following.

Lemma 2. [6] Let v be a vertex on a core P where $|P| > 1$, and let the vertices adjacent to v be $u_1, u_2, \cdots, u_{\delta(v)}$. Let T_{u_i} denote the subtree rooted at u_i not containing v. The following conditions hold for a vertex $w \in T_{u_i}$, $1 \leq i \leq \delta(v)$: (1) if $u_i \notin P$, then $d(w, P) = d(w, v)$; (2) if $u_i \in P$, then $d(w, P) < d(w, v)$.

Proof. Let v be a vertex on a core P. Clearly, $d(v) > d(P)$ since v is a single vertex. If $u_i \notin P$, i.e., the core does not pass through u_i, then for any vertex $w \in T_{u_i}$, w must go through u_i to reach the closest vertex on P (in this case v on P, thus $d(w, P) = d(w, v)$).

If $u_i \in P$, then the core passes through u_i and any vertex $w \in T_{u_i}$ is at a distance of $d(w, P) \le d(w, u_i) < d(w, v)$ from the core. $\qquad\square$

Therefore, there is a saving in distance from $w \in T_{u_i}$ to P by extending a core P from v to u_i. Let (u, v)-path denote the path from u to v in G.

Definition 3. Let Q be a path ending at s. The total saving distance from $d(Q)$ by extending Q to include the vertices on the (s, v)-path is $sav(s, v) = \sum_{w \in (s,v)-path, w \ne s} d(parent(w), w) \times |T_w|$, where T_w is the subtree rooted at w not containing s, and $|T_w|$ is the size (number of vertices) of T_w. If all the edges in G have unit length, $d(parent(w), w) = 1$. Otherwise, $d(parent(w), w)$ is equal to the arbitrary positive length assigned to edge $(parent(w), w)$.

Lemma 4. *A core P of a tree G must be a path connecting two leaves of G.*

Proof. Suppose P is a core and P does not contain two leaves of the tree, then there exists a maximal path Q in G such that Q contains two leaves and $P \subset Q$. It follows from lemma 2 and definition 3 that $d(Q) < d(P)$. Thus, P cannot be a core, a contradiction. $\qquad\square$

An end-point v of a core of a tree G can be found by first rooting G at an arbitrary vertex r and then finding the rooted core of G with respect to r.

Lemma 5. *Let G be a tree rooted at an arbitrary vertex r. For a leaf vertex v, if $sav(r, v)$ is equal to the maximum possible value, then v is an end-point of a core.*

Proof. Let P be a core of G and let x be an arbitrarily chosen vertex on P. Then there are $\delta(x)$ maximal subtrees, $T_1, T_2, \cdots, T_{\delta(x)}$, rooted at the children of x. Let $v_1 \in T_1$ and $v_2 \in T_2$ denote the end-points of P such that $sav(x, v_1) \ge sav(x, v_2)$. Clearly, for all $w \in T_1$, $sav(x, w) \le sav(x, v_1)$; for all $w \in T_2$, $sav(x, w) \le sav(x, v_2)$; and for all $w \in T_i$, $3 \le i \le \delta(x)$, $sav(x, w) \le sav(x, v_2) \le sav(x, v_1)$.

Let r be a root vertex and let v be the end-point on the rooted core P_r such that $sav(r, v)$ is maximized. We show that for any choice of a root vertex r, v is either v_1 or v_2.

Suppose $r \in T_1$ then v is either v_1 or v_2 depending on the position of r; because as r moves from x toward v_1, $sav(r, v_1)$ decreases and $sav(r, v_2)$ increases. If $r \notin T_1$, then v is v_1 because moving r away from x and from v_1 increases $sav(r, v_1)$. $\qquad\square$

Consequently, a core P of G can be found by re-rooting G at v (an end-point of P) and repeating the procedure for rooted core on G with respect to v.

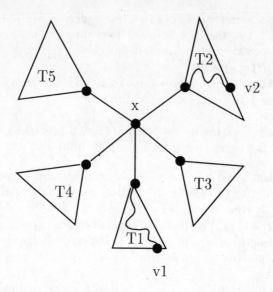

Fig. 1. $sav(x, v_1) \geq sav(x, v_2) \geq sav(x, w)$ for $w \in T_i$, $3 \leq i \leq \delta(x)$. In this example, $\delta(x) = 5$.

4   Finding a Core

We give an overview of the algorithm before describing each step in more detail. *Algorithm Core_of_a_Tree(G)*:

1. root the tree G at an arbitrary vertex r.
2. identify an end-point v of a core of G (solve rooted core with respect to r).
3. re-root G at v.
4. find a core P of G by extending a path from v (solve rooted core with respect to v).

Steps 1 and 2 can be combined into one tree traversal from the leaves to a root r chosen by the algorithm. Since the algorithm may be started by any subset of vertices S in G where $|S| \geq 1$, S must activate the leaves of G to start the tree traversal.

Assume each vertex is either *active* or *passive*. Each initiator in S activates its neighbors by sending an *INIT* message on all of its incident edges. A passive vertex receiving an *INIT* on edge e becomes active and will propagate the *INIT* message on all its incident edges except e. An *INIT* message is ignored if received at an already active vertex. If an active vertex is a leaf, it starts the tree traversal to choose a root r. While traversing from a leaf ℓ to choose a root r, $sav(u, \ell)$ for each vertex $u \in V$ is computed along the way as well. When r is chosen/reached, r can then follow a path of maximum savings at each intermediate vertex to find v, an end-point of a core.

When a leaf ℓ is activated, it sends a $PARENT(|T_\ell|, sav = 1)$ message to its only neighbor to establish a parent-child relation (the sender being the child). When an internal vertex u has received a $PARENT(|T_i|, sav_i)$ message from all but one of its edges, it marks the edge on which $max(sav_i)$ is received. If the maximum savings is reported on several edges, then mark one of these edges arbitrarily. This marking is used later by the root to find an end-point of a core. Vertex u will also compute $|T_u| = 1 + \sum |T_i|$, and $sav(u, \ell) = |T_u| + max(sav_i)$. Then u sends a $PARENT(|T_u|, sav(u, \ell))$ on the edge from which no $PARENT$ message was received, if any. Since T is a tree, there can be at most two vertices contending to become a root, and the vertex with the smaller processor identity wins.

To re-root G at v (Step 3), the root r reverses the parent-child relation from r to v by following the marked path. Step 4 is accomplished as follows. When v becomes the new root, it broadcasts a $FIND\_CORE$ message over G. Every leaf receiving a $FIND\_CORE$ will start a backward traversal to find the other end-point of a core with respect to v. The procedure is identical to Steps 1 and 2, and the path which is marked (P) is a core of G.

5   Correctness and Complexity

Lemma 6. *Algorithm Core_of_a_Tree terminates in finite time and a core of a tree network G is computed correctly.*

Proof. (Sketch) Initially, the passive vertices in the tree network G are activated by the initiators in a depth-parallel exploration fashion. Since there is at least one initiator and each passive vertex being activated will only propagate its first $INIT$ message, this phase of the algorithm will terminate in finite time. The choosing of r, finding of an end-point v of a core, re-rooting of G at v and the finding of the core P (with v as one of its end-points) each involves the traversal on a tree in one direction and thus will terminate in finite time also. From lemmas 2, 4 and 5, it follows that the computed path P is a core of the given tree network G.   □

Theorem 7. *Given a tree G with n vertices and diameter D, Algorithm Core_of_a_Tree finds a core of G in $O(D)$ time using $O(n)$ messages where message length is $O(\log b)$ bits.*

Proof. In Steps 1 and 2, at most two $INIT$ messages are sent on each edge and at most n $PARENT$ messages are sent. The time and number of messages required are $2D$ and $3n - 2$ respectively. In Step 3, the reversing of the parent-child relation from r to v takes at most D time and $n - 1$ messages. This is due to the fact that in depth-parallel traversal, the messages propagate as fast as possible; and since the network is asynchronous, it is possible for a message to be passed on more than D edges in D units of time. In step 4, the broadcast of $FIND\_CORE$ takes D time and $n - 1$ messages. A core of P is then found during backward tree traversal requiring D time and $n - 1$ messages. Therefore, the entire algorithm takes $4D$ time using $5n - 4$ messages.   □

6 Conclusion

In this paper, we presented a simple distributed algorithm which finds a core of a tree network in $O(D)$ time using $O(n)$ messages, where D and n are the diameter and the number of vertices of the tree network G respectively. Modifying the algorithm for trees with arbitrary positive edge lengths (weights) is straightforward. Recall that in definition 3, $d(parent(w), w) = 1$. For edges of arbitrary positive lengths, we simply substitute the actual edge lengths for $d(parent(w), w)$ in the computation of the saving distance. Our algorithm can also be applied to find a constrained core where the core must pass through a pre-specified vertex v.

Some interesting open problems are to design distributed algorithms for finding p-median, p-center, a core of a specified size, and other central structures of tree networks. Extending these problems to arbitrary networks is also of interest.

References

1. Albacea, E. A.: Parallel algorithm for finding a core of a tree network. Information Processing Letters **51** (1994) 223–226
2. Bar-Ilan, J., Peleg, D.: Approximation algorithms for selecting network centers. Workshop on Algorithms and Data Structures (1991) 343–354
3. Hakim, S. L.: Optimal distribution of switching centers in a communication network and some related graph theoretical problems. Opns. Res. **13** (1965) 462–475
4. Korach, E.: Distributed algorithms for finding centers and medians in networks. ACM Trans. on Programming Languages and Systems **6(3)** (1984) 380–401
5. Minieka, E., Patel, N. H.: On finding the core of a tree with a specified length. J. Algorithms **4** (1983) 345–352
6. Morgan, C. A., Slater, P. J.: A linear algorithm for a core of a tree. J. Algorithms. **1** (1980) 247–258
7. Peng, S., Lo, W.: A simple optimal parallel algorithm for a core of a tree. J. of Parallel and Distributed Computing **20** (1994) 388–392
8. Shier, D. R.: A min-max theorem for p-center problems on a tree. Transportation Sci. **11** (1977) 243–252
9. Slater, P. J.: Locating central paths in a graph. Transportation Sci. **16** (1982) 1–18

Stepwise Synthesis of Reactive Programs*

Petr Kozák

Institute of Information Theory and Automation, Czech Academy of Sciences,
Pod vodárenskou věží 4, 182 08 Prague 8, Czech Republic. E-mail: kozak@utia.cas.cz
WWW Home Page: ftp://ftp.utia.cas.cz/pub/staff/DES/kozak.html

Abstract. A new method for synthesis of reactive programs is proposed. The model formulation and synthesis phases are combined in consecutive steps. The suggested stepwise synthesis overcomes certain common difficulties encountered in applications of synthesis methods. The application of the method is documented using the example of communication protocol design.

1 Introduction

A reactive program (the opposite of a transformational program) does not produce a final result but maintains some ongoing interaction with its environment [8]. Examples of reactive programs include operating and communication systems, process control programs. The environment of a reactive program can be viewed as another program (process, system) acting concurrently with the reactive program. The reactive program itself is often composed of concurrent modules.

The concepts of environments and concurrency play the key role in the development methods for reactive programs. Many approaches to the formal specification and development of reactive programs have been proposed [8]. The concepts of environment and system (program) communication have been extensively studied also within the system theory (control theory) [4, 2]. The environment (called plant) is controlled by a program (supervisor or controller). The reactive programs are called discrete event systems (DES) in this context [4, 2].

The control-theoretic approach to the reactive programs differs from the computer-science-theoretic approach in two key features.

- The environment, supervisor and requirements are *modelled separately* therefore the means for *observation and control* (i.e. for communication) are studied in great detail.
- The central problem to be solved is the *synthesis of programs* as opposed to the verification which the computer-science-theoretic formal approaches to the program development focus mainly on.

---

* The work was partially supported by the AVČR grant #A2075505.

One of the advantages of the control-theoretic approach is that it aims to answer systematically the question how an optimal (in some specified sense, e.g. minimal restrictive) supervisor can be computed. The separate modelling of the main problem components enables to explore the behaviour of a fixed system under different requirements or under different control strategies.

On the other hand, there are serious difficulties the theory has been fighting with. The enormous complexity of practical problems is attacked using modular, decentralized, hierarchical, etc. methods. See [4, 2] for the latest development. Another problem is the design (formulation) of models of the environment and requirements (estimation of models and specification) [10].

The present paper proposes a new way how to formulate and solve the synthesis problems of reactive programs. The overall synthesis problem is divided into a sequence of logically consecutive subproblems. The subproblems are reformulated and refined using the solutions and/or failure results of the previous subproblems. The initial problem is formulated using simplified models and specifications. The task of the designer is to navigate the synthesis process performed by a computer-aided control design package into an area where a suitable solution can be found. The proposed stepwise synthesis enables the most effective involvement of human designer into the process.

The stepwise synthesis method can be used in several tasks of the software development cycle namely in formulation and validation of requirements, design and implementation. However, the utilization in the design and implementation requires further deeper elaboration in the direction of hierarchical modelling and synthesis in the sense of [11]. The future research will be aimed to incorporating the hierarchical synthesis and results related to timed models (e.g. [5]).

2   DES Supervisory Control

This section presents the results of the (untimed) DES supervisory control necessary for the explanation of the stepwise synthesis and formulation and solution of the example in the next section. Tutorials, extensions as well as recent results can be found in [4, 2].

The set of finite sequences (including the empty sequence ϵ) over an arbitrary finite set Σ is denoted Σ^*. The set of all prefixes of $L \subseteq \Sigma^*$ is $\mathrm{pref}(L) = \{v \in \Sigma^* \mid \exists v' \in \Sigma^*, vv' \in L\}$.

The *uncontrolled behaviour of the plant* is given as a nonempty set L of finite sequences over a finite *set of event labels* Σ such that $L = \mathrm{pref}(L)$. The set L represents all sequences of events the plant can generate if it is not controlled by any supervisor. It is interpreted such that the plant can stop the generation of events at any time. This model of system behaviour does not give exact time moments of event occurrences. The time is represented here only by the order of events.

Let $\Sigma_c \subseteq \Sigma$ be a set of *controllable event labels*. It represents the labels of events which may be dynamically disabled and enabled by a supervisor. The *centralized supervisor* for the given plant is defined as the mapping $\gamma : L \to 2^{\Sigma_c}$.

The sets $\gamma(v)$ (for $v \in L$) are interpreted as the sets of disabled events after observation of v.

The *closed-loop system* generated by the feedback interconnection of L and γ is defined as

$$\mathcal{S}(L/\gamma) = \{v \in L \mid \forall v' \in \text{pref}(v), \forall \sigma \in \Sigma, \ v'\sigma \in \text{pref}(v) \ \Rightarrow \ \sigma \notin \gamma(v')\} \ .$$

Consider the sets $\emptyset \neq A \subseteq E \subseteq L$ and $L_m \subseteq L$ such that $A = \text{pref}(A)$ and $E = \text{pref}(E)$. The *Supervisory Control Problem (SCP)* is to find a centralized supervisor γ for the given plant such that the closed-loop system satisfies the following two conditions

$$A \subseteq \mathcal{S}(L/\gamma) \subseteq E \ , \tag{1}$$
$$\text{pref}(\mathcal{S}(L/\gamma) \cap L_m) = \mathcal{S}(L/\gamma) \ . \tag{2}$$

The *legal language* E represents legal sequences. The *minimal acceptable language* A represents sequences which generation must be possible. The *marked language* L_m can be interpreted as the set of sequences representing completed tasks. Specification (2) means that at least one task must be completable at any time. In other words, the system is never blocked to do "something reasonable".

If the problem is solvable then there exists a unique supremal (in the sense of set inclusion) solution OPT of the problem. In the case of regular languages, the computation of OPT has complexity $O(m^2 n^2)$, where m (n) is the number of states of deterministic automaton generating L (E), respectively. If $\text{pref}(E \cap L_m) = E \cap L_m$ then the computation has complexity $O(m\,n)$. Results for certain other classes as Petri nets, VDES ... are also available [4, 2].

The control problem often has additional requirements, e.g. a particular structure of supervisor is required (for instance the supervisor consists of a set of subsupervisors each with limited means of observation and control) etc. The resulting supervisor often provides a solution which is strict subset of OPT and is in fact only an *approximation* of OPT with respect to the additional requirements. Typically there is no supremal approximation in the sense of set inclusion. Additional criteria are to be specified for selecting a single approximation in this case.

The supervisor can be composed from several decentralized subsupervisors. Suppose that I is the set of supervisor names and that each supervisor $i \in I$ can observe only event labels $\Sigma_{o,i} \subseteq \Sigma$ and control only $\Sigma_{c,i} \subseteq \Sigma_c$. Each subsupervisor $i \in I$ is defined as the mapping $\gamma_i : P_i(L) \rightarrow 2^{\Sigma_{c,i}}$, where $P_i : \Sigma^* \rightarrow \Sigma_{o,i}^*$ is the natural projection which erases events in $\Sigma \setminus \Sigma_{o,i}$ from the resulting sequences.

The sets $\gamma_i(v)$ (for $v \in P_i(L)$) are interpreted as sets of events disabled by the ith subsupervisor after observation of v. The decentralized supervisor γ is defined for all $v \in L$ such that $\gamma(v) = \bigcup_{i \in I} \gamma_i(P_i(v))$.

The paper [6] introduces a special class of decentralized supervisors called *(fully decentralized supervisor)* which can be effectively computed. Each subsupervisor of the fully decentralized supervisor is supposed to have the following unique form: $\gamma_i(v) = \{\sigma \in \Sigma_{c,i} \mid \exists w \in L, P_i(w) = v \wedge \sigma \in \gamma(w)\}$, for all $v \in P_i(L)$, where γ is the optimal centralized supervisor.

The plant model given by Σ and L can be also constructed in a modular fashion using e.g. synchronous product. Given two systems (Σ_1, L_1) and (Σ_2, L_2), their synchronous product is

$$L = \{v \in (\Sigma_1 \cup \Sigma_2)^* \mid P_1(v) \in L_1 \wedge P_2(v) \in L_2\},$$

where P_1 and P_2 are natural projections into the local event sets. If $\Sigma_1 = \Sigma_2$ then $L = L_1 \cap L_2$.

3 Stepwise Synthesis

Since 1981, the DES supervisory control has developed into a well established area with several fundamental results, many developed algorithms, several packages supporting the computations and modest experience with applications e.g. [1, 7]. At present time, there is an urgent need for combination of the methods into a practically oriented framework supported by (possibly heuristic) rules for utilization of the theory.

The DES models successful in simulation may be big and ill structured with respect to their utilization in the synthesis methods. The models built for verification are much more suitable for the synthesis methods and are often based on the same mathematical theories as the models for synthesis. These models are often built step by step by refinement.

The present paper proposes a combination of several tasks in a stepwise development process. Each step consists of two phases.

1. Formulation of a synthesis problem,

2. Running a synthesis procedure.

The second phase can be fully automated and gives the human designer detailed information about the reasons of failure and/or about the structure and properties of result of previous synthesis. This information can be used in the problem formulation phase of the next step. In the first phase, the designer can examine the model and the information provided by the previous step using simulation, visualization or inspection to some states of his/her interest. This gives the designer good insight into the process and helps to reformulate or refine the problem effectively. The interleaving of the synthesis by the examination and problem reformulation seems to be the most promising scheme for utilization of the synthesis design methods.

The following rules have been found essential for the synthesis process.

R1 *The initial problem should formulate the overall problem in an extremely simple way even if it is not visibly solvable and/or does not reflect all required details.*

R2 *The initial problem should be formulated as a centralized problem with full observation.*

R3 *All models (of plant and specifications) should be kept as simple as possible,* *i.e. with small sets of event labels and states.*

R4 *The models should be built from subsystems e.g. using modularity, decentralization .... This provides the synthesis procedures with extremely helpful information.*

R5 *The structure of specifications should follow the structure of the plant model whenever possible, e.g. it is better to mark some states as illegal instead of building an additional automaton describing the corresponding legal behaviour. In other words, the specifications should be formulated such that they make the problem size "smaller" and not "bigger".*

R6 *Do always minimal changes of the problem formulation.*

R7 *Keep always the specifications as little restrictive as possible, e.g. add always as many selfloops as possible.*

R8 *Allow the plant model to generate always as many event sequences as possible.*

R9 *Try always to find (or at least to verify the existence of) the supremal centralized solution with full observation first.*

R10 *Try "standard" solutions (e.g. supremal centralized, fully decentralized, supremal normal, infimal decentralizable, ... [4, 2]) first.*

R11 *In the case of need, try "tricks" like decomposition of languages using some order of events etc.*

R12 *Make documentation for each step as complete as possible including the rationale for the step and intuitive verbal formulation.*

R13 *Instead of generating a single sequence of synthesis steps, it is possible to return back and investigate alternatives.*

R14 *Solve an untimed version of the problem first.*

In the following, the rules are documented using the example of communication protocol synthesis. Rudie and Wonham showed that the choice of model is critical for the computation of a solution. Their paper [10] presents an example of the alternating bit protocol synthesis and examines several problem formulations with the conclusion that without anticipating some structural properties of the solution by the problem formulation it may not be possible to find (synthesize) the solution in an automated way.

The following example shows that the proposed stepwise synthesis guided with the presented rules leads to the protocol in four natural steps. The presented method of interleaving the model development and synthesis phases overcomes the difficulties described in [10] and gives the designer a practically useful way how to solve problems in a natural and relatively easier way.

The presented example is chosen to be simple, small sized and well known. However, the presented method can be applied to much more involved problems.

Example. The computations can be performed using e.g. the procedures of the TCT developed at the University of Toronto [9].

Step 1. The first problem formulation only reflects the one-way communication between two agents, the sender **S** and the receiver **R** using a (reliable) communication channel **C** (Fig. 1). The plant is the synchronous product of the three subsystems. All events are controllable. The legal language **E** requires alternating sequence of send (S) and receive (R) events.

The problem is solvable but it does not model the losses of messages.

Step 2. The event set is extended by an uncontrollable event "the message is lost or timeout" (L). The new channel model incorporates L event (Fig. 2). The legal language is the same as in the previous problem. The minimal acceptable behaviour **A** requires that the projection of the solution deleting L events equals to the legal behaviour.

The problem is not solvable. The possibility of resending a message is necessary. Therefore it is necessary to distinguish each message, e.g. by a number. However, for a channel with the capacity one message, just two numbers are sufficient.

Step 3. Numbering introduces events S0, S1 R0, and R1 instead of S and R. The plant model is changed accordingly (Fig. 3). The legal language allows a message to be resent.

The supremal centralized solution with full observation exists! The corresponding supervisor disables S1 at states 1, 2, 3 and the event S0 at states 4, 5, and 6. The set of observable events must include R0, and R1. Therefore the supervisor event set contains the events of both **S** and **R**. But this is unrealistic in the present problem formulation as it requires sending information between the supervisor and both **S** and **R**.

Step 4. The preceding difficulty with observation leads to introducing two-way communication implemented using the acknowledgement, i.e. send acknowledgement (A0, A1) and receive acknowledgement (RA0, RA1) events. The intention is to find two supervisors, one observing and controlling only the events of the sender and the other only the events of the receiver.

The sender and receiver models are changed accordingly (Fig. 4). The second channel for "acknowledgement" is introduced. The legal language is now formulated using the synchronous product of two languages **E1**, **E2** (one for communication in each direction).

The supremal centralized solution with full observation exists and can be expressed in a modular way using two subsupervisors. The supervisor of the sender corresponds to the legal language **E1** and disables S1 at states 1, 2, 3 and S2 at 4, 5, and 6. The supervisor of the receiver corresponds to the legal language **E2** and disables A1 at states 2, 3, 4, 8 and A0 at 5, 6, 7 and 1.

The fully decentralized solution exists and follows easily from the centralized solution by determining the local event sets as intended. The set of sequences this solution enables is equivalent to the set of sequences of the alternating bit protocol [3, 10].

4   Conclusion

The presented "mixed" problem formulation and synthesis represents one of few practically feasible ways how the theoretical synthesis procedures can be applied to practical problems.

References

1. S. Balemi, G.J. Hoffmann, P. Gyugyi, H. Wong-Toi, and G.F. Franklin. Supervisory control of a rapid thermal multiprocessor. *IEEE Trans. Autom. Control*, 38(7):1040–1059, July 1993.

2. S. Balemi, P. Kozák, and R. Smedinga, editors. *Discrete Event Systems: Modeling and Control*, volume 13 of *Progress in Systems and Control Theory*. Birkhäuser Verlag, Basel, Switzerland, 1993.

3. K.A. Barlett, R.A. Scantlebury, and P.T. Wilkinson. A note on reliable full-duplex transmission over half-duplex links. *J. ACM*, 12(5):260–261, May 1969.

4. G. Cohen and J.P. Quadrat, editors. *11th Int. Conf. on Analysis and Optimization of Systems, Discrete Event Systems*, volume 199 of *LNCS*, Berlin, Germany, June 1994. Springer-Verlag.

5. P. Kozák. Control of real-time discrete event systems with hybrid controllability of events. In *Proc. of 32nd IEEE Conf. Decision and Control*, pages 223–228, San Antonio, TX, USA, December 1993.

6. P. Kozák and W.M. Wonham. Fully decentralized solutions of supervisory control problems. Technical Report # 9310, Systems Control Group, Dept. of El. Eng., Univ. of Toronto, Canada, August 1993. to appear *IEEE Trans. Autom. Control*, 40(11), November 1995.

7. P. Kozák and W.M. Wonham. Synthesis of database management protocols. Technical Report # 9311, Systems Control Group, Dept. of El. Eng., Univ. of Toronto, Canada, August 1993. submitted.

8. Z. Manna and A. Pnueli. *The Temporal Logic of Reactive and Concurrent Systems*. Springer-Verlag, New York, NY, USA, 1992.

9. S.D. O'Young. TCT_talk: User's guide. Technical Report # 8915, Systems Control Group, Dept. of El. Eng., Univ. of Toronto, Canada, October 1989.

10. K. Rudie and W.M. Wonham. Supervisory control of communicating processes. In L. Logrippo, R.L. Probert, and H. Ural, editors, *Proc. of 10th Int. Symp. on Protocol Specification, Testing, and Verification*, pages 243–257, Ottawa, Canada, June 1990. Elsevier Science Publisher (North-Holland). Expanded version appears as Systems Control Group Report #8907,Dept. of El. Eng., Univ. of Toronto, Canada, 1989.

11. H. Zhong and W.M. Wonham. On the consistency of hierarchical supervision in discrete-event systems. *IEEE Trans. Autom. Control*, 35(10):1125–1134, October 1990.

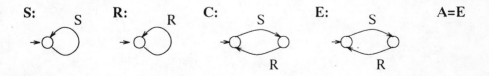

Fig. 1. Step 1

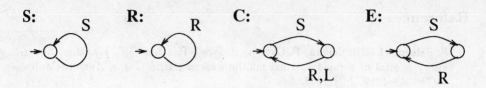

Fig. 2. Step 2

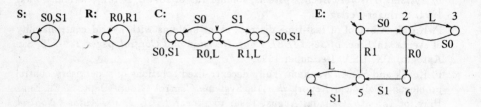

Fig. 3. Step 3

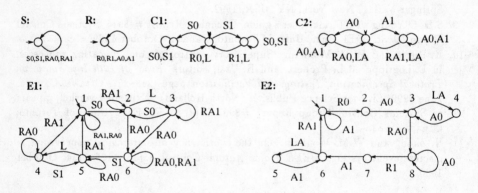

Fig. 4. Step 4

A Simple and Efficient Incremental LL(1) Parsing

Warren X. Li

Department of Computer Science.
The University of Western Australia
Nedlands 6009, W.A., Australia
Email: warren@cs.uwa.edu.au

Abstract. Incremental parsing is widely used in language-based editors and incremental compilation and interpretive environments. Reparsing of modified input strings is the most frequently performed operation in these environments and its efficiency can greatly affect the success of such environments. This paper describes the introduction of nonterminals as lookahead symbols into an LL parse table to support minimal LL reparsing. This enhancement is then used to produce an efficient incremental LL parser.

1 Introduction

Incremental parsing is widely used in language-based editors and incremental compiling and interpreting environments. An incremental parser deals with the re-construction of a parse tree while a modification from xyz to $x\bar{y}z$ has been made. Given a parse tree T for a string xyz, generated by a context-free grammar G, and a string $\bar{y}$, an incremental parser intends to build a new parse tree $\bar{T}$ for the string $x\bar{y}z$ with as few steps as possible.

We take the following LL(1) grammar $G1$ as our example grammar in this paper.

$$
\begin{array}{lll}
(0)\ E \to TE' & (1)\ E' \to +TE' & (2)\ E' \to \lambda \\
(3)\ T \to FT' & (4)\ T' \to *FT' & (5)\ T' \to \lambda \\
(6)\ F \to (E) & (7)\ F \to id &
\end{array}
$$

The parse tree for the string $id + id + id$ is shown in Figure 1 (a). Suppose the string $id + id + id$ is changed to $id * id + id$. In this instance, we have $x = id$, $y = +$, $z = id + id$ and $\bar{y} = *$. Since the modification only changes y, the subtrees related to x and z may be retained. We use a "divide" operation to break the tree T into a number of trees.

A "divide" at a terminal node t divides a parse tree to a number of trees produced by following procedures; (1) let n be t, and repeat step 2 and step 3 until no such n exists, (2) move n to its right sibling (if one exists), otherwise to the right sibling of the closest ancestor that has a right sibling, (3) prune the subtree rooted at n from the tree T. The "divide" operation is similar to the "cut" operation in the reference [10].

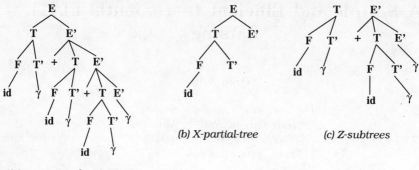

(a) parse tree for id+id+id

(b) X-partial-tree

(c) Z-subtrees

Fig. 1. The *X-partial-tree* and *Z-subtrees* from the modification $id+id+id$ to $id*id+id$

An *X-partial-tree* for xyz is defined as the remaining tree after the "divide" operation is applied at the last terminal node of x (the first *id* node for the above example). The *X-partial-tree* for the above example is shown in Figure 1 (b). In fact, X-partial-tree is an incompleted parse tree at the moment when the last terminal of x is parsed. With an *X-partial-tree*, we can obtain the content of parse stack. They are those leave after the last terminal of x e.g. $T'E'$ for the above example. The content of parse stack is also called *X-sequence*. *Z-subtrees* for xyz are defined as the trees pruned from the "divide" operation on the last terminal of y, excluding the trees that are epsilon or only have an epsilon child. The *Z-subtrees* for the above example is depicted in the Figure 1 (c). Z-subtrees are those subtrees that are considered for re-use. The symbols on the roots of Z-subtrees are called *Z-sequence* (TE' in this example).

An incremental parser can directly use X-partial-tree as its initial structure to start with. How to re-use Z-subtrees or the components of Z-subtrees is a focus point for incremental LL parsers. Existing incremental LL(1) parsers [5,9,10] try to re-use Z-subtrees or the components of Z-subtrees by the traditional LL(1) parsing method, i.e. a parser has to look at the next terminal lookahead to decide actions. Often they have to build the subtrees that have already existed in Z-subtrees.

Look at the root symbols of Z-subtrees. They are a sequence of nonterminals and terminals. Imagine that if we have a parsing method that decides actions (expanding or reusing) by only looking these nonterminals, it will be much efficient. We introduce a new LL(1) parsing method which permits both terminals and nonterminals as lookahead symbols. The theory of the new parsing method is directly extended from the existing LL(1) parsing method. By applying the new parsing theory, an efficient incremental LL(1) parser has been developed. In the following discussion, we adhere to usual notations, i.e. $A, B, C, \cdots \in N$; $a, b, c, \cdots \in T$; $X, Y, Z, \cdots \in N \cup T$; $x, y, z, \cdots \in T^*$; and $\alpha, \beta, \gamma \cdots \in (N \cup T)^*$.

2 Construction of parsing table containing nonterminals

To construct the parsing table that contains nonterminals in columns, we need to modify the definitions of $First$ and $Follow$ in order to accommodate nonterminals. We use the definitions in the reference [4] in our discussion. The modified ones are called $First'$ and $Follow'$ defined as follows. S is assumed as the start symbol.

$$First'(\alpha) = \{X \in N \cup T \mid \alpha \overset{*}{\Rightarrow} X\beta\} \bigcup (if\ \alpha \overset{*}{\Rightarrow} \lambda\ then\ \{\lambda\}\ else\ \phi)$$
$$Follow'(A) = \{X \in N \cup T \mid S \overset{+}{\Rightarrow} \gamma AX\beta\} \bigcup (if\ S \overset{*}{\Rightarrow} \gamma A\ then\ \{\lambda\}\ else\ \phi)$$

The algorithms to collect the $First'$ sets and the $Follow'$ sets are similar to the traditional ones (they can be found in a number of references such as [4,1,3]). We omit them here. For the grammar $G1$, the $First'$ sets and the $Follow'$ sets are given as follows.

$$First'(E) = \{T, F, (, id\}$$
$$First'(E') = \{\lambda, +\}$$
$$First'(T) = \{F, (, id\}$$
$$First'(T') = \{*, \lambda\}$$
$$First'(F) = \{(, id\}$$
$$Follow'(E) = \{(, id\}$$
$$Follow'(E') = \{(, id\}$$
$$Follow'(T) = \{), +, \$, E'\}$$
$$Follow'(T') = \{), +, \$, E'\}$$
$$Follow'(F) = \{*, T', E',), +, \$\}$$

Again, the algorithm to construct the parsing table M' containing nonterminals is similar to the one that builds LL(1) parsing table M. The parsing table for the grammar $G1$ is shown in Figure 2. As you can see, nonterminals are included in the columns of the parsing table M'.

Nonterminal	id	+	*	(	)	$	E	E'	T	T'	F
E	0			0					0		0
E'		1			2	2					
T	3			3							3
T'		5	4		5	5		5			
F	7			6							

Fig. 2. LL(1) parsing table containing nonterminals

With the parsing table M', we can easily extend the traditional LL(1) parsing algorithm to parse an input string containing both terminals and nonterminals.

3 An efficient incremental LL(1) parser

The incremental LL(1) parser uses the new parsing method to parse the string $x\bar{y}$ z. The incremental parsing algorithm starts with X-*partial-tree* (with X-*sequence* as the content of parse stack). $\bar{y}$ has to be parsed with traditional way. After $\bar{y}$ is parsed, the algorithm then tries to re-use Z-subtrees or the components of Z-subtrees by the new parsing method.

For the incremental LL(1) parsing algorithm, a case need to be specially considered. That is when $M'(X, Y) = error$ where $Y \in N$. It does not always mean a syntax error. It may mean the tree rooted at Y is no longer a subtree of the new tree $\bar{T}$ for $x\bar{y}z$. But some components of the tree Y can be still possibly re-used, and so they should be tried for re-use. An *undo* operation is used to dissolve the tree Y into a number of subtrees rooted at the children of Y. Suppose the tree rooted at Y is produced by the production $Y \rightarrow Y_1 \cdots Y_m$. Then subtrees rooted with the symbols $Y_1, \cdots, Y_m$ are re-considered by the incremental LL(1) parser.

The incremental LL(1) parsing algorithm is given as follows. It employs two stacks, P-Stack, the parsing stack and I-Stack, the input symbol stack.

Algorithm. An Incremental LL(1) parsing algorithm.

Input. An parsing table M' for a CFG G, a parse tree T for a string xyz, and a string $\bar{y}$.
Output. Left parse of G and a parse tree $\bar{T}$ for $x\bar{y}z$.
Method.

1. get X-partial-tree and Z-subtrees by dividing the tree T;
   push X-sequence to P-Stack and Z-sequence to I-Stack
   push $\bar{y}$ to I-Stack on top.
2. repeat
   let X be the top of P-Stack and Y be the top of I-Stack
   (a) case $X = Y$, (matching)
       the tree rooted at Y is re-used; pop X from P-Stack and Y from I-Stack.
   (b) case $M'(X, Y) = k$, (predict production k)
       let production k be $X \rightarrow X_1 \cdots X_n$;
       pop X from P-Stack and push $X_1 \cdots X_n$ to P-Stack with X_1 on top;
       build the node X with the production k.
   (c) case $M'(X, Y) = error$,
       if $Y \in N$ then
           undo Y: let $Y \rightarrow Y_1 \cdots Y_m$, pop Y from I-Stack,
           push $Y_1 \cdots Y_m$ (excluding $Y_j \rightarrow \lambda$) to I-Stack with Y_1 on top.
       else $(Y \in T)$
           syntax error; halt or call error recovery procedure.

Example 1. For the modification from $id + id + id$ to $id * id + id$ for the grammar $G1$, the reparsing steps are shown in Figure 3. The new parse tree for $id * id + id$ built by the Algorithm is shown in Figure 4, in which the circled areas have been reused.

P-Stack	I-Stack	Action
T'E'\$	*TE'\$	predict 4 $(T' \to *FT')$
FT'E'\$	*TE'\$	match
FT'E'\$	TE'\$	undo T $(T \to FT')$
FT'E'\$	FE'\$	match (re-use)
T'E'\$	E'\$	predict 5 $(T' \to \lambda)$
E'\$	E'\$	match (re-use)
\$	\$	match

Fig. 3. Re-parsing steps for the modification from $id + id + id$ to $id * id + id$

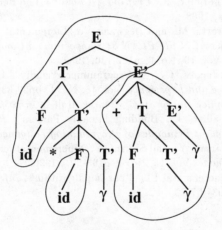

Fig. 4. The reuse of subtrees

4 Conclusion

In this paper, we have introduced a new parsing method that permits an input string to contain both terminals and nonterminals. We have defined the $First'$ set and the $Follow'$ set that include terminals and nonterminals. The new parse table M' containing nonterminals can be built by the similar way to the traditional one. Last we have developed an efficient incremental LL(1) parsing algorithm.

The parsing table M' contains $m(m + n)$ entries where m is the number of nonterminals and n is the number of terminals in a grammar. It can be built by slightly modifying the existing LL(1) parsing table generators such as the LLGen[6], LLama[7].

The incremental LL(1) parser always tries subtrees as reusing units without looking their terminal descendants (unlike all other incremental LL(1) parsers), therefore maximise the re-use of subtrees. So, it is time efficient.

Also the incremental LL(1) parser is directly derived from the traditional LL(1) parser. It is simpler than any other incremental LL(1) parser.

References

1. Aho, A., Sethi, R. and Ullman, J, *Compilers: Principles, Techniques, and Tools,* Addison-Wesley Publishing Company, 1986.
2. Aho, A. and Ullman, J, *The Theory of Parsing, Translation and Compiling,* Vol. 1 and 2, Prentice-Hall, Englewood Cliffs, NJ, 1972 and 1973.
3. Aho, A. and Ullman, J, *Principles of Compiler Design,* Addison-Wesley Publishing Company, 1979.
4. Fischer, C. and LeBlanc, R., *Crafting A Compiler* The Benjamin/Cummings Publishing Company, 1988.
5. Delisle, N., Schwartz, M., and Begwani, V., "Incremental compilation in magpie", *Proceedings of the ACM SIGPLAN'84 Symposium on Compiler Construction,* SIGPLAN Notices, Vol. 19, No. 6, p122-130, 1982.
6. Grune, D. and Jacobs, C., "A Programmer-Friendly LL(1) Parser Generator", *Software-Practice and Experience,* Vol. 18, No. 1, pp29-38, January 1988.
7. Holub, A., *Compiler Design in C,* Prentice-Hall International, 1990.
8. Jalili, F. and Gallier, J., "Building Friendly Parsers", *Proceedings of the Ninth ACM Symposium on Principles of Programming Languages,* 1982.
9. Murching, A., Parsad, Y., and Srikant, Y., "Incremental recursive descent parsing", *Computer Languages* Vol. 15, No. 4, p193-204, 1990.
10. Yang, W., "An incremental LL(1) parsing algorithm", *Information Processing Letters* Vol. 48 (1993) 67-72,

Fundamentals of context-sensitive rewriting*

Salvador Lucas

Departamento de Sistemas Informáticos y Computación
Universidad Politécnica de Valencia
Camino de Vera s/n, E-46071 Valencia, Spain.
e.mail: slucas@dsic.upv.es

Abstract. Recently we have introduced a novel class of rewrite relations we call *context-sensitive rewriting* that proves useful to mechanize a particular class of inference systems. In this paper, we give a more accurate characterization of some properties of context-sensitive rewriting. We also show that several reduction strategies used in λ-calculus namely weak reduction and lazy (*call by name*) reduction, can be viewed as an instance of the context-sensitive rewriting.

Keywords: term rewriting systems, regularity, functional programming.

1 Introduction

The theory of Term Rewriting Systems (TRSs) has proven useful to mechanize the execution of functional programs [3] by imposing directionality on the use of equations in proofs [1, 2]. Directed equations, called 'rewrite rules', are used to replace equals by equals, but only in the indicated direction. In this scheme, computation consists of rewriting terms to a normal form, i.e. an expression that cannot be rewritten any further [1]. The notion of sequence of rewrites traditionally defines an operational view of computation. The equational origin of term rewriting techniques leads to consider an expression $t \rightarrow s$ as 't equals s' rather than 't becomes s' [8]. As a consequence, the property of 'being closed under context application' (a particular form of the algebraic property of regularity) is essential in the definition of the rewriting relation.

In [6] we have introduced a novel class of rewrite relations, we call *context--sensitive* rewriting, whose definition is based on regularity. Roughly speaking, given a term t, the subterm of t at the occurrence u is a redex of the context--sensitive rewrite relation iff the symbols in t which label the occurrences above u satisfy a particular condition we call *replacement condition*.

In this paper, we introduce some properties of the replacement condition, which give a more powerful characterization of the context-sensitive rewriting process. In particular, we show that the evaluation of the replacement condition can be made compositionally. We also show that context-sensitive rewriting satisfies some desirable properties such as stability which allows us to ensure that a

---

* This work has been partially supported by CICYT under grant TIC 95-0433-C03-03.

(context-sensitive) reducible term also rewrites to another when we instantiate its variable occurrences. This property plays an important role in studying the computational properties of rewriting such as confluence and termination. We also show that several common reduction strategies used in λ-calculus [4, 5], such as weak reduction and lazy reduction, can be viewed as an instance of the context-sensitive rewriting.

The paper is organized as follows. In Section 2, we briefly recall the technical concepts and results used in the remainder of the paper. In Section 3, we shows the basic properties of the context-sensitive rewrite relation. At the end of this section, we illustrate the application of this technique to weak reduction and lazy λ-calculus. We conclude by pointing to some further research.

2   Preliminaries

Let us first introduce the main notations used in the paper. For full definitions we refer to [2, 5]. Throughout the paper, V denotes a countable set of variables and Σ denotes a set of function symbols $\{f, g, \ldots\}$, each with a fixed arity given by a function $ar : \Sigma \to \mathcal{N}$. By $\mathcal{T}(\Sigma, V)$ we denote the set of terms. Given a term t, $Var(t)$ is the set of variable symbols in t.

Terms are viewed as labelled trees in the usual way. Occurrences $u, v, \ldots$ are represented by chains of positive natural numbers used to address subterms of t, and they are ordered by the prefix ordering: $u \leq v$ if there exists a w such that $u.w = v$. By $u \parallel v$ we denote that the occurrences u, v are disjoint, i.e. $u \nleq v$ and $v \nleq u$. $O(t)$ denotes the set of occurrences of a term t. $t|_u$ is the subterm at occurrence u of t. $t[s]_u$ is the term t with the subterm at the occurrence u replaced with s. We refer to any term C that is the same as t everywhere except below u, i.e. there exists a term s such that $C[s]_u = t$, as the *context* within the replacement occurs.

A rewrite rule is an ordered pair (l, r), written $l \to r$, with $l, r \in \mathcal{T}(\Sigma, V)$, $l \notin V$ and $Var(r) \subseteq Var(l)$. l is said the left-hand side (*lhs*) of the rule and r is the right-hand side (*rhs*). A TRS is a pair $\mathcal{R} = (\Sigma, R)$ where R is a set of rewrite rules. For a given TRS $\mathcal{R} = (\Sigma, R)$, a term t rewrites to a term s (at the occurrence u), written $t \to_{\mathcal{R}} s$, if $t|_u = \sigma(l)$ and $s = t[\sigma(r)]_u$, for some rule $l \to r$ in R, occurrence u in t and substitution σ. $\to_{\mathcal{R}}$ is the one-step rewrite relation for $\mathcal{R}$.

$\mathcal{N}_k^+$ is an initial segment $\{1, 2, \ldots k\}$ of the set of positive natural numbers $\mathcal{N}^+$ where $\mathcal{N}_0^+ = \emptyset$.

A homogeneous algebra $\mathcal{A}$ is a pair (A, F) where A is a set (the carrier) and F is a set of mappings $\{f, g, \ldots\}$. The mapping $ar : F \to \mathcal{N}$ associates with each function f in F its arity, i.e. $ar(f) = k$ iff f is a mapping from $A^k \to A$.

3   Context-sensitive rewriting

3.1   Regularity

First we summarize the main algebraic concepts that support the context-sensitive rewriting. More details and missing proofs can be found in [6, 7].

Definition 3.1 (Regularity) *Let* R *be a relation on* A *and* $f : A^k \to A$ *be a mapping. We say that* R *is regular wrt* f *with index* j, $1 \leq j \leq k$ *(we also say that* R *is* j-regular *wrt* f) *iff for all* $a, b, a_1, \ldots, a_k \in A$. a R $b \Rightarrow$ $f(a_1, \ldots, a_{j-1}, a, \ldots, a_k)$ R $f(a_1, \ldots, a_{j-1}, b, \ldots, a_k)$. *The set* $m_R(f) \subseteq \mathcal{N}_k^+$ *of all indexes* j *such that* R *is* j-regular *wrt* f *is called the* regularity map *of* R *wrt* f.

The concept of regularity can be isolated of considering any particular relation by just taking a set of indices for each function in the algebra. This leads to the relation-independent concept of *algebraic regularity map*.

Definition 3.2 (Algebraic regularity map) *Let* $\mathcal{A} = (A, F)$ *be an algebra. A mapping* $m : F \to 2^{\mathcal{N}}$ *is an* algebraic regularity map *(r-map) for* $\mathcal{A}$ *iff for all* $f \in F$. $m(f) \subseteq \mathcal{N}_{ar(f)}^+$. *The set of all r-maps of* $\mathcal{A}$ *is denoted by* $M_{\mathcal{A}}$.

We express in a compact mode the regularity property of a relation R wrt each function in a given algebra $\mathcal{A} = (A, F)$, according to definition 3.1. The map $m_R : F \to 2^{\mathcal{N}}$ is called the *regularity map* (or simply the r-map) of R wrt $\mathcal{A}$ iff for all $f \in F$. $m_R(f)$ is the regularity map of R wrt f. We also say that R is m_R-regular wrt $\mathcal{A}$.

The following example shows the regularity maps of a given relation with respect to several algebras. Let us consider the relation R of 'being multiple of' in the set $\mathcal{Q}^+$ of positive rational numbers, i.e. $\forall\, a, b \in \mathcal{Q}^+$. a R $b \Leftrightarrow \exists c \in \mathcal{N}$. $a = b \times c$. Then the r-map of R wrt $(\mathcal{Q}^+, \{+\})$ verifies $m_R(+) = \emptyset$, the r-map of R wrt $(\mathcal{Q}^+, \{/\})$ verifies $m_R(/) = \{1\}$ and the r-map of R wrt $(\mathcal{Q}^+, \{\times\})$ verifies $m_R(\times) = \{1, 2\}$.

Now we introduce a partial order on r-maps.

Definition 3.3 (Partial order on regularity maps) *Let* $\mathcal{A} = (A, F)$ *be an algebra. Let* $M_{\mathcal{A}}$ *be the set of r-maps for* $\mathcal{A}$ *and let* $m, m' \in M_{\mathcal{A}}$. *We define a partial order* $\sqsubseteq$ *on* $M_{\mathcal{A}}$ *as follows:* $m \sqsubseteq m' \Leftrightarrow \forall f \in F$. $m(f) \subseteq m'(f)$.

It is immediate to see that $(M_{\mathcal{A}}, \sqsubseteq)$ is a complete lattice. The map $m_{\top}$ which assigns to each function $f \in F$ the whole segment $\mathcal{N}_{ar(f)}^+$ is the top element and the map $m_{\bot}$ which assigns to each function $f \in F$ the empty set $\emptyset$ is the bottom element.

3.2 Basic properties of context-sensitive rewriting

In this section, we show some powerful properties of context-sensitive rewriting. The idea behind the concept of context-sensitive rewriting is to impose a syntactic replacement condition which prevents one from performing some reduction steps. This is achieved by using a map on the signature we call replacement map. A mapping $\mu : \Sigma \to 2^{\mathcal{N}}$ is a *replacement map* (or Σ-map) for the signature Σ iff for all $f \in \Sigma$. $\mu(f) \subseteq \mathcal{N}^{+}_{ar(f)}$.

We use the replacement map to give a condition on the occurrences of a given term where the rewrite rules can be applied.

Definition 3.4 (Replacement condition) *Let Σ be a signature and μ be a Σ-map. Let $t \in \mathcal{T}(\Sigma, V)$ be a term. The replacement condition is a relation $\gamma_{\mu,t}$ defined on the set of occurrences $O(t)$ as follows:*

$\gamma_{\mu,t}(\varepsilon)$.

$\gamma_{\mu,f(t_1,\ldots,t_i,\ldots,t_k)}(i.u) \Leftrightarrow (i \in \mu(f)) \wedge \gamma_{\mu,t_i}(u)$.

We say that the occurrence u of a term t satisfies the replacement condition $\gamma_{\mu,t}$ iff $\gamma_{\mu,t}(u)$. We also say that u is a replacing occurrence of t or that the subterm $t|_u$ is a replacing subterm.

In the following, we write $\gamma_t(u)$ when the replacement map is clear from the context. Also, let us denote as $O^\mu(t)$ the set of *replacing* occurrences of a term t: $u \in O^\mu(t) \Leftrightarrow u \in O(t) \wedge \gamma_t(u)$.

Roughly speaking, the replacement condition for a term t wrt μ imposes a restriction based on the function symbols which label the path between the root of t and the subterm at occurrence u. To make clear the meaning of this restriction, we present some basic properties of the replacement condition we defined above.

Proposition 3.5 (Compositionality in evaluating the replacement condition) *Let Σ be a signature, $t \in \mathcal{T}(\Sigma, V)$ and $u \in O(t)$. Then the following statement holds: $u = u_1.u_2 \Rightarrow (\gamma_t(u) \Leftrightarrow (\gamma_t(u_1) \wedge \gamma_{t|_{u_1}}(u_2)))$.*

This Proposition allows us to realize the evaluation of replacement conditions in a compositionally mode. As an immediate consequence of this result, we have the following corollaries.

Corolary 3.6 *Let Σ be a signature, $t \in \mathcal{T}(\Sigma, V)$ and $u, v \in O(t)$. The following statements hold:*

1. $(u \leq v \wedge \gamma_t(v)) \Rightarrow \gamma_t(u)$,
2. $(u \leq v \wedge \neg\gamma_t(u)) \Rightarrow \neg\gamma_t(v)$.

Corolary 3.7 *Let Σ be a signature, $t \in \mathcal{T}(\Sigma, V)$ and $u \in O(t)$. The following statement holds: $\gamma_t(u) \Rightarrow (u = u_1.u_2 \Rightarrow \gamma_{t|_{u_1}}(u_2))$*

We can demonstrate some useful properties related with the persistence of the evaluation of the replacement condition with respect to substitution application and subterm replacement.

Proposition 3.8 (Persistence with respect to substitution application)
Let Σ be a signature, $t \in \mathcal{T}(\Sigma, V)$ and $u \in O(t)$. Let $\sigma : V \to \mathcal{T}(\Sigma, V)$ be a substitution. Then, $\gamma_t(u) \Leftrightarrow \gamma_{\sigma(t)}(u)$.

Proposition 3.9 (Persistence with respect to subterm replacements)
Let Σ be a signature, $t, t' \in \mathcal{T}(\Sigma, V)$ and $u, v \in O(t)$. Then,

1. $u \le v \Rightarrow (\gamma_t(u) \Leftrightarrow \gamma_{t[t']_v}(u))$ *and*
2. $u \parallel v \Rightarrow (\gamma_t(u) \Leftrightarrow \gamma_{t[t']_v}(u))$.

The above results allow us to devise more efficient methods for the evaluation of the replacement condition in context-sensitive systems.

The order $\sqsubseteq$ on algebraic regularity maps can easily be translated to compare *replacement* maps for a given signature Σ. By abuse of notation, we will use the same symbol $\sqsubseteq$ to denote both orderings. The next result establishes that a replacement condition that holds for a given replacement map is also verified wrt a greater replacement map.

Proposition 3.10 *Let Σ be a signature, $t \in \mathcal{T}(\Sigma, V)$ and $u \in O(t)$. Let μ, μ' be two Σ-maps such that $\mu \sqsubseteq \mu'$. Then we have $\gamma_{\mu,t}(u) \Rightarrow \gamma_{\mu',t}(u)$*

Now we introduce the context-sensitive rewriting by means of their one-step reduction relation.

Definition 3.11 (One-step context-sensitive rewrite relation) *Let $\mathcal{R} = (\Sigma, R)$ be a TRS and μ be a Σ-map. A term t μ-rewrites to a term s, written $t \hookrightarrow_{\mathcal{R}(\mu)} s$, if $t \to_{\mathcal{R}} s$ reducing the subterm of t at the replacing occurrence $u \in O^\mu(t)$. $\hookrightarrow_{\mathcal{R}(\mu)}$ is the one-step context-sensitive rewrite relation of $\mathcal{R}$ wrt μ. $\hookrightarrow^*_{\mathcal{R}(\mu)}$ is the context-sensitive rewrite relation of $\mathcal{R}$ wrt μ.*

In the following, when no necessary, we assume that the TRS $\mathcal{R} = (\Sigma, R)$ and Σ-map μ are given, and we drop references to them by solely writing $\hookrightarrow$ instead of $\hookrightarrow_{\mathcal{R}(\mu)}$ to denote the one-step context-sensitive rewrite relation.

Let us now consider a first example of context-sensitive rewriting. Let $\alpha :$ f$(x) \to x$ be a rule and $t =$ g(f(a), f(b)) be a term. a) If μ(g) $= \emptyset$ then t cannot be reduced, because neither the occurrence $u = 1$ nor $u = 2$ satisfies the replacement condition wrt μ. b) If μ(g) $= \{1\}$, then we can reduce f(a) but we cannot reduce f(b). c) If μ(g) $= \{2\}$, then we can reduce f(b) but we cannot reduce f(a). d) If μ(g) $= \{1, 2\}$, then we can be reduce both f(a) and f(b).

The following proposition illustrates the (one-step) context-sensitive version of the 'being closed under context application' property. The context-sensitive rewriting is 'closed under *replacing* context application'.

Proposition 3.12 (Restricted context replacement) *Let $C, t, s \in \mathcal{T}(\Sigma, V)$. Let $u \in O^\mu(C)$. If $t \hookrightarrow s$ then $C[t]_u \hookrightarrow C[s]_u$.*

Note that for the *top* Σ-map μ_T the replacement condition is satisfied for every term t and occurrence u. This is to say that, given a TRS $\mathcal{R}$, the one-step context-sensitive rewrite relation for μ_T and the standard one-step rewrite relation coincide, i.e. $\hookrightarrow_{\mathcal{R}(\mu_T)}=\to_{\mathcal{R}}$. Now we show that the context-sensitive rewriting is stable under substitution.

Proposition 3.13 (Stability of $\hookrightarrow$) *Let* $\mathcal{R} = (\Sigma, R)$ *be a TRS, μ be a Σ-map and $\sigma : V \to \mathcal{T}(\Sigma, V)$ be a substitution. Then $t \hookrightarrow s \Rightarrow \sigma(t) \hookrightarrow \sigma(s)$.*

The following proposition establishes that, given a TRS, the one-step context--sensitive rewrite relation induced by a replacement map includes the relation induced by a lesser replacement map.

Proposition 3.14 (Monotonicity of $\hookrightarrow$ with respect to $\sqsubseteq$)
Let $\mathcal{R} = (\Sigma, R)$ be a TRS and μ, μ' be Σ-maps. Then $\mu \sqsubseteq \mu' \Rightarrow \hookrightarrow_{\mathcal{R}(\mu)} \subseteq \hookrightarrow_{\mathcal{R}(\mu')}$.

3.3 Context-sensitive rewriting and Inference Systems

In [7] we have proven that a TRS $\mathcal{R} = (\Sigma, R)$ and a Σ-map μ generate an inference system (IS) which transition relation and the context-sensitive rewrite relation $\hookrightarrow_{\mathcal{R}(\mu)}$ coincide. Roughly speaking, the axioms of the IS are instances of the rewrite rules and a *contextual* inference rule is defined for each k-ary symbol $f \in \Sigma$ and each argument $i \in \mu(f)$. The *basic inference system* associated to $\mathcal{R}$ and μ, denoted by $I(\mathcal{R}, \mu)$, is defined as follows:

1. $\alpha : l \to r \in R$ iff
   $$(\mathsf{a}_\alpha)\frac{}{l \diamond r} \text{ is an (scheme of) axiom of } I(\mathcal{R}, \mu)$$

2. For each $f \in \Sigma$, $k = ar(f)$, $i \in \mu(f)$ and terms $t_1, \ldots, t_k, s_i$
   $$(\mathsf{r}[f, i])\frac{t_i \diamond s_i}{f(t_1, \ldots, t_i, \ldots, t_k) \diamond f(t_1, \ldots, s_i, \ldots, t_k)} \text{ is a rule of } I(\mathcal{R}, \mu)$$

The relation defined by $I(\mathcal{R}, \mu)$ on $\mathcal{T}(\Sigma, V)$ (that is, its *deductive closure*) is denoted by $\to_{I(\mathcal{R}, \mu)}$.

This is the class of ISs that context-sensitive rewriting mechanizes, i.e. those ISs such that $\to_{I(\mathcal{R}, \mu)}=\hookrightarrow_{\mathcal{R}(\mu)}$. Conversely, given an IS such that every rule fits the pattern $r[f, i]$, we define a TRS by taking the axioms of the IS as rewrite rules and we attach a replacement map according to the existing contextual inference rules $r[f, i]$.

Now, if we want to define an abstract machine that computes the transition relation of such an IS we can modify a standard rewriting machine (such as the graph reduction machine [10]) to deal with the restrictions imposed by the replacement condition. Roughly speaking, in order to execute a program with respect to a set of rewrite rules, the *evaluator* of a rewriting machine must follows the following algorithm (until a normal form is reached) [10]:

1. selecting the next redex to be reduced and
2. reducing it.

To accomodate this to a context-sensitive rewriting system we must to take into account the replacement condition in the first step.

3.4 Examples and applications

Let us consider the λ-calculus. A λ-term $M ::= x \mid \lambda x.M \mid MN$ is represented as a tree by considering each λx as an unary symbol, application as a binary symbol @ and each variable as a symbol of arity zero [5]. This is expressed by means of the signature $\Sigma_\lambda = C_V \cup \Lambda_x \cup \{@\}$, where $\Lambda_x = \{\lambda_x \mid x \in V\}$ and C_V is a set of arbitrary constants (one for each variable symbol). The immediate β-reduction of λ-calculus $\to_\beta$, can be obtained from the following inference system [4, 5], which we refer to as IS_β (in spite of the introduction of Σ_λ, we express IS_β in the standard λ-notation):

$$(red) \; \frac{}{(\lambda x.P)Q \triangleright P[x := Q]}$$

We can see that any instance of the axiom scheme (red) can be taken as a rewrite rule $(\lambda x.P)Q \to P[x := Q]$. In the sequel, R_λ is the set of rules which are instances of the (red) axiom scheme.

$$(r\lambda) \; \frac{M \triangleright M'}{\lambda x.M \triangleright \lambda x.M'} \qquad (r1) \; \frac{M \triangleright M'}{MN \triangleright M'N} \qquad (r2) \; \frac{M \triangleright M'}{NM \triangleright NM'}$$

Note that the *context passing* rules $(r\lambda)$, $(r1)$ and $(r2)$ fit the pattern r[f,i].

Example 3.15 (Weak β-reduction) *Let us consider the weak β-reduction, a restriction on the β-reduction of λ-calculus. For this reduction, an abstraction $\lambda x.M$ is irreducible, even if M contains a redex. This corresponds to drop the rule $(r\lambda)$ in IS_β, thus obtaining IS_w whose only rules are $r1$ and $r2$. We can simulate this behavior with context-sensitive rewriting by considering the following TRS $\mathcal{R} = (\Sigma_\lambda, R_\lambda)$ and the Σ_λ-map μ_w defined as follows: $\mu_w(@) = \{1, 2\}$, $\mu_w(f) = \emptyset$ for all $f \in \Sigma_\lambda - \{@\}$.*

Example 3.16 (Lazy λ-calculus) *Now consider the lazy λ-calculus, another restriction on the β-reduction used by the majority of functional languages to avoid the 'eagerness' in evaluating functional applications. To delay the evaluation of an application MN we need only one context passing rule, namely $(r1)$ to constitute IS_z, the inference system for lazy λ-calculus. We can simulate this behavior with context-sensitive rewriting by considering the following TRS $\mathcal{R} = (\Sigma_\lambda, R_\lambda)$ and the Σ_λ-map μ_z defined as follows: $\mu_z(@) = \{1\}$, $\mu_z(f) = \emptyset$ for all $f \in \Sigma_\lambda - \{@\}$.*

The R. Milner's π-calculus [9] is a computational scheme which models concurrency. In [7] we define a TRS and a replacement map whose context-sensitive rewriting can be seen as a mechanization of the π-calculus process execution.

4 Further research

We have introduced a powerful characterization of the context-sensitive rewriting process. We have examined several computational properties of context-sensitive relations and demonstrated that they are stable under substitution and closed under replacing context application.

A first approach to the characterization of confluence of context-sensitive rewriting can be found in [6]. A desirable direction for further research will be the definition of syntactic criteria to ensure the confluence and termination of induced context-sensitive rewriting when we attach a replacement map to a given term rewriting system.

5 Acknowledgements

I would like to thank María Alpuente and Germán Vidal for their encouragement and support. Also, I am grateful to Asunción Casanova, Javier Oliver and Javier Piris for their helpful comments and corrections.

References

1. N. Dershowitz. A Taste of Rewrite Systems. In P.E. Lauer, editor, *Proc of Functional Programming, Concurrency, Simulation and Automated Reasoning*, volume 693 of *Lecture Notes in Computer Science*, pages 199-228, Berlin, 1993.
2. N. Dershowitz and J.P. Jouannaud. Rewrite Systems. In J. van Leeuwen, editor, *Handbook of Theoretical Computer Science*, volume B: Formal Models and Semantics, pages 243-320. Elsevier, Amsterdam and The MIT Press, Cambridge, MA, 1990.
3. H. Ehrig and B. Mahr. Fundamentals of Algebraic Specification. volume 6 of *EATCS Monographs on Theoretical Computer Science*. Springer-Verlag, Berlin, 1985.
4. J.R. Hindley and J.P. Seldin. Introduction to Combinators and λ-Calculus. Cambridge University Press, 1986.
5. R. Lalement. Computation as Logic. Masson-Prentice Hall International, 1993.
6. S. Lucas. Computational properties in context-sensitive rewriting. In *Proc. of 1995 Joint Conference on Declarative Programming, GULP-PRODE'95*. To appear.
7. S. Lucas and J. Oliver. Context-sensitive rewriting. Technical report DSIC-II/23/94.
8. J. Meseguer. Conditional Rewriting Logic as an Unified Model of Concurrency. *Journal of Theoretical Computer Science*, 96:73-155, 1992.
9. R. Milner. The polyadic π-calculus: A tutorial. In F.L. Brauer, W Bauer and H Schwintenberg, editors, *Logic and Algebra of Specifications*, Springer-Verlag, Berlin, 1993.
10. S. L. Peyton-Jones. The Implementation of Functional Programming Languages. Prentice-Hall, 1987.
11. D. Plaisted. Equational Reasoning and Term Rewriting Systems. In D. Gabbay and J. Siekmann, editors, *Handbook of Logic in Artificial Intelligence and Logic Programming*, Oxford University Press, volume 1, 1994.

Constraint Logic Programming with Fuzzy Sets

Luděk Matyska and Hynek Bureš

Institute of Computer Science, Masaryk University, Burešova 20, CZ-602 00 Brno,
Czech Republic
e-mail: {ludek,cd2bcg16}@ics.muni.cz

Abstract. Constraint Logic Programming language embodying extensional finite Fuzzy Sets is presented. Basic fuzzy set operations ($=$, $\in$,
$\neq$, and $\notin$) are defined as *constraints* over fuzzy sets and their elements.
Simple list-like representation of sets is presented, with fset/2 as the
interpreted set constructor and {} as the empty set. Members of the
fuzzy sets are fuzzy elements (terms with mu/2 as the main functor),
with explicit membership value associated with each individual member.
The language is implemented using the concept of attributed variables;
brief discussion of the usability of attributed variables for this kind of
meta-programming is also given.

1 Introduction

Sets form a fundamental mathematical entity which is often used in declarative
specifications of many algorithms. Classical logic programming does not provide
set-manipulation predicates and is thus extremely inconvenient as a specification tool in these cases. The Goedel programming language [6] can serve as an
example of a logic programming system with a very restricted set-manipulating
predicates, almost unusable in a truly declarative way. There are several other
logic programming systems with embedded set-manipulations [10, 2], none beyond the research and development stage.

Fuzzy sets, on the other hand, are most often used in connection with uncertainty and vagueness handling [13]. Fuzzy logic [5], as a derived concept, was
introduced to Logic Programming almost ten years ago resulting in the development of several "Fuzzy Prolog" systems [7]. These systems replace the inference
mechanism of Prolog by its fuzzy variant, which is able to handle the concept of
partial truth. All these systems associate a truth value with each clause in the
program. This is a computationally very expensive approach, as the underlying
theory requires that the resolvent with the maximal truth value is to be selected
at each resolution step.

It is possible to overcome some of the problems of using fuzzy logic in the
framework of Logic Programming by restricting ourselves to logic programming
with fuzzy sets. The underlying basic inference mechanism remains the same as
in ordinary logic programming and the strength of fuzzy set manipulation is used
only when really needed — as all the operations must be explicitly coded. The
possibility to manipulate fuzzy sets directly and declaratively widely enlarges
areas of potential applications of logic programming systems. Natural language

analysis and understanding, fuzzy (deductive) databases or fuzzy front-ends to (deductive) databases together with expert system development are just few examples of potential use of logic programming with fuzzy sets.

The CLP(FS) system, built on top of SICStus Prolog and ECL^{i}PS^e, represents the first step towards the full implementation of the Constraint Logic Programming language over Fuzzy Sets. The four basic set manipulation predicates, namely equality and disequality over sets and membership and non-membership, are implemented in a quasi-eager way. Fuzzy sets are introduced as a special kind of sets with a prescribed structure of individual term, membership function being represented simply as a real value from the interval $(0, 1)$.

The paper is organized as follows. In the next section, brief description of the underlying theory of set implementation is presented. This is followed by a description of implementation techniques used. Finally, the future research directions are sketched.

2 Theory

The first point is to define *representation* of extensional finite sets. The representation similar in many approaches to the list representation was chosen. It is based on the following:

- availability of a constant {} for empty sets;
- existence of a binary function symbol, set, with the following intended interpretation: set(t,s) is a set created by adding (term) t as a new element to the set s.

The extensional notation for sets is provided by a collection G of ground terms; G is the smallest collection such that

- {} belongs to G;
- set(t,s) belongs to G for any ground term t if s belongs to G.

Any term s from G is called a *set term*. A non-ground term t is called a set term if there exists an instantiation σ of the variables in t such that the ground term tσ belongs to G.

To provide the intended meaning of the set/2 functor, it must satisfy the following requirements:

1. *Left permutivity*, i.e., set(A,set(B,C)) = set(B,set(A,C))
2. *Left absorption*, i.e., set(A,set(A,C)) = set(A,C)

To deal with *fuzzy sets*, the membership value has to be associated with each individual item of the set. This is possible by defining explicit association of individual membership values with individual items. For this purpose, new binary functor mu/2[1] is introduced: mu(I,M), the element I is a term and membership

---

[1] The name was chosen to reflect the greek character μ, usually used to represent membership function/values.

value M is a term or a variable which can be, eventually, evaluated to the real number in the interval $(0, 1)$. M is *constrained* on both the type — it must be a real number — and the value — its value must lie in the prescribed interval. An extensional notation for fuzzy elements is provided by a collection $\mathcal{M}$ of ground terms mu(I,M) where I is a ground term and M is a real number from interval $(0, 1)$. Any term in $\mathcal{M}$ will be called a *fuzzy element*. A non-ground term m is called a fuzzy element if there exists an instantiation σ such that the ground term mσ is in $\mathcal{M}$.

For fuzzy sets, new binary functor fset is introduced, similar in all aspects to the set functor with the one exception — the term t in the construct fset(t,s) must be a fuzzy element. All terms in the collection F of ground terms constructed using the fset instead of the set functor, will be called *fuzzy set terms*, as well as all the non-ground terms f for which substitution σ exists such that fσ is ground and belongs to F. The fset must also fulfill the left absorption and left permutivity rules.

The most important and in the same time the most difficult part of the incorporation of sets into the framework of logic programming lies in the definition of set unification. The lack of order of set elements causes that the main feature of the standard unification, i.e., the "uniqueness" of the most general unifier, does not hold any more. In general, there can be more than one most general unifier. The unification of fuzzy elements requires no further modification of the unification procedure. Fuzzy element can be unified with another fuzzy element only, i.e., mu(I,M) = F succeeds if and only if F = mu(I$'$, M$'$) $\wedge$ I = I$'$ $\wedge$ M = M$'$ and fails otherwise. The unification of the membership values is dealt within the framework of the original CLP($\mathcal{R}$) framework (i.e., appropriate constraints are generated and eventually solved via the CLP($\mathcal{R}$) arithmetic solver); two implicit constraints are always generated by the intended interpretation, namely M > 0 $\wedge$ M <= 1 for each fuzzy term mu(I,M).

Another important point is the *canonical representation* of sets. We will say that the set A={t_1, t_2, ..., t_n} is in canonical form (i.e., A = fset(t_1, fset(t_2, ..., t_n)...)), if $t_i <_C t_{i+1}$ holds for each $i \in \langle 1, n - 1 \rangle$ and $<_C$ is some order on terms such that {} is the largest element.

The second most important set operation, namely the set membership, may be expressed via set unification: $A \in X$ is equivalent to $X = \{A|X\}$. Using partial evaluation techniques, more specific algorithm may be found [12].

Any set-manipulation language pretended for real use must define at least the negative counter-parts of the set unification and the set membership operations presented above. From the semantical point of view the introduction of two new functors, namely $\neq$ and $\notin$ over sets poses no additional complication in the context of constraint logic programming, by introducing both dis-equalities as *constraints*. In fact, it is more convenient to deal with *all* basic set-manipulation operations as constraints in the context of constraint logic programming. The sets are taken to be *interpreted objects* of the language and they are dealt with by the appropriate *constraint solver*. The approach, together with the theoretical foundations, was firstly presented in Dovier's works [2]. In order to deal with fuzzy sets, the basic domain must be at least three-sorted — it must include not only Herbrand Universe with new interpreted terms (three in our case: {}, fset/2, and mu/2), but also real numbers with appropriate function and predicate symbols.

Following basic constraints over sets are thus introduced: $t = s$, $t \in s$, $t \neq s$, and $t \notin s$. The other group of available constraints is associated with real numbers and is (at least) a subset of interpreted functors and predicates of the CLP($\mathcal{R}$) language. The set constraint solver comprises of algorithms simplifying (and eventually solving) the original constraints. The simplified constraints are satisfiable — there exists some substitution σ of its variables which grounds them while satisfying all the constraints.

Let us denote a collection of elementary constraints as C; it can be splitted to disjoint sets

$$C = C_= \cup C_{\neq} \cup C_{\in} \cup C_{\notin} \cup C^F, \tag{1}$$

where the elements of C_ν are all of the form $t_1 \, \nu \, t_2$, with t_1, t_2 terms, ν a symbol in $\{=, \neq, \in, \notin\}$, and C^F is either $\emptyset$ or $\{False\}$.

The actual simplification algorithms for individual elementary constraints may be found elsewhere [12, 1]. Collection of constraints, defined in (1), is said to be in canonical form if

- $C^F = \{False\}$, or
- $C_{\in} = C^F = \emptyset$, $C_=$, $C_{\neq}$, and $C_{\notin}$ are in canonical form.

The main result here is that the collection of constraints in canonical form is solvable if $C^F = \emptyset$. This means that the algorithms together represent complete procedure for the solver of the set relations. The canonical form of the collection of constraints is computed as the minimum fix-point of application of all individual canonicalisation algorithms. The solver always terminates in a finite number of steps and this assures that the resulting canonical collection of constraints is always finite.

The finiteness of the solver procedure assures its implementability and usefulness as a solver for basic set-related constraints in the CLP scheme. The connection between this algebraic treatment of sets and the logic counterpart in the appropriate CLP language is simply established by selecting one of the constraint collections returned by solve (different from $\{False\}$) and using the substitutions induced by $C_=$.

3 Implementation

Although the existence of the theory behind some programming language is a very good pre-requisite for any working *and* usable programming system, the theory itself is not sufficient if there is no efficient implementation.

There are many possibilities how to implement a Constraint Logic Programming language, the most prominent ones based on the modification of some 'standard' abstract machine for appropriate logic programming language (usually Prolog) [2]. While this approach may be the best in terms of the quality of the system produced (measured by its efficiency, speed of execution, etc.), it is not the best approach to be used during the development of new system. However, languages of logic programming are themselves very good tools for meta-programming and (meta-)interpreter writing. This appropriateness is further enhanced by recent introduction of a new kind of objects: the attributed variables [8, 9]. They were introduced to allow *semantic unification* to be easily implemented.

At the object-level, attributed variables behave exactly the same way as ordinary logical variables. They have, however, an *attribute* attached to them. In general, attribute may be any (ground or non-ground) term. The attributes are accessible at the meta-level through a set of predicates, the most important are predicates for the extended unification. These predicates are called whenever the attributed variable is unified with either another attributed variable or any term. The user supplied code of these two predicates actually performs the unification, with the actual call to explicit instantiation (or binding) of the two terms to be unified.

The first version of CLP(FS) was implemented using a clone of SICStus Prolog with a simple implementation of attributed variables [9]. This implementation platform was chosen because CLP($\mathcal{R}$) system was also implemented on the top of these attributed variables.

As the details of the actual implementation are given elsewhere [1], we will focus only on the problems encountered. The sets are represented as attributed variables whose attribute holds not only the actual canonical representation of the set, but also a list of active dis-equality and not-membership constraints. This was due to the fact that there may be only one attribute attached to a variable. If two orthogonal concepts are to be implemented via attributed variables (like set manipulation and goal delaying), their attributes must be combined *by hand* and all the predicates for extended unification rewritten. This effectively inhibits the meta-meta-programming, i.e. implementation of one meta-level on top of another (as we intended to implement CLP(FS) on top of CLP($\mathcal{R}$)). As a result, only restricted form of fuzzy sets is currently available: the relations between membership values are simply delayed and are woken only when the values are fully instantiated.

Recently, meta-variables were introduced in ECL^{i}PS^e [3] as an extension of attributed variables. The number of attributes attached to meta-variable is not limited and different unification handler may be specified for individual attributes. This opens the path towards stacking meta-levels one on top of the other, as is proven by preliminary results with the re-implementation of the CLP(FS) system.

4 Future Work

The re-implemetation of the CLP(FS) system into the ECL^{i}PS^e with meta variables is already under way. The set unification, set membership and the negative counter-parts are already implemented in a crude way, the complete set of input/output manipulating predicates will follow. We plan to re-implement CLP($\mathcal{R}$) system to allow truly declarative semantics over reals to be used for the membership value manipulation. In the meantime, the membership values are implemented using the finite domain library of ECL^{i}PS^e, with values lying in the range 1..100 (membership value 100 coresponds to the non-fuzzy (crisp) element).

The resulting CLP(FS,$\mathcal{R}$) system will be used in the development of an expert system for medical diagnosis [4].

In a far looking horizon, an enhancement of extended unification predicates is being developed, allowing to use the meta-variables in a truly declarative way (the planned extension will deal with the current asymmetry of extended unification predicates, which sometimes leads to constraint floundering).

References

1. H. Bureš: *Constraint Logic Programming with Fuzzy Sets*. Master thesis, Faculty of Informatics, Masaryk University, Brno, Czech Republic, 1995 (in czech).
2. A. Dovier, E. G. Omodeo, E. Pontelli, and G. Rosii. {log}: A logic programming language with finite sets. In *Proceedings 8th International Conference on Logic Programming*, pages 111–124. MIT Press, Cambridge, MA, 1991.
   A. Dovier and E. Pontelli. A WAM-based implementation of logic language with sets. In *Proc. Int. Symp. Logic. Prog.* MIT Pres, 1994.
   A. Dovier and G. Rossi. Embedding extensional finite sets in CLP. In *Proceedings International Symposium on Logic Programming*, MIT Press, Cambridge, MA, 1993.
3. M. Meier et al.: ECL^{i}PS^e, Extensions Manual. ECRC, München, Germany, 1995.
4. J. Feit, L. Matyska: *Expert system for liver biopsy diagnosis*, in preparation.
5. P. Hajek. Fuzzy logic as logic. In *Proc. SOFSEM95*. Springer-Verlag, 1995.
6. P. M. Hill and J. W. Lloyd. *The Gödel Programming Language*. MIT Press, New York, 1994.
7. C. J. Hinde. Fuzzy Prolog. *Int. J. Man. Machine Studies*, 24:569–595, 1986.
8. C. Holzbaur. *Specification of Constraint Based Inference Mechanisms through Extended Unification*. PhD thesis, University of Vienna, Freyung 6, A-1010 Vienna, Austria, 1990.
9. C. Holzbaur. DMCAI CLP 1.2. Technical report, University of Vienna, Freyung 6, A-1010 Vienna, Austria, 1992.
10. B. Legeard and E. Legros. CLPS: A set constraints logic programming language. Technical report, Laboratoire d'Automatique de Besançon, February 1991.
11. L. Matyska. Constraint logic programming. In *SOFSEM93*, Hrdoňov, 1993. VÚSEI AR Bratislava.
12. L. Matyska: Logic Programming with Fuzzy Šets. TR, Department of Computer Science, City University, London, England, 1993.
13. L. A. Zadeh. The role of fuzzy logic in the management of uncertainty in expert systems. In M. M. Gupta, A. Kandel, W. Brandler, and J. B. Kiszka, editors, *Approximate Reasoning in Expert Systems*, pages 3–32. North-Holland, Amsterdam, 1985.

Parallel Processing of Image Database Queries

Francois Meunier[1] and Petr Zemanek[2]

[1] Institut National des Telecommunications, 9 rue Ch. Fourier, 91011 Evry, France
[2] Dept. of Computer Science and Engineering, FEE CTU, Karlovo nam. 13, 121 35 Prague, Czech Republic

Abstract. This paper treats data structures for image representation and parallel algorithms for operations associated with databases of images. In our approach, images are converted from input pixel form to *linear quadtrees* that allow efficient storage of image data and that are suitable for a large number of operations. We have designed and implemented algorithms for *set operations* - union, intersection, difference, and for *relational database operations* - selection, projection and join. These operations are essential for data retrieval in spatial database queries. All the algorithms mentioned above were developed on *MasPar* SIMD (Single Instruction Multiple Data) parallel computer equipped with 1024 processors.

1 One-Dimensional Representation of Lines and Polygons

In the challenging process of development of large computer applications, we are positioned in the ability to manipulate data reflecting the specific nature of the real world. One of the specific phenomena that has to be considered when dealing with real objects, is the *spatial properties* of these objects. The spatial properties - like shape of an object, coloring of an object and its parts, volume of an object, changes in the shape as a function of time, etc. - are to be stored and manipulated using specific techniques and methods.

There exist a number of techniques for digital representation of spatial data. In this paper we present a model suitable for data representation allowing efficient *parallel processing* of spatial data. We will work with two-dimensional spatial objects, but extension to three or more dimensions is straightforward.

There are several procedures to represent relative locations of any two- or three-dimensional object by a one-dimensional object. Probably the most efficient means to fulfill this task are *space-filling curves*, that is one dimensional paths through multidimensional tiled space.

A good sequential ordering of tiles traversed by space-filling curve should have certain properties that provide some conveniences in single dimension addressing for two- or three-dimensional sets of regularly shaped tiles. The path should pass only once through each tile in the space, and neighbors in space should be adjacent on the path. The path should be usable even if there is a mixture of different sized spatial units, and should work equally well in two or three dimensions, and for connecting to adjacent blocks of space.

In reality there are no curves having all specified properties, but there are some with valuable properties for our purposes. The original space-filling curve was exhibited in 1890 by Italian mathematician Guiseppe Peano [2], (see Fig.1). It facilitates retrieving of neighbors, and although neighboring points are not always neighbors on the curve, they generally are. The encoding of space-filling curves uses one coordinate, called a *key*, to stand for two or more coordinates. The keys are easily obtained (see [4]) by interleaving of binary digits of Cartesian coordinates x and y.

The idea of variable spatial resolution implies varying sized units at a given resolution level. The choice of the shape of the units is a different matter. There are practical advantages in using the square figure. The square is practically handy if the process of creating blocks of varying size is one of decomposing space from a general level to more detail level.

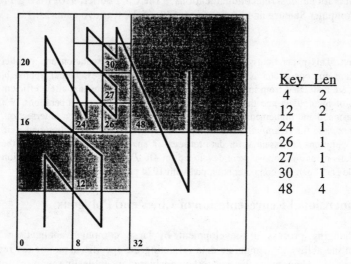

Key	Len
4	2
12	2
24	1
26	1
27	1
30	1
48	4

Fig. 1. Linear location coding for quadtrees - Peano keys

For example, as Fig.1 illustrates, any polygon can be successively approximated by sets of blocks at different levels. If the process involves systematic splitting of space in two-dimensional space by a rule of four, then the structure is known as a *quadtree*. A three-dimensional equivalent is known as an *octtree* [3].

2 Operations with Linear Quadtrees

In the previous chapter we presented a solution on storing quadtrees with a linear model based on Peano-filling curves. Using the relational notation, a set of quadtrees can be represented by the *relational schema* [1]:

Quadtree_Relation (Object_Identification, Peano_key, Side_length)

in which a tuple represents one quadrant, *Object_Identification* represents the object number (logically connected to other attributes), *Peano_key* is the Peano key of the quadrant foot, and *Side_length* is the length of the side of the quadrant square. In spatial applications, a tuple representing a quadrant can model different situations.

When working with Peano relations, we have to work only with tuples that may describe a correctly defined object. In order to obtain a consistent description, three steps are necessary, each of them consisting of checking what are known as *consistent conformance levels* [2]:

1/ Good positioning of quadrants: *first conformance level*
2/ Absence of overlapping quadrants: *second conformance level*
3/ Maximal quadrant compaction: *third conformance level*

Having two spatial objects *A* and *B* represented as linear lists, we realize the *union* of these two objects as follows. We merge the lists representing *A* and *B* into one list ordered by Peano keys of the nodes from *both* lists. In the resulting list we delete all nodes that are overlapped by another node and we aggregate all quadruples of nodes that may form one node.

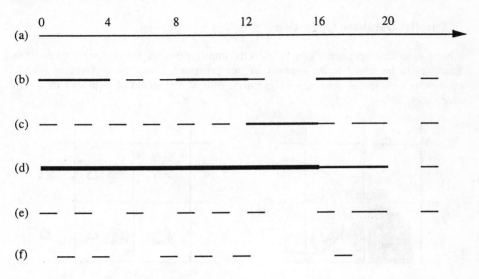

Fig. 2. Set operations on linear quadtrees
(a) - linear (Peano) coordinate, (b) - quadtree nodes of spatial object *A*,
(c) - quadtree nodes of spatial object *B*, (d) *union* of objects *A* and *B*,
(e) - *intersection* of objects *A* and *B*, (f) - *difference A - B*.

Because of the memory requirements, it is not suitable to merge both input lists into one list and operate on this list. We propose more efficient solution that does not merge two lists into one. Instead of merging two lists into one, our algorithm takes nodes from both lists in order defined by Peano keys of nodes from both lists. The operations defined by *First Conformance Level* and *Second Conformance Level* are performed on each node separately.

Intersection of two objects represented as linear lists of quadtree nodes is performed using the same input handling technique as in the set union operation. We scan nodes from both input lists according to the Peano ordering of quadtree nodes. If a node from one list does not contain next node from the other list, we skip this node (we do not attach it to the output). If input node from one input list is contained in the input node from the second input list, we attach the contained node to the output list. If both the input nodes are the same, we attach this node also to the output.

Set *difference* of two spatial objects represented as linear quadtrees is performed as follows. Difference of any sets *A* and *B* is not symmetrical operation. Suppose we want to realize *(A - B)*. We scan nodes from both input lists according to the Peano ordering of quadtree nodes. If a node from the *A* list does not contain any node from the *B* list, we attach this node to the output list. If a node from the *B* list does not contain any node from the *A* list, we skip this node from the *B* list.

If there are two nodes in both input lists that have the same Peano key and the same side length, we skip both these nodes. If a node from one input list is contained in a node from the other list, but the side lengths of these two nodes are different, the node with greater side length is disaggregated into four nodes and these four nodes replace disaggregated node in the corresponding input list.

3 Parallel Database Operations

Above described operations can be directly implemented as *serial* - we expect linear quadtrees to be stored in the memory of one processor. If we are performing *parallel operations* with spatial objects, we manipulate with objects stored in memories of several processors.

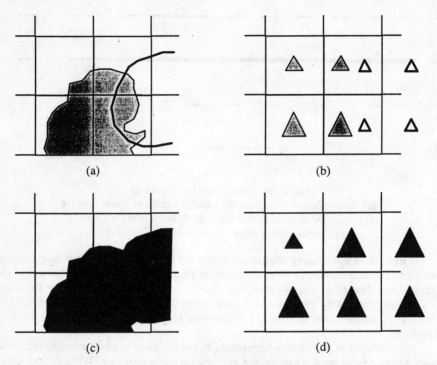

(a)   (b)

(c)   (d)

Fig. 3. Parallel set operations on spatial objects represented as linear quadtrees.
(a) - two spatial objects, (b) - quadtree representation, (c) - union of objects,
(d) - quadtree representation of the union

In our approach, we will work with parallel computers that do not have any shared memory, like *MasPar* SIMD parallel computer (see [4]). All data (i.e. spatial objects represented as linear quadtrees) will be stored in distributed memory. Input image we divide into nonoverlapping parts of same size and each processor will store and process the same portion of input image, i.e., the lists that represent spatial objects that are located in given part of input image (see Fig.3).

Above described approach has been also implemented in the *pixel* to *linear quadtree* conversion algorithm (see [4]). We have divided the input pixel image into square pixel portions of the same size and we have generated lists (linear quadtrees) representing objects (or their parts) that have been found in given parts of input pixel image. The result of the mentioned algorithm was the set of lists stored in the memory of every processor. Some objects may also have been stored in the memories of several processors.

If there are several images to be processed (like when we are processing set operations), we divide these images using the same technique (see Fig.3). The raster that is used for image division among the processors is the same for all processed images.

Above described approach has been also implemented in the *pixel* to *linear quadtree* conversion algorithm (see [4]). We have divided the input pixel image into square pixel portions of the same size and we have generated lists (linear quadtrees) representing objects (or their parts) that have been found in given parts of input pixel image. The result of the mentioned algorithm was the set of lists stored in the memory of every processor. Some objects may therefore have been stored in the memories of several processors.

The result of any of the parallel operations with spatial objects represented as linear quadtrees will again be a spatial object represented as linear quadtree and stored in memories of corresponding processors. Note that there is no interprocess communication during any of the parallel operations presented below. If we process, e.g., union of two spatial objects A and B that are stored as objects

$$A = A_{p(1)}, ..., A_{p(n)} \quad \text{and} \quad B = B_{q(1)}, ..., B_{q(m)}$$

in the memories of processors $p(1)$ to $p(n)$ and $q(1)$ to $q(m)$, respectively, we do in parallel following operations:

$$C_{r(k)} = Union(A_{p(i)}, B_{q(j)})$$

in all processors where $r(k) = p(i)$ for any i $(i = 1,..,n)$ or $r(k) = q(j)$ for any j $(j = 1,...,m)$ (see Fig.3). The algorithm for union of linear quadtrees presented above is simultaneously performed in all processors that have the representation of any part of spatial objects A or B in their memory. Result of the union operation is a linear quadtree that is stored in the memories of all processors that have stored the spatial object A or B.

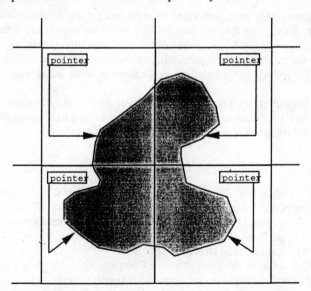

Fig. 4. Result of a selection on object name - `plural` pointer to `plural` object

In the serial processing of database queries we have one object or one set of tuples as a result of the first or second selection, respectively. In our approach to parallel processing, we store an input image divided into parts of equal size in memories of several processors and all processors work simultaneously on all of these parts. Because we *select* one spatial objects among objects in *one image*, the result of a selection on given object type (name) is a set of all parts of the selecting object. On MasPar parallel computer are these parts referenced by a set of pointers - a `plural` pointer to `plural` data. This pointer points to all parts of the desired object stored in corresponding processors (see Fig.4).

In Peano tuple algebra, we are interested in *projection* according to object identification to obtain a relation representing only the different names of objects in given image. This task is performed in parallel in all processors.

We have implemented *relational join* on Peano keys. Join is performed simultaneously in all processors. We scan (in parallel) lists representing spatial objects in all processors. As the result we obtain set of pointers referencing all resulting objects.

Below we present experimental results with developed algorithms. Results were obtained from experiments with parallel image data processing on MasPar computer with 1024 processors where each processor had 16 kB RAM memory.

Image size (pix.)	256x256	512x512	1024x1024	2048x2048
Number of objects	3 072	7 168	11 264	15 360
Quadtree building	*130*	*530*	*2 050*	*7 280*
Union	31	54	73	78
Intersection	2,2	5,4	6,9	7,2
Difference	12	18	23	25
Selection (Key)	0,5	0,7	0,8	0,7
Selection (Object)	0,2	0,4	0,6	0,7
Join and projection	37	62	85	88

All measurements were performed on input images that contained same image for each processor. This image had the size *(n/32 x n/32)* where *n* is the size of the whole original image. Because there is no interprocess communication in any algorithm, we can easily estimate the results for serial processing on the same type of processor. There is only one computation having execution time dependent on input image size - the quadtree building.

It can be seen from presented experimental results that database operations on spatial objects can be solved in very reasonable time using parallel computers. This fact may influence the design of spatial information systems in near future.

References

1. Elmasri, R., Navathe, S.B.: Fundamentals of Database Systems.
   Redwood City (CA), Benjamin Cummings Publishing Company. 873 p.
2. Laurini, R., Thompson, D.: Fundamentals of Spatial Information Systems.
   London, Academic Press 1992. 680 p.
3. Samet, H.: Applications of Spatial Data Structures.
   Reading (MA), Addison-Wesley Publishing Company 1990. 480 p.
4. Zemanek, P.: Parallel Database Operations with Spatial Objects.
   Report 95-05-01. Evry (France), Institut National des Telecommunications 1995. 92 p.

Maximum Flow Problem in Distributed Environment

Lenka Motyčková

e-mail:lenka@fi.muni.cz, Department of Computer Science, Masaryk University, Brno, Czech Republic

Abstract. Our contribution here is to design efficient distributed algorithms for the maximum flow problem. The idea behind our distributed version of highest-label preflow-push algorithm is to disseminate label values together with safety information from every node. When the algorithm terminates, the computed flow is stored distributedly in incident nodes for all edges, that is, each node knows the values of flow which belong to its adjacent edges. We compute maximum flow in $O(n^2 \log^3 n)$ time with communication complexity $O(n^2 (\log^3 n + \sqrt{m}))$, where n and m are the number of nodes and edges respectively in a network graph.

1 Introduction

The *maximum flow* problem is well known problem being solved for years by sequential algorithms. Recently several parallel algorithms appeared and new methods were proposed that are more suitable for parallel proceeding.

The *maximum flow* problem is defined as follows. Suppose we are given a directed graph $G(E, V)$ in which each edge $(u, v) \in E$ has a nonnegative capacity $c(u, v) \geq 0$. We distinguish two nodes in a graph: a source s and a sink t. A flow in G is a real-valued function $f: V \times V \to R$ that satisfies the following properties: capacity constraint, skew symmetry, and flow conservation.

The quantity $f(u, v)$, which can be positive or negative, is called the *net flow* from vertex u to vertex v. The value of a flow f is defined as $|f| = \sum_{v \in V} f(s, v)$, that is the total *net flow out* of the source.

The *maximum flow problem* is to find a flow of the biggest value.

Goldberg introduces in [8] generic preflow-push algorithm which has a simple sequential implementation that runs in $O(n^2 m)$ time, thereby improving upon $O(nm^2)$ bound of the Edmonds-Karp algorithm. Cheriyan and Maheshwari [6] were able to improve the time bound of this method to $O(n^2 \sqrt{m})$.

Problems for the maximum flow are P-complete, so it is unlikely that they can be solved in NC. Even though the speedup of computation when a parallel machine is used is substantial. Parallelism was one of the motivations for the development of the recent network flow methods.

The first parallel algorithm for the maximum flow problem is due to Shiloach and Vishkin [13]; this algorithm runs in $O(n^2 \log n)$ time and uses n processors and $O(n^2)$ memory. Goldberg [8] gave an algorithm that runs in the same time and processor bounds but uses $O(m)$ memory. This is the first of the push-relabel maximum flow algorithms. A parallel implementation of a scaling version of the push relabel method due to Ahuja and Orlin [12] decreases the number of processors to $O(m/n)$.

The similar problem of *multicommodity flow* has been solved recently for distributed model. Many NP-hard problems can be approximately solved using multicommodity flow algorithms. Equality between multicommodity max-flow and min-cut does not hold for all multicommodity flow instances in this (more complicated) case. Approximation algorithms due to Awerbuch and Leighton [2], [3] are based on edge-balancing approach. Their $(1 + \varepsilon)$- algorithm runs in $O(m^3 K^{5/2} L\varepsilon^{-3} \log K)$ steps resp. $O(KL^2 m\varepsilon^{-3} \ln^3(m/\varepsilon))$, where K is the number of commodities, L is the length of the longest flow path.

Our contribution here is to design the efficient asynchronous distributed algorithms for the problem of maximum flow. At the start of our algorithm, each processor only knows about its immediate neighbors and capacities of adjacent edges. We assume that nodes of a network are connected by bidirectional communication channels so that the network is represented by undirected graph. An undirected network graph can be transformed into general network by regarding each two-way channel as two one-way channels, one in each direction. In other words, we replace each two-way edge in the network by two one-way edges with the same capacity. When the algorithm terminates, computed flow is stored distributedly in incident nodes for all edges, that is each node knows about values of flow which were computed for its adjacent edges. Our maximum flow algorithm works in $O(n^2 \log^3 n)$ time having a communication complexity of $O(n^2(\log^3 n + \sqrt{m}))$.

2 Distributed Algorithms

2.1 Computing maximum flow - general algorithms

In the classical Ford-Fulkerson's algorithm there is some ambiguity in choosing a next node to label. Cheung [5] uses three diferent graph traversal techniques to develop distributed max flow algorithms. Clasification of distributed algorithms in terms of communication complexity differs from efficiency criterion of sequential algorithms. An algorithm using largest augmentation path presented by Cheung is the most efficient compared to algorithms using depth-first search or breadth-first search in terms of number of messages. Cheung shows that the number of messages transmitted involved in his algorithm using largest augmentation search and breadth-first search which have a worst case upper bound $O((1 + \log f^*)nm^2)$ and $O(n^6)$ respectively.

Distributed algorithms based on Edmods-Karp method start by giving each edge a flow of zero. We asume that for every arc (u, v) the opposite arc (v, u) also exist with null capacity. The variables with residual capacities are maintained in adjacent nodes. In each iteration we try to find a flow-augmenting path by proceeding from node to node along unsaturated edges. If we manage to reach the sink by this method, we proceed as follows: we trace the flow augmenting path back to the source and increase the flow along this path by the appropriate amount. The procedure is repeated until we obtain a maximum flow.

By applying effective methods of graph traversal to analyze efficiency of distributed max flow algorithms we improve the previous results of Cheung [5]. Algorithms based on classical method using breadth-first search are proved to be effective in number of iterations. In each iteration we apply the breadth-first search to residual graph, and send flow over the shortest path from the source to sink

Awerbuch et. al [4] present distributed breadth-first-search working in an asynchronous network in $O(n \log^3 n)$ time using $O(m \log^3 n)$ messages. When we apply Awerbuch's algorithm in maximum flow algorithm we achieve the overall complexities for maximum flow problem: $T = O(mn^2 \log^3 n)$, $C = O(m^2 n \log^3 n)$

By small modification of breadth-first search procedure we obtain largest augmentation search algorithm. Instead of length of the path from the root to a node we considere a bottleneck capacity of this path. Each node has a label (i, c_i), which means that we have found a path with capacity c_i and its last by one node is i. Let $\{i, j\}$ be an edge for which i is already labeled and j is not labeled. Then we label successor j by $r_j = min(c_i, c_{ij})$ (c_{ij} stands for capacity of an edge). At the end of a procedure finding the largest augmentation path in residual graph a node j is labeled by (i, r_j), i.e. $c_j = r_j$, where r_j is maximal value offered by neighbors of j. In other words among all neighboring nodes already labeled we select the one associated with the node having the largest throughput capacity with respect to the current flow. Using this procedure to augment the flow in each iteration we obtain the algorithm with time and communication complexity $T = mn \ln f*$, $C = mn^2 \ln f*$ respectively.

Goldberg and Tarjan [10] present distributed algorithm for finding a blocking flow in an acyclic network which works on an asynchronous model in $O(n)$ message passing rounds using $O(nm)$ messages. Space requirements are $O(m)$ space bound per vertex. Dinic [7] showed that the maximum flow problem can be solved by solving a sequence of $O(n)$ blocking flow problems on layered networks.

In the next section we show that for distributed model more suitable is preflow - push method which allows more parallel activities.

2.2 Distributed Preflow-Push Algorithm

The algorithm does not maintain the flow-conservation property throughout its execution. A new notion is introduced of a *preflow*, which is a function $f : V \times V \rightarrow R$ that satisfies skew symmetry, capacity constraints and the following relaxation of flow conservation: $f(V, u) \geq 0 \ \forall u \in V - \{s\}$. That is, the net flow into each vertex other than the source is nonnegative. We call the net flow into a vertex u the *excess flow* into u, given by $e(u) = f(V, u)$. We say that a vertex $u \in V - \{s, t\}$ is *overflowing* if $e(u) > 0$. A preflow is a flow if $e_f(w) = 0$ for every node $w \notin \{s, t\}$.

A function $h : V \rightarrow N$ is a *height function* if $h(s) = |V|$, $h(t) = 0$ and $h(u) \leq h(v) + 1$ for every residual edge $(u, v) \in E_f$. The basic operation $Push(u, v)$ can be applied if u is overflowing node, $c_f \geq 0$ and $h(u) = h(v) + 1$. It is a *saturating push* if edge (u, v) becomes saturated $(c_f(u, v) = 0)$ afterward; otherwise it is a *nonsaturating push*. The basic operation *Lift(u)* applies if u is overflowing and if $c_f(u, v) \geq 0$ implies $h(u) \leq h(v)$ for all nodes v. We say that a vertex v is *active* if $v \notin \{s, t\}$ and $e_f(v) > 0$. An adge is *admissible* if $(v, w) \in E_f$ and $d(v) = d(w) + 1$.

A distributed algorithm proceeds by alternating two basic types of operations *Push* and *Lift* which are performed in parallel by nodes in network. It is efficient to combine push and lift operations locally in one node. The discharge operation accomplishes this: it is aplicable to an active node v. Discharge iteratively reduces the excess at v by pushing it through admissible edges going out of v if such edge exists; otherwise discharge lifts v. The operation stops when the excess at v is reduced to zero or v is lifted.

All active nodes can be processed at once. Distributed algorithm works in pulses. A pulse consists of a maximal interval of time during which the height of processed nodes does not change.

The distributed version of Goldberg's algorithm [9] takes $O(n^2)$ rounds of message-passing and a total of $O(n^3)$ messages in the synchronous network. The processor at a vertex v needs $O(n\Delta_v)$ storage.

2.3   The Highest-Label Preflow-Push Algorithm

The highest-label preflow-push algorithm is currently the most efficient method for solving the maximum flow problem in practice as it performs the least number of nonsaturating pushes. A parallel algorithms which process all largest height nodes in parallel work in $O(n^2)$ pulses [8]. Each pulse consists of two stages: in the first stage the active nodes of maximal height push the flow out. In the second stage the vertices that still have positive excess are lifted. The highest-label preflow-push algorithm starts at the highest level and pushes all the axcess at this level to the next lower level and repeats this process.

A straightforward implementation of preflow-push strategy in asynchronous distributed model leads to an algorithm in which every node communicates to all its neighbors in every pulse to inform them about its height and flow sent over adjacent links. Only a subset of nodes is active in a given pulse; other nodes only communicate their heights without pushing flow to its neighbors. Such implementation is quite expensive in a number of messages sent. Nevertheless in asynchronous model we need these extra messages to distinguish subsequent pulses of the algorithm. Nodes communicate their heights in every pulse at least and acknowledge their readiness to enter the next round at the same time. With this algorithm we make an asynchronous network to work synchronously. The similarity between α-synchronizer and distributed implementation of preflow-push algorithm introduces the idea of improving on efficiency of net-flow algorithm. More efficient algorithm - highest-label preflow-push algorithm requires the knowledge of the highest label used over an entire network in each pulse. The algorithm is based on knowledge of a subset of nodes with highest labels.

To identify such a subset in every pulse of the algorithm we make use of synchronizing mechanism which is used in asynchronous network to enable the basic function of preflow-push algorithm. By adding more information to the messages of static synchronizer we distribute the knowledge of maximum labels assigned to nodes during the previous pulse. In order to disseminate this information over the network we use an efficient data structure that enables fast communication between nodes.

Every node is initially activated at the beginning of preflow-push algorithm by other node when shipping a flow over a link between them. Activation pattern defines father-son relation between nodes and consequently a spanning tree (execution forest) of a network. In order to enable fast communication we break the induced spanning tree into layers. Each node is assigned to a level and in addition each node v is assigned a supervisor, Supervisor(v), which is either the root of the spanning tree or the nearest ancestor of v at level $Level(v) + 1$. Let $D(v)$ be the length of the path from v to the root of the spanning tree. Define $Level(v) = \max \{i|2^i \text{divides } D(v)\}$. Define Supervisor($v$) to be either the root of the spanning tree, or the closest ancestor of v whose level is one higher than the level of v, whichever is closer.

For this structure [4] holds that the path from a vertex v to Supervisor (v) has either 2^l or 3.2^l links where l stands for level of v.

In every pulse the information on readiness of all nodes to enter another pulse is convergecast over the execution forest. Each node on the path from v to Supervisor(v) serves as a relay for the communication between v and Supervisor(v). The idea here is to aggregate a large number of messages together in supervisor and represent them by a single message. A key tool for achieving this aggregation is the data structure that defines a hierarchy on the nodes of the spanning tree. Thus we can ommit direct communication between every pair of neighboring nodes. Moreover during this synchronization we collect the highest label value over all nodes in every pulse. Together with start signal for the next pulse nodes receive the highest label and decide whether to push flow in the next pulse or not.

2.4 Analysis of the Algorithm

Costs for initial labelling all nodes are $O(n^2)$ messages and $O(n)$ time. Number of pulses is bounded by $O(n^2)$ according to [8]. The running time of the resulting algorithm is $O(n^2)$ times the time needed for one discharge operation including the time needed to discover the subset of nodes taking part in the next discharge operation. The message complexity of discharge operation is dominated by number of saturating pushes $O(n)$. The time we need to identify all nodes taking part in the next parallel discharge operation is included in costs of synchronizing mechanism. The resulting complexity is $O(n^2 \log^3 n)$ in time and communication expencies are bounded by $O(n^2(\log^3 n + \sqrt{m}))$ messages.

3 Conclusion

The idea behind our distributed version of highest-label preflow-push algorithm is to disseminate values of labels together with safety information from every node. Using this method we are able to define the highest label in every pulse without significantly increasing time and communication expencies. A node decides on its actions performed in the next step based on safety information communicated by its neighborhood and its local label compared to the communicated highest value.

An interesting point here is that using Awerbuch's modification of the static synchronizer to the dynamic version we obtain the distributed highest-label preflow-push algorithm working in dynamic network. Rollback technique is appropriate for maximum-flow algorithm as well as for network synchronization.

Applications include product distribution, traffic planning and scheduling problems, especially network routing or graph partitioning of a network graph.

References

1. B.Awerbuch, Boaz Patt-Shamir, D.Peleg, M.Saks: Adapting to Asynchronous Dynamic Networks. 24-th STOC, 1992
2. B.Awerbuch, T.Leighton: A Simple Local-Control Approximation Algorithm for Multicommodity Flow. 25-th STOC, 1993
3. B.Awerbuch, T.Leighton: Improved Approximation Algorithms for the Multi-Commodity Flow Problem and Local Competitive Routing in Dynamic Networks. 26-th STOC, 1994
4. B.Awerbuch, D.Peleg: Network Synchronization with Polylogarithmic Overhead. 31-st FOCS, 1990
5. To-Yat Cheung: Graph Traversal Techniques and the Maximum Flow Problem in Distributed Computation. IEEE Trans. on Softw.Eng., $9(4)$ (1983) 504–512
6. J.Cheriyan and S.N. Maheshwari. Analysis of Preflow Push Algorithms for Maximum Network Flow. SIAM j. Comput., 18:1057-1086, 1989
7. E.A.Dinic. Algorithm for Solution of a Problem of Maximum Flow in Networks with Power Estimation. Soviet.Math.Dokl. 11, 1970
8. A.V. Goldberg. Processor Efficient Implementation of a Maximum Flow Algorithm. Information Processing Let., pg.179-185, 1991
9. A.V., Goldgberg, R.E., Tarjan. A New Approach to the Maximum Flow Problem. J. ACM, 35:921-940, 1988, also in Proc. 18th ACM Symp. on Theory of Comp., 136-146, 1986.
10. A.V.Goldberg, R.E.Tarjan. A Parallel Algorithm for Finding a Blocking Flow in an Acyclic Network. Information processing Letters 31, 1989
11. N.Linial, M.Saks. Decomposing Graphs Into Regions of Small Diameter. In Proc. 2nd ACM-SIAM Symp.on Discr.Algorithms, Jan.1991
12. R.K.Ahuja, J.B. Orlin. A Fast and Simple Algorithm for the Maximum Flow Problem. Sloan Working Paper 1905-87, Sloan School of Management, M.I.T., 1987
13. Y.Shiloach, U. Vishkin. An $O(n^2 \log n)$ Parallel Max-Flow Algorithm. J. Algorithms, 3: 128-146, 1982

Fuzzy Set Theory and Medical Expert Systems: Survey and Model

Nguyen Hoang Phuong

Institute of Computer Science
Academy of Sciences of the Czech Republic
Pod vodárenskou věží 2, 182 07 Praha 8, Czech Republic
Fax:(+42)(2)8585789, e-mail:phuong@uivt.cas.cz

Abstract:
In recent years, fuzzy set theory and Fuzzy Logic are applied successfuly in medical expert systems as CADIAG, MILORD etc. This paper intends to provide a short survey on application of fuzzy set theory in medicine, especialy, fuzzy logic in medical expert systems. An improved fuzzy inference model of CADIAG-2 for medical diagnosis combining negative and positive evidence is presented. This model can be used for obtain more smooth transition between confirmed and disconfirmed diagnoses.

Keywords: Fuzzy set theory and fuzzy logic, fuzzy inference model, negative and positive evidence.

1   Introduction

A theory of fuzzy sets was proposed by Zadeh in 1965 [10] and it was extended for medical diagnosis by Adlassnig [3]. Adlassnig indicated some main properties of fuzzy set theory for medical diagnosis and treatment as "1) it defines inexact medical entities as fuzzy sets, 2) it provides a linguistic approach with an excellent approximation to texts and 3) fuzzy logic offers reasoning methods capable of drawing approximate inferences". Until now, several hundreds papers based on fuzzy set theory in medicine were published in different aspects of application: diagnosis, differential diagnosis, therapy, image analysis, pattern recognition, patient monitoring, medical data analysis, data bank, text analysis . . . and of theory: fuzzy logic, multi-valued logic, fuzzy relations, fuzzy set theory, fuzzy classification etc . . . One can see more details in [7]. This paper will focuss on third property of fuzzy set theory as Adlassnig claimed above. We will analyse and improve Max-Min compositions of rules of CADIAG-2. CADIAG-2 is a famous medical diagnostic rule-based expert system based on methods of fuzzy set theory [2], [4], [5], [6], [8], [3]. The paper is organized as follows: Section 2 presents briefly a list of medical expert systems using fuzzy set theory and fuzzy logic. Section 3 presents an impvoved fuzzy inference model of CADIAG-2 for medical diagnosis combining negative and positive evidence. This model can be used to obtain more smooth transition between confirmed and disconfirmed diagnoses. Finally, some conclusions will be reported.

2   Review of medical fuzzy expert systems

The imprecise nature of medical concepts and their relationships requires a development of fuzzy set theory, especially, of fuzzy set conceptual models and fuzzy inference models for medical fuzzy expert systems. Until now, many medical expert systems based on fuzzy set theory were developed and applied in practical applications. Here we will briefly summare some fuzzy systems and fuzzy models for medical diagnosis.

ABVAB:

One expert system for diagnosis of abnormal vaginal bleeding. ABVAB is an application of the expert system shell SYSTEM Z-II. The inference of the ABVAB based on fuzzy logic and data of the system is represented as fuzzy numbers and fuzzy linguistic variable.

CADIAG-2

CADIAG-2 is diagnostic system for internal medicine using fuzzy set theory for medical diagnosis. In general, CADIAG-2 based on relationships between symptoms (or symptom-combinations) with two parameters:

o - frequency of occurrence of symptom S_i with disease D_j

c - confirmation degree of symptom S_i for disease D_j

Based on these fuzzy relationships, the MaxMin inferences are used to deduce the fuzzy value $\mu_{R_{PD}}(P_q, D_j)$ which indicates the degree of confirmation of disease D_j by patient P_q from the observed symptoms. This MaxMin composition is the follow:

1) Composition for $S_i D_j$ (hypotheses and confirmation)

$$R_{PD}^1 = R_{PS} \circ R_{SD}^c$$

defined by

$$\mu_{R_{PD}^1}(P_q, D_j) = max_{S_i} min[\mu_{R_{PS}}(P_q, S_i); \mu_{R_{SD}^c}(S_i, D_j)]$$

2) Composition for $S_i D_j$ (exclusion (by present symptoms))

$$R_{PD}^2 = R_{PS} \circ (1 - R_{SD}^o)$$

defined by

$$\mu_{R_{PD}^2}(P_q, D_j) = max_{S_i} min[\mu_{R_{PS}}(P_q, SC_i); 1 - \mu_{R_{SD}^o}(S_i, D_j)]$$

3) Composition for $S_i D_j$ (exclusion (by absent symptoms))

$$R_{PD}^3 = (1 - R_{PS}) \circ R_{SD}^o$$

defined by

$$\mu_{R_{PD}^3}(P_q, D_j) = max_{S_i} min[1 - \mu_{R_{PS}}(P_q, S_i); \mu_{R_{SD}^o}(S_i, D_j)]$$

In analogous way, compositions for SCD (symptom-combinations) ... are established. Using support scores, CADIAG-2 is able to infer diagnoses as confirmed, excluded and possible diagnoses D_j.

Parameters o and c are considered to be linguistic variables as always, almost always,elements.Until now, CADIAG-2 was applied in several practical applications.

CADIAG-2/CONSULT
This is a consultation assisted component of CADIAG-2.

CADIAG-2/GALL
This is an application of CADIAG-2 in Gall-Blladder diagnosis.

CADIAG-2/PANCREAS
One application of CADIAG-2 in pancreas diseases.

CADIAG-2/RHEUMA
One application of CADIAG-2 in Rheumatology.

CADIAG-2/STUDY
A computer aid learning in medicine.

CLINAID:
One knowledge based system for diagnosis and administration. The system uses probabilistic theory and fuzzy set theory.

DIABETO-III
An expert system for diagnosis and treatment of diabete. As CLINAID, DIABETO-III based on Probabilistic and fuzzy set theory.

FLOPS:
One Fuzzy Logic Production Expert System shell. Knowledge of the system is represented as Fuzzy numbers and sets.

MILORD
has developed as an expert system shell based on Management of Linguistically Expressed Uncertainty. The system allows one to perform different calculi of uncertainty on an expert defined set of linguistic terms expressing uncertainty. Each calculus corresponds to specific conjunction, disjunction, and implication operator. Knowledge in MILORD consists of Facts, Rules, Modules, Strategies and Contexts. The internal representation of each linguistic uncertainty value is a fuzzy subset of the interval [0,1]. MILORD was applied to the diagnosis and treatment of pneumonia and to Rheumatology Diagnosis.

SPHINX:
SPHINX - a fuzzy, interactive diagnostic expert system for internal medicine. The consultation takes the form of the input of symptomatic and patient history information. Based on these inputs, a possible diagnostic orientation is determined using fuzzy heuristics. The absence of some symptoms with cause the rejection of certain diagnosis, then SPHINX suggests futher diagnostic steps interately until a diagnosis is suggested.

PROTIS:
One medical support system for treating diabetes. Knowledge of the system is represented in fuzzy deduction rules.

PNEUMON IA:
MILORD was applied to the diagnosis and treatment of pneumonia.

Z-III:

An expert system shell Z-III - one extention of Z-II. The Z-III system has the ability to handle both exact and inexact, fuzzy or non-fuzzy reasoning. In Z-III, rule-based representation of knowledge is used. Fuzzy concepts are in the form of natural language and associated with three linguistic fuzzy terms describing the upper, medium and lower levels of the concepts. Hedges such as "very", "more or less" and "quite" could be used to describe the fuzzy values. Two medical expert systems in the field of obstetrics have been built successfully using Z-III.

ZUMA:

One intelligent editor of CADIAG-2.

This section described briefly some medical expert systems based on fuzzy set theory. One can see references of systems described in this section more details in [7] and [1]. These systems express in part a success of aplication of fuzzy logic in medical expert systems [11].

3 An improved fuzzy inference model for CADIAG-2

In this section, the improved fuzzy inference model of CADIAG-2 is presented. Inference engine of CAGIAG-2 is based on Max-Min compostions of rules of CADIAG-2 described briefly in 2. Our approach is combining the strengths of opposite evidences (symptoms and symptom-combinations) for disease D_j. The measure value of strengths of opposite evidences μ_{D_j}, where $-1 \leq \mu_{D_j} \leq 1.0$, is a combination of a global strength of confirmation $\mu_{D_j}^+$ (a measure of confirmation with D_j) and a global strength of disconfirnation $\mu_{D_j}^-$ (a measure of exclusion with D_j) and it is defined as follows:

$$\mu_{D_j} = \mu_{D_j}^+ - \mu_{D_j}^-$$

where

a) $\mu_{D_j}^+$ is a global strength of confirmation and defined by

$$\mu_{D_j}^+ = max[\mu_{R_{PD}^1}(P_q, D_j); \mu_{R_{PD}^4}(P_q, D_j)]$$

- $\mu_{R_{PD}^1}(P_q, D_j), \mu_{R_{PD}^4}(P_q, D_j)$ are fuzzy values of compositions for $S_i D_j$ (symptom-disease) and $SC_i D_j$ (symptom-combination disease), respectively, of CADIAG-2 for hypotheses and confirmation and are defined in (Adlassnig, 1986)

b) $\mu_{D_j}^-$ is a global strength of disconfirmation and defined by

$$\mu_{D_j}^- = max[\mu_{R_{PD}^2}(P_q, D_j); \mu_{R_{PD}^3}(P_q, D_j);$$

$$\mu_{R_{PD}^5}(P_q, D_j); \mu_{R_{PD}^6}(P_q, D_j)]$$

where

- $\mu_{R_{PD}^2}(P_q, D_j)$ are the fuzzy values of composition for $S_i D_j$ (exclusion(by present symptoms))

- $\mu_{R_{PD}^3}(P_q, D_j)$ are the fuzzy values of composition for $S_i D_j$ (exclusion(by absent symptoms))

- $\mu_{R^5_{PD}}(P_q, D_j)$ are the fuzzy values of composition for $SC_i D_j$ (exclusion(by present symptom-combinations))
- $\mu_{R^6_{PD}}(P_q, D_j)$ are the fuzzy values of composition for $SC_i D_j$ (exclusion(by absent symptom-combinations))

To obtain a conclusion, the following criteria for diagnosis are proposed:
1. If the values $\mu_{D_j} = 1.0$, then absolutely confirmed diagnoses D_j for patient P_q are identified.
2. If the values $\mu_{D_j} = -1.0$, then absolutely disconfirmed diagnoses D_j for patient P_q are identified.
3. If the values μ_{D_j} such that $-\varepsilon \leq \mu_{D_j} \leq \varepsilon$, then a "unknown" about diagnoses D_j is suggested.
4. If the values μ_{D_j} such that $-1 \leq \mu_{D_j} \leq -\varepsilon$, then "unlikely" diagnoses D_j for patient P_q are identified.
5. If the values μ_{D_j} such that $\varepsilon \leq \mu_{D_j} \leq 1$, then "likely" diagnoses D_j for patient P_q are identified.
(ε - a heuristic low value and it takes value 0.01)
This model is tested for an artifical patient database described in [9]. The advantage of applying the combination of opposite strengths of evidences is that this approach can give us a more smooth transition between absolutely confirmed diagnoses and absolutely disconfirmed diagnoses, i. e. we can identify unlikely diagnoses for which $\mu_{D_j}^- > \mu_{D_j}^+$.

4 Conclusions

The above survey indicates that the application of fuzzy set theory to medical problems, especially, application of fuzzy logic in medical expert systems has been modest but achieved many successes. For example, as Zadeh claimed in [11] that " among them is CADIAG-2, the well-know large-scale medical diagnostic system". On the other hand, we presented briefly an approach to combining negative and positive evidence in CADIAG-2 which can improve MaxMin inference of rules of CADIAG-2 for obtaining more smooth transition between confirmed and disconfirmed diagnoses. One can see this approach in more details in [9].

Acknowledgments

Thanks are due to Prof. P. Hájek for drawing the idea and his advice about combining negative and positive knowledge elaborated in this paper. This work was supported by grant through COPERNICUS Project No. 10053 (MUM).

References

1. Adlassnig, K.-P. 1982. A Survey on Medical Diagnosis and Fuzzy Subsets. Approximate Reasoning in Decision Analysis, 203-217.

2. Adlassnig, K.-P. et al. 1984. CADIAG-2/PANCREAS: An Artificial Intelligence system based on fuzzy set theory to diagnose pancreatic disease. Proc. Third Intern. Conf. on System Science in Health Care, Springer-Verlag, Berlin, 396-399.

3. Adlassnig, K.-P.1986. Fuzzy Set Theory in Medical Diagnosis. IEEE Transaction on Systems, Man, and Cybernetics, SMC-16, 260-265.

4. Adlassnig, K.-P. et al. 1986. Approach to a hospital based application of a medical expert system. Med. Inform., Vol. 11, No 3, 205-223.

5. Adlassnig, K.-P. et al. 1989. CADIAG-2/GALL: An experimental expert system for the diagnosis of gallbladder and biliary tract diseases, Artificial Intelligence in Medicine 1, 71-77.

6. Adlassnig, K.-P. 1990. Update on CADIAG-2: A fuzzy medical expert system for general internal medicine. Progress in Fuzzy Sets and Systems. W.H.Janko et al. (eds.), 1-6

7. Bohm, R. 1990. Die Theorie der unscherfen und ihre Anwendungen in der Medizin, Diplomarbeit, Universitat Wien, 1990.

8. Kolarz, G., Adlassnig K.-P. 1986. Problems in establishing the medical expert systems CADIAG-1 and CADIAG-2 in rheumatology, Jour. of Medical Systems, 10, 395-405.

9. Nguyen, H.P. 1995. Approach to Combining Negative and Positive Evidence in CADIAG-2. Proc. of EUFIT'95, 1653-1658.

10. Zadeh, L.A. 1965. Fuzzy sets, Information and Control, Vol. 8, 338-353.

11. Zadeh, L.A. 1994. Why the success of Fuzzy Logic is not Paradoxical, IEEE Expert, Vol. 9, No. 4, 43-46.

The Fusion Object-Oriented Method: an Evaluation*

Alain Pirotte[1], Thierry van den Berghe[1], Esteban Zimanyi[2]

[1] University of Louvain, IAG, 1 place des Doyens, 1348 Louvain-la-Neuve, Belgium,
e-mail: pirotte@info.ucl.ac.be, vandenberghe@qant.ucl.ac.be
[2] University of Brussels, INFODOC, 50 Av. F. Roosevelt, C.P. 175-2, 1050 Brussels,
Belgium, e-mail: ezimanyi@ulb.ac.be

Abstract. This paper presents a critical evaluation, from a computer science point of view, of the *Fusion* method[3] for object-oriented development and it sketches some guidelines for improvement. It focuses on three critical observations: (1) weakness of the ontology of the object model, (2) lack of formality, and (3) failure of the iterative process to construct comprehensive requirements and analysis models. A longer version of the paper [3] illustrates our observations with examples and develops our suggestions for improvement.

Keywords: object-oriented software development, analysis and design methods, *Fusion*, evaluation

1 A Very Short Introduction to Fusion

Software development remains a complex and expensive task. Although the research and development activity has been steadily growing in the field, progress has been very slow over the years.

Fusion [1] is one of several interesting recent methods for object-oriented (OO) software development (see, e.g., [2], for a collection of short descriptions). Very generally, those OO methods break system development into several stages along the system lifecycle. Further they provide guidelines along two dimensions: (1) they define representation *languages* or formalisms (e.g., data models), with their syntax, often graphical, and semantics to describe the structural, behavioral, and functional aspects of the system being built at various stages of its development, and (2) they propose guidelines on the *process* to be followed for how and when to build descriptions in the representation languages, to proceed between languages along the system lifecycle, and to perform various checks of correspondence and adequacy.

Fusion adopts the division of the development process into analysis, design, and implementation. *The goal of analysis is to capture as many of the requirements on the system as possible. This is accomplished by constructing several*

---

* This work is part of the EROOS (Evaluation and Research on Object-Oriented Strategies) project, principally based at the University of Louvain and the University of Brussels.

[3] We follow the current usage, which tends to prefer "method" to "methodology".

models of the system describing what a system does rather than how it does it.[4] Specifically, the analysis models of *Fusion* comprise:

- an object model, that superficially resembles a usual OO database model, with object and relationship classes, and generalization and aggregation mechanisms;
- a system interface, that identifies external agents in the environment of the system, and input and output events generated, respectively, by the external agents and by the system;
- an interface model, comprising (1) an operation model, with the specification of system operations that can be invoked by input events and executed by the system, and (2) a lifecycle model, prescribing the allowed sequences of events in the form of regular expressions.

The design stage decides *how to represent the system operations by the interaction of related objects and how those objects gain access to each other.* Specifically, the design models comprise:

- an object interaction graph for each system operation of the interface model, that records how functionality is distributed among objects;
- visibility graphs, where communication paths between objects are detected;
- class descriptions, specifying the internal state of object classes and the external interface for methods;
- inheritance graphs, extending the generalization structure of analysis to design objects.

Implementation gives some guidelines for translating the lifecycle model into a finite-state automaton and for coding class definitions. Consistency of the various models and performance are also briefly considered.

Fusion also maintains a multi-purpose data dictionary, which turns out to play a central role (1) for cross-checking models for completeness and consistency, (2) for recording information about the development process and about the relationships between the *Fusion* models and the underlying real world, but also (3) for making explicit those descriptions that cannot be expressed in full because of the limited power of some models.

2   Poor Ontology of the Object Model

Many problems originate from the poor definition of the basic ingredients, objects and relationships, of analysis (or, as is sometimes said, of the *ontology* of the models, i.e., a precise syntactic and semantic definition of what is taken for granted, namely the languages available for expressing the structural, behavioral, and functional models). There is constant ambiguity, in *Fusion* and also in other OO methods, between, on the one hand, objects that reflect entities in the

---

[4] Italics signal quotes from the *Fusion* reference [1].

real world (similar to entities in the entity-relationship (ER) model and to object classes in OO conceptual database models) and, on the other hand, design objects, which are computational structures with attributes, processing capabilities, and access mechanisms. This ambiguity is transmitted .to structuring mechanisms, like aggregation, which appears alternatively as modeling part-of relationships of composite objects during analysis or as encapsulating composite design objects to control complexity.

For example, the following assertions are inappropriate for real world objects:

- *during analysis, the values of attributes are not allowed to be objects*; some OO models do describe attributes as objects, but what is presumably meant here is that some attributes of design objects will be pointers to other objects;
- *during analysis, we are seldom interested in how an object can be identified*; we disagree: proper identification is essential for analysis objects; what is presumably meant here is that specific additional identification means will be defined during design or implementation.

On the other hand, the statement that *the analysis concept of object does not include any notion of method interface* is consistent with an explicit migration of the status of objects between analysis and design.

Fusion entertains a similar confusion about the status of relationships, as shown by the following quotes: *A relationship represents a set of tuples, ... some subset of the Cartesian product of the classes it relates.* This is clearly the style of relationships in ER and conceptual OO models. But the following is also written: *Relationships model correspondences between objects (communication, physical associations, containment, actions). ... The notions of operation and event are often connected with some relationship between classes.* Also: *Relationships may be misinterpreted as data flows ... especially if they model real-world actions.*

ER relationships represent structural information that persists for some time. Modeling events as relationships is unorthodox in conceptual modeling. In fact, *Fusion* blends various semantic styles in a single syntax for relationships.

As another example, *Fusion* uses the same abstraction mechanism for representing both aggregation and classification of relationships. *Aggregations are similar to relationships since both are formed by taking tuples of class instances. Aggregations models "part of" or "has a" relationship. It can be used to model physical containment.* However *Fusion*, unlike the classical approach followed in OO Databases and conceptual modeling, does not consider different types of aggregation according to the following dimensions: (1) *exclusive* (the component exclusively belongs to the aggregate) or *shared* (the component may be part of several aggregates); and (2) *dependent* (the existence of the component depends on the existence of the aggregate) or *independent* (the component exists irrespective of the aggregate).

On the other hand, the following statements are also written. *An aggregation can be used to "wrap up" a relationship. Aggregations can also be used as a convenient structuring device by treating a relationship as an entity. In these situations there need not to be connotation of being physically part of.* This use of aggregation for representing classification of relationships (i.e. allow a relationship to participate in other relationships) is inadequate.

As a result, the object model of *Fusion* is weak and it has little direct influence on design. It is not just a question of lack of formality. The ontology of object and relationships is so blurred that a systematic extraction and transformation of information from the object model of analysis into design would be extremely difficult.

A powerful contribution of *Fusion* analysis to the future system is the specification of system operations, with pre- and post-conditions, and assertions specifying the input-output relationships to be realized by the operations. System operations are later refined as object interaction graphs during design, and eventually implemented as class methods in an OO programming language. Throughout that process, the object model serves as a general informal documentation of the domain and of its relationships with the system being built.

Another symptom of the ancillary role played by the object model is that the system object model that comes out of the system interface definition is not necessarily a connected graph. This seems inappropriate if it must provide a comprehensive guide for a smooth evolution into design and implementation.

Put differently, *Fusion* fails to disguise its programming language bias. Clearly, there are at least two OO cultures: the programming language culture and the information or conceptual modeling culture. *Fusion*, like other similar OO methods, is firmly based in the world of programming and computation. Serious business in *Fusion* starts with the design phase. To caricature, analysis seems to have been grafted as an afterthought.

This is not to say that reconciling the two cultures in a single method is not desirable nor feasible. But then the world of analysis would be more resolutely independent from that of design and implementation, and the resulting method would exhibit a larger and more explicit transition in moving from an implementation independent conceptual realm (analysis) into the realm of operational solutions (design and implementation). It seems that the database culture has better mastered the related dual role of the conceptual schema in the database design process, first, as a basis of agreement, between designers and specialists of the application domain, on a perception of the relevant portion of the application domain and, second, as a specification for the subsequent logical and physical database design phases.

Rethinking the ontology of the object model would involve a substantial redesign of the *Fusion* method.

3   Lack of Formality

Fusion could be more formal, or at least more precise, in a number of places. The first criticism to *Fusion* (namely, weak ontology and programming bias) is a severe one, because it touches the heart of the method. The criticism of lack of formality is less severe, because it seems that precision could be relatively easily improved in a number of places.

The clearest symptom is the importance taken by the data dictionary (*without a data dictionary, the Fusion models would have little semantic content*). Examples abound. Even the Object Interaction Graphs, maybe the most sucessful model in *Fusion*, are a caricature of the associated procedural description to be found in the data dictionary. Object Interaction Graphs appear like attractive pictorial descriptions packaging those procedural aspects for which a simple diagram could be imagined. Similar remarks apply for the visibility relationships.

An improved *Fusion* method would exhibit (1) a more precise integration and coherence between the various models, (2) mechanisms for describing the whole system at different abstraction levels, from a (detailed) very specific level to a (general) high abstraction level, and (3) formal correspondences between levels.

4   Iterative Process

Presenting the analysis/design/implementation process as inevitably iterative appears like a humble recognition of the difficulty of the overall enterprise. But iterativeness does not preclude a gradual enrichment and refinement of models which would eventually evolve into complete (in some sense to be defined) descriptions of the system and the relevant part of its environment at various levels of abstraction.

On the contrary, *Fusion* does not produce analysis models that would eventually provide a stand-alone description of the complete system, independent of design and implementation decisions. The problem is compounded by the absence of a systematic requirements engineering phase upstream of analysis. Instead, new requirements are continually injected during analysis and design. This appears to be, at least partly, a cultural problem of the method area. In software engineering, by contrast, it is now firmly believed that requirements engineering is a crucial and unescapable phase for the adequacy and correctness of the whole process.

An alternative strategy, that would acknowledge the inevitable iterativeness, could gradually retrofit into a comprehensive requirements model the various pieces of requirements as they are discovered in the iterative process. Eventually, the implemented system would thus be documented by complete and consistent requirements, analysis and design models, which would model the implemented system at various levels of abstraction. This would thus enhance the possibility of reuse and the flexibility of evolution to reflect changes in the application domain and/or in the requirements of the implemented system in its operational environment.

5   Summary and Conclusions

The major problem with *Fusion* is that it fails to clearly separate two different uses of the object concept: (1) a representation of the structure and behavior of entities in the application domain, and (2) a programming realization of the structure of system components. This failure, compounded by a weak ontology for the analysis object model, causes *Fusion*'s real business to start with design, which is itself heavily influenced by the target OO programming language. As a purported method for global system development, *Fusion* is clearly not in line with the current ideas which reduce the emphasis on design and implementation and emphasize instead the understanding of organizational environment and needs, and the requirements collection and analysis processes. ˙

A longer version of our paper [3] discusses other issues with *Fusion*, like the difficulty of defining the system object model, i.e., the frontier between the system and its environment, or the appropriate modeling of behavior at various levels of granularity. It illustrates our observations with examples and develops our suggestions for improvement.

This paper takes a computer science point of view in that it is more critical than our more general appraisal of the role of *Fusion* and other recent OO methods in the evolution of user practices. Object orientation provides a better description of system components and their interactions than the previous generations of so-called structured methods. In spite of our criticisms in this paper, we believe that the recent OO methods, and *Fusion* in particular, also bring with them the promise of a more formal semantics for the various models and of a clearer distinction and integration of the structural, behavioral, and functional components of system modeling.

For these reasons, *Fusion* and other OO methods have become worthy of serious interest from the computer science community, which was not (or much less) the case for previous generations of methods. Although much progress is still needed, these new methods eventually aim at capitalizing on two advantages of object orientation: (1) naturalness of real world modeling for the requirements modeling and analysis stages, and (2) modularity, encapsulation, and inheritance for the design and implementation stages.

References

1. D. Coleman, P. Arnold, S. Bodoff, C. Dollin, H. Gilchrist, F. Hayes, and P. Jeremaes. *Object-Oriented Development: The Fusion Method.* Prentice Hall, 1994.
2. A. Hutt, editor. *Object Analysis and Design – Description of Methods.* J. Wiley, 1994. Document of the Object Management Group.
3. A. Pirotte, T. Van Den Berghe, and E. Zimányi. Problems and improvements of the Fusion Object-Oriented Method. Forthcoming, Sept. 1995.

Integration of Object-Oriented Analysis and Algebraic Specifications

Zuzana Repaská

Comenius University, Mlynská dolina, 842 15 Bratislava, Slovakia

Abstract. In this paper, we focus on the integration of semiformal and formal methods that use OMT methodology and Algebraic specifications. An aim of this paper is to discuss advantages and problematic parts of the integration and to suggest opportunities of providing more elegant and lucid integration by exploiting different enrichments of the Algebraic specifications or their combination with other formalisms.

1 Introduction

Semiformal or formal method can be used for an application domain (AD) description during software system development. With respect to advantages and disadvantages of both methods (the semiformal method is graphical, but it uses natural language partially; the formal method uses only formal means, but is hard to understand for an ordinary customer) it is worthwhile to investigate opportunities of their integration. The aim is to integrate the semiformal and the formal AD model. The semiformal model (SFM) is created for a customer and the formal model (FM) for software developers.

The integration can be approached in two different ways. The first approach integrates two existent methods (e.g. Polack et al. 1993). In the second approach an appropriate semiformal method is created for an existent formal method. We have chosen the first approach. We aimed the integration of Object-Oriented (O-O) method - OMT (Object Modeling Technique, Rumbaugh et al. 1991) - and Algebraic specifications (ASs) - the ASs of SL syntax (Privara and Nižňanský 1991). Both satisfy the common principle of abstract data types. The integration is accomplished and fully described in our master thesis (Repaská 1994).

In this paper we describe techniques and tools we have developed for the SFM transformation. Difficult parts of the transformation are also discussed and possibilities of their elimination are suggested. The paper is organized as follows. In Sect.2 overview of the integration is given. The SFM of the AD consists of three models. They are an object model (OM), a dynamic model (DM) and a functional model (FCM). Therefore, the OM formalization (OMF) is provided in Sect.3. The DM formalization (DMF) is described in Sect.4 and the FCM formalization (FCMF) is presented in Sect.5. In Sect.6, integration improvement opportunities are summarized. Reader is expected to be familiar with both the OMT (Rumbaugh et al. 1991) and the ASs (Privara and Nižňanský 1991).

2   Integration of the OMT and Algebraic Specifications

O-O methodologies and ASs satisfy the common principle of abstract data types, i.e. data and operations defined on them are regarded as a whole. Data can be approached only using operations. The aim of the integration of the above mentioned methods is to propose techniques and means for the transformation of the SFM to the FM.

Each AD model consists of a "visual" part (VP) and a "natural language" part (NLP). The VP is concerned with diagrams built exploiting different graphical notational concepts. The NLP is concerned with the information which have to be explained using the natural language. The VP of an actual model can be usually automatically transformed to the ASs. However the transformation of the NLP depends on the human creativity. Regarding each model, we shall gradually describe the transformation of the VP concepts and the NLP concepts, discuss problematic aspects of the transformation and suggest possibilities of their elimination.

3   Object Model Formalization

The ASs are declarative language. Thus they are able to express static relationships of the AD which are captured in the OM elegantly.

Class - the VP. The class concept formalization is straightforward. The class coincides with the AS module. Therefore sorts and operations describing properties of the class and its objects will be captured in one specification module (see Fig.1). The inherent class formalization (*ClassSort*, i.e. sort formalizing the class) which always works is done by the creation of one sort constructor ($\{\_;\ldots;\_\}$). The constructor comprises all the information that a class object holds. We shall call this constructor a "poor" constructor.

```
spec module CLASS
    sort Attr1Sort...AttrnSort ClassSort ...
    constr {_;...;_} : (Attr1Sort...AttrnSort) ClassSort ...
    op operation1, ... ,operationn : (ClassSort ...) ...
end CLASS
```

Fig. 1. Schema of the class concept formalization

Generalization - the VP. The information about class parents becomes the part of the "poor" constructor during the OMF.

However the ASs provide more elegant concepts of the class and generalization formalization, i.e. they allow to avoid the application of the "poor" constructor. With the help of human creativity, a parametric specification (PS), a top-down and a bottom-up sort hierarchy and a set of constructors reflecting the structure of objects can be utilized.

Association - the VP. An ordinary association relates two or more classes. In order to be formalized it becomes unidirectional. An association constraint - the multiplicity - is included to the special PS named *ASSOC* (see Fig.2). Supposing only requirements on participants (*EQEL, BOUND*), the association is modelled at the abstract level exploiting the AS of bounded sets (*BOUNDSET*). The operations and sorts modelling the association are proposed to describe not only the association constraint (e.g. *testAssociat*), but also properties of manipulations with the association and its links (e.g. *insert-Assoc*) and properties of the association traversing (e.g. *card-Assoc*). To obtain the AS of the association between classes the PS *ASSOC* has to be instantiated using the ASs of the classes.

```
gen module  ASSOC[X Y Z]
    par      (* sort: Elem  op: eq *)
      X : EQEL  rename  Elem to Left  eq to eq-Left  end
      Y : EQEL  rename  Elem to Right  eq to eq-Right  end
      Z : BOUND       (* sort: Natural Boolean  op: testBound *)
    use BOUNDSET[Y actual  Elem is Right  end  Z]  rename
                  (* sort and operation formalizing the association with multiplicity *)
              BoundSet to Association  testBoundSet to testAssociat
                  (* manipulations with the association links *)
              empty to empty-Assoc  insert to insert-Assoc  delete to delete-Assoc
                  (* current state of the association *)
              member to member-Assoc  card to card-Assoc  eq-Set to eq-Assoc  end
    end  ASSOC
```

Fig. 2. The association formalization

Other constrained associations (e.g. a qualified or an ordered association) are modelled the similar way as the ordinary association is. For every constrained association the precise mathematical interpretation was found, the special PS was created, useful sorts and operations were proposed and specifications of sets, lists, tuples, etc. were exploited.

As the graphical concepts of different association types can be combined, their corresponding PSs can be also composed during the OMF.

Constraint - the NLP. A constraint (e.g. on objects or attributes) is formalized with the help of the formalization of the VP of the OM and incorporated to the class specification.

Operation of many arguments - disadvantage. Operations of the ASs (such as the "poor" constructor) which have to capture the state of a system or its components make the specification less readable. The operations have a lot of arguments and need a lot of additional access and maintenance operations. Using the ASs with implicit state (c.f. Sect.6) such operations can be decomposed to elementary access operations that have implicit modification operations (see Fig.3).

```
sort   Attr1Sort... AttrnSort
elem_access   attribute1 : AttrSort ... attributen : AttrnSort
```

Fig. 3. The transformation of the "poor" constructor to the ASs with implicit state

4   Dynamic Model Formalization

The ASs are not quite suitable for describing the dynamic behaviour of objects. This causes some difficulties in the course of the DMF. However, some relationships between the ASs and the state diagrams were found in order to make the integration possible.

Event - the VP. The concept of an event is formalized as a special sort (*Event*) having the constructor of four arguments (see Fig.4). They are an event name (*EventName*), a sender (*From*) and a receiver (*To*) of the event and an event attribute (*Attribute*). The amount of the arguments can vary and sort *Event* can have more constructors (some events do not carry attributes, etc.).

```
sort   EventName From To Attribute Event
constr Send_from_to_with_ : (EventName From To Attribute) Event
       Send_from_to_ : (EventName From To) Event ...
```

Fig. 4. The event formalization

Transition - the VP. The key part of the DMF is the formalization of a transition. The transition becomes an axiom describing the properties of the event which causes the transition, i.e. the axiom covers all the changes and conditions (guards) connected with firing of the transition.

As an example (see Fig.5), the schema of the formalization of one type of the transition is given. This transition is caused by the event with a known attribute and receiver. The transition is conditional and connected with an action. The event causes the change of a state. An activity is performed in the new state.

Send event *to* receiver *with* attribute =
       activity(action(update-state(receiver,newstate),attribute,...),attribute,...)
  when is-in-state(receiver)=true condition(receiver,attribute)=true **end**

Fig. 5. Example of the transition formalization

Event receiver, guard and action - the NLP. An event receiver, a guard and an action are expressed in the natural language in the SFM because they strongly utilize information captured in the OM. Using the results of the OMF they can be elegantly formalized.

Object "life", parallelism - disadvantages. The ASs do not have explicit means for describing the "life" of objects (i.e. their creation and destruction) and their parallel activities. When we want to formalize the parallel behaviour of objects, we must approach the transformation of objects state diagrams so that activities would be performed in a "serial" order. This causes large and unexpected changes in the DM and subsequently in other AD models.

The parallelism can be elegantly captured by various formalisms (e.g. by Petri nets). Thus the solution for the elegant transformation to the ASs appears to be in integration of the ASs and one of parallelism formalisms (c.f. Sect.6). The ASs will describe static and the parallel formalism will describe dynamic properties of the AD. Some of the parallel formalisms allow to solve difficulties of describing the object "life", e.g. if objects represent tokens in Petri nets.

Operations with similar semantics - disadvantage. During the DMF, operations with the very similar meaning are arising. Utilizing the ASs with "meta" level features (c.f. Sect.6) such operations can be captured by one "meta" operation, e.g. the "meta" operation checking the object state (see Fig.6).

op is-in-state : (Class ((Class) Boolean)) Boolean ...
axiom
    is-in-state(class,checkf) = checkf(class)

Fig. 6. Checking an state in the ASs with "meta" level features

5 Functional Model Formalization

The functional model formalization is the key part of the SFM transformation because a lot of information expressed in natural language has to be formalized. Moreover, it is required that this formalization is as abstract as possible.

The VP. With respect to the consistency of the AD models, the formalization of the VP (i.e. of a process, a data flow, a data store and an actor) has been already accomplished. Utilizing the FCM, the process formalization can be improved.

Primitive process - the NLP. The process described in natural language has to be formalized with the help of the OMF and the DMF. Usually the process description comprises a lot of conditions on input values and results of an object diagram traversing.

Disadvantage. No powerful hints or advice can be provided for the FCMF. Even more, inconsistencies and incompleteness can be discovered in the AD model during the FCMF. Then the model has to be revised and the AD deeper analyzed.

The specialist who carry out the formalization has to exploit his creativity and abstract thinking to create the AD specification. Such a specification is lucid and use all provided formal concepts.

6 Integration Improvement Opportunities

We can suppose two approaches of the integration improvement. First of them is concerned with the OMT methodology, i.e. a semiformal method itself. It would be worthwhile to deal with the notational concepts used for the AD modelling. Clarification of the notational concepts semantics and closely defining which parts of the AD they are intended to model would certainly make the integration easier. The aim of the second approach is to suggest the ASs enrichments. The ASs enrichments were already discussed together with the disadvantages they are able to eliminate. The enrichments are in research and we supply only their brief characteristics and advantages in this section.

The ASs with "meta" level features. The ordinary ASs allow to create "meta" specification, i.e. the PS. However, they miss higher-order operations, i.e. operations that can have other operations as parameters. Higher-order operations help to remove the operations with similar semantics.

The ASs with implicit state (Dauchy and Gaudel 1994). The state of a specification is a Σ-algebra. (Non)elementary access operations allow to observe the state. Modification operations cause state changes, i.e. changes of the Σ-algebras. These ASs are able to capture the system changes in a convenient way.

The ASs integrated with parallel formalism. The integration of formalisms for expressing both static and dynamic properties of a modelled system allows to carry out the SFM formalization without significant changes in the DM. We were influenced by the integration of Petri nets and Smalltalk (Vondrak 1994).

References

Dauchy, P., Gaudel, M.C.: Algebraic Specifications with Implicit State. Rapport de Recherche no 887, Université de Paris-Sud, 02/1994

Polack, F., Whiston, M., Mander, K.: The SAZ Project: Integrating SSADM and Z. In Proc. of the First Intern. Symposium of Formal Methods, Springer-Verlag, 1993

Privara, I., Nižňanský, J.: Špecifikačný jazyk PROGRESS - SL.2. Technical Report UAI-4/1991, VUSEI-AR, 1991

Repaská, Z.: Formalizácia objektovo-orientovanej analýzy softwarového systému algebraickými špecifikáciami. Master Thesis, Comenius University, 1994

Rumbaugh, J., Blaha, M., Premerlani, W., Eddy, F., Lorensen, W: Object-Oriented Modeling and Design. Prentice Hall, 1991

Vondrak, I.: Interaction Coordination Nets. Technical Report of the Research Grant, Technical University of Ostrava, 1994

On the Implementation of Some Residual Minimizing Krylov Space Methods

M. Rozložník, Z. Strakoš

Institute of Computer Science, Academy of Sciences of the Czech Republic
Pod vodárenskou věží 2, 182 07 Praha 8, Czech Republic
e-mail: miro@uivt.cas.cz, strakos@uivt.cas.cz

Abstract. Several variants of the GMRES method for solving linear nonsingular systems of algebraic equations are described. These variants differ in building up different sets of orthonormalized vectors used for the construction of the approximate solution. A new $A^T A$-variant of GMRES is proposed and the efficient implementation of the algorithm is discussed.

1 Introduction

Let $Ax = b$ be a system of linear algebraic equations, where A is a real nonsingular N by N matrix and b an N-dimensional real vector. Many iterative methods for solving this system start with an initial guess x^0 for the solution and seek the n-th approximate solution x^n in the linear variety

$$x^n \in x^0 + K_n(A, r^0), \tag{1}$$

where $r^0 = b - Ax^0$ is the initial residual and $K_n(A, r^0)$ is the n-th Krylov subspace generated by A, r^0,

$$K_n(A, r^0) = span\{r^0, Ar^0, \ldots, A^{n-1}r^0\}. \tag{2}$$

Among the broad variety of the Krylov space methods (surveys can be found, e.g., in [3], [7], [6]) we will concentrate on the GMRES method [5] which minimizes the Euclidean norm of the residual

$$\|b - Ax^n\| = \min_{u \in x^0 + K_n(A, r^0)} \|b - Au\|, \tag{3}$$

or, equivalently, for which the n-th residual r^n is orthogonal to the shifted n-th Krylov subspace $K_n(A, Ar^0) \equiv AK_n(A, r^0)$

$$r^n \perp AK_n(A, r^0). \tag{4}$$

In this paper, we describe several variants of the GMRES method. For any method, which minimizes the residual, the approximate solution is constructed via some set of orthogonal vectors (note that these vectors may not span the subspaces $K_n(A, r^0)$ from (1) and may be orthogonal with respect to some other than the Euclidean innerproduct). Our exposition is based on the following observation: *the choice of this set of orthogonal vectors together with the way in which the orthogonality is enforced determine the numerical stability of the algorithm.* We point out the effective and stable versions and indicate the weak points of the unstable ones.

2 Variants of the GMRES Method

After a brief summarization of the classical approach due to Saad and Schultz, we recall the variant proposed by Walker and Lu Zhou and propose a new variant based on the $A^T A$-orthonormal basis of the Krylov space $K_n(A, r^0)$. Implementation details and optimal formulation of the algorithms suitable for the development of the computer code are discussed in Section 3.

The classical formulation of GMRES proposed by Saad and Schultz [5] is based on the orthonormal basis $V_{n+1} = [v_1, \ldots, v_{n+1}]$ of the Krylov space $K_{n+1}(A, r^0)$ which is computed via the Arnoldi recurrence

$$v_1 = r^0/\varrho, \ \varrho = \|r^0\|, \ AV_n = V_{n+1}H_{n+1,n}, \ V_{n+1}^T V_{n+1} = I_{n+1}. \tag{5}$$

Using the substitution

$$x^n = x^0 + V_n y^n \tag{6}$$

the vector of coefficients y^n is found as the solution of the transformed least squares problem

$$\|\varrho e_1 - H_{n+1,n} y^n\| = \min_{y \in R^n} \|\varrho e_1 - H_{n+1,n} y\|. \tag{7}$$

The last one is solved by the QR factorization of the upper Hessenberg matrix $H_{n+1,n}$ using the Givens rotations [5], [4].

A simpler implementation of GMRES not requiring the QR factorization of the upper Hessenberg matrix containing the Arnoldi coefficients was proposed by Walker and Lu Zhou [8]. This variant, denoted here as WLZ, computes orthonormal basis $Q_n = [q_1, \ldots, q_n]$ of the shifted Krylov subspaces $AK_n(A, r^0) \equiv K_n(A, Ar^0)$. This can be done via the recursive column by column QR factorization of the matrix $[Ar^0, AQ_{n-1}]$

$$[Ar^0, AQ_{n-1}] = Q_n S_n, \ Q_n^T Q_n = I_n, \tag{8}$$

where S_n is upper triangular. Then, the substitution (6) is replaced by

$$x^n = x^0 + [r^0, Q_{n-1}] t^n. \tag{9}$$

The optimality condition (4), rewritten as $Q_n^T r^n = 0$, gives

$$Q_n^T r^0 - Q_n^T A[r^0, Q_{n-1}] t^n = 0. \tag{10}$$

Combining (10) with (8), we receive the upper triangular linear system for determining the unknown vector t^n,

$$S_n t^n = Q_n^T r^0. \tag{11}$$

In this variant, both the residual vector and its norm can be easily updated step by step. Indeed, using (9), (8) and (11),

$$r^n = r^0 - Q_n Q_n^T r^0 = r^{n-1} - (q_n, r^0) q_n, \tag{12}$$
$$\|r^n\|^2 = \|r^{n-1}\|^2 - (q_n, r^0)^2. \tag{13}$$

From orthogonality, $Q_n^T r^0$ resp. (q_n, r^0) can be replaced, in (11) - (13) by $[(q_1, r^0), (q_2, r^1), \ldots, (q_n, r^{n-1})]^T$ resp. (q_n, r^{n-1}). The basis used for determining the approximate solution is, however, not orthogonal, which may affect ther numerical stability of this variant [8].

To determine the approximate solution, the WLZ variant still requires, however, solving an upper triangular system. One can look for a variant computing a simple step by step update of the approximate solution. This can be done by generating the $A^T A$-orthonormal basis $W_n = [w_1, \ldots, w_n]$ of $K_n(A, r^0)$. Indeed, let W_n be a result of the recursive column by column QR factorization of the matrix $[r^0, A W_{n-1}]$, assuming the innerproduct $(g, h)_{A^T A} = g^T A^T A h$,

$$[r^0, A W_{n-1}] = W_n G_n, \quad W_n^T A^T A W_n = I_n \tag{14}$$

where G_n is upper triangular. Then, using

$$x^n = x^0 + W_n f^n, \tag{15}$$

the optimality condition (4) implies

$$f^n = (A W_n)^T r^0, \tag{16}$$

and the approximate solution, as well as the residual vector and the norm of the residual can be easily updated step by step

$$x^n = x^{n-1} + (A w_n, r^0) w_n \tag{17}$$
$$r^n = r^{n-1} - (A w_n, r^0) A w_n \tag{18}$$
$$\|r^n\|^2 = \|r^{n-1}\|^2 - (A w_n, r^0)^2 \tag{19}$$

Analogously to the WLZ variant, $(A W_n)^T r^0$ resp. $(A w_n, r^0)$ can be replaced in (16) - (19) by $[(A w_1, r^0), (A w_2, r^1), \ldots, (A w_n, r^{n-1})]^T$ resp. $(A w_n, r^{n-1})$. Throughout the paper, we will denote this new formulation of GMRES as the $A^T A$-variant.

3 Implementation details

The implementation of the WLZ variant, given in [8] has the following numerical drawback. Iterative updating the norm of the normalized residual by the formula

$$\varrho_j^2 = \varrho_{j-1}^2 \{1 - (q_j, \hat{r}^0)^2 / \varrho_{j-1}^2\} \tag{20}$$

is unreliable and may lead to an early termination of the computation caused by the underestimating of the norm of the residual due to accumulation of round-off. Roughly speaking, the accumulated error in computing ϱ_j^2 by (20) can be bounded by $\gamma_1 j N \varepsilon$, where ε denotes the machine precision unit and γ_1 is constant independent on j, N and ε. Once ϱ_j^2 becomes of the order of $j N \varepsilon$, one cannot trust the result of (20) anymore. One may replace (20)

$$\varrho_j = \varrho_{j-1} sin(cos^{-1}(\xi_j/\varrho_{j-1})) \tag{21}$$

as proposed in [8], but to our opinion, this does not behave any better. For $\varrho_j^2 \gg j N \varepsilon$, however, the results produced by the implementation in [8] are satisfactory accurate.

If the square of the relative norm of the residual (within possible restarts) drops significantly close to the level $j N \varepsilon$, then the algorithm WLZ1 must be modified by adding the recursive computation of the residual vector. This can be done by using (12). Having the normalized residual vector $\hat{r}^{j-1}$, one can further replace, with no additional costs, $(q_j, \hat{r}^0)$ by $(q_j, \hat{r}^{j-1})$, which improves the numerical behavior of the algorithm. To see that, note that the actually computed basis vectors $q_1, q_2, \ldots, q_j$ are not orthogonal (for simplicity of exposition we assume that they are exactly normalized). From (12) it is clear that the approximate solution x^n computed from (11) and (9) corresponds to computing r^n by the orthogonalization of r^0 against $q_1, q_2, \ldots, q_n$ via the classical Gram-Schmidt algorithm. We may therefore expect that this process is strongly affected by rounding errors and the optimality condition (4) is not satisfactorily enforced. One may therefore look for a formulation corresponding to computing r^n via the modified Gram-Schmidt, namely,

$$r^n = (I - q_n q_n^T)(I - q_{n-1} q_{n-1}^T) \ldots (I - q_1 q_1^T) r^0, \tag{22}$$

which would guarantee that the optimality condition (4) is satisfied to much higher accuracy. Following [2], [1] we denote

$$\tilde{q}_j = (I - q_1 q_1^T) \ldots (I - q_{j-1} q_{j-1}^T) q_j, \quad j = 2, \ldots, n, \quad \tilde{q}_1 = q_1 \tag{23}$$

and $\tilde{Q}_n = [\tilde{q}_1, \ldots, \tilde{q}_n]$. Then

$$(I - q_n q_n^T)(I - q_{n-1} q_{n-1}^T) \ldots (I - q_1 q_1^T) = I - Q_n \tilde{Q}_n^T. \tag{24}$$

Using (9),(8),

$$r^n = b - A x^n = r^0 - A[r^0, Q_{n-1}] t^n = r^0 - Q_n S_n t^n. \tag{25}$$

Comparing (22), (25) and using (24), we receive

$$Q_n(\tilde{Q}_n^T r^0 - S_n t^n) = 0. \tag{26}$$

Using the linear independence of the basis vectors $q_1, q_2, \ldots, q_n$, (26) implies

$$S_n t^n = \tilde{Q}_n^T r^0. \tag{27}$$

The i-th element of the vector $\tilde{Q}_n^T r^0$ is expressed as

$$(\tilde{q}_i, r^0) = ((I - q_1 q_1^T) \ldots (I - q_{i-1} q_{i-1}^T) q_i, r^0) = (q_i, r^{i-1}).$$

Consequently, we have shown that replacing $Q_n^T r^0$ resp. (q_n, r^0) in (11)-(13) by $[(q_1, r^0), (q_2, r^1), \ldots, (q_n, r^{n-1})]^T$ resp. (q_n, r^{n-1}), one may hope for much better numerical behavior of the algorithm. The iterative updating (20) of the residual norm ϱ_j will, however, face essentially the same numerical difficulty as described above, even if $(q_j, \hat{r}^0)$ is replaced by $(q_j, \hat{r}^{j-1})$. For a stable implementation we therefore suggest to base the stopping criterion on the norm of the residual computed by (12) with (q_n, r^0) replaced by (q_n, r^{n-1}).

The $A^T A$ variant requires computing the $A^T A$-orthonormal basis $w_1, w_2, \ldots, w_n$ of $K_n(A, r^0)$ which represents a serious complication. We will concentrate on the modified Gram-Schmidt orthogonalization here and show that this difficulty can be eliminated to some extent. The usual MGS implementation is rather inefficient due to the kernel operation (At, Aw_i) which requires an extra matrix-vector multiplication in every substep of the MGS orthogonalization. If we consider an additional computing of the orthonormal vectors $u_1, u_2, \ldots, u_n$, where $u_j = Aw_j$, by the MGS process, then this algorithm can be replaced in the price of doubling the recurrences by

$$
\begin{aligned}
&w_1 = r^0/\|r^0\|_{A^T A}; \; u_1 = Aw_1; \\
&\text{for } j = 1, 2, \ldots, n \\
&\quad u = Au_j; \; t = u_j; \\
&\quad \text{for } i = 1, 2, \ldots, j \\
&\qquad t = t - (u, u_i)w_i; \\
&\qquad u = u - (u, u_i)u_i; \\
&\quad \text{end;} \\
&\quad u_{j+1} = u/\|u\|; \; w_{j+1} = t/\|u\|; \\
&\text{end;}
\end{aligned}
\tag{28}
$$

Summarizing, we propose the following implementation of the $A^T A$-variant (for some modifications and details see [4])

ALGORITHM $A^T A$
x^0 is an initial guess;
set $r^0 = b - Ax^0$; if $\|r^0\|$ small enough then accept x^0 and quit;
$\alpha = \|Ar^0\|$; $w_1 = r^0/\alpha$; $u_1 = Aw_1$;
for $j = 1, 2, \ldots, n$
$\quad \xi_j = (u_j, r^{j-1})$;
$\quad r^j = r^{j-1} - \xi_j u_j$;
$\quad$ if $\|r^j\|$ small enough then $x^j = x^0 + \sum_{i=1}^{j} \xi_j w_j$; quit;
$\quad u = Au_j$; $t = u_j$;
$\quad$ for $i = 1, 2, \ldots, j$
$\qquad \eta_i = (u, u_i)$;
$\qquad u = u - \eta_i u_i$;
$\qquad t = t - \eta_i w_i$;
$\quad$ end;
$\quad u_{j+1} = u/\|u\|$; $w_{j+1} = t/\|u\|$;
end;
$\xi_{n+1} = (u_{n+1}, r^n)$;
$x^j = x^0 + \sum_{i=1}^{j} \xi_j w_j$.

4 Conclusions

Computing the $A^T A$-orthonormal basis of $K_n(A, r^0)$ via (28) requires one more SAXPY operation per every substep of the MGS orthogonalization process and about twice as storage as the MGS used in the SS or WLZ variants. On the other hand, the $A^T A$-implementation is considerably simpler than the implementations of the other variants. It offers a simple step by step update of both the approximation to the solution and the residual vector. Moreover, the extra work can be easily done in parallel to the other arithmetic, and algorithms can be performed in less sequential steps than the implementations of the SS and WLZ variants. Therefore, for parallel computer architectures, the code based on the $A^T A$-variant may become competitive to codes based on the SS or WLZ variants. The $A^T A$-variant of GMRES is closely related to several other methods used for years (e.g. the method ORTHODIR [9]). The newly proposed $A^T A$ variant of GMRES is clearly superior to these well known and still frequently used relatives with respect to the numerical stability and the accuracy of the computed solution.

References

1. Björck, Å: Solving linear least squares problems by Gram-Schmidt orthogonalization. BIT **7** (1967) 1-21
2. Björck, A, Paige, C.C.: Loss and recapture of orthogonality in the modified Gram-Schmidt algorithm SIAM J. Matrix Anal. Appl. **13**, 1 (1992) 176-190
3. Freund, R.W., Golub G.H., Nachtigal, N.M.: Iterative solution of linear systems. Acta Numerica **1** (1992) 1-44
4. Rozložník, M., Strakoš, Z.: Variants of the residual minimizing Krylov space methods. Research Report 592, ICS AS CR, Prague 1994, 1-26
5. Saad, Y, Schultz, M.H.: GMRES: A Generalized minimal residual algorithm for solving nonsymmetric linear systems. SIAM J. Sci. Stat. Comput. **7** (1986) 856-869
6. Stoer, J.: Solution of large linear systems of equations by conjugate gradient type methods. In Mathematical Programming - The State of the Art (A. Bachem, M. Grotschel and B. Korte eds.), Springer, Berlin 1983, 540-565
7. Stoer, J., Freund, R.W.: On the solution of large indefinite systems of linear equations by conjugate gradients algorithm. In Computing Methods in Applied Sciences and Engineering V (R.Glowinski, J.L.Lions eds.), North Holland - INRIA, 1982, 35-53
8. Walker, H.F. , Zhou Lu: A Simpler GMRES. Research Report 10/92/54, Dept. of Mathematics and Statistics, Utah State University, Logan, 1992
9. Young, D.M., Jea, K.C.: Generalized conjugate gradient acceleration of nonsymmetrizable iterative methods. Linear Algebra Appl. **34** (1980) 159-194

A Formal Lazy Replication Regime for Spreading Conversion Functions Over Objectbases

Clara Smith
LINTI, Universidad Nacional de La Plata,
and Consejo Nacional de Investigaciones
Científicas y Técnicas, Argentina.
e-mail: csmith@ada.info.unlp.edu.ar

Carlos A. Tau
LINTI, Universidad Nacional de La Plata,
and L.B.S. Informática.
La Plata, Buenos Aires, Argentina.
Fax: +54 21 258816

Abstract. This paper introduces a functional-flavored formalization of objectbase evolution processes. It also determines features of the failure equivalence concept between the two main approaches for the fulfillment of database conversions: immediate and lazy updates.

1 Introduction

Schema evolution commands produce a significant impact on the bases, as objects have to accomodate theirselves to the new specifications. The updates are usually expressed using *system* or *user-defined* conversion functions. The objective of this study is to clarify and formally specify objectbase evolution concepts and change replication regimes, within a mathematical framework. Our work combines some of the strongest features of the objectbase literature and formal methods of specification and design. The source objectbase model, SIGMA, is the result of our grade thesis [ST93] at the Informatics Department, Universidad Nacional de La Plata, Buenos Aires, Argentina. SIGMA's formal description, including semantic domains, interpretation functions and denotations for the Object Manipulation Language (OML) appear in [Tau94] [Tau95]. Despite the *ad hoc* choice of SIGMA, should be noticed that the notions introduced in this article fit any current typical objectbase model, due to the simplicity and precision achieved on the definitions.

The rest of the paper is organized as next: Section 2 briefly recalls core SIGMA components. It explains how adjustments and adaptations are applied to concrete objectbase stores in order to suit new schema organizations, using the renowned immediate and lazy update replication policies. Furthermore, we analyze two equivalences between both approaches: observational and failure equivalence. Section 3 introduces the *conversion queue*, a representation for retaining updates at hand. The *mix_map* regime for implementing lazy base updates is also presented. Section 4 shows how the mix_map regime can be considered failure equivalent to the immediate approach. Finally, our conclusions are exposed in section 5.

2 Mapping Conversions on the Bases

A SIGMA **schema** is defined as a 5-tuple $<sid, T, I, A, R>$; where *sid* is the schema identifier, T is a certain set of types and relationships selected to conform the schema, I is a parallel set of well-formed implementations for types in T, R is a set of general integrity constraints defined for the schema, and A is a function providing customizations for types in T. SCH = (ID x T x I x CUSTOM x AXIOMS) is a semantic domain for SIGMA schemas, where CUSTOM and AXIOMS are primitive domains for custom-built axioms and integrity constraints respectively [Tau95], and ID is a primitive domain for names [Wir86]. A SIGMA **base** is defined as a 4-tuple $<bid, \pi, \sigma, \zeta>$, where *bid* is the base identifier, π is an object composition environment (with *is-part-of* and client references among objects), σ is the concrete object store, and ζ is the type-extention (or **class**) **system**. The semantic domain BASE = (ID x COMP_ENV x STORE x CLASS_SYS) for SIGMA bases and its constituent domains are strictly analyzed and defined in [Tau95]. Finally, we describe an **objectbase system** as a sequence of schemas, each of which governs a list of bases. This domain is expressed as OBASE_SYS = (SCH x (BASE)*)*.

One single SIGMA schema may serve as the conceptual reference for several bases. Therefore, there is a need to spread every schema evolution over each subordinate base, without exception, as they have to be updated to be brought up to a consistent state with respect to the new governor schema. This kind of propagation is usually expressed using a *map* operation, that receives a conversion function and a group of bases and *effectuates* every update. Its functional definition follows:

map :: FUNCTION $\rightarrow$ BASE* $\rightarrow$ BASE*

map cf [ ] = [ ]

map cf b:tail = *apply*(cf, b):*map*(cf tail)

The symbol **:** above stands for item chaining. *Apply* is a high order function that receives a function and an object (a base in this case), and executes the function using such object as a real parameter. Update mappings are also present in [Mon92].

Following the main two strategies for the accomplishment of database renewals, namely immediate and lazy updates [Kim89] [Tre93] [Fer94], we can give at least two meanings from an implementation viewpoint to the map effect: *immediate map* and *lazy map*. The former instantaneously replicates the conversions in every subordinate base, while the latter keeps pending changes until a base activation is solicited. But from a formal viewpoint, map should be interpreted within a unique final semantics: the immediate one. The lazy map effect is guaranteed to be the same as the immediate map effect if we are sure all bases will be touched once again during their lifetime.

Definition 2.1 *Lazy maps are always equivalent to immediate maps, as bases accomodate theirselves to changes when they are going to be observed (activated).*

This definition (which improves the one given in [Fer94]) determines that every base conforms to the schema change, due to the fact that we are merely spectators of base conversions. If we care about the application of conversion functions in a more detailed way, we will probably conclude things look not so plain. To illustrate, suppose each of the several serviceable parts of an objectbase system has its own identity, which we shall call **agent**. This term is used broadly, but we will refer to agents when talking about a discrete set of (possibly atomic) actions. Each action is either an interaction with a neighbour agent, or it may occur independently of them. Agents are always observable to the system. Definition 2.1 states an observational

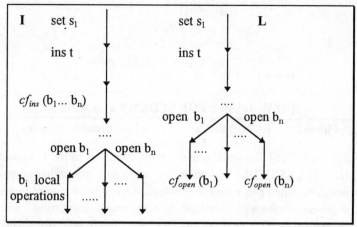

Figure 1 - Traces for a Type Insertion: Immediate and Lazy Policies

equivalence that is perhaps the simplest of all we can deal with: it equates two agents if and only if they can perform exactly the same sequences of observable actions. It can also be called **trace equivalence** (written $\approx$) [Mil89].

Let a schema designer write the sequence *...; set s_1; insert t; ...* in a transaction body, in which first schema s_1 is activated, and then a type t is placed in s_1. Next, suppose s_1-governed bases, say b_1 ... b_n, are activated. Both agents I and L in figure 1 outline what it may occur during the transition from one consistent base configuration to another in identical copies of a single objectbase system, using immediate and lazy map policies respectively. As conversion functions are unobservable to end users, we conclude $I \approx L$.

The main disadvantage of trace equivalence is that it may equate a deadlocking agent to one which does not deadlock. This certainty indicates that trace equivalence concept, applied to our agents, is too weak. An interesting and stronger equivalence is Hoare's **failure equivalence** ($\approx_f$) [Mil89], that equates two agents if both have the same set of failures. A failure is a pair *(t,{l})* where *t* is a trace and *{l}* is a set of action labels, meaning *t* can be performed and thereby reach a state in which no further activity is possible if the environment will only permit actions in *{l}*. It turns out that I and L do not possess the same failures. Trace I has, among others, the failure *(set ins,{l})* $\forall$ *{l}* such that $cf_{ins} \notin \{l\}$. This one does not belong to L's failure set, thus $I \approx_f L$ is false. Therefore, this couterexample shows how the lazy execution of a conversion function cannot be considered failure equivalent to the execution of the same conversion function treated immediately.

3 Lazy Maps Need Conversion Queues

In the worst case, evolutions may be deferred for lazy applications. Besides, a schema may undergo several changes before its bases are touched. We will associate to each base a *conversion queue* to maintain pending updates. Such a queue is merely an entry that contains FIFO-arranged references to conversion functions.

$$ass\_schemas(\beta) \rightarrow l\epsilon$$
$$get(l\epsilon, sch\_named(s)) \rightarrow \xi$$
$$ass\_bases(\beta,\xi) \rightarrow l\mu$$
$$include(\ (new\_base\ b\ \xi)\ l\mu) \rightarrow l\mu'$$
$$(\textbf{replace } <\xi,l\mu> \textbf{ in } \beta \textbf{ with } <\xi, l\mu'>) \rightarrow \beta'$$

$$(\textbf{NEW\_BASE b FOR SCHEMA } s\ \beta) \rightarrow \beta'$$

Figure 2 - Operational Semantics for the Base Creation Operation

We embody a CQUEUE primitive domain for queues with the BASE domain to configure (BASE x CQUEUE), a domain for bases and conversion queues. Under this representation, when generating a new base we just point out its name and the handpicked governor schema's identifier. Its new empty conversion queue will be attached automatically, it is imperceptible and intangible to end base-users. Figure 2 depicts an operational semantics [Plo81] for such SIGMA's OML command. The symbol $\rightarrow$ in the equation means *reduces to*, or should be more specifically understood as an evaluation relation [Hen90]. The formula has the following interpretation: *ass_schemas* picks up the various current valid schemas ($l\epsilon$) for the objectbase (β). Next, once verified the schema name, *ass_bases* takes all s-governed bases ($l\mu$). *Include* does the item piercing job. A definition for *new_base* follows:
new_base:: ID $\rightarrow$ SCH $\rightarrow$ (BASE x CQUEUE)
new_base b ξ = ($<$b, π_0, σ_0, $\zeta_0>_\xi$, [ ]$_b$); where:
$\pi_0 = \lambda(x,y).unused$ (empty ξ–composition environment), $\sigma_0 = \lambda x.unused$ (vacant ξ–store), $\zeta_0 = \lambda id.\textbf{if } type(\xi,id) \textbf{ then } <type\_of(x)=id,\{\}> \textbf{ else } unbound$, (unoccupied ξ–class system); and [ ]$_b$ is b allied empty conversion queue. Moreover, $type(\xi,id)$ returns the semantic object true (*tt*) if id is the name for a type in ξ. *Type_of*(x) retrieves the type name of an object x. We use the **replace in with** constructor to partially replace some sorts in a specification and generate a new one.

Definition 3.1: *Let mix_map be a lazy replication policy defined over SIGMA bases and conversion queues. Its formal functionality is specified as:*
mix_map :: FUNCTION $\rightarrow$ (BASE x CQUEUE)* $\rightarrow$ (BASE x CQUEUE)*
mix_map cf [ ] = [ ]
mix_map cf (b,cq):tail = (b, *push* cf cq):*mix_map*(cf tail)

4 Immediate vs. Mix_Map: Failure Equivalence

We consider a **complex agent** as a set of actions organized in a unit of atomicity. This notion is related to the one of transaction [Cat94]; both can be simply blended.

Definition 4.1: *Complex agents are deduced from user-transaction traces, and inserted in system traces as follows:*
• For the immediate map policy, given an update *uc* for a schema *s* in a transaction body, a complex agent is built as *<uc s; map cf$_{uc}$ ass_bases(s)>*, where the second

component stands for the effective instantaneous map (section 2) of the suitable conversion function onto the s-governed bases. The system trace is expanded with this complex agent. For base activation commands, no complex agents need to be built, as any immediate base activation ignores the remaining bases. .

• For the mix_map regime, i) due to an update uc applied over a schema s, the system derives a complex agent of the form $<uc\ s\ ;\ mix\_map\ cf_{uc}\ assoc\_bases(s)>$. $Assoc\_bases$ is a redefinition of ass_bases, its outcome fits the domain defined for pairs base-queue in section 3. ii) From an activation command ac, the system obtains a complex agent configured as $<ac\ b\ ;\ dequeue\ b\ cq_b>$. Function $dequeue$ clears cq_b via the performance of its queued renewals over b.

Proposition 4.2: *A system trace built up from a user-transaction trace using the immediate policy is failure equivalent to a system trace under the mix_map regime, built up from the same user-transaction using complex agents.*

Proof sketch: the proof uses the induction principle over the trace structure and the number of schema updates and base openings ocurring in the trace.

One schema update. Let T be a user transaction and let uc be the unique update command (for a given schema s) in T. Two system traces, say I and M, are built identically for the immediate and mix_map policies respectively, except for the agent involving uc. Trace I holds a duple of the form $<uc\ s;\ map\ cf_{uc}\ ass\_bases(s)>$ as a complex agent, expanding uc's original place. M contains the complex agent $<uc\ s;\ mix\_map\ cf_{uc}\ assoc\_bases(s)>$, replacing uc's earliest location. Thus, traces I and M are identical in structure for those commands which are not updates. For the only update in T they both have a complex agent in the same place, and complex agents are atomic. Thus, I and M have the same set of failures. Therefore $I \approx_f M$.

One base opening. Let T be a user transaction, let ac be the unique base activation command in T. System traces I and M are built exactly alike for the immediate and mix_map regimes, except for the agent involving ac. For trace I, the agent is atomic and it is namely ac, as the base opening is executed directly over the desired base, without any mapping over other bases. Trace M holds, covering ac's position, the complex agent $<ac\ b,\ dequeue\ b\ cq_b)>$. Thus, I and M are identical in structure for those commands that are not base openings. For the only ac in T, I holds the atomic agent ac and M maintains the complex agent built above, and complex agents are atomic. We conclude $I \approx_f M$.

Multiple schema updates and multiple openings. Let $uc_1, ..., uc_n$ be a sequence of updates for a given schema s arbitrarily found in T, and let $ac_1, ..., ac_m$ be base activation commands arbitrarily spread over T. If the failure equivalence between both regimes is proven for n updates and also holds for m openings, then:

i) The equivalence is proven also in case of an additional update uc_{n+1} included in T following the first n updates. Traces I and M upto the agent immediately before uc_{n+1} are by hypothesis failure equivalent. For every uc_i in T, trace I holds the complex agents $<uc_i\ s;\ map\ cf_{uci}\ ass\_bases(s)>$, and M contains the complex agents $<uc_i\ s;\ mix\_map\ cf_{uci}\ assoc\_bases(s)>$ in places where T originally has a uc_i.

ii) In addition, the trace equivalence between I and M is also proven in case of an additional opening ac_{m+1}, as by hypothesis I and M are failure equivalent upto the agent placed just before ac_{m+1}. Trace I holds the original ac_i agents, and M possesses $<ac\ b_i;\ dequeue\ b_i\ cq_{bi}>$ as complex agents for each ac_i.

Therefore, traces I and M for a transaction T involving certain $uc_1, ..., uc_{n+1}$ update commands and $ac_1, ..., ac_{m+1}$ base openings are failure equivalent. ☐

5 Conclusions

Immediate and lazy (mix) maps can be used as alternate policies for the concretion of objectbase evolutions. For a particular situation, the most convenient regime may be applied, and the other left for a better occasion. Conversion queues act as an appropriate bank for change sequences, as they do not interfere with the original objectbase model's base format. This observation suggest a notable facility for adapting the use of conversion queues in current objectbase systems. We think the endeavor to give rigorous definitions and earnestly remark the formalities related to the trace equivalence concept in the framework of objectbase updates is valuable: we believe the relevance of this type of equivalence is significant because it strongly cares in the efficacy of the system.

References

[Cat94] - *The Object Database Standard: ODMG-93 Release 1.1*. R. Cattell, ed. Morgan Kaufmann Series in Database Management, San Francisco, CA, 1994.

[Fer94] - *Implementing Lazy Database Updates for an Object Database System*. F. Ferrandina, T. Meyer, R. Zicari. Proceedings of the 20th VLDB Conference, 261-272. Chile, 1994.

[Hen90] - *The Semantics of Programming Languages*. M. Hennessy. J. Wiley & Sns., 1990.

[Kim89] - *Features of the ORION OODBMS*. W. Kim, N Ballou et al. In Object-Oriented Concepts, Databases and Applications, W. Kim, F. Lochovsky, eds. ACM Press, 1989.

[Mil89] - *Communication and Concurrency*. R. Milner. M. Hoare series, Prentice Hall, 1989.

[Mon92] - *Lazy Evaluation of Intensional Updates in Constraint Logic Programming*. D. Montesi, R. Torlone. Proceedings of the 2nd International Computer Science Conference, 502-508. Hong Kong, 1992.

[Plo81] - *A Structural Approach to Operational Semantics*. G. Plotkin. Lecture Notes, Aarhus University, 1981.

[ST93] - *A Unified Model for Object-Oriented Databases*. C. Smith, C. Tau. Grade Thesis. Informatics Department, Universidad Nacional de La Plata, Argentina. February 1993.

[Tau94] - *Formalization of Object Manipulation Concepts in the Denotational Semantics Framework*. C. Tau, C. Smith, C. Pons, A. Monteiro, G Baum. 20th VLDB Conference Poster Paper Collection, 47-56. Santiago, Chile, September 1994.

[Tau95] - *Formally Speaking About Schemata, Bases, Classes and Objects*. C. Tau, C. Smith, C. Pons, A. Monteiro. 4th International Symposium on Database Systems for Advanced Applications, Singapore. World Scientific Publishing Co., 308-317. April 1995.

[Tre93] - *Schema Transformation Without Database Reorganization*. M Tresch, M. Scholl. ACM SIGMOD RECORD 22 (1), 1993.

[Wir86] - *Structured Algebraic Specifications: A Kernel Language*. M. Wirsing. Theoretical Computer Science, 123-249, 1986.

Hopfield Languages

Jiří Šíma*

Department of Theoretical Informatics
Institute of Computer Science
Academy of Sciences of the Czech Republic
Pod vodárenskou věží 2, 182 07 Prague 8
Czech Republic
e-mail: sima@uivt.cas.cz

1 Introduction

Neural networks are alternative computational models. Both, their computational power and their efficiency have been traditionally investigated [3] [4], [6] within the framework of computer science.

One less commonly studied task which we will be addressing is the comparison of the computational power of neural networks with the traditional finite models of computation, such as recognizers of regular languages. It appears that a finite discrete recurrent neural network can be used for language recognition in parallel mode: at each time step one bit of an input string is presented to the network via an input neuron and an output neuron signals whether the input string which has been read, so far, belongs to the relevant language. In this way, a language can be recognized by a neural acceptor. It is clear that the neural acceptors recognize only regular languages.

A similar definition of a neural acceptor appeared in [1], [2] where the problem of language recognition by neural networks has been explored in the context of finite automata. It was shown in [1] that every m-state finite automaton can be realized as a discrete neural net with $O(m^{\frac{3}{4}})$ neurons and that at least $\Omega((m \log m)^{\frac{1}{3}})$ neurons are necessary for such construction. This upper and lower bound was improved in [2] by showing that $O(m^{\frac{1}{2}})$ neurons suffice and that most of the finite automata require $\Omega(m^{\frac{1}{2}})$ neurons when the values of weights in the network are polynomial with respect to the network size.

In [5] the present author related the size of neural acceptors to regular expressions that on one hand are known to posses the same expressive power as finite automata, but on the other hand they represent a tool whose descriptional efficiency can exceed that of deterministic finite automata. It was thus proved that any regular language described by a regular expression of a length n can be recognized by a neural acceptor consisting of $O(n)$ neurons. Subsequently, it was shown that in general this result cannot be improved because there is a regular language given by a regular expression of length n requiring neural acceptors

* This research was supported by GA ČR Grant No. 201/95/0976.

of size $\Omega(n)$. Therefore the respective neural acceptor construction from regular expressions is size-optimal.

In the present paper we introduce the concept of Hopfield languages as the languages that are recognized by so–called Hopfield acceptors based on symmetric neural networks (Hopfield networks). Hopfield networks have been studied widely outside of the framework of formal languages, because of their convergence properties. From the formal language theoretical view point we will prove an interesting fact, namely that the class of Hopfield languages is strictly contained in the class of regular languages. Hence, they represent a natural proper subclass of regular languages. Furthermore, we will formulate a necessary and sufficient so-called Hopfield condition stating when a regular language is a Hopfield language. We will show a size-optimal construction of a Hopfield acceptor for a regular language satisfying the Hopfield condition. Thus, we will obtain a complete characterization of the class of Hopfield languages.

Finally, we will study the closure properties of Hopfield languages. We will show that the class of Hopfield languages is closed under the union, intersection, concatenation and complement and that it is not closed under the iteration.

All previous results jointly point to the fact that neural acceptors present quite an efficient tool not only for the recognition of regular languages and of their respective subclasses, but also for their description.

2 Neural Acceptors

In this section we will formalize the concept of a neural acceptor and state the respective basic results and definitions that we will need in the sequel.

Definition 1. A *neural acceptor* is a 7-tuple $N = (V, inp, out, E, w, h, s_{init})$, where V is the set of n neurons including the input neuron $inp \in V$, and the output neuron $out \in V$, $E \subseteq V \times (V - \{inp\}) - \{\langle inp, out \rangle\}$ is the set of edges, $w : E \longrightarrow \mathcal{Z}$ ($\mathcal{Z}$ is the set of integers) is the *weight* function (we use the abbreviation $w(\langle j, i \rangle) = w_{ij}$), $h : V - \{inp\} \longrightarrow \mathcal{Z}$ is the *threshold* function (the abbreviation $h(i) = h_i$ is used), and $s_{init} : V - \{inp\} \longrightarrow \{0, 1\}$ is the *initial* state of the network. The graph (V, E) is called the *architecture* of the neural network N and $n = |V|$ is the *size* of the neural acceptor.

Definition 2. Let $x = x_1 x_2 \cdots x_m \in \{0, 1\}^m$, followed formally by some $x_{m+i} \in \{0, 1\}$, $i \geq 1$ (due to the notation consistency), be the *input* for the neural acceptor. The *state* of the neural network at the time t is a function $s_t : V \longrightarrow \{0, 1\}$. At the beginning of a neural network computation the state s_0 is set to $s_0(i) = s_{init}(i)$ for $i \in V - \{inp\}$ and $s_0(inp) = x_1$. Then at each time step $1 \leq t \leq m+1$, the network computes its new state s_t from the old state s_{t-1} as follows:

$$s_t(i) = \begin{cases} x_{t+1} & \text{if } i = inp \\ S\left(\sum_{\langle j, i \rangle \in E} w_{ij} s_{t-1}(j) - h_i \right) & \text{if } i \in V - \{inp\} \end{cases}$$

where $S(z) = 1$ for $z \geq 0$ and $S(z) = 0$ otherwise. For the neural acceptor N and its input $x \in \{0,1\}^m$ we denote the state of the output neuron $out \in V$ in the time step $m + 1$ by $N(x) = s_{m+1}(out)$. Then $L(N) = \{x \in \{0,1\}^\star \mid N(x) = 1\}$ is the language *recognized* by the neural acceptor N.

The next theorem characterizes the computational and descriptive power of neural acceptors [5].

Theorem 3.
(i) *Any language $L = L(N)$ recognized by a neural acceptor N is regular.*
(ii) *For every regular language L denoted by a regular expression $L = [\alpha]$ there exists a neural acceptor N of the size $O(|\alpha|)$ such that L is recognized by N.*
(iii) *There exist regular languages $L_n = [\alpha_n]$, $n \geq 1$ such that any neural acceptor N that recognizes the language $L_n = L(N)$ requires at least $\Omega(|\alpha_n|)$ neurons.*

An example of the neural acceptor for the regular language $[(1(0+0(1+0)))^\star]$ is in figure 1 (neuron types are depicted inside the circles representing neurons; thresholds are depicted as weights of edges with constant inputs -1).

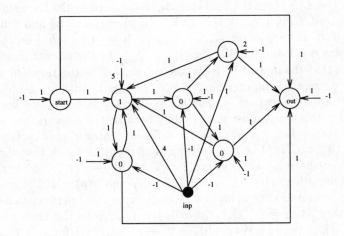

Fig. 1. Neural acceptor for $[(1(0 + 0(1 + 0)))^\star]$.

Furthermore, we restrict ourselves to a special type of neural acceptors — so–called Hopfield acceptors that are based on symmetric neural networks (Hopfield networks). In these networks the weights are symmetric and therefore, the architecture of such acceptors is given by an undirected graph. Using the concept of Hopfield acceptors we will define a class of Hopfield languages that are recognized by these particular acceptors.

Definition 4. The neural acceptor $N = (V, inp, out, E, w, h, s_{init})$ that is based on a symmetric (Hopfield) neural network (in which for every $i, j \in V - \{inp\}$ it holds $\langle i, j \rangle \in E \longleftrightarrow \langle j, i \rangle \in E$, and $w_{ij} = w_{ji}$), is called a *Hopfield acceptor*. The language $L = L(N)$ recognized by a Hopfield acceptor N is called a *Hopfield language*.

3 Necessary Condition

In this section we will show that the class of Hopfield languages is strictly contained in the class of regular languages. We will formulate the necessary condition — the so-called Hopfield condition which states when a regular language is a Hopfield language. Intuitively, Hopfield languages cannot include words with those potentially infinite substrings which allow the Hopfield acceptor to converge and to forget relevant information about the previous part of the input string which is recognized.

Definition 5. A regular language L is said to satisfy a *Hopfield condition* iff for every $v_1, v_2 \in \{0, 1\}^*$ and $x \in \{0, 1\}^2$ there exists $m_0 > 0$ such that either $(\forall m \geq m_0 \ v_1 x^m v_2 \in L)$ or $(\forall m \geq m_0 \ v_1 x^m v_2 \notin L)$.

Theorem 6. *Every Hopfield language satisfies the Hopfield condition.*

Proof. Let $L = L(N)$ be a Hopfield language recognized by the Hopfield acceptor $N = (V, inp, out, E, w, h, s_{init})$. Denote $V - \{inp\} = \{1, \ldots, n\}$ and define $w_{ij} = 0$ for $\langle j, i \rangle \notin E$. Let $\mathbf{w}_0 = (w_{1,inp}, \ldots, w_{n,inp})$, $\mathbf{h} = (h_1, \ldots, h_n)$ be the integer vectors of size $n \times 1$ and let $W = (w_{ij})_{i,j \in V - \{inp\}}$ be the integer matrix of size $n \times n$. Note that the matrix W is symmetric, since N is the Hopfield acceptor.

Let us present an input string $v_1 x^{m_0}$, $m_0 \geq 1$, with $v_1 \in \{0, 1\}^*$ and $x \in \{0, 1\}^2$ to the acceptor N. For m_0 sufficiently large the network's computation over this input must start cycling because the network has only 2^{n+1} of possible states. Let $s_1, \ldots, s_p$ be the different states in this cycle and $x_1 = s_1(inp), \ldots, x_p = s_p(inp)$ be the corresponding input bits such that the state s_i is followed by the state $s_{\pi(i)}$, where $\pi : \{1, \ldots, p\} \longrightarrow \{1, \ldots, p\}$ is the index shifting permutation: $\pi(i) = i + 1$ for $1 \leq i < p$ and $\pi(p) = 1$. Let $\sigma = \pi^{-1}$ be the inverse permutation of π, and let π^r be the composed permutations, for any $r \geq 1$. Further let $\mathbf{c}_i = (s_i(1), \ldots, s_i(n))$, $i = 1, \ldots, p$ be the binary vectors of size $n \times 1$. Then $(\mathbf{w}_0 x_i + W \mathbf{c}_i - \mathbf{h})_j \geq 0 \longleftrightarrow c_{\pi(i)j} = 1$ for $j = 1, \ldots, n$ and $1 \leq i \leq p$ follows from Definition 2.

For each state of the cycle we define an integer

$$E_i = \mathbf{c}_i^T \mathbf{w}_0 x_{\sigma(i)} + \mathbf{c}_{\pi(i)}^T \mathbf{w}_0 x_i + \frac{1}{2} \left(\mathbf{c}_i^T W \mathbf{c}_{\pi(i)} + \mathbf{c}_{\pi(i)}^T W c_i \right) - \left(\mathbf{c}_i^T + \mathbf{c}_{\pi(i)}^T \right) \mathbf{h}$$

where $1 \leq i \leq p$ and the symbol ^{T} denotes the transposition of a vector. Obviously, $E_{\pi^r p(i)} = E_i$ for $r \geq 1$ and $1 \leq i \leq p$. Using the fact that the matrix W is symmetric we obtain

$$E_{\pi(i)} - E_i = \mathbf{c}_{\pi^2(i)}^T \mathbf{w}_0 x_{\pi(i)} - \mathbf{c}_i^T \mathbf{w}_0 x_{\sigma(i)} + \left(\mathbf{c}_{\pi^2(i)}^T - \mathbf{c}_i^T \right) \left(W \mathbf{c}_{\pi(i)}^T - h \right).$$

Moreover, $x_{\pi(i)} = x_{\sigma(i)}$ for $i = 1, \ldots, p$ because $|x| = 2$. So we can write

$$E_{\pi(i)} - E_i = \left(\mathbf{c}_{\pi^2(i)}{}^T - \mathbf{c}_i{}^T\right)\left(\mathbf{w}_0 x_{\pi(i)} + W\mathbf{c}_{\pi(i)}^T - h\right) \quad i = 1, \ldots, p.$$

We know that $\left(\mathbf{w}_0 x_{\pi(i)} + W\mathbf{c}_{\pi(i)}^T - h\right)_j \geq 0 \longleftrightarrow c_{\pi^2(i)j} = 1,\ 1 \leq j \leq n$. This implies $E_{\pi(i)} - E_i \geq 0$ for $i = 1, \ldots, p$, since then $\left(\mathbf{c}_{\pi^2(i)}{}^T - \mathbf{c}_i{}^T\right)_j \times$ $\times \left(\mathbf{w}_0 x_{\pi(i)} + W\mathbf{c}_{\pi(i)}^T - h\right)_j \geq 0$ for $j = 1, \ldots, n$. But from $E_{\pi^p(i)} = E_i$ it follows that $E_{\pi(i)} - E_i = 0$ for $i = 1, \ldots, p$ and hence

$$\left(\mathbf{c}_{\pi^2(i)}{}^T - \mathbf{c}_i{}^T\right)_j \left(\mathbf{w}_0 x_{\pi(i)} + W\mathbf{c}_{\pi(i)}^T - h\right)_j = 0.$$

Then we cannot have both $c_{\pi^2(i)j} = 0$ and $c_{ij} = 1,\ 1 \leq j \leq n$, at the same time because in this case the inequality

$$\left(\mathbf{c}_{\pi^2(i)}{}^T - \mathbf{c}_i{}^T\right)_j \left(\mathbf{w}_0 x_{\pi(i)} + W\mathbf{c}_{\pi(i)}^T - h\right)_j > 0$$

is strict. The complementary case of $c_{\pi^2(i)j} = 1$ and $c_{ij} = 0$ simultaneously is impossible as well. Since then the number of 1's in $\mathbf{c}_{\pi^2(i)}$ would be greater than the number of 1's in $\mathbf{c}_i$, which contradicts $c_{\pi^p(i)} = c_i$.

Therefore we can conclude that $\mathbf{c}_{\pi^2(i)} = \mathbf{c}_i$ for $i = 1, \ldots, p$ and consequently $\pi^2(i) = i$. This implies that the cycle length $p \leq 2$. Hence for every $v_2 \in \{0,1\}^*$ either $(\forall m \geq m_0\ v_1 x^m v_2 \in L)$ or $(\forall m \geq m_0\ v_1 x^m v_2 \notin L)$. This completes the proof that L satisfies the Hopfield condition. $\qquad\square$

For example it follows from Theorem 6 that the regular languages $[(000)^*]$, $[(1010)^*]$ are not Hopfield languages because they do not satisfy the Hopfield condition.

4 The Hopfield Condition Is Sufficient

We will prove in this section that the necessary Hopfield condition from Definition 5, stating when a regular language is a Hopfield language, is sufficient as well. A construction of a Hopfield acceptor is shown for a regular language satisfying the Hopfield condition. It follows from Theorem 3 (iii) that this construction is size-optimal.

Theorem 7. *For every regular language $L = [\alpha]$ satisfying the Hopfield condition there exists a Hopfield acceptor N of the size $O(|\alpha|)$ such that L is recognized by N. Hence L is a Hopfield language.*

Proof. The architecture of the Hopfield acceptor for the regular language $L = [\alpha]$ satisfying the Hopfield condition is created by using the general construction from the proof of Theorem 3 (ii) [5]. As a result we obtain an oriented network N' that corresponds to the structure of the regular expression α where each neuron n_s of N' (besides the special neurons *inp*, *out*, *start*) is associated with one symbol $s \in \{0, 1\}$ from α (i.e., is of the type s). The task of n_s is to check whether s agrees with the input.

We will transform N' into an equivalent Hopfield network N. Supposing that α contains iterations of binary substrings with at most two-bits, the standard technique [4], [6] of transformation acyclic neural networks to equivalent Hopfield networks can be employed. The idea consists in adjusting weights to prevent propagating a signal backwards while preserving the original function of neurons. The transformation·starts in the neuron $\overline{o}ut$, it is carried out in the opposite direction to oriented edges and ends up in the neuron $start$. For a neuron whose outcoming weights have been already adjusted, its threshold and incoming weights are multiplied by a sufficiently large integer which exceeds the sum of absolute values of outcoming weights. This is sufficient to suppress the influence of outcoming edges on the neuron. After the transformation is accomplished all oriented paths leading from $start$ to out are evaluated by decreasing sequences in weights.

Here, the problem lays in realizing general iterations using only the symmetric weights. Consider a subnetwork I of N' corresponding to an iteration from α. The subnetwork I arose from a subexpression β^+ of α in the proof of Theorem 3 (ii) [5]. After the above-mentioned transformation is performed, any path leading from the incoming edges of I to the outcoming ones is evaluated by a decreasing sequence of weights in order to avoid the backward signal spreading. But the signal should be propagated from any output of the subnetwork I back to each subnetwork input, as the iteration requires. On one hand, an integer weight associated with such a connection should be small enough in order to suppress the backward signal propagation. On the other hand, this weight should be sufficiently large to influence the subnetwork input neuron. However, these two requirements are contradictory.

Consider a simple cycle C in the subnetwork I consisting of an oriented path passing through I and of one backward edge leading from the end of this path (i.e., the output of I) to its beginning (i.e., the input of I). Let the types of neurons in the cycle C establish an iteration a^+ where $a \in \{0, 1\}^*$ and $|a| > 2$. Moreover, suppose that $x \in \{0, 1\}^2$ and $a = x^k$ for some $k \geq 2$. In the Hopfield condition set v_2 to be a postfix of L associated with a path leading from C to out. Similarly set v_1 to be a prefix of L associated with a path leading from $start$ to C such that for every $m \geq 0$ it holds $v_1 x^{mk} v_2 \in L$ and $v_1 x^{mk+1} v_2 \notin L$ which contradicts the Hopfield condition. Therefore $a \neq x^k$. This implies that strings a^i, $i \geq 2$ contain a substring of the form $by\bar{b}$ where $b, y, \bar{b} \in \{0, 1\}$ and $b \neq \bar{b}$. Hence the string a has the form either $a = a_1 by\bar{b}a_2$, $a_1, a_2 \in \{0, 1\}^*$, or $a = y\bar{b}a_2b$ (e.g., $a = 10101$). For notation simplicity we confine ourselves to the former case while the latter remains similar. Furthermore, we consider $a = a_1 by\bar{b}a_2$ with a minimal $|a_2|$.

We shift the decreasing sequence of weights in C to start and to end in the neuron n_y while relevant weights in N' are modified by the above-mentioned procedure to ensure a consistent linkage of C within N'. For example, this means that all edges leading from the output neuron of I in C to the input neurons of I are evaluated by sufficiently large weights to realize the corresponding iterations.

Now the problem lays in signal propagation from the neuron n_b to the neuron n_y. Assume $b = 1$. To support the small weight in the connection between n_b and n_y a new neuron id that copies the state of the input neuron inp is connected to the neuron n_y via a sufficiently large weight which strengthens the small weight in the connection from n_b. Obviously, both the neuron n_b ($b = 1$) and the new neuron id are active at the same time and both enable the required signal propagation from n_b to n_y together. On the other hand, when the neuron $n_{\bar{b}}$ ($\bar{b} = 0$) is active, the neuron id is passive due to the fact that it is copying the input. This prevents the neuron n_y to become active at that time.

However, for some symbols $b' = b \in \{0, 1\}$ in α there can be neurons $n_{b'}$ outside the cycle C (but within the subnetwork I) to which the edges from n_y lead. This situation corresponds to y concatenated with a union operation within β. In this case the active neurons $n_{b'}$, id would cause the neuron n_y to fire. To avoid this, we add another new neuron $n_{y'}$ that behaves identically as the neuron n_y for the symbol $y' = y \in \{0, 1\}$. Thus, the same neurons that are connected to n_y are linked to $n_{y'}$ and the edges originally outcoming from n_y to $n_{b'}$ for all corresponding b' are reconnected to lead only from $n_{y'}$.

A similar approach is used in the opposite case when $b = 0$. The above-described procedure is applied for each simple cycle C in the subnetwork I corresponding to the iteration β^+. These cycles are not necessary disjoint but the decomposition of $a = a_1 b y \bar{b} a_2$ with minimal $|a_2|$ ensures their consistent synthesis. Similarly the whole transformation process is performed for each iteration in α. In this case some iteration can be a part of another iteration and the magnitude of weights in the inner iteration will need to be accommodated to embody this into the outer iteration. It is also possible that the neuron id has to support both iterations in the same point. Finally, the number of simple cycles in α is $O(|\alpha|)$. Hence, the size of the resulting Hopfield acceptor remains of order $O(|\alpha|)$.

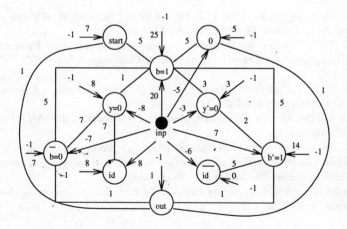

Fig. 2. Hopfield acceptor for $[(1(0 + 0(1 + 0)))^*]$.

In figure 2 the preceding construction is illustrated by an example of the Hopfield acceptor for the regular language $[(1(0+0(1+0)))^*]$ (compare with figure 1). A simple cycle consisting of neurons $n_b, n_y, n_{\bar{5}}$ is clarified here in details. Notice the decreasing sequence of weights $(7,5,1)$ in this cycle starting and ending in the neuron n_y as well as the neuron id, which enables the signal propagation from n_b to n_y. The neuron $n_{y'}$, with the same function as n_y, has been also created because the neuron $n_{b'}$ $(b' = b)$ was originally connected to n_y (see figure 1). □

Corollary 8. *Let L be a regular language. Then L is a Hopfield language iff L satisfies the Hopfield condition.*

5 Closure Properties

In this section we investigate the closure properties of the class of Hopfield languages.

Theorem 9. *The class of Hopfield languages is closed under the union, concatenation, intersection, and complement. It is not closed under the iteration.*

Proof. The closeness of Hopfield languages under the union and concatenation follows from Corollary 8. To obtain the Hopfield acceptor for complement negate the function of the output neuron *out* by multiplying the associated weights (and the threshold) by -2 and by adding 1 to the threshold. Hence, the Hopfield languages are closed under the intersection as well. Finally, due to Theorem 7, $[1010]$ is a Hopfield language whereas $[(1010)^*]$ is not a Hopfield language because it does not satisfy the Hopfield condition from Theorem 6. □

References

1. Alon, N., Dewdney, A. K., Ott, T. J. 1991. Efficient Simulation of Finite Automata by Neural Nets. Journal of ACM, 38, 495-514.
2. Indyk, P. 1995. Optimal Simulation of Automata by Neural Nets. Proc. of the 12th Annual Symposium on Theoretical Aspects of Computer Science STACS'95 LNCS 900, 337-348.
3. Orponen, P. 1994. Computational Complexity of Neural Networks: A Survey. Nordic Journal of Computing, 1, 94-110.
4. Parberry, I. 1994. Circuit Complexity and Neural Networks. The MIT Press, Cambridge, Massachusetts.
5. Šíma, J., Wiedermann, J. 1995. Neural Language Acceptors. To appear in Proc. of the Second International Conference Developments in Language Theory, Magdeburg, World Scientific Publishing Co., Singapore.
6. Wiedermann, J. 1994. Complexity Issues in Discrete Neurocomputing. Neural Network World, 4, 99-119.

Inconsistency Conflict Resolution *

Július Štuller

Institute of Computer Science, Academy of Sciences of the Czech Republic,
182 07 Pod vodárenskou věží 2, Prague 8, Czech Republic
e-mail : stuller@uivt.cas.cz

Abstract. Multiple databases may store data about the same slice of
the reality. Naturally one may try to get the overall complex information
as a result of integrating data from these different databases. And, also
naturally, one is immediately facing the problems of the inconsistency
(in the sense of the classical logic), which are amplified if one admit the
temporal dimension (leading to the temporal logic) and the uncertainty
(leading, for instance, to the fuzzy logic or the possibilistic logic).
We present an overview of some inconsistency problems and a general
framework within which they can be treated giving generic solutions for
some well-defined classes of these problems.

1 Denotational Inconsistencies

In the database community for a long time the problems illustrated by the
following two examples are well known :

Example 1. How many different people are listed below ?

- Novák
- M. Novák
- Mirko Novák
- Dr. Novák
- General Director of H.E.M. Informatics

Example 2. How many different objects types are listed below ?

- SSN
- social security number
- PIN

The database designers have learned to **solve** these problems, or at least to
minimize them *proportionally to the strictness in not allowing the synonyms.*
We call these problems the **denotational inconsistencies (DI)** either at the

- *extensional level* (**EDI**) - Example No. 1
- *intensional level* (**IDI**) - Example No. 2

---

* This work was partly supported by the Project No. 10053 *Managing uncertainty
in Medicine* (**MUM**) of the Program COPERNICUS of the Commission of the
European Community

Another kind of inconsistency is illustrated in the following example.

Example 3. At a certain university there are several information systems (IS) :

- IS about students
- IS about Ph.D. students
- IS about staff
- IS about researchers

The university rector wants to invite all university community to annual feast. For opening ceremony he must choose the right hall - with sufficient capacity to accommodate all the people, but also no too much large to assure a good ambience. Will the sum of students, staff and researchers give the correct capacity?

Here the problem comes from *interleaving* (not disjunctive) **classes** at the *conceptual level* design. Again the *appropriate* **classification** can **minimize** such inconsitencies (noted **ICDI**).

Proposition 1. *The existence of the generalization/specialization hierarchies leads to the ICDI.*

Corollary 2. *In real system design we cannot guarantee the elimination of ICDI.*

Corollary 3. *In general we cannot guarantee the complete elimination of DI.*

2 Hierarchical Inconsistencies

Example 4. A private Hospital, owned by Miloš, has a director, say Peter. Its Clinic of Surgery, headed by George, has five departments :

- Aestetic Surgery, headed by Ladislav
- Heart Surgery, headed by Ivan
- Neurosurgery, headed by Marcel
- Bone Surgery, headed by Emil
- Stomatology-Orthodonty, headed by Vašek

The Hospital is well equipped and so every manager has in his own computerized database the exact image of his own knowledge about his organizational unit.
On a regular weekly meeting of the Hospital directorate Miloš asks in what department is currently undergoing medical treatment the actor John Travolta after his last car accident.
Here are the answers :

- (**E1**) Emil : He already left our Clinic.
- (**V1**) Vašek : Since Friday he is not in my department (the Stomatology).
- (**L1**) Ladislav : Since Friday he is in my department (the Aestetic Surgery).
- (**G1**) George : He is at the Stomatology-Orthodonty.

Unsatisfied Miloš requires clear answers.

Vašek and Ladislav, being not sure (of their overloaded memories), verify in their private computerized databases, and surprisingly, repeat the same answers.

Peter, as a director (and a good diplomatist), has to save the situation.

After checking his own computerized database (which corresponds simply to the possibility to access, in addition to his private database also the appropriate portions of private databases of all his, direct and indirect, subordinates) he tries to resume the previous answers :

1. Until Friday the patient John Travolta was at the Stomatology-orthodonty.
2. Emil will not listen to Clinic gossips and will take care only of his own department patients.
3. There is somewhere an error because our patient John Travolta is confined simultaneously to two beds in two different departments, namely :
   Stomatology-Orthodonty and Aestetic surgery, which is naturally impossible.
4. We must immediately remove this controversial situation.

Fortunately, George explains there is no controversial situation.

There is just an *hierarchical* **inconsistency** emerging in the process of the **integration** of local (here *private* : Ladislav's, Vašek's and George's) **databases (information systems, knowledge-bases** or simply **knowledges**).

Ladislav and Vašek have no knowledge of the latest change, by which George, as the Director of the Clinic, decided to transfer back John Travolta from Ladislav's department of Aestetic surgery to Vašek's department of Stomatology-Orthodonty for a new stomatological operation.

Definition 4. Two assertions (propositions) will be called **inconsistent** iff their conjunction is false .

Notation

> **P, Q** : *assertions (propositions)*
> **and** : symbol of *conjunction*
> $\Rightarrow$: *then* (implication)
> $\Leftrightarrow$: *iff* (if and only if)
> **T** : symbol for *true*
> **F** : symbol for *false*
> $>$: (strictly) *greater than*
> $<$: (strictly) *smaller than*

The Definition 4 can be rewritten formally in the following short form :

P and **Q** are *inconsistent* $\Leftrightarrow$ **(P and Q) = F**

(In the following the symbol **DB** will denote a *database*, or an *information system*, or, more generally, a *knowledge-base*, or even an abstract or concrete *knowledge*, computerized or not, about certain slice of reality.)

The conclusion we can draw from the last example is simply the following. Peter could rely upon his (global) DB and would not need George explanation if Peter's DB was supplemented with the following **inconsistency resolution** *mechanism* (**IRM** - here noted **IRM-h** , *h* coming from *hierarchical*) :

Proposition 5. *Let a query to DB of* **X** *give an answer* **q(X)** *inconsistent with the answer* **q(Y)** *to a query to DB of* **Y** *.*
Suppose **X** *is superior (in the institution organizational hierarchy) to* **Y** *.*
Then valid (true) is the answer **q̇(X)** *.*

Remark. We must be able to compare **X** and **Y**. In other words, the employees of the Hospital must form an (partially) ordered set.

Note 6. The comparison can be done, for instance, with the help of a function, say **h** - from *hierarchy*, which will associate with every employee an element from an (partially) ordered set. The **IRM-h** can be then rewritten in the shorter form:

Proposition 7. *Let a query to DB of* **X** *and to DB of* **Y** *give inconsistent answers* **q(X)** *and* **q(Y)** *. Then :* $h(X) > h(Y) \Rightarrow q(X) = T$ *.*

3 Temporal Inconsistencies

Example 5. The previous inconsistency resolution mechanism will not help Peter if the answer of George (**G1**) was replaced by the following second answer of Vašek (**V2**) : Since Sunday he is again in my department (the Stomatology).

Even in this case one can naturally find the solution in the form of the following **temporal** inconsistency resolution mechanism (**TIRM**) :

Proposition 8. *Let a query to DB of* **X** *give an answer* **q(X)** *temporally inconsistent with the answer* **q(Y)** *to a query to DB of* **Y** *.*
Then valid is the answer containing the **most recent time information** *.*

Remark. We must be able to determine the "most recent time information" in the answers. (For usual time expressions containing only time points and time intervals it is true.)

Example 6. Suppose the answer of Ladislav was **L2** instead of **L1** and that the second answer of Vašek was **V3** instead of **V2** :

- (**L2**) Ladislav : He is in my department (the Aestetic Surgery).
- (**V3**) Vašek : He is again in my department (the Stomatology-Orthodonty).

None of the two previous inconsistency resolution mechanisms (**IRM-h** or **TIRM**) could help Peter.
But if we make the additional assumption (not so unrealistic) that the data in DB are timestamped indicating *when* they were entered into the DB, we can associate with the two last answers the timestamps $\tau(\mathbf{L2})$ and $\tau(\mathbf{V3})$.

And again one can naturally find the right solution helping Peter in the form of the following inconsistency resolution mechanism *"by timestamps"* (**IRM-τ**) :

Proposition 9. *Let a query to DB of* **X** *give an answer* **q(X)** *inconsistent with the answer* **q(Y)** *to a query to DB of* **Y** .
Suppose the timestamp associated with the appropriate information in DB of **X**, *denoted by* $\tau(\mathbf{q(X)})$, *is strictly superior to the timestamp associated with the appropriate information in DB of* **Y**, *denoted by* $\tau(\mathbf{q(Y)})$.
Then valid is the answer **q(X)** .

Remark. The timestamps must form an (partially) ordered set.
Usual representation of time points by (nonnegative) numbers (reals, rationals, decimals or integers) fulfill this requirement (considering the natural ordering).

Note 10. The timestamps can be assigned to the answers, for instance, by a function, say τ - from *timestamp*, which will associate to every answer the corresponding timestamp (i. e. a number) from an (partially) ordered set.

4   Generalizations

The inconsistency resolution mechanisms **IRM-h** (Proposition 5) and **IRM-τ** (Proposition 9) can be easily generalized to the following inconsistency resolution mechanism *"by labels"* (**IRM-λ**) .
(The only prerequisite is that the information in DB must be "labeled" - i. e. "timestamped" as in the case of **IRM-τ** or , as in the case of **IRM-h**, there must exist "hierarchy levels", associated with information sources, etc.)

Proposition 11. *Let a query to DB of* **X** *give an answer* **q(X)** *inconsistent with the answer* **q(Y)** *to a query to DB of* **Y** .
Suppose the label associated with the appropriate data in DB of **X**, *denoted by* $\lambda(\mathbf{q(X)})$, *is strictly superior to the label associated with the appropriate data in DB of* **Y**, *denoted by* $\lambda(\mathbf{q(Y)})$.
Then valid is the answer **q(X)** .

Remark. The labels must form an (partially) ordered set.

Note 12. The labels can be assigned to the answers, similarly as the timestamps or the hierarchies, for instance, by a function, say λ - from *label*, which can be thought as a generalization of the corresponding functions τ (Note 10) and **h** (Note 6), and which will associate to every answer the corresponding label from an (partially) ordered set.
The **IRM-λ** can be then rewritten in the following shorter form :

Proposition 13. *Let a query to DB of* **X** *and to DB of* **Y** *give inconsistent answers* **q(X)** *and* **q(Y)** . *Then :* $\lambda(\mathbf{X}) > \lambda(\mathbf{Y}) \Rightarrow \mathbf{q(X)} = \mathbf{T}$.

Remark. The condition of "superiority" can be replaced by that of "inferiority" (for instance, if the labels represent positions in the organizational hierarchy, and if the management of the Clinic of Surgery was fully decentralized, then the correct information about John Travolta medical treatment should be the Vašek's one and no that of George ...).

But we can go even further.

First, we can consider the case of more than two, say **n** , inconsistent answers. In this case, the corresponding *generalized* inconsistency resolution mechanism *"by labels"* (**GIRM-**λ) can have the following form :

Proposition 14. *Let a query to DB of X_i , $i = 1, 2, \ldots, n$, give answers $\mathbf{q}(X_i)$ which are inconsistent . Suppose there exists maximum (minimum) of the labels associated with the appropriate information in DB of X_i, denoted by $\lambda(\mathbf{q}(X_i))$, and that this maximum (minimum) is attained by an unique label, say $\lambda(\mathbf{q}(X_m))$. Then valid is the answer $\mathbf{q}(X_m)$.*

Remark. The labels must form an (partially) ordered set.

Note 15. If the labels form (at least) semi-lattice (with respect to the operation of maximum , or minimum) , the **GIRM-**λ can be simplified as follows :

Proposition 16. *Let the maximum (minimum) of the labels associated with the appropriate information to a query $\mathbf{q}$ in DB of X_i , $i = 1, 2, \ldots, n$, (denoted by $\lambda(\mathbf{q}(X_i))$), giving the inconsistent answers $\mathbf{q}(X_i)$, be attained by an unique label, say $\lambda(\mathbf{q}(X_m))$. Then valid is the answer $\mathbf{q}(X_m)$.*

Further, we can consider several different types of labels, combine them, make hierarchies of labels, combine **GIRM-**λ and **TIRM**, etc., which lead us to *complex* (**vector**) *labels* and *various possibilities of their ordering ...*
Finally, we can leave the scope of *classical* **two valued logic** and associate with every answer to a query to DB a number representing *uncertainty* (which leads us, depending on the choice of numbers, to i. e. **many-valued logic**, *finite* or *infinite* , **possibilistic** and **fuzzy logic, belief functions** , etc) [1].

5 Conclusions

As can be seen from the previous simple examples it is hardly conceivable to find universal **IRM**. Nevertheless, for certain *classes of inconsistencies* (**temporal, hierarchically organized**, *centralized* or *decentralized*, **local databases**) we have sketched the appropriate **IRM**.
In every case we are persuaded that the *"logic of the inconsistency conflict"* must be written into the **IRM** .

References

1. Hájek, P.: On Logics of Approximate Reasoning. Neural Network Word, **6**, 1993, 733-744.

A Methodology for Performance and Scalability Analysis

Efthimios Tambouris and Peter van Santen

Electrical Engineering and Electronics Department, Brunel University, Uxbridge UB8 3PH, Middlesex, UK.

Abstract. A methodology for obtaining the performance and scalability of large scale *parallel systems* (parallel algorithm-machine combinations) is proposed. This methodology distinguishes and integrates performance and scalability analysis. It provides a framework to estimate scalability, and evaluate and compare different scalability metrics. The main objectives are to minimise the effort required for analysing scalability, provide mechanisms for evaluating alternatives, and reduce the cost of backtracking from bad choices.

1 Introduction

Scalability is a property that is difficult to define. Informally, the scalability of a parallel algorithm on a parallel machine is a measure of its capacity to effectively utilise an increasing number of processors [4]. A literature survey suggests that both the performance and scalability of parallel systems do not have generally accepted formal definitions [2][4][5][7]. Nevertheless, our research found that both performance and scalability are characterised by a small number of different features, that together capture the *scaling behaviour* of the parallel system. This paper introduces a methodology that uses a number of performance models, methods and scalability metrics to simplify the determination of a parallel system's scaling behaviour covering all primary aspects of importance to the analysis of performance and scalability.

2 Scaling Behaviour of Parallel Systems

Based on a study of the published literature the following set of criteria were determined for the scaling behaviour of a system: the degree of concurrency of the algorithm, the cost optimality of the system, performance models and the performance as a function of input size and processor numbers.

The algorithm's degree of concurrency indicates the maximum number of tasks that can be executed simultaneously at any time interval. Cost optimality determines whether the cost of solving a problem on a parallel computer is proportional to the execution time of the fastest-known sequential algorithm on a single processor. Proposed performance models are space complexity functions for the sequential and parallel algorithms and time complexity functions for both the sequential algorithm and the parallel system. The space complexity function of an algorithm determines the space used by data objects while the time complexity function of a parallel algorithm is used to evaluate the parallel execution time. The limiting behaviour of these complexities as size increases is referred to as asymptotic [1], it is of interest for analysis purposes, such as determining the limiting input size that can be solved by an algorithm. Order analysis which allows us to approximate a complex function by considering dominant factors only is used in first order approximation analysis within the methodology. When estimating the system's scalability using asymptotic complexity functions the O, Θ and Ω order analysis notation is used.

The scalability of a system can be analysed by estimating how its performance varies as a function of the input size growth and the numbers of processors. The growth of the input size may follow one of three objectives: to preserve a fixed-execution time, to use all available memory, or to maintain fixed efficiency. The scalability metrics proposed for each are based on speedup, defined as the ratio of the time to run a program on one processor to the time to run it on p processors. Scaled speedup is a metric of a system's scalability when the input size is increased to fill all available memory and for most parallel systems the curve obtained is linear [3][6]. For poorly scalable systems however the parallel execution time increases rapidly[9]. Fixed-time speedup is a metric of a system's scalability with the input size adjusted to preserve a fixed execution time. Its speedup curve is similar to that for a fixed-size speedup of a system with overheads [3][9]. Isoefficiency is a metric of a system's scalability that determines the rate at which work must increase with respect to p to maintain fixed efficiency [2]. For most parallel systems isoefficiency, derived analytically, is equivalent to the experimentally determined isospeed metric [7].

3 The Methodology

Scalability metrics are based on the comparison of the parallel system to be analysed with the best known sequential algorithm run on a sequential architecture.

The six step methodology proposed here is suitable for evaluating the performance of complex scientific algorithms for large scale parallel architectures since it is based on the identification of basic computational and communication patterns frequently used in many scientific algorithms. The performance of a parallel system is estimated using these patterns of operations from which performance bottle-necks can be identified. A simple matrix multiplication algorithm on a nCUBE2 hypercube is used as a example to demonstrate the use of the methodology.

3.1 Step 1. Analysis of the parallel system.

In the first step we identify the basic computational and communication operations for both the sequential and parallel algorithms. Examples of computational operations are matrix operations such as transposition, addition, multiplication, etc while communication operations examples include single-node broadcast and scatter, all to all broadcast and scatter, permutations, etc. Sequential algorithms consist of computational operations only, parallel algorithms however contain both computation and communication operations.

In our example, the simple sequential algorithm for multiplying two $n \times n$ matrices A and B consists of one computational operation. For the parallel algorithm we assume that the two matrices A and B are partitioned into p blocks of size $n/\sqrt{p} \times n/\sqrt{p}$ mapped onto a $\sqrt{p} \times \sqrt{p}$ mesh of processors. Implemented on the nCUBE2 this mesh can be mapped onto the hypercube and consists of one communication and one computational phase per processor. Each processor determines the elements which are to reside locally and acquires them. All to all broadcasts of n^2/p elements of matrix A among the $\sqrt{p}$ processors of each row of processors and of n^2/p elements of matrix B among $\sqrt{p}$ processors of each column are required. Hence, the communication phase of the algorithm consists of two, all to all broadcast communication operations. The computation phase involves the computation of all elements which are local to and are performed on a processor; this is referred to as a single computational operation.

3.2   Step 2. Construction of asymptotic performance models.

Space complexity is derived directly from the memory requirements of the algorithm(s). Order analysis [1] is used to determine the time complexity, a function of the input size only, for sequential algorithm(s). The time complexity of parallel algorithm(s), a function of both the input size and the number of processors, is determined by the model of parallel computation adopted (e.g. PRAM, BSP, logP, or network model).

For our example, the space complexity of the sequential algorithm is $\Theta(n^2)$ whereas for the parallel algorithm the memory requirements per processor is $\Theta(n^2/\sqrt{p})$ giving a total space complexity of $\Theta(n^2\sqrt{p})$ for the system. The time complexity of the sequential algorithm T_1 (here equivalent to the amount of work W) is n^3 time units assuming that an addition and multiplication pair takes one unit time to complete. In the parallel algorithm the computation is accomplished in n^3/p time units. Assuming a network model of computation based on the hypercube interconnection topology, the all to all broadcast of n^2/p elements among processors can be accomplished in $2t_s \log p + 2t_w n^2/\sqrt{p}$ (see [2]) where t_s is the start-up cost and t_w the per-word cost. Let T_o represent all sources of overheads, then T_p, the total parallel execution time is given by: $\frac{W}{p} + \frac{T_o}{p}$ where $W = n^3$ and $T_o = 2t_s p \log p + 2t_w n^2 \sqrt{p}$. By substitution we find $T_p = n^3/p + 2t_s \log p + 2t_w n^2/\sqrt{p}$.

3.3   Step 3. First order approximation of scaling behaviour.

During this step a first approximation of the system's scaling behaviour is established using performance and scalability analysis methods. Methods to be considered include analysis of the algorithm's degree of concurrency, the system's cost optimality, and isoefficiency analysis.

In our example, the algorithm's concurrency analysis is as follows: each processor is allocated at least one element and since there are a total of n^2 elements $p_{max} = n^2$ i.e. the minimum growth rate of n is $\Theta(p^{0.5})$. Since $W = n^3$ it follows that the minimum rate of W is $\Theta(p^{1.5})$.

For the system to maintain a fixed-value efficiency E, the work W should grow at the same rate as KT_o where $K = E/(1 - E)$ as $E = \frac{T_1}{pT_p} \Rightarrow E = \frac{W}{W+T_o} \Rightarrow E = \frac{1}{1+W/T_o}$. Solving for W we find $W = KT_o$. In our example, $T_o = \Theta(p \log p)$ hence $W = \Theta(p \log p)$. Because $\Theta(p \log p)$ increases at a rate less than the minimum derived from to the algorithm's concurrency i.e. $\Theta(p^{1.5})$, for the system to maintain a fixed-value efficiency, W should increase at $\Theta(p^{1.5})$.

Finally, for the system to be cost-optimal its overhead function T_o should not exceed the work W asymptotically. Hence, the condition for cost-optimality is that the work W grows at a rate of $\Theta(p^{1.5})$.

3.4   Step 4. Analysis of results.

After completing the first three steps we are able to analyse and evaluate the parallel system for implementation difficulties and potential performance bottlenecks. If the performance or scalability results are not satisfactory those parameters effecting the deterioration can be re-evaluated and analysed by re- visiting steps 1 to 3.

In our example analysis shows that work has to increase as $\Theta(p^{1.5})$ for the system to obtain a performance proportional to the number of processors used. The $\Theta(p^{1.5})$ growth rate is determined from the algorithm's degree of concurrency, while the communication which involves transferring data suggests a slower growth rate of $\Theta(p \log p)$. Optimisation of the communication will not improve the asymptotic performance of the system.

3.5   Step 5. Refinement of models and timing measurements.

This step involves the refinement of time and space complexity models for each computational and communication step. The time complexity model is constructed from the program's control flow ensuring that the resulting expression has the correct functional form. Parameters of the performance models relating to H/W characteristics (i.e. speed of processors, communication links, etc.) are measured by executing the appropriate operations on a parallel architecture with a small number of processors. These measurements are obtained through timing, usage of a programming environment, or by collecting timing data with a hardware monitor while the program is running. A method such as least-squares approximation is applied to the measurements so the values of the parameters which best fit the theoretical model can be derived.

The asymptotic models constructed in step 2 for the algorithms in our example result in sufficient accuracy. Consequently, no further refinement of the models is needed. The hardware parameters used $t_w = 3$ and $t_s = 150$ are based on results from measurements of the nCUBE2 [2].

3.6   Step 6. Scaling behaviour estimation.

Here we determine the remaining metrics that could not be estimated in step 3 so the complete scaling behaviour of the system can be analysed. Metrics to be determined include fixed-size, scaled, fixed-time speedups, and the isospeed metric. Two approaches may be followed. The first involves using a S/W or H/W monitor to directly *measure* the values of the metrics, while the second involves the use of performance models to *estimate* the metric's value.

In the first approach we have a trade-off between the accuracy of results and the effort required to obtain timing measurements, especially if a hardware monitor is not available. In the second approach the performance models already constructed are used, to estimate the metrics. This approach allows for the analytical performance of parallel systems to be evaluated before code development and is the one selected for obtaining scalability metrics.

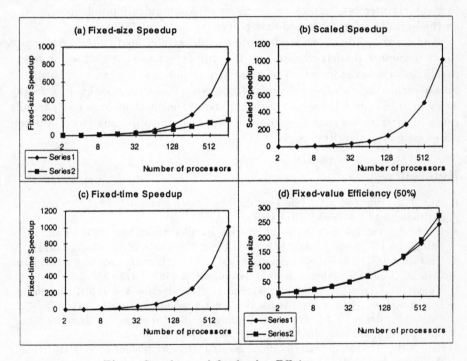

Fig. 1. Speedup and fixed-value Efficiency curves

In our example we determined the system's scaling behaviour over the range 2 to 1, 024 processors. Fig. 1(a) shows the fixed- size speedup for medium ($n = 1,000$; series 1) and small ($n = 100$, series 2) input size values. Fig. 1(b) shows the scaled speedup curve with an input size per processor of $n = 1,000$. The scaled speedup curve is better than the fixed-size but the parallel execution time grows rapidly e.g. 1.6×10^{13} time units for $p = 128$ and 1.1×10^{15} time units for $p = 1,024$. Fig. 1(c) shows the fixed-time speedup for 10^9 time units (the time for one processor to solve a problem of size $n = 1,000$). Finally, the results from isospeed analysis are shown in fig. 1(d) which shows the growth rate of n w.r.t. p for a 50% efficiency (series 1). The same figure includes the results from first order approximation isoefficiency analysis (step 3) to achieve the same level of efficiency (series 2).

4 Conclusions

This paper proposes a methodology for estimating the scaling behaviour (i.e. the performance and scalability) of parallel systems. The methodology provides mechanisms for: (a) obtaining performance and estimating scalability at low overall effort, (b) identifying performance bottle-necks, (c) evaluating the effect of optimising a computational or communication phase of the algorithm, and (d) evaluating the effect of changing the parameters of the target architecture (e.g. adding memory, improving processor or communication link speeds, etc.) on the overall performance and scalability.

The accuracy of the scaling behaviour is directly related to the accuracy of the performance models constructed. It is important to note that a number of parallel systems exist for which accurate performance models can be constructed thus allowing their scaling behaviour to be estimated with reasonable accuracy e.g. structured algorithms on multicomputers. The methodology was partially demonstrated with a simple example. Its application to the analysis of a power state- estimator algorithm is given in [8].

References

1. Aho A.V., Hopcroft J.E., Ullman J.D.: The Design and Analysis of Computer Algorithms. Addison-Wesley USA (1974)
2. Gupta A.: Analysis and Design of Scalable Parallel Algorithms for Scientific Computing. Ph.D. Thesis, Computer Science Dept, University of Minnesota (1995)
3. Gustafson J.L. : The Consequences of Fixed Time Performance Measurement. Proc. 25th Int. Conf. on System Sciences, Hawaii, vol. 2, (1992) 113-124
4. Kumar V., Grama A., Gupta A., Karypis G.: Introduction to Parallel Computing. Design and Analysis of Algorithms. Benjamin/Cummings, USA (1994)
5. Singh J.P., Hennessy J.L, Gupta A.: Scaling Parallel Programs for Multiprocessors: Methodology and Examples. Computer July (1993) 42-50
6. Sun X-H., Ni L.M. : Scalable Problems and Memory-bounded Speedup. ICASE Report 92-59 (1992)
7. Sun X-H., Rover D.T. : Scalability of Parallel Algorithm-Machine Combinations. Technical Report IS-5057, Ames Laboratories, Iowa State University, Ames, IA (1991). Also in IEEE Trans. Par. Distr. Sys. (1994) May
8. Tambouris E., Van Santen P., Marsh J.: Performance Evaluation of a Processor Farm Model for Power Systems State-Estimators on a Distributed-Memory Computer. Comp. Sys. Eng. **5** (4-6) (1994) 479-487
9. Worley P.H. : The Effect of Time Constrains on Scaled Speedup. SIAM J. Sc. Stat. Comp. **11** (5) (1991) 1-35

On the efficiency of superscalar and vector computer for some problems in scientific computing[*]

M. Tůma and M. Rozložník

Institute of Computer Science, Academy of Sciences of the Czech Republic
Pod vodárenskou věží 2, 182 07 Praha 8, Czech Republic
e-mail: tuma@uivt.cas.cz, miro@uivt.cas.cz

Abstract. Some details of arithmetic of two representatives of computers (a superscalar workstation and a vector uniprocessor) available in the Czech Republic for scientific computing are described. Consequently, their efficiency and precision on a set of linear algebraic tasks solved by different solvers is compared.

1 Introduction

One very important question in scientific computing is how to guarantee efficient performance of a given computer on a set of fundamental operations. On the other hand, efficiency on a set of basic, often linear algebra operations, plays usually the key role in the choice of computer for scientific computations.

Although a lot of effort has been devoted to developing benchmarks for scientific computing [5], [9], [2] there is still a lack of comparison for computers avilable using a broader spectrum of the important basic algorithms.

We devote our attention to some properties of computer arithmetic of two computers which present different philosophy of performing arithmetic operations. Their choice was motivated by the hardware platforms available for the scientific computations in the Czech Republic: computer Cray Y-MP EL installed in the Institute of Physics of the Czech Academy of Sciences, the representative of vector processing (we concentrate on the vector parallelism only), SGI Crimson with the superscalar processor R4000, the representative of the group of advanced uniprocessor workstations installed at many places in the Czech Republic. The comparison of their efficiency and precision is based on the set of numerical experiments. Our investigation includes not only CPU timings, but also precision of solutions and residuals.

We concentrate on the one of the fundamental problems of the computational linear algebra: solving large linear algebraic systems with symmetric and positive definite, indefinite or nonsymmetric system matrix. This task is crucial for successful tackling of many physical, chemical and economical applications. For

---

[*] This work was supported in part by the Grant Agency of the Czech Republic with grant No. 201/93/0067.

instance, core of both interior point and simplex linear programming methods is completely dependent on the sparse linear solvers. The most dominant part of the CPU time spent for the numerical solution of partial differential equations describing various phenomena in physics and chemistry is usually spent in linear solver of the discretized equation.

Efficient solution of large linear systems needs a careful choice of the algorithm with respect to the problem size, problem characteristics and the computer architecture available. Therefore, we use different algorithmic techniques to solve the same problem.

2 Precision of numerical computations

Let Ψ denote the **machine precision** defined as $1^+ - 1$, where 1^+ is the successor of 1 in the machine arithmetic. We set $\Psi = \beta^{-p}$. Superscalar workstation SGI Crimson performs the arithmetic calculations according to IEEE standard, where $\beta = 2$ and $p = 53$. The arithmetic of vector machine Cray Y-MP EL satisfies $\beta = 2$ and $p = 50$. Let us define the roundoff unit $\mathbf{u}$ as the highest number which does not change 1 if added to it. This roundoff unit depends on the machine precision and the way in which is the result rounded. The workstations use rounding to the nearest, which results in $\mathbf{u} = \frac{1}{2}\Psi$. The Cray Y-MP EL uses rounding with chopping which implies $\mathbf{u} = \Psi$. These machine constants and the computer clock frequencies are tabulated in Table 1.

Values	Cray Y-MP EL	SGI Crimson
Ψ	1.8D-15	2.2D-16
$\mathbf{u}$	1.8D-15	1.1D-16
Clock frequency	33.3 MHz	50 MHz

Table 1: *Comparison of the machine precision, roundoff unit and clock frequency for the computers Cray Y-MP EL and SGI Crimson*

The difference in the precision of the basic hardware of the two computers can be easily faced in practice. Using Cray Y-MP EL for the computations, we often need to use an additional procedure to make the results of numerical algorithms more precise, when the problem dimension is reasonably large. J. Demmel in [4] quotes a result of the linear system solver where the iterative solution improvement had to be used to get acceptable solution. The differences in precision of the computed results are clearly seen from our experiments in subsequent sections.

The basic benchmarks for the solution of generated dense linear systems are being published in the regularly updated report [5]. We show the performance results for our computers for the test problems of dimensions 100 and 1000 (denoted as L100 and L1000) in Table 2. In addition, we give the theoretical peak performance corresponding to the CPU results with the problem which is either totally vectorized (for Cray Y-MP) and for which the superscalar processor reaches its maximum speed for the whole problem. Details about the compiler options can be found in [5]. We present the results in the millions of floating-point operations per second (MFLOPS).

Performance	Cray Y-MP EL	SGI Crimson
L100	32 MFLOPs	16 MFLOPs
L1000	107 MFLOPs	32 MFLOPs
Peak performance	133 MFLOPs	50 MFLOPs

Table 2: *Comparison of computer performance for the dense linear systems computations*

Benchmarks based on the dense linear system solvers are easy to construct, but they often say very little about the application problems. The problems which we use for the tests are often much closer to the reality. Nevertheless, they also cannot be exhausting, as well as any isolated idea used in computer benchmarks construction (cf. [3], [9]).

Probably the biggest advantage of the Cray Y-MP EL over an advanced workstation is its vector processor, which enables to manipulate the vectors of data in an effective way. This is advantageous especially in dense matrix manipulations, where operations with dense vectors and submatrices constitute prevailing part of the overall operations. Moreover, the processing of sparse vectors and matrices (vectors and matrices with many zero elements taking into account only the nonzeros), which have elements indirectly addressed, is also supported by hardware. The Cray computer uses so-called hardware gather-scatter enabling to vectorize also the sparse calculations.

The workstation SGI Crimson does not have an vector processing unit. Nevertheless, its superscalar RISC unit is very efficient. It enables to pipeline one scalar addition with one scalar multiplication in the so-called superscalar mode. Moreover, its integer arithmetic unit is more efficient than the Cray's one.

All the programs used were written in Fortran 77 using double precision. Some of the solvers were written by the authors, including the sparse matrix codes. Other were taken from the Linpack and Lapack (see [1], [6]). For timings we used the standard function *etime()*, programs were optimized using the highest compiler options. Test matrices were taken from the Harwell-Boeing collection. We will shortly quote the application areas to give the idea about the scope of the comparison: linear programming, economical modelling, air-pollution including chemical kinetics and transport equations, computer simulations, electrical engineering problems, structural engineering, power network calculations, chemical engineering, astrophysics, nuclear reactor computations and flow modelling. The right-hand side vectors were computed using the known solution with unit components.

3 Linear system solvers

3.1 Symmetric positive definite case

Consider the system of linear algebraic equations

$$Ax = b,$$

where $A \in R^{N,N}$ is a symmetric and positive definite (SPD) matrix and $b \in R^N$ is a right-hand side vector. Standard strategy for the SPD computations is the symmetric form of the Gaussian elimination (For discussion on the iterative and direct methods, sparsity and computer architectures see [10]). Among the most effective implementations of the dense algorithms are the ones in Linpack ([6]) and Lapack ([1]) libraries. We used the procedures DPOFA and DPOSL from Linpack library. The algorithms are usually incorporated in basic libraries delivered by computer producers. The results given in the Table 3 clearly show that in the dense case, the procedures can be easily vectorized and the CPU times obtained from the Cray Y-MP EL are better that the CPU times from the workstation, especially for larger problems.

MATRIX	Dimension N	Nonzeros NONZ	CPU time		Error norm		Residual norm	
			Cray	Crimson	Cray	Crimson	Cray	Crimson
1138BUS	1138	2596	27.88	66.29	1.05–06	7.60–10	2.85–08	4.61–11
494BUS	494	1080	4.44	4.75	1.25–08	2.16–11	1.42–09	1.29–11
662BUS	662	1568	8.36	11.7	8.51–09	3.89–12	1.62–10	9.75–13
685BUS	685	1967	9.00	13.07	1.50–09	3.85–13	3.11–10	8.29–12
BRNO974	974	12340	19.61	41.03	1.14–09	1.52–12	2.93–08	1.49–10
GR3030	900	4322	16.45	31.61	6.35–11	2.94–14	5.44–12	4.92–14

Table 3: Results of comparison for the dense implementation of the symmetric Gaussian elimination of SPD matrices

For most of the matrices, the nonzero elements constitute only a small proportion of all the matrix elements. Nowadays, an enormous effort is devoted to sparse implementations of the computer algorithms, which enable to make use of the structure of nonzeros in the original matrix. In SPD case we can determine the structure of nonzeros in the matrix obtained from the symmetric Gaussian elimination in advance. This leads to efficient implementations which make use of the indirectly addressed nonzero elements processed during the algorithm. For the sake of the comparison we used our implementation which does not promote any special advantages of Cray or workstation based on the column decomposition (see [7]). It is out of scope of this paper to compare various enhancements (e.g. block building) of the basic algorithmic schemes and their influence on the code performance (see [8]). The results are provided in Table 4.

MATRIX	Dimension N	Nonzeros NONZ	CPU time		Error norm		Residual norm	
			Cray	Crimson	Cray	Crimson	Cray	Crimson
1138BUS	1138	2596	0.42	0.07	0.23–09	0.65–12	0.19–05	0.66–08
494BUS	494	1080	0.16	0.03	0.40–10	0.62–12	0.17–09	0.18–11
662BUS	662	1568	0.30	0.05	0.18–09	0.14–13	0.89–10	0.23–12
685BUS	685	1967	0.34	0.05	0.25–10	0.94–13	0.12–09	0.36–11
BRNO974	974	12340	2.30	0.57	0.12–08	0.59–12	0.28–07	0.56–10
GR3030	900	4322	0.79	0.15	0.74–11	0.33–14	0.21–11	0.53–14

Table 4: Results of comparison for the sparse implementation of the symmetric Gaussian elimination of SPD matrices

Our results show that the timings for the workstation are invariably better. For the discussion what are the algorithmic features promoting this fact see [10]. Moreover, all the results are better for the sparse algorithm on all the test matrices. We face the problem of reasonable benchmarks again, since the dense linear solver test is often not sufficient to reveal the real computer performance.

As for the precision (norm of the error of the solution $\hat{x} - x$) and residual size (norm of $b - A\hat{x}$), where $\hat{x}$ is the computed approximation to the solution vector, we can notice that they differ as the theory predicts. In particular, results from Cray Y-MP EL are usually less precise and iterative improvement is sometimes necessary for larger and/or ill-conditioned problems.

3.2 Systems with symmetric indefinite and nonsymmetric matrices

The typical source of these problems are bases of the linear programming problems, economical and chemical engineering and discretized flow problems. Table 5 provides results of the direct sparse nonsymmetric solver for the symmetric indefinite and nonsymmetric matrices.

MATRIX	Dimension N	Nonzeros NONZ	CPU time Cray	CPU time Crimson	Error norm Cray	Error norm Crimson	Residual norm Cray	Residual norm Crimson
BCSSTK09	1083	9760	34.91	7.71	0.91–08	0.75–11	0.13–03	0.37–06
BP800	822	4534	2.48	0.45	0.17–09	0.29–11	0.14–09	0.34–12
FS5413	541	4285	2.92	0.59	0.79–06	0.80–09	0.94–06	0.12–08
GRE1107	1107	5664	13.53	3.47	0.17–06	0.29–09	0.19–11	0.58–13
JPWH991	991	6027	11.94	2.65	0.18–09	0.19–13	0.44–10	0.62–13
MAHINDAS	1258	7682	5.72	1.21	0.24–07	0.45–09	0.58–07	0.74–09
NNC666	666	4044	21.05	9.02	0.75–04	0.33–06	0.10–09	0.21–11
NOS7	729	2673	9.71	2.13	0.22–03	0.50–08	0.63–05	0.66–08
ORSIRR1	1030	6858	9.21	1.97	0.51–08	0.41–11	0.19–06	0.34–09
PORES2	1224	9613	33.84	9.49	0.10–07	0.15–11	0.32–05	0.21–07
SHERMAN1	1000	3750	2.47	0.51	0.23–09	0.75–12	0.10–11	0.58–14
WEST0989	989	3537	4.09	0.57	0.26–07	0.35–09	0.73–08	0.21–09

Table 5: Results of comparison for the sparse implementation of the Gaussian elimination for symmetric indefinite and nonsymmetric matrices

Also as in the SPD case, the results are in favor of the superscalar computer. The partial reason is the increased portion of the integer calculations due to pivoting. Moreover, the timings are strongly influenced by the structure of nonzeros of the matrix. For the Cray Y-MP EL computer, the dense implementation provided better timings for some small problems. This never happened for the SGI computer.

4 Conclusions

The paper contains a comparison of the two representatives of computers available for scientific computations in the Czech Republic. We concentrated on the precision, issue of density and sparsity in computer benchmarks, fitting the algorithm to the architecture for the fundamental linear algebra problem arising in important applications in various branches of industry.

Although algorithms with dense matrices are very often used in the benchmarks and they promote a good speedup on the vector computers, the real-world problems provide rather matrices with many nonzero elements - sparse matrices. Processing of dense blocks is only a subtask of a complicated direct sparse solver. The necessary indirect addressing decreases the potential for the vectorization. In this case, the superscalar architecture is often preferable. The results are then often not in favor for the Cray Y-MP EL computer and the proportion price/performance is much better for the superscalar workstation. We also note the problems with precision for the Cray Y-MP computers.

In any case, extrapolation of the results to other members of the Cray Y-MP and SGI families must be done very carefully and detailed discussion is outside the scope of this paper. We have compared the computers which are available for the computations in the Czech Republic, demonstrated some of their characteristics and pointed out that the choice of a computer for scientific computing is a complicated multidimensional problem.

References

1. Anderson, E., Bai, Z., Bischof, J., Demmel, J., Dongarra, J.J., Du Croz, J., Greenbaum, A., Hammarling, S., McKenney, A., Ostrouchov, S., Sorensen, D.: Lapack user's guide. SIAM Philadelphia, 1992
2. Berry, M., Cybenko, G., Larson, J.: Scientific benchmarks characterizations. Parallel Computing **17** (1991), 1173–1194.
3. Daydé, M.J., Duff, I.S.: Porting industrial codes and developing sparse linear solvers on parallel computers, Technical Report RAL 94-019, Rutheford Appleton Laboratory, 1994.
4. Demmel, J.W.: Trading off parallelism and numerical stability. In: Linear Algebra for Large-Scale and Real-Time Applications (M.S.Moonen et al. eds.), Kluwer Academic Publishers 1993, 49-68
5. Dongarra, J.J.: Performance of various computers using standard linear equations software. Technical Report CS-89-85, University of Tennessee, Update 1.2.1995
6. Dongarra, J.J., Bunch, J.R., Moler, C.B., Stewart, G.W.: Linpack user's Guide. SIAM, Philadelphia 1979
7. Liu, J.W.H.: The role of elimination trees in sparse factorization. SIAM J. Matrix Anal. Appl. **11** (1990), 134–172
8. Ng, E.G., Peyton, B.W.: Block sparse Cholesky algorithms on advanced uniprocessor architectures, SIAM J. Sci. Comput. **14** (1993), 1034–1056.
9. Pointer,L: Perfect: Performance evaluation for cost-effective tansformations. Report 2. CSRD Report No. 964, University of Illinois 1990
10. Strakoš, Z., Tůma, M.: Current trends in numerical linear algebra: from theory to practice. In: Proceedings of SOFSEM'94, 1994, 229–247

Logic Programming in RPL and RQL

Peter Vojtáš and Leonard Paulík

Mathematical Institute of Slovak Academy of Sciences, *
Jesenná 5, 041 54 Košice, Slovakia

Abstract. The aim of this contribution is to show that RPL-Rational Pavelka Logic and RQL-Rational Quantification Logic (Hájek's substantial simplification of Pavelka's propositional and Novák's predicate fuzzy calculi) are suitable logical systems for handling uncertainty in logic programming and expert systems. We define corresponding procedural and declarative semantics, prove the soundness of graded SLD-refutation with fixed → and & and discuss some further couples of connectives suitable for logic programming and appropriate declarative semantics.

1 Introduction (and Motivation)

Every expert system contains some deduction engine, the rôle of Prolog in expert systems and their deduction process is emphasized in D. Meritt's book [M]. This is one of our motivations.

For expert systems to work in the real world they must also be able to deal with uncertainty. One of the simplest schemes is to associate a numeric value with each piece of information in the system. The numeric value represents the certainty with which the information is known. We will treat these aspect of (un)certainty by using many valued and/or fuzzy logic. So far this is our motivation of studying connections between logic programming and many valued logic.

Another point is, that usual many valued calculi of Lukasiewicz (see e.g. [G]) are not suitable for this purpose because they are oriented to handle connection between syntax and semantics for 1-Tautologies and standard proofs. Our situation requires to handle cases where an information (fact or rule in Prolog) has some degree of certainty (confidence factor) and the deduction is graded with some numerical value. This corresponds to case where the set of axioms is no more a crisp set of formulas (propositions, resp.) but rather a fuzzy set of formulas. We are enough lucky that there were already developed tools in logic to handle this phenomena namely Pavelka's propositional logic [P], Novák's predicate fuzzy logic [N] (extending Pavelka's ideas) and a substantial simplification of both in works of P. Hájek [H1, H2] where RPL-Rational Pavelka Logic and RQL-Rational Quantification Logic are introduced and developed.

* e-mail:{vojtas,lepaulik}@kosice.upjs.sk, tad/fax (+42 95)6 228 291

This work was supported by the grant 2/1224/95 of the Slovak Grant Agency for Science.

D. Dubois, J. Lang and H. Prade in [DLP] offer an extensive survey of research of the use of fuzzy sets in deductive approach to approximate reasoning. We consider similar deduction as in certainty factor approach of Shortliffe and Buchanan ([SB]) and our results cover also the correctness of MYCIN-deduction. We do not discuss relationship between truth and (un)certainty. Many theoretical result on and/or implementation of, fuzzy logic programming described in the Chapter 4.3 of [DLP] use a resolution threshold, this is not our case. Our approach is closest to that of Ding, Shen and Mukaidono ([DSM], as quoted in [DLP], the original source we were not able to consult). They propose a linear resolution strategy which is not guided by weights and it gives the first refutation found, whatever its confidence degree may be. We do the same but moreover we discuss all pairs and/or triples of connectives used in a sound way.

In this contribution we study theoretical aspects of logic programming in RPL and RQL and their analogues for other connectives. We consider the connection between procedural and declarative semantics. We find out its dependence on semantical choice for conjunction and implication, and on monotonicity of conjunction, and discuss several cases.

We would like to express our thanks to Peter Hájek for getting acquainted with [H4] (handwritten by D. Harmancová) and for being present at [H3].

In what follows, our main reference source for Prolog is [L] and for Pavelka-like logical systems are [H1-2] and [G]. Moreover let us note that though we are concerning both propositional and predicate calculus in this short contribution we restrict ourselves to predicate logic, where propositional logic works in same way as dealing with ground atoms. Further we restrict ourselves to definite programs.

2 Declarative Semantics

Let L be a first order language. The fuzzy Herbrand interpretation differs from the crisp one based of Herbrand universe U_L and Herbrand base B_L and interpretation of constants and function symbols (see e.g. [L]) just in interpretation of predicate symbols. For each n-ary predicate symbol in L we assign in I_L^F a mapping from U_L^n into $[0,1]$ (the unit interval). So since in fuzzy Herbrand interpretations the assignment to constants and function symbols is fixed (and same as in crisp case), it is possible to identify a fuzzy Herbrand interpretation with a fuzzy subset of the Herbrand base, and we write $I_L^F(p(a_1, \ldots, a_n)) = x \in [0,1]$ (x is a real number from the unit interval, not necessarily rational).

To calculate truth values of arbitrary formulas let us define truth functions $\neg^{\cdot}$, $\rightarrow^{\cdot}$ and $\&^{\cdot}$ (corresponding to $\neg$, $\rightarrow$ and $\&$). Note that in Lukasiewicz logics $\varphi \& \psi$ stands for $\neg(\varphi \rightarrow \neg\psi)$ in contrast to $\varphi \wedge \psi$ which stands for $\neg((\neg\varphi \rightarrow \neg\psi) \rightarrow \neg\psi)$, both being equivalent only in two valued case. For arbitrary $x, y \in [0,1]$ put $\neg^{\cdot} x = 1 - x, x \rightarrow^{\cdot} y = \min(1, 1 - x + y)$ and $x \&^{\cdot} y = \max(0, x + y - 1)$. The truth value φ_I of φ w.r.t. a fuzzy Herbrand interpretation I and an evaluation of variables $e : Var_L \rightarrow U_L^F$ is defined as $(p(a_1, \ldots, a_n, X_1, \ldots, X_l))_I[e] = I(p(a_1, \ldots, a_n, e(X_1), \ldots, e(X_l)))$, $(\neg\varphi)_I[e] = \neg^{\cdot}(\varphi_I[e])$, $(\varphi \rightarrow \psi)_I[e] = \varphi_I[e] \rightarrow^{\cdot}$

$\psi_I[e]$, and $((\forall x)\varphi)_I[e] = \inf\{\varphi_I[e'] : \ e'$ varies through all evaluation which can differ from e only at $x\}$. Finally set $\varphi_I = (\forall \varphi)_I = \inf\{\varphi_I[e] : e$ evaluation$\}$ (the truth value of φ (or its generalization) w.r.t. I).

A fuzzy theory is a rational valued fuzzy set of formulas, i.e. a (possibly partial) mapping T associating a formula φ a positive rational number $T(\varphi) \in [0,1]$. Partiality of the mapping T we understand as of being defined constantly zero outside of the domain $\text{dom}(T)$.

Definition 1. A fuzzy Herbrand interpretation I is a model of a fuzzy theory T if for all formulas $\varphi \in \text{dom}(T)$ we have $\varphi_I \geq T(\varphi)$.

3 Procedural Semantics

A $(\rightarrow, \&)$-definite program clause is a formula of the form $\forall(A \leftarrow B_1 \& \cdots \& B_n)$ (often denoted by $A \leftarrow B_1, \ldots, B_n$) where $A, B_1, \ldots, B_n$ are atoms and commas in the antecedent denote the (sharp) conjunction $\&$. Similarly we define $(\rightarrow, \&)$-facts and goals.

Let us define an equivalence relation $\approx$ on the set of all formulas by $\varphi \approx \psi$ if φ is a variant of ψ.

A fuzzy theory P is called a fuzzy $(\rightarrow, \&)$-definite program if

1. $\text{dom}(P)$ is a set of $(\rightarrow, \&)$-definite program clause
2. $\text{dom}(P)/_\approx$ is finite
3. for $\varphi \approx \psi$ and $\varphi \in \text{dom}(P)$ we have $\psi \in \text{dom}(P)$ and $P(\varphi) = P(\psi) > 0$.

Following P. Hájek ([H1],[H2]) we define a graded formula being a pair $(\varphi; r)$, where φ is a formula and $r \in [0,1]$ is a rational number. Especially, $(A \leftarrow; r)$, $(A \leftarrow B_1, \ldots, B_n; r)$, and $(\leftarrow B_1, \ldots, B_n; r)$ are a graded fact, a graded clause, and a graded goal, respectively.

Definition 2. Let $G = (\leftarrow A_1, \ldots, A_m, \ldots, A_k; r)$ and $C = (A \leftarrow B_1, \ldots, B_l; q)$ be a graded goal and a graded clause, respectively. Then a graded goal G' is f-derived from G and C using mgu θ if the following conditions hold:

1. A_m is an atom, called the selected atom in G
2. θ is a mgu of A_m and A
3. $G' = (\leftarrow(A_1, \ldots, A_{m-1}, B_1, \ldots, B_l, A_{m+1}, \ldots, A_k)\theta; r \ \& \ q)$.

Definition 3. Let P be a fuzzy $(\rightarrow, \&)$-definite program and let H be a $(\rightarrow, \&)$-definite goal. A pair $(\theta; r)$ consisting of a substitution θ and a rational number r is a *graded computed answer* (GCA) for P and H if there is a sequence $G_0, \ldots, G_n$ of graded goals, a sequence $D_1, \ldots, D_n$ of suitable variants of clauses from the domain of P and a sequence $\theta_1, \ldots, \theta_n$ of mgu's such that

1. $G_0 = (H; 1)$
2. G_{i+1} is f-derived from G_i and $(D_{i+1}; P(D_{i+1}))$
3. $\theta = \theta_1 \circ \cdots \circ \theta_n$ restricted to variables of H
4. $G_n = (\square; r)$

($G_0, \ldots, G_n$ is called a *graded SLD-refutation*).

4   Soundness of Graded SLD-Refutation

Definition 4. A pair $(\theta; r)$ consisting of a substitution θ and a rational number r is a *fuzzy Herbrand correct answer* for a fuzzy $(\rightarrow, \&)$-definite program P and a $(\rightarrow, \&)$-definite goal $H = \leftarrow A_1, \ldots, A_n$ if for all fuzzy Herbrand interpretations I which is a model of P we have $(\forall(A_1 \& \cdots \& A_k)\theta)_I \geq r$.

Theorem 5. *Let P be a fuzzy $(\rightarrow, \&)$-definite program and H be a $(\rightarrow, \&)$-definite goal $\leftarrow A_1, \ldots, A_k$. Let $(\theta; r)$ be a graded computed answer for P and H, then $(\theta; r)$ is a fuzzy Herbrand correct answer.*

Proof. Let $G_0 = (H; 1), \ldots, G_i = (H_i; p_i), \ldots, G_n = (\square; r)$ be a sequence of graded goals, $D_1, \ldots, D_n$ a sequence of suitable variants of clauses from $\text{dom}(P)$ and $\theta_1, \ldots, \theta_n$ a sequence of mgu's witnessing the computed answer $(\theta; r)$. We prove the theorem by induction on the length of the refutation.

Suppose $n = 1$. Then H is a goal $\leftarrow A_1$, there is $A \leftarrow$ in domain of P and $A_1\theta_1 = A\theta_1$, $\theta = \theta_1$. Let I be a model of P then $(A_1\theta)_I = (\forall A_1\theta_1)_I = (\forall A\theta_1)_I \geq (\forall A)_I = P(A\leftarrow) = r$.

Suppose that the result holds for computed answers which are witnessed by a computation of length $n - 1$. Let D_1 be $A \leftarrow B_1, \ldots, B_l$ and A_m selected atom of H and $A\theta_1 = A_m\theta_1$. Let us denote $\vartheta = \theta_2 \circ \cdots \circ \theta_n$ and (having in mind that $\&$ is commutative and associative), $A^* = (A_1 \& \cdots \& A_{m-1} \& A_{m+1} \& \cdots \& A_k)\theta_1$, $B^* = (B_1 \& \cdots \& B_l)\theta_1$, and $q = P(D_2) \mathbin{\&} \cdots \mathbin{\&} P(D_n) = p_2 \mathbin{\&} \cdots \mathbin{\&} p_n$. As $(H_1; 1)$, $(H_2; 1 \mathbin{\&} p_2), \ldots, (H_i; p_2 \mathbin{\&} \cdots \mathbin{\&} p_i), \ldots (\square; q)$ with $D_2, \ldots, D_n$ and $\theta_2, \ldots, \theta_n$ is a graded SLD-refutation for P and $H_1 = \leftarrow A^* \& B^*$ of length $n - 1$, for every I model of P we have $(\forall(A^* \& B^*)\vartheta)_I \geq q$. We can consider an evaluation e as a substitution (because we are working only with Herbrand universes) so we can extend ϑ and θ outside of their domains using e getting ϑ_e, θ_e. Denote $A^e = A^*\vartheta_e$, $B^e = B^*\vartheta_e$ and $A_m^e = A_m\theta_e$. We have (for I a model of P)

$$(A^e \& B^e)_I = (A^*\vartheta \& B^*\vartheta)_I[e] \geq (\forall(A^*\vartheta \& B^*\vartheta)_I \geq q \tag{1}$$

$$(A_m^e \leftarrow B^e)_I \geq (A_m\theta_1 \leftarrow B^*)_I = (A\theta_1 \leftarrow B^*)_I \geq (\forall(A \leftarrow B_1 \& \cdots \& B_l))_I \geq \tag{2}$$

$$\geq P(\forall(A \leftarrow B_1 \& \cdots \& B_l)) = p_1 = 1 \mathbin{\&} P(D_1). \tag{3}$$

So every model I of P is also a model of $T = P \cup \{(A^e \& B^e; q), (B^e \rightarrow A_m^e; p_1)\}$. As $(B^e \rightarrow A_m^e) \rightarrow (A^e \& B^e \rightarrow A^e \& A_m^e)$ is a 1-Tautology of L_∞ (see (T21) on p. 90 of [G]) its truth value for all interpretations is 1. So using modus ponens for graded proof of [H2] (from (φ, x) and $(\varphi \rightarrow \psi, y)$ derive $(\psi, x \mathbin{\&} y)$) we see that

$$(B^e \rightarrow A_m^e ; p_1) \tag{4}$$

$$((B^e \rightarrow A_m^e) \rightarrow (A^e \& B^e \rightarrow A^e \& A_m^e) ; 1) \tag{5}$$

$$(A^e \& B^e \rightarrow A^e \& A_m^e ; p_1 \mathbin{\&} 1) \tag{6}$$

$$(A^e \& B^e ; q) \tag{7}$$

$$(A^e \& A_m^e ; q \mathbin{\&} p_1 \mathbin{\&} 1) \tag{8}$$

is a graded proof in T in sense of P. Hájek ([H2]) and as $r = p_1 \;\&\; q$, we have that in all models I of P (which are also models of T) and for all evaluations e $(A^e \& A_m^e)_I \geq r$ and hence $(\forall (A_1 \& \cdots \& A_m \& \cdots \& A_k)\theta)_I = \inf_e (A^e \& A_m^e)_I \geq r$.

$\square$

Note moreover that the use of & in graded SLD-refutation was necessary, because e.g. using $x \wedge^{\cdot} y = \min(x, y)$ in a derivation we get a wrong answer. E.g. for RPL fuzzy program $P = \{(A \leftarrow B; \frac{1}{2}), (B \leftarrow; \frac{1}{2})\}$ and for the goal $\leftarrow A$ we get the answer $(yes; \frac{1}{2})$ although the interpretation $\{(A; 0), (B; \frac{1}{2})\}$ is a model of P. The point is that $\&$ is the only logical connective under which modus ponens with $\rightarrow^{\cdot}$ is sound (see ([P]). The soundness of modus ponens depends on the implication and conjunction that are chosen. Calculating modus ponens with $\wedge^{\cdot} = \min(x, y)$ the corresponding implication is $(x \Rightarrow^{\cdot} y) = 1$ if $x \geq y$ and $(x \Rightarrow^{\cdot} y) = y$ otherwise. In this case $\{(A; 0), B; \frac{1}{2})\}$ is no more a model of P and all works.

We say a tuple (seq, et) of implication and conjunction being sound if the modus ponens "from $(A; x)$ and $(A \text{ seq } B; y)$ infer $(B; \text{et}^{\cdot}(x, y))$" is a sound rule, we denote this by MP(seq, et). The tuple (seq, et) fulfills the monotonicity condition (denoted MON(seq, et)) if in all fuzzy interpretations the formula "$(A \text{ seq } B) \text{ seq } ((A \text{ et } C) \text{ seq } (B \text{ et } C))$" has value 1. We see that immediate translation of the proof of the Theorem 5 gives

Theorem 6. *Let* MP&MON(seq, et) *holds and* P *be a fuzzy* (seq, et)-*definite program;* H *a goal and* $(\theta; r)$ *a graded computed answer for* P *and* H. *Then* $(\theta; r)$ *is a Herbrand correct answer.*

Proof. Similar to that of Theorem 5. $\square$

Note, that in [VPL] we discussed other pairs of connectives fulfilling this requirements.

5 When et_1 Evaluating MP Differs from et_2 in the Body

In MYCIN like deduction (as of [SB]) the clause (or rule) looks like

$A \text{ qes } B_1 \text{ et}_2 \ldots \text{et}_2 B_n$ (equivalently, if $B_1 \text{ et}_2 \ldots \text{et}_2 B_n$ then A)

where *if–then* is *seq* (and *qes* is the leftarrow version of *seq*) and corresponding conjunction et_1 fulfilling MP(seq, et_1) possibly differs from et_2 in the body of clause. We have to handle the prolog deduction of this case by separate procedural semantics (the SLD-refutation is the crisp one just the evaluation differs).

Definition 7. Let P be a fuzzy (seq, et_2)-definite program, MP(seq, et_1) and H a goal. A pair $(\theta; r)$ is a combined graded computed answer (abbreviated as CGCA), if we get it by recursive application of following rule.
Assume:
$P(A \text{ qes } B_1 \text{ et}_2 \ldots \text{et}_2 B_n) = x$ and θ_0 is an mgu for H and A

$(\theta_1; r_1)$ is a CGCA for $B_1\theta_0$

$$\vdots$$

$(\theta_n; r_n)$ is a CGCA for $B_n\theta_0\theta_1\ldots\theta_{n-1}$

then

$\theta = \theta_0 \circ \cdots \circ \theta_n$ and

$r = \mathrm{et}_1(\mathrm{et}_2(r_1,\ldots,r_n),x)$

(note that if H is $\leftarrow B_1,\ldots,B_n$ and B_i,θ_i,r_i are as above then the answer is $\mathrm{et}_2(r_1,\ldots,r_n)$ (think of A being empty and $\Box \leftarrow B_1$ $\mathrm{et}_2,\ldots \mathrm{et}_2$ B_n having cf=1).

Theorem 8. *Let* $\mathrm{MP}(\mathrm{seq},\mathrm{et}_1)$ *and* $\mathrm{MON}(\mathrm{seq},\mathrm{et}_2)$ *holds and let P be a fuzzy* $(\mathrm{seq},\mathrm{et}_2)$-*definite program, let H be a goal and* $(\theta;r)$ *a CGCA. Then* $(\theta;r)$ *is a Herbrand correct answer.*

Proof. Similar as that of Theorem 5. □

References

[DSM] Ding L., Shen Z. L., Mukaidono M.: Fuzzy linear resolution as the inference engine of intelligent systems. in Ras Z. W. (Ed.): Methodologies for Intelligent Systems, Volume 4, Elsevier Science Publ., Amsterdam, 1989, Volume 4, 1–8

[DLP] Dubois D., Lang J., Prade H.: Fuzzy sets in approximate reasoning, Part 2: Logical approaches. Fuzzy Sets and Systems **40** (1991) 203–244

[G] Gottwald, S.: Mehrwertige Logik. Akademie Verlag, Berlin, 1988

[H1] Hájek, P.: Fuzzy logic and arithmetical hierarchy I. Fuzzy Sets and Systems (to appear)

[H2] Hájek, P.: Fuzzy logic and arithmetical hierarchy II. Preprint, 1995

[H3] Hájek, P.: Grundlagen der Fuzzy Logik. Vorträge, Technische Universität, Wien, 24.–28. 4. 1995

[H4] Hájek, P.: Lectures on Fuzzy Logic. Handwritten notes of lectures, Prague, Fall 1994

[L] Lloyd, J.W.: Foundation of Logic Programming. Springer Verlag, Berlin, 1987

[M] Meritt, D.: Building Expert Systems in Prolog. Springer Verlag, Berlin, 1989

[N] Novák, V.: On the syntactico-semantical completeness of first-order fuzzy logic I, II. Kybernetika **26** (1990) 47–26, 134–152

[P] Pavelka, J.: On fuzzy logic I, II, III. Zeitschr. f. Math. Logik und Grundl. der Math. **25** (1979) 45–52, 119–134, 447–464

[SB] Shortliffe, E. H., Buchanan, B. G.: A model of inexact reasoning in medicine. Math. Biosci. **23** (1975) 351–379

[VPL] Vojtáš, P., Paulík, L., Lieskovský, M: Expert systems and different logic systems. Accepted for the proceeding of AIT'95, Brno, Published by Tech. Univ., Brno, 1995

Recognition of Handwritten Characters using Instance-Based Learning Algorithms

Jan Žižka and Irena Šnajdárková

Department of Automatic Control and Instrumentation
Technical University of Brno, Božetěchova 2
612 66 Brno, Czech Republic

E-mail: zizka@dame.fee.vutbr.cz
Fax: (++42 5) 41211141, Telephone: (++42 5) 7275275

Abstract. The paper deals with the application of Machine Learning methods to the computerized recognition of separated handwritten or printed characters. The recognition system makes use of Instance-Based Learning Algorithms (IBL). First, some portion of bit-mapped representation of input data is used as training examples (i.e., instances of individual characters) – this phase is called *interactive learning*. During the following phase, the system is able to recognize characters with the possibility of additional on-line training whenever an unknown pattern appears on the input. Two approaches are implemented: (1) storing all the training instances (IB1), and (2) memorizing only a reduced set of them (IB2), thus substantially decreasing storage requirements and speeding-up the recognition process. Depending on the input data quality and the number of training examples, the classification accuracy ranges from 82% (irregular children's writing) to 97% (standard handwriting) to 100% (printed texts).

1 Introduction

One of the important Artificial Intelligence applications is character recognition. There exist some systems for printed character recognition, however, efficient and reliable processing of handwritten characters still presents a difficulty. The problem is caused by the broad variety of styles, shapes, and sizes of handwritten characters. This paper summarizes an experience with the application of the Machine Learning algorithm family known as *instance-based learning* (IBL) to handwritten character recognition. The prototype can learn and classify characters (converted into bit-maps using a scanner) written by humans. Separation of individual characters is not included in the system. The system's output is an extended ASCII file, therefore the method proposed here can be used for automatic conversion of scanned handwritten text into a computer form. The method employed in the prototype can easily learn and classify arbitrary characters (letters, numbers, ligatures), including any national alphabets – printed characters is just one possibility. No context analysis is performed.

2 Instance-Based Learning

Instance-based learning algorithms rank among the group of methods characterized by incremental, supervised learning (learning from examples) where the source of instances is the external environment (Aha, 1990). IBL algorithms passively accept instances from an exterior process rather than request or choose specific ones for input. Each instance is described by a set of attribute-value pairs. This representation has clear advantages because it is simple and not difficult to analyze. On the other hand, missing relationships among sets of attributes does not help in making accurate predictions. IBL algorithms are derived from the classification methods known as *nearest neighbor algorithms* (NN algorithms), see for example (Winston, 1992). Other sources of inspiration were also *case based learning* and *exemplar based learning*, cf. (Shapiro, 1992). To avoid possible terminological confusion, IBL algorithms use the term *instance* instead of *case* or *exemplar*. IBL algorithms can also tolerate missing attribute values.

Instances, described by n attributes, create points in an n-dimensional instance space. Each attribute is defined over a set of totally-ordered (numeric) or unordered (symbolic) values. IBL algorithms use an input sequence of *training instances* and learn *concepts*, i.e., functions that map instances to certain categories. IBL can learn multiple concepts simultaneously.

IBL algorithms generally consist of the following four functions: (1) *normalization*, (2) *similarity*, (3) *prediction*, (4) *memory update*. According to the specific implementation of the functions, various learning algorithms can be obtained, e.g., IB1 to IB4, TIBL and others; see (Aha, Kibler, and Albert, 1991) and (Zhang, 1992). The first component, the normalizer, normalizes (pre-processes) each numeric attribute's values to force the similarity function to assume that each of attributes has the same range of values. Whenever new information appears on the input, re-normalization is required. For example, in the IB1 algorithm, which closely resembles the k-nearest neighbor decision rule, the linear normalization function uses the lowest and the highest values of some attribute a, which describes an instance x_a:

$$Norm(x_a, a) = \frac{(x_a - a_{min})}{(a_{max} - a_{min})} \tag{1}$$

The second function, similarity, returns a numerical value, which expresses the degree to which some new instance is similar to all instances in the description of the partial concept. A simple similarity function for numeric-valued attributes can use, for example, the inverse of the Euclidean distance of two instances x and y, where n is the number of attributes:

$$Sim(x, y) = [\sum_{i=1}^{n} (x_i - y_i)^2]^{-0.5} \tag{2}$$

However, in the particular application described in this paper, *Hamming distance* –

which is the number of features (typically, pixel values), in which the observed pattern differs from a prototype class – gave also excellent results.

The third function, prediction, uses a k-most similar instance decision rule to predict values. The prediction function for numeric values computes a weighted-similarity of its k-most similar instances' target values (Aha, 1990):

$$Tval(K, t, k) = \sum_{i=1}^{k} \frac{Sim[K_i] \times K_{it}}{\sum_{j=1}^{k} Sim[K_j]} \tag{3}$$

where K_i is one of the k-most similar stored instances, K_{it} is instance K_i's value for target attribute t, and $Sim[K_i]$ is K_i's pre-computed similarity with the current test instance x_i. The similarity-weighted function combines the predictions of similar instances based on their similarity to the instance given to the algorithm. In practice, $k = 1$ often provides very good or acceptable results. Generally, k-NN algorithms with $k > 1$ increases – to the certain degree – the accuracy of classification, however, the optimal value of k is application-dependent. Higher values of k often lead to poor performance.

Finally, the IB1's memory update (learning) function stores *all* processed training instances into the target's partial concept description.

Modifications of the basic IB1 algorithm include the IB2 algorithm, which stores only a subset of the training data (instances that are misclassified), thus substantially decreasing the memory requirements. IB2 differs from IB1 in the learning phase (correctly classified instances are filtered). Consequently, IB2 is very sensitive to noise – if there are noisy instances, exceptions, or instances that are too close to concepts' boundaries, the classification is often wrong. This disadvantage is removed by the IB3 algorithm, which is capable of tolerating noise. IB3 stores records of all correct and incorrect classifications. Instances to be stored require confirmation that they are so called *significant classifiers* before their use for classification purpose. If noise is present in the data, classification is more accurate and memory demands are lower in comparison with IB1 and IB2. IB4 algorithm increases the learning performance in cases where instances are described by many irrelevant attributes; attributes are weighted.

The system described in this paper includes only the first three algorithms; there was no need of irrelevant attributes processing.

3 Recognition of Separated Handwritten Characters

After binarization of the text by a scanning device, the system reads the bit-mapped representation of a page (a part of text) and looks for *lines*. Lines are simply rectangular areas containing sequences of characters. A page can be viewed as being horizontally split by lines. As soon as the lines are determined, rectangular subareas (which split a line vertically) containing isolated characters are detected within each line (no frames are needed to mark off these areas). It is possible to parameterize the detection phase by setting up the numbers of points (bit-map elements) that may be ignored or considered when boundaries of lines and characters are looked for. Similarly, minimum and maximum size of a character can be set up.

The next phase consists of learning. Each detected character is normalized into the bit-map area having the size 16×16 points. Exceptionally, if a character is not separated correctly, it is possible to adjust manually its boundaries. By pushing the corresponding key on the keyboard, the bit-mapped representation is assigned a letter/number code. A normalized character is represented by 256 points. Each point can be assigned either "0" or "1" (white or dark point). Because characters can be obtained with different resolutions (dots-per-inch) – typically, 75dpi, 150dpi, 300dpi, 600dpi –, normalization is inevitable. For each point within the normalized map, it is necessary to find a corresponding part of the character image. It can be done using the ratio of white and dark image's points (the ratio can be set up as a parameter).

Characters may be classified by different ways. The system, which is described here, uses five methods how to compare the normalized bit-map with the character's image bit-map (this method is known as *template matching*): (1) comparison of corresponding "1s" and "0s" (implemented by $\neg XOR$). This method gave the best results. (2) comparison of only "1s" (*AND*); (3) comparison of only "0s" ($\neg OR$); (4) the Euclidean distance from the circle around a character, and (5) the Euclidean distance from the normalized circle around a character. The classification is according to the best match (or minimum mismatch) using the Hamming distance.

Alternatively, intelligent learning phase (based on the IB2 algorithm) may be used – only selected patterns are stored. The system offers the best assumed classification. Only if it is wrong then the pattern is stored which substantially saves memory (for 300 training instances, only 20–30% of memory requirements – compared with IB1 – was observed with the same classification precision). Consequently, IB2 was also several times faster than IB1 during classification.

Fig. 1 and **Fig. 2** show two examples of handwriting (section of testing data):

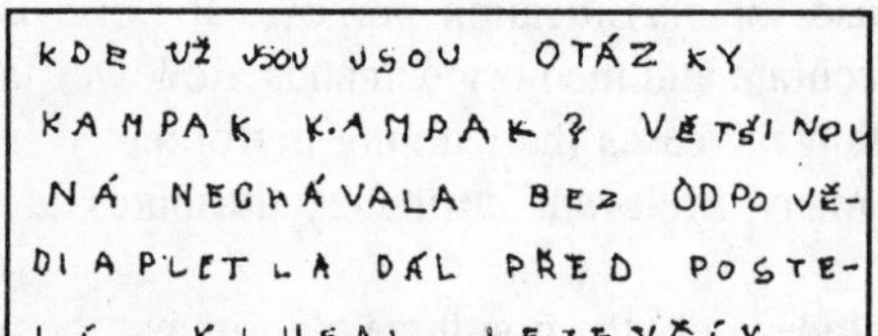

Fig. 1 A sample of children's writing 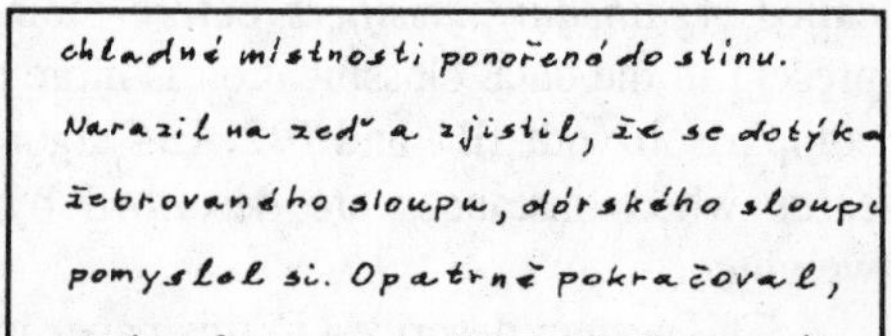　　　Fig. 2 A sample of adult's writing

The following **Fig. 3** illustrates the learning process using IB2. The page was automatically split into lines; lines – being processed so far – were split into characters. In the top right corner, the image of the letter "t" is displayed in the form as it was obtained from a scanning device (in this case, the resolution was 150dpi).

The bottom right corner shows the normalized bit-map of "t". The screen snapshot illustrates the moment when the system verifies its last classification.

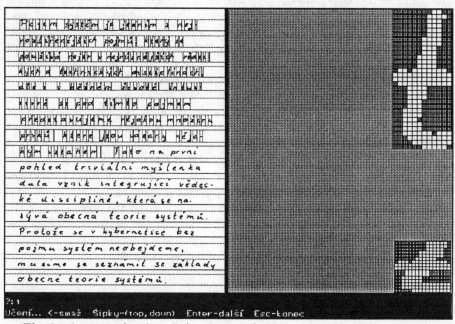

Fig. 3. An example taken during the learning phase using the IB2 algorithm

4 Comparison with other Systems

There are few systems available for the written text recognition. Most of them are capable of printed text recognition only. The system named Form File (Improx) can process also handwritten characters, which must be placed within frames 5×7 mm and must be of the same size, having the form of capital block letters. This system requires a special hardware adapter with a RISC processor and, consequently, is very fast (up to 400 characters per second, according to the manufacturer data). Unlike the IBL-based prototype, it uses a dictionary. It is difficult to compare the speed of the IBL-based system with Form File because only 386/486 PCs running under MS-DOS were available for testing; 386/DX2 40 MHz processor enabled the speed of 10-20 characters per second for the IB2 algorithm, depending on specific data. However, during the tests with IBL algorithms, substantially larger class of characters was processed (not only the very restricted class of capital block letters with limited variability in comparison with small characters), so it is impossible to provide any significant comparison having no common platform.

Unlike artificial neural networks, see e.g. (Kwan and Cai, 1994), IBL algorithms need only a fraction of time to train and it is possible to analyze them and understand the way how they learn and work.

5 Conclusions

The family of IBL algorithms demonstrated excellent capabilities for being applied to handwritten character recognition. Depending on the quality of scanned text, handwritten characters in testing data were classified with 82–97% accuracy while printed characters presented no difficulty – they were easily classified with 100% accuracy. The prototype can learn and classify characters having different features (sizes, fonts, styles, shapes, and so like). Better results were achieved when characters were scanned with the resolution 150dpi or higher, particularly during the learning phase. However, very good results were obtained also for 75dpi and even the resolution 40dpi is acceptable. The method used in the prototype is also not too much sensitive to noise in the input data, so it is possible to classify distorted characters as well. The advantage of the solution presented here is that no special forms or frames are needed. The implementation demonstrated that a very broad variety of handwritten characters can be easily recognized. Accuracy of classification naturally increases with the number of stored instances and the system can be given additional training any time – this is automatically done each time when an unknown or ambiguous character appears on the input. It is supposed that by integrating the IBL-based system with a dictionary, the recognition precision would be further improved.

References

Aha, D. W.: A Study of Instance-based Algorithms for Supervised Learning Tasks: Mathematical, Empirical, and Psychological Evaluations. PhD dissertation, Dept. of Information and Computer Science, Univ. of California, Irvine (November 1990)

Aha, D. W., Kibler, D., Albert, M. K.: Instance-based Learning Algorithms. Machine Learning 6 (1991) 37-66

Kurtzberg, J. M.: Feature Analysis for Symbol Recognition by Elastic Matching. IBM Journal of Research and Development 31 (1987) 57-78

Kwan, H. K., Cai, Y.: A Fuzzy Neural Network and its Application to Pattern Recognition. IEEE Transactions on Fuzzy Systems, Vol. 2, No. 3 (1994) 185-193

Shapiro, S. C. (Ed.): Encyclopedia of Artificial Intelligence. Second edition. John Wiley & Sons, Inc. (1992)

Winston, Patrick H.: Artificial Intelligence. Third edition. Addison-Wesley Publishing Company (1992)

Zhang, J.: Selecting Typical Instances in Instance-Based Learning. Proc. of the Ninth International Workshop on Machine Learning, Aberdeen, Scotland (July 1-3, 1992) 470-479

Author Index

Bac*, C.	272	Mørk, S.	206
Berghe, T. van den	437	Motyčková, L.	425
Bernard, G.	272	Nguyen, Q.H.	272
Betts*, A.J.G.	166	Paton*, N.W.	146
Bicarregui*, J.C.	184	Paulík, L.	487
Börger*, E.	236	Phuong, N.H.	431
Borovanský, P.	363	Pirotte, A.	437
Bureš, H.	413	Plátek, M.	379
Cappelli, A.	369	Ravn, A.P.	206
Chapman, B.	292	Repaská, Z.	443
Charvát*, K.	334	Rischel*, H.	206
Conan, D.	272	Rozložník, M.	449, 481
Cuellar, J.	206	Santen, P. van	475
De Castro, C.	369	Scalas, M.R.	369
Gellersen, H.-W.	375	Siegelmann*, H.T.	83, 95
Giles, C.L.	95	Šíma, J.	461
Grimson*, J.	120	Šnajdárková, I.	493
Hájek*, P.	31	Smith, C.	455
Holan, T.	379	Strakoš, Z.	449
Horne, B.G.	95	Štuller, J.	469
Jeffery*, K.G.	103	Taconet, C.	272
Jennings, E.	385	Tambouris, E.	475
Kozák, P.	391	Tau, C.A.	455
Kuboň, V.	379	Tel*, G.	50
Li, W.X.	399	Tůma, M.	481
Limpouch*, A.	334	Vojtáš, P.	487
Lucas, S.	405	Wiedermann*, J.	1
Marshall*, V.A.	350	Wildgruber, I.	206
Matthews, B.M.	184	Zemánek, P.	419
Matyska, L.	413	Zima*, H.P.	292
Maurer*, H.	315	Zimanyi, E.	437
Mehrotra, P.	292	Žižka, J.	493
Meunier, F.	419		

* invited speaker

Springer-Verlag
and the Environment

W̲e at Springer-Verlag firmly believe that an international science publisher has a special obligation to the environment, and our corporate policies consistently reflect this conviction.

W̲e also expect our business partners – paper mills, printers, packaging manufacturers, etc. – to commit themselves to using environmentally friendly materials and production processes.

T̲he paper in this book is made from low- or no-chlorine pulp and is acid free, in conformance with international standards for paper permanency.

Lecture Notes in Computer Science

For information about Vols. 1–935

please contact your bookseller or Springer-Verlag

Vol. 936: V.S. Alagar, M. Nivat (Eds.), Algebraic Methodology and Software Technology. Proceedings, 1995. XIV, 591 pages. 1995.

Vol. 937: Z. Galil, E. Ukkonen (Eds.), Combinatorial Pattern Matching. Proceedings, 1995. VIII, 409 pages. 1995.

Vol. 938: K.P. Birman, F. Mattern, A. Schiper (Eds.), Theory and Practice in Distributed Systems. Proceedings, 1994. X, 263 pages. 1995.

Vol. 939: P. Wolper (Ed.), Computer Aided Verification. Proceedings, 1995. X, 451 pages. 1995.

Vol. 940: C. Goble, J. Keane (Eds.), Advances in Databases. Proceedings, 1995. X, 277 pages. 1995.

Vol. 941: M. Cadoli, Tractable Reasoning in Artificial Intelligence. XVII, 247 pages. 1995. (Subseries LNAI).

Vol. 942: G. Böckle, Exploitation of Fine-Grain Parallelism. IX, 188 pages. 1995.

Vol. 943: W. Klas, M. Schrefl, Metaclasses and Their Application. IX, 201 pages. 1995.

Vol. 944: Z. Fülöp, F. Gécseg (Eds.), Automata, Languages and Programming. Proceedings, 1995. XIII, 686 pages. 1995.

Vol. 945: B. Bouchon-Meunier, R.R. Yager, L.A. Zadeh (Eds.), Advances in Intelligent Computing - IPMU '94. Proceedings, 1994. XII, 628 pages. 1995.

Vol. 946: C. Froidevaux, J. Kohlas (Eds.), Symbolic and Quantitative Approaches to Reasoning and Uncertainty. Proceedings, 1995. X, 420 pages. 1995. (Subseries LNAI).

Vol. 947: B. Möller (Ed.), Mathematics of Program Construction. Proceedings, 1995. VIII, 472 pages. 1995.

Vol. 948: G. Cohen, M. Giusti, T. Mora (Eds.), Applied Algebra, Algebraic Algorithms and Error-Correcting Codes. Proceedings, 1995. XI, 485 pages. 1995.

Vol. 949: D.G. Feitelson, L. Rudolph (Eds.), Job Scheduling Strategies for Parallel Processing. Proceedings, 1995. VIII, 361 pages. 1995.

Vol. 950: A. De Santis (Ed.), Advances in Cryptology - EUROCRYPT '94. Proceedings, 1994. XIII, 473 pages. 1995.

Vol. 951: M.J. Egenhofer, J.R. Herring (Eds.), Advances in Spatial Databases. Proceedings, 1995. XI, 405 pages. 1995.

Vol. 952: W. Olthoff (Ed.), ECOOP '95 - Object-Oriented Programming. Proceedings, 1995. XI, 471 pages. 1995.

Vol. 953: D. Pitt, D.E. Rydeheard, P. Johnstone (Eds.), Category Theory and Computer Science. Proceedings, 1995. VII, 252 pages. 1995.

Vol. 954: G. Ellis, R. Levinson, W. Rich. J.F. Sowa (Eds.), Conceptual Structures: Applications, Implementation and Theory. Proceedings, 1995. IX, 353 pages. 1995. (Subseries LNAI).

VOL. 955: S.G. Akl, F. Dehne, J.-R. Sack, N. Santoro (Eds.), Algorithms and Data Structures. Proceedings, 1995. IX, 519 pages. 1995.

Vol. 956: X. Yao (Ed.), Progress in Evolutionary Computation. Proceedings, 1993, 1994. VIII, 314 pages. 1995. (Subseries LNAI).

Vol. 957: C. Castelfranchi, J.-P. Müller (Eds.), From Reaction to Cognition. Proceedings, 1993. VI, 252 pages. 1995. (Subseries LNAI).

Vol. 958: J. Calmet, J.A. Campbell (Eds.), Integrating Symbolic Mathematical Computation and Artificial Intelligence. Proceedings, 1994. X, 275 pages. 1995.

Vol. 959: D.-Z. Du, M. Li (Eds.), Computing and Combinatorics. Proceedings, 1995. XIII, 654 pages. 1995.

Vol. 960: D. Leivant (Ed.), Logic and Computational Complexity. Proceedings, 1994. VIII, 514 pages. 1995.

Vol. 961: K.P. Jantke, S. Lange (Eds.), Algorithmic Learning for Knowledge-Based Systems. X, 511 pages. 1995. (Subseries LNAI).

Vol. 962: I. Lee, S.A. Smolka (Eds.), CONCUR '95: Concurrency Theory. Proceedings, 1995. X, 547 pages. 1995.

Vol. 963: D. Coppersmith (Ed.), Advances in Cryptology - CRYPTO '95. Proceedings, 1995. XII, 467 pages. 1995.

Vol. 964: V. Malyshkin (Ed.), Parallel Computing Technologies. Proceedings, 1995. XII, 497 pages. 1995.

Vol. 965: H. Reichel (Ed.), Fundamentals of Computation Theory. Proceedings, 1995. IX, 433 pages. 1995.

Vol. 966: S. Haridi, K. Ali, P. Magnusson (Eds.), EURO-PAR '95 Parallel Processing. Proceedings, 1995. XV, 734 pages. 1995.

Vol. 967: J.P. Bowen, M.G. Hinchey (Eds.), ZUM '95: The Z Formal Specification Notation. Proceedings, 1995. XI, 571 pages. 1995.

Vol. 968: N. Dershowitz, N. Lindenstrauss (Eds.), Conditional and Typed Rewriting Systems. Proceedings, 1994. VIII, 375 pages. 1995.

Vol. 969: J. Wiedermann, P. Hájek (Eds.), Mathematical Foundations of Computer Science 1995. Proceedings, 1995. XIII, 588 pages. 1995.

Vol. 970: V. Hlaváč, R. Šára (Eds.), Computer Analysis of Images and Patterns. Proceedings, 1995. XVIII, 960 pages. 1995.

Vol. 971: E.T. Schubert, P.J. Windley, J. Alves-Foss (Eds.), Higher Order Logic Theorem Proving and Its Applications. Proceedings, 1995. VIII, 400 pages. 1995.

Vol. 972: J.-M. Hélary, M. Raynal (Eds.), Distributed Algorithms. Proceedings, 1995. XI, 333 pages. 1995.

Vol. 973: H.H. Adelsberger, J. Lažanský, V. Mařík (Eds.), Information Management in Computer Integrated Manufacturing. IX, 665 pages. 1995.

Vol. 974: C. Braccini, L. DeFloriani, G. Vernazza (Eds.), Image Analysis and Processing. Proceedings, 1995. XIX, 757 pages. 1995.

Vol. 975: W. Moore, W. Luk (Eds.), Field-Programmable Logic and Applications. Proceedings, 1995. XI, 448 pages. 1995.

Vol. 976: U. Montanari, F. Rossi (Eds.), Principles and Practice of Constraint Programming — CP '95. Proceedings, 1995. XIII, 651 pages. 1995.

Vol. 977: H. Beilner, F. Bause (Eds.), Quantitative Evaluation of Computing and Communication Systems. Proceedings, 1995. X, 415 pages. 1995.

Vol. 978: N. Revell, A M. Tjoa (Eds.), Database and Expert Systems Applications. Proceedings, 1995. XV, 654 pages. 1995.

Vol. 979: P. Spirakis (Ed.), Algorithms — ESA '95. Proceedings, 1995. XII, 598 pages. 1995.

Vol. 980: A. Ferreira, J. Rolim (Eds.), Parallel Algorithms for Irregularly Structured Problems. Proceedings, 1995. IX, 409 pages. 1995.

Vol. 981: I. Wachsmuth, C.-R. Rollinger, W. Brauer (Eds.), KI-95: Advances in Artificial Intelligence. Proceedings, 1995. XII, 269 pages. (Subseries LNAI).

Vol. 982: S. Doaitse Swierstra, M. Hermenegildo (Eds.), Programming Languages: Implementations, Logics and Programs. Proceedings, 1995. XI, 467 pages. 1995.

Vol. 983: A. Mycroft (Ed.), Static Analysis. Proceedings, 1995. VIII, 423 pages. 1995.

Vol. 984: J.-M. Haton, M. Keane, M. Manago (Eds.), Advances in Case-Based Reasoning. Proceedings, 1994. VIII, 307 pages. 1995.

Vol. 985: T. Sellis (Ed.), Rules in Database Systems. Proceedings, 1995. VIII, 373 pages. 1995.

Vol. 986: Henry G. Baker (Ed.), Memory Management. Proceedings, 1995. XII, 417 pages. 1995.

Vol. 987: P.E. Camurati, H. Eveking (Eds.), Correct Hardware Design and Verification Methods. Proceedings, 1995. VIII, 342 pages. 1995.

Vol. 988: A.U. Frank, W. Kuhn (Eds.), Spatial Information Theory. Proceedings, 1995. XIII, 571 pages. 1995.

Vol. 989: W. Schäfer, P. Botella (Eds.), Software Engineering — ESEC '95. Proceedings, 1995. XII, 519 pages. 1995.

Vol. 990: C. Pinto-Ferreira, N.J. Mamede (Eds.), Progress in Artificial Intelligence. Proceedings, 1995. XIV, 487 pages. 1995. (Subseries LNAI).

Vol. 991: J. Wainer, A. Carvalho (Eds.), Advances in Artificial Intelligence. Proceedings, 1995. XII, 342 pages. 1995. (Subseries LNAI).

Vol. 992: M. Gori, G. Soda (Eds.), Topics in Artificial Intelligence. Proceedings, 1995. XII, 451 pages. 1995. (Subseries LNAI).

Vol. 993: T.C. Fogarty (Ed.), Evolutionary Computing. Proceedings, 1995. VIII, 264 pages. 1995.

Vol. 994: M. Hebert, J. Ponce, T. Boult, A. Gross (Eds.), Object Representation in Computer Vision. Proceedings, 1994. VIII, 359 pages. 1995.

Vol. 995: S.M. Müller, W.J. Paul, The Complexity of Simple Computer Architectures. XII, 270 pages. 1995.

Vol. 996: P. Dybjer, B. Nordström, J. Smith (Eds.), Types for Proofs and Programs. Proceedings, 1994. X, 202 pages. 1995.

Vol. 997: K.P. Jantke, T. Shinohara, T. Zeugmann (Eds.), Algorithmic Learning Theory. Proceedings, 1995. XV, 319 pages. 1995.

Vol. 998: A. Clarke, M. Campolargo, N. Karatzas (Eds.), Bringing Telecommunication Services to the People – IS&N '95. Proceedings, 1995. XII, 510 pages. 1995.

Vol. 999: P. Antsaklis, W. Kohn, A. Nerode, S. Sastry (Eds.), Hybrid Systems II. VIII, 569 pages. 1995.

Vol. 1000: J. van Leeuwen (Ed.), Computer Science Today. XIV, 643 pages. 1995.

Vol. 1004: J. Staples, P. Eades, N. Katoh, A. Moffat (Eds.), Algorithms and Computation. Proceedings, 1995. XV, 440 pages. 1995.

Vol. 1005: J. Estublier (Ed.), Software Configuration Management. Proceedings, 1995. IX, 311 pages. 1995.

Vol. 1006: S. Bhalla (Ed.), Information Systems and Data Management. Proceedings, 1995. IX, 321 pages. 1995.

Vol. 1007: A. Bosselaers, B. Preneel (Eds.), Integrity Primitives for Secure Information Systems. VII, 239 pages. 1995.

Vol. 1008: B. Preneel (Ed.), Fast Software Encryption. Proceedings, 1994. VIII, 367 pages. 1995.

Vol. 1009: M. Broy, S. Jähnichen (Eds.), KORSO: Methods, Languages, and Tools for the Construction of Correct Software. X, 449 pages. 1995. Vol.

Vol. 1010: M. Veloso, A. Aamodt (Eds.), Case-Based Reasoning Research and Development. Proceedings, 1995. X, 576 pages. 1995. (Subseries LNAI).

Vol. 1011: T. Furuhashi (Ed.), Advances in Fuzzy Logic, Neural Networks and Genetic Algorithms. Proceedings, 1994. (Subseries LNAI).

Vol. 1012: M. Bartošek, J. Staudek, J. Wiedermann (Eds.), SOFSEM '95: Theory and Practice of Informatics. Proceedings, 1995. XI, 499 pages. 1995.

Vol. 1013: T.W. Ling, A.O. Mendelzon, L. Vieille (Eds.), Deductive and Object-Oriented Databases. Proceedings, 1995. XIV, 557 pages. 1995.

Vol. 1014: A.P. del Pobil, M.A. Serna, Spatial Representation and Motion Planning. XII, 242 pages. 1995.

Vol. 1015: B. Blumenthal, J. Gornostaev, C. Unger (Eds.), Human-Computer Interaction. Proceedings, 1995. VIII, 203 pages. 1995.

Vol. 1017: M. Nagl (Ed.), Graph-Theoretic Concepts in Computer Science. Proceedings, 1995. XI, 406 pages. 1995.